Computation, Causation, and Discovery

Computation, Causation, and Discovery

Edited by Clark Glymour and Gregory F. Cooper

AAAI PRESS / THE MIT PRESS

MENLO PARK, CALIFORNIA, CAMBRIDGE, MASSACHUSETTS, LONDON, ENGLAND

Copublished and distributed by The MIT Press, Massachusetts Institute of
Technology, Cambridge, Massachusetts and London, England.

Library of Congress Cataloging-in-Publication Data

Computation, causation, and discovery / edited by Clark N. Glymour and
Gregory F. Cooper.
       p.   cm.
  Includes bibliographical references and index.
  ISBN 0-262-57124-2 (pbk. : alk. paper)
  1. Prediction theory. 2. Causation. 3. Data mining. I. Glymour, Clark N. II.
Cooper, Gregory Floyd.
QA279.2.C66   1999
519.5'4—dc21   98-34234
                                              CIP

Printed on acid-free paper in the United States of America.

For Holly and Madelyn — C.N.G.

and to Patty, Nathan, and Emma — G.F.C.

Contents

Part Three: Controversy Over Search

Part Four: Estimating Causal Effects

Preface

Clark Glymour

In science, business, policy making, anywhere data are used in prediction, two sorts of problems that require very different methods of analysis standardly arise but are often confused. *Problems of diagnosis and classification* concern how to reliably and accurately predict some features of a kind of system from other features of that kind of system. *Problems of causal prediction* concern how to reliably predict the changes in some features of a kind of system that will result if an intervention changes other features. This book is about the problem of learning to make causal predictions, which is the problem of causal discovery.

Familiar examples illustrate classification and recognition problems: data on payment history, income, age, and past credit-card default are to be used to find a procedure to predict credit-card default; data on shape, size, coloring and motion characteristics of the aircraft of various nations are to be used to find a procedure to predict whether an aircraft is friendly or hostile; data from infrared spectra of various minerals are to be used to find a procedure to predict the classification of unknown minerals. In these problems the prediction itself does not concern any alteration of any feature of the system; it simply uses some of the features of the system to recognize or classify other features. Of course, once you know an aircraft is hostile you may want to alter its features dramatically and suddenly, and you may know how to do so, but that is extra knowledge not provided by the data analysis itself. Statistics and machine learning have long been concerned with methods that use data to obtain classification and recognition rules (of many forms) that can in turn be used to make such predictions rapidly and accurately. There are many well-known methods for this kind of problem: linear and logistic regression, probabilistic decision trees, classification and regression trees, and neural network learning techniques are all methods that can be applied to appropriate data to extract procedures for diagnosis or classification.

Causal discovery is relevant to making predictions that include the following sort of thing: What will a change in commission rates do to the total sales, or to the net profits of a company; what will a reduction in cigarette smoking among older smokers do to their life expectancy; what will a change in the formula a college uses for awarding scholarships do to its drop-out rate; what will a change in children's lead absorption do to their IQs? The changes in question are possible interventions that would directly alter some of the features of systems, and perhaps—and this is the question—indirectly alter other features. These are problems about discovering the cause and effect relations between some of the features of a system, or features of a collection of systems.

The second class of problems, those this book is about, are much more difficult. Solutions to classification and recognition problems turn on finding informative associations among features. But those very associations underdetermine causal relations: Two variables, A and B, may be associated in a sample or in a database because in a sufficiently large proportion of units, A causes B; or B causes A; or one or more other features cause both A and B; or because A and B have no causal connection of any kind but, for a sufficiently large proportion of units, the values of A and B influence whether that unit is in the sample or database; or simply because the sample or database includes two or more kinds of systems for which A and B have different probability distributions. Associations can be produced in all of these ways and their combinations.

The standard solution to these difficulties has been to call for randomized, controlled experiments. Depending on their design, randomized experiments may remove many of these reasons for uncertainty about the process that generated an association, although some of these same difficulties may arise in a disguised form—for example, when some people drop out of a randomized clinical trial because of the intended effect (the value of the outcome variable for them) of the treatment and because of treatment side effects. But in any case, randomized controlled experiments are comparatively rare and comparatively expensive: in business, medicine, social science, biological science—in a great variety of contexts where predictions are needed about the effects of interventions or of policy changes—randomized, controlled experiments may be infeasible. The relevant experiments may be too costly, beyond our technical capacity, unethical, or illegal. Of the enormous number of databases that have been assembled in the hope that they can somehow be used to provide better causal predictions, very few contain only outcomes of randomized controlled experiments.

Until very recently, these problems more or less neatly divided methodologists into a skeptical group who held that without randomized controlled experiments, reliable causal inference is impossible, period, end of story; and an optimistic group who held that either prior "theory" or various *ad hoc* search procedures can be used to discover causal relations from associations in nonexperimental data. (In contrast, perhaps sensitive to the difficulties, practitioners who have available only nonexperimental data often fudge the question of whether they are offering conclusions or hypotheses about associations or about causal structures, and equally fudge the question of what sorts of predictions their hypotheses entail. The language of science has changed to aid the ambiguity; thus conclusions of epidemiological studies are often stated, not in terms either of associations or of causes, but in terms of "risk factors," which sometimes mean one thing and sometimes the other.)

Over the last fifteen years a third viewpoint has emerged from a series of investigations in statistics and computer science. Its fundamental methodological idea is that principled causal inference from sample data is not an all or nothing affair: if the data for a system of variables are generated from an unknown causal structure, without experimental controls, it may be impossible to uncover all of that structure, but, depending on the data, on the true unknown structure, and on the assumptions the investigator is willing to make, it may nonetheless be possible to uncover aspects of the structure sufficient for predicting the outcomes of specific interventions. Fully recognizing all of the difficulties of causal discovery from uncontrolled, nonexperimental data, these developments explore an intricate interplay between assumptions about the data-generating process, patterns of associations in the data, aspects of causal processes that are consistent with the assumptions and can explain the patterns in the data, and predictions about the outcomes of interventions that can be made from incomplete causal knowledge.

These developments turn on four sets of ideas: (1) a great variety of causal structures, and the patterns of associations they imply, can be represented by *directed graphs* with an accompanying set of parameters—with values for its parameters specified, a graph implies a definite probability distribution over all of the variables it represents; (2) assuming available a graphical representation of a causal structure and values for the relevant parameters, the effects of "ideal" interventions—manipulations that fix the values of one or more variables without otherwise altering the causal structure—can be calculated, and similar calculations can sometimes be carried out when features of the graph and its parameters are uncertain; (3) new techniques permit the estimation of parameters in causal graphs from appropriate sample data; (4) the reliabilities and computational efficiencies of various algorithms for extracting features of directed graphs from sample data can be studied mathematically, tested with simulated data, and tested with real-world data when the relevant causal structures are independently known.

Unlike traditional statistics, this work focuses on search among an enormous number of possible structures, rather than on testing a specific model, or selecting from among a small list of alternative models. It provides the theory for data mining for causal relationships. An important aspect of some of the work related to search concerns the representation of equivalence classes of causal relationships under various characterizations of equivalence. Some of the recent work is striking in developing Bayesian approaches to search, and in combining Bayesian approaches with constraint-based approaches to search, both permitting various combinations of prior belief to interact with data. Not last, but almost first in the presentation in this collection, recent research has unfolded theorems about the consequences of manipulations of causal structures, theorems that allow for simultaneous conditioning on observations and on interventions, and simultaneous modeling of measured variables, unmeasured variables, and data selection processes.

This book is intended to provide an up-to-date introduction to these developments. The book is intended for anyone interested in either data mining, database management, machine learning, social science, economics, epidemiology, or any other area or application where data are used to inform decision makers about the likely consequences of alternative courses of action. The work presented here covers a sample of developments over the last five years, developments which have built on foundational ideas first introduced twenty years ago. In the theoretical contributions to the book, we have tried to include papers that are sufficiently detailed so that their mathematical techniques can be understood by the interested reader and applied elsewhere. We have also included a sample of applications from a wide range of subjects. And since the developments reported here challenge assumptions that dominate professional statistics, we have included a criticism of search techniques by two distinguished statisticians, and a rebuttal.

The book has five parts and an introductory chapter. The first chapter gives an overview of graphical representations and many of the subtleties involved in using them to describe causal relations. Part one, which consists of chapters 2 and 3, discusses how to use graphical representations of causal relations and their associated probability relations to predict the results of interventions. Part two, which consists of chapters 4, 5, 6, and 7, lay out Bayesian approaches to search, search using significance tests for constraints, search and representation when there may be confounding and sample selection bias in the data, and representation and search when the causal structures under study may have feedback. Part three contains a critical exchange about search methods. Briefly, Wasserman and Robins argue that epidemiologists have prior degrees of belief about causal structures which make use of the computerized search methods inappropriate. They suggest alternative methods of inference. Scheines, Spirtes, and Glymour reply that the degrees of belief and practices ascribed to epidemiologists are not coherent, and that the proposed alternative methods are demonstrably unreliable. Part four consists of three chapters (12, 13, and 14) on estimating parameters in graphical causal models. The chapters address interesting medical and epidemiological issues, including a reanalysis of much-discussed data on the influence of lead on children's intelligence. The final part contains chapters that apply the techniques described in this book to various empirical problems from economics, medicine, physics, and elsewhere.

This book leaves a great deal out of a rapidly developing subject. In particular, there are a variety of interesting search techniques that we have not included, either because of a lack of space or because they were not known when this book was planned, or because their developers did not have time to prepare a chapter. They include variations of Bayesian search methods, for example by Korb and his collaborators; minimum description length search techniques developed by Wedelin; a search using cross entropy developed by Cheng; and model averaging techniques developed by Madigan.

References

Cheng, J., Bell, D. A., Liu, W. 1997. Learning Beliefs Networks from Data: An Information Theory Based Approach. In *Proceedings of the Sixth ACM International Conference on Information and Knowledge Management.* New York: Association for Computing Machinery.

Cheng, J., Bell, D. A., Liu, W. 1997. An Algorithm for Bayesian Network Construction from Data. Paper presented at the Sixth International Workshop on Artificial Intelligence and Statistics, Ft. Lauderdale, Florida.

Dai, H., Korb, K. B., Wallace, C. S., and Wu, X. 1997. A Study of Causal Discovery with Weak Links and Small Samples. In *Proceedings of the Fifteenth International Joint Conference on Artificial Intelligence.* San Francisco: Morgan Kaufmann.

Korb, K. B., and Wallace, C. S. 1997. In Search of the Philosopher's Stone: Remarks on Humphreys and Freedman's Critique of Causal Discovery. *The British Journal for the Philosophy of Science,* 48(3): 543-553.

Wallace, C.S., and Korb, K.B. (forthcoming) A Study of Causal Discovery by MML Sampling. In *Causal Models and Intelligent Data Analysis,* ed. M. Slater. Berlin: Springer-Verlag.

Wallace, C. S., Korb, K. B., and Dai, H. 1996 Causal Discovery Via MML. In *Proceedings of the Thirteenth International Conference on Machine Learning,* ed. L. Saitta, 516-524. San Francisco: Morgan Kaufmann.

Wedelin, D. 1996 Efficient Estimation and Model Selection in Large Graphical Models. *Statistics and Computing,* 6(2): 123–138. (www.cs.chalmers.se/~dag/index.html).

Acknowledgments

We are indebted to many people, not the least to the contributors for their patience while this volume was prepared. We are extremely grateful to David Mike Hamilton for his help and his patience. This book would not have appeared without the aid and support of Kenneth Ford, editor of the AAAI Press. When, thanks to the first editor, editorial entropy had been maximized, Jennifer Schmidt saved the enterprise from complete collapse by taking over responsibility for assembling and organizing the contributions.

– Clark Glymour
– Gregory Cooper

Computation, Causation, and Discovery

An Overview of the Representation and Discovery of Causal Relationships Using Bayesian Networks

Gregory F. Cooper

To assist readers who are new to the area of causal discovery from observational data, this chapter describes some important concepts. The emphasis is on informal insight rather than formal rigor. The chapter introduces Bayesian networks as a representation of causal relationships. Other representations of causality are mentioned, but are not discussed in detail. Some basic properties of causal and noncausal Bayesian networks are described. Several fundamental methods and assumptions for learning causal Bayesian networks from observational data are introduced, and strengths and weaknesses of the methods are also discussed.

1. Bayesian Networks

A *Bayesian network* consists of a structural model and a set of probabilities (Castillo, Gutierrez, and Hadi 1997; Jensen 1996; Neapolitan 1990; Pearl 1988; Spirtes, Glymour, and Scheines 1993). The structural model is a directed acyclic graph[1] in which nodes represent variables and arcs represent probabilistic dependence. For convenience, I will use the terms *node* and *variable* interchangeably in this chapter. Each node can represent a continuous or discrete variable. For each node there is a probability distribution on that node given the state of its parents. A Bayesian network specifies graphically how the node probabilities factor to specify a joint probability distribution over all the nodes (variables).

Let S be the graphical structure of a Bayesian network G and let P be the

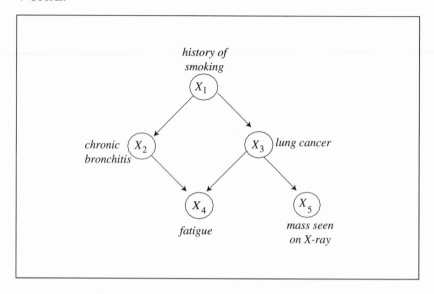

Figure 1. A hypothetical Bayesian network structure.

joint probability distribution represented by G. By definition, S is a directed, acyclic graph. A node in S denotes a variable that models a feature of a process, event, state, object, agent, etc., all of which I will denote generically as an entity. For example, the presence or absence of fatigue is a feature of a patient, and the patient is an entity. S may contain both measured (i.e., recorded) and hidden (i.e., unrecorded) variables. Hidden variables are variables for which we have no data.

Figure 1 illustrates the structure of a hypothetical medical Bayesian network, which contains five nodes. Table 1 shows the probabilities that are associated in this example with the structure in figure 1.

1.1. The Markov Condition

The independence relationships represented by the structure of a Bayesian network are given by the *Markov condition*:

Any node is conditionally independent of its nondescendants, given its parents.

A descendant of a node X is a node Y that can be reached by a directed path from X to Y. The Markov condition can be used to define equivalence classes of network structures. Two Bayesian network structures are *Markov equivalent* if and only if they contain the same set of variables and they represent the same conditional independence relationships on those variables, as

$P(X_1 = \text{no}) = 0.80$ $P(X_1 = \text{yes}) = 0.20$

$P(X_2 = \text{absent} \mid X_1 = \text{no}) = 0.95$ $P(X_2 = \text{present} \mid X_1 = \text{no}) = 0.05$
$P(X_2 = \text{absent} \mid X_1 = \text{yes}) = 0.75$ $P(X_2 = \text{present} \mid X_1 = \text{yes}) = 0.25$

$P(X_3 = \text{absent} \mid X_1 = \text{no}) = 0.99995$ $P(X_3 = \text{present} \mid X_1 = \text{no}) = 0.00005$
$P(X_3 = \text{absent} \mid X_1 = \text{yes}) = 0.997$ $P(X_3 = \text{present} \mid X_1 = \text{yes}) = 0.003$

$P(X_4 = \text{absent} \mid X_2 = \text{absent}, X_3 = \text{absent}) = 0.95$ $P(X_4 = \text{present} \mid X_2 = \text{absent}, X_3 = \text{absent}) = 0.05$
$P(X_4 = \text{absent} \mid X_2 = \text{absent}, X_3 = \text{present}) = 0.50$ $P(X_4 = \text{present} \mid X_2 = \text{absent}, X_3 = \text{present}) = 0.50$
$P(X_4 = \text{absent} \mid X_2 = \text{present}, X_3 = \text{absent}) = 0.90$ $P(X_4 = \text{present} \mid X_2 = \text{present}, X_3 = \text{absent}) = 0.10$
$P(X_4 = \text{absent} \mid X_2 = \text{present}, X_3 = \text{present}) = 0.25$ $P(X_4 = \text{present} \mid X_2 = \text{present}, X_3 = \text{present}) = 0.75$

$P(X_5 = \text{absent} \mid X_3 = \text{absent}) = 0.98$ $P(X_5 = \text{present} \mid X_3 = \text{absent}) = 0.02$
$P(X_5 = \text{absent} \mid X_3 = \text{present}) = 0.40$ $P(X_5 = \text{present} \mid X_3 = \text{present}) = 0.60$

Table 1. The probabilities associated with figure 1.

These probabilities are for illustration only; they are not intended to accurately reflect frequencies of events in any actual patient population.

given by the Markov condition. For example, consider a two-node Bayesian network. The network structure $X \rightarrow Y$ is Markov equivalent to $X \leftarrow Y$, because both networks represent the same conditional independence relationships between X and Y (namely, none). Neither network is Markov equivalent to a structure with no arc between X and Y, which we will represent as X no_arc Y.

The Markov condition also permits the factorization of a joint probability distribution on model variables X_1, X_2, ... , X_n into the following product (Pearl 1988):

$$P(X_1, X_2, ..., X_n) = \prod_{i=1}^{n} P(X_i \mid parents(X_i)) \qquad (1)$$

where $parents(X_i)$ denotes the set of nodes with arcs into X_i. If X_i has no parents, then the set $parents(X_i)$ is empty, and therefore $P(X_i \mid parents(X_i))$ is just $P(X_i)$.

Consider the example given by figure 1. Equation 1 permits the derivation of a joint probability on the five model variables as follows:

$P(X_1, X_2, X_3, X_4, X_5)$
$= P(X_5 \mid X_3) P(X_4 \mid X_2, X_3) P(X_3 \mid X_1) P(X_2 \mid X_1) P(X_1)$

Thus, for example, $P(X_1 = \text{yes}, X_2 = \text{present}, X_3 = \text{present}, X_4 = \text{present}, X_5 = \text{present}) = 0.20 \times 0.25 \times 0.003 \times 0.75 \times 0.60 = 0.0000675$. The factorization entailed by a Bayesian network often allows a compact representation of the complete joint probability distribution. For instance, in the previous example, the exhaustively enumerated joint distribution requires 32 probabilities. In contrast, table 1 contains only 11 independent probabilities (the other 11 in table 1 can be derived from the axioms of probability theory). Often, unless a Bayesian network structure contains a high density of arcs, the amount of space savings is substantial.

Consider a node X in a Bayesian network. The *Markov blanket* of X is defined as the set of nodes consisting of the parents of X, the children of X, and the parents of the children of X. It follows from the Markov condition that if we condition on values of each node in the Markov blanket of X, then X is probabilistically independent of all other nodes in the network other than X and its Markov blanket.

1.2. The *d*-Separation Criterion

A graphical criterion called *d-separation* captures exactly all the conditional independence relationships that are implied by the Markov condition (Geiger, Verma, and Pearl 1996; Meek 1995; and Pearl 1988), which was defined in section 1.1. The following is a definition of *d*-separation (Pearl 1995):

> Let A, B, and C be disjoint subsets of the nodes in S. Let p be any acyclic path between a node in A and a node in B, where an acyclic path is any succession of arcs, regardless of their directions, such that no node along those arcs appears more than once. We say a node w has converging arrows along a path if two arcs on the path point to w. Subset C is said to block p if there is a node w on p satisfying one of the following two conditions: (1) w has converging arrows (along p) and neither w nor any of its descendants are in C, or (2) w does not have converging arrows (along p) and w is in C. Subset C is said to *d*-separate A from B in S if and only if C blocks every acyclic path from a node in A to a node in B.

If A and B are not *d*-separated given C, then we say they are *d-connected* given C. For example, in the Bayesian network structure in figure 1, X_2 and X_3 are *d*-separated given X_1, which implies that X_2 and X_3 are conditionally independent given X_1. If we do not condition on X_1, then X_2 and X_3 are not *d*-separated, because the path from X_2 to X_3 through X_1 is not blocked. As another example, X_4 is *d*-separated from X_1 by X_2 and X_3. As a final example, suppose we remove X_1 from figure 1 to create a new example network, then X_2 and X_3 would be *d*-separated, without any conditioning. Note, however, that once we condition on X_4, then X_2 and X_3 are not *d*-separated; in section 4.5.3 I provide a causal justification for such *d*-connectivity.

1.3. Probabilistic Inference Using a Bayesian Network

In this section, I discuss how a given Bayesian network can be used to derive the posterior probability distribution of one or more variables in the network given that we condition on the values *observed* for other variables in the network. Such inferences presume, of course, that the network has already been constructed, either manually or with the aid of automated learning methods, such as those I describe later in this chapter. While this section focuses on inferences given only observations, in section 2 I discuss how to derive a posterior probability distribution of a variable when we observe some of the variables and *manipulate* other variables.

Since a Bayesian network encodes a joint probability distribution, as given by equation 1, it contains all the information needed to compute any marginal or conditional probability on the nodes in the network. Using the sample network given by figure 1 and table 1, we can derive the following five probabilities (and many more):

$P(X_1 = yes \mid X_4 = present)$
$P(X_1 = yes \mid X_4 = absent$ and $X_5 = present)$
$P(X_4 = present$ and $X_5 = present \mid X_1 = no)$
$P(X_1 = yes$ and $X_4 = absent \mid X_2 = present$ and $X_5 = present)$
$P(X_2 = present$ and $X_3 = present)$

Let S and T be sets of variables with assigned values. For example, S might be $\{X_1 = yes\}$ and T might be $\{X_4 = present\}$. Suppose we wish to know $P(S \mid T)$. Conceptually, we can view inference as a simple procedure in which the marginals $P(S \cup T)$ and $P(T)$ are computed, and $P(S \cup T)/P(T)$ is returned. Consider deriving the marginal probability $P(T)$. Let U be the variables in the network that do not appear in set T. Using equation 1, we can sum over all U to obtain $P(T)$ as follows:

$$P(T) = \sum_U \prod_{i=1}^{n} P(X_i \mid parents(X_i)) \tag{2}$$

where the sum is taken over all unique combinations of value assignments to the variables in U, and in the product if X_i appears in T, then X_i is assigned the value given by T. For the example in which T is $\{X_4 = present\}$, the application of equation 2 yields:

$P(T) =$
$\quad P(X_1 = no) \, P(X_2 = absent \mid X_1 = no) \, P(X_3 = absent \mid X_1 = no)$
$\qquad P(X_4 = present \mid X_2 = absent, X_3 = absent) \, P(X_5 = absent \mid X_3$
$\qquad = absent)$
$\quad + P(X_1 = yes) \, P(X_2 = absent \mid X_1 = yes) \, P(X_3 = absent \mid X_1 = yes)$
$\qquad P(X_4 = present \mid X_2 = absent, X_3 = absent) \, P(X_5 = absent \mid X_3$
$\qquad = absent)$

$+ P(X_1 = no) \, P(X_2 = present \mid X_1 = no) \, P(X_3 = absent \mid X_1 = no)$
$\quad P(X_4 = present \mid X_2 = present, X_3 = absent) \, P(X_5 = absent \mid X_3$
$\quad = absent)$

$$\vdots$$

$+ P(X_1 = yes) \, P(X_2 = present \mid X_1 = yes) \, P(X_3 = present \mid X_1 = yes)$
$\quad P(X_4 = present \mid X_2 = present, X_3 = present)$
$\quad P(X_5 = present \mid X_3 = present)$

which by equation 1 is equal to

$\quad P(X_1 = no, X_2 = absent, X_3 = absent, X_4 = present, X_5 = absent)$
$+ P(X_1 = yes, X_2 = absent, X_3 = absent, X_4 = present, X_5 = absent)$
$+ P(X_1 = no, X_2 = present, X_3 = absent, X_4 = present, X_5 = absent)$

$$\vdots$$

$+ P(X_1 = yes, X_2 = present, X_3 = present, X_4 = present, X_5 = present)$

That is, we sum over every possible joint instantiation of the variables, while holding the variables in T constant to their assigned values. A serious practical problem with using equation 2 is that its time complexity is exponential in the number of variables in U. Thus, often this simple, brute-force inference algorithm is not computationally tractable. Researchers have developed general inference algorithms that can take advantage of independence relationships represented in a Bayesian network to often perform inference much more efficiently than equation 2 (Jensen 1996). Indeed, for some networks, inference can be performed in time that is polynomial in the number of nodes in the network. For example, if a network has only one path between any two nodes, then algorithms have been developed that perform inference in time that is linear in the size of the Bayesian network (Kim and Pearl 1983, Pearl 1988). Nonetheless, it has been shown that inference is NP-hard (Cooper 1990). Thus, we would not expect to find an inference algorithm that is efficient (i.e., polynomial-time in the size of the network) in the worst cases for all Bayesian networks. High computational complexity results from having multiple pathways between nodes in a network. For a network with multiple pathways, typically the number of pathways between nodes increases with the number of arcs, making exact inference more computationally expensive. When exact inference is prohibitively time consuming, stochastic approximation algorithms can be applied (Henrion 1990). These algorithms may yield useful estimates of exact inference results, although in the worst cases stochastic approximation algorithms are unlikely to yield usefully precise estimates (Dagum and Luby 1993).

2. An Operational Test of Causality

The usefulness of causal knowledge stems from its ability to predict how manipulation of the world will (or did) change the world. The immediate goals for acquiring causal knowledge include causal *explanation* of past manipulations and outcomes (e.g., legal liability often is based on the probable causes of an untoward effect), *insight* into the existence of causal mechanisms acting currently (e.g., the side effects caused by a newly introduced drug), and *prediction* of outcomes that will follow from manipulations (e.g., the cure rate of a disease when a particular surgery is performed). In this book, we emphasize insight and prediction.

This book does not attempt to develop a comprehensive, formal definition of causality. Intuitively, however, causal knowledge is knowledge that predicts how actions are likely to change the world. Operationally, for example, we might test for the existence of a causal relationship by using randomized controlled experiments (RCEs), where saying that X *causes* Y means that a hypothetically ideal RCE would conclude that there is some manipulation of X (possibly in concert with the manipulation of other variables; see section 4.3) that leads to a change in the probability distribution of values that Y will take on. Since no claim is being made that such a test can detect all causal relationships, the test is not being proposed here as a definition of causality.

The notion of a *manipulation* is closely related to the concept of an *act* in decision theory (Savage 1954). In most formulations, the application of normative decision theory requires a specification of the probabilities of possible effects of alternative causes. Heckerman and Shachter (1995) develop a formal connection between causality and decision theory.

In what follows, I informally describe a test for causality in terms of manipulations performed within RCEs. I first outline here a prototypical RCE; although variations certainly exist, they are not discussed. An RCE is performed with an explicitly defined population of units (e.g., patients with *chest pain*) in some explicitly defined context or set of contexts (e.g., currently receiving no chest-pain medication and residing in a given geographical area). Thus, causal relationships that are discovered are relative to a population of units and a context. In an RCE, for a given experimental unit, the value to set the cause in question, which I denote as X, is randomly selected using a uniform distribution over the possible values of X. The state of X is then manipulated to have the selected value. The RCE defines explicitly the details of how these manipulations are made (e.g., the quantity of chest-pain medication to take and the time course of taking the medication). For each unit, after the new value of X is set (e.g., either *receive chest-pain medication* or *receive no chest-pain medication*), the value of Y is measured at some designated time later (e.g., either *has chest pains* or *does not have chest*

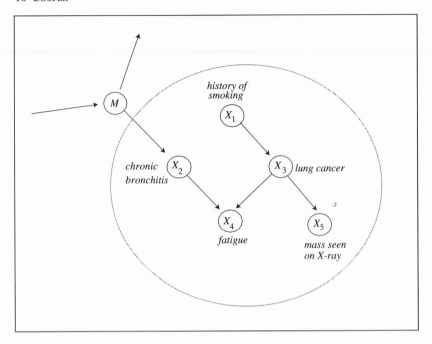

Figure 2. Chronic bronchitis is the variable being manipulated.

pains). The greater the experimental data support a statistical dependency between X and Y, the more the data support that X causally influences Y.

The population units under consideration may have properties, as represented by variable values, that are intrinsic to the meaning of those units. If such values of such a unit were changed as a result of manipulations, then the unit would no longer be in the population under study. For example, if we are interested in causal processes within an intact *e. coli* cell (the population units of interest), but a manipulation completely destroys the cell membrane of *e. coli* cells, then we could not use such a manipulation to study the causal processes of interest.

The notion of a manipulation deserves further description. A manipulation can be represented with a variable that is external to the system being modeled, such that the manipulation variable has an arc to the variable within the system that is being manipulated. We assume that such an external variable is not caused by or confounded with any variable in the modeled system. The marginal probability distribution over the values of the manipulation variable should be positive; that is, it should contain no probabilities of zero or one. With an RCE we can test experimentally that variable X (or variable set X) has a causal influence (on one or more other variables) if it is possible for a manipulation variable to influence (i.e., have an arc into) just X (or X), without influencing the state of the remaining modeled system variables. The manipulation variable has the same value set as the manipulated variable. The relationship between the two variables is deterministic, so that the manipulated variable always takes on the same value as the manipulation variable; this deterministic linkage ensures that the manipulated variable will not be influenced by any other variable within the modeled system. In essence, manipulation is a special type of causal relationship that we assume exists in order to define and discover more subtle causal relationships within some system of interest.

Figure 2 shows *chronic bronchitis* as the variable being manipulated. The variable named M denotes the manipulation variable, which is outside the encircled system of five modeled variables $X_1, X_2, \ldots, X_5$. Note that the manipulation of X_2 by M means that all other arcs into X_2 (i.e., the arc from X_1 in the example) are causally inconsequential and therefore are removed. The arcs into and out of the manipulation variable M indicate that variables outside the modeled system may causally influence and be influenced by M, as long as they are not causally related to the variables in the modeled system.

The manipulation theorem, which is stated and proved in Spirtes, Glymour, and Scheines (1993) (see also chapters 2 and 3), provides a simple graphical procedure for inferring the posterior probability distribution of variables under manipulation M given observations O. The procedure is as follows: We remove all the arcs into each manipulated variable and set the variable to the value given by the manipulation. We then perform regular Bayesian network inference, as outlined in section 1.3, conditioned on the observations given by O and the instantiated values of the manipulated variables. For example, for the causal network shown in figure 2, suppose we wish to infer the expected distribution of fatigue, given that an individual has a mass seen on X-ray and we cure him or her of any existing bronchitis. In this case, we set *chronic bronchitis* to the value absent and remove its arc from *history of smoking*. We set *mass seen on X-ray* to the value *yes*. We then apply regular Bayesian probabilistic inference methods (see section 1.3) to compute the posterior probability of *fatigue*.

While we can use RCEs to provide (at least conceptually) a test of causality, in practice even a limited RCE might not be safe, ethical, logistically feasible, financially worthwhile, or even theoretically possible, all of which are reasons for using observational data to attempt to infer causal relationships. Because (1) RCEs have limitations and (2) causal discovery from RCEs is well addressed in the literature (see, for example, Bulpitt 1996 and Friedman, Furberg, and DeMets 1996), this book focuses on learning causal relationships from observational data. The ability to use observational data for causal discovery significantly extends our analytical capabilities beyond using experimental data alone.

3. The Possibility of Causal Discovery
from Observational Data

Observational data is passively observed, as contrasted with experimental data in which one or more variables is manipulated (often randomly) and the effects on other variables are measured. Observational data is more readily available than experimental data. As observational databases become increasingly available, the opportunities for causal discovery increase.

Traditional statistical thinking says that "correlation does not imply causation." Observational data, however, can be informative regarding which causal relationships do or do not exist. Perhaps the simplest example of such a constraint is the inductive principle that if two variables X and Y are not correlated (or, more generally, are not statistically dependent according to some measure), then X does not cause Y, and Y does not cause X. While this principle can fail, it also can serve as a powerful guide in the search for causal relationships. The story, however, is much richer and more interesting than that simple principle. In particular, a key idea in this book is that among a set of variables, the statistical relationships that are obtained from observational data sometimes can strongly suggest likely causal relationships among a subset of those variables. For example, suppose that in fact X causes Y. By measuring just X and Y, we indeed cannot determine whether X causes Y. So, in that limited sense, correlation does not imply causation. If, however, there is a variable W that is known not to be caused by X or Y, then by examining the statistical independence and dependence relationships among W, X, and Y that are obtained from observational data, it sometimes is possible to infer that X very likely causes Y. Section 7 illustrates how. In some instances, even though we may not be able to induce that X causes Y, we may be able to determine, for example, that Y does not cause X, and thereby constrain the possible causal relationships between X and Y.

In order to show how it is possible to discover causal relationships from observational data, we first need a representation of causality. In the next section, I show how Bayesian networks provide such a representation, which I discuss in some detail.

4. Causal Bayesian Networks

A causal Bayesian network (or *causal network* for short) is a Bayesian network in which each arc is interpreted as a direct causal influence between a parent node and a child node, relative to the other nodes in the network. In this section, I discuss nodes, arcs, and their combination within causal networks.

4.1. The Entity Being Modeled

Assume that there is an entity about which we are representing causal relationships. That entity might be a single system or it might be a set of systems. An example of a single system is a manufacturing plant in which we are trying to detect causal relationships in order to improve productivity. An example of a set of entities (units) is a set of patients. There are many medical causal relationships that are of interest, including discovering preventable causes of serious disease. When we model the causal relationships of a set of entities, the component entities may or may not share all of the same causal relationships. The chapters in this book focus primarily on entities that share the same causal relationships. If the entities do not share a common set of causal relationships, then our model of those relationships should be a causal mixture model (see section 4.5.6).

4.2. Nodes

A node represents a variable that characterizes some aspect of the entity being modeled causally. The variable may contain continuous or discrete values. If it contains discrete values, then those values may be ordered or unordered.

The meaning of a node is given by its definition, which for simplicity we will assume is equal to its name; in general, the name is any unique label that identifies the definition. For example, *history of smoking* is the name of node X_1 in figure 1. If a name of a variable is not sufficiently precise, then it may not be possible to know the value to give the variable. Consider again *history of smoking*. This name does not indicate whether we mean smoking cigarettes, cigars, or other materials. The name also does not indicate the amount of smoking required for *history of smoking* to be given the value *yes,* or the time period over which such an amount of smoking must occur. A variable with a name that is insufficiently precise is said to fail the clarity test (Howard and Matheson 1984). But such failure or success is not absolute. Generally, we want all variables in a causal model to have names that pass the clarity test well enough for the purposes to which we plan to apply our model. For the example, the name/definition *patient has smoked one to two packs of cigarettes per day during the past 10 years of his or her lifetime, but did not smoke prior to that time* arguably passes the clarity test well enough for many clinical purposes, even though we have not precisely defined, for example, what we mean by a cigarette.

The value of a variable may represent any aspect of the modeled entity. A value may represent a state of the entity, a change in the state of the entity, or some sequence of changes. The value may or may not contain explicit temporal information. The value of any particular variable may be measured or missing. If the value of a variable will always be missing, then we say this is a *hidden* or *latent variable;* otherwise, we say it is a *measured variable.* We may have no description or identification of hidden variables in a network other than by their causal and probabilistic relations to observed variables.

4.3. Causal Arcs

Let X be a subset of the modeled variables. Suppose that there are two different manipulations of the variables in X, called *manipulate$_i$* and *manipulate$_j$,* such that $P(Y \mid manipulate_i(X)) \neq P(Y \mid manipulate_j(X))$. Now let X' be a subset of X such that $P(Y \mid manipulate_i(X')) \neq P(Y \mid manipulate_j(X'))$, and for every proper subset X'' of X' it is the case that either $X'' = \varnothing$ or $P(Y \mid manipulate_i(X'')) = P(Y \mid manipulate_j(X''))$.[2] Note that in general there may be more than one set X' that satisfies these relationships. We say that each variable X in X' *causally influences* Y and we place an arc from X to Y in the causal Bayesian network. In words, X is a necessary member of a set of variables whose manipulation is sufficient to change the distribution of Y. (Mackie [1974] contains a detailed discussion of causal sufficiency and necessity.) Note that this characterization of causal influence is relative to the set of modeled variables. The causal influence could be direct or it could be mediated through other measured model variables. Note also that the characterization of causality given here requires that we are able to manipulate just the variables in **X** and just the variables in each subset of **X,** without manipulating (disturbing) other variables. The probabilities used in this analysis may be interpreted from either a frequentist or a Bayesian perspective.

Suppose that there is some variable Z, such that X only causally influences Y through Z. We express this relationship in causal network notation as $X \rightarrow Z \rightarrow Y$. Here X is no longer a direct cause of Y in the network, but rather is an indirect cause. We say that Z is a direct (or immediate) effect of X, and Y is an indirect (nonlocal) effect of X. Similarly, we say that Z is a direct (or immediate) cause of Y and X is an indirect (nonlocal) cause of Y.

If X is a direct cause of Y (relative to a set of modeled variables), that does not mean there are no unmodeled hidden variables (representing hidden processes) that link X to Y. Indeed, there almost always will be. We are not required to represent such hidden variables in a causal graph, however, because their influence is captured by the probability distribution of Y given X. Similarly, if a hidden variable only influences one of the measured variables, as for instance variable Z, we need not represent the hidden variable explicitly, because its influence is represented by the conditional probability distribution of Z given its parents. Thus, a causal network provides a causal abstraction that typically represents certain types of hidden processes only implicitly. If, however, a hidden variable causally influences two or more measured variables, then in general it should be represented in a causal network.

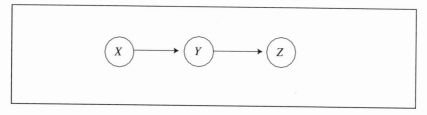

Figure 3. Causal network structure.

4.4. Causal Markov Condition

The causal Markov condition is the Markov condition described in section 1.1 in which arcs are given a causal interpretation. More formally, as adapted from Spirtes, Glymour, and Scheines (1993), the causal Markov condition is as follows:

> Let S be a causal Bayesian network with node set V. Let P be a probability distribution over the nodes in V. The Markov condition is satisfied if and only if for every node X in V it holds that, according to P, node X is independent of its noneffects (nondescendants) in S given its direct causes (parents) in S.

The intuition underlying the causal version of the Markov condition is as follows. Assume that the structure S of a causal network G is causally valid. A descendant Y of X in S is on a causal path from X. Thus, we would expect there to be the possibility of a probabilistic dependency between X and Y. Now, consider the nondescendants of X; that is, consider all entities represented by the variables in G that are not directly or indirectly caused by X. Let C represent a set of nodes, such that each node in C is a direct and/or indirect cause of one or more parents of X, which we denote as *parents*(X). Since *parents*(X) represents all of the direct causes of X, if we do not change the state of these parents, but rather hold just them fixed, we expect that X will be probabilistically independent of each node in C; thus, C will give us no information about the distribution of X. Furthermore, given values for *parents*(X), we expect that the direct and indirect effects of C (and so on) also are probabilistically independent of X, given just *parents*(X), unless such an effect happens also to be an effect of X.

The basic intuition underlying the causal Markov condition is that causality is local in time and space. The philosophy literature contains considerable discussion of this issue (Cartwright 1989; Reichenbach 1956; Salmon 1984; Suppes 1970). To illustrate the notion, we now describe two types of locality. According to the causal Markov condition, if we know the local measured causes of X, then nonlocal, indirect causes provide no additional information about the value of X. Consider the causal network in figure 3. Since Y is a local cause of Z, if Y is fixed to some value then changes in the value of X will

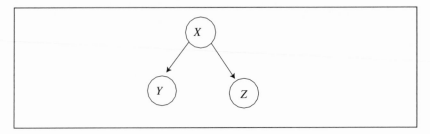

Figure 4. A causal network structure with divergent arcs.

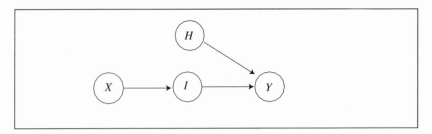

Figure 5. A causal relationship that is probabilistic due to a hidden variable (H).

not causally influence *Z*. Thus, proximal causes block or screen off more distal, indirect causes.

Consider next the causal network depicted in figure 4. According to the causal Markov condition, if the value of cause variable *X* is fixed, the value of effect variable *Y* provides no information about the value of effect variable *Z* and vice versa. More generally, if there is no directed causal path between two variables, then conditioning on just their common causal ancestors renders the two variables independent.

Causal relationships may be inherently probabilistic (see the end of this section) or probabilistic due to hidden variables. Regarding the latter, consider the causal network depicted in figure 5 in which *X*, *Y*, and *I* are measured variables, and *H* is a hidden variable. In this situation, *X* and *Y* are independent given *I*. Suppose *Y* is a deterministic function of *H* and *I*, and the probability distribution over *H* contains no probabilities of 0 or 1. Because of the causal influence of *H* on *Y*, the value of *Y* is not a deterministic function of the value of *I*; thus, if we are not modeling *H* explicitly (i.e., it is a hidden causal factor), then we use a probability function to specify a distribution over the values of *Y* given each value of *I*.

The causal independence relationships implied by the causal Markov condition should be interpreted relative to (1) the measured and unmeasured variables represented explicitly in the model, and (2) the values of those variables. I discuss both of these provisos next.

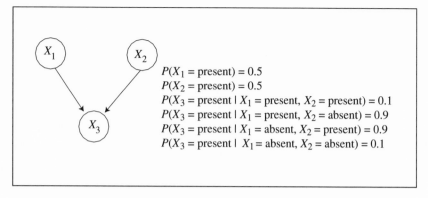

$P(X_1 = \text{present}) = 0.5$
$P(X_2 = \text{present}) = 0.5$
$P(X_3 = \text{present} \mid X_1 = \text{present}, X_2 = \text{present}) = 0.1$
$P(X_3 = \text{present} \mid X_1 = \text{present}, X_2 = \text{absent}) = 0.9$
$P(X_3 = \text{present} \mid X_1 = \text{absent}, X_2 = \text{present}) = 0.9$
$P(X_3 = \text{present} \mid X_1 = \text{absent}, X_2 = \text{absent}) = 0.1$

Figure 6. A causal network structure in which X_1 and X_2 taken together (but not alone) have a causal influence on X_3.

$P(X_1 = \text{present}) = 0.5$
$P(X_3 = \text{present}) = 0.5$

Figure 7. The causal network structure in figure 6, with X_2 marginalized out.

Figure 6 illustrates the first proviso. Suppose there is a causal process that can be represented by the figure. Given the joint probability distribution implied by the probabilities in figure 6, if we consider just variables X_1 and X_3 (i.e., by marginalizing out X_2), we obtain the causal network in figure 7.

As shown in figure 6, when taken together, both X_1 and X_2 causally influence X_3. Figure 7 shows that if we only consider the relationship between X_1 and X_3, then X_1 does not (by itself) have a causal influence on X_3. Consider an RCE that involves just the two variables X_1 and X_3. If we manipulate X_1 and measure X_3, the RCE will show no causal influence of X_1 on X_3. This simple example illustrates yet another way in which causality must be interpreted relative to the set of variables that are in the model. The absence of a statistical dependency between two variables does not mean they are causally unrelated to one another when unmeasured variables are considered.

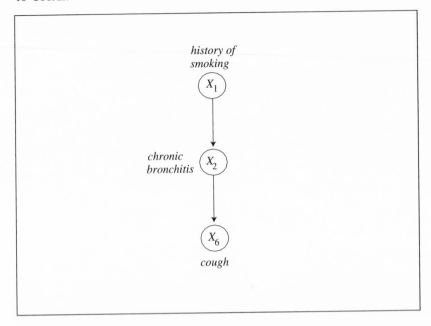

Figure 8. A simple three-node causal network structure.

Note that this example contains a special type of distribution that violates the faithfulness assumption discussed in section 6.1; for most distributions, marginalizing out X_2 would not lead to a situation in which X_1 has no causal influence on X_3. Still, the distribution of X_3 given X_1 may be significantly different when X_2 is in the model than when it is not. For example, there exist distributions for which X_1 having the value present, when considered alone, makes X_3 highly likely to have the value present; however, when a variable X_2 has the value present, then X_1 having the value present makes X_3 highly likely to have the value absent. *The general point, then, is that the causal relationships in a model should be interpreted relative to the variables in that model* (Aliferis and Cooper 1998).

The network structure depicted in figure 8 illustrates the second proviso previously mentioned, which involves the values of variables. Suppose that the three variables can take on a value from the following respective companion sets:

history of smoking: {none, moderate, severe}
chronic bronchitis: {absent, moderate, severe}
cough: {absent, present}

It could well be that given this value representation, then the Markov condition applied to the above network would imply the correct independence relationships: namely, the value of *cough* is independent of the value of *history*

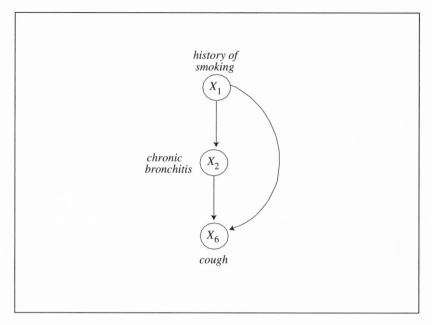

Figure 9. An example in which X_6 is not independent of X_1 given X_2 because the possible values of X_2 are too coarse to sustain that independence.

of smoking, given that we know the value of *chronic bronchitis.*

Consider, however, the following representation of the values, which for chronic bronchitis are coarser than before:

history of smoking: {none, moderate, severe}
chronic bronchitis: {absent, present}
cough: {absent, present}

Suppose we condition on *chronic bronchitis* having the value present. It may be the case that a severe degree of smoking suggests (with high likelihood) a severe degree of *chronic bronchitis,* which in turn suggests a high likelihood of a *cough* being present. Similarly, a moderate degree of *smoking* suggests a moderate degree of *chronic bronchitis,* which suggests an intermediate likelihood of a *cough.* In this situation, *cough* is not independent of *history of smoking,* given that all we know is that *chronic bronchitis* has the value present; the causal network in figure 9 expresses the independence relationships that exist (namely, none) given the coarser variable-value representation being used for *chronic bronchitis.*

Is the arc from *history of smoking* to *cough* causal in figure 9? In a sense, yes. If we maintain (i.e., fix) *chronic bronchitis* to the value present and we manipulate *history of smoking* between values of none, moderate, and severe, then we would expect (given this story) that the likelihood of *cough* will vary

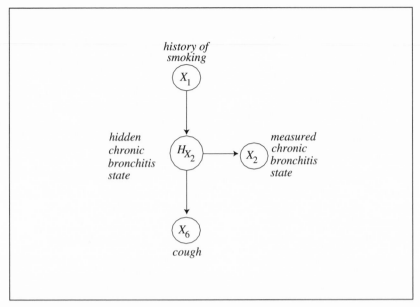

Figure 10. An alternative representation of the
causal network structure shown in figure 9.

with the value of *history of smoking*. The reason is that even though we maintain *chronic bronchitis* to just the value present, it can (and probably will) still vary between being moderate and severe. That is, in maintaining *chronic bronchitis* to be present, we only ensure that the value present holds, we do not ensure that any more specific value of the variable holds or does not hold.

Figure 9 illustrates only one specific situation in which the values of network variables are important; there are other more complex situations. The general point, however, is that there is no fixed, directed acyclic graph structure for which the causal Markov condition will be valid, if we allow the value sets of the variables to vary. In other words, the interpretation of the arcs in a causal network is relative to the sets of values associated with the nodes in the network. Thus, those sets of values should in essence be considered a part of the causal network structure. When we "read" causal relationships from the directed acyclic graph, our interpretation of the arcs in that graph should be relative to the value representation of the nodes in the graph.

An alternative representation of the causal network in figure 9 is shown in figure 10, where H_{X_2} has the value set {absent, moderate, severe} and X_2 has the value set {absent, present}. Variable X_2 is a deterministic function of H_{X_2}, but not vice versa. The basic idea underlying the representation in figure 10 is that measured variables can be abstractions of unmeasured variables (Aliferis and Cooper 1998). According to the causal Markov condition, conditioning on X_2 does not render X_1 and X_6 independent.

I close this section with a brief discussion of one additional issue regarding the causal Markov condition. Current quantum theory and experimental data provide support for the notion that at the quantum level, causality is not temporally and spatially local (Herbert 1985). Thus, at that level, there may be no local variables that render a variable X independent of other variables. Such a situation would not imply that the Markov condition is violated, but rather that quantum events are less independent than we intuitively expect them to be. The utility of the Markov condition might thereby be diminished in the discovery of causal relationships at the quantum level. I note also that quantum events can be coupled tightly to macroscopic events (Herbert 1985; Zurek 1991); thus, it may be that the Markov condition would hold for macroscopic systems less often than we intuitively expect. Nonetheless, our common experience suggests that local conditioning as given by the causal Markov condition often does hold in the macroscopic world, at least approximately. The methods described in this book employ the causal Markov condition as a reasonable working assumption. It is an open problem to investigate the frequency with which we expect the condition to hold in the macroscopic world and yet it does not.

4.5. Causal Relationships

This section introduces several important concepts regarding causal relationships, including temporal representation, transitivity, multivariate causes, confounding, selection bias, and compound relationships.

4.5.1. Temporal Representation

Often the temporal relationship between a cause and an effect is left implicit in a causal network. Consider the nodes *history of smoking* and *chronic bronchitis* in figure 8. For simplicity, assume that we are using the causal network to predict *chronic bronchitis* given a *history of smoking*. Suppose that $P(chronic\ bronchitis = \text{present} \mid history\ of\ smoking = \text{severe}) = 0.3$. What does this probability mean exactly?

We view *history of smoking* as taking on the value severe some time in the past. But when in the past? And what was the value of *history of smoking* from which we manipulated it to the value severe? These details are unspecified here. A problem may arise if *history of smoking* has a modeled cause C. In that case, the value of C may change the distribution over the possible ways that *history of smoking* takes on the value severe. Thus, depending on the value of C, we may have a different distribution for *chronic bronchitis* conditioned on *history of smoking*. The problem is one of an insufficient representation of the values of *history of smoking*. It is the same type of phenomenon that I discussed in association with figures 9 and 10, except specialized here to be the temporal dimension of the value set. A solution is to represent the temporal dimension of the values of *history of smoking* in finer detail, so that conditioning on *history of smoking* makes *chronic bronchitis* independent of ancestors of *history of smoking*.

Researchers have begun to develop temporal Bayesian networks that permit detailed explicit modeling of temporal causal relationships among variables (Aliferis 1998; Aliferis and Cooper 1995; Aliferis and Cooper 1998; Berzuini, Bellazi, Quaglini, and Spieglehalter 1992; Dagum and Galper 1993; Provan and Clarke 1993). These representations provide the basis for future learning algorithms that can induce detailed causal temporal patterns from data.

4.5.2. Transitivity

Causality is not necessarily transitive. Although X may cause I and I may cause Y, it could be that X does not cause Y. Violations of transitivity require special probability distributions in order to exhibit nontransitivity. Consider the following example for which X is a binary variable that takes the values x_1 and x_2, Y is a binary variable that takes the values y_1 and y_2, and variable I can take on any one of the values i_1, i_2, i_3, or i_4.

$$P(X = x_1) = 3/4$$
$$P(I = i_1 \mid X = x_1) = 2/9 \quad P(I = i_1 \mid X = x_2) = 2/9$$
$$P(I = i_2 \mid X = x_1) = 4/9 \quad P(I = i_2 \mid X = x_2) = 1/9$$
$$P(I = i_3 \mid X = x_1) = 1/9 \quad P(I = i_3 \mid X = x_2) = 4/9$$
$$P(I = i_4 \mid X = x_1) = 2/9 \quad P(I = i_4 \mid X = x_2) = 2/9$$
$$P(Y = y_1 \mid I = i_1) = 2/3$$
$$P(Y = y_1 \mid I = i_2) = 1/2$$
$$P(Y = y_1 \mid I = i_3) = 1/2$$
$$P(Y = y_1 \mid I = i_4) = 1/3$$

In the distribution defined by this causal Bayesian network, X and I are dependent, and I and Y are dependent, yet X and Y are independent because $P(Y = y_1 \mid X = x_1) = P(Y = y_1 \mid X = x_2) = 1/2$.

4.5.3. Multivariate Causes and Explaining Away

When a node X has more than one parent node, those parent nodes often have a characteristic pattern of being dependent conditioned on X. To illustrate, consider the causal network in figure 11, in which we assume X_2 and X_3 are marginally independent and are both causes of X_4. While X_2 and X_3 are marginally independent when we do not condition on X_4, they often are dependent when we condition on X_4. Since *chronic bronchitis* and *lung cancer* are causally independent (as assumed here), it is appropriate that they are marginally independent. Consider conditioning on *fatigue*. If *fatigue* is present, then the presence of *chronic bronchitis* and *lung cancer* each become

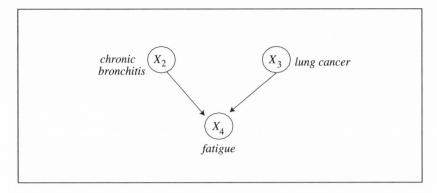

Figure 11. The structure of a causal network that illustrates explaining away.

more likely. This likelihood of *lung cancer* will decrease, however, if we learn that *chronic bronchitis* is present, because *chronic bronchitis* provides an explanation for the *fatigue* (i.e., chronic bronchitis "explains away" fatigue). Thus, conditioned on *fatigue,* the events *chronic bronchitis* and *lung cancer* are not probabilistically independent.

The appearance of "explaining away" is one example of how parent nodes can be dependent given that we condition on the child node (Wellman and Henrion 1993). Other types of conditional dependency can exist. Although in causal Bayesian networks there is not a requirement that parents be dependent conditioned on some value of their child, often they are (Pearl 1988); for example, in linear models and in noisy-or-gate models, they must be.

4.5.4. Confounding

If two variables are probabilistically dependent due (at least in part) to one or more shared causes (either direct or indirect), then the two variables are said to be confounded and their common causes are called the *confounders*. The confounders can be either measured or unmeasured variables. The causal network structure in figure 12, which is taken from figure 1, shows *history of smoking* as a confounder of *chronic bronchitis* and *lung cancer.*

Confounding is important, because when two variables X and Y are statistically dependent, often the most likely possibilities are that (1) one variable causally influences the other, (2) the two variables are confounded, or (3) both 1 and 2 hold. If the confounders are measured, we can condition on them and remove the statistical dependency between X and Y that is due to confounding. If the confounders are not measured, then we need other methods for detecting or eliminating them.

An RCE is one way to eliminate a confounder. For example, if we manipulate *chronic bronchitis,* then we break the arc from *history of smoking* into *chronic bronchitis,* because our manipulation means that *history of smoking*

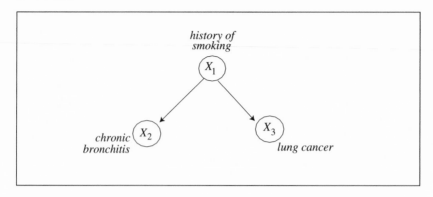

Figure 12. History of smoking is the confounder of chronic bronchitis and lung cancer.

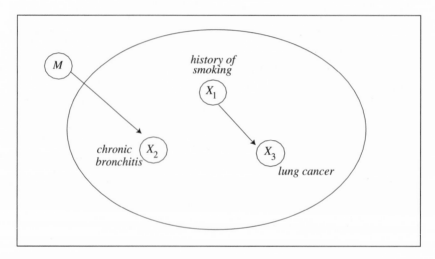

Figure 13. An RCE is one way to eliminate a confounder.

no longer has a causal influence on *chronic bronchitis*. Thus, we would obtain the causal network shown in figure 13. Data generated by a process that
is represented by figure 13 is expected to support *chronic bronchitis* as being
independent of *lung cancer,* which would support that *chronic bronchitis* is
not a cause of *lung cancer.*

Section 7 contains a discussion of assumptions under which observational
data is sufficient to determine that two variables are statistically dependent due
to confounding.

4.5.5. Selection Bias

If V' denotes an arbitrary instantiation of all the variables in $V,$ then we want

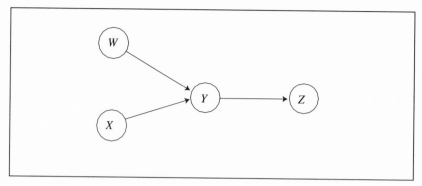

*Figure 14. Units may share this causal network structure
but differ in the distribution of Z given Y.*

that V' is sampled for inclusion in D with probability $Pr(V'\mid G)$, where G is the causal Bayesian network to be discovered, which represents the data generating causal process. If selection bias exists, then V' is sampled with a probability other than $Pr(V'\mid G)$.

Suppose that an individual with only a fever (X) is likely to stay home and take aspirin. Similarly, a person with only abdominal pain (Y) is likely to stay home and take an over-the-counter medication for relief. Suppose, however, that an individual with both fever and abdominal pain is likely to be concerned about the possibility of a serious illness, and therefore, is prone to go to his or her local emergency room, where we have been collecting our data. In this situation, X and Y may be dependent, due to selection bias, even though X does not causally influence Y, Y does not causally influence X, and X and Y have no common confounder. Such bias can persist, regardless of how large the sample size. Selection bias can be avoided in RCEs by measuring the outcomes that follow in time for each unit in the experiment (e.g., the outcomes for each patient in a clinical trial). The presence or absence of selection bias sometimes can be inferred from observational data (Cooper 1995b). Chapter 6 provides a detailed handling of selection bias when using constraint-based methods for causal discovery from observational data.

4.5.6. Causal Mixtures

Recall that in section 4.1 I stated that usually the units under study are assumed to share a common set of causal relationships, both in terms of causal structure and the parameterization of that structure. It could be, however, that the members of a given population of units do not all share the same causal relationships. For example, all units may share the same causal network structure (figure 14), but one subpopulation of units may have a different distribution between Y and Z than does the remaining subpopulation.

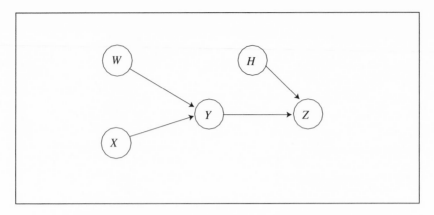

Figure 15. A hidden variable H can represent a mixture of subpopulations
that differ according to the parameterization of Z given its cause Y.

We can represent such a mixture by using a hidden binary variable H, which is included in the causal network structure shown in figure 15. More generally, hidden variables seem adequate to represent mixtures that involve just the parameters relative to a common structure (rather than mixtures of causal network structures).

The structure depicted in figure 15 represents at least two possible situations. In one, which I just discussed, there is a mixture of units represented by H, with each subpopulation having a common distribution (possibly deterministic) of Z given Y. In the other situation, all the population units are homogeneous and each unit has the same distribution of Z given Y; the variable H serves only to represent the inherent uncertainty expressed by that distribution.

In an extreme case, one subset of the population might have the causal network structure shown in figure 16a, and the remaining subset might have the network shown in figure 16b. Causal structure includes both the arcs among nodes and the value range of each node. In general, admitting mixtures weakens our ability to learn causal relationships from observational data. The discovery of mixtures of causal structures is a challenging, largely open problem.

One approach to admitting mixtures is to have a graphical language that expresses them as members of an equivalence class of causal networks that are statistically indistinguishable. Another approach would be to search over subsets of the cases to locate for each subset a causal network (or set of networks) that is most likely given the subset. A Bayesian version of this approach would require specifying a prior probability over the various ways of forming subsets of the cases in the database. This approach makes possible

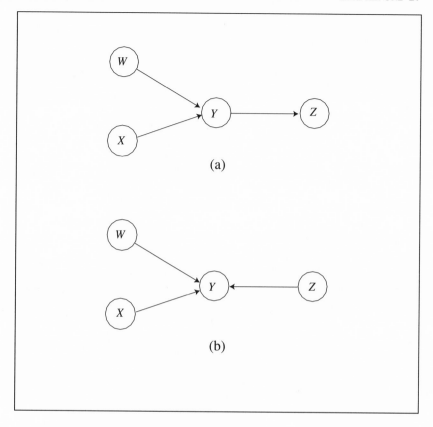

Figure 16 a and b. The causal network structures for two subpopulations.

the scoring of causal relationships for subsets of the population; from such analyses we could derive the posterior probabilities of causal relationships for the population as a whole. A challenge in applying this Bayesian approach is to find ways to make it computationally tractable.

4.5.7. Compound Relationships

The statistical dependency between two measured variables X and Y may be due to a complex combination of the following mechanisms: (1) direct causality, (2) indirect causality, (3) confounding, and (4) selection bias. The Bayesian network structure in figure 17 illustrates one such possibility, which involves all four mechanisms. The shaded node S represents a special instantiated variable that indicates selection of a unit for observation based on the values of the parents of S, namely X and Y in the current example. There are of course many other combinations of the four mechanisms. For

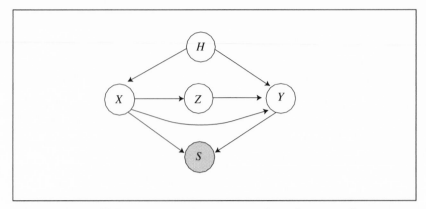

Figure 17. Bayesian network structure involving direct causality, indirect causality, confounding, and selection bias.

example, suppose we limit consideration to just the five nodes in the figure 17 network. Consider every directed acyclic graph on those nodes for which X and Y are d-connected (conditioned on no other variables). Each such graph represents a set of mechanisms which can render X and Y statistically dependent.

5. Causal Discovery

Up to this point, I have described the causal Bayesian network as a representation of causal relationships, and I have discussed some of its properties. In the remainder of this chapter, I discuss two approaches for discovering causal Bayesian networks from observational data. One approach, which is described in sections 6 and 7, uses tests of conditional independence and dependence among subsets of model variables to constrain the causal relationships among the model variables. Another approach, which is described in section 8, computes the probability that causal relationships exist among the variables. Section 9 introduces several basic search algorithms that have been used with these two fundamental approaches to causal discovery. These sections are not intended to provide a comprehensive overview of research on causal discovery methods (see, for example, Angrist, Imbens, and Rubin 1996; Balke and Pearl 1994; Bollen 1989; Bowden and Turkington 1984; Heise 1975; Manski 1995; Meyer 1995; Pearl 1996; Pratt and Schlaifer 1988; Robins 1986, 1989; Rubin 1974; Simon 1953; and Wright 1921 for samples of relevant prior work), but rather to introduce basic concepts for the graphical causal discovery methods that are emphasized in this book.

An assumption that typically is made with the causal discovery approaches described in this book is that the samples (i.e., cases, records, instances, etc.) in the observational database are *independently sampled* and *identically distributed*. Independent sampling means that given a causal Bayesian network model, the probability of one sample is independent of any other samples that have been obtained. In theory, a lack of independence among cases could be modeled using hidden variables (see Spirtes, Glymour, and Scheines 1993, section 9.4), but this makes learning causal relationships more difficult and is seldom done. Samples are identically distributed if the probability of seeing a given case at one point in time is the same as seeing that case at another point in time; that is, the joint probability distribution defined by the causal Bayesian network is time invariant. The assumption of identically distributed cases can be relaxed by using temporal causal Bayesian networks that explicitly allow the representation of changes in distributions over time. While progress is being made on the representation of temporal Bayesian networks (see section 4.5.1), relatively little research has been done yet in learning such representations from time series data.

If a set of causal structures can equally account for the same observational data, then no observational data can distinguish among them. This fundamental concept is a type of *statistical indistinguishability*. If no members of a set of causal structures are statistically indistinguishable, then they are called *statistically distinguishable,* or equivalently, *statistically identifiable*. Different types of statistical indistinguishability are established based on different meanings of the phrase "can equally account for" in the preceding sentence. Returning to a previous simple example, consider the causal networks $X \rightarrow Y$ and $X \leftarrow Y$. If we do not restrict the distributions considered, then both networks can represent any joint probability distribution on the two variables, and thus, they each can equally well account for the same observational data. Therefore, we would say that the two networks are statistically indistinguishable given only observational data. By contrast, the causal network X no_arc Y is in general statistically distinguishable from $X \rightarrow Y$, because with observational data X and Y will be statistically independent in the former network, whereas in the latter network they will not. For a more detailed discussion of statistical distinguishability in causal discovery, see chapter 4 of Spirtes, Glymour, and Scheines (1993). A key theme underlying the topics in this book is that there are interesting classes of causal networks that under assumptions are statistically distinguishable, based on observational data. Section 6 introduces one such set of assumptions. Section 10 provides some support for these assumptions, although further evaluation is an important open problem.

6. Assumptions for
Constraint-Based Causal Discovery

In this section I discuss the assumptions typically made in constraint-based methods for discovering causal knowledge from observational data. Almost always the methods assume that the causal processes generating the data can be modeled as a Bayesian network; in this chapter, for brevity, I sometimes state that the Bayesian network itself generated the data. Since, as described in section 1.1, the Markov condition is inherent in the Bayesian network representation, the discovery methods assume the causal Markov condition. Recently, researchers have begun to extend the Bayesian network representation of causal relationships; one extension is the representation of causal feedback cycles with directed *cyclic* graphs (see chapter 7).

Constraint-based causal discovery involves a two-step procedure in which (1) statistical tests are used to establish conditional dependence and independence relationships among the variables in a model, and (2) those relationships are used to constrain the types of causal relationships that exist among the model variables.

The remainder of section 6 summarizes and illustrates typical assumptions that have been used in applying constraint-based causal discovery methods. Chapters 2, 3, 5, and 6 describe these assumptions and their use in additional detail. Chapters 8, 9, 10, and 11 contain arguments for and against some of these assumptions holding for causal discovery in the real world.

6.1. Causal Faithfulness Assumption

Let G be a causal Bayesian network, V be the nodes in G, S be the network structure of G, and P be the joint probability distribution generated by G. The *causal faithfulness assumption* is as follows:

> For all disjoint sets A, B, and C in V, if in S we have that A is not d-separated from B given C, then in P we have that A and B are conditionally dependent given C, where A and B are not empty but C may be.

The causal faithfulness assumption says that the only way variables will be probabilistically independent is if their independence is due to the Markov condition, or equivalently, to the d-separation condition. In other words, if variables are d-connected (i.e., not d-separated) in G then they are dependent in P. Thus, the network structure S reveals all the independence relationships among all the variables in V relative to the underlying distribution P. Note that P must be estimated from data D; we generally do not know P exactly.

For example, in the network in figure 1, consider just nodes X_1 and X_2, which are d-connected by the arc between them. The faithfulness assumption would be violated if the probabilities given in figure 1 were changed so that X_1 and X_2 are marginally independent, but the arc from X_1 to X_2 remained. In the actual joint probability distribution that follows from the probabilities given in figure 1, the faithfulness assumption is not violated.

The Markov condition relates causal structure to probabilistic independence and the faithfulness assumption relates causal structure to probabilistic dependence. Together, they provide a highly informative mapping between the independence and dependence relationships of model variables as given by the their probability distribution and the d-separation/d-connection relationships of the corresponding nodes in a Bayesian network structure. Thus, we can use statistically inferred independence and dependence relationships (see section 7) to constrain the structure of the Bayesian network that is generating the data.

The following result regarding the faithfulness assumption has been proved for discrete (Meek 1995b) and for multivariate Gaussian (Spirtes, Glymour, and Scheines 1993) Bayesian networks. Consider any *smooth* distribution[3] Q over the possible parameters in a Bayesian network. The parameters are just the probabilities represented in the network. Now consider drawing a particular set of parameters from distribution Q. The results in Meek (1995b) and Spirtes, Glymour, and Scheines (1993) show that the probability of drawing a distribution that is not faithful is Lebesgue measure zero. These results do not mean that drawing such a distribution is impossible, but rather, under the assumption of a smooth distribution, such an outcome is exceedingly unlikely.

Most current constraint-based causal discovery methods, including those described in this book, are based on the faithfulness assumption. Alternative assumptions, such as the minimality assumption, also have been considered (Yao and Tritchler 1996; Spirtes, Glymour, and Scheines 1993). These alternative approaches are not, however, discussed further in this chapter.

While the faithfulness assumption is plausible in many circumstances, there are circumstances in which it is invalid. In the remainder of this section I outline some basic reasons that the faithfulness assumption can fail.

Deterministic relationships can interfere with causal discovery from observational data. Consider the following causal Bayesian network structure

$$X \rightarrow Y \rightarrow Z$$

for which all three variables are binary and

$P(X = \text{yes}) = p,$
$P(Y = \text{yes} \mid X = \text{yes}) = q,$
$P(Y = \text{no} \mid X = \text{no}) = q,$
$P(Z = \text{yes} \mid Y = \text{yes}) = q,$ and
$P(Z = \text{no} \mid Y = \text{no}) = q.$

For the moment, assume $p = 1$ and $q = 1$. Thus, the three variables are deterministically related, and indeed, they always have the same value *yes*. Since there is no variation in the values of variables, we cannot determine from observational data what would happen if variation (in the form of manipulation) were to take place.

Consider next that $p = 0.5$ and again $q = 1$. The Markov condition applied to the network structure of the example does not imply (through d-separation) that X is independent of Y given Z, and thus, by the faithfulness assumption such independence should not hold. But, for the distribution defined, X is independent of Y given Z. Knowing the value of Z tells us the value of X exactly, and therefore, conditioning on Y makes no difference. In the example, the faithfulness assumption is valid for any value of q that is not equal to 0, 0.5, or 1. Practically, however, as q gets close to 0, 0.5, or 1, the usefulness of the assumption being technically valid begins to decrease, because with finite data samples the variables will appear to be deterministically related (for $q = 0$ or $q = 1$) or independent (for $q = 0.5$), and thus the faithfulness assumption will appear to be violated.

Violation of the faithfulness assumption does not, however, require the presence of deterministic relationships, as shown previously by the example given in figures 6 and 7. Here each of X_1 and X_2 considered alone is marginally independent of X_3. When X_1 and X_2 are taken together, however, there is a dependency between them and X_3. Other nondeterministic distributions that violate the faithfulness assumption are described in Spirtes, Glymour, and Scheines (1993), including distributions based on special cases of Simpson's paradox, which I briefly describe next.

Qualitatively, Simpson's original example (Simpson 1951) is as follows. Consider a population of people. Among males in the population there is a positive statistical association between receiving a particular treatment and surviving. Similarly, among females there is a positive statistical association between receiving a particular treatment and surviving. However, when considering the population as a whole (both males and females), there is no statistical association between the treatment and survival. Suppose, in reality, that treatment causally influences survival and that gender confounds treatment and survival. Then, the example distribution violates the faithfulness condition, relative to a Bayesian causal network that represents the causal reality. Two additional points are worth noting here. First, not surprisingly, very special distributions are required to exhibit Simpson's paradox. Second, in the example just given, the statistical associations among the variables representing *gender, treatment,* and *survival* are based on observational data. The example does not indicate that the paradox would persist under manipulation in an RCE, and indeed, it would not.

Goal-oriented systems, both animate and inanimate, provide another general class of situations in which violations of the faithfulness conditions may tend to occur. Consider a generic clinical situation that is modeled in figure 18. As-

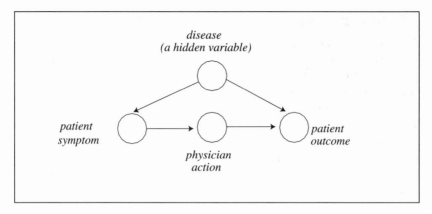

Figure 18. Model of a general clinical situation.

sume that the patient outcome is *near-term mortality*. A disease causes a patient symptom, which the physician observes and which influences the physician's action to obtain a cure. Suppose that if the disease is severe enough to cause a patient's death, then the symptom appears and the physician initiates a treatment action. Assume further that the treatment always prevents near-term mortality. Based on information about their patients, physicians take actions that maintain patient outcomes to be the preferred state of surviving. This physician goal-oriented behavior leads to near-term survival of all patients; thus, the physician action variable and the patient outcome variable will be independent, which violates the faithfulness assumption. This example does contain probabilities of one and zero. More significantly, however, is that the example illustrates a system (here a physician) whose goal (implicitly) is to violate distributions that would follow from the faithfulness assumption. Although the goal may not be completely achieved in practice, the induced distribution may be close enough to being unfaithful that it makes causal discovery difficult; this point is supported by an experiment described in chapter 15 that involves the photosynthetic rate and internal CO_2 concentration in plant leaves. The faithfulness assumption would more plausibly hold for systems (or subsystems) that are not goal-oriented.

In the context of all possible distributions on a set of variables, there are relatively few unfaithful distributions. Thus, a violation of the faithfulness assumption is not likely unless we have reason to believe that such special distributions are present (Meek 1995b; Spirtes, Glymour, and Scheines 1993). This section has described several cases in which the likelihood of occurrence of such special distributions is heightened. The existence of such unfaithful distributions can lead to errors by causal discovery methods that assume faithfulness.

6.2. The Assumption of Valid Statistical Testing

In attempting to discover causal relationships from observational data, we do not have a probability distribution for the underlying causal process that is generating the data, we just have the data. Thus, we need some way of linking inference of independence and dependence relationships from data to the underlying probability distribution on which the Markov condition and faithfulness assumption are based. The following assumption regarding valid statistical testing does just that:

> Consider the sets of variables A, B, and C in V. If in the underlying distribution P we have that A and B are conditionally dependent given C, then A and B are conditionally dependent given C according to test T applied to the data in D. Similarly, if in P we have that A and B are conditionally independent given C, then A and B are conditionally independent given C according to test T applied to the data in D.

We are assuming that test T can be used to uncover the probabilistic dependence and independence relationships among the measured variables, as given by P. Note that T implicitly includes the value of any statistical significance threshold (e.g., an alpha level) that is required in applying the test.

The smaller the number of cases in D, the more skeptical we should be of whether statistical testing is valid. When using classical statistical tests of independence, such as the chi-square test, it is not clear, even for a large database, precisely which value to use as a statistical threshold. The Bayesian causal discovery methods (see section 8) avoid categorical tests of independence and dependence, and instead use a continuous measure for scoring networks that inherently encodes the uncertainty of small data samples. Closely related methods, based on using minimum description length scores or entropic measures, also avoid categorical tests (Bouckaert 1995, Herskovits and Cooper 1991, Lam and Bacchus 1994, Wedelin 1993).

As mentioned in section 6.1, there is an interplay between the faithfulness assumption and the assumption of valid statistical testing. As distributions approach being unfaithful, we require more data in order for statistical tests to reliably detect dependence among network variables. Chapters 8–11 provide further discussion of this issue.

6.3. Missing Data

Constraint-based causal discovery programs may make one of several assumptions about how to handle missing data. I discuss several possible approaches in this section.

Consider a database D that contains records (e.g., patient cases). Often there is missing data in D; that is, each variable is not measured for each record. One approach to dealing with missing data is to remove all records from D in which any of these variables has a missing value. The problem with this approach is two-fold. First, we may end up with a very small database (possibly even zero records) for learning. Second, the data may not be missing randomly, in which case the distribution among the complete records may not accurately reflect the distribution in the unselected population of interest. Although sometimes we may be able to detect such selection bias, it can interfere with uncovering causal relationships that exist.

Another solution to the problem of missing data is to assign the value *missing* to a variable in a record for which that variable was not measured. This approach may, however, lead to the loss of independence relationships that otherwise would hold were all the data measured. Consider the causal network structure $X \rightarrow Y \rightarrow Z$ as a valid representation of the causal relationships among the three variables when each is measured. Conditioned on Y having the explicit value *missing,* the value of X may provide some information about the value of Z, and thus, X and Z may test as being dependent conditioned on Y.

A third solution to the problem is to *fill in* each missing value of each variable with some admissible value for the variable. There are numerous methods for assigning missing values (Little and Rubin 1987). Hopefully, of course, the substituted values correspond closely to the actual, underlying values, but in general there is no guarantee that this will be the case.

6.4. Types of Variables and Distributions

In principle, constraint-based discovery methods apply when there are continuous variables, or even a mixture of continuous and discrete variables, as long as there are reliable statistical tests of independence and dependence. Numerous statistical tests of independence exist for discrete variables. For multivariate Gaussian Bayesian networks, tests also exist (Spirtes, Glymour, and Scheines 1993). Developing statistical tests that apply to a wide variety of distributions on continuous variables (or mixed continuous and discrete variables) is an open problem.

7. Constraint-based Methods for Evaluating Causal Bayesian Networks

In this section I first provide a simple illustration of the constraint-based causal discovery method. Then I briefly discuss two representative algorithms for constraint-based causal discovery.

Figure 19 extends figure 1 by adding a causal arc from a node representing

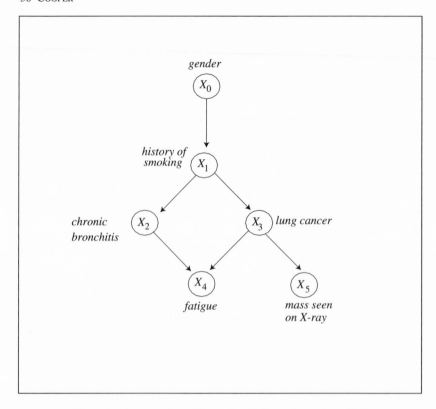

Figure 19. An extension of figure 1 with the node gender added.

gender (X_0) to a node representing *history of smoking* (X_1). Does smoking cause lung cancer? For the purpose of this simple example, suppose we know, or are willing to assume, that gender causally influences whether an individual smokes. Consider the four causal Bayesian networks in table 2 as representing among the three variables the set of causal relationships that we believe are tenable. Suppose that smoking actually does cause lung cancer. Given the assumptions in section 6, we can infer the *d*-separation conditions in row 2 of table 2, which are unique relative to the *d*-separation conditions of the other three possible causal hypotheses being considered. Thus, under the assumptions made, we can conclude that *history of smoking* is causally influencing whether a patient gets *lung cancer*. We can quantify that causal relationship by using the data to estimate *P(lung cancer | history of smoking)*. In general, if we know that the set of variables in *T* causes variable *Y* without confounding or selection bias, then we are warranted in equating *P(Y | ma-nipulate(T))* with *P(Y | T)*, which we can estimate from available observational data.

Row no.	Structure of a causal network C	d-separation conditions as inferred by statistical tests	
		$DS(X_0, X_3)$	$DS(X_0, X_3 \mid X_1)$
1	$X_0 \longrightarrow X_1 \qquad X_3$	+	+
2	$X_0 \longrightarrow X_1 \longrightarrow X_3$		+
3	$X_0 \longrightarrow X_1 \longleftarrow X_3$	+	
4	H with arrows to X_1 and X_3; $X_0 \longrightarrow X_1 \quad X_3$	+	

Table 2. The four causal Bayesian networks being hypothesized in the example as representing the causal relationships among the three variables shown. DS(A, B) means that variables A and B are d-separated unconditionally. DS(A, B | C) means A and B are d-separated given variable C.

If alternatively, lung cancer causes smoking (row 3 of table 2) or there is a hidden cause of both lung cancer and smoking (row 4), then we could detect (from the d-separation patterns in of table 2) that smoking is not causing lung cancer.

Table 2 illustrates the fundamental idea underlying how constraint-based methods can discover causal knowledge from observational data, although the example is simple and limited in scope. A modest generalization of that procedure is described by Cooper (1997), where it is assumed that we have a variable like X_0 in table 2 that (among other properties) is not caused by any other measured variable; such a privileged variable has been termed an *instrumental variable* (Bowden and Turkington 1984). A major generalization of this constraint-based procedure is described, along with proofs of convergence, by Spirtes, Glymour, and Scheines (1993). Chapter 13 discusses a Bayesian method for using instrumental variables for causal inference.

Given the assumptions in section 6, is it possible to discover causal knowledge from observational data alone, without background domain knowledge? The answer is yes. If hidden variables (confounders) are excluded as possibilities, then at least three measured variables are needed. The simplest set of causal relationships that admit causal discovery from observational data is shown in figure 20. We can infer both of the following causal relationships: W causes Y, and X causes Y.

If hidden confounders may exist and we cannot assume an instrumental variable, then at least four measured variables are needed to discover a

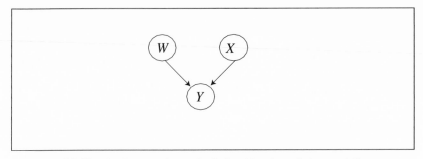

Figure 20. The simplest set of causal relationships that admit causal discovery from observational data, assuming no hidden confounders.

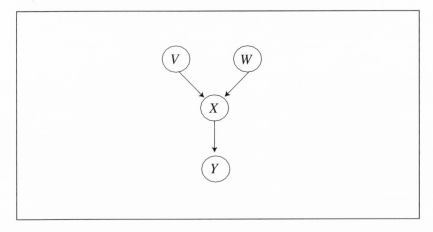

Figure 21. Simplest set of causal relationships that admit causal discovery from observational data, allowing for the possibility of hidden confounders.

causal relationship; the simplest set of causal relationships that admit causal discovery from observational data is shown in figure 21. From data generated by a causal process that can be modeled by the network shown in figure 21, we can infer only one causal relationship: X causes Y.

PC and FCI are constraint-based algorithms that considerably generalize the type of causal discovery that is illustrated in figure 21. Both algorithms are described in detail in Spirtes, Glymour, and Scheines (1993) and they have been implemented as computer programs which are commercially available (see Scheines, Spirtes, Glymour, and Meek 1995 and chapter 5). See also Pearl and Verma (1991) and chapter 3 for related research. PC and FCI assume a Bayesian network causal model, the faithfulness condition, and valid statistical testing. Current implementations of the algorithms typically involve deleting cases in which any variable has a missing value. PC assumes that hidden variables and selection bias do not exist, while FCI allows hidden variables and selection bias. Under the assumptions that each algorithm makes, the algorithms are provably correct. PC and FCI allow the user to specify categorical background knowledge about causal relationships, as for example that one measured variable is not caused by any other measured variable. Both algorithms output a graphical pattern that expresses the causal constraints among the variables. Simple arcs express direct causality, as expected. Other edge types between nodes provide weaker constraints on the types of causal relationships between two variables, as for example an edge type indicating that the data are insufficient to resolve whether X causes Y or Y causes X. Chapter 6 describes the FCI algorithm and some of its extensions.

8. Bayesian Methods for Evaluating Causal Bayesian Networks

In 1991 Cooper and Herskovits described a general Bayesian formulation for learning causal structure (including latent variables) and parameters from observational data using Bayesian networks (Cooper and Herskovits 1992, 1991a, 1991b). To my knowledge, this was the first such description. Their Bayesian formulation assumed only that causal relationships are modeled as Bayesian networks; the basic ideas are similar to those presented later in this section. Cooper and Herskovits also specialized the general formulation by introducing a set of assumptions that make computation more tractable. Since that initial research, Bayesian causal discovery has become an active field of research in which numerous advances have been—and are continuing to be—made (Buntine 1991, 1996; Chickering and Heckerman 1996; Cooper 1995; Heckerman 1996; Heckerman, Geiger, and Chickering 1995; Meek 1995b).

Bayesian methods for causal discovery differ in several ways from constraint-based methods. First, the methods take a user-specified prior probability over Bayesian network structures and over parameters. If the user has little prior information, or it is not feasible to specify this information, then noninformative priors can be used. Given a set of modeling assumptions, the Bayesian approach combines one's prior probabilities with observational data to produce a posterior probability that conveys what one's causal beliefs should be in light of the data. Unlike constraint-based methods, no statistical testing thresholds need to be specified, but instead prior probabilities are needed.

Consider deriving the posterior probability that variable X causes variable Y given observational database D on measured variables V. Let S denote an arbitrary causal network structure containing all of the variables in V and

possibly additional hidden variables. Let K denote our background knowledge that may influence our beliefs about the causal relationships among the
variables in V. Such background knowledge could come from RCEs, scientific laws, common sense, expert opinion, accumulated personal experience,
as well as other sources. We can derive the posterior probability that X causes Y as

$$P(X \rightarrow Y \mid D, K) = \sum_{S: \{X \rightarrow Y\} \in S} P(S \mid D, K)$$
(3)

where the sum is taken over all causal network structures that contain an arc
from X to Y and that have a nonzero prior probability. Based on the properties of probabilities, the term within the sum in equation 3 may be rewritten
as follows:

$$P(S \mid D, K) = \frac{P(S, D \mid K)}{P(D \mid K)}$$

$$= \frac{P(S, D \mid K)}{\sum_S P(S, D \mid K)}$$
(4)

Since relative to the entire set of causal structures being considered, the
probability $P(D \mid K)$ is a constant, equation 4 shows that the posterior probability of causal structure S is proportional to $P(S, D \mid K)$, which we can view
as a score of S in the context of D. The probability terms on the right side of
equation 4 may be expanded as follows:

$$P(S, D \mid K) = P(S \mid K) P(D \mid S, K)$$

$$= P(S \mid K) \int P(D \mid S, \theta_s, K) P(\theta_s \mid S, K) d\theta_s$$
(5)

where (1) $P(S \mid K)$ is our prior belief that S captures correctly the causal relationships among the variables in V, (2) θ_S are the probabilities (parameters)
that relate the nodes in S to their parents, (3) $P(D \mid S, \theta_S, K)$ is the likelihood
of data D being produced given that the causal process generating the data is
isomorphic to the causal Bayesian network given by S and θ_S, and (4) $P(\theta_S \mid S, K)$ expresses our prior belief about the probability distributions that serve
to model the underlying causal process. The integral in equation 5 integrates
out the parameters θ_S in a Bayesian network with structure S to derive $P(D \mid S, K)$, which is called the *marginal likelihood*. Combining equations 3, 4, and
5, we obtain equation 6.

$$P(X \rightarrow Y \mid D, K) =$$

$$\frac{\sum_{S: \{X \rightarrow Y\} \in S} P(S \mid K) \int P(D \mid S, \theta_s, K) P(\theta_s \mid S, K) d\theta_s}{\sum_S P(S \mid K) \int P(D \mid S, \theta_s, K) P(\theta_s \mid S, K) d\theta_s}$$
(6)

The only assumption made in equation 6 is that causal relationships are represented as Bayesian networks. Thus, the causal Markov condition is assumed. If we require that the parameter distributions given by $P(\theta_S \mid S, K)$ be continuous and contain no delta functions, then the probability of a nonfaithful distribution is infinitesimally small (Lebesgue measure zero) (see chapter 4). If we wish, however, we can express parameter priors that violate the faithfulness assumption. More likely, we might express priors that admit some distributions that are faithful and some that are not. In all cases, equation 6 will derive a valid posterior. In general, however, unfaithful distributions make identification of causal relationships more difficult for both constraint-based and Bayesian methods.

A full Bayesian approach to causal discovery considers, at least in principle, all causal models that are a priori possible. Thus, for example, the sums in equation 6 are over all possible causal structures, and the integrals are over all possible parameters for each possible causal structure. The result of such a global analysis of causality is that the derived posterior probabilities summarize a comprehensive, normative belief about the causal relationships among a set of variables.

Although equation 6 makes few assumptions, and the Bayesian theory underlying it is quite general, to render evaluation of the equation tractable, additional assumptions typically must be made, as I next describe.

One primary problem with Bayesian methods is computational tractability. Exact computation using equation 6 requires summing over a number of causal graphs that is exponential in the number of graph variables (see section 9.1). In the limited set of simulation experiments done to date, however, the application of Bayesian methods with heuristic search techniques has often been effective in rapidly and accurately recovering much of the causal generating structure on measured variables (Aliferis and Cooper 1994; Herskovits and Cooper 1990, Heckerman, Geiger, and Chickering 1995). Thus, there is hope that sometimes—perhaps even often—we can heuristically locate quickly the most probable structures that are denoted in the sums in equation 6, and then use this limited set of structures to provide a good approximation to equation 6 (Madigan and Rafferty 1994).

Under assumptions described in chapter 4, the integral in equation 6 can be computed efficiently in closed form when there are no hidden variables or missing data. When there are hidden variables or missing data, the Bayesian approach can model them explicitly and normatively; however, exact computation of the integral with current methods usually is intractable, even when causal graphs contain only a few variables. The use of sampling methods and asymptotic approximations have shown promise (Chickering and Heckerman 1996) in estimating the integral when there is missing data or hidden variables, and chapter 4 discusses several such methods.

Another challenge of applying Bayesian methods for causal discovery is the assessment of informative priors on possible causal structures and on parameters for those structures. On the one hand, the ability to represent such prior information is a great strength of the Bayesian approach. With it, we can potentially express prior causal knowledge that comes from many sources other than the observational data D. While good progress has been made in facilitating the expression of priors on Bayesian network structures and parameters (Heckerman, Geiger, and Chickering 1995), assessing such prior probabilities (particularly when there is a large set of variables) can still be difficult and sometimes infeasible; thus, assessment remains an important, open problem. Currently, it is common to specify some form of a noninformative prior on the causal structures (e.g., a uniform prior over all possible structures) and on the parameters of those structures. Noninformative priors typically require that the user specify only a few parameters; still, it sometimes is not obvious what those few parameters should be. In that case, performing a sensitivity analysis over the parameters may be a good idea.

In summary, even though exact application of Bayesian methods often is intractable, approximate solutions may be acceptable. The ability to specify structural and parameter priors is a significant strength of the Bayesian approach to causal discovery, because it allows us to incorporate into a causal analysis relevant knowledge beyond the observational data. When informative priors are not available, or are impractical to assess, noninformative priors may be used, such that the causal analysis is driven largely by the available observational data.

9. Model Search

In this section, I first describe the size of the space of causal Bayesian network structures as a function of the number of nodes in the network. Since the space is large, I provide a selected overview of methods that have been developed for searching the space.

9.1. The Size of the Model Space

Sections 6, 7, and 8 describe methods for evaluating a causal Bayesian network given a set of observational data. In this section, I describe how to use those evaluations in searching for causal models. The emphasis here is on model selection wherein we attempt to find the single best causal model that represents the relationships among the measured variables. I also briefly discuss model averaging that uses more than one model. In practice, both tasks require considering a large space of possible causal networks. In particular, as a function of the number of measured variables, the number of possible causal structures containing just those variables grows exponentially. Thus,

number of measured variables	number of causal Bayesian network structures
1	1
2	3
3	25
4	543
5	29,281
6	3,781,503
7	1.1×10^9
8	7.8×10^{11}
9	1.2×10^{15}
10	4.2×10^{18}

Table 3. The number of causal Bayesian network structures as a function of the number of variables in the network.

an exhaustive enumeration of all structures is not feasible in most domains. Table 3 shows a few sample values for the number of possible causal Bayesian network structures (i.e., directed acyclic graphs) that contain a given number of nodes; for a number of nodes greater than six, the number of structures is given in scientific notation with only two digits of accuracy in the mantissa.

The size of the space of causal Bayesian networks clearly is enormous when there are more than a few variables. Even so, it is possible that some clever algorithm could efficiently find the most probable structure, even in the worst case. However, two results suggest that in the worst case, such searches are indeed likely to be exponential time.

Bouckaert (1995) has shown that a constraint-based version of learning Bayesian networks with no hidden variables is NP-hard. Let V be a set of n binary variables and let P be a joint probability distribution over V. Assume that an oracle is available that reveals in $O(1)$ time whether a conditional independence statement holds in P. Let k be a positive constant. Consider algorithms that consult the oracle to determine whether or not there exists a causal Bayesian network structure that represents P that has at most k arcs. Bouckaert shows that this problem is NP-complete. Thus, finding the causal network structure with the minimal number of arcs is NP-hard. It can be shown that if the Markov condition and the faithfulness assumption hold, then the generating causal network contains a minimal number of arcs to represent P. Thus, if that condition and assumption hold, determining the structure of an underlying causal network using constraint-based methods must be NP-hard.

Chickering (1996a) has shown that a version of Bayesian learning of Bayesian networks is NP-hard. An instance of the decision problem consists of a set of variables V, a database D, a Bayesian network structure S, the likelihood-equivalence Bayesian scoring metric $M(S, D)$ that computes equation 5 (see chapter 4 for a definition of likelihood equivalence), and a real value p. The decision question is as follows: Does there exist a network structure S defined over the variables in V, where each node in S has at most k parents (for k greater than 1), such that $M(S, D) \geq p$? Chickering shows that this problem is NP-complete. Thus, finding the causal network structure with the maximum score is NP-hard. The proof of NP-completeness uses a reduction that relies on informative priors.

Thus far in this section I have considered Bayesian networks on measured variables only. Chapter 4 discusses several methods for estimating equation 5 when S contains hidden (latent) variables or missing data.

9.2. Search Algorithms

Since searching the usually enormous space of causal Bayesian networks appears infeasible, researchers have developed a number of approaches to cope with the task. In the remainder of this section I provide a brief survey of a selected set of those approaches. No attempt is made to provide complete coverage of all the algorithms that have been developed. As concrete examples, three search algorithms (PC, K2, and OccamsWindow) are described in more detail than the others.

9.2.1. Search Algorithms for Constraint-Based Causal Discovery

In this section, I provide a brief summary of the PC search algorithm that was developed by Spirtes, Glymour, and Scheines (1993) (figure 22). In figure 22, steps 1 and 4 are performed in $O(n^2)$ time. PC has relatively efficient techniques for performing steps 2 and 3. In the worst case, however, steps 2 and 3 require time that is exponential in n. The worst cases occur when the nodes in the generating graph are highly connected, and therefore, F is a dense graph. In particular, the computational time complexity of PC is bounded from above by

$$n^2(n-1)^{k-1}/(k-1)!$$

where k is the maximum number of edges directly connected to a node in graph F that is produced by Step 2 (Spirtes, Glymour, and Scheines 1993). Thus, when k is bounded, the complexity is polynomial in the number of nodes. This analysis provides a loose upper bound on the worst-case time complexity; the expected time complexity will depend on the details of the underlying causal model and the data it produces.

---

procedure PC;

{Input: A set of *n* nodes, and a function T to test conditional independence of sets of nodes.}

{Output: A set of arcs that indicate causal relationships between variables, and a set of undirected edges that indicate relationships between variables in which causal directionality is left undetermined.}

{Assumptions: The data generating process is a causal Bayesian network, the faithfulness assumption holds, the test T is correct, and there are no missing data or hidden variables.}

Step 1. Form a complete undirected graph *C* on the *n* nodes.

Step 2. Using T, begin with low order conditional independence tests and progressively remove edges from *C* whenever two nodes are marginally or conditionally independent. Let F denote the resulting undirected graph.

Step 3. For each triple of nodes (X, Y, Z) such that (X, Y) and (Y, Z) are each adjacent in F, but (X, Z) is not, do the following: Orient $X - Y - Z$ as $X \rightarrow Y \leftarrow Z$ if and only if X and Z are dependent when conditioned on each subset of the nodes (excluding X and Z) that contains Y. Let F' denote the resulting partially directed graph.

Step 4. Repeat, until no more edges in F' can be oriented:

    a. If in F' it is the case that $X \rightarrow Y$ appears, $Y - Z$ appears, and X and Z are not connected (by an undirected edge or an arc), then orient $Y - Z$ as $Y \rightarrow Z$.

    b. If there is a directed path from X to Y, and $X - Y$ is in F', then orient $X - Y$ as $X \rightarrow Y$.

end {PC};

Figure 22. The PC algorithm.

The output of Step 4 in PC is called a *pattern,* which is a term introduced by Verma and Pearl (1990). Arcs represent causal relationships. Undirected edges indicate relationships in which causal directionality is left undetermined by PC. The PC algorithm does not always orient all undirected edges that can be oriented. For a discussion of rules for obtaining a complete orientation, see Meek (1995), as well as the discussion of essential graphs in section 9.2.2.

Figure 23 shows an example of applying PC. In this example, I assume that the causal network that generated the data is shown at the top of figure 23. In Step 1 in the figure all four nodes are connected by edges. In Step 2, *A* and *B* are marginally independent, so the edge between them is removed. Also in Step 2, *A* and *D* are independent given *C,* and therefore the edge between them is removed. Similarly, *B* and *D* are independent given *C.* The final graph in Step 2 contains just three edges, which form a skeleton indicating variables that have direct causal relationships. In Step 3 of the example, it happens that the independence conditions on *A, B,* and *C* that fol-

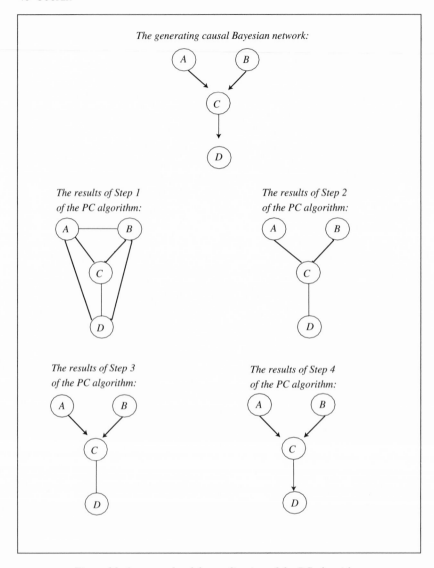

Figure 23. An example of the application of the PC algorithm.

low from the generating network are consistent only with an arc from *A* to *C* and an arc from *B* to *C*. No other arcs can be generated in Step 3. In Step 4a we orient an arc from *C* to *D* and quit.

In figure 23, I have shown one of the simplest possible applications of PC. For more complex applications of PC, see Spirtes, Glymour, and Scheines (1993), which also describes extensions to the algorithm. As mentioned in section 7, FCI is a constraint-based causal discovery algorithm that admits both measured and hidden variables. A detailed description and analysis of FCI also is given by Spirtes, Glymour, and Scheines (1993).

9.2.2. Search Algorithms for Bayesian Causal Discovery

In this section I describe several heuristic search algorithms that have been used along with Bayesian scoring metrics to search for the most probable causal network given a set of observational data. Many of these algorithms have close parallels to search algorithms used in statistics for constructing predictive models (e.g., logistic regression models), although I do not focus here on that comparison. I also describe a method for model averaging. All the algorithms I describe use $P(S, D \mid K)$ from equation 5 as a *scoring metric* to rank causal network structures, since $P(S, D \mid K)$ is proportional to $P(S \mid D, K)$ given a database D.

Special Case Algorithms. Researchers have developed special case search algorithms that are efficient for restricted causal network structures. When we can assume that each node in the generating network has at most one parent, then a polynomial time algorithm exists for finding the most probable structure (or set of structures) (Heckerman, Geiger, and Chickering 1995). Unfortunately, such restrictions rarely apply, and thus the need for other search methods.

Greedy Search Algorithms. Greedy search algorithms work by adding, removing, and/or reversing a few arcs (typically one) at each step of the search. The search halts when there is no greedy step that improves the scoring metric. A forward stepping algorithm, for example, typically begins with a network that contains no arcs, and then it adds incrementally that arc whose addition most increases the probability of the resulting structure. When the addition of no single arc can increase the scoring metric, the algorithm stops adding arcs. A backward stepping algorithm usually begins with a fully connected network and then removes one arc at a time, until no single arc can be removed to increase the scoring metric. Combinations of forward and backward stepping algorithms have been developed as well (Heckerman, Geiger, and Chickering 1995; Spirtes and Meek 1995).

Some greedy search algorithms have assumed a causal ordering of the nodes, such that the potential parents of a node X are just the nodes that are lower in the ordering than X (Cooper 1990). Time precedence, for instance, sometimes can provide such information; in general, however, an ordering will not be available. Researchers have therefore explored greedy algorithms that do not require an ordering (Buntine 1991; Heckerman, Geiger, and Chickering 1995). A problem with greedy search algorithms is they may halt at local maxima of the scoring metric, rather than at a global maxima (Xiang, Wong, and Cercone 1996) Various procedures, such as multiple search restarts from random graphs, can be used in an attempt to ameliorate the lo-

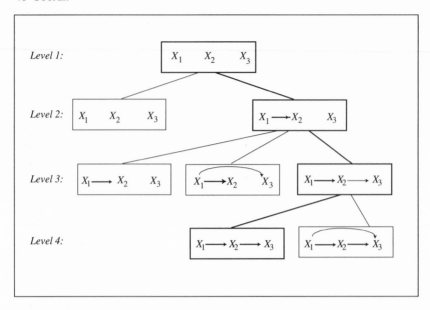

Figure 24. An example of the application of the K2 forward stepping search algorithm. The path taken in the search is shown in bold.

cal maxima problem by taking the maximum of a set of local maxima.

I now illustrate a simple application of a forward stepping search algorithm called K2 (Cooper and Herskovits 1992). The K2 algorithm makes assumptions that allow it to search for the parents of each node separately. Figure 24 shows an example in which the search starts at level 1 with no arcs. Suppose the node ordering is given by the list (X_1, X_2, X_3), so that the potential parents of a node are given by the nodes to its left in the list. The search starts with the first node in the list. At level 1, K2 searches for the parents of node X_1, which can have no parents, according to the node ordering. So, the search advances to level 2. Here the algorithm searches for the parents of X_2 by considering no arcs (left box) and one arc (right) from X_1. Suppose the causal network structure on the right has the highest score, where the score for a structure S is given by $P(S, D \mid K)$. Since there are no additional arcs to consider as possible parents of X_2, the algorithm fixes X_1 as a parent of X_2 (shown as a bold arc) and then it continues onward to consider X_3. For node X_3, K2 considers each possible single arc addition, of which there are two, as well as the addition of no arc. Suppose the rightmost causal network structure receives the highest score. In that case, K2 fixes X_2 as a parent of X_3. Next, it considers all additional single arcs it could add into X_3, of which there is only one, which is from X_1. Suppose the rightmost structure at level 4 has a score lower than $X_1 \to X_2 \to X_3$. In that case the algorithm halts and returns $X_1 \to X_2 \to X_3$.

Greedy Search Algorithms on Essential Graphs. Markov equivalence is a relationship based on independence that establishes a set of equivalence classes of causal network structures relative to a set of measured variables. In particular, these structures are statistically indistinguishable based on independence relationships among the measured variables. Let U be a set of causal network structures representing one such equivalence class. If for every S in U, an arc between two nodes is oriented only in one direction, then retain the arc; otherwise replace it with an undirected edge. The resulting graph was independently developed and investigated by several researchers (Andersson, Madigan, and Perlman 1997; Chickering 1995; Meek 1995), who use the terms *maximally oriented graph, completed pdag representation,* and *essential graph* to describe it. This chapter uses the term essential graph. Essential graphs are a special case of chain graphs (Wermuth and Lauritzen 1990), both of which can contain arcs as well as undirected edges. For example, consider a two node model with variables X and Y. There are three causal network structures that contain just these two measured variables (X no_arc Y, $X \to Y$, and $X \leftarrow Y$), but only two essential graphs (X no_arc Y and $X — Y$) because in this case $X \to Y$ and $X \leftarrow Y$ are Markov equivalent.

Researchers have developed greedy algorithms for searching over essential graphs (Anderson, Madigan, and Perlman 1998; Chickering 1996; Meek 1995; Spirtes and Meek 1995). For a given set of n measured variables, there are fewer essential graphs than causal network structures (directed acyclic graphs). For example, for n equal to 4, there are 543 causal network structures, but only 185 essential graphs.[4] Since the essential graph space is smaller, it is potentially easier to search. Thus, searching the space of essential graphs appears to be a promising method for causal Bayesian network selection.

Model Averaging. Suppose we perform an inference, as for example to derive the probability that in light of observation U the manipulation of variables W and X to particular values will cause variable Y to have a particular value. The normative Bayesian approach to performing this inference is model averaging. Model averaging involves performing the inference for each possible causal model and multiplicatively weighting the inference result (a probability) by the posterior probability of the causal model. The Bayesian inference is just the sum of these weighted inferences.

The large space of possible causal network structures generally makes it infeasible to perform complete model averaging. Researchers, therefore, have investigated heuristic methods for performing selective model averaging. These methods heuristically search for high probability causal network structures; the networks encountered during the search are used for model averaging.

Madigan and colleagues developed an algorithm called Occam's Window

---

procedure OccamsWindow;

Step 1.   Initialize a set A of models {e.g., place in A a Bayesian network with no arcs}

Step 2.   Consider each possible legal, one-step, greedy modification to each member of A. Modifications include single arc additions, deletions, and reversals that induce no cycles.

Step 3.   Choose the modification in Step 2 that leads to the highest scoring structure S (if any) that satisfies the following conditions:
  • The highest scoring structure already in A is not more than 20 times greater than $P(S, D \mid K)$.
  • There is no model S' in A that is a subgraph of S such that $P(S', D \mid K) > P(S, D \mid K)$.

Step 4.   If step 3 produces a new structure S, then add S to A and go to Step 2; otherwise, continue to step 5.

Step 5.   Perform model averaging using the structures in A.

end; {OccamsWindow}

Figure 25. The Occam's Window algorithm.

(Madigan and Raftery 1994), which can be applied to search for a set of causal Bayesian network structures with which to do model averaging. A high-level description of the algorithm is shown in figure 25. Researchers also have investigated a method for performing heuristic model averaging using essential graphs rather than Bayesian networks (Madigan, Andersson, Perlman, and Volinsky 1996).

Combining Constraint-based and Bayesian Methods. Researchers have developed hybrid search algorithms that have two stages (Singh and Valtorta 1993, Spirtes and Meek 1995). The first stage involves selecting a causal network structure using a constraint-based search method. The second stage involves using that structure to start a Bayesian search. The main idea underlying these algorithms is that constraint-based methods provide a relatively quick first approximation structure, which is then refined by the Bayesian methods.

Other combinations of constraint-based and Bayesian methods are possible, and the general approach appears promising. For instance, chapter 14 describes a method that uses a constraint-based method for constructing the structure of a causal model and a Bayesian method for parameter estimation. As another example, as mentioned in section 9.1, an unconstrained search for hidden variables using a Bayesian scoring method generally is intractable. It may be more effective to use constraint-based methods to limit the space of latent variable networks that are searched. Recently researchers have investigated a latent-variable version of the essential graph search method mentioned earlier in this section (Spirtes, Richardson, and Meek 1997). In this recent research, a representation called a partial ancestral graph (PAG) is used to model equivalence classes of causal Bayesian networks that may include latent variables. A greedy search is performed in the space of PAGs. For each greedy step, the corresponding PAG is converted to a mixed ancestral graph (MAG), which is a completely oriented PAG. The MAG is then evaluated using a Bayesian information criterion (BIC) scoring metric, which can be viewed as an asymptotic approximation to a Bayesian scoring metric. The MAG with the highest score is converted back to a PAG, and the search continues until no local addition to the leading PAG improves the BIC score. Starting with that leading PAG, a similar procedure is applied using backward stepping search. When backward searching is completed, the final, leading PAG is returned. Preliminary simulation experiments, while very limited in scope, are encouraging (Spirtes, Richardson, and Meek 1997). The use of a Bayesian scoring metric to search an abstraction space of causal network models (e.g., PAGs) appears to be a promising direction of research.

10. A Selected Summary of Prior Results

Inducing causal relationships from observational data is challenging for many reasons, including the possible presence of latent variables, selection bias, missing data, limited amounts of records, a large search space, and statistical indistinguishability. Even so, as this chapter has shown, there are circumstances in which we can induce causal relationships from observational data. Characterizing all the circumstances and their consequences regarding causal discovery remains an open problem. Nonetheless, presently we do have some useful understanding of the conditions that make causal discovery possible. While it is beyond the scope of this chapter to provide a complete survey of present understanding, in the remainder of section 10 I provide a selected summary of some key results.

10.1. Convergence Results

The PC algorithm assumes the Markov condition, the faithfulness condition, valid statistical testing, no latent variables, and no selection bias. Under these assumptions, in the large sample limit, PC will recover all causal relationships that can be recovered from observational data. Bouckaert (1995) has shown that under those assumptions Bayesian learning methods will recover the same causal relationships as PC in the large sample limit. This result assumes that the Bayesian method does not include prior probabilities of 0 or 1 on structures or parameters, and that model search is exhaustive.

The FCI constraint-based discovery method models latent variables and selection bias. In the large sample limit, FCI has been proved to converge to a model that contains no incorrect causal statements if the modeling assumptions it makes are correct (Spirtes, Glymour, and Scheines 1993). Within the FCI language for representing causal constraints, it also has been shown that the algorithm is complete (Spirtes, Glymour, and Scheines 1993). The degree to which the FCI language itself is complete, relative to all possible causal constraints that can be expressed, remains an open question. There are known examples in which independence constraints alone are insufficient to discover a causal constraint that can be discovered from observational data (Verma and Pearl 1990). As a simple example, since FCI does not model the number of values of latent variables, it clearly is unable to learn what may be learnable about that number. Bayesian methods, conversely, are able to model and learn about the number of values of hidden variables (Chickering and Heckerman 1996; Cooper 1995; Cooper and Herskovits 1992; Geiger, Heckerman, and Meek 1996). Bayesian methods, however, are computationally demanding, although as mentioned in section 8, approximation methods appear promising (see chapter 4). Current Bayesian methods evaluate a specific causal Bayesian network, or somewhat more generally, an essential graph that represents an equivalence class of Bayesian networks. More abstract causal constraints (e.g., X either causes Y or causes Z) can be constructed from the evaluation of a set of causal Bayesian networks. It remains an open problem, however, to investigate the extent to which abstract constraints can be evaluated (scored) directly using Bayesian methods.

10.2. Simulation Studies

In this section, I describe the results of studies in which a database of cases was generated from a Bayesian network by simulation and then given as input to an algorithm that attempted to discover causal relationships. Since the ALARM Bayesian network has been widely used for simulation studies, I focus on experiments that have used data generated from that network.

Beinlich constructed the ALARM network as a research prototype to model potential anesthesia problems in the operating room (Beinlich, Suermondt, Chavez, and Cooper 1989; Cooper and Herskovits 1992). ALARM contains 46 arcs and thirty-seven nodes, and each node has from two to four possible values.

Cases were generated from ALARM using a Monte Carlo simulation technique (Henrion 1988). Although all the studies mentioned here have used the same network structure for ALARM, variations of the probability parameters have been applied. Each ALARM case corresponds to a value assignment to each of the thirty-seven variables. The simulation technique is an unbiased generator of cases, in the sense that the probability that a particular case is generated is equal to the probability of the case according to the Bayesian network.

Cooper and Herskovits applied K2 with a database of 3,000 ALARM cases (Cooper and Herskovits 1992). K2 also was given an ordering on the thirty-seven nodes that is consistent with the partial order of the nodes as specified by the ALARM network. From the 3,000 cases, K2 constructed a network identical to ALARM, except that one arc was missing and one arc was added. A subsequent analysis revealed that the missing arc is not strongly supported by the 3,000 cases. The extra arc was added because of the greedy nature of the search algorithm. Total search time was approximately five minutes when using a circa 1990 personal computer.

Heckerman, Geiger, and Chickering (1995) developed and investigated a greedy search algorithm that generalized K2 by removing the assumption of a node ordering. A Bayesian scoring metric similar to that used by K2 was applied as well. Although the algorithm was able to estimate the ALARM joint distribution accurately, as measured by cross entropy, the estimated structural model had on average forty-five arc differences from the ALARM network; arc difference is defined as

$$\sum_{i=1}^{n} \delta_i ,$$

where δ_i is the symmetric difference of the parents of node x_i in ALARM and the parents of x_i in the learned network. This difference is conservative because it counts arcs that are reversed from ALARM, even when those arc orientations are statistically indistinguishable. When a much slower simulated annealing search algorithm was applied to the same data set, only about twenty differences existed on average.

Algorithms that perform a greedy search over a space of essential graphs have been applied to ALARM data sets (Chickering 1996; Meek 1998; Spirtes and Meek 1995). The best results to date of any search algorithm on ALARM data has been achieved by Meek's greedy equivalence search (GES) algorithm (Meek 1998). The GES algorithm first performs a forward stepping greedy search followed by a backward stepping greedy search. When given a data set containing 10,000 ALARM cases, and run on a UNIX workstation, the algorithm returns in about 5 hours a network that contains only one error, namely, a missing edge between two variables that are only very weakly statistically associated in ALARM. When an arc and its reversal are statistically indistinguishable in the generating ALARM network, and one of those arc orientations is in ALARM, the evaluation of GES counted the presence of either orientation as acceptable (no error). These results are impressive and suggest that the GES algorithm deserves considerably more study.

Chapter 6 describes a preliminary experiment in which 10,000 cases generated from ALARM were used to evaluate the FCI algorithm when there are latent variables. Selection bias also was examined, but those results are not summarized here. The primary metrics of evaluation were the percentage of ancestor and nonancestor relationships correctly predicted, according to the ALARM network. A node X is an ancestor of node Y if there is a directed path from X to Y. When there were no latent variables, FCI correctly predicted all of the ancestor relationships (pairs) and 97 percent of the nonancestor relationships. When node 29 was considered a latent variable, FCI correctly predicted all ancestor relationships and 91 percent of the nonancestor relationships. When both nodes 29 and 22 were considered as latent variables, FCI still correctly predicted all the ancestor relationships and 92 percent of the nonancestor relationships. Although these results provide useful insight into the performance of FCI, we have much more to learn about how causal discovery algorithms perform when there are latent variables.

In this section, I have given only a sampling of simulation results that have been reported. Other simulation studies include an extensive set of experiments using constraint-based methods that are described in Spirtes, Glymour, and Scheines (1993), and experiments applying K2 to random graphs, as described by Aliferis and Cooper (1994). I conclude this section with a summary of the latter results.

Aliferis and Cooper generated sixty-seven Bayesian networks in a randomized fashion (see Aliferis and Cooper 1994 for details), such that each network contained from two to fifty nodes, two or three values per node, and zero to ten parents per node. For each network, the number of cases generated was randomly (uniformly) selected to be in the range from 0 to 2,000. The probability parameters for each network also were randomly generated. The K2 search algorithm and metric were applied to each of the sixty-seven datasets, where K2 was given a node ordering consistent with the generating Bayesian network. In brief, on average K2 found 92 percent of all the arcs in the generating network and erroneously added 5 percent more arcs than existed in the generating network.

In experiments based on simulated databases, we know the causal network that generated the data, and thus, we know the underlying causal reality. We therefore can judge the causal discovery performance of an algorithm relative to that generating causal network. There are, however, two major weaknesses of such studies. First, we assume the existence of a causal process that can be modeled by a Bayesian network. Thus, we evaluate the internal validity of discovery methods relative to an assumed model of causality. We are not testing external validity relative to the real world. Second, assuming a Bayesian network model, we still need to parameterize the network with a set of probabilities that are used to stochastically generate a database. It can be difficult to know what these probabilities should be, particularly in the presence of latent variables. One strategy is to choose random probabilities to parameterize a given Bayesian network structure. As a form of sensitivity analysis, we can generate multiple random parameterizations, and for each one we generate a database that is used to evaluate a causal discovery algorithm. Unfortunately, it may be highly unlikely that a given random parameterization will closely resemble any real-world causal process.

An arguably better approach is to have an expert generate a causal Bayesian network based on personal knowledge and knowledge from the literature. The ALARM network is one example. Such networks have the advantage that we know their structure precisely and their probabilities are likely to resemble those of the real-world processes being modeled. One disadvantage of the approach is that manually generating such networks is labor intensive. Another disadvantage is that it relies on human knowledge of a causal process, which may be incomplete or incorrect.

A related, and relatively unexplored approach, would be to use causal Bayesian networks that represent human-constructed entities (e.g., a jet engine). For example, Spirtes, Glymour, and Scheines (1993, p. 243) describe such a study in which the PC algorithm correctly identifies the subcomponents of a qualification test taken in the military. Such experiments do not, of course, inform us directly about the performance of causal discovery methods when using data on natural systems.

10.3. Studies Using Real Databases

Using observational data, we would like to discover new and useful causal knowledge about the real world. Evaluating the performance of causal discovery methods in achieving that goal is significantly more difficult than evaluating most statistical and machine-learning algorithms, such as classification algorithms. The difficulty stems from being unable to simply use a test set of reserved cases for evaluation. Since manipulation is intrinsic to the notion of causality (at least as I use the term *causality*), the evaluation of a causal hypothesis involves knowledge of what follows from such a manipulation. Sources of such knowledge include expert subjective knowledge and RCEs, which I now discuss in turn.

Several studies have examined causal discovery that is evaluated based on human judgment, which often is rendered in an original paper in the literature. Examples include causal discovery in the areas of publication productivity, education and fertility, American occupational structure, the influences on college plans, and abortion opinions (Spirtes, Glymour, and Scheines 1993). Although an account of these studies is beyond the scope of this chapter, on the whole the causal relationships discovered often (but not always) are consistent with human judgment. Where there is deviation, we generally do not know whether it is due to incorrect algorithmic output, inadequate human knowledge, or both.

Ideally we would have available the results of large, well-performed RCEs to validate causal relationships that are suggested from observational data by causal discovery algorithms. Conducting RCEs can be problematic for the reasons outlined in section 2. More feasibly, we might look for prior studies in which observational data was obtained on a set of variables in a given domain and RCE data was obtained on the same or a similar set of variables in the domain. Preferably, the context and entity population sample would be exactly the same, but an informative study could certainly occur in the absence of such an ideal. If the causal relationships suggested using an observational database coincide closely with the causal relationships suggested by the corresponding RCE, then we have positive support for methods for causal discovery from observational data. If such comparisons were carried out over many databases and domains, we would begin to get a clear picture of the strengths and weaknesses of present methods for causal discovery from observational data.

Spirtes, Glymour, and Scheines (1993) use the discovery methods described in this book to analyze observational biological data of Spartina biomass. They applied the PC algorithm to field data collected by Linthurst (1979). Linthurst collected observational data on 14 possible factors that influence the growth of Spartina biomass, as well as the actual biomass. At each of nine sites in the Cape Fear Estuary five data samples were measured. Using this data, the PC algorithm output only pH as a cause of biomass. Original laboratory experiments performed by Linthurst showed pH to be a causal factor influencing biomass. The experiments also showed salinity to be a causal factor at fairly neutral pH levels that were sparsely represented in the field data. Aeration did not significantly influence biomass in the laboratory. Linthurst did not experimentally examine all the other 11 possible factors, so we do not know whether any of them would show a causal effect on biomass. Overall, the known experimental results support the output of the PC algorithm as being essentially correct for the Spartina biomass domain.

As another example, chapter 15 describes a study that involves causal models found by a constraint-based discovery algorithm that are compared to current knowledge and theory of gas exchange in plant leaves. The results reveal some strengths and weaknesses of the discovery method for this domain.

Clearly, more studies are needed that compare the causal relationships derived from observational investigations with those derived from experimental investigations. As researchers locate parallel observational and experimental databases, additional studies will be possible.

Acknowledgments

I thank Constantin Aliferis, John Aronis, Clark Glymour, David Heckerman, Chris Meek, Peter Spirtes, and Stefano Monti for helpful comments on earlier drafts of this chapter. The writing of this chapter and portions of the research presented here were supported in part by grants BES-9315428 and IRI-9509792 from the National Science Foundation and by grant LM05291 from the National Library of Medicine. Any opinions, findings, and conclusions or recommendations expressed in this material are those of the author and do not necessarily reflect the views of the National Science Foundation or the National Library of Medicine.

Notes

1. A *graph* consists of *nodes* (typically represented as circles—in the structural equation modeling literature [Bollen 1989], usually measured variables are represented with squares and unmeasured variables with circles; in the causal network structures in the current chapter, we simply use circles for all variables) with *edges* between some pairs of the nodes. Nodes are also called vertices. If every edge has a direction associated with it (typically represented with an *arc* →), the graph is a *directed graph*. A *directed path* from node X to node Y is a sequence of nodes, beginning with X and ending with Y, such that there is an arc from each node to its successor in the sequence. A directed path from a node to itself is called a *directed cycle*. A directed graph that contains no directed cycles is called a *directed acyclic graph*. A *parent* of node X is a node W for which there is an arc from W to X. Node X is then said to be a *child* of W. If there is a directed path from V to X, then V is an *ancestor* of X. Correspondingly, X is said to be a *descendant* of V. The *nondescendants* of a node X are all the other nodes in the graph that are not descendants of X. A subgraph G' of a graph G is a graph that contains just a subset of the nodes in G and all the edges in G among that subset of nodes.

2. The notation *manipulate$_i$*(X') corresponds to the same manipulations as *manipulate$_i$*(X) for that subset of X represented by X'. Similarly, *manipulate$_i$*(X'') corresponds to the same manipulations as *manipulate$_i$*(X) for that subset of X represented by X''. An analogous correspondence holds for *manipulate$_j$*(X), *manipulate$_j$*(X'), and *manipulate$_j$*(X'').

3. With a smooth distribution, we exclude discontinuities and delta functions in the probability density functions.

4. Joel Martin provided this count of essential graphs, based on exhaustive enumeration (personal communication, March 1994).

References

Aliferis, C. F. 1998. A Temporal Representation and Reasoning Model for Medical Decision-Support Systems, Ph.D dissertation, University of Pittsburgh, Intelligent Systems Program, Pittsburgh, Penn.

Aliferis, C. F., and Cooper, G. F. 1998. Causal Modeling with Modifiable Temporal Belief Networks, Center for Biomedical Informatics. Technical Report 01, University of Pittsburgh, Pittsburgh, Penn.

Aliferis, C. F., and Cooper, G. F. 1995. A New Formalism for Temporal Modeling in Medical Decision-Support Systems. In *Proceedings of the Symposium on Computer Applications in Medical Care*. Philadelphia, Penn: Hanley and Belfus.

Aliferis, C. F., and Cooper, G. F. 1994. An Evaluation of an Algorithm for Inductive Learning of Bayesian Belief Networks Using Simulated Data Sets. In *Proceedings of the Conference on Uncertainty in Artificial Intelligence,* 8–14. San Francisco: Morgan Kaufmann Publishers.

Andersson, S. A.; Madigan, D.; and Perlman, M. D. 1997. A Characterization of Markov Equivalence Classes for Acyclic Digraphs. *Annals of Statistics.* 25(2): 505-541.

Angrist, J. D.; Imbens, G. W.; and Rubin, D. B. 1996. Identification of Causal Effects Using Instrumental Variables. *Journal of the American Statistical Association* 91(434): 444–472.

Balke, A., and Pearl, J. 1994. Counterfactual Probabilities: Computational Methods, Bounds, and Applications. In *Proceedings of the Conference on Uncertainty in Artificial Intelligence,* 46–54. San Francisco: Morgan Kaufmann Publishers.

Beinlich, I. A.; Suermondt, H. J.; Chavez, R. M.; and Cooper, G. F. 1989. The ALARM Monitoring System: A Case Study with Two Probabilistic Inference Techniques for Belief Networks. Paper presented at the Second European Conference on Artificial Intelligence in Medicine, London, August.

Berzuini, C.; Bellazi, R.; Quaglini, S.; and Spieglehalter, D. J. 1992. Bayesian Networks for Patient Monitoring. *Artificial Intelligence in Medicine* 4(3): 243–260.

Bollen, K. A. 1989. *Structural Equation Models with Latent Variables.* New York: Wiley.

Bouckaert, R. 1995. Bayesian Belief Networks: From Construction to Inference, Ph.D. dissertation, Computer Science Department, University of Utrecht, Netherlands.

Bowden, R. J., and Turkington, D. A. 1984. *Instrumental Variables.* Cambridge, U.K.: Cambridge University Press.

Bulpitt, C. J. 1996. *Randomized Controlled Clinical Trials.* Norwell, Mass.: Kluwer Academic.

Buntine, W. 1996. A Guide to the Literature on Learning Probabilistic Networks from Data. *IEEE Transactions on Knowledge and Data Engineering* 8(2): 1–17.

Buntine, W. 1991. Theory Refinement in Bayesian Networks. In *Proceedings of the Conference on Uncertainty in Artificial Intelligence,* 52–60. San Francisco: Morgan Kaufmann Publishers.

Cartwright, N. 1989. *Nature's Capacities and Their Measurement.* New York: Oxford University Press.

Castillo, E.; Gutierrez, J. M.; and Hadi, A. S. 1997. *Expert Systems and Probabilistic Network Models.* New York: Springer-Verlag.

Chickering, M. 1996a. Learning Bayesian Networks Is NP-Complete. In *Learning from Data: Lecture Notes in Statistics*, eds. D. Fisher D. and H. Lenz, 121–130. New York: Springer- Verlag.

Chickering, D. M. 1996b. Learning Equivalence Classes of Bayesian Network Structures. In *Proceedings of the Conference on Uncertainty in Artificial Intelligence,* 150–157. San Francisco: Morgan Kaufmann Publishers.

Chickering, M. 1995. A Transformational Characterization of Equivalent Bayesian Network Structures. In *Proceedings of the Conference on Uncertainty in Artificial Intelligence,* 87–98. San Francisco: Morgan Kaufmann Publishers.

Chickering, D. M., and Heckerman, D. 1996. Efficient Approximations for the Marginal Likelihood of Incomplete Data Given a Bayesian Network. In *Proceedings of the Conference on Uncertainty in Artificial Intelligence,* 158–168. San Francisco: Morgan Kaufmann Publishers.

Cooper, G. F. 1997. A Simple Constraint-Based Algorithm for Efficiently Mining Observational Databases for Causal Relationships. *Journal of Data Mining and Knowledge Discovery* 1(2): 203–224.

Cooper, G. F. 1995a. A Method for Learning Belief Networks That Contain Hidden Variables. *Journal of Intelligent Information Systems* 4 (4):1–18.

Cooper, G. F. 1995b. Causal Discovery from Data in the Presence of Selection Bias. Paper presented at the International Workshop on Artificial Intelligence and Statistics, January 4–7, Ft. Lauderdale, Florida.

Cooper, G. F. 1990. The Computational Complexity of Probabilistic Inference Using Bayesian Belief Networks. *Artificial Intelligence* 42(2–3): 393–405.

Cooper, G. F., and Herskovits, E. 1992. A Bayesian Method for the Induction of Probabilistic Networks from Data. *Machine Learning* 9(4): 309–347.

Cooper, G. F., and Herskovits, E. H. 1991a. A Bayesian Method for Constructing Bayesian Belief Networks from Databases. In *Proceedings of the Conference on Uncertainty in Artificial Intelligence,* 86–94. San Francisco: Morgan Kaufmann Publishers.

Cooper, G. F., and Herskovits, E. H. 1991b. A Bayesian Method for the Induction of Probabilistic Networks from Data, SMI-91-1, Section of Medical Informatics, University of Pittsburgh, Pittsburgh, Penn.

Dagum, P., and Galper, A. 1993. Forecasting Sleep Apnea with Dynamic Network Models. In *Proceedings of the Conference on Uncertainty in Artificial Intelligence,* 64–71. San Francisco: Morgan Kaufmann Publishers.

Dagum, P., and Luby, M. 1993. Approximating Probabilistic Inference in Bayesian Belief Networks Is NP-Hard. *Artificial Intelligence* 60(1): 141–153.

Friedman, L. M.; Furberg, C. D.; and DeMets, D. L. 1996. *Fundamentals of Clinical Trials.* 3d ed. St. Louis, Mo.: Mosby.

Geiger, D.; Heckerman, D.; and Meek, C. 1996. Asymptotic Model Selection for Directed Networks with Hidden Variables. In *Proceedings of the Conference on Uncertainty in Artificial Intelligence,* 283–290. San Francisco: Morgan Kaufmann Publishers.

Geiger, D.; Verma, T.; and Pearl, J. 1990. Identifying Independence in Bayesian Networks. *Networks* 20(5): 507–534.

Heckerman, D. 1996. A Tutorial on Learning with Bayesian Networks, MSR-TR-95-06, Microsoft Research, Redmond, Wash. Available at http://www.research.microsoft.com/research/dtg/heckerma/heckerma.html

Heckerman, D., and Shachter, R. 1995. A Definition and Graphical Representation of Causality. In *Proceedings of the Conference on Uncertainty in Artificial Intelligence,* 262– 273. San Francisco: Morgan Kaufmann Publishers.

Heckerman, D.; Geiger, D.; and Chickering, D. 1995. Learning Bayesian Networks: The Combination of Knowledge and Statistical Data. *Machine Learning* 20(3): 197–243.

Heise, D. R. 1975. *Causal Analysis.* New York: Wiley.

Henrion, M. 1990. An Introduction to Algorithms for Inference in Belief Nets. In *Uncertainty in Artificial Intelligence 5,* eds. M. Henrion, R. D. Shachter, L. N. Kanal, and J. F. Lemmer, 129–138. Amsterdam, The Netherlands: North-Holland.

Henrion, M. 1988. Propagating Uncertainty in Bayesian Networks by Logic Sampling. In *Uncertainty in Artificial Intelligence 2,* eds. J. F. Lemmer and L. N. Kanal, 149–163. Amsterdam, The Netherlands: North-Holland.

Herbert, N. 1985. *Quantum Reality.* Garden City, N.Y.: Anchor.

Herskovits, E. H., and Cooper, G. F. 1991. KUTATO: An Entropy-Driven System for the Construction of Probabilistic Expert Systems from Databases. In *Uncertainty in Artificial Intelligence 6,* ed. P. P. Bonissone, M. Henrion, L. N. Kanal, and J. F. Lemmer. Amsterdam: Elsevier North Holland.

Howard, R. A., and Matheson, J. E. 1984. Readings on the Principles and Applications of Decision Analysis, Strategic Decisions Group, Menlo Park, California.

Jensen, F. V. 1996. *An Introduction to Bayesian Networks.* New York: Springer-Verlag.

Kim, J. H., and Pearl, J. 1983. A Computational Model for Combined Causal and Diagnostic Reasoning in Inference Systems. In *Proceedings of the Eighth International Joint Conference on Artificial Intelligence,* 190–193. San Francisco: Morgan Kaufman.

Lam, W., and Bacchus, F. 1994. Learning Bayesian Belief Networks, An Approach Based on the MDL Principle. *Computational Intelligence* 10(3): 269–293.

Linthurst, R. A. 1979. Aeration, Nitrogen, pH, and Salinity as Factors Affecting Spartina Alterniflora Growth and Dieback, Ph.D. dissertation, North Carolina State University, Dept. of Biology, Raleigh, N.C.

Little, R. J. A., and Rubin, D. B. 1987. *Statistical Analysis with Missing Data.* New York: Wiley.

Mackie, J. L. 1974. *The Cement of the Universe.* Oxford, U.K.: Oxford University Press.

Madigan, D., and Raftery, A. 1994. Model Selection and Accounting for Model Uncertainty in Graphical Models Using Occam's Window. *Journal of the American Statistical Association* 89(428): 1535–1546.

Madigan, D.; Andersson, S. A.; Perlman, M. D.; and Volinsky, C. T. 1996. Bayesian Model Averaging and Model Selection for Markov Equivalence Classes of Acyclic Digraphs. *Communications in Statistics—Theory and Methods* 25(11): 2493–2519.

Manski, C. F. 1995. *Identification Problems in the Social Sciences.* Cambridge, Mass.: Harvard University Press.

Meek, C. 1998. Selecting Graphical Models: Causal and Statistical Modeling, Ph.D. dissertation, Department of Philosophy, Carnegie Mellon University.

Meek, C. 1995a. Causal Inference and Causal Explanation with Background Knowledge. In *Proceedings of the Conference on Uncertainty in Artificial Intelligence,* 403–410. San Francisco: Morgan Kaufmann Publishers.

Meek, C. 1995b. Strong Completeness and Faithfulness in Bayesian Networks. In *Proceedings of the Conference on Uncertainty in Artificial Intelligence,* 411–418. San Francisco: Morgan Kaufmann Publishers.

Meyer, B. D. 1995. Natural and Quasi-Experiments in Economics. *Journal of Business and Economic Statistics* 13(2): 151–161.

Neapolitan, R. 1990. *Probabilistic Reasoning in Expert Systems.* New York: Wiley.

Pearl, J. 1996. On the Foundation of Structural Equation Models, or When Can We Give Causal Interpretation to Structural Coefficients?, Technical Report, R-244-S, Cognitive Systems Laboratory, Department of Computer Science, University of California.

Pearl, J. 1995. Causal Diagrams for Empirical Research. *Biometrika* 82:669–709.

Pearl, J. 1988. *Probabilistic Reasoning in Intelligent Systems.* San Francisco, Calif.: Morgan Kaufmann.

Pearl, J., and Verma, T. S. 1991. A Theory of Inferred Causality. In *Proceedings of the Second International Conference on the Principles of Knowledge Representation and Reasoning,* 441–452. San Francisco: Morgan Kaufmann Publishers.

Pratt, J., and Schlaifer, R. 1988. On the Interpretation and Observation of Laws. *Journal of Econometrics* 39(1–2): 23–52.

Provan, G. M., and Clarke, J. R. 1993. Dynamic Network Construction and Updating Techniques for the Diagnosis of Acute Abdominal Pain. *IEEE Transactions on Pattern Analysis and Machine Intelligence* 15(3): 299–306.

Reichenbach, H. 1956. *The Direction of Time.* Berkeley, Calif.: University of California Press.

Robins, J. 1989. The Analysis of Randomized and Nonrandomized AIDS Treatment Trials Using a New Approach to Causal Inference in Longitudinal Studies. In *Health Services Research Methodology: A Focus on AIDS,* eds. L. Sechrest, H. Freeman, and A. Mulley, 113–159. Washington, D.C.: U.S. Public Health Service.

Robins, J. M. 1986. A New Approach to Causal Inference in Mortality Studies with Sustained Exposure Periods—Application to Control of the Healthy Worker Survivor Effect. *Mathematical Modelling* 7(2): 1393–1512.

Rubin, D. 1974. Estimating Causal Effects of Treatments in Randomized and Nonrandomized Studies. *Journal of Educational Psychology* 66(5): 688–701.

Salmon, W. 1984. *Scientific Explanation and the Causal Structure of the World.* Princeton, N.J.: Princeton University Press.

Savage, L. J. 1954. *Foundations of Statistics.* New York: Wiley.

Scheines, R.; Spirtes, P.; Glymour, C.; and Meek, C. 1995. TETRAD II: *Tools for Causal Modeling* (with software). Hillsdale, N.J.: Lawrence Erlbaum.

Simon, H. 1953. Causal Ordering and Identifiability. In *Studies in Econometric Method,* eds. W. C. Hood and T. C. Koopmans, 49–74. New York: Wiley.

Simpson, C. 1951. The Interpretation of Interaction in Contingency Tables. *Journal of the Royal Statistical Society* B13:238–241.

Singh, M., and Valtorta, M. 1993. An Algorithm for the Construction of Bayesian Network Structures from Data. In *Proceedings of the Conference on Uncertainty in Artificial Intelligence,* 259–265. San Francisco: Morgan Kaufmann Publishers.

Spirtes, P., and Meek, C. 1995. Learning Bayesian Networks with Discrete Variables from Data. In *Proceedings of the First International Conference on Knowledge Discovery and Data Mining,* 294–299. Menlo Park, Calif.: AAAI Press.

Spirtes, P.; Glymour, C.; and Scheines, R. 1993. *Causation, Prediction, and Search* New York: Springer-Verlag. Available at hss.cmu.edu/html/ departments/philosophy/TETRAD.BOOK/book.html.

Spirtes, P.; Glymour, C.; and Scheines, R. 1991. An Algorithm for Fast Recovery of Sparse Causal Graphs. *Social Science Computer Review* 9 (1): 62–72.

Spirtes, P.; Richardson, T.; and Meek, C. 1997. Heuristic Greedy Search Algorithms for Latent Variable Models. Paper presented at the InternationalWorkshop on Artificial Intelligence and Statistics, January 4–7, Ft. Lauderdale, Florida.

Suppes, P. 1970. *A Probabilistic Theory of Causality.* Amsterdam, The Netherlands: North Holland.

Verma, T. S., and Pearl, J. 1990. Equivalence and Synthesis of Causal Models. Paper presented at the Conference on Uncertainty in Artificial Intelligence, July 27–29, Cambridge, Mass.

Wedelin, D. 1993. Efficient Algorithms for Probabilistic Inference, Combinatorial Optimization, and the Discovery of Causal Structure from Data, Ph.D. dissertation, Department of Computer Science, Chalmers University of Technology, Sweden.

Wellman, M. P., and Henrion, M. 1993. Explaining "Explaining Away." *IEEE Transactions on Pattern Analysis and Machine Intelligence* 15(3): 287–292.

Wermuth, N., and Lauritzen, S. L. 1990. On Substantive Research Hypotheses, Conditional Independence Graphs, and Graphical Chain Models. *Journal of the Royal Statistical Society* B 52(1): 21–72.

Wright, S. 1921. Correlation and Causation. *Journal of Agricultural Research* 20(1): 557– 585.

Xiang, Y.; Wong, S. K. M.; and Cercone, N. 1996. Critical Remarks on Single Link Search in Learning Belief Networks. In *Proceedings of the Conference on Uncertainty in Artificial Intelligence,* 564–571. San Francisco: Morgan Kaufmann Publishers.

Yao, Q., and Tritchler, D. 1996. Likelihood-Based Causal Inference. In *Learning from Data: Lecture Notes in Statistics*, eds. D. Fisher D. and H. Lenz, 35–44. New York: Springer- Verlag.

Zurek, W. 1991. Decoherence and the Transition from Quantum to Classical. *Physics Today* 44 (10):36–44.

PART ONE

Causation, Representation and Prediction

Directed graphs and associated parameters can encode probability distributions, but what makes these representations about *causal* relations is that they also contain information about how the influence of interventions or manipulations of some variables propagates to other variables.

The first of the two chapters in this section was written in 1991 but has not been previously published. The chapter introduces the basic ideas used to compute the propagation of influence by means of causal graphs, and relates the representation, assumptions and procedures to a formalism—the "Rubin framework"— sometimes used in statistics for similar purposes. This chapter led to published work on procedures for calculating the propagation of influence when the causal and probabilistic structure is only partially known.

The second chapter in this section, by Judea Pearl, offers a diagnosis of the many conceptual confusions about causal prediction in the literature of social statistics, and also offers a solution. The diagnosis is that there is no standard language, no formal notation, to distinguish conditioning on a variable from intervening to fix its value. Of course, a notation is only good if the distinctions it allows can be used to good purpose, and Pearl uses the notation to formulate rules for causal prediction, which are illustrated in a variety of clear and striking examples.

CHAPTER TWO

Prediction and Experimental Design with Graphical Causal Models

*Peter Spirtes, Clark Glymour, Richard Scheines,
Christopher Meek, Stephen Fienberg, and Elizabeth Slate*

One of the aims of an empirical study may be to predict the effects a general policy would have if put in force, or to predict relevant differences resulting from alternative policies. The interest might be in predicting the differential yield if a field is planted with one species of wheat rather than another; or the difference in number of polio cases per capita if all children are vaccinated against polio as against if none are; or the difference in recidivism rates if parolees are given $600 per month for six months as against if they are given nothing; or the reduction of lung cancer deaths in middle-aged smokers if they are given help in quitting cigarette smoking; or the decline in gasoline consumption if an additional dollar tax per gallon is imposed. Such inference problems are puzzling because a policy of treatment creates a potential distribution different from the distribution sampled in observations or experiments, and alternative policies of treatment create alternative potential distributions with alternative statistics. The inference task is to move from a sample of one of these distributions, the one corresponding to passive observation or experimental manipulation, to conclusions about the distribution that would result if a policy were imposed.

A further feature makes prediction especially difficult. Empirical studies are often unable to control or randomize all of the relevant variables, with the result that the dependency among variables relevant to prediction may be confounded by unmeasured common causes. In that case, the effect of a policy that manipulates one of the variables cannot be expected to be predictable from sample statistics. There are many examples of predictions whose disappointment may be in part due to confounding. The second Surgeon General's report on smoking and health (1979, p. 43) found that mortality ratios (compared to permanent nonsmokers) for those who quit smoking declined with

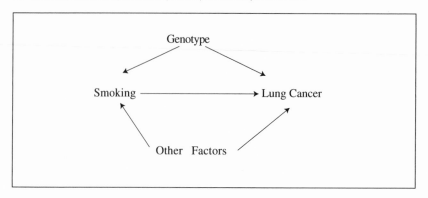

Figure 1. The Brownlee hypothesis.

the number of years since quitting, equaling lifelong nonsmokers after 15 years. Brownlee (1965), following Fisher (1959) conjectured that such decreases might at least in part be due to self-selection of quitters caused by genetic or cultural factors. The Brownlee hypothesis can be represented by a simple picture (figure 1).

If accepted, the picture leads one to expect that the sample mortality ratios reported by the Surgeon General will not be good predictors of the effects of intervention against cigarette smoking. Shortly after the Surgeon General's report there appeared the results of randomized intervention studies that followed subjects for six and ten years respectively. The studies (Rose, et al. 1982; MRFIT 1983) found that intervention that reduced cigarette smoking in middle aged males did not reduce their mortality rate.

Prediction of the effects of a policy from sample data requires knowledge of the causal processes that generated the sample. There are two questions. First, what must be known, and second, when *can* it be known? Rubin (1974, 1977, 1978) and following him Holland (1986) and Pratt and Schlaifer (1984, 1988) have developed a theory that addresses the first question, and Pratt and Schlaifer (1988) have applied it to attempt to answer the second question as well. Their account has been applied to the question of randomization in experimental design (Rubin 1978), to estimation of the difference in expected values of an outcome variable if alternative treatments were to be given to an entire population (Rubin 1977), to determining from a causal structure when the law giving the distribution of a variable Y if a variable or set of variables X were to be forced to have a specified value is "observable," i.e., equal to the observed conditional distribution of Y on that value of X (Pratt and Schlaifer 1988), to advice about when regression coefficients are "structural" (Pratt and Schlaifer 1984, 1988), and to other topics.

Our aims are, first, to show how the results announced in the Rubin framework may be rigorously derived from simple axioms on graphical causal models and thereby connected with another line of statistical work on causality deriving from Kiiveri and Speed (1982), Wermuth and Lauritzen (1983), Pearl (1989) and others. We will, furthermore, generalize results in Rubin's framework and characterize in graphical terms the conditions under which those results apply.

2. Rubin's Framework and Pratt and Schlaifer's Rules

Rubin's framework has a simple and appealing intuition. In experimental or observational studies we sample from a population. Each unit in the population, whether a child or a national economy or a sample of a chemical, has a collection of properties. Among the properties of the units in the population, some are *dispositional*—they are propensities of a system to give a response to a treatment. A glass vase, for example, may be fragile, meaning that it has a disposition to break if struck sharply. A dispositional property isn't exhibited unless the appropriate treatment is applied—fragile vases don't break unless they are struck. Similarly, in a population of children, for each reading program each child has a disposition to produce a certain post-test score (or range of test scores) if exposed to that reading program. In experimental studies when we give different treatments to different units, we are attempting to estimate dispositional properties of units (or their averages, or the differences of their averages) from data in which only some of the units have been exposed to the circumstances in which that disposition is manifested. Rubin associates with each such dispositional quantity, Q, and *each value x* of relevant treatment variable, X, a random variable, Q_{xf}, whose value for each unit in the population is the value Q *would have* if that unit were to be given treatment x, or in other words if X were forced to equal x. If unit i is actually given treatment $x1$ and a value of Q is measured for that unit, the measured value of Q equals the value of Q_{x1f}.

Experimentation may give a set of paired values $<x, y> = <x, y_{xf}>$, where y_{xf} is the value of the random variable Y_{xf}. But for a unit i that is given treatment $x1$, we also want to know the value of Y_{x2f}, Y_{x3f}, and so on for each possible value of X, representing respectively the values for Y that unit i is disposed to exhibit if unit i were exposed to treatment $x2$ or $x3$, that is, if the X value for these units were forced to be $x2$ or $x3$ rather than $x1$. These unobserved values depend on the causal structure of the system. For example, the value of Y that unit i is disposed to exhibit on treatment $x2$ might depend on the treatments given to other units. We will suppose that there is no dependence of this kind, but we will investigate in detail other sorts of connections between causal structure and Rubin's counterfactual random variables.

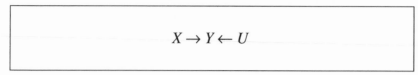

Figure 2. Causal graph of example 1.

A typical inference problem in Rubin's framework is to estimate the distribution of Y_{xf} for some value x of X, over all units in the population, from a sample in which only some members have received the treatment x. A number of variations arise. Rather than forcing a unique value on X, we may contemplate forcing some specified distribution of values on X, or we may contemplate forcing different specified distributions on X depending on the (unforced) values of some other variables Z; our experiment may be purely observational so that an observed value q of variable Q for unit i when X is observed to have value x is not necessarily the same as Q_{xf}. Answers to various problems such as these can be found in the papers cited. For example, in our paraphrasing, Pratt and Schlaifer claim the following:

> When all units are systems in which Y is an effect of X and possibly of other variables, and no causes of Y other than X are measured, in order for the conditional distribution of Y on $X = x$ to equal Y_{xf} for all values of x of X, it is sufficient and "almost necessary" that X and each of the random variables Y_{xf} (where xf ranges over all possible values of X) be statistically independent.

Pratt and Schlaifer's principle requires us to treat *some* counterfactual variables as the same as their observed counterparts, to let the manipulated variable X_f be independent of *some* counterfactual variables, and to let *some* other counterfactual variables have their distributions be determined by manipulated variables in the same way as in the unmanipulated, sampled distribution. What principles guide these choices? What determines that some counterfactual variables are the same as their observed counterparts while others are not? Which choices are to be made in applying the framework, and why?

Pratt and Schlaifer's claim may be clarified with several examples, which will also serve to illustrate some tacit assumptions in the application of the framework. Suppose X and U, which are unobserved, are the only causes of Y, and they have no causal connection of any kind with one another, a circumstance that we will represent by the diagram in figure 2.

For simplicity we suppose the dependencies are all linear, and that for all possible values of X, Y and U, and all units, $Y = X + U$. Let X_f represent values of X that could possibly be *forced* on all units in the population. X is an observed variable; X_f is not. X is a random variable; X_f is not. We further simplify Pratt and Schlaifer's set-up by giving each unit a precise value rather than a distribution of values. Consider the values in table 1.

X	Y	U	X_f	$U_{Xf=1}$	$Y_{Xf=1}$
1	1	0	1	0	1
1	2	1	1	1	2
1	3	2	1	2	3
2	2	0	1	0	1
2	3	1	1	1	2
2	4	2	1	2	3

Table 1. Values for example 1.

Suppose for simplicity each row (ignoring X_f, which is not a random variable) is equally probable. Here the X and Y columns give possible values of the measured variables. The U column gives possible values of the unmeasured variable U. X_f is a variable whose column indicates values of X that might be forced on a unit; we have not continued the table beyond $X_f = 1$. The $U_{Xf=1}$ column represents the range of values of U when X is forced to have the value 1; the $Y_{Xf=1}$ gives the range of values of Y when X is forced to have the value 1. Notice that in the table $Y_{Xf=1}$ is uniquely determined by the value of X_f and the value of $U_{Xf=1}$ and is independent of the value of X. Table 1 illustrates Pratt and Schlaifer's claim: $Y_{Xf=1}$ is independent of X and the distribution of Y conditional on $X = 1$ equals the distribution of $Y_{Xf=1}$.

We constructed the table by letting $U = U_{Xf=1}$, and $Y_{Xf=1} = 1 + U_{Xf=1}$. In other words, we obtained the table by assuming that save for the distribution of X, the causal and probabilistic structures are completely unaltered if a value of X is forced on all units. By applying the same procedure with $Y_{Xf=2} = 2 + U_{Xf=2}$, the table can be extended to obtain values when $X_f = 2$ that satisfy Pratt and Schlaifer's claim.

Consider a different example in which, according to Pratt and Schlaifer's rule, the law relating Y to X is *not* observable. In this case X causes Y and U causes Y, and there is no causal connection of any kind between X and U, as before, but in addition an unmeasured variable V is a common cause of both X and Y, a situation we represent in figure 3.

Consider the distribution in table 2, with the same conventions as in table 1. Again, assume all rows are equally probable, ignoring the value of Xf, which is not a random variable. Notice that $Y_{Xf=1}$ is now *dependent* on the value of X. And, just as Pratt and Schlaifer require, the conditional distribution of Y on $X = 1$ is *not* equal to the distribution of $Y_{Xf=1}$.

Table 2 was constructed so that when $X = 1$ is forced, and hence $Xf = 1$,

X	V	U	Y	Xf	$V_{Xf=1}$	$U_{Xf=1}$	$Y_{Xf=1}$
0	0	0	0	1	0	0	1
0	0	1	1	1	0	1	2
0	0	2	2	1	0	2	3
0	0	3	3	1	0	3	4
1	1	0	2	1	1	0	2
1	1	1	3	1	1	1	3
1	1	2	4	1	1	2	4
1	1	3	5	1	1	3	5

Table 2. Values for example 2.

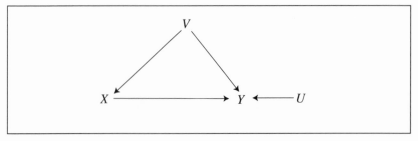

Figure 3. Causal graph for example 2.

the distributions of $U_{Xf=1}$, and $V_{Xf=1}$ are independent of Xf. In other words, while the system of equations $\{Y = X + V + U; X = V\}$ was used to obtain the values of X and Y, the assumptions $U_{Xf} = U$, $V_{Xf} = V$ and the single equation $Y_{Xf} = Xf + V_{Xf} + U_{Xf}$ were used to determine the values of $U_{Xf=1}$, $V_{Xf=1}$ and $Y_{Xf=1}$. The forced system was treated as if it were described by figure 4.

For another example, suppose $Y = X + U$, but there is also a variable V that is dependent on both Y and X, so that the system can be depicted in figure 5.

Table 3 displays values obtained by assuming $Y = X + U$ and $V = Y + X$, and these relations are unaltered by a manipulation of X.

Again assume all rows are equally probable. Note that $Y_{Xf=1}$ is independent of X, and $Y_{Xf=1}$ has the same marginal distribution as Y conditional on $X = 1$. So Pratt and Schlaifer's principle is again satisfied, and in addition the law relating X and Y is "observable." The table was constructed by supposing the manipulated system satisfies the very same system of equations as the un-manipulated system, and in effect that the diagram of dependencies in figure 4 is unaltered by forcing values on X.

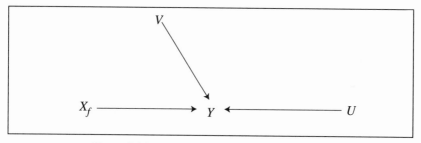

Figure 4. Manipulated causal graph for example 2.

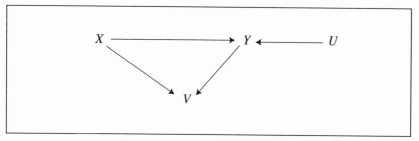

Figure 5. Causal graph for example 3.

X	Y	V	U	Xf	$V_{Xf=1}$	$U_{Xf=1}$	$Y_{Xf=1}$
0	0	0	0	1	2	0	1
0	1	1	1	1	3	1	2
0	2	2	2	1	4	2	3
1	1	2	0	1	2	0	1
1	2	3	1	1	3	1	2
1	3	4	2	1	4	2	3

Table 3. Values for example 3.

Consider finally an example due to Rubin. In an experiment in which treatments T are assigned on the basis of a randomly sampled value of some variable X which shares one or more unmeasured common causes, V, with Y, we wish to predict the average difference τ in Y values if all units in the population were given treatment $T = 1$ as against if all units were given treatment $T = 2$. The situation in the experiment can again be represented by a diagram (figure 6).

The pretest (X), reading program assignment (T), posttest (Y) case is a

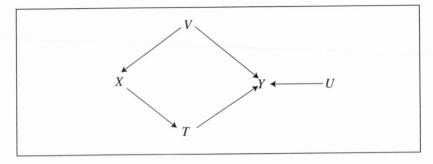

Figure 6. Unmanipulated causal graph for Rubin's example.

model. Provided the experimental sample is sufficiently representative, Rubin says that an unbiased estimate of τ can be obtained as follows: Let k range over values of X, let $\overline{Y1k}$ be the average value of Y conditional on $X = k$ and $T = 1$, and analogously for $\overline{Y2k}$. Let $n1k$ be the number of units in the sample with $T = 1$ and $X = k$, and analogously for $n2k$. The numbers $n1$ and $n2$ represent the total number of units in the sample with $T = 1$ and $T = 2$ respectively. Then estimate the expected value of Y if treatment 1 is forced on all units by

$$\sum_{k=1}^{K} \frac{n1k + n2k}{n1 + n2} \overline{Y1k}$$

and estimate τ by:

$$\sum_{k=1}^{K} \frac{n1k + n2k}{n1 + n2} \left[\overline{Y1k} + \overline{Y2k}\right]$$

The basis for this choice may not be apparent. In the distribution of experimental units, the expected value of Y *conditional on $T = 1$* is

$$\sum_k P(X \mid T = 1)\, P(Y \mid T = 1, X = k).$$

But in calculating the expected value of Y if *treatment 1 is forced on all units,* Rubin substitutes the formula

$$\sum_k P(X)\, P(Y \mid T = 1, X = k)$$

Now, $P(X \mid T)$ is equal to $P(X)$ if and only if X and T are independent. In other words, in calculating the distribution of Y when T is forced to have value 1 (or when forced to have value 2), Rubin treats X and T as independent. In effect, he assumes the manipulated systems would have the structure shown in figure 7.

We trust these examples help to clarify the idea behind Pratt and Schlaifer's principle, but they don't themselves answer the chief questions. Pratt and Schlaifer's principle is satisfied when (1) we treat *some* counterfactual variables as the same as their observed counterparts, (2) let the manipulated variable Xf be independent of *some* counterfactual variables, and (3) let *some* other

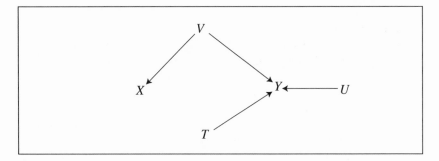

Figure 7. Manipulated causal graph for Rubin's example.

counterfactual variables have their distributions determined by Xf, U_{Xf} and V_{Xf} in the same way that the distribution of Y is determined by X, U and V. What principles guide these choices? If, to modify Rubin's example, treatment were assigned not on the basis of pretest X but on the basis of some variable such as family income which presumably is a cause of X, could we predict the conditional distribution of Y on X values if all children were given a particular reading program? Presumably there is some principle that determines which variables are changed in their marginal distributions upon a manipulation, which are not changed, and which formerly dependent variables are made independent. We will give such a principle in the context of graphical causal models.

3. Graphical Causal Models

Under appropriate conventions, the diagrams we have drawn are not only depictions of hypothetical causal dependencies, they are also perfectly definite statistical hypotheses. We will assume that causal relations among variables are represented by a directed acyclic graph. The variables of interest are vertices of the graph, and a directed edge $X \rightarrow Y$ indicates that X is a cause of Y whose influence is not entirely mediated by other variables in the graph. Following Kiiveri and Speed (1982) and Pearl (1988) we will assume that if units satisfying such causal relations are to be sampled randomly, the distribution thus determined satisfies the Markov condition, or more strongly, the Faithfulness condition.

Markov condition: A graph G and a probability distribution P on the vertices $\mathbf{V}$ of G satisfy the Markov condition if and only if for every V in $\mathbf{V}$, and every set $\mathbf{X}$ of vertices in $\mathbf{V}$ such that no member of $\mathbf{X}$ is a descendant of V, V and $\mathbf{X}$ are independent conditional on the parents of V.

Faithfulness condition: P is faithful to G provided for all disjoint sets of variables $\mathbf{X}$, $\mathbf{Y}$, and $\mathbf{Z}$, $\mathbf{X}$ and $\mathbf{Z}$ are independent conditional on $\mathbf{Y}$ in P if and only if **X** and **Z** are independent conditional on **Y** in every distribution satisfying the Markov condition for *G*.

The Faithfulness condition says that the Markov condition applied to *G* completely axiomatizes the conditional independence relations in *P*. For linear causal systems with multinormally distributed variables it can be shown that the set of linear coefficients and exogenous variances for which the Markov condition is satisfied by a graph but faithfulness is not satisfied has zero Lebesque measure. As we will see, Pratt and Schlaifer assume a condition that is at least as strong as Faithfulness.

For any distribution satisfying the Markov condition on a graph *G* with vertex set *V*, the joint density can be factored

$$\prod_{i=1}^{n} P(V_i \mid \pi_i) \tag{1}$$

where π_i denotes the (possibly empty) set of parents of vertex V_i (Kiiveri and Speed 1982). Directed independence graphs represent hypotheses about marginal independence and marginal conditional independence relations as well as nonmarginal relations. We will use "conditional independence" to include both marginal and nonmarginal relations. For multinomial distributions the maximum likelihood estimate of the distribution subject to the conditional independence constraints represented by the causal graph can be obtained by substituting the marginal sample frequencies into formula (1).

In keeping with the discussion of section 1, we are interested in making predictions about distributions that are produced by forcing a distribution on a variable(s) in a way that breaks causal links *into* that variable, and only such links, in the causal structure actually sampled. We make one assumption about distributions produced by such forcing:

Manipulation condition: If the original distribution is

$$\prod_{i=1}^{n} P(V_i \mid \pi_i)$$

then a manipulation of *X* to force P_X on *X*—in such a way that changes in distributions of other variables are due entirely to changes in the distribution of *X*—gives the same distribution save that $P(X \mid \pi_X)$ is replaced by P_X.

In view of the factorization principle for probability distributions satisfying the Markov condition, the Manipulation condition implies that in a system originally represented by graph *G*, the directed graph *G'* representing the system upon forcing a distribution *P(X)* is obtained by deleting from *G* all of the edges directed into *X*. A generalization of the Manipulation condition says that if we force a distribution on *X* depending on the unforced values of a variable *Z*, the original conditional distribution of *X* on its parents should be replaced by the forced conditional distribution of *X* on *Z*, and the original graph replaced by a graph that is otherwise the same save that there is an edge from *Z* into *X* and there are no other edges directed into *X*.

In each of the examples illustrating Pratt and Schlaifer's condition, the tables of values accord with the Manipulation condition—indeed, that is how we calculated them. Likewise, Rubin's analysis of treatment assignment determined by a covariate gives exactly the result that would be obtained by applying the Manipulation condition. That seems to us good reason to think that the structure the Rubin framework is after is caught by the Markov, Faithfulness and Manipulation conditions. A model-free theory of causal inference and experimental design follows from these axioms, and in practice the entire story is contained in the diagrams. If the causal structure of the experimental system is known, determining observability is as simple as drawing a picture and then erasing one or more lines.

While we will show how to obtain equivalents in graphical terms of Rubin's and Pratt and Schlaifer's results, it should be pointed out that the framework is more general. The results we have described in the Rubin framework give rules for predicting particular features of a joint distribution provided the causal structure is known and satisfies various conditions. The Markov and Manipulation conditions specify, for any causal structure given by an acyclic directed graph, any appropriate joint distribution, and any distribution or conditional distribution to be imposed on any subset of the variables, the resulting joint distribution of all of the variables.

4. Sampling and Conditional Probabilities

If the conditional probability relations for variables in units with the same structure are known, then by the Manipulation condition we can derive the probability distribution that will be obtained for any variable Y upon forcing a distribution on a set of variables X in a fashion that satisfies the antecedent of the condition. Hence an estimate of the conditional probability relations leads to a prediction. In both observational and experimental studies we sample from a population; the difference is that in experimental studies we force a distribution on some of the variables. Rubin (1978) emphasizes, correctly we believe, the importance of sample selection and assignment mechanisms. However we sample, to apply the Manipulation condition to predict the effects on variable Y of manipulations or policies directed to variables X, we need to know if the conditional probabilities can be consistently estimated from the sample. Suppose there is a population whose units are each described by a directed graph G of causal structure; let the values of the variables be distributed as P faithfully to G. Under what methods of sampling will the conditional probabilities for sampled variables be as in P?

We will assume that a sample is always obtained by specifying a property S that, like other variables of concern, has a distribution of values in the population. In the simplest case, S can be viewed as a binary variable with the value 1 indicating that a unit has the sample property. In principle one might wish to select a sample by using a variable with several values (e.g., age group) and drawing fixed numbers or proportions from each group. So our general questions concern when conditioning on any value of S leaves unaltered the conditional probabilities or conditional independence relations for variables in the vertex set of G. We will not consider questions about the sampling distributions obtained by imposing various constraints on the distribution of values of S in a sample. Our treatment assumes that S is not logically connected with any of the variables in G, but trivial variations of the theorems apply when S is identical with one of those variable.

The graph G can be expanded to a graph $G(S)$ that includes S and whatever causal relations S and the other variables realize. We assume a distribution $P(S)$ faithful to $G(S)$ whose marginal distribution summing over S values will of course be P. We suppose that the sampling distribution is determined by the conditional distribution $P(\_ \mid S)$. Our questions are then, more precisely, when this conditional distribution has the same conditional probabilities and conditional independence relations as P. We require, moreover, that the answer be given in terms of the properties of the graph $G(S)$. To give the full answer we require some simple graph theoretic definitions and a lemma.

Any sequence of vertices joined by edges of any orientation, e.g.

$A \rightarrow B \leftarrow C \leftarrow D \rightarrow E,$

is an *undirected* path, and any vertex in which two edges meet in such a path is a *collider* on the path, e.g., B in the path illustrated. An undirected path is said to be *into* a terminus, e.g., E, if it contains an edge into E, and *out of* a terminus, e.g., A, if it contains an edge out of A. A *parent* of vertex V in graph G is any vertex U such that $U \rightarrow V$ in G; a *descendant* of U is any vertex V (including U) such that there is a directed path from U to V.

In directed graph G, variables X, Y are *d-connected* relative to a set $\mathbf{Z}$ of variables not containing X or Y provided there exists a sequence p of edges (an undirected path) connecting X, Y such that no noncollider on p is in $\mathbf{Z}$ and every collider on $\mathbf{Z}$ has a descendant in $\mathbf{Z}$. (Pearl 1988; Lauritzen, et al. 1990) any undirected path with the properties of p is said to be a *d-connecting path* for X, Y with respect to $\mathbf{Z}$. X and Y are *d*-separated by $\mathbf{Z}$ if and only if X and Y are not *d*-connected given $\mathbf{Z}$. For any three disjoint sets of variables $\mathbf{X}$, $\mathbf{Y}$, and $\mathbf{Z}$, $\mathbf{X}$ and $\mathbf{Y}$ are *d*-separated by $\mathbf{Z}$ if and only if every member of $\mathbf{X}$ is *d*-separated from every member of $\mathbf{Y}$ by $\mathbf{Z}$.

Assume for the moment that all variables are discrete.

LEMMA For any directed acyclic graph G and probability distribution P on the vertices of G, P is faithful to G if and only if for all vertices X, Y and every set $\mathbf{Z}$ of vertices, $\mathbf{Z}$ *d*-separates X, Y if and only if X, Y are conditionally independent on $\mathbf{Z}$.

That d-separability characterizes the Markov condition was proved by Verma. See Pearl (1988).

Theorem 1

Let X, S, Y be distinct discrete variables in G, P a distribution faithful to G. Then $Y \perp\!\!\!\perp S \mid X$ if and only if $\{X\}$ d-separates Y and S in $G(S)$.

(We use Dawid's notation, so that $Y \perp\!\!\!\perp S \mid X$ signifies that Y, S are independent conditional on X). The theorem follows immediately from the lemma since for discrete variables $P(Y \mid X) = P(Y \mid X, S)$ if and only if Y, S are independent conditional on X. A parallel lemma can be proved for linear systems with partial correlations substituted for conditional independence, and a corresponding theorem then follows (Spirtes, Glymour, and Scheines 1993).

Theorem 1 generalizes to any number of conditioning variables $X1, ..., Xn$. The theorem is essentially the observation that for any covariate Z, $P(Y \mid XZ) = P(Y \mid XZS)$ if and only if in P the variables Y and S are independent conditional on $\{XZ\}$. It entails, for example, that if we wish to estimate the conditional probability of Y on X from a sample of units with an S property (say, $S = 1$) and a Z property, we should try to ensure that there is (1) no direct connection between Y and S; (2) no trek between Y and S that does not contain X or Z, and; (3) no pair of treks between Y and Z and between S and Z that are both into Z, and similarly for Y and X.

Our sampling property should not be the direct or indirect cause or effect of Y save through a mechanism that is blocked by holding X and Z constant, and neither X nor Z should be the effect, direct or indirect of both Y and the sampling property. (The latter clause in effect guarantees that Simpson's paradox is avoided in a faithful distribution).

These examples are of course not exhaustive. Theorem 1 entails a partial justification of the conventional wisdom: "prospective" sampling is more reliable than "retrospective" sampling if by the former is meant a procedure that selects by a property associated with Y, the effect, only through X, the cause, and by the latter is meant a procedure that selects by a property associated with X only through Y.

5. Prediction and Experimental Design

The Markov and Manipulation conditions provide the basis for prediction from samples obtained by experiment, quasi-experiment or observation provided appropriate facts about the causal structure of the sampled population are known. We will consider several issues of design taken up by Rubin or by Pratt and Schlaifer.

5.1 Randomization

Suppose as before that the goal is to estimate the conditional probability $P(Y \mid X)$ in distribution P. In drawing a random sample of units from P we in effect sample according to a property S that is entirely disconnected, graphically, from the variables of interest in the system. If we succeed in doing that, then we ensure that S has no causal connections that can bias the estimate of the conditional probability. Of course because of sample variation an actual sample so obtained might give a poor estimate of the conditional probability in the population. Substantive knowledge about the causal relations of the sampling property could in principle substitute for randomization.

5.2 Observability

Pratt and Schlaifer are concerned with the following question: If X and Y are measured, and no other relevant variables are measured, when is the conditional distribution of Y on any value x of X equal to the distribution Y would have if X were forced to have value x? If the equality holds, they say the law relating the distributions of Y and X is "observable." One of their "sufficient and almost necessary" conditions for observability is that X and Y_{xf} be independently distributed for any value xf of Xf. The condition can only be applied if we know the joint distribution of X and Y_{xf}. The Manipulation condition gives the following result:

Theorem 2

Assuming the Faithfulness and Manipulation conditions, and assuming that all conditional probabilities are positive, the law giving the dependency of Y on X will be "observable" if and (almost) only if in the sampled systems no undirected path *into* X d-connects X, Y with respect to the empty set of vertices. Equivalently, if and (almost) only if (1) Y is not a cause of X, and (2) there is no common cause of X and Y.

The sufficiency claimed in theorem 2 is a special case of theorem 3 below and requires only the Markov and Manipulation conditions. "Necessity" is used in the vague sense of Pratt and Schlaifer's claim: unless the distribution satisfies special constraints, the condition is necessary assuming Faithfulness.

In comparing the conditional distribution of Y on X in our experimental or observational sample with the distribution of Y_{Xf}, we are comparing factors in distributions for two graphs. The original graph, G, represents the causal structure of the observed or experimental system; the other graph, G', is the original graph, *minus all of the edges directed into X*. Y_{Xf} will be distributed in the same way as Y conditional on X if and only if when we use the factorization formula (1) on the two graphs, we find in each case the same formula for the conditional distribution of Y on X. Theorem 2 gives the sufficient graphical condition for the sameness of the conditional distribution of Y on X in G and in G'.

Theorem 2 is illustrated in the three tables of section 2 and the accompanying causal graphs. For example if G is given by figure 2, then G' is given by the same figure, and the conditional distribution of Y on X is trivially the same in both cases. If G is given by the graph in figure 3 , then G' is given by figure 4 and the conditional distribution of Y on X for G is

$$\sum_{uv} P(Y \mid X, U, V) P(X \mid V) P(U) P(V)$$

while for G' it is $\sum_{uv} P(Y \mid X, U, V) P(X) P(U) P(V)$ where probabilities of the same arguments have the same values for G and G'. Save for odd cases, the two expressions are equal only if $P(X) = P(X \mid V)$, which will not be the case if P is a distribution faithful to G. The Faithfulness condition captures part of what is meant by Pratt and Schlaifer's claim that their rule is "almost necessary."

5.3 Covariates and Predicting Conditional Distributions in Manipulated Populations

Pratt and Schlaifer consider the case in which, besides X and Y, some further variables $\mathbf{Z}$ are measured. Their discussion is a generalization of Rubin's (1977) discussion of experiments in which treatment assignments depend on some variable that is a cause of the outcome variable or shares a common cause with the outcome variable. (Rubin's X is Pratt and Schlaifer's Z; Rubin's T is Pratt and Schlaifer's X; we will keep with Pratt and Schlaifer's notation.) We know from theorem 2 that if in the sampled or experimental systems Z is a cause of both X and Y, or a cause of X and shares a common cause with Y, then the distribution of Y if a value x is forced on X will not be the same as the conditional probability of Y on X. The dependency of Y on X will not be "observable." Rubin's observation is in effect that in this situation we can nonetheless use the conditional probability of Y given $Z = z$ and $X = x$ to estimate the distribution of Y given $Z = z$ when X is forced to have the value x. Pratt and Schlaifer say in this case that the law relating Y to X is "observable with concomitant Z." With an estimate in hand for each value z of Z of the distribution of Y conditional on $Z = z$ when X is forced to have the value x, by summing over the values of the concomitant Z, Rubin estimates the average value Y when X is forced to have the value x. Pratt and Schlaifer also claim sufficient and "almost necessary" conditions for observability with concomitants, namely that for any value x of X the distribution of X be independent of the conditional distribution of Y_x on the value of z of Z_{xf} when X is forced to have the value x. We will give a general sufficient condition in graphical terms, a condition which follows necessarily from the Markov and Manipulation conditions.

Theorem 3

Assuming the Markov and Manipulation conditions and positivity for all conditional probabilities, for all values of X and of $\mathbf{Z}$, the distribution of Y conditional on $X = x$ and $\mathbf{Z}$ equals the distribution of Y conditional on $\mathbf{Z}$ when X is forced to have the value x if no path d-connecting X, Y relative to $\mathbf{Z}$ is *into X*.

The proof is given in a later section. Pratt and Schlaifer say their condition is "almost necessary." What they mean, we take it, is that there are cases in which their condition fails to hold but they arise only if a special constraint is satisfied by the conditional probabilities. Parallel remarks apply to the graphical condition given in theorem 3.

Theorem 4

Assuming the Markov and Manipulation conditions and positivity for all conditional probabilities, is X is not in $\mathbf{Z}$, for all values of X and of $\mathbf{Z}$, the distribution of Y conditional on $\mathbf{Z}$ equals the distribution of Y conditional on $\mathbf{Z}$ when X is forced to have the value x if either X has no descendant in $\{Y\} \cup \mathbf{Z}$, or X is not d-connected to Y given $\mathbf{Z}$.

6. Causal Inference

Some disputes are less about how much one variable affects another and more about whether one variable affects another at all. For example in the 1950s R. A. Fisher and many epidemiologists were not so much concerned with estimating how much of the incidence of lung cancer was due to smoking, or how much the rate of lung cancer would decline if people stopped smoking; they were principally concerned with whether smoking has a causal role in producing lung cancer. (Cook 1979). Consider questions of the following kind: Does X influence Y at all? Does X influence Y by any mechanism that cannot be blocked by controlling Z? Answers to such questions are to be obtained from a sample of units that may or may not have been subjected to some experimental treatment. As before, the first issue is to characterize sampling procedures that do not bias answers to such questions.

In theorem 5 let $\mathbf{Z}$ be any set of variables in G not including X and Y.

Theorem 5

Exactly one of $< X \perp\!\!\!\perp Y \mid \mathbf{Z};\ X \perp\!\!\!\perp Y \mid \mathbf{Z} \cup \{S\}>$ is false if and only if the corresponding member and only that member of $<\mathbf{Z}$ d-separates X, Y; $\mathbf{Z} \cup \{S\}$ d-separates X, $Y>$ is false.

Theorem 5 is an obvious application of previous results. Suppose in the ambient distribution P that X and Y are independent conditional on $\mathbf{Z}$. When will sample property S make it appear that X and Y are instead dependent conditional on $\mathbf{Z}$? The answer is exactly when X, Y are dependent conditional on $\mathbf{Z} \cup \{S\}$ in $P(S)$. This circumstance—conditional independence in P and conditional dependence in $P(S)$—can occur for faithful distributions when and only when there exists an undirected path q from X to Y with special properties. Then for conditional independence in P and conditional independence in $P(S)$ there must exist an undirected path q in the causal graph such that (1) no noncollider on q is in $\mathbf{Z} \cup \{S\}$; (2) every collider on q has a descendant in $\mathbf{Z} \cup \{S\}$; and (3) some collider on q does not have a descendant in $\mathbf{Z}$.

The converse error involves conditional dependence in P and conditional independence in $P(S)$. That can happen in a faithful distribution when and only when there exists an undirected path U from X to Y such that (1) every collider on U has a descendant in $\mathbf{Z}$; and (2) no noncollider in U is in $\mathbf{Z}$, and S is a noncollider on every such path. Again, asymptotically both of these errors can be avoided by sampling randomly, that is by a property S that is causally unconnected with the variables of interest.

7. Conclusion

The Rubin framework for comparing distributional properties between manipulated and unmanipulated (or differently manipulated) populations is a first step towards a principled understanding of prediction and experimental design, and we hope the derivation of the claims of that framework from axioms on directed graphical models represents a further step towards the same goal. It is important to recognize, however, how small these steps are, and how far they leave us from the goal.

The property Pratt and Schlaiffer call "observability" is better termed *conditional probability invariance under manipulation*, since their principles are neither necessary nor sufficient for predicting features of a distribution of manipulated systems from distributional properties of a population of unmanipulated systems. The insufficiency is due to the fact that Pratt and Shlaiffer's and Rubin's conditions presume counterfactual—that is, in most cases, causal—knowledge about the systems under study, but provide no information as to when the marginal distribution of measured variables and background knowledge determine enough about causal structure to conclude that particular conditional probabilities are the same in the manipulated and unmanipulated distributions. Assuming either the Markov or the Faithfulness conditions, there are connections between causal structure and marginal distributional structure; the implications of these connections for conditional probability invariance under manipulation are described in Spirtes, Glymour, and Scheines (1993).

That conditional probability invariance is unnecessary for the prediction of features of manipulated distributions can be illustrated in a simple linear case. Suppose the causal structure is that shown in figure 8, and all dependencies are linear. Suppose only A, S and C are observed. For concreteness,

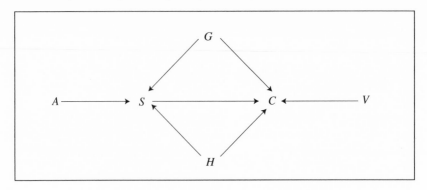

Figure 8. Hypothetical causal graph for smoking.

we can interpret *A* as cigarette advertising exposure, *S* as cigarette smoking, *C* as age at death, although it is not very likely these variables are linearly related. Let b be the linear coefficient of *S* in the equation for *C*. For a standardized model, *b* is proportional to the partial correlation of *C*, *S* controlling for all unmeasured causes. If *S* is manipulated according to the Manipulation condition, the graph is the same save that the $G \rightarrow S$ and $H \rightarrow S$ edges are omitted, the linear equations are correspondingly altered, and *S* becomes independent of *A*, *G* and *H*. The conditional density of *C* given *S* is not the same in the manipulated and unmanipulated distributions, and the "law" relating *S* and *C* is not "observable," in Pratt and Schlaiffer's terminology.

Now suppose one knew the following about the causal structure: *A* has no effect on *C* save possibly through *S*. Then *b* is determined by the ratio of the correlation of *A* and *C* to the correlation of *S* and *C*. But *b* determines the difference in mean values of *C* for two manipulations that assign different values to *S*. An unbiased estimate of the differential effects of alternative smoking behaviors on mortality could be obtained without any knowledge of the unobserved common causes (see Fox 1984, p. 234–236).

Finally, it should be noted that while the Manipulation condition captures the intuitions of the Rubin framework in graphical terms, in many cases it is not a correct representation of the relation between a distribution of unmanipulated units and the distribution that would result from a manipulation. In the Rose and MRFIT studies of smoking and mortality, for example, the Manipulation condition arguably did not apply because the counseling and support treatment given to one group merely added another cause of smoking behavior in the members of that treatment group. Other causes of smoking behavior in the treatment and nontreatment groups were not disengaged, as they might have been if, for example, members of one group had been forced not to smoke and members of the other had been forced to continue smoking.

8. Proof of Theorem 3

The proof of theorem 3 requires a series of lemmas. Let P be the distribution over a set of variables containing X in a population, and P' be the corresponding distribution when X is manipulated to have the value x. Y is *observable conditional on* $\mathbf{Z}$, *when X is manipulated* iff $P(Y \mid \mathbf{Z}) = P'(Y \mid \mathbf{Z})$. We will show that if P is faithful to the graph G of the causal process that generated P then Y is observable conditional on $\{X\} \cup \mathbf{Z}$ when X is manipulated if in G there are no paths that d-connect X to Y given $\mathbf{Z}$ that are into X, and Y is observable conditional on $\mathbf{Z}$ when X is manipulated if in G, X either has no descendants in $\{Y\} \cup \mathbf{Z}$ or X is not d-connected to Y given $\mathbf{Z}$.

For a distribution P over a set of variables V

$$P(\mathbf{V}) = \prod_{V \in \mathbf{V}} P(V \mid \pi_v)$$

is a *graphical factorization* of P according to G if and only for each V in $\mathbf{V}$, π_V is the set of parents of V in G, and the terms (conditional probabilities) in the product are ordered so that for each term $P(V \mid \pi_V)$, V does not occur in any term to its left.

Let $\mathbf{S}$ be a subset of $\mathbf{V}$. Consider the marginal distribution that results by summing $P(\mathbf{V})$ over $\mathbf{S}$.

$$P(\mathbf{V} \setminus \mathbf{S}) = \sum_s \left(\prod_{v \in \mathbf{V}} P(V \mid \mathbf{X}(V)) \right)$$

We will describe an algorithm that divides $\mathbf{S}$ into two disjoint subsets $\mathbf{IV}$(informative variables) and $\mathbf{IV}'$ such that $P(\mathbf{V}\setminus\mathbf{S})$ is equal to the product of a summation over $\mathbf{IV}$ and a summation over $\mathbf{IV}'$.

If T is a set of terms (conditional probabilities) in a given recursive factorization F of $P(\mathbf{V})$, let $Var(T)$ be the set of variables appearing in T. Similarly, if $\mathbf{S}$ is a set of variables included in $\mathbf{V}$, let $Terms(\mathbf{S})$ be the set of terms containing variables in $\mathbf{S}$. If the summation over $\mathbf{S}$ is equal to a product of two summations over $\mathbf{IV}$ and $\mathbf{IV}'$ respectively, then $Var(Terms(\mathbf{IV})) \cap Var(Terms(\mathbf{IV}'))$ is included in $\mathbf{V}\setminus\mathbf{S}$. If P is factorized according to graph F and $\mathbf{S}$ is a set of variables being summed over, the following algorithm generates the smallest set of variables $\mathbf{IV}$ such that $P(\mathbf{V}\setminus\mathbf{S})$ is factored into a product of a summation over $\mathbf{IV}$ of a product of terms in $Terms(\mathbf{IV} \cup \{Y\})$ and a summation over $\mathbf{IV}'$ of a product of terms in $Terms(\mathbf{V})\setminus Terms(\mathbf{IV} \cup \{Y\})$, where Y occurs only in $Var(Terms(\mathbf{IV} \cup \{Y\}))$.

Algorithm Factor (F, V, S, Y, IV, IV')

1. If Y is in $\mathbf{S}$, then Y is in $\mathbf{IV}(F, \mathbf{V}, \mathbf{S}, Y)$.
2. $\pi_y \cap \mathbf{S}$ and $\mathbf{Children}(Y) \cap \mathbf{S}$ are in $\mathbf{IV}(F, \mathbf{V}, \mathbf{S}, Y)$.
3. If W is in $\mathbf{IV}$, then $\pi_w \cap \mathbf{S}$ and $\mathbf{Children}(W) \cap \mathbf{S}$ are in $\mathbf{IV}(F, \mathbf{V}, \mathbf{S}, Y)$.

4. If Z is in $\mathbf{V} \backslash \mathbf{S} \cup \{Y\}$ and some member of π_Z is in $\mathbf{IV}(F, \mathbf{V}, \mathbf{S}, Y)$, then every member of $\pi_V \cap \mathbf{S}$ is in $\mathbf{IV}(F, \mathbf{V}, \mathbf{S}, Y)$.

5. $\mathbf{IV}'(F, \mathbf{V}, \mathbf{S}, Y) = \mathbf{S} \backslash \mathbf{IV}(F, \mathbf{V}, \mathbf{S}, Y)$

LEMMA 1. If P is factorized according to graph F then the set $\mathbf{IV}(F, \mathbf{V}, \mathbf{S}, Y)$ generated by algorithm factor($F, V, \mathbf{S}, Y, \mathbf{IV}, \mathbf{IV}'$) is the smallest set such that

$$P(\mathbf{V} \backslash \mathbf{S}) =$$

$$\left(\sum_{\mathbf{IV}(F,\mathbf{V},\mathbf{S},Y)} \left(\prod_{t \in Terms(\mathbf{IV}(F,\mathbf{V},\mathbf{S},Y) \cup \{Y\})}^{t} \right) \right) \times \left(\sum_{\mathbf{IV}'(F,\mathbf{V},\mathbf{S},Y)} \left(\prod_{t \in Terms(\mathbf{V}) \backslash Terms(\mathbf{IV}(F,\mathbf{V},\mathbf{S},Y) \cup \{Y\})}^{t} \right) \right)$$

where Y occurs only in $Var(Terms(\mathbf{IV}(F, \mathbf{V}, \mathbf{S}, Y) \cup \{Y\}))$.

Proof. Because all terms containing Y are in $Terms(\mathbf{IV}(F, \mathbf{V}, \mathbf{S}, Y) \cup \{Y\})$, those terms are under the scope of the summation over $\mathbf{IV}(F, \mathbf{V}, \mathbf{S}, Y)$, and all variables in $\mathbf{S}$ appearing in those terms are in $\mathbf{IV}(F, \mathbf{V}, \mathbf{S}, Y)$. If W is in $\mathbf{IV}(F, \mathbf{V}, \mathbf{S}, Y)$, any term containing W is in $Terms(\mathbf{IV}(F, \mathbf{V}, \mathbf{S}, Y) \cup \{Y\})$ and hence all of the variables in $\mathbf{S}$ occurring in any term containing W are in $\mathbf{IV}(F, \mathbf{V}, \mathbf{S}, Y)$. Finally, if $Z \neq Y$ is in $\mathbf{V} \backslash \mathbf{S}$, a term containing Z is in $Terms(\mathbf{IV}(F, \mathbf{V}, \mathbf{S}, Y))$ if and only if it contains a variable in $\mathbf{IV}(F, \mathbf{V}, \mathbf{S}, Y)$, and then all of the other variables in that term that are in $\mathbf{S}$ are also in $\mathbf{IV}(F, \mathbf{V}, \mathbf{S}, Y)$. Any set smaller than $\mathbf{IV}(F, \mathbf{V}, \mathbf{S}, Y)$ leaves some variable in $\mathbf{S}$ appearing in $Var(Terms(\mathbf{IV}(F, \mathbf{V}, \mathbf{S}, Y) \cup \{Y\}))$ and $Var(Terms(\mathbf{V}) \backslash Terms(\mathbf{IV}(F, \mathbf{V}, \mathbf{S}, Y) \cup \{Y\}))$. Q.E.D.

LEMMA 2. If G is a directed acyclic graph over a set of variables $\mathbf{V}$, $\mathbf{S}$ and $\mathbf{S}'$ are subsets of $\mathbf{V}$ such that $\mathbf{S}' \backslash \mathbf{S} = \{Y\}$, P is a distribution faithful to G, and F is a graphical recursive factorization of P, $\mathbf{IV}(F, \mathbf{V}, \mathbf{S}', Y)$ $\backslash \mathbf{IV}(F, \mathbf{V}, \mathbf{S}, Y) = \{Y\}$.

Proof. This follows directly from the way that Algorithm factor($F, \mathbf{V}, \mathbf{S}, Y, \mathbf{IV}$) constructs $\mathbf{IV}(F, \mathbf{V}, \mathbf{S}', Y)$ and $\mathbf{IV}(F, \mathbf{V}, \mathbf{S}, Y)$. Q.E.D.

If F is a factorization of $P(\mathbf{V})$ with respect to directed acyclic graph G, then $\mathbf{ND}(\mathbf{K})$ corresponds to the set of variables in $\mathbf{V}$ that have no descendant in $\mathbf{K}$ in G.

LEMMA 3. If F is a recursive factorization of $P(\mathbf{V})$, $\mathbf{S}$ is a subset of $\mathbf{V}$, $\mathbf{ND}(Y)$ is included in $\mathbf{S}$, $\mathbf{V}' = \mathbf{V} \backslash \mathbf{ND}(Y)$ then

$$\sum_{\mathbf{S}} \left(\prod_{V \in \mathbf{V}} P(V \mid \pi_V) \right) = \sum_{\mathbf{S} \backslash \mathbf{ND}(Y)} \left(\prod_{V \in \mathbf{V}'} P(V \mid \pi_V) \right)$$

Proof. $\mathbf{S}$ can be partitioned into $\mathbf{S} \backslash \mathbf{ND}(Y)$ and $\mathbf{S} \cap \mathbf{ND}(Y)$. Because $\mathbf{ND}(Y)$ is included in $\mathbf{S}$, $\mathbf{S} \cap \mathbf{ND}(Y) = \mathbf{ND}(Y)$. Also if V is in $\mathbf{V}'$ then no variable occurring in the term $P(V \mid \pi_V)$ occurs in $\mathbf{ND}(Y)$. Hence there is a recursive factorization F' such if V is in $\mathbf{ND}(Y)$ and W is not in $\mathbf{ND}(Y)$, then $P(V \mid \pi_V)$ occurs to the right of $P(W \mid \pi_W)$ in F'.

$$\sum_{S}\left(\prod_{V \in \mathbf{V}} P(V \mid \pi_V)\right) =$$

$$\sum_{S \setminus \mathbf{ND(Y)}}\left(\prod_{V \in \mathbf{V'}} P(V \mid \pi_V) \times \left(\sum_{\mathbf{ND(Y)}}\left(\prod_{V \in \mathbf{ND(Y)}} P(V \mid \pi_V)\right)\right)\right)$$

We will now show that

$$\sum_{\mathbf{ND(Y)}}\left(\prod_{V \in \mathbf{ND(Y)}} P(V \mid \pi_V)\right) = 1$$

Let $P(W \mid \pi_W)$ be the rightmost term in the factorization F'. If $\mathbf{ND(Y)}$ is not empty then by definition W does not occur in any term to its left and is in $\mathbf{ND(Y)}$. Rewrite

$$\sum_{\mathbf{ND(Y)}}\left(\prod_{V \in \mathbf{ND(Y)}} P(V \mid \pi_V)\right)$$

as

$$\sum_{\mathbf{ND(Y)} \setminus W}\left(\left(\prod_{V \in \mathbf{ND(Y)} \setminus W} P(V \mid \pi_V)\right) \times \sum_{W} P(W \mid \pi_W)\right)$$

The latter expression can now be written as

$$\sum_{\mathbf{ND(Y)} \setminus W}\left(\prod_{V \in \mathbf{ND(Y)} \setminus W} P(V \mid \pi_V)\right)$$

because

$$\sum_{W} P(W \mid \pi_W)$$

is equal to one. Repeat this process for each successive rightmost in $\mathbf{ND(Y)}$.
Q.E.D.

We will abbreviate $\{X\} \cup \{Y\} \cup \mathbf{Z}$, by $XY\mathbf{Z}$, and $\{X\} \cup \mathbf{Z}$ by $X\mathbf{Z}$, etc.

LEMMA 4. If F is a recursive factorization of $P(\mathbf{V})$, and $\mathbf{V'} = \mathbf{V} \setminus \mathbf{ND}(Y\mathbf{Z})$ then

$$P(Y \mid \mathbf{Z}) = \frac{\left(\sum_{\mathbf{IV}(F, \mathbf{V'}, \mathbf{V'} \setminus Y\mathbf{Z}, Y)}\left(\prod_{t \in Terms(\mathbf{IV}(F, \mathbf{V'}, \mathbf{V'} \setminus Y\mathbf{Z}, Y) \cup \{Y\})} t\right)\right)}{\left(\sum_{\mathbf{IV}(F, \mathbf{V'}, \mathbf{V'} \setminus \mathbf{Z}, Y)}\left(\prod_{t \in Terms(\mathbf{IV}(F, \mathbf{V'}, \mathbf{V'} \setminus \mathbf{Z}, Y) \cup \{Y\})} t\right)\right)}$$

Proof. By definition, $P(Y \mid \mathbf{Z}) = P(Y\mathbf{Z})/P(\mathbf{Z})$. By definition,

$$P(Y\mathbf{Z}) = \left(\sum_{\mathbf{V} \setminus Y\mathbf{Z}}\prod_{V \in \mathbf{V}} P(V \mid \pi_V)\right)$$

If $\mathbf{V'} = \mathbf{V} \setminus \mathbf{ND}(Y\mathbf{Z})$ then by lemma 3,

$$P(Y\mathbf{Z}) = \left(\sum_{V \setminus Y\mathbf{Z}} \prod_{V \in \mathbf{V}'} P\left(V \mid \pi_V\right) \right)$$

By lemma 1,

$$P(Y\mathbf{Z}) = \left(\sum_{\mathbf{IV}'(F,\mathbf{V}',\mathbf{V}' \setminus Y\mathbf{Z},Y)} \left(\prod_{t \in \mathit{Terms}(\mathbf{V}') \setminus \mathit{Terms}\left(\mathbf{IV}(F,\mathbf{V}',\mathbf{V}' \setminus Y\mathbf{Z},Y) \cup \{Y\}\right)}^{t} \right) \right) \times$$

$$\left(\sum_{\mathbf{IV}(F,\mathbf{V}',\mathbf{V}' \setminus Y\mathbf{Z},Y)} \left(\prod_{t \in \mathit{Terms}(\mathbf{IV})(F,\mathbf{V}',\mathbf{V}' \setminus Y\mathbf{Z},Y \cup \{Y\})}^{t} \right) \right)$$

Also by lemma 1,

$$P(\mathbf{Z}) = \left(\sum_{\mathbf{IV}'(F,\mathbf{V}',\mathbf{V}' \setminus \mathbf{Z},Y)} \left(\prod_{t \in \mathit{Terms}(\mathbf{V}') \setminus \mathit{Terms}\left(\mathbf{IV}(F,\mathbf{V}',\mathbf{V}' \setminus \mathbf{Z},Y) \cup \{Y\}\right)}^{t} \right) \right) \times$$

$$\left(\sum_{\mathbf{IV}(F,\mathbf{V}',\mathbf{V}' \setminus \mathbf{Z},Y)} \left(\prod_{t \in \mathit{Terms}(\mathbf{IV}(F,\mathbf{V}',\mathbf{V}' \setminus \mathbf{Z},Y) \cup \{Y\})}^{t} \right) \right)$$

By lemma 2, $\mathbf{IV}(F, \mathbf{V}', \mathbf{V}' \setminus \mathbf{Z}, Y) \setminus \mathbf{IV}(F, \mathbf{V}', \mathbf{V}' \setminus \mathbf{Z}Y, Y) = \{Y\}$.
Hence $\mathbf{IV}'(F,\mathbf{V}',\mathbf{V}' \setminus \mathbf{Z},Y) = \mathbf{IV}'(F,\mathbf{V}',\mathbf{V}' \setminus \mathbf{Z}Y,Y)$, and
$\mathit{Terms}(\mathbf{IV}(F,\mathbf{V}',\mathbf{V}' \setminus \mathbf{Z},Y) \cup \{Y\}) = \mathit{Terms}(\mathbf{IV}(F, \mathbf{V}', \mathbf{V}' \setminus \mathbf{Z}Y, Y) \cup \{Y\})$.
It follows that

$$\frac{\left(\displaystyle\sum_{\mathbf{IV}'(F,\mathbf{V}',\mathbf{V}' \setminus Y\mathbf{Z},Y)} \left(\prod_{t \in \mathit{Terms}(\mathbf{V}') \setminus \mathit{Terms}\left(\mathbf{IV}(F,\mathbf{V}',\mathbf{V}' \setminus Y\mathbf{Z},Y) \cup \{Y\}\right)}^{t} \right) \right)}{\left(\displaystyle\sum_{\mathbf{IV}'(F,\mathbf{V}',\mathbf{V}' \setminus \mathbf{Z},Y)} \left(\prod_{t \in \mathit{Terms}(\mathbf{V}') \setminus \mathit{Terms}\left(\mathbf{IV}(F,\mathbf{V}',\mathbf{V}' \setminus \mathbf{Z},Y) \cup \{Y\}\right)}^{t} \right) \right)} = 1$$

Q.E.D.

LEMMA 5. If G is a directed acyclic graph over a set of variables $\mathbf{V}$ containing Y and $\mathbf{Z}$, where Y is not a member of $\mathbf{Z}$, $P(\mathbf{V})$ is faithful to G, F is a graphical recursive factorization of $P(\mathbf{V})$ according to G, $\mathbf{V}' = \mathbf{V} \setminus \mathbf{ND}(Y\mathbf{Z})$, and W is in $\mathbf{IV}'(F, \mathbf{V}', \mathbf{V}' \setminus \mathbf{Z}, Y)$ then W is d-separated from Y given $\mathbf{Z}$.

Proof. By lemma 1, $\mathbf{IV}(F, \mathbf{V}', \mathbf{V}' \setminus \mathbf{Z}, Y)$ is a set such that

$$P(\mathbf{V}') =$$

$$\left(\sum_{\mathbf{IV}(F,\mathbf{V}',\mathbf{V}' \setminus \mathbf{Z},Y)} \left(\prod_{t \in \mathit{Terms}\left(\mathbf{IV}(F,\mathbf{V}',\mathbf{V}' \setminus Y\mathbf{Z},Y) \cup \{Y\}\right)}^{t} \right) \right) \times$$

$$\left(\sum_{\mathbf{IV}'(F,\mathbf{V}',\mathbf{V}' \setminus \mathbf{Z},Y)} \left(\prod_{t \in \mathit{Terms}(\mathbf{V}') \setminus \mathit{Terms}\left(\mathbf{IV}(F,\mathbf{V}',\mathbf{V}' \setminus \mathbf{Z},Y) \cup \{Y\}\right)}^{t} \right) \right)$$

Hence $P(\mathbf{V}')$ can be factored into a product of two functions

$g(\mathbf{IV}(F, \mathbf{V}', \mathbf{V}'\backslash\mathbf{Z}, Y) \cup \{Y\}, \mathbf{Z})$ and $h(\mathbf{IV}'(F, \mathbf{V}', \mathbf{V}'\backslash\mathbf{Z}, Y), \mathbf{Z})$.
It follows that $\mathbf{IV}(F, \mathbf{V}', \mathbf{V}'\backslash\mathbf{Z}, Y) \cup \{Y\}$ is independent of $\mathbf{IV}'(F, \mathbf{V}', \mathbf{V}'\backslash\mathbf{Z}, Y)$ given $\mathbf{Z}$. Hence every member of $\mathbf{IV}'(F, \mathbf{V}', \mathbf{V}'\backslash\mathbf{Z}, Y)$ is d-separated from every member of $\mathbf{IV}'(F, \mathbf{V}', \mathbf{V}'\backslash\mathbf{Z}, Y) \cup \{Y\}$, including Y, by $\mathbf{Z}$.

LEMMA 6. If G is a directed acyclic graph over a set of variables $\mathbf{V}$ containing Y and $\mathbf{Z}$, where Y is not a member of $\mathbf{Z}$, $P(\mathbf{V})$ is faithful to G, F is a graphical recursive factorization of $P(\mathbf{V})$ according to G, $\mathbf{V}' = \mathbf{V}\backslash\mathbf{ND}(Y\mathbf{Z})$, and W is in $\mathbf{IV}'(F, \mathbf{V}', \mathbf{V}'\backslash Y\mathbf{Z}, Y)$ then W is d-separated from Y given $\mathbf{Z}$.

Proof. By lemma 5, every member of $\mathbf{IV}'(F, \mathbf{V}', \mathbf{V}'\backslash\mathbf{Z}, Y)$ is d-separated from Y by $\mathbf{Z}$. By lemma 2, $\mathbf{IV}(F, \mathbf{V}, \mathbf{V}'\backslash Y\mathbf{Z}, Y)\backslash\mathbf{IV}(F, \mathbf{V}, \mathbf{V}'\backslash\mathbf{Z}, Y) = \{Y\}$. Hence $\mathbf{IV}(F, \mathbf{V}, \mathbf{V}'\backslash Y\mathbf{Z}, Y) \cup \{Y\} = \mathbf{IV}(F, \mathbf{V}, \mathbf{V}'\backslash\mathbf{Z}, Y) \cup \{Y\}$, $\mathbf{IV}'(F, \mathbf{V}', \mathbf{V}'\backslash Y\mathbf{Z}, Y) = \mathbf{IV}'(F, \mathbf{V}', \mathbf{V}'\backslash\mathbf{Z}, Y)$, and every member of $\mathbf{IV}'(F, \mathbf{V}', \mathbf{V}'\backslash Y\mathbf{Z}, Y)$ is d-separated from Y by $\mathbf{Z}$. Q.E.D.

LEMMA 7. If G is a directed acyclic graph over a set of variables $\mathbf{V}$ containing Y and $\mathbf{Z}$, $P(\mathbf{V})$ is faithful to G, F is a graphical recursive factorization of $P(\mathbf{V})$ according to G, $\mathbf{V}' = \mathbf{V}\backslash\mathbf{ND}(Y\mathbf{Z})$, and X is in $\mathbf{IV}(F, \mathbf{V}', \mathbf{V}'\backslash\mathbf{Z}, Y)\backslash Y$ then X is d-connected to Y given $\mathbf{Z}$.

Proof. Let $\mathbf{V}'(n)$ be the set of variables in $\mathbf{V}'$ such that the longest undirected path from Y to each W in $\mathbf{V}'(n)$ is n. The proof will be by induction over n.
Base Case: If $n = 1$, then the members of $\mathbf{V}'(n)$ are parents or children of Y, which are d-connected to Y given any subset of $\mathbf{V}'$ not containing Y.
Induction Case: Suppose for all $i \leq n$, if W in $\mathbf{V}'(i)$ and W in
$\mathbf{IV}(F, \mathbf{V}', \mathbf{V}'\backslash\mathbf{Z}, Y)\backslash Y$
then W is d-connected to Y given $\mathbf{Z}$. Let X be a member of $\mathbf{V}'(n + 1)$ and $\mathbf{IV}(F, \mathbf{V}', \mathbf{V}'\backslash\mathbf{Z}, Y)\backslash Y$. Because X is in $\mathbf{IV}(F, \mathbf{V}', \mathbf{V}'\backslash\mathbf{Z}, Y)$ it is not in $\mathbf{Z}$. There are three cases.

If X is a member of $\mathbf{IV}(F, \mathbf{V}', \mathbf{V}'\backslash\mathbf{Z}, Y)\backslash Y$ because it is the child of some variable T in $\mathbf{IV}(F, \mathbf{V}', \mathbf{V}'\backslash\mathbf{Z}, Y)$, then by the induction hypothesis T is d-connected to Y given $\mathbf{Z}$ by some path U. If X occurs on U then X is d-connected to Y given $\mathbf{Z}$; if X does not occur on U then the concatenation of U with the edge from X to T is a path from X to Y that d-connects X and Y given $\mathbf{Z}$ because T is not a collider along the concatenated path and T is not in $\mathbf{Z}$.

If X is a member of $\mathbf{IV}(F, \mathbf{V}', \mathbf{V}'\backslash\mathbf{Z}, Y)\backslash Y$ because it is the parent of some variable T in $\mathbf{IV}(F, \mathbf{V}', \mathbf{V}'\backslash\mathbf{Z}, Y)$ then by the induction hypothesis T is d-connected to Y given $\mathbf{Z}$ by some path U. If X occurs on U then X is d-connected to Y given $\mathbf{Z}$; if X does not occur on U then let U' be the concatenation of U with the edge from X to T. If T is not a collider on U' then U' d-connects X to Y given $\mathbf{Z}$. If T is a collider on U', then it has a descendant in $Y\mathbf{Z}$ because every member of $\mathbf{IV}(F, \mathbf{V}', \mathbf{V}'\backslash\mathbf{Z}, Y)\backslash Y$ has a descendant in $Y\mathbf{Z}$. If T has Y as a descendant but no member of $\mathbf{Z}$ as a descendant, there is a directed path from

T to Y that does not contain X (because X is a parent of T.) The concatenation of the directed path from T to Y and the edge from T to X d-connects X and Y given $\mathbf{Z}$. If T has some member of $\mathbf{Z}$ as a descendant, then U' d-connects X and Y given $\mathbf{Z}$ because T is a collider on U' and has a descendant in $\mathbf{Z}$.

If X is a member of $\mathbf{IV}(F,\ \mathbf{V'},\ \mathbf{V'}\backslash\mathbf{Z},\ Y)\backslash Y$ because it is the parent of some variable T in $\mathbf{Z}$ and not in $\mathbf{IV}(F,\ \mathbf{V'},\ \mathbf{V'}\backslash\mathbf{Z},\ Y)$, but some other parent M of T is in $\mathbf{IV}(F,\ \mathbf{V'},\ \mathbf{V'}\backslash\mathbf{Z},\ Y)$, then by the induction hypothesis M is d-connected to Y given $\mathbf{Z}$ by some path U. If X occurs on U, then X is d-connected to Y given $\mathbf{Z}$. If T occurs on U but X does not, let U' be the subpath of U from T to Y. U' d-connects T and Y given $\mathbf{Z}$; hence T is a collider on U. The concatenation of U' and the edge from X to T is a path that d-connects X and Y given $\mathbf{Z}$. If neither X nor T occurs on U, let U'' be the concatenation of U with the edges from M to T and T to X. M is not a collider along U'' and is not a member of $\mathbf{Z}$. T is a collider along U'' and is a member of $\mathbf{Z}$. Hence U'' d-connects X and Y given $\mathbf{Z}$. Q.E.D.

LEMMA 8. If G is a directed acyclic graph over a set of variables $\mathbf{V}$ containing Y and $\mathbf{Z}$, $P(\mathbf{V})$ is faithful to G, F is a graphical recursive factorization of $P(\mathbf{V})$ according to G, $\mathbf{V'} = \mathbf{V}\backslash\mathbf{ND}(Y\mathbf{Z})$, and X is in $\mathbf{IV}(F,\ \mathbf{V'},\ \mathbf{V'}\backslash Y\mathbf{Z},\ Y)\backslash Y$ then X is d-connected to Y given $\mathbf{Z}$.

Proof. By lemma 2, $\mathbf{IV}(F,\mathbf{V'},\mathbf{V'}\backslash\mathbf{Z},Y)\backslash Y = \mathbf{IV}(F,\ \mathbf{V'},\ \mathbf{V'}\backslash Y\mathbf{Z},\ Y)\backslash Y$. Hence the proof is the same as that of lemma 7, substituting $\mathbf{IV}(F,\ \mathbf{V'},\ \mathbf{V'}\backslash Y\mathbf{Z},\ Y)\backslash Y$ for $\mathbf{IV}(F,\ \mathbf{V'},\ \mathbf{V'}\backslash\mathbf{Z},\ Y)\backslash Y$. Q.E.D.

In a directed acyclic graph G containing Y and $\mathbf{Z}$, if Y is not in $\mathbf{Z}$, then V is in $\mathbf{IV}(Y,\mathbf{Z})$ (informative variables for Y given $\mathbf{Z}$) if and only if V is not in $\mathbf{Z}$, V is d-connected to Y given $\mathbf{Z}$, and V is not in $\mathbf{ND}(Y\mathbf{Z})$. W is in $\mathbf{IP}(\mathbf{Y},\ Z)$ (W has a parent who is an informative variable for Y given $\mathbf{Z}$) if and only if W is a member of $\mathbf{Z}$, and W has a parent in $\mathbf{IV}(Y,\mathbf{Z})$.

LEMMA 9. If G is a directed acyclic graph over $\mathbf{V}$, P is a distribution faithful to G, and $\mathbf{V'} = \mathbf{V}\backslash\mathbf{ND}(Y\mathbf{Z})$ then

$$P(Y\mid\mathbf{Z}) = \frac{\displaystyle\sum_{\mathbf{IV}(Y\mathbf{Z})}\ \prod_{W\,\in\,\mathbf{IV}(Y,\mathbf{Z})\cup\mathbf{IP}(Y,\mathbf{Z})\cup\{Y\}} P(W\mid\pi_W)}{\displaystyle\sum_{\mathbf{IV}(Y\mathbf{Z})\cup\{Y\}}\ \prod_{W\,\in\,\mathbf{IV}(Y,\mathbf{Z})\cup\mathbf{IP}(Y,\mathbf{Z})\cup\{Y\}} P(W\mid\pi_W)}$$

Proof. By lemma 4,

$$P(Y\mid\mathbf{Z}) = \frac{\displaystyle\left(\sum_{\mathbf{IV}(F,\mathbf{V'},\mathbf{V'}\backslash Y\mathbf{Z},Y)}\left(\prod_{t\,\in\,Terms(\mathbf{IV}(F,\mathbf{V'},\mathbf{V'}\backslash Y\mathbf{Z},Y)\cup\{Y\})}t\right)\right)}{\displaystyle\left(\sum_{\mathbf{IV}(F,\mathbf{V'},\mathbf{V'}\backslash\mathbf{Z},Y)}\left(\prod_{t\,\in\,Terms(\mathbf{IV}(F,\mathbf{V'},\mathbf{V'}\backslash\mathbf{Z},Y)\cup\{Y\})}t\right)\right)}$$

Let F be a graphical factorization of $P(\mathbf{V'})$. First we will show that in the numerator that W is in $\mathbf{IV}(F,\ \mathbf{V'},\ \mathbf{V'}\backslash Y\mathbf{Z},\ Y)$ if and only if it is in $\mathbf{IV}(Y,\mathbf{Z})$, and

$P(W \mid \pi_W)$ is in *Terms*($\mathbf{IV}(F, \mathbf{V}', \mathbf{V}'\backslash Y\mathbf{Z}, Y) \cup \{Y\}$) if and only if $P(W \mid \pi_W)$ is in $\mathbf{IV}(Y, \mathbf{Z}) \cup \mathbf{IP}(Y, \mathbf{Z}) \cup \{Y\}$; then we will prove the same for the denominator.

If W is in $\mathbf{IV}(F, \mathbf{V}', \mathbf{V}'\backslash Y\mathbf{Z}, Y)$ then W is not in $\mathbf{ND}(Y\mathbf{Z})$ and by lemma 7 W is d-connected to Y given $\mathbf{Z}$; hence W is in $\mathbf{IV}(Y, \mathbf{Z})$. If W is not in $\mathbf{IV}(F, \mathbf{V}', \mathbf{V}'\backslash Y\mathbf{Z}, Y)$ then either it is in $\mathbf{Z}$, $\mathbf{ND}(Y\mathbf{Z})$, or $\mathbf{IV}'(F, \mathbf{V}', \mathbf{V}'\backslash Y\mathbf{Z}, Y)$. In the first two cases, it is not in $\mathbf{IV}(Y, \mathbf{Z})$ by definition; in the last case it is not in $\mathbf{IV}(Y, \mathbf{Z})$ by lemma 5. Hence W is in $\mathbf{IV}(F, \mathbf{V}', \mathbf{V}'\backslash Y\mathbf{Z}, Y)$ if and only if it is in $\mathbf{IV}(Y, \mathbf{Z})$.

$P(W \mid \pi_W)$ is in *Terms*($\mathbf{IV}(F, \mathbf{V}', \mathbf{V}'\backslash Y\mathbf{Z}, Y) \cup \{Y\}$) if and only if some variable in $P(W \mid \pi_W)$ is in $\mathbf{IV}(F, \mathbf{V}', \mathbf{V}'\backslash Y\mathbf{Z}, Y) \cup \{Y\}$. Hence either $W = Y$, or W is in $\mathbf{IV}(F, \mathbf{V}', \mathbf{V}'\backslash Y\mathbf{Z}, Y)$, or W is in $\mathbf{Z}$ and has a parent in $\mathbf{IV}(F, \mathbf{V}', \mathbf{V}'\backslash Y\mathbf{Z}, Y) \cup \{Y\}$. W is in $\mathbf{IV}(F, \mathbf{V}', \mathbf{V}'\backslash Y\mathbf{Z}, Y)$ if and only if W is in $\mathbf{IV}(Y, \mathbf{Z})$, and W is in $\mathbf{Z}$ and has a parent in $\mathbf{IV}(F, \mathbf{V}', \mathbf{V}'\backslash Y\mathbf{Z}, Y) \cup \{Y\}$if and only if W is in $\mathbf{IP}(Y, \mathbf{Z})$. Hence, $P(W \mid \pi_W)$ is in *Terms*($\mathbf{IV}(F, \mathbf{V}', \mathbf{V}'\backslash Y\mathbf{Z}, Y) \cup \{Y\}$) if and only if $P(W \mid \pi_W)$ is in $\mathbf{IV}(Y, \mathbf{Z}) \cup \mathbf{IP}(Y, \mathbf{Z}) \cup \{Y\}$.

The proof for the denominator is the same using lemmas 6 and 8 in place of 5 and 7. Q.E.D.

LEMMA 10. If G is a directed acyclic graph containing X, Y, and $\mathbf{Z}$, X and Y are not in $\mathbf{Z}$, $X \neq Y$, and G' the corresponding graph when X is manipulated, and $V \neq X$, and no path that d-connects X to Y given $\mathbf{Z}$ is into X, then V is in $\mathbf{IV}(Y, X\mathbf{Z})$ in G if and only if V is in $\mathbf{IV}(Y, X\mathbf{Z})$ in G'.

Proof. It is trivial that if V is in $\mathbf{IV}(Y, X\mathbf{Z})$ in G' then V is in $\mathbf{IV}(Y, X\mathbf{Z})$ in G, because G' is a subgraph of G.

Suppose then that $V \neq X$, no path that d-connects X to Y given $\mathbf{Z}$ is into X, and V is in $\mathbf{IV}(Y, X\mathbf{Z})$ in G. By definition, V is not in $\mathbf{Z}$. Then in G there is a path that d-connects V to Y given $X\mathbf{Z}$, and V has a descendant in $XY\mathbf{Z}$. We will show that in G' there is a path that d-connects V to Y given $X\mathbf{Z}$.

Suppose first that there is a path U in G that d-connects Y to V given $X\mathbf{Z}$ that does not contain an edge into X. It follows that there is a corresponding path U' in G'. Every noncollider on U' is not in $\mathbf{Z}$. If every collider on U' has a descendant in $X\mathbf{Z}$ then U' d-connects V and Y given $\mathbf{Z}$ in G'. Otherwise let R be the collider on U' closest to Y that does not have a descendant in $X\mathbf{Z}$ in G'; in G every directed path D from R to a member of $X\mathbf{Z}$ contains X. Let Q be the point of intersection of D and the subpath of U from R to Y that is closest to Y on U. The concatenation of the subpath of D from Q to X and the subpath of U from Q to Y is into X and d-connects X and Y given $\mathbf{Z}$ in G, contrary to our assumption.

Suppose then that every path U in G that d-connects V to Y given $X\mathbf{Z}$ is into X. It follows that X is a collider along U. If there is no collider along the subpath of U from X to Y such that every directed path from the collider to a member of $\mathbf{Z}$ contains X, then in G the subpath of U from X to Y d-connects

X to Y given $\mathbf{Z}$, and is into X, contrary to our assumption. Otherwise this reduces to the previous case.

We will now prove that if V is in $\mathbf{IV}(Y, X\mathbf{Z})$ in G then V has a descendant in $XY\mathbf{Z}$ in G'. Suppose that V is in $\mathbf{IV}(Y, X\mathbf{Z})$. V has a descendant in $XY\mathbf{Z}$ in G. Suppose that V does not have a descendant in $XY\mathbf{Z}$ in G'. It follows that in G every directed path from V to a member of $XY\mathbf{Z}$ contains X. Because in G there is directed path from V to some member of $XY\mathbf{Z}$, in G there is a directed path from V to X that contains no member of $\mathbf{Z}$. Let $U1$ be a directed path from V to X that contains no member of $\mathbf{Z}$ in G. We have already proved that V and Y are d-connected given $\mathbf{Z}$ in G', so there is some path $U2$ that d-connects V and Y in G that does not contain X, such that every collider on $U2$ is the source of a directed path to a member of $\mathbf{Z}$ that does not contain X. Let Q be the vertex on $U2$ closest to Y such that Q is on both $U1$ and $U2$. The concatenation of the subpath of $U1$ from Q to X and the subpath of $U2$ from Q to Y is a path that d-connects X and Y given $\mathbf{Z}$ in G, and is into X, contrary to our assumption. Q.E.D.

THEOREM 3. If P is a distribution faithful to the directed acyclic graph G of the causal process that generated P, G contains X, Y, and $\mathbf{Z}$, X and Y are not in $\mathbf{Z}$, $X \neq Y$, G' is the graph resulting from manipulating X, and P' the distribution resulting from the manipulation of X, then Y is observable conditional on $X\mathbf{Z}$ when X is manipulated if in G there are no paths that d-connect X to Y conditional on $\mathbf{Z}$ that are into X.

Proof. Suppose G is a directed acyclic graph, G' is the graph resulting from manipulating G, and in G there are no paths that d-connect X and Y with respect to $\mathbf{Z}$ that are into X.

By lemma 10, $\mathbf{IV}(Y, X\mathbf{Z})$ is the same in G and G'.

Because the parent relationship is the same in G and G' except for the parents of X, it follows that $\mathbf{IP}(Y, X\mathbf{Z})$ is the same in G and G' with the possible exception of X. X is not in $\mathbf{IP}(Y, X\mathbf{Z})$ in G' because X has no parents in G'. Suppose that X is in $\mathbf{IP}(Y, X\mathbf{Z})$ in G. It follows that X has a parent V not in $X\mathbf{Z}$ that is in $\mathbf{IV}(Y, X\mathbf{Z}) \cup \{Y\}$ in G. Hence V is d-connected to Y given $X\mathbf{Z}$ in G by some path U. If U contains X then X is a collider on U because otherwise U does not d-connect Y and V given $X\mathbf{Z}$. It follows then that X is d-connected to Y given $\mathbf{Z}$ by the subpath of U from X to Y that is into X, contrary to our assumption. If U does not contain X then the concatenation of U with the edge from V to X is a path from X to U that d-connects X and Y given $\mathbf{Z}$ that is into X, contrary to our assumption. Hence X is not in $\mathbf{IP}(Y, X\mathbf{Z})$ in G, and $\mathbf{IP}(Y, X\mathbf{Z})$ is the same in G and G'.

By hypothesis, $P'(W \mid \pi_W) = P(W \mid \pi_W)$ for all W in $\mathbf{V}$, except for $W = X$. By lemma 4, $P(Y \mid X\mathbf{Z}) = P'(Y \mid X\mathbf{Z})$. Q.E.D.

Theorem 4 requires a further lemma.

LEMMA 11. If G is a directed acyclic graph containing X, Y, and $\mathbf{Z}$, X

and Y are not in $\mathbf{Z}$, $X \neq Y$, and G' is the corresponding graph when X is manipulated, X is not in $\mathbf{IV}(Y, \mathbf{Z})$, and $V \neq X$ then V is in $\mathbf{IV}(Y, \mathbf{Z})$ in G if and only if V is in $\mathbf{IV}(Y, \mathbf{Z})$ in G'.

Proof. It is trivial that if V is in $\mathbf{IV}(Y, \mathbf{Z})$ in G' then V is in $\mathbf{IV}(Y, \mathbf{Z})$ in G, because G' is a subgraph of G.

X is not in $\mathbf{IV}(Y, \mathbf{Z})$ in either G or G'. Suppose then that $V \neq X$, and V is in $\mathbf{IV}(Y, X\mathbf{Z})$ in G. First we will show that V and Y are d-connected given $\mathbf{Z}$ in G'; then we will show that if V and Y are d-connected given $\mathbf{Z}$ in G' then V has a descendant in $Y\mathbf{Z}$ in G'. It will follow that V is in $\mathbf{IV}(Y, \mathbf{Z})$ in G'.

First we will show that V is d-connected to Y given $\mathbf{Z}$ in G'. Suppose, contrary to the hypothesis, that V is not d-connected to Y given $\mathbf{Z}$ in G'. In G, either there is a path $U(V,Y)$ d-connecting V and Y given $\mathbf{Z}$ that contains an edge into X, or there is some path $U(V,Y)$ d-connecting V and Y given $\mathbf{Z}$ that contains a collider W for which every directed path to a member of $\mathbf{Z}$ contains X.

Suppose first that some path $U(V, Y)$ d-connecting V and Y given $\mathbf{Z}$ contains a collider W for which every directed path to a member of $\mathbf{Z}$ contains X. Let $U(W, X)$ be the directed path from W to X, and $U(W, Y)$ be the subpath of $U(V, Y)$ from W to Y. If $U(W, X)$ does not intersect $U(W, Y)$ except at W then the concatenation of $U(W, X)$ and $U(W, Y)$ d-connects X and Y given $\mathbf{Z}$. If $U(W, X)$ does intersect $U(W, Y)$ at some vertex not equal to W, let Q be the vertex on $U(W, Y)$ closest to Y where they intersect. Let $U(Q, Y)$ be the subpath of $U(W, Y)$ from Q to Y, and $U(Q, X)$ the subpath of $U(W, X)$ from Q to X. Q is not in $\mathbf{Z}$ because no member of $\mathbf{Z}$ is on $U(W, X)$. The concatenation of $U(Q, X)$ and $U(Q, Y)$ is an undirected path that d-connects X and Y given $\mathbf{Z}$ in G'.

Suppose next that there is a path $U(V, Y)$ d-connecting V and Y given $\mathbf{Z}$ that contains an edge into X. Let $U(X, Y)$ be the subpath of $U(V, Y)$ from X to Y. If there is a collider W on $U(X, Y)$ such that every directed path from W to a member of $\mathbf{Z}$ contains X, this reduces to the previous case. Hence $U(X, Y)$ d-connects X and Y given $\mathbf{Z}$.

Next we will show that if V is d-connected to Y given Z in G', then V has a descendant in $Y\mathbf{Z}$. Because V is d-connected to Y given $\mathbf{Z}$ in G' by some path $U(V, Y)$, either U is into V, or V has Y or a collider on U as a descendant. Every collider on U has a descendant in $\mathbf{Z}$, so if U is not into V, then V has a descendant in $Y\mathbf{Z}$. Suppose then that $U(V, Y)$ is into V. In G, V has a descendant in $Y\mathbf{Z}$. Hence V has a descendant in $Y\mathbf{Z}$ in G' unless every directed path from V to a member of $Y\mathbf{Z}$ contains X. In G, there exists a path from V to a member of $Y\mathbf{Z}$; if in addition every directed path from V to a member of $Y\mathbf{Z}$ contains X it follows that X has a descendant in $Y\mathbf{Z}$ in G. Let $U(V, X)$ be a directed path from V to X. If $U(V, X)$ does not intersect $U(V, Y)$ then the concatenation of $U(V, X)$ and $U(V, Y)$ d-connects X and Y given $\mathbf{Z}$. If $U(V, X)$

does intersect $U(V, Y)$ let Q be the vertex on $U(V, Y)$ closest to Y that is a point of intersection. Let $U(Q, X)$ be the subpath of $U(V, X)$ from Q to X, and $U(Q, Y)$ be the subpath of $U(V, Y)$ from Q to Y. Then the concatenation of $U(Q, X)$ and $U(Q, Y)$ d-connects X and Y given $\mathbf{Z}$. Hence X is in $\mathbf{IV}(Y, \mathbf{Z})$, contrary to our assumption. Q.E.D.

THEOREM 4. If P is a distribution faithful to the directed acyclic graph G of the causal process that generated P, G contains X, Y, and $\mathbf{Z}$, X and Y are not in $\mathbf{Z}$, $X \neq Y$, G' is the graph resulting from manipulating X, and P' the distribution resulting from the manipulation of X, then Y is observable conditional on $\mathbf{Z}$ when X is manipulated if X is not in $\mathbf{IV}(Y, \mathbf{Z})$.

Proof. Suppose G is a directed acyclic graph, G' is the graph resulting from manipulating G, and in G, and X is not in $\mathbf{IV}(Y, \mathbf{Z})$.

By lemma 11, $\mathbf{IV}(Y, \mathbf{Z})$ is the same in G and G'.

Because the parent relationship is the same in G and G' except for the parents of X, and X is not in $\mathbf{Z}$, it follows that $\mathbf{IP}(Y, \mathbf{Z})$ is the same in G and G'.

By hypothesis, $P'(W \mid \pi_W) = P(W \mid \pi_W)$ for all W in $\mathbf{V}$, except for $W = X$. By lemma 9, $P(Y \mid X\mathbf{Z}) = P'(Y \mid X\mathbf{Z})$. Q.E.D.

Acknowledgements

We gratefully acknowledge support to the first three authors under grant ONR-N00014-91-J-1361 from the Navy Personnel Research and Development Center and the Office of Naval Research, and from the National Science Foundation under grant IRI-9102169.

References

Asmussen, S. and Edwards, D. 1983. Collapsibility and Response Variables in Contingency Tables. *Biometrika* 70(3): 567–578.

Bishop, Y., Fienberg, S., and Holland, P. 1975. *Discrete Multivariate Analysis: Theory and Practice.* Cambridge, Mass.: The MIT Press.

Brownlee, K. 1965. A Review of "Smoking and Health." *Journal of the American Statistical Association* 60(311): 722–739.

Cook, R. D. 1980. Smoking and Lung Cancer. In *R. A. Fisher: An Appreciation,* ed. S. Fienberg and D. Hinkley. Berlin: Springer-Verlag.

Fisher, R. 1959. *Smoking. The Cancer Controversy. Some Attempts to Assess the Evidence.* Edinburgh: Oliver and Boyd.

Fox, J. 1984. *Linear Statistical Models and Related Methods.* New York: John Wiley and Sons.

Greenland, S. 1989. Modeling and Variable Selection in Epidemiologic Analysis. *American Journal of Public Health* 79(3): 340–349.

Holland, P. 1986. Statistics and Causal Inference. *Journal of the American Statistical Association* 81(396): 945–960.

Kiiveri, H., Speed, T. 1982. Structural Analysis of Multivariate Data: A Review. In *Sociological Methodology*, ed. S. Leinhardt. San Francisco: Jossy Bass.

Lauritzen, S.; Dawid, P.; Larsen, B.; and Leimer, H. 1990. Independence Properties of Markov Fields. *Networks* 20(5): 491–505.

MRFIT Research Group. 1982. Multiple Risk Factor Intervention Trial: Risk Factor Changes and Mortality Results. *Journal of the American Medical Association* 248(12): 1465–1477.

Pearl. J. 1988. *Probabilistic Reasoning in Intelligent Systems*. San Francisco: Morgan Kaufman Publishers.

Pratt, J. and Schlaifer, R. 1984. On the Nature and Discovery of Structure. *Journal of the American Statistical Association* 79(385): 9–21.

Pratt, J. and Schlaifer, R. 1988. On the Interpretation and Observation of Laws. *Journal of Econometrics* 39(1/2): 23–52.

Rose, G., Hamilton, P., Colwell, L. and Shipley, M. 1982. A Randomized Controlled trial of Antismoking Advice: 10-year Results. *Journal of Epidemiology and Community Health* 36(12): 102–108.

Rubin, D. 1974. Estimating Causal Effects of Treatments in Randomized and Nonrandomized Studies. *Journal of Educational Psychology* 66(1): 688–701.

Rubin, D. 1977. Assignment to Treatment Group on the Basis of a Covariate. *Journal of Educational Statistics* 2(1): 1–26.

Rubin, D. 1978. Bayesian Inference for Causal Effects. *Annals of Statistics* 6(1): 34––58.

Simpson, E. 1951. The Interpretation of Interaction in Contingency Tables. *Journal of the Royal Statistical Society* B, 13(2): 238–241.

Spirtes, P. 1994. In Place of Regression. In *Patrick Suppes: Scientific Philosopher, V.I.*, ed. P. Humphrey, 339-365. Dortrecht, Netherlands: Kluwer Academic Publishers.

Spirtes, P., and Glymour, C. 1988. Latent Variables, Causal Models and Overidentifying Constraints. *Journal of Econometrics* 39(1): 175–198.

Spirtes, P., Glymour, C., and Scheines, R. 1991. An Algorithm for Fast Recovery of Sparse Causal Graphs. *Social Science Computer Review* 9(1): 62–72.

Spirtes, P., Glymour, C., and Scheines, R. 1993. Causality, Prediction and Search. Berlin: Springer-Verlag.

Surgeon General of the United States. 1979. *Smoking and Health*. Washington, D.C.: U.S. Government Printing Office.

Verma, T. and Pearl, J. 1990. Equivalence and Synthesis of Causal Models. In Proceedings of the Conference on Uncertainty in Artificial Intelligence, July 1990. Mountain View, Calif.: Association for Uncertainty in Artificial Intelligence.

Wermuth, N. and Lauritzen, S. 1983. Graphical and Recursive Models for Contingency Tables. *Biometrika* 72(3): 537–552.

Whittaker, J. 1990. Graphical Methods in Applied Multivariate Statistics. New York: John Wiley and Sons.

CHAPTER THREE

Graphs, Structural Models, and Causality

Judea Pearl

1. Introduction

The tools introduced in this chapter are aimed at helping researchers communicate qualitative assumptions about cause-effect relationships, elucidate the ramifications of such assumptions, and derive causal inferences from a combination of assumptions, experiments, and data. (More about these topics will be covered in my forthcoming book on causality.)

The basic philosophy of the proposed method can best be illustrated through the classical example due to Cochran (Wainer 1989). Consider an experiment in which soil fumigants (X) are used to increase oat crop yields (Y) by controlling the eelworm population (Z) but may also have direct effects (both beneficial and adverse) on yields besides the control of eelworms. We wish to assess the total effect of the fumigants on yields when this typical study is complicated by several factors. First, controlled randomized experiments are infeasible—farmers insist on deciding for themselves which plots are to be fumigated. Second, farmers' choice of treatment depends on last year's eelworm population (Z_0), an unknown quantity which is strongly correlated with this year's population—thus we have a classical case of confounding bias, which interferes with the assessment of treatment effects, regardless of sample size. Fortunately, through laboratory analysis of soil samples, we can determine the eelworm populations before and after the treatment and, furthermore, because the fumigants are known to be active for a short period only, we can safely assume that they do not affect the growth of eelworms surviving the treatment. Instead, eelworms' growth depends on the population of birds (and other predators), which is correlated, in turn, with last year's eelworm population and hence with the treatment itself.

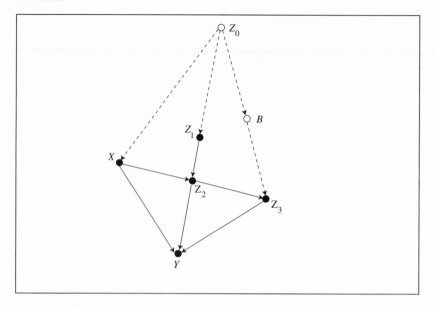

Figure 1. A causal diagram representing the effect of fumigants (X) on yields (Y).

The method proposed in this chapter permits the investigator to translate complex considerations of this sort into a formal language, thus facilitating the following tasks:

1. Explicate the assumptions underlying the model.
2. Decide whether the assumptions are sufficient for obtaining consistent estimates of the target quantity: the total effect of the fumigants on yields.
3. If the answer to item 2 is affirmative, the method provides a closed-form expression for the target quantity, in terms of distributions of observed quantities.
4. If the answer to item 2 is negative, the method suggests a set of observations and experiments which, if performed, would render a consistent estimate feasible.

The first step in this analysis is to construct a causal diagram such as the one given in figure 1 which represents the investigator's understanding of the major causal influences among measurable quantities in the domain. For example, the quantities Z_1, Z_2, and Z_3 represent, respectively, the eelworm population (both size and type) before treatment, after treatment, and at the end of the season. Z_0 represents last year's eelworm population; because it is an unknown quantity, it is denoted by a hollow circle, as is the quantity B, the population of birds and other predators. Links in the diagram are of two kinds: those that connect unmeasured quantities are designated by dashed arrows, those connecting measured quantities by solid arrows. The substantive assumptions embodied in the diagram are negative causal assertions which are conveyed through the links missing from the diagram. For example, the missing arrow between Z_1 and Y signifies the investigator's understanding that pretreatment eelworms cannot affect oat plants directly; their entire influence on oat yields is mediated by post-treatment conditions, namely Z_2 and Z_3. The purpose of this chapter is not to validate or repudiate such domain-specific assumptions but, rather, to test whether a given set of assumptions is sufficient for quantifying causal effects from nonexperimental data, for example, estimating the total effect of fumigants on yields.

The causal diagram in figure 1 is similar in many respects to the path diagrams devised by Wright (1921): both reflect the investigator's subjective and qualitative knowledge of causal influences in the domain, both employ directed acyclic graphs, and both allow for the incorporation of latent or unmeasured quantities. The major differences lie in the method of analysis. First, whereas path diagrams have been analyzed mostly in the context of additive linear models, causal diagrams permit arbitrary nonlinear interactions. In fact, the analysis of causal effects will be entirely nonparametric, entailing no commitment to a particular functional form for equations and distributions. Second, causal diagrams will be used not only as a passive language to specify assumptions but also as an active computational device through which the desired quantities will be derived. For example, the proposed method allows an investigator to inspect the diagram of figure 1 and conclude immediately that:

1. The total effect of X on Y can be estimated consistently from the observed distribution of X, Z_1, Z_2, Z_3, and Y.
2. The total effect of X on Y (assuming discrete variables throughout) is given by the formula[1]

$$P(y \mid \hat{x}) =$$
$$\sum_{z_1}\sum_{z_2}\sum_{z_3} P(y \mid z_2, z_3, x) P(z_2 \mid z_1, x) \sum_{x'} P(z_3 \mid z_1, z_2, x') P(z_1, x') \tag{1}$$

where $P(y \mid \hat{x})$ stands for the probability of achieving a yield level of $Y = y$ given that the treatment is set to level $X = x$ by external intervention.
3. A consistent estimation of the total effect of X on Y would not be feasible if Y were confounded with Z_3; however, confounding Z_2 and Y will not invalidate the formula for $P(y \mid \hat{x})$.

These conclusions can be obtained either by analyzing the graphical properties of the diagram or by performing a sequence of symbolic derivations, governed by the diagram, which gives rise to causal effect formulas such as equation 1.

The formal semantics of the causal diagrams used in this chapter will be defined in section 2, following review of directed acyclic graphs (DAGs) as a language for communicating conditional independence assumptions (subsection 2.1). Subsection 2.2 reviews the scientific basis for inducing causal relations from raw statistical data. Subsection 2.3 introduces a causal interpretation of DAGs based on nonparametric structural equations and demonstrates their use in predicting the effect of interventions. An alternative formulation is then described where interventions are treated as variables in an augmented probability space (shaped by the causal diagram) from which causal effects are obtained by ordinary conditioning. Using either interpretation, it is possible to quantify how probability distributions will change as a result of external interventions and to identify conditions under which randomized experiments are not necessary. Section 3 will demonstrate the use of causal diagrams to control confounding bias in observational studies. I will establish two graphical conditions ensuring that causal effects can be estimated consistently from nonexperimental data. The first condition, named the back-door criterion, is semantically equivalent to the ignorability condition of Rosenbaum and Rubin (1983) and thus renders the latter operational. The second condition, named the front-door criterion, involves covariates that are affected by the treatment, and thus introduces new opportunities for causal inference. In section 4, I introduce a symbolic calculus that permits the stepwise derivation of causal effect formulas of the type shown in equation 1. Using this calculus, section 5 characterizes the class of graphs that permit the quantification of causal effects from nonexperimental data or from surrogate experimental designs. Ties with alternative approaches to causation, primarily those based on counterfactual analysis, are provided in sections 6 and 8.

2. Graphical Models and the Manipulative Account of Causation

In this section, I will define the formal semantics of the causal diagrams used in this chapter.

2.1 Graphs and Conditional Independence

The usefulness of directed acyclic graphs (DAGs) as economical schemes for representing conditional independence assumptions is well acknowledged in the literature (Pearl 1988, Whittaker 1990). This usefulness stems from the existence of graphical methods for identifying the conditional independence relationships that are implied by definition 1.

Definition 1

Let $V = \{X_1,..., X_n\}$ be an ordered set of variables, and let $P(v)$ be the joint probability distribution on these variables. A set of variables PA_j is said to be Markovian parents of X_j if PA_j is a minimal set of predecessors of X_j that renders X_j independent of all its other predecessors. In other words, PA_j is any subset of $\{X_1, \ldots, X_j - 1\}$ satisfying

$$P(x_j \mid pa_j) = P(x_j \mid x_1, \ldots, x_j - 1) \tag{2}$$

such that no proper subset of PA_j satisfies equation 2.

Definition 1 assigns to each variable X_j a select set of variables PA_j that are sufficient for determining the probability of X_j ; knowing the values of other preceding variables is redundant once we know the values pa_j of the parent set PA_j. This assignment can be represented in the form of a DAG G in which variables are represented by nodes and arrows are drawn from each node of the parent set PA_j toward the child node X_j. Definition 1 also suggests a simple recursive method for constructing such a DAG: At the ith stage of the construction, select any minimal set of X_i's predecessors that satisfies equation 2, call this set PA_i (connoting "parents"), and draw an arrow from each member in PA_i to X_i. The result is a DAG, called a *Bayesian network* (Pearl 1988), in which an arrow from X_i to X_j assigns X_i as a Markovian parent of X_j, consistent with definition 1.

The construction implied by definition 1 defines a Bayesian network as a carrier of conditional independence information that is obtained along a specific order O. Clearly, every distribution satisfying equation 2 must decompose (using the chain rule of probability calculus) into the product

$$P(x_1, \cdots, x_n) = \prod_i P(x_i \mid pa_i) \tag{3}$$

which is no longer order-specific since, given P and G, we can test whether P decomposes into the product given by equation 3 without making any reference to variable ordering. Conversely, for every distribution decomposed as equation 3 one can find an ordering O that would produce G as a Bayesian network. If a probability distribution P admits the product decomposition dictated by G, as given in equation 3, we say that G and P are compatible.

A convenient way of characterizing the set of distributions compatible with a DAG G is to list the set of (conditional) independencies that each such distribution must satisfy. These independencies can be read off the DAG by using a graphical criterion called *d*-separation (Pearl 1988). To test whether X is independent of Y given Z in the distributions represented by G, we need to examine G and test whether the nodes corresponding to variables Z *d*-separate all paths from nodes in X to nodes in Y. By path we mean a sequence of consecutive edges (of any directionality) in the DAG.

Definition 2 (*d*-separation)

A path p is said to be *d*-separated (or blocked) by a set of nodes Z iff:
1. p contains a chain $i \rightarrow j \rightarrow k$ or a fork $i \leftarrow j \rightarrow k$ such that the middle

node j is in Z, or
2. p contains an inverted fork $i \rightarrow j \leftarrow k$ such that neither the middle node j nor any of its descendants (in G) are in Z.

If X, Y, and Z are three disjoint subsets of nodes in a DAG G, then Z is said to d-separate X from Y, denoted $(X \perp\!\!\!\perp Y \mid Z)_G$, iff Z d-separates every path from a node in X to a node in Y.

To distinguish between the graphical notion of d-separation, $(X \perp\!\!\!\perp Y \mid Z)_G$, and the probabilistic notion of conditional independence (Dawid 1979), we will use the notation $(X \perp\!\!\!\perp Y \mid Z)_P$ for the latter. The connection between the two is given in theorem 1.

Theorem 1

(Verma and Pearl 1988; Geiger, Verma, and Pearl 1990) For any three disjoint subsets of nodes (X, Y, Z) in a DAG G, and for all probability functions P, we have
1. $(X \perp\!\!\!\perp Y \mid Z)_G \Rightarrow (X \perp\!\!\!\perp Y \mid Z)_P$ whenever G and P are compatible, and
2. If $(X \perp\!\!\!\perp Y \mid Z)_P$ holds in all distributions compatible with G, then $(X \perp\!\!\!\perp Y \mid Z)_G$.

For example, the DAG in figure 1 induces the decomposition

$P(z_0, x, z_1, b, z_2, z_3, y) =$
$P(z_0)P(x \mid z_0)P(z_1 \mid z_0)P(b \mid z_0)P(z_2 \mid x, z_1)P(z_3 \mid z_2, b)P(y \mid x, z_2, z_3)$

and it implies (among others) the d-separation condition $(X \perp\!\!\!\perp \{B, Z_3\}\mid\{Z_0, Z_2\})_G$ because all paths between X and $\{B, Z_3\}$ are blocked by $\{Z_0, Z_2\}$. However, G does not imply $(X \perp\!\!\!\perp \{B, Z_3\}\mid\{Z_0, Z_2, Y\})_G$ because the path (X, Y, Z_3) contains a node (Y) drawing converging arrows which is also in the conditioning set $\{Z_0, Z_2, Y\}$.

An alternative test for d-separation has been devised by Lauritzen et al. (1990), based on the notion of ancestral graphs. To test for $(X \perp\!\!\!\perp Y \mid Z)_G$, delete from G all nodes except those in $\{X, Y, Z\}$ and their ancestors, connect by an edge every pair of nodes that share a common child, and remove all arrows from the arcs. $(X \perp\!\!\!\perp Y \mid Z)_G$ holds iff Z is a cutset of the resulting undirected graph, separating nodes of X from those of Y.

An important property that follows from the d-separation characterization is a criterion for determining whether two given DAGs are observationally equivalent, that is, whether every probability distribution that is compatible with one of the DAGs is also compatible with the other.

Theorem 2

(Verma and Pearl 1990) Two DAGs are observationally equivalent iff they have the same sets of edges and the same sets of v-structures, that is, two converging arrows whose tails are not connected by an arrow.

Observational equivalence places a limit on our ability to infer causal directionality from probabilities alone. Two networks that are observationally equivalent cannot be distinguished without resorting to manipulative experimentation or temporal information. For example, reversing the direction of the arrow between Z_0 and B in figure 1 does not introduce any new v-structure. Therefore, this reversal yields an observationally equivalent network, and the directionality of the link $Z_0 \to B$ cannot be determined from probabilistic information. The arrows $Z_2 \to Y$ and $Z_2 \to Z_3$, however, are of different nature; there is no way of reversing their directionality without creating a new v-structure. Thus, we see that some probability functions P (such as the one generated by the process described in figure 1), unaccompanied by temporal information, can constrain the directionality of some arrows, and hence the directionality of the causal relationships among the corresponding variables. The precise meaning of such directionality constraints will be discussed in the next subsection. Additional properties of DAGs and their applications to evidential reasoning in expert systems are discussed in Pearl (1988), Lauritzen and Spiegelhalter (1988), Spiegelhalter et al. (1993), Pearl (1993a), and Shafer (1997).

2.2 Graphs and Causal Discovery

The interpretation of DAGs as carriers of independence assumptions does not necessarily imply causation and will in fact be valid for any set of Markovian independencies along any ordering (not necessarily causal or chronological) of the variables. However, the patterns of independencies portrayed in a DAG are typical of causal organizations, and some of these patterns can only be given meaningful interpretation in terms of causation. Consider, for example, the following intransitive pattern of dependencies among three events: E_1 and E_3 are dependent, E_3 and E_2 are dependent, yet E_1 and E_2 are independent. If you ask a person to supply an example of three such events, the example invariably portrays E_1 and E_2 as two independent causes and E_3 as their common effect, namely, $E_1 \to E_3 \leftarrow E_2$. Fitting this dependence pattern by using E_3 as the cause and E_1 and E_2 as the effects, although mathematically feasible, is very unnatural indeed (the reader is encouraged to try this exercise).

Such thought experiments teach us that certain patterns of dependency, totally void of temporal information, are conceptually characteristic of certain causal directionalities and not others. Reichenbach (1956) has suggested that this directionality is a characteristic of Nature, reflective of the second law of thermodynamics. Pearl and Verma (1991) have offered a more subjective explanation, attributing the directionality to choice of language and to certain assumptions (e.g., Occam's razor) prevalent in scientific induction. Regardless of the origins of this asymmetry, exploring whether it provides a significant source of causal information (or at least causal clues) in human learning is an interesting topic for research (Waldemann, Holyoak, and Fratiannea 1995).

The distinction between transitive and intransitive dependencies has become the basis for several algorithms aimed at extracting causal structures from raw statistical data (Pearl 1988, 387–397; Pearl and Verma 1991; Spirtes, Glymour, and Schienes 1993). Clearly, because these algorithms rely solely on conditional independence relationships, the structures found are valid only if one is willing to accept forms of guarantees that are weaker than those obtained through controlled randomized experiments. Pearl and Verma (1991) expressed these guarantees in terms of two notions, minimality and stability. Minimality guarantees that any other structure compatible with the data is necessarily less specific, and hence less falsifiable and less trustworthy, than the one(s) inferred. Stability ensures that any alternative structure compatible with the data must be less stable than the one(s) inferred; in other words, slight fluctuations in experimental conditions will render the alternative structure incompatible with the data. With these forms of guarantees, discovery algorithms can provide criteria for identifying genuine and spurious causes, with or without temporal information.

Minimality can be easily illustrated in the example above. If we assume that X, Y and Z are the only relevant variables and that the joint distribution $P(x, y, z)$ embodies no other independence except $X \perp\!\!\!\perp Y$, then P is compatible with several DAGs, some of which contain an arrow from X to Z and some from Z to X. However, only one of those DAGs $G : X \to Z \leftarrow Y$ is minimal; the rest are complete DAGs (containing an arrow between any pair of nodes) hence they can fit any distribution whatsoever (including P). The rationale for preferring G on any complete DAG G' is basic to scientific induction; having the potential of fitting any data means that G' is empirically nonfalsifiable, that P is overfitted, hence, that G' is less trustworthy than G. Thus, the rationale for inferring the causal arc $X \to Z$ from P rests on finding the arrow $X \to Z$ in all DAGs (only G in our example) that are preferred on minimality grounds.

This minimality argument rests on the closed-world assumption, and would fail if hidden variables were permitted. For example, the DAG $X \leftarrow a \to Z \leftarrow b \to Y$, with a and b unobserved, imposes the same set of independencies on the observed variables X, Y, Z as the DAG $X \to Z \leftarrow Y$, yet the former does not present X as a cause of Z. The remarkable thing about minimality, however, is that it uniquely determines the directionality of some arrows even when we dispose of the closed-world assumption and allow for the presence of hidden variables. Adding another variable W to our example, with an arrow pointing from Z to W, would demonstrate this uniqueness (the arrow from Z_2 to Y in figure 1 is another example). Among all DAGs that fit P, including DAGs containing unobserved variables, those which do not include an arrow from Z to W are nonminimal, i.e., each fits a superset of the probability distributions (on the observables) compatible with G. It is this feature that encouraged Pearl and Verma (1991) to label certain links in the DAG as "genuine causes," to be distinguished from "potential causes" and "spurious associations." The latter identifies certain associations as non-causal (i.e., no link exists between the corresponding nodes in all minimal DAG's that fit the data) implying that the observed association must be attributed to a hidden common cause between the corresponding variables. Criteria and algorithms for identifying genuine causes, potential causes, and spurious associations are described in Pearl and Verma (1991) and Spirtes, Glymour, and Schienes (1993).

The notion of stability (also called "DAG-isomorphism" and "nondegeneracy" [Pearl 1988, p. 391] and "faithfulness" [Spirtes, Glymour, and Schienes 1993]) amounts to assuming that P embodies only independencies that can be represented in a DAG, excluding independencies that are sensitive to the precise numerical values of the conditional probabilities. This assumption is usually justified by the fact that strict equalities among parameters are rare, i.e., they have zero measure in any probability space in which parameters are allowed to vary independently of one another (Spirtes, Glymour, and Schienes 1993). The license for imposing such a constraint over the parameter distribution rests with the notion of autonomy (Aldrich 1989), which is at the heart of causal modeling. As will be further discussed in the next section, the distinctive feature of causal models is that each variable is determined by a set of other variables through a functional relationship (called "mechanism") which remains invariant when those other variables are subjected to external influences. Only by virtue of this invariance do causal models allow us to predict the effect of changes and interventions. This invariance means that mechanisms can vary independently of one another which, in turn, implies that under slightly varying conditions accidental independencies will be destroyed and only structural independencies will remain.

Bayesian methods offer alternative ways of identifying causal structures in data. These methods assign prior probabilities to the parameters and structure of the network and use Bayes' rule to score the degree to which a given network fits the data (Cooper and Herskovits 1991; Heckerman, Geiger, and Chickering 1994). These methods have the advantage of operating well under small-sample conditions, but they encounter difficulties in coping with hidden variables. It is important to stress that the guarantees provided by these Bayesian approaches also rest on the principles of minimality and stability. The assumption of parameter-independence, which is made in all practical Bayesian approaches to model discovery, induces preferences toward models with fewer parameters, hence minimality. Likewise, parameter-independence can be justified only when mechanisms are free to change independently of one another, namely, when the system is autonomous, hence, stable.

2.3 Graphs as Models of Interventions

Causal models, assuming they are properly validated, are more informative than probability models because they also encode effects of actions. In other words, a joint distribution tells us how probable events are and how probabilities would change with subsequent observations, but a causal model also tells us how these probabilities would change as a result of external interventions, such as those encountered in policy analysis and treatment management.

The connection between the causal and associational readings of DAGs is formed through the mechanism-based account of causation, which owes its roots to early works in econometrics (Frisch 1948; Haavelmo 1943; Simon 1953). In this account, assertions about causal influences, such as those specified by the links in figure 1, stand for autonomous physical mechanisms among the corresponding quantities, and these mechanisms are represented as functional relationships perturbed by random disturbances. Echoing this tradition, Pearl and Verma (1991) have interpreted the causal reading of a DAG in terms of functional, rather than probabilistic relationships; in other words, each child-parent family in a DAG G represents a deterministic function

$$X_i = f_i(\mathbf{pa}_i, \varepsilon_i); \ i = 1, \ldots, n \qquad (4)$$

where $\mathbf{pa}_i$ are the parents of variable X_i in G, and ε_i, $1 \leq i \leq n$, are mutually independent, arbitrarily distributed random disturbances. These disturbance terms represent independent exogenous factors that the investigator chooses not to include in the analysis. If any of these factors is judged to be influencing two or more variables (thus violating the independence assumption), then that factor must enter the analysis as an unmeasured (or latent) variable, to be represented in the graph by a hollow node, such as Z_0 and B in figure 1. For example, the causal assumptions conveyed by the model in figure 1 correspond to the following set of equations:

$$\begin{aligned}
&Z_0 = f_0(\varepsilon_0) && Z_2 = f_2(X, Z_1, \varepsilon_2) \\
&B = f_B(Z_0, \varepsilon_B) && Z_3 = f_3(B, Z_2, \varepsilon_3) \\
&Z_1 = f_1(Z_0, \varepsilon_1) && Y = f_Y(X, Z_2, Z_3, \varepsilon_Y) \\
&X = f_X(Z_0, \varepsilon_X)
\end{aligned} \qquad (5)$$

The equational model in equation 4 is the nonparametric analogue of the so-called structural equations model (Wright 1921; Goldberger 1973), with one exception: the functional form of the equations as well as the distribution of the disturbance terms will remain unspecified. The equality signs in structural equations convey the asymmetrical counterfactual relation of "is determined by," thus forming a clear correspondence between causal diagrams and Rubin's model of potential outcome (Rubin 1974; Holland 1988; Pratt and Schlaifer 1988; Rubin 1990). For example, the equation for Y states that regardless of what we currently observe about Y, and regardless of any changes that might occur in other equations, if $(X, Z_2, Z_3, \varepsilon_Y)$ were to assume the values $(x, z_2, z_3, \varepsilon_Y)$, respectively, Y would take on the value dictated by the function f_Y. Thus, the corresponding potential response variable in Rubin's model $Y(x)$ (read: the value that Y would take if X were x) becomes a deterministic function of Z_2, Z_3 and ε_Y and can be considered a random variable whose distribution is determined by those of Z_2, Z_3 and ε_Y. The relation between graphical and counterfactual models is further analyzed in section 8 and Pearl (1994a), Balke and Pearl (1994), and Galles and Pearl (1997, 1998). Formal proof of the equivalence of the potential-outcome framework and structural equation models is given in Galles and Pearl (1998).

Characterizing each child-parent relationship as a deterministic function, instead of the usual conditional probability $P(x_i \mid \mathbf{pa}_i)$, imposes equivalent independence constraints on the resulting distributions and leads to the same recursive decomposition that characterizes DAG models (see equation 3). This occurs because each ε_i is independent on all nondescendants of X_i. However, the functional characterization $X_i = f_i(\mathbf{pa}_i, \varepsilon_i)$ also provides a convenient language for specifying how the resulting distribution would change in response to external interventions. This is accomplished by encoding each intervention as an alteration on a select subset of functions, while keeping the others intact. Once we know the identity of the mechanisms altered by the intervention and the nature of the alteration, the overall effect of the intervention can be predicted by modifying the corresponding equations in the model and using the modified model to compute a new probability function.

The simplest type of external intervention is one in which a single variable, say X_i, is forced to take on some fixed value x_i. Such an intervention, which we call atomic, amounts to lifting X_i from the influence of the old functional mechanism $X_i = f_i(\mathbf{pa}_i, \varepsilon_i)$ and placing it under the influence of a new mechanism that sets the value x_i while keeping all other mechanisms unperturbed. Formally, this atomic intervention, which we denote by $set(X_i = x_i)$, or $set(x_i)$ for short,[2] amounts to removing the equation $X_i = f_i(\mathbf{pa}_i, \varepsilon_i)$ from the model and substituting $X_i = x_i$ in the remaining equations. The new model thus created represents the system's behavior under the intervention $set(X_i = x_i)$ and, when solved for the distribution of X_j, yields the causal effect of X_i on X_j, denoted $P(x_j \mid \hat{x}_i)$. More generally, when an intervention forces a subset X of variables to attain fixed values x, then a subset of equations is to be pruned from the model given in equation 4, one for each member of X, thus defining a new distribution over the remaining variables, which completely characterizes the effect of the intervention.[3] This leads to definition 3.

Definition 3. (Causal Effect)

Given two disjoint sets of variables, X and Y, the causal effect of X on Y, denoted $P(y \mid \hat{x})$, is a function from X to the space of probability distributions on Y. For each realization x of X, $P(y \mid \hat{x})$ gives the probability of

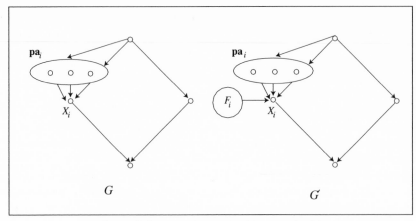

*Figure 2. Representing external intervention F_i
by an augmented network $G' = G \cup \{F_i \rightarrow X_i\}$.*

$Y = y$ induced by deleting from the model (equation 4) all equations corresponding to variables in X and substituting $X = x$ in the remaining equations.

Clearly the graph corresponding to the reduced set of equations is an edge subgraph of G from which all arrows entering X have been pruned (Spirtes, Glymour, and Schienes 1993). An alternative, but often more appealing, account of intervention treats the force responsible for the intervention as a variable within the system (Pearl 1993c). This is facilitated by representing the identity of the function f_i itself as a (value of a) variable F_i and writing

$$X_i = I(\mathbf{pa}_i, f_i, \varepsilon_i) \tag{6}$$

where I is a 3-argument function defined by

$I(a, b, c) = f_i(a, c)$ whenever $b = f_i$.

Thus, the impact of any external intervention that alters f_i can be represented graphically as an added parent node F_i of X_i, and the effect of such an intervention can be analyzed by Bayesian conditionalization, that is, by conditioning our probability on the added variable having attained the value f_i.

The effect of an atomic intervention $set(X_i = x_i')$ is encoded by adding to G a link $F_i \rightarrow X_i$ (see figure 2), where F_i is a new variable taking values in $\{set(x_i'), idle\}$, x_i' ranges over the domain of X_i, and $idle$ represents no intervention. Thus, the new parent set of X_i in the augmented network is $\mathbf{pa}'_i = \mathbf{pa}_i \cup \{F_i\}$, and it is related to X_i by the conditional probability

$$P(x_i \mid \mathbf{pa}'_i) = \begin{cases} P(x_i \mid \mathbf{pa}_i) & \text{if } F_i = idle \\ 0 & \text{if } F_i = set(x_i') \text{ and } x_i \neq x_i' \\ 1 & \text{if } F_i = set(x_i') \text{ and } x_i = x_i' \end{cases} \tag{7}$$

The effect of the intervention $set(x'_i)$ is to transform the original probability function $P(x_1, \ldots, x_n)$ into a new probability function $P(x_1, \ldots, x_n \mid \hat{x}'_i)$, given by

$$P(x_1, \ldots, x_n \mid \hat{x}') = P'(x_1, \ldots, x_n \mid F_i = set(x'_i)) \qquad (8)$$

where P' is the distribution specified by the augmented network $G' = G \cup \{F_i \rightarrow X_i\}$ and equation 7, with an arbitrary prior distribution on F_i. In general, by adding a hypothetical intervention link $F_i \rightarrow X_i$ to each node in G, we can construct an augmented probability function $P'(x_1, \ldots, x_n, F_1, \ldots, F_n)$ that contains information about richer types of interventions. Multiple interventions would be represented by conditioning P' on a subset of the F_i's—taking values in their respective $set(x'_i)$—while the preintervention probability function P would be viewed as the posterior distribution induced by conditioning each F_i in P' on the value *idle*.

Regardless of whether we represent interventions as a modification of an existing model (definition 3) or as a conditionalization in an augmented model (equation 8), the result is a well-defined transformation between the preintervention and the postintervention distributions. In the case of an atomic intervention $set(X_i = x'_i)$, this transformation can be expressed in a simple algebraic formula that follows immediately from equation 4 and definition 3:[4]

$$P(x_1, \cdots, x_n \mid \hat{x}'_i) = \begin{cases} \prod_{j \neq i} P(x_j \mid \mathbf{pa}_j) = \dfrac{P(x_1, \cdots, x_n)}{P(x_i \mid \mathbf{pa}_i)} & \text{if } x_i \\ 0 \text{ if } x_i \neq x'_i \end{cases} \qquad (9)$$

This formula reflects the removal of the term $P(x_i \mid \mathbf{pa}_i)$ from the product of equation 3, since $\mathbf{pa}_i$ no longer influences X_i. Graphically, the removal of this term is equivalent to removing the links between $\mathbf{pa}_i$ and X_i while keeping the rest of the network intact. Clearly, then, an intervention $set(x_i)$ can affect only the descendants of X_i in G. The immediate implication of equation 9 is that, given a causal diagram in which all parents of intervened variables are observable, one can infer post-intervention distributions from preintervention distributions; hence, under such assumptions we can estimate the effects of interventions from passive (i.e., nonexperimental) observations. The aim of this chapter, however, is to derive causal effects in situations such as figure 1, where some members of $\mathbf{pa}_i$ may be unobservable, thus preventing estimation of $P(x_i \mid \mathbf{pa}_i)$. The next two sections provide simple graphical tests for deciding when $P(x_j \mid \hat{x}_i)$ is estimable in a given model.

3. Controlling Confounding Bias

Whenever we undertake to evaluate the effect of one factor (X) on another (Y), the question arises as to whether we should adjust our measurements for possible variations in some other factors Z, sometimes called "covariates," "concomitants" or "confounders" (Cox 1958, p. 48). The illusive nature of such adjustment has been recognized as early as 1899, when Karl Pearson discovered what is now called Simpson's paradox: Any statistical relationship between two variables may be reversed by including additional factors in the analysis. For example, we may find that students who smoke obtain higher grades than those who do not smoke but, adjusting for age, smokers obtain lower grades in every age group and, further adjusting for family income, smokers again obtain higher grades than nonsmokers in every income-age group, and so on.

Despite a century of analysis, Simpson's reversal continues to "trap the unwary" (Dawid 1979), and the practical question that it poses—whether an adjustment for a given covariate is appropriate—has resisted mathematical treatment. The counterfactual analyses of Rubin (1974), Rosenbaum and Rubin (1983), and Pratt and Schlaifer (1988) have led to a criterion named "ignorability" which recasts the covariate-selection problem in counterfactual vocabulary, but falls short of providing a workable solution to the problem. Ignorability reads: "Z is an admissible set of covariates if, given Z, the value that Y would obtain had X been x is independent of X." Since counterfactuals are not observable, and judgments about conditional independence of counterfactuals are not readily assertable from ordinary understanding of causal processes, ignorability has remained a theoretical construct, with only minor impact on practice. Epidemiologists, for example are still debating the meaning of "confounding," and often adjust for wrong sets of covariates (Weinberg 1993).

Subsection 3.1 presents a general and formal solution of the adjustment problem using the language of causal graphs. Subsection 3.2 extends this result to nonstandard covariates which require several steps of adjustment. Subsection 3.3 illustrates the use of these criteria in an example.

3.1 The Back-door Criterion

Assume we are given a causal diagram G together with nonexperimental data on a subset V_0 of observed variables in G and we wish to estimate what effect the intervention $set(X_i = x_i)$ would have on some response variable X_j. In other words, we seek to estimate $P(x_j \mid \hat{x}_i)$ from a sample estimate of $P(V_0)$.

In Pearl (1993b) it is shown that there exists a simple graphical test, named the "back-door criterion," that can be applied directly to the causal diagram, to test if a set $Z \subseteq V_0$ of variables is sufficient for identifying $P(x_j \mid \hat{x}_i)$.[5]

Definition 4. (Back-door)

A set of variables Z satisfies the back-door criterion relative to an ordered pair of variables (X_i, X_j) in a DAG G if

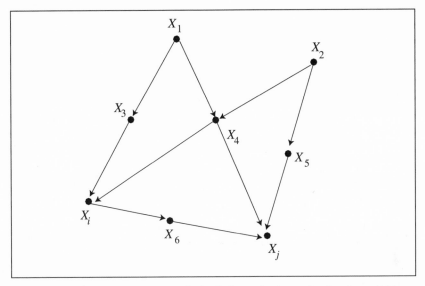

Figure 3. A diagram representing the back-door criterion; adjusting for variables {X_3, X_4} (or {X_4, X_5}) yields a consistent estimate of $P(x_j \mid \hat{x}_i)$.

1. no node in Z is a descendant of X_i, and
2. Z blocks every path between X_i and X_j which contains an arrow into X_i. Similarly, if X and Y are two disjoint subsets of nodes in G, then Z is said to satisfy the back-door criterion relative to (X, Y) if it satisfies the criterion relative to any pair (X_i, X_j) such that $X_i \in X$ and $X_j \in Y$.

The name "back-door" echoes condition 2, which requires that only paths with arrows pointing at X_i be d-blocked; these paths can be viewed as entering X_i through the back door. In figure 3, for example, the sets $Z_1 = \{X_3, X_4\}$ and $Z_2 = \{X_4, X_5\}$ meet the back-door criterion, but $Z_3 = \{X_4\}$ does not because X_4 does not block the path $(X_i, X_3, X_1, X_4, X_2, X_5, X_j)$. We summarize this finding in a theorem, after formally defining "identifiability."

Definition 5. (Identifiability)

The causal effect of X on Y is said to be identifiable if the quantity $P(y \mid \hat{x})$ can be computed uniquely from any positive distribution of the observed variables. Identifiability means that $P(y \mid \hat{x})$ can be estimated consistently from an arbitrarily large sample randomly drawn from the joint distribution.

Restricting identifiability to positive distributions substantially simplifies the analysis, as it avoids pathological cases associated with deterministic relationships (e.g., zero denominator in equation 9). Extensions to some nonpositive distributions are feasible, but will not be treated here. Note that, to

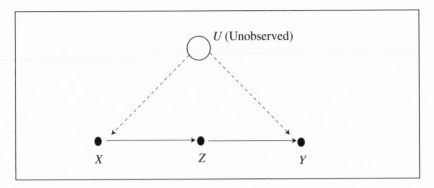

Figure 4. A diagram representing the front-door criterion.

prove nonidentifiability, it is sufficient to present two sets of structural equations that induce identical distributions over observed variables but different causal effects.

Theorem 3

If a set of variables Z satisfies the back-door criterion relative to (X, Y), then the causal effect of X on Y is identifiable and is given by the formula

$$P(y \mid \hat{x}) = \sum_{z} P(y \mid x, z) P(z)$$
(10)

Equation 10 represents the standard adjustment for concomitants Z, and it is valid when X is "conditionally ignorable given Z" (Rosenbaum and Rubin 1983). Reducing ignorability conditions to the graphical criterion of definition 4 replaces judgments about counterfactual dependencies with systematic procedures that can be applied to causal diagrams of any size and shape. The graphical criterion also enables the analyst to search for an optimal set of concomitants, namely, a set Z that minimizes measurement cost or sampling variability. The use of a similar graphical criterion for identifying path coefficients in linear structural equations is demonstrated in Pearl (1998). Applications to epidemiological research are given in Greenland, Pearl, and Robins (1999).

3.2 The Front-door Criteria

Condition 1 of definition 4 reflects the prevailing practice that "the concomitant observations should be quite unaffected by the treatment" (Cox 1958, 48 1958). This subsection demonstrates how concomitants that are affected by the treatment can be used to facilitate causal inference. The emerging criterion, which we will name the front-door criterion, will constitute the second building block of the general test for identifying causal effects which will be formulated in section 4. Consider the diagram in figure 4, which obtains from figure 3 in case variables $X_1, \ldots, X_5$ are unobserved. Although Z does not satisfy any of the back-door conditions, measurements of Z can nevertheless enable consistent estimation of $P(y \mid \hat{x})$. This will be shown by reducing the expression for $P(y \mid \hat{x})$ to formulae computable from the observed distribution function $P(x, y, z)$.

The joint distribution associated with figure 4 can be decomposed (equation 3) into

$$P(x, y, z, u) = P(u)P(x \mid u)P(z \mid x)P(y \mid z, u) \tag{11}$$

From equation 9, the intervention $set(x)$ removes the factor $P(x \mid u)$ and induces the post-intervention distribution

$$P(y, z, u \mid \hat{x}) = P(y \mid z, u)P(z \mid x)P(u) \tag{12}$$

Summing over z and u gives

$$P(y \mid \hat{x}) = \sum_z P(z \mid x) \sum_u P(y \mid z, u)P(u) \tag{13}$$

To eliminate u from the right-hand side of equation 13, we use the two conditional independence assumptions encoded in the graph of figure 4

$$P(u \mid z, x) = P(u \mid x) \tag{14}$$

$$P(y \mid x, z, u) = P(y \mid z, u) \tag{15}$$

which yields the equality

$$\sum_u P(y \mid z, u)P(u)$$
$$= \sum_x \sum_u P(y \mid z, u)P(u \mid x)P(x)$$
$$= \sum_x \sum_u P(y \mid x, z, u)P(u \mid x, z)P(x)$$
$$= \sum_x P(y \mid x, z)P(x) \tag{16}$$

and allows the reduction of equation 13 to the desired form:

$$P(y \mid \hat{x}) = \sum_z P(z \mid x) \sum_{x'} P(y \mid x', z)P(x') \tag{17}$$

Since all factors on the right-hand side of equation 17 are consistently estimable from nonexperimental data, it follows that $P(y \mid \hat{x})$ is estimable as well. Thus, we are in possession of an identifiable nonparametric estimand for the causal effect of an X on a Y whenever we can find a mediating variable Z that meets the conditions of equations 14 and 15.

Equation 17 can be interpreted as a two-step application of the back-door formula. In the first step we find the causal effect of X on Z and, since there is no back-door path from X to Z, we simply have $P(z \mid \hat{x}) = P(z \mid x)$

Next, we compute the causal effect of Z on Y, which we can no longer equate with the conditional probability $P(y \mid z)$ because there is a back-door path $Z \leftarrow X \leftarrow U \rightarrow Y$ from Z to Y. However, since X blocks (d-separates) this path, X can play the role of a concomitant in the back-door criterion, which allows us to compute the causal effect of Z on Y in accordance with equation 10. Finally, we combine the two causal effects via

$$P(y \mid \hat{x}) = \sum_z P(y \mid \hat{z})P(z \mid \hat{x})$$

which reduces to equation 17. We summarize this result by a theorem, after formally defining the assumptions.

Definition 6

A set of variables Z is said to satisfy the front-door criterion relative to an ordered pair of variables (X, Y) if
1. Z intercepts all directed paths from X to Y.
2. There is no back-door path from X to Z.
3. All back-door paths from Z to Y are blocked by X.

Theorem 4

If Z satisfies the front-door criterion relative to (X, Y), and $P(x, z) > 0$, then the causal effect of X on Y is identifiable and is given by the formula

$$P(y \mid \hat{x}) = \sum_z P(z \mid x)\sum_{x'} P(y \mid x', z)P(x') \tag{18}$$

The conditions stated in definition 6 are overly restrictive; some of the back-door paths excluded by conditions 2 and 3 can in fact be allowed, as long as they are blocked by some concomitants. For example, the variable Z_2 in figure 1 satisfies a front-door-like criterion relative to (X, Z_3) by virtue of Z_1 blocking all back-door paths from X to Z_2 as well as those from Z_2 to Z_3. To allow the analysis of such intricate structures, including nested combinations of back-door and front-door conditions, a more powerful symbolic machinery will be introduced in section 4, one that will sidestep algebraic manipulations such as those used in the derivation of equation 16. But first let us look at an example illustrating possible applications of the front-door condition.

3.3 Example: Smoking and the Genotype Theory

Consider the century-old debate on the relation between smoking (X) and lung cancer (Y) (Spirtes, Glymour, and Schienes, 1993, 291–203). According to many, the tobacco industry has managed to stay anti-smoking legislation by arguing that the observed correlation between smoking and lung cancer could be explained by some sort of carcinogenic genotype (U) which involves inborn craving for nicotine.

The amount of tar (Z) deposited in a person's lungs is a variable that promises to meet the conditions listed in definition 6 above, thus fitting the structure of figure 4. To meet condition 1, we must assume that smoking cigarettes has no effect on the production of lung cancer except the one me-

	Group Type	P(x, z) Group Size (% of Population)	P(Y = 1 | x, z) % of Cancer Cases in Group
X = 0, Z = 0	Nonsmokers, No tar	47.5	10
X = 1, Z = 0	Smokers, No tar	2.5	90
X = 0, Z = 1	Nonsmokers, Tar	2.5	5
X = 1, Z = 1	Smokers, Tar	47.5	85

Table 1. Frequency data from hypothetical study on smoking and lung cancer.

diated through tar deposits. To meet conditions 2 and 3, we must assume that, even if a genotype is aggravating the production of lung cancer, it nevertheless has no effect on the amount of tar in the lungs except indirectly, through cigarette smoking. Finally, condition $P(x, z) > 0$ of theorem 4 requires that we allow that high levels of tar in the lungs could be the result not only of cigarette smoking but also of other means (e.g., exposure to environmental pollutants) and that tar may be absent in some smokers (perhaps due to an extremely efficient tar-rejecting mechanism). Satisfaction of this last condition can be tested in the data.

To demonstrate how we can assess the degree to which cigarette smoking increases (or decreases) lung cancer risk, we will assume a hypothetical study in which the three variables, X, Y, and Z, were measured simultaneously on a large, randomly selected sample from the population. To simplify the exposition, we will further assume that all three variables are binary, taking on true (1) or false (0) values. A hypothetical data set from a study on the relations among tar, cancer, and cigarette smoking is presented in table 1.

It shows that 95% of smokers and 5% of nonsmokers have developed high levels of tar in their lungs. Moreover, 81% of subjects with tar deposits have developed lung cancer, compared to only 14% among those with no tar deposits. Finally, within each of these two groups, tar and no tar, smokers show a much higher percentage of cancer than nonsmokers.

These results seem to prove that smoking is a major contributor to lung cancer. However, the tobacco industry might argue that the table tells a different story—that smoking actually decreases, not increases, one's risk of lung cancer. Their argument goes as follows. If you decide to smoke, then your chances of building up tar deposits are 95%, compared to 5% if you decide not to smoke. To evaluate the effect of tar deposits, we look separately at two groups, smokers and nonsmokers. The table shows that tar deposits have a protective effect in both groups: in smokers, tar deposits lower cancer rates from 90% to 85%; in nonsmokers, they lower cancer rates from 10% to 5%. Thus, regardless of whether I have a natural craving for nicotine, I should be seeking the protective effect of tar deposits in my lungs, and smoking offers a very effective means of acquiring them.

To settle the dispute between the two interpretations, we now apply the front-door formula (equation 18) to the data in table 1. We wish to calculate the probability that a randomly selected person will develop cancer under each of the following two actions: smoking (setting $X = 1$) or not smoking (setting $X = 0$).

Substituting the appropriate values of $P(z \mid x)$, $P(y \mid x, z)$, and $P(x)$ gives

$$P(Y = 1 \mid set(X = 1))$$
$$= .05(.10 \times .50 + .90 \times .50) + .95(.05 \times .50 + .85 \times .50)$$
$$= .05 \times .50 + .95 \times .45 = .4525$$
$$P(Y = 1 \mid set(X = 0)) = .95(.10 \times .50 + .90 \times .50) + .05(.05 \times .50 + .85 \times .50)$$
$$= .95 \times .50 + .05 \times .45 = .4975 \tag{19}$$

Thus, contrary to expectation, the data prove smoking to be somewhat beneficial to one's health.

The data in table 1 are obviously unrealistic and were deliberately crafted so as to support the genotype theory. However, the purpose of this exercise was to demonstrate how reasonable qualitative assumptions about the workings of mechanisms, coupled with nonexperimental data, can produce precise quantitative assessments of causal effects. In reality, we would expect observational studies involving mediating variables to refute the genotype theory by showing, for example, that the mediating consequences of smoking, such as tar deposits, tend to increase, not decrease, the risk of cancer in smokers and nonsmokers alike. The estimand of equation 18 could then be used for quantifying the causal effect of smoking on cancer.

4. A Calculus of Intervention

This section establishes a set of inference rules by which probabilistic sentences involving interventions and observations can be transformed into other such sentences, thus providing a syntactic method of deriving (or verifying) claims about interventions. We will assume that we are given the structure of a causal diagram G in which some of the nodes are observable while the others remain unobserved. Our main problem will be to facilitate the syntactic derivation of causal effect expressions of the form $P(y \mid \hat{x})$, where X and Y stand for any subsets of observed variables. By derivation we mean step-wise reduction of the expression $P(y \mid \hat{x})$ to an equivalent expression involving standard probabilities of observed quantities. Whenever such reduction is feasible, the causal effect of X on Y is identifiable (see definition 5).

4.1 Preliminary Notation

Let X, Y, and Z be arbitrary disjoint sets of nodes in a DAG G. We denote by $G_{\overline{x}}$ the graph obtained by deleting from G all arrows pointing to nodes in X. Likewise, we denote by $G_{\underline{x}}$ the graph obtained by deleting from G all arrows emerging from nodes in X. To represent the deletion of both incoming and outgoing arrows, we use the notation $G_{\overline{x}\underline{z}}$ (see figure 5 for illustration). Finally, the expression $P(y \mid \hat{x}, z) \triangleq P(y, z \mid \hat{x}) / P(z \mid \hat{x})$ stands for the probability of $Y = y$ given that $Z = z$ is observed and X is held constant at x.

4.2 Inference Rules

The following theorem states the three basic inference rules of the proposed calculus. Proofs are provided in section 7.

Theorem 5

Let G be the directed acyclic graph associated with a causal model as defined in equation 4, and let $P(\bullet)$ stand for the probability distribution induced by that model. For any disjoint subsets of variables X, Y, Z, and W we have:

Rule 1 Insertion/deletion of observations

$$P(y \mid \hat{x}, z, w) = P(y \mid \hat{x}, w) \text{ if } (Y \perp\!\!\!\perp Z \mid X, W)_{G_{\overline{x}}} \tag{20}$$

Rule 2 Action/observation exchange

$$P(y \mid \hat{x}, \hat{z}, w) = P(y \mid \hat{x}, z, w) \text{ if } (Y \perp\!\!\!\perp Z \mid X, \mathrm{W})_{G_{\overline{x}\underline{z}}} \tag{21}$$

Rule 3 Insertion/deletion of actions

$$P(y \mid \hat{x}, \hat{z}, w) = P(y \mid \hat{x}, w) \text{ if } (Y \perp\!\!\!\perp Z \mid X, \mathrm{W})_{G_{\overline{x}, \overline{z}(w)}} \tag{22}$$

where $Z(W)$ is the set of Z-nodes that are not ancestors of any W-node in $G_{\overline{x}}$.

Each of the inference rules above follows from the basic interpretation of the "$\hat{x}$" operator as a replacement of the causal mechanism that connects X to its preaction parents by a new mechanism $X = x$ introduced by the intervening force. The result is a submodel characterized by the subgraph $G_{\overline{x}}$ (named "manipulated graph" in Spirtes, Glymour, and Schienes [1993]), which supports all three rules.

Rule 1 reaffirms d-separation as a valid test for conditional independence in the distribution resulting from the intervention $set(X = x)$, hence the graph $G_{\overline{x}}$. This rule follows from the fact that deleting equations from the system does not introduce any dependencies among the remaining disturbance terms (see equation 4).

Rule 2 provides a condition for an external intervention $set(Z = z)$ to have the same effect on Y as the passive observation $Z = z$. The condition amounts to $\{X \cup W\}$ blocking all back-door paths from Z to Y (in $G_{\overline{x}}$), since $G_{\overline{x}\underline{z}}$ retains all (and only) such paths.

Rule 3 provides conditions for introducing (or deleting) an external interven-

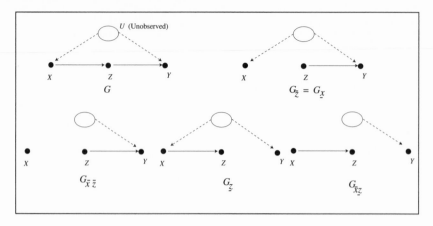

Figure 5. Subgraphs of G used in the derivation of causal effects.

tion $set(Z = z)$ without affecting the probability of $Y = y$. The validity of this rule stems, again, from simulating the intervention $set(Z = z)$ by the deletion of all equations corresponding to the variables in Z (hence the graph $G_{\overline{X}, \overline{Z(W)}}$).

Corollary 1.

A causal effect q: $P(y_1, ..., y_k \mid \hat{x}_1, ..., \hat{x}_m)$ is identifiable in a model characterized by a graph G if there exists a finite sequence of transformations, each conforming to one of the inference rules in theorem 5, which reduces q into a standard (i.e., hat-free) probability expression involving observed quantities.

Whether the three rules above are sufficient for deriving all identifiable causal effects remains an open question (see Vovk 1996). However, the task of finding a sequence of transformations (if such exists) for reducing an arbitrary causal effect expression can be systematized and executed by efficient algorithms (Galles and Pearl 1995; Pearl and Robins 1995). As the next subsection illustrates, symbolic derivations using the hat notation are much more convenient than algebraic derivations that aim at eliminating latent variables from standard probability expressions (as in section 3.2).

4.3 An Example of Symbolic Derivation of Causal Effects

We will now demonstrate how rules 1-3 can be used to derive all causal effect estimands in the structure of figure 4 above. Figure 5 displays the subgraphs that will be needed for the derivations that follow.

Task-1, compute $P(z \mid \hat{x})$. This task can be accomplished in one step, since

G satisfies the applicability condition for rule 2; namely, $X \perp\!\!\!\perp Z$ in $G_{\underline{x}}$ because the path $X \leftarrow U \rightarrow Y \leftarrow Z$ is blocked by the converging arrows at Y) and we can write

$$P(z \mid \hat{x}) = P(z \mid x) \tag{23}$$

Task-2, compute $P(y \mid \hat{z})$. Here we cannot apply rule 2 to exchange $\hat{z}$ with z because $G_{\underline{z}}$ contains a back-door path from Z to $Y : Z \leftarrow X \leftarrow U \rightarrow Y$. Naturally, we would like to block this path by measuring variables (such as X) that reside on that path. This involves conditioning and summing over all values of X,

$$P(y \mid \hat{z}) = \sum_x P(y \mid x, \hat{z}) P(x \mid \hat{z}) \tag{24}$$

We now have to deal with two expressions involving $\hat{z}$, $P(y \mid x, \hat{z})$ and $P(x \mid \hat{z})$. The latter can be readily computed by applying rule 3 for action deletion:

$$P(x \mid \hat{z}) = P(x) \text{ if } (Z \perp\!\!\!\perp X)_{G_{\overline{z}}} \tag{25}$$

since X and Z are d-separated in $G_{\overline{z}}$. (Intuitively, manipulating Z should have no effect on X, because Z is a descendant of X in G.)

To reduce the former, $P(y \mid x, \hat{z})$, we consult rule 2:

$$P(y \mid x, \hat{z}) = P(y \mid x, z) \text{ if } (Z \perp\!\!\!\perp Y \mid X)_{G_{\underline{z}}} \tag{26}$$

noting that X d-separates Z from Y in $G_{\underline{z}}$. This allows us to write equation 24 as

$$P(y \mid \hat{z}) = \sum_x P(y \mid x, z) P(x) = E_x P(y \mid x, z) \tag{27}$$

which is a special case of the back-door formula (equation 10). The legitimizing condition, $(Z \perp\!\!\!\perp Y \mid X) G_{\underline{z}}$, offers yet another graphical test for the ignorability condition of Rosenbaum and Rubin (1983).

Task-3, compute $P(y \mid \hat{x})$. Writing

$$P(y \mid \hat{x}) = \sum_z P(y \mid z, \hat{x}) P(z \mid \hat{x}) \tag{28}$$

we see that the term $P(z \mid \hat{x})$ was reduced in equation 23 but that no rule can be applied to eliminate the "hat" symbol ^ from the term $P(y \mid z, \hat{x})$. However, we can add a "hat" symbol to this term via rule 2

$$P(y \mid z, \hat{x}) = P(y \mid \hat{z}, \hat{x}) \tag{29}$$

since the applicability condition $(Y \perp\!\!\!\perp Z \mid X)_{G_{\overline{x}\underline{z}}}$, holds true (see figure 5). We can now delete the action $\hat{x}$ from $P(y \mid \hat{z}, \hat{x})$ using rule 3, since $Y \perp\!\!\!\perp X \mid Z$ holds in $G_{\overline{x}\overline{z}}$. Thus, we have

$$P(y \mid z, \hat{x}) = P(y \mid \hat{z}) \tag{30}$$

which was calculated in equation 27. Substituting equations 27, 30, and 23 back into equation 28 finally yields

$$P(y \mid \hat{x}) = \sum_z P(z \mid x) \sum_{x'} P(y \mid x', z) P(x') \tag{31}$$

which is identical to the front-door formula of equation 17.

Task-4, compute $P(y, z \mid \hat{x})$

$P(y, z \mid \hat{x}) = P(y \mid z, \hat{x})P(z \mid \hat{x})$

The two terms on the right-hand side were derived before in equations 23 and 30, from which we obtain

$P(y, z \mid \hat{x})$
$$= P(y \mid \hat{z})P(z \mid x)$$
$$= P(z \mid x)\sum_{x'} P(y \mid x', z)P(x') \tag{32}$$

Task-5, compute $P(x, y \mid \hat{z})$

$P(x, y \mid \hat{z})$
$$= P(y \mid x, \hat{z})P(x \mid \hat{z})$$
$$= P(y \mid x, z)P(x') \tag{33}$$

The first term on the right-hand side is obtained by rule 2 (licensed by G_z) and the second term by rule 3 (as in equation 25). Note that in all the derivations the graph G has provided both the license for applying the inference rules and the guidance for choosing the right rule to apply.

4.4 Causal Inference by Surrogate Experiments

Suppose we wish to learn the causal effect of X on Y when $P(y \mid \hat{x})$ is not identifiable and, for practical reasons of cost or ethics, we cannot control X by randomized experiment. The question arises whether $P(y \mid \hat{x})$ can be identified by randomizing a surrogate variable Z, which is easier to control than X. For example, if we are interested in assessing the effect of cholesterol levels (X) on heart disease (Y), a reasonable experiment to conduct would be to control subjects' diet (Z), rather than exercising direct control over cholesterol levels in subjects' blood.

Formally, this problem amounts to transforming $P(y \mid \hat{x})$ into expressions in which only members of Z obtain the hat symbol. Using theorem 5 it can be shown that the following conditions are sufficient for admitting a surrogate variable Z:

(1) X intercepts all directed paths from Z to Y, and,

(2) $P(y \mid \hat{x})$ is identifiable in $G_{\bar{z}}$.

Indeed, if condition 1 holds, we can write $P(y \mid \hat{x}) = P(y \mid \hat{x}, \hat{z})$; because $(Y \perp\!\!\!\perp Z \mid X)_{G_{\overline{xz}}}$. But $P(y \mid \hat{x}, \hat{z})$ stands for the causal effect of X on Y in a model governed by $G_{\bar{z}}$ which, by condition 2, is identifiable. Translated to our cholesterol example, these conditions require that there be no direct effect of diet on heart conditions and no confounding effect between cholesterol levels and heart disease, unless we can measure an intermediate variable between the two.

Figures 8e and 8h [which will be introduced later on in this chapter] illustrate models in which both conditions hold. For figure 8e, for example, we obtain this estimand

$$P(y \mid \hat{x}) = P(y \mid x, \hat{z}) = P(y, x \mid \hat{z})/P(x \mid \hat{z}) \qquad (34)$$

This can be established directly by first applying rule 3 to add $\hat{z}$,

$$P(y \mid \hat{x}) = P(y \mid \hat{x}, \hat{z}) \text{ because } (Y \perp\!\!\!\perp Z \mid X)_{G_{\overline{XZ}}}$$

then applying rule 2 to exchange $\hat{x}$ with x:

$$P(y \mid \hat{x}, \hat{z}) = P(y \mid x, \hat{z}) \text{ because } (Y \perp\!\!\!\perp X \mid Z)_{G_{\underline{X}\overline{Z}}}$$

According to equation 34, only one level of Z suffices for the identification of $P(y \mid \hat{x})$, for any values of y and x. In other words, Z need not be varied at all, just held constant by external means, and, if the assumptions embodied in G are valid, the right-hand side of equation 34 should attain the same value regardless of the level at which Z is being held constant. In practice, however, several levels of Z will be needed to ensure that enough samples are obtained for each desired value of X. For example, if we are interested in the difference $E(Y \mid \hat{x}) - E(Y \mid \hat{x}')$, where x and x' are two treatment levels, then we should choose two values z and z' of Z which maximize the number of samples in x and x', respectively, and estimate

$$E(Y \mid \hat{x}) - E(Y \mid \hat{x}') = E(Y \mid x, \hat{z}) - E(Y \mid x', \hat{z}')$$

5. Graphical Tests of Identifiability

Figure 6 shows simple diagrams in which $P(y \mid \hat{x})$ cannot be identified due to the presence of a bow pattern, i.e., a confounding arc (dashed) embracing a causal link between X and Y. A confounding arc represents the existence in the diagram of a back-door path that contains only unobserved variables and has no converging arrows. For example, the path X, Z_0, B, Z_3 in figure 1 can be represented as a confounding arc between X and Z_3. A bow-pattern represents an equation $Y = f_Y (X, U, \varepsilon_Y)$ where U is unobserved and dependent on X. Such an equation does not permit the identification of causal effects since any portion of the observed dependence between X and Y may always be attributed to spurious dependencies mediated by U.

The presence of a bow-pattern prevents the identification of $P(y \mid \hat{x})$ even when it is found in the context of a larger graph, as in figure 6b. This is in contrast to linear models, where the addition of an arc to a bow-pattern can render $P(y \mid \hat{x})$ identifiable (Pearl 1998). For example, if Y is related to X via a linear relation $Y = bX + U$, where U is an unobserved disturbance possibly correlated with X, then

$$b = \frac{\partial}{\partial x} E(Y \mid \hat{x})$$

is not identifiable. However, adding an arc $Z \to X$ to the structure (that is,

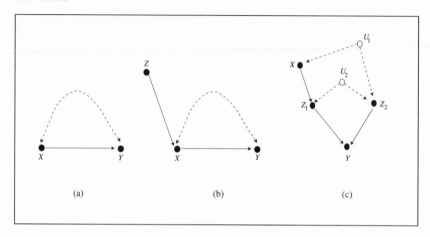

Figure 6. (a) A bow-pattern: a confounding arc embracing a causal link X → Y, thus preventing the identification of P(y | x̂) even in the presence of an instrumental variable Z, as in (b). (c) A bow-less graph still prohibiting the identification of P(y | x̂).

finding a variable Z that is correlated with X but not with U) would facilitate the computation of $E(Y \mid \hat{x})$ via the instrumental-variable formula (Bowden and Turkington 1984, Angrist, Imbens, and Rubin 1996):

$$b \overset{\Delta}{=} \frac{\partial}{\partial x} E(Y \mid \hat{x}) = \frac{E(Y \mid z)}{E(X \mid z)} = \frac{R_{yz}}{R_{xz}} \tag{35}$$

In nonparametric models, adding an instrumental variable Z to a bow-pattern (figure 6b) does not permit the identification of $P(y \mid \hat{x})$. This is a familiar problem in the analysis of clinical trials in which treatment assignment (Z) is randomized (hence, no link enters Z), but compliance is imperfect. The confounding arc between X and Y in figure 6b represents unmeasurable factors which influence both subjects' choice of treatment (X) and subjects' response to treatment (Y). In such trials, it is not possible to obtain an unbiased estimate of the treatment effect $P(y \mid \hat{x})$ without making additional assumptions on the nature of the interactions between compliance and response, as is done, for example, in the general approach to instrumental variables developed in Angrist, Imbens, and Rubin (1996) and Imbens and Angrist (1994). While the added arc $Z \to X$ permits us to calculate bounds on $P(y \mid \hat{x})$ (Robins 1989, section 1g; Manski 1990) and the upper and lower bounds may even coincide for certain types of distributions $P(x, y, z)$ (Balke and Pearl 1994, 1997; Pearl 1995b), there is no way of computing $P(y \mid \hat{x})$ for every positive distribution $P(x, y, z)$, as required by definition 5.

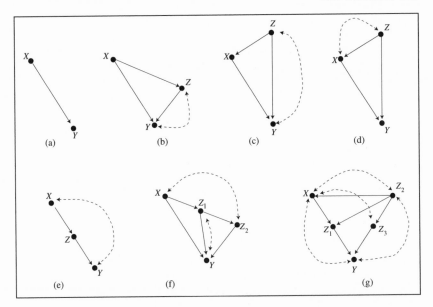

Figure 7. Typical models in which the effect of X on Y is identifiable. Dashed arcs represent confounding paths, and Z represents observed covariates.

In general, the addition of arcs to a causal diagram can impede, but never assist, the identification of causal effects in nonparametric models. This is because such addition reduces the set of d-separation conditions carried by the diagram and, hence, if a causal effect derivation fails in the original diagram, it is bound to fail in the augmented diagram as well. Conversely, any causal effect derivation that succeeds in the augmented diagram (by a sequence of symbolic transformations, as in Corollary 1) would succeed in the original diagram.

Our ability to compute $P(y \mid \hat{x})$ for pairs (x, y) of singleton variables does not ensure our ability to compute joint distributions, such as $P(y_1, y_2 \mid \hat{x})$. Figure 6c, for example, shows a causal diagram where both $P(z_1 \mid \hat{x})$ and $P(z_2 \mid \hat{x})$ are computable, but $P(z_1, z_2 \mid \hat{x})$ is not. Consequently, we cannot compute $P(y \mid \hat{x})$. Interestingly, this diagram is the smallest graph that does not contain a bow-pattern and still presents an uncomputable causal effect.

Another interesting feature demonstrated by figure 6c is that computing the effect of a joint intervention is often easier than computing the effects of its constituent singleton interventions.[6] Here, it is possible to compute $P(y \mid \hat{x}, \hat{z}_2)$ and $P(y \mid \hat{x}, \hat{z}_1)$, yet there is no way of computing $P(y \mid \hat{x})$. For example, the former can be evaluated by invoking rule 2 in $G_{\underline{xz_2}}$, giving

$$P(y \mid \hat{x}, \hat{z}_2) =$$

$$\sum_{z_1} P(y \mid z_1, \hat{x}, \hat{z}_2) P(z_1 \mid \hat{x}, \hat{z}_2) =$$

$$\sum_{z_1} P(y \mid z_1, x, z_2) P(z_1 \mid x) \qquad (36)$$

However, rule 2 cannot be used to convert $P(z_1 \mid \hat{x}, z_2)$ into $P(z_1 \mid x, z_2)$ because, when conditioned on Z_2, X and Z_1 are d-connected in $G_{\underline{x}}$ (through the dashed lines). A general approach to computing the effect of joint interventions is developed in Pearl and Robins (1995).

5.1 Identifying Models

Figure 7 shows simple diagrams in which the causal effect of X on Y is identifiable. Such models are called identifying because their structures communicate a sufficient number of assumptions (missing links) to permit the identification of the target quantity $P(y \mid \hat{x})$. Latent variables are not shown explicitly in these diagrams; rather, such variables are implicit in the confounding arcs (dashed). Every causal diagram with latent variables can be converted to an equivalent diagram involving measured variables interconnected by arrows and confounding arcs. This conversion corresponds to substituting out all latent variables from the structural equations of equation 4 and then constructing a new diagram by connecting any two variables X_i and X_j by (1) an arrow from X_j to X_i whenever X_j appears in the equation for X_i and (2) a confounding arc whenever the same ε term appears in both f_i and f_j. The result is a diagram in which all unmeasured variables are exogenous and mutually independent. Several features should be noted from examining the diagrams in figure 7.

First, since the removal of any arc or arrow from a causal diagram can only assist the identifiability of causal effects, $P(y \mid \hat{x})$ will still be identified in any edge-subgraph of the diagrams shown in figure 7. Likewise, the introduction of mediating observed variables onto any edge in a causal graph can assist, but never impede, the identifiability of any causal effect. Therefore, $P(y \mid \hat{x})$ will still be identified from any graph obtained by adding mediating nodes to the diagrams shown in figure 7.

Second, the diagrams in figure 7 are maximal, in the sense that the introduction of any additional arc or arrow onto an existing pair of nodes would render $P(y \mid \hat{x})$ no longer identifiable.

Third, although most of the diagrams in figure 7 contain bow-patterns, none of these patterns emanates from X (as is the case in figure 8a and 8b below). In general, a necessary condition for the identifiability of $P(y \mid \hat{x})$ is the absence of a confounding arc between X and any child of X that is an ancestor of Y.

Fourth, diagrams in figure 7a and 7b contain no back-door paths between X and Y, and thus represent experimental designs in which there is no confounding bias between the treatment (X) and the response (Y); hence, $P(y \mid \hat{x})$ $= P(y \mid x)$. Likewise, diagrams in figure 7c and 7d represent designs in which observed covariates, Z, block every back-door path between X and Y (i.e., X is "conditionally ignorable" given Z in the language of (Rosenbaum and Rubin 1983)); hence, $P(y \mid \hat{x})$ is obtained by standard adjustment for Z (as in equation 10):

$$P(y \mid \hat{x}) = \sum_z P(y \mid x, z) P(z)$$

Fifth, for each of the diagrams in figure 7, we can readily obtain a formula for $P(y \mid \hat{x})$, by using symbolic derivations patterned after those in section 4.3. The derivation is often guided by the graph topology. For example, diagram in figure 7f dictates the following derivation. Writing

$$P(y \mid \hat{x}) = \sum_{z_1, z_2} P(y \mid z_1, z_2, \hat{x}) P(z_1, z_2 \mid \hat{x})$$

we see that the subgraph containing $\{X, Z_1, Z_2\}$ is identical in structure to that of diagram in figure 7e, with (Z_1, Z_2) replacing (Z, Y), respectively. Thus, $P(z_1, z_2 \mid \hat{x})$ can be obtained from equation 32. Likewise, the term $P(y \mid z_1, z_2, \hat{x})$ can be reduced to $P(y \mid z_1, z_2, x)$ by rule 2, since $(Y \perp\!\!\!\perp X \mid Z_1, Z_2)_{G_{\underline{x}}}$. Thus, we have

$$P(y \mid \hat{x}) = \sum_{z_1, z_2} P(y \mid z_1, z_2, x) P(z_1 \mid \hat{x}) \sum_{x'} P(z_2 \mid z_1, x') P(x') \qquad (37)$$

Applying a similar derivation to the diagram in figure 7g yields

$$P(y \mid \hat{x}) = \sum_{z_1} \sum_{z_2} \sum_{x'} P(y \mid z_1, z_2, x') \, P(x' \mid z_2) \, P(z_1 \mid z_2, x) P(z_2) \qquad (38)$$

Note that the variable Z_3 does not appear in the expression above, which means that Z_3 need not be measured if all one wants to learn is the causal effect of X on Y.

Sixth, in the diagrams of figure 7e, 7f, and 7g, the identifiability of $P(y \mid \hat{x})$ is rendered feasible through observed covariates, Z, that are affected by the treatment X (i.e., Z being descendants of X). This stands contrary to the warning, repeated in most of the literature on statistical experimentation, to refrain from adjusting for concomitant observations that are affected by the treatment (Cox 1958; Rosenbaum 1984; Pratt and Schlaifer 1988; Wainer 1989). It is commonly believed that if a concomitant Z is affected by the treatment, then it must be excluded from the analysis of the total effect of the treatment (Pratt and Schlaifer 1988). The reason given for the exclusion is that the calculation of total effects amounts to integrating out Z, which is functionally equivalent to omitting Z to begin with. The diagrams in figure 7e, 7f, and 7g show cases where one wants to learn the total effects of X and,

124 PEARL

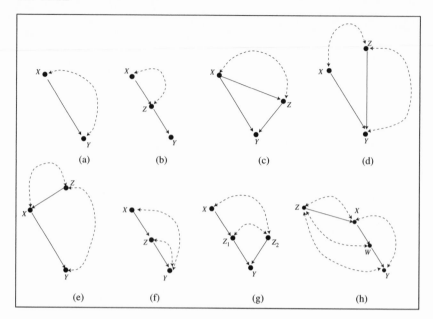

Figure 8. Typical models in which P(y | x̂) is not identifiable.

still, the measurement of concomitants that are affected by X (e.g., Z, or Z_1) is necessary. However, the adjustment needed for such concomitants is non-standard, involving two or more stages of the standard adjustment of equation 10, (see equations 17, 37, and 38).

Finally, in the diagrams of figure 7b, 7c, and 7f, Y has a parent whose effect on Y is not identifiable yet the effect of X on Y is identifiable. This demonstrates that local identifiability is not a necessary condition for global identifiability. In other words, to identify the effect of X on Y we need not insist on identifying each and every link along the paths from X to Y.

5.2 Nonidentifying Models

Figure 8 presents typical diagrams in which the total effect of X on Y, $P(y | x̂)$, is not identifiable. Noteworthy features of these diagrams are as follows.

First, all graphs in figure 8 contain unblockable back-door paths between X and Y, that is, paths ending with arrows pointing to X which cannot be blocked by observed nondescendants of X. The presence of such a path in a graph is, indeed, a necessary test for nonidentifiability (see theorem 3). It is not a sufficient test, though, as is demonstrated by figure 7e, in which the back-door path (dashed) is unblockable and yet $P(y | x̂)$ is identifiable.

Second, a sufficient condition for the nonidentifiability of $P(y \mid \hat{x})$ is the existence of a confounding path between X and any of its children on a path from X to Y, as shown in figure 8b and 8c. A stronger sufficient condition is that the graph contain any of the patterns shown in figure 8 as an edge-subgraph.

Finally, the graph in figure 8g (same as figure 6c) demonstrates that local identifiability is not sufficient for global identifiability. For example, we can identify $P(z_1 \mid \hat{x})$, $P(z_2 \mid \hat{x})$, $P(y \mid \hat{z}_1)$, and $P(y \mid \hat{z}_2)$, but not $P(y \mid \hat{x})$. This is one of the main differences between nonparametric and linear models; in the latter, all causal effects can be determined from the structural coefficients, each coefficient representing the causal effect of one variable on its immediate successor.

6. Discussion

The basic limitation of the methods proposed in this chapter is that the results must rest on the causal assumptions shown in the graph, and that these cannot usually be tested in observational studies. In related papers (Pearl 1995a, 1995b) we show that some of the assumptions, most notably those associated with instrumental variables (figure 6b) are subject to falsification tests.[7] Moreover, considering that any causal inferences from observational studies must ultimately rely on some kind of causal assumptions,[8] the methods described in this chapter offer an effective language for making those assumptions precise and explicit, so they can be isolated for deliberation or experimentation and, once validated, be integrated with statistical data.

A second limitation concerns an assumption inherent in identification analysis, namely, that the sample size is so large that sampling variability may be ignored. The mathematical derivation of causal-effect estimands should therefore be considered a first step toward supplementing these estimands with confidence intervals and significance levels, as in traditional analysis of controlled experiments. We should remark, though, that having obtained nonparametric estimands for causal effects does not imply that one should refrain from using parametric forms in the estimation phase of the study. For example, if the assumptions of Gaussian, zero-mean disturbances and additive interactions are deemed reasonable, then the estimand given in equation 17 can be converted to the product $E(Y \mid \hat{x}) = R_{xz} \beta_{zy \cdot x} x$ where $\beta_{zy \cdot x}$ is the standardized regression coefficient, and the estimation problem reduces to that of estimating regression coefficients (e.g., by least-squares). More sophisticated estimation techniques can be found in Rubin (1978), Robins (1989, section 17), and Robins et al. (1992, 331–333).

Several extensions of the methods proposed in this chapter are noteworthy.

First, the analysis of atomic interventions can be generalized to complex policies in which a set X of treatment variables is made to respond in a specified way to some set Z of covariates, say through a functional relationship $X = g(Z)$ or through a stochastic relationship whereby X is set to x with probability $P^*(x \mid z)$. In Pearl (1994b) it is shown that computing the effect of such policies is equivalent to computing the expression $P(y \mid \hat{x}, z)$.

A second extension concerns the use of the intervention calculus (theorem 5) in nonrecursive models, that is, in causal diagrams involving directed cycles or feedback loops. The basic definition of causal effects in terms of "wiping out" equations from the model (definition 3) still carries over to nonrecursive systems (Strotz and Wold 1960, Sobel 1990), but then two issues must be addressed. First, the analysis of identification must ensure the stability of the remaining submodels (Fisher 1970). Second, the d-separation criterion for DAGs must be extended to cover cyclic graphs as well. The validity of d-separation has been established for nonrecursive linear models (Spirtes 1995) as well as nonlinear systems involving discrete variables (Pearl and Dechter 1996). However, the computation of causal effect estimands will be harder in cyclic networks, because symbolic reduction of $P(y \mid \hat{x})$ to hat-free expressions may require the solution of nonlinear equations.

Finally, a few comments regarding the notation introduced in this chapter. Traditionally, statisticians have approved of only one way of combining domain knowledge with statistical data: the Bayesian method of assigning subjective priors to distributional parameters. To incorporate causal information within the Bayesian framework, plain causal statements such as "Y is affected by X" must be converted into sentences capable of receiving probability values, e.g., counterfactuals. Indeed, this is how Rubin's model has achieved statistical legitimacy: causal judgments are expressed as constraints on probability functions involving counterfactual variables (see the graphs, structural equations, and counterfactuals section that follows).

Causal diagrams offer an alternative language for combining data with causal information. This language simplifies the Bayesian route by accepting plain causal statements as its basic primitives. These statements, which merely identify whether a causal connection between two variables of interest exists, are commonly used in natural discourse and provide a natural way for scientists to communicate experience and organize knowledge. It can be anticipated, therefore, that the language of causal graphs will find applications in problems requiring substantial domain knowledge.

The language is not new. The use of diagrams and structural equations models to convey causal information has been quite popular in the social sciences and econometrics. Statisticians, however, have generally found these models suspect, perhaps because social scientists and econometricians have failed to provide an unambiguous definition of the empirical content of their models, that is, to specify the experimental conditions, however hypothetical, whose outcomes would be constrained by a given structural equation. As a result, even such basic notions as "structural coefficients" or "missing links" become the object of serious controversy (Freedman 1987) and misinterpretations (Wermuth 1992; Whittaker 1990, p. 302; Cox and Wermuth 1993).

To a large extent, this history of controversy and miscommunication stems from the absence of an adequate mathematical notation for defining basic notions of causal modeling. For example, standard probabilistic notation cannot express the empirical content of the coefficient b in the structural equation $Y = bX + \varepsilon_Y$ even if one is prepared to assume that ε_Y (an unobserved quantity) is uncorrelated with X. Nor can any probabilistic meaning be attached to the analyst's excluding from the equation certain variables that are highly correlated with X or Y.

The notation developed in this chapter gives these notions a clear empirical interpretation, because it permits one to specify precisely what is being held constant and what is merely measured in a controlled experiment. (The need for this distinction was recognized by many researchers, most notably Pratt and Schlaifer [1988] and Cox [1992]). The meaning of b is simply

$$\frac{\partial}{\partial x} E(Y \mid \hat{x})$$

namely, the rate of change (in x) of the expectation of Y in an experiment where X is held at x by external control. This interpretation holds regardless of whether ε_Y and X are correlated (e.g., via another equation: $X = aY + \varepsilon_X$) and, moreover, the notion of randomization need not be invoked. Likewise, the analyst's decision as to which variables should be included in a given equation can be based on a hypothetical controlled experiment: A variable Z is excluded from the equation for Y if it has no influence on Y when all other variables, s_{YZ}, are held constant, that is, $P(y \mid \hat{z}, \hat{s}_{YZ}) = P(y \mid \hat{s}_{YZ})$. Specifically, variables that are excluded from the equation $Y = bX + \varepsilon_Y$ are not conditionally independent of Y given measurements of X, but rather causally irrelevant to Y given settings of X. The operational meaning of the so called "disturbance term," ε_Y, is likewise demystified: ε_Y is defined as the difference $Y - E(Y \mid \hat{s}_y)$; two disturbance terms, ε_X and ε_Y, are correlated if $P(y \mid \hat{x}, \hat{s}_{XY}) \neq P(y \mid x, \ \hat{s}_{XY})$, and so on (see Pearl 1998).

The distinctions provided by the "hat" notation clarify the empirical basis of structural equations and should make causal models more acceptable to empirical researchers. Moreover, since most scientific knowledge is organized around the operation of "holding X fixed," rather than "conditioning on X," the notation and calculus developed in this chapter should provide an effective means for scientists to communicate subject-matter information and to infer its logical consequences.

7. Proof of Theorem 5

Rule 1 follows from the fact that deleting equations from the model in equation 4 results, again, in a recursive set of equations in which all ε terms are mutually independent. The d-separation condition is valid for any recursive model; hence it is valid for the submodel resulting from deleting the equations for X. Finally, since the graph characterizing this submodel is given by $G_{\bar{x}}$, $(Y \perp\!\!\!\perp Z \mid X, W)_{G_{\bar{x}}}$ implies the conditional independence $P(y \mid \hat{x}, z, w) = P(y \mid \hat{x}, w)$ in the post-intervention distribution.

Second, the graph $G_{\bar{x}\underline{z}}$ differs from $G_{\bar{x}}$ only in lacking the arrows emanating from Z, hence it retains all the back-door paths from Z to Y that can be found in $G_{\bar{x}}$. The condition $(Y \perp\!\!\!\perp Z \mid X, W)_{G_{\bar{x}\underline{z}}}$ ensures that all back-door paths from Z to Y (in $G_{\bar{x}}$) are blocked by $\{X, W\}$. Under such conditions, setting $(Z = z)$ or conditioning on $Z = z$ has the same effect on Y. This can best be seen from the augmented diagram $G'_{\bar{x}}$, to which the intervention arcs $F_Z \rightarrow Z$ were added, where F_z stands for the external intervention as in figure 2. If all back-door paths from F_z to Y are blocked, the remaining paths from F_z to Y must go through the children of Z, hence these paths will be blocked by Z. The implication is that Y is independent of F_z given Z, which means that the observation $Z = z$ cannot be distinguished from the intervention $F_z = set(z)$.

Third (after D. Galles), consider the augmented diagram $G'_{\bar{x}}$ to which the intervention arcs $F_z \rightarrow Z$ are added. If $(F_z \perp\!\!\!\perp Y \mid W, X)_{G'_{\bar{x}}}$, then $P(y \mid \hat{x}, \hat{z}, w) = P(y \mid \hat{x}, w)$. If $(Y \perp\!\!\!\perp Z \mid X, W)_{G_{\bar{x}\;\overline{z}(w)}}$, and $(F_z \perp\!\!\!\!\!\!/\;\; Y \mid W, X)_{G'_{\bar{x}}}$, there must be an unblocked path from a member $F_{Z'}$ of F_Z to Y that passes through either a head-to-tail junction at Z', or a head-to-head junction at Z'. If there is such a path, let P be the shortest such path. We will show that P will violate some premise, or there exists a shorter path, either of which leads to a contradiction.

If the junction is head-to-tail, that means that $(Y \perp\!\!\!\!\!\!/\;\; Z' \mid W, X)_{G'_{\bar{x}}}$, but $(Y \perp\!\!\!\perp Z' \mid W, X)_{G'_{\bar{x}\;\overline{z}(w)}}$. So there must be an unblocked path from Y to Z' that passes through some member Z'' of $Z(W)$ in either a head-to-head or a tail-to-head junction. This is impossible. If the junction is head-to-head, then some descendant of Z'' must be in W for the path to be unblocked, but then Z'' would not be in $Z(W)$. If the junction is tail-to-head, there are two options: the path from Z' to Z'' ends in an arrow pointing to Z'', or an arrow pointing away from Z''. If it ends in an arrow pointing away from Z'', then there must be a head-to-head junction along the path from Z' to Z''. In that case, for the path to be unblocked, W must be a descendant of Z'', but then Z'' would not be in $Z(W)$. If it ends in an arrow pointing to Z'', then there must be an unblocked path from Z'' to Y in $G_{\bar{x}}$ that is blocked in $G_{\bar{x}\;\overline{z}(w)}$. If this is true, then there is an unblocked path from $F_{Z''}$ to Y that is shorter than P, the shortest path.

If the junction through Z' is head-to-head, then either Z' is in $Z(W)$, in which case that junction would be blocked, or there is an unblocked path from Z' to Y in $G_{\overline{X}\,\underline{Z}(w)}$ that is blocked in $G_{\overline{X}}$. Above, we proved that this could not occur. So $(Y \perp\!\!\!\perp Z \mid X,\ W)_{G'_{\overline{X}\,\underline{Z}(w)}}$ implies $(F_Z \perp\!\!\!\perp Y \mid W,\ X)_{G'_{\overline{X}}}$, and thus $P(y \mid \hat{x},\ \hat{z},\ w) = P(y \mid \hat{x},\ w)$.

8. Graphs, Structural Equations, and Counterfactuals

This chapter uses two representations of causal models: graphs and structural equations. By now, both representations have been considered controversial for almost a century. On the one hand, economists and social scientists have embraced these modeling tools, but they continue to debate the empirical content of the symbols they estimate and manipulate (Cartwright 1995; LeRoy 1995; McDonald 1997); as a result, the use of structural models in policy-making contexts is often viewed with suspicion. Statisticians, on the other hand, reject both representations as problematic (Freedman 1987) if not meaningless (Wermuth 1992; Holland 1995), and instead resort to the Neyman-Rubin counterfactual notation whenever they are pressed to communicate causal information (Rubin 1990). This section presents an explication that unifies these three representation schemes in order to uncover commonalities, mediate differences, and make the causal-inference literature more generally accessible.

The primitive object of analysis in Rubin's counterfactual framework is the unit-based response variable, denoted $Y(x,\ u)$ or $Y_x(u)$, read: "the value that Y would obtain in unit u, had X been x." This variable has natural interpretation in structural equations models. Consider a set T of equations

$$X_i = f_i(PA_i,\ U_i) \quad i = 1, \ldots, n \tag{39}$$

where the U_i stands for latent exogenous variables (or disturbances), and the PA_i are the explanatory (observed) variables in the ith equation (pa_i is a realization of PA_i). Equation 39 is similar to equation 4, except we no longer insist on the equations being recursive or on the U_i's being independent. Let U stand for the vector $(U_1, \ldots, U_n)$, let X and Y be two disjoint subsets of observed variables, and let T_x be the submodel created by replacing the equations corresponding to variables in X with $X = x$, as in definition 3. The structural interpretation of $Y(x,\ u)$ is given by

$$Y(x, u) \underset{=}{\Delta} Y_{T_x}(u) \tag{40}$$

namely, $Y(x,\ u)$ is the (unique) solution of Y under the realization $U = u$ in the submodel T_x of T. While the term "unit" in the counterfactual literature normally stands for the identity of a specific individual in a population, a unit may also be thought of as the set of attributes that characterize that individual, the experimental conditions under study, the time of day, and so on, which are represented as components of the vector u in structural modeling. Equation 40 forms a connection between the opaque English phrase "the value that Y would obtain in unit u, had X been x" and the physical processes that transfer changes in X into changes in Y. The formation of the submodel T_x represents a minimal change in model T needed for making x and u compatible; such a change could result either from external intervention or from a natural yet unanticipated eventuality.

Given this interpretation of $Y(x, u)$, it is instructive to contrast the methodologies of causal inference in the counterfactual and the structural frameworks. If U is treated as a random variable, then the value of the counterfactual $Y(x, u)$ becomes a random variable as well, denoted as $Y(x)$ or Y_x. The counterfactual analysis proceeds by imagining the observed distribution $P(x_1, \ldots, x_n)$ as the marginal distribution of an augmented probability function $P*$ defined over both observed and counterfactual variables. Queries about causal effects, written $P(y \mid \hat{x})$ in the structural analysis, are phrased as queries about the marginal distribution of the counterfactual variable of interest, written $P*(Y(x) = y)$. The new entities $Y(x)$ are treated as ordinary random variables that are connected to the observed variables via consistency constraints (Robins 1987) such as

$$X = x \Rightarrow Y(x) = Y \tag{41}$$

and a set of conditional independence assumptions which the investigator must supply to endow the augmented probability, $P*$, with causal knowledge, paralleling the knowledge that a structural analyst would encode in equations or in graphs.

For example, to communicate the understanding that in a randomized clinical trial (see figure 6b) the way subjects react (Y) to treatments (X) is statistically independent of the treatment assignment (Z), the analyst would write $Y(x) \perp\!\!\!\perp Z$. Likewise, to convey the understanding that the assignment process is randomized, hence independent of any variation in the treatment selection process, structurally written $U_X \perp\!\!\!\perp U_Z$, the analyst would use the independence constraint $X(z) \perp\!\!\!\perp Z$.

A collection of constraints of this type might sometimes be sufficient to permit a unique solution to the query of interest, for example, $P*(Y(x) = y)$; in other cases, only bounds on the solution can be obtained. Section 6 explains why this approach is conceptually appealing to some statisticians, even though the process of eliciting judgments about counterfactual dependencies has so far not been systematized. When counterfactual variables are not viewed as by-products of a deeper, process-based model, it is hard to ascertain whether *all* relevant judgments have been articulated, whether the judgments articulated are redundant, or whether those judgments are self-consistent. The elicitation of such judgments can be systematized using the following translation from graphs.

Graphs provide qualitative information about the structure of both the equations in the model and the probability function $P(u)$. The former is encoded as missing arrows, the latter as missing dashed arcs. Each parent-child family (PA_i, X_i) in a causal diagram G corresponds to an equation in the model (39). Hence, missing arrows encode exclusion assumptions, that is, claims that adding excluded variables to an equation will not change the outcome of the hypothetical experiment described by that equation. Missing dashed arcs encode independencies among disturbance terms in two or more equations. For example, the absence of dashed arcs between a node Y and a set of nodes $Z_1,..., Z_k$ implies that the corresponding error variables, U_Y, U_{Z_1} ,..., U_{Z_k}, are jointly independent in $P(u)$.

These assumptions can be translated into the counterfactual notation using two simple rules; the first interprets the missing arrows in the graph, the second, the missing dashed arcs.

1. *Exclusion restrictions:* For every variable Y having parents PA_Y, and for every set of variables S disjoint of PA_Y, we have

$$Y(pa_Y) = Y(pa_Y, s) \qquad (42)$$

2. *Independence restrictions:* If $Z_1,..., Z_k$ is any set of nodes not connected to Y via dashed arcs, we have

$$Y(pa_Y) \perp\!\!\!\perp \left\{ Z_1\left(pa_{z_1}\right), \cdots, Z_k\left(pa_{z_k}\right) \right\} \qquad (43)$$

Given a sufficient number of such restrictions on P^*, it is possible to compute causal effects $P^*(Y(x) = y)$ using standard probability calculus together with the logical constraints (e.g., equation 41 that couple counterfactual variables with their measurable counterparts). These constraints can be used as axioms, or rules of inference, in attempting to transform causal effect expressions, $P^*(Y(x) = y)$, into expressions involving only measurable variables. When such a transformation is found, the corresponding causal effect is identifiable, since P^* reduces then to P. The axioms needed for such transformation (Galles and Pearl 1997, 1998) are:

Null-Action: $Y(\emptyset) = Y$ \qquad (44)

Effectiveness: $Y(y, x) = y$ \qquad (45)

Composition: $Y(x) = Y(x, Z(x))$ for any Z disjoint of $\{X, Y\}$ \qquad (46)

The first two axioms are technical; the first identifies an expression with a null argument with a variable (Y) under nonexperimental conditions. The second assures that a variable (Y) will attain the value (y) that is imposed by the action that manipulates that variable. The essence of counterfactual expressions and the main tool of symbolic inference rests with the axiom of composition.[9] This axiom asserts:

If $Y(x, z) = y$ and $Z(x) = z$, then $Y(x) = y$

and, conversely:

If $Y(x) = y$ and $Z(x) = z$, then $Y(x, z) = y$

In words: "The value that Y would obtain had X been x is the same as that obtained had X been x and Z been z, where z is the value that Z would obtain had X been x."

Properties 44-46 are theorems in the structural interpretation of $Y(x, u)$ as given in equation 40. However, in the Neyman-Rubin model, where $Y(x, u)$ is taken as a primitive notion, these properties must be considered axioms which define the abstract counterfactual conditioning operator "had X been x." It is easy to verify that composition and null-action imply the consistency rule of equation 41; substituting $X = \{\emptyset\}$ in equation 46 yields $Y = Y(z)$ if $Z = z$, which is equivalent to equation 41.

As an example, let us compute the causal effects associated with the model shown in figure 4. The parents sets are given by:

$$PA_X = \{\emptyset\}, PA_Z = \{X\}, PA_Y = \{Z\} \tag{47}$$

Consequently, the exclusion restrictions translate into:

$$Z(x) = Z(y, x) \tag{48}$$
$$X(y) = X(z, y) = X(z) = X \tag{49}$$
$$Y(z) = Y(z, x) \tag{50}$$

The absence of a dashed arc between Z and $\{Y, X\}$ translates into the independence restrictions:

$$Z(x) \perp\!\!\!\perp \{Y(z), X\} \tag{51}$$

Task-1, compute $P^*(Z(x) = z)$ (Equivalently $P(z \mid \hat{x})$)
From equation 51 we have $Z(x) \perp\!\!\!\perp X$, hence

$$P^*(Z(x) = z) = P^*(Z(x) = z \mid x) = P^*(z \mid x) = P(z \mid x) \tag{52}$$

Task-2, compute $P^*(Y(z) = y)$ (Equivalently $P(y \mid \hat{z})$)

$$P^*(Y(z) = y) = \Sigma_x P^*(Y(z) = y \mid x)P^*(x) \tag{53}$$

From equation 51 we have

$$Y(z) \perp\!\!\!\perp Z(x) \mid X \tag{54}$$

hence

$$\begin{aligned}
P^*(Y(z) = y \mid x) &= P^*(Y(z) = y \mid x, Z(x) = z) \quad \text{by equation 52} \\
&= P^*(Y(z) = y \mid x, z) \quad \text{by equation 41} \\
&= P^*(y \mid x, z) \quad \text{by equation 41} \\
&= P(y \mid x, z)
\end{aligned} \tag{55}$$

Substituting equation 55 in equation 53, gives

$$P^*\left(Y(z) = y\right) = \sum_x P(y \mid x, z)P(x) \tag{56}$$

which is the celebrated covariate-adjustment formula for causal effect, as in equation 10.

Task-3, compute $P^*(Y(x) = y)$ (Equivalently $P(y \mid \hat{x})$)
For any arbitrary variable Z, we have (by composition equation 46)

$$Y(x) = Y(x, Z(x))$$

In particular, since $Y(x, z) = Y(z)$ (from equation 50), we have

$$Y(x) = Y(x, Z(x)) = Y(Z(x))$$

and

$$P*(Y(x) = y) = P*(Y(Z(x)) = y)$$

$$= \sum_z P*(Y(Z(x)) = y \mid Z(x) = z) \ P*(Z(x) = z)$$

$$= \sum_z P*(Y(z) = y \mid Z(x) = z) \ P*(Z(x) = z)$$

$$= \sum_z P*(Y(z) = y) \ P*(Z(x) = z)$$

since $Y(z) \perp\!\!\!\perp Z(x)$. $P*(Y(z) = y)$ and $P*(Z(x) = z)$ were computed in equation 56 and 52, respectively, hence

$$P*(Y(x) = y) = \sum_z P(z \mid x) \sum_{x'} P(y \mid z, x') P(x')$$

in agreement with the front-door formula of equation 18.

We see that axioms 44-46 are sufficient for deriving powerful results like the back-door and front-door formulas, which were shown to be valid relative to structural equation semantics of equation 4. The question naturally arises whether these axioms are complete, that is, whether they are sufficient for deriving every valid property of structural equations. Recent result by Galles and Pearl (1997, 1998) confirms the completeness of axioms 44-46 relative to recursive structural equations. In nonrecursive systems, additional axioms are required. The practical implication of this completeness result is that there is no harm in interpreting counterfactual sentences as statements about solutions of structural equations—such an interpretation does not introduce any new assumption or new property beyond those embedded in the abstract counterfactual analysis governed by axioms 44-46.

There is a substantial advantage, however, to the structural equation model versus the counterfactual model in notational clarity. The reader will appreciate this advantage by attempting to judge whether assumption 51 holds in a given practical situation. This assumption reads: "the value that Z would attain had X been x is jointly independent on both X and on the value of Y had Z been z." The meaning of such a cumbersome sentence is greatly simplified through its causal interpretation, read: "Z shares no common cause with either X or Y." Still, researchers who find counterfactual vocabulary more comfortable than graphs or plain causal expressions can now use the translation given by equations 42 and 43 as a definition of graphs, structural equations and the physical processes which they represent.

Acknowledgments

Much of this investigation was inspired by Peter Spirtes's lecture in Uppsala, Sweden, where I first saw manipulations represented in mutilated graphs. Phil Dawid, David Freedman, James Robins and Donald Rubin have provided genuine encouragement and valuable advice. For example, Phil has suggested the first part of definition 3. The investigation also benefited from discussions with Joshua Angrist, Peter Bentler, David Cox, Arthur Dempster, David Galles, Arthur Goldberger, Sander Greenland, David Hendry, Paul Holland, Guido Imbens, Ed Leamer, Rod McDonald, John Pratt, Paul Rosenbaum, Keunkwan Ryu, Glenn Shafer, Michael Sobel, David Tritchler, and Nanny Wermuth. This research was partially supported by grants from AFOSR and NSF.

Notes

1. The reader need not be intimidated if, at this point, the formula appears unfamiliar. After reading section 4, the reader should be able to derive such formulas with greater ease than solving a pair of algebraic equations. Note that x' is merely an index of summation that ranges over the values of X.

2. An equivalent notation, using $do(x)$ instead of $set(x)$, was first used in (Goldszmidt and Pearl 1992), and is currently winning a broader popular support.

3. An explicit translation of interventions to "wiping out" equations from the model was first proposed by Strotz and Wold (1960) and later used in Fisher (1970) and Sobel (1990). Graphical ramifications of this translation were explicated first in Spirtes, Glymour, and Schienes (1993) and later in Pearl (1993c). A related mathematical model, using event trees, has been introduced by Robins (1986, 1422–1425).

4. Equation 9 can also be obtained from the G-computation formula of Robins (1986, p. 1423) and the Manipulation Theorem of Spirtes, Glymour, and Schienes (1993) (according to this source, such formula was "independently conjectured by Fienberg in a seminar in 1991"). Additional properties of the transformation defined in equation 9 are given in Pearl (1993c).

5. This criterion may also be obtained from theorem 7.1 of Spirtes, Glymour, and Schienes (1993). An alternative criterion, using a single d-separation test will be established in section 4 (see equation 26).

6. This was brought to my attention by James Robins, who has worked out many of these computations in the context of sequential treatment management. Equation 36, for example, can be obtained from Robin's G-computation algorithm (Robins, p. 1423, 1986).

7. The testable implications of the model of figure 6b can be expressed in a simple inequality (Pearl 1995a and b): $\max_x \Sigma_y \max_z P(y, x|z) \leq 1$.

8. See Pearl (1996) for a review of attempts by philosophers to reduce causality to probabilities.

9. James Robins has informed me that he has been using composition since 1986 (Robins 1986) and has considered it to be true by definition. Composition can also be shown (Galles and Pearl 1997) to follow from Lewis's (1973) closest-world definition of counterfactuals.

References

Aldrich, J. 1989. Autonomy. In *History and Methodology of Econometrics,* ed. N. Marchi and C. Gibert, 15–34. New York: *Oxford University Press.*

Angrist, J. D.; Imbens, G. W.; and Rubin, D. B. 1996. Identification of Causal Effects Using Instrumental Variables (with Comments). *Journal of the American Statistical Society* 91(434): 444–472.

Balke, A., and Pearl, J. 1997. Bounds on Treatment from Studies with Imperfect Compliance. *Journal of the American Statistical Association* 92(439): 1171–1176.

Balke, A., and Pearl, J. 1994. Counterfactual Probabilities: Computational Methods, Bounds, and Applications. In *Uncertainty in Artificial Intelligence 10,* eds. R. Lopez de Mantaras and D. Poole, 46–54. San Francisco, Calif.: Morgan Kaufmann Publishers.

Bowden, R. J., and Turkington, D. A. 1984. *Instrumental Variables.* Cambridge, Mass.: Cambridge University Press.

Cartwright, N. 1995. Probabilities and Experiments. *Journal of Econometrics* 67(1): 47–95.

Cooper, G. F., and Herskovits, E. 1991. A Bayesian Method for Constructing Bayesian Belief Networks from Databases. In *Proceedings of the Conference on Uncertainty in Artificial Intelligence,* 86–94. San Francisco: Morgan Kaufmann Publishers.

Cox, D. R. 1992. Some Statistical Aspects. *Journal of the Royal Statistical Society* A155(2): 291–301.

Cox, D. R. 1958. *The Planning of Experiments.* New York: John Wiley.

Cox, D. R., and Wermuth, N. 1993. Linear Dependencies Represented by Chain Graphs. *Statistical Science* 8(3): 204–218.

Dawid, A. P. 1979. Conditional Independence in Statistical Theory. *Journal of the Royal Statistical Society* A41(1): 1–31.

Fisher, F. M. 1970. A Correspondence Principle for Simultaneous Equation Models. *Econometrica* 38(1): 73–92.

Freedman, D. 1987. As Others See Us: A Case Study in Path Analysis (with Discussion). *Journal of Educational Statistics* 12(2): 101–223.

Frisch, R. 1948. Statistical versus Theoretical Relations in Economic Macrodynamics: League of Nations Memorandum. In *Autonomy of Economic Relations,* Olso, Norway: Universitetets Socialokonomiske Institutt.

Galles, D., and Pearl, J. 1998. An Axiomatic Characterization of Causal Counterfactuals. *Foundations of Science,* 3(1): 151-182.

Galles, D., and Pearl, J. 1997. Axioms of Causal Relevance. *Artificial Intelligence* 97(1–2): 9–43.

Galles, D., and Pearl, J. 1995. Testing Identifiability of Causal Effects. In *Uncertainty in Artificial Intelligence 11*, eds. P. Besnard and S. Hanks, 185–195. San Francisco, Calif.: Morgan Kaufmann Publishers.

Geiger, D.; Verma, T. S.; and Pearl, J. 1990. Identifying Independence in Bayesian Networks. *Networks* 20(5): 507–534.

Goldberger, A. S. 1973. *Structural Equation Models in the Social Sciences.* New York: Seminar.

Goldszmidt, M., and Pearl, J. 1992. Rank-Based Systems: A Simple Approach to Belief Revision, Belief Update, and Reasoning about Evidence and Actions. In *Proceedings of the Third International Conference on Knowledge Representation and Reasoning,* eds. B. Nebel, C. Rich, and W. Swartout, 661–672. San Francisco: Morgan Kaufmann Publishers.

Greenland, S.; Pearl, J.; and Robins, J. M. 1999. Causal Diagrams for Epidemiologic Research. *Epidemiology* 10(1): 37–48.

Haavelmo, Trygve. 1943. The Statistical Implications of a System of Simultaneous Equations. *Econometrica* 11(1)(January): 1–12.

Heckerman, D.; Geiger, D.; and Chickering, D. M. 1994. Learning Bayesian Networks: The Combination of Knowledge and Statistical Data. In *Uncertainty in Artificial Intelligence 10,* 293–301. San Francisco, Calif.: Morgan Kaufmann Publishers.

Holland, P. W. 1995. Some Reflections of Freedman's Critiques. *Foundations of Science* 1(1): 50–57.

Holland, P. W. 1988. Causal Inference, Path Analysis, and Recursive Structural Equations Models. In Sociological Methodology, ed. C. Clogg, 449–484. Washington, D.C.: American Sociological Association.

Imbens, G. W., and Angrist, J. D. 1994. Identification and Estimation of Local Average Treatment Effects. *Econometrica* 62(2): 467–476.

Lauritzen, S. L., and Spiegelhalter, D. J. 1988. Local Computations with Probabilities on Graphical Structures and Their Applications to Expert Systems. *Proceedings of the Royal Statistical Society* B50(2): 154–227.

Lauritzen, S. L.; Dawid, A. P.; Larsen, B. N.; and Leimer, H. G. 1990. Independence Properties of Directed Markov Fields. *Networks* 20(5): 491–505.

Leroy, S. F. 1995. Causal Orderings. In *Macroeconometrics: Developments, Tensions, Prospects,* ed. K. D. Hoover, 211–228. Boston: Kluwer Academic.

Lewis, D. 1973. *Counterfactuals.* Cambridge, Mass.: Harvard University Press.

McDonald, R. P. 1997. Haldane's Lungs: A Case in Path Analysis. *Multivariate Behavioral Research* 32(1): 1–38.

Manski, C. F. 1990. Nonparametric Bounds on Treatment Effects. *American Economic Review, Papers and Proceedings* 80(2): 319–323.

Pearl, J. 1998. Graphs, Causality, and Structural Equation Models. *Sociological Methods and Research* 27(2): 226–284.

Pearl, J. 1996. Structural and Probabilistic Causality. In *The Psychology of Learning and Motivation, Volume 34,* eds. D. R. Shanks, K. J. Holyoak, and D. L. Medin, 393–435. San Diego, Calif.: Academic Press.

Pearl, J. 1995a. Causal Inference from Indirect Experiments. *Artificial Intelligence in Medicine* 7(6): 561–582.

Pearl, J. 1995b. On the Testability of Causal Models with Latent and Instrumental Variables. In *Uncertainty in Artificial Intelligence 11,* eds. P. Besnard and S. Hanks, 435–443. San Francisco, Calif.: Morgan Kaufmann Publishers.

Pearl, J. 1994a. A Probabilistic Calculus of Actions. In *Uncertainty in Artificial Intelligence 10,* eds. R. Lopez de Mantaras and D. Poole, 454–462. San Francisco, Calif.: Morgan Kaufmann Publishers.

Pearl, J. 1994b. From Bayesian Networks to Causal Networks. In *Bayesian Networks and Probabilistic Reasoning,* ed. A. Gammerman, 1–31. London: Alfred Walter.

Pearl, J. 1993a. Aspects of Graphical Models Connected with Causality. Paper Presented at the Forty-Ninth Session of the International Statistical Institute, Florence, Italy, 25 August – 2 September.

Pearl, J. 1993b. Belief Networks Revisited. *Artificial Intelligence* 59(1–2): 49–56.

Pearl, J. 1993c. Comment: Graphical Models, Causality, and Intervention. *Statistical Science* 8(3)(August): 266–269.

Pearl, J. 1992. *Probabilistic Reasoning in Intelligence Systems*. San Francisco, Calif.: Morgan Kaufmann.

Pearl, J. 1988. *Probabilistic Reasoning in Intelligent Systems*. San Francisco: Morgan Kaufmann Publishers.

Pearl, J., and Dechter, R. 1996. Identifying Independencies in Causal Graphs with Feedback. In *Uncertainty in Artificial Intelligence 12,* eds. E. Horvitz and F. Jensen, 240–246. San Francisco, Calif.: Morgan Kaufmann.

Pearl, J., and Robins, J. 1995. Causal Effects of Dynamic Policies. In *Uncertainty in Artificial Intelligence 11,* eds. P. Besnard and S. Hanks, 444–453. San Francisco, Calif.: Morgan Kaufmann Publishers.

Pearl, J., and Verma, T. 1991. A Theory of Inferred Causation. In *Principles of Knowledge Representation and Reasoning: Proceedings of the Second International Conference,* eds. J. A. Allen, R. Fikes, and E. Sandewall, 441–452. San Francisco, Calif.: Morgan Kaufmann Publishers.

Pratt, J. W., and Schlaifer, R. 1988. On the Interpretation and Observation of Laws. *Journal of Econometrics* 39:23–52.

Reichenbach, H. 1956. *The Direction of Time*. Berkeley, Calif.: University of California Press.

Robins, J. M. 1989. The Analysis of Randomized and Non-Randomized AIDS Treatment Trials Using a New Approach to Causal Inference in Longitudinal Studies. In *Health Service Research Methodology: A Focus on AIDS,* eds. L. Sechrest, H. Freeman, and A. Mulley, 113–159. Washington D.C.: U. S. Public Health Service, National Center for Health Services Research.

Robins, J. M. 1987. A Graphical Approach to the Identification and Estimation of Causal Parameters in Mortality Studies with Sustained Exposure Periods. *Journal of Chronic Diseases* 40 (Supplement 2): 139S–161S.

Robins, J. M. 1986. A New Approach to Causal Inference in Mortality Studies with a Sustained Exposure Period—Applications to Control of the Healthy Workers Survivor Effect. *Mathematical Modelling* 7: 1393–1512.

Robins, J. M.; Blevins, D.; Ritter, G.; and Wulfsohn, M. 1992. G-Estimation of the Effect of Prophylaxis Therapy for Pneumocystis Carinii Pneumonia on the Survival of AIDS Patients. *Epidemiology* 3(4): 319–336.

Rosenbaum, P. R. 1984. The Consequences of Adjustment for a Concomitant Variable that has Been Affected by the Treatment. *Journal of the Royal Statistical Society* A147(5): 656–666.

Rosenbaum, P., and Rubin, D. 1983. The Central Role of Propensity Score in Observational Studies for Causal Effects. *Biometrica* 70(1): 41–55.

Rubin, D. B. 1990. Neyman (1923) and Causal Inference in Experiments and Observational Studies. *Statistical Science* 5(4): 472–480.

Rubin, D. B. 1978. Bayesian Inference for Causal Effects: The Role of Randomization. *Annals of Statistics* 7(1): 34–58.

Rubin, D. B. 1974. Estimating Causal Effects of Treatments in Randomized and Nonrandomized Studies. *Journal of Educational Psychology* 66(5): 688–701.

Shafer, G. 1997. Advances in the Understanding and Use of Conditional Independence. *Annals of Mathematical and Artificial Intelligence.* 21(1): 1–11.

Simon, H. A. 1953. *Causal Ordering and Identifiability. Studies in Econometric Method,* eds. W. C. Hood and T. C. Koopmans, 49–79. New York: John Wiley.

Sobel, M. E. 1990. Effect Analysis and Causation in Linear Structural Equation Models. *Psychometrika* 55(3): 495–515.

Spiegelhalter, D. J.; Lauritzen, S. L.; Dawid, P. A.; and Cowell, R. G. 1993. Bayesian Analysis in Expert Systems. *Statistical Science* 8(3):219–247.

Spirtes, P. 1995. Directed Cyclic Graphical Representation of Feedback. In *Uncertainty in Artificial Intelligence 11,* eds. P. Besnard and S. Hanks, 491–498. San Francisco, Calif.: Morgan Kaufmann Publishers.

Spirtes, P.; Glymour, C.; and Schienes, R. 1993. *Causation, Prediction, and Search.* New York: Springer-Verlag.

Strotz, Robert H., and Wold, H. O. A. 1960. Recursive Versus Nonrecursive Systems: An Attempt at Synthesis (Part I of a Triptych on Causal Chain Systems). *Econometrica* 28(2)(April): 417–427.

Verma, T. S., and Pearl, J. 1990. Equivalence and Synthesis of Causal Models. In *Uncertainty in Artificial Intelligence 6,* 220–227, eds P. Bonnison, M. Henrion, L. N. Kanal, and S. Lemmer. Amsterdam, The Netherlands: Elsevier Science.

Verma, T. S., and Pearl, J. 1988. Causal Networks: Semantics and Expressiveness. In *Uncertainty in Artificial Intelligence 4,* eds. R. Shachter, T. S. Levitt, and L. N. Kanal, 69–76. Amsterdam, The Netherlands: Elsevier Science.

Vovk, V. G. 1996. Another Semantics for Pearl's Action Calculus. In *Computational Learning and Probabilistic Reasoning,* ed. A. Gammerman, 125–144. New York: John Wiley and Sons.

Wainer, H. 1989. Eelworms, Bullet Holes, and Geraldine Ferraro: Some Problems with Statistical Adjustment and Some Solutions. *Journal of Educational Statistics* 14(2): 121–140.

Waldmann, M. R.; Holyoak, K. J.; and Fratianne, A. 1995. Causal Models and the Acquisition of Category Structure. *Journal of Experimental Psychology* 124(2): 181–206.

Weinberg, C. R. 1993. Toward a Clearer Definition of Confounding. *American Journal of Epidemiology* 137(1): 1–8.

Wermuth, N. 1992. On Block-Recursive Regression Equations (with Discussion). *Brazilian Journal of Probability and Statistics* 6(1): 1–56.

Whittaker, J. 1990. Graphic Models in Applied Multivariate Statistics. Chichester, U.K.: Wiley.

Wright, S. 1921. Correlation and Causation. *Journal of Agricultural Research* 20: 557–585.

PART TWO

Search

The chapters of this section describe two basic approaches to search for causal models. One class of search procedures assigns a score to models based on previous knowledge, features of each model, and the data, and searches for models with the best score. Bayesian search procedures, described in the chapter by Heckerman, Meek and Cooper, are of this kind. Another class of search procedure makes decisions about patterns in the data, and using whatever prior information is provided by the investigator, finds the collection of models that best explains those patterns. Papers on learning linear models, learning with sample selection bias, and learning linear feedback systems illustrate this approach.

The distinction among search procedures is neither exclusive nor exhaustive. Bayesian and pattern- or constraint-based procedures have been fruitfully combined, for example, using constraint based search to find an initial class of models which Bayesian procedures then modify. Some other approaches to search are briefly described in the preface to this book.

Not all of the procedures described here search for the same thing, or search under the same assumptions. The chapter by Spirtes, Meek, and Richardson, includes a procedure for searching for a special kind of latent variable model, a "unidimensional measurement model," and the chapter by Richardson and Spirtes describes a procedure for searching for models with cyclic graphs, often called "nonrecursive" models in the social science literature. Both procedures are best suited to linear models.

Evaluating search procedures involves a variety of interdependent considerations, including the existence or absence of proofs of asymptotic correctness, complexity analyses, and various kinds of error frequencies on simulated data varying in number and kind of variables.

CHAPTER FOUR

A Bayesian Approach to Causal Discovery

David Heckerman, Christopher Meek, and Gregory Cooper

1. Introduction

In this chapter, we examine the Bayesian approach to the discovery of causal models in the family of directed acyclic graphs (DAGs). The Bayesian approach is related to the constraint-based approach, which is discussed in chapters 1, 5, and 6 of this book. In particular, both methods rely on the causal Markov condition. Nonetheless, the two approaches differ significantly in theory and practice. An important difference between them is that the constraint-based approach uses categorical information about conditional-independence constraints in the domain, whereas the Bayesian approach weighs the degree to which such constraints hold. As a result, the Bayesian approach has three distinct advantages over its constraint-based counterpart. First, conclusions derived from the Bayesian approach are not susceptible to incorrect categorical decisions about independence facts that can occur with data sets of finite size. Second, using the Bayesian approach, finer distinctions among model structures—both quantitative and qualitative—can be made. Third, information from several models can be combined to make better inferences and to better account for modeling uncertainty.

In sections 2 and 3, we review the Bayesian approach to model averaging and model selection and its application to the discovery of causal DAG models. In section 4, we discuss methods for assigning priors to model structures and their parameters. In section 5, we compare the Bayesian and constraint-based methods for causal discovery for a small domain with complete data, highlighting some of the advantages of the Bayesian approach. In section 6, we note computational difficulties associated with the Bayesian approach when data sets are incomplete—for example, when some variables are hidden—and discuss more efficient approximation methods including Monte-Carlo and asymptotic approximations. In section 7, we illustrate the Bayesian approach on the data set of Sewall and Shah (1968) concerning the college plans of high-school students. Using this example, we show that the Bayesian approach can make finer distinctions among model structures than can the constraint-based approach.

2. The Bayesian Approach

In a constraint-based approach to the discovery of causal DAG models, we use data to make *categorical* decisions about whether or not particular conditional-independence constraints hold. We then piece these decisions together by looking for those sets of causal structures that are consistent with the constraints. To do so, we use the causal Markov condition (Spirtes, Glymour, and Scheines 1993) to link lack of cause with conditional independence.

In the Bayesian approach, we also use the causal Markov condition to look for structures that fit conditional-independence constraints. In contrast to constraint-based methods, however, we use data to make *probabilistic* inferences about conditional-independence constraints. For example, rather than conclude categorically that, given data, variables X and Y are independent, we conclude that these variables are independent with some probability. This probability encodes our uncertainty about the presence or absence of independence. Furthermore, because the Bayesian approach uses a probabilistic framework, we no longer need to make decisions about individual independence facts. Rather, we compute the probability that the independencies associated with an entire causal structure are true. Then, using such probabilities, we can average a particular hypothesis of interest—such as, "Does X cause Y?"—over all possible causal structures.

Let us examine the Bayesian approach in some detail. Suppose our problem domain consists of variables $\mathbf{X} = \{X_1,..., X_n\}$. In addition, suppose that we have some data $D = \{\mathbf{x}_1,..., \mathbf{x}_N\}$, which is a random sample from some unknown probability distribution for $\mathbf{X}$. For the moment, we assume that each case $\mathbf{x}$ in D consists of an observation of all the variables in $\mathbf{X}$. We assume that the unknown probability distribution can be encoded by some causal model with structure $\mathbf{m}$. As in Spirtes, Glymour, and Scheines (1993), we assume that the structure of this causal model is a DAG that encodes conditional independencies via the causal Markov condition. We are uncertain about the structure and parameters of the model; and—using the

Bayesian approach—we encode this uncertainty using probability.

In particular, we define a discrete variable **M** whose states **m** correspond to the possible true models and encode our uncertainty about **M** with the probability distribution $p(\mathbf{m})$. In addition, for each model structure **m**, we define a continuous vector-valued variable Θ_m, whose values θ_m correspond to the possible true parameters. We encode our uncertainty about Θ_m using the (smooth) probability density function $p(\theta_m \mid \mathbf{m})$. The assumption that $p(\theta_m \mid \mathbf{m})$ is a probability density function entails the assumption of faithfulness employed in constraint-based methods for causal discovery (Meek 1995).

Given random sample D, we compute the posterior distributions for each **m** and θ_m using Bayes' rule:

$$p(\mathbf{m} \mid D) = \frac{p(\mathbf{m})p(D \mid \mathbf{m})}{\sum_{m'} p(\mathbf{m}')p(D \mid \mathbf{m}')} \tag{1}$$

$$p(\theta_m \mid D, \mathbf{m}) = \frac{p(\theta_m \mid \mathbf{m})p(D \mid \theta_m, \mathbf{m})}{p(D \mid \mathbf{m})} \tag{2}$$

where

$$p(D \mid \mathbf{m}) = \int p(D \mid \theta_m, \mathbf{m})\, p(\theta_m \mid \mathbf{m})\, d\theta_m \tag{3}$$

is called the *marginal likelihood*. Given some hypothesis of interest, h, we determine the probability that h is true given data D by averaging over all possible models and their parameters:

$$p(h \mid D) = \sum_m p(\mathbf{m} \mid D)p(h \mid D, \mathbf{m}) \tag{4}$$

$$p(h \mid D, \mathbf{m}) = \int p(h \mid \theta_m, \mathbf{m})\, p(\theta_m \mid D, \mathbf{m})\, d\theta_m \tag{5}$$

For example, h may be the event that the next case $\mathbf{X}_{N+1}$ is observed in configuration $\mathbf{x}_{N+1}$. In this situation, we obtain

$$p(\mathbf{x}_{N+1} \mid D) = \sum_m p(\mathbf{m} \mid D) \int p(\mathbf{x}_{N+1} \mid \theta_m, \mathbf{m})\, p(\theta_m \mid D, \mathbf{m})\, d\theta_m \tag{6}$$

where $p(\mathbf{x}_{N+1} \mid \theta_m, \mathbf{m})$ is the likelihood for the model. As another example, h may be the hypothesis that "X causes Y." We consider such a situation in detail in section 5.

Under certain assumptions, these computations can be done efficiently and in closed form. One assumption is that the likelihood term $p(\mathbf{x} \mid \theta_m, \mathbf{m})$ factors as follows:

$$p(\mathbf{x} \mid \theta_m, \mathbf{m}) = \prod_{i=1}^{n} p(x_i \mid \mathbf{pa}_i, \theta_i, \mathbf{m}) \tag{7}$$

where each *local likelihood* $p(x_i \mid \mathbf{pa}_i, \theta_i, \mathbf{m})$ is in the exponential family. In this expression, $\mathbf{pa}_i$ denotes the configuration of the variables corresponding to parents of node x_i, and θ_i denotes the set of parameters associated with the local likelihood for variable x_i. One example of such a factorization occurs when each variable $X_i \in \mathbf{X}$ is discrete, having r_i possible values $x_i^1, \ldots, x_i^{r_i}$, and each local likelihood is a collection of multinomial distributions, one distribution for each configuration of $\mathbf{Pa}_i$—that is,

$$p\left(x_i^k \mid \mathbf{pa}_i^j, \boldsymbol{\theta}_i, \mathbf{m}\right) = \theta_{ijk} > 0 \tag{8}$$

where

$$\mathbf{pa}_i^1, \ldots, \mathbf{pa}_i^{q_i} \left(q_i = \prod\nolimits_{X_i \in \mathbf{Pa}_i} r_i\right)$$

denote the configurations of

$$\mathbf{Pa}_i \text{ and } \boldsymbol{\theta}_i = \left(\left(\theta_{ijk}\right)_{k=2}^{r_i}\right)_{j=1}^{q_i}$$

are the parameters. The parameter θ_{ij1} is given by

$$1 - \sum\nolimits_{k=2}^{r_i} \theta_{ijk}$$

We shall use this example to illustrate many of the concepts in this chapter. For convenience, we define the vector of parameters $\theta_{ij} = (\theta_{ij2}, \ldots, \theta_{ijr_i})$ for all i and j. A second assumption for efficient computation is that the parameters are mutually independent. For example, given the discrete-multinomial likelihoods, we assume that the parameter vectors θ_{ij} are mutually independent.

Let us examine the consequences of these assumptions for our multinomial example. Given a random sample D that contains no missing observations, the parameters remain independent:

$$p(\boldsymbol{\theta}_m \mid D, \mathbf{m}) = \prod_{i=1}^{n} \prod_{j=1}^{q_i} p(\boldsymbol{\theta}_{ij} \mid D, \mathbf{m}) \tag{9}$$

Thus, we can update each vector of parameters θ_{ij} independently. Assuming each vector θ_{ij} has a conjugate prior[1] —namely, a Dirichlet distribution $\mathrm{Dir}(\theta_{ij} \mid \alpha_{ij1}, \ldots, \alpha_{ijr_i})$—we obtain the posterior distribution for the parameters

$$p\left(\boldsymbol{\theta}_{ij} \mid D, \mathbf{m}\right) = \mathrm{Dir}\left(\boldsymbol{\theta}_{ij} \mid \alpha_{ij1} + N_{ij1}, \ldots, \alpha_{ijr_i} + N_{ijr_i}\right) \tag{10}$$

where N_{ijk} is the number of cases in D in which $X_i = x_i^k$ and $\mathbf{Pa}_i = \mathbf{pa}_i^j$. Note that the collection of counts N_{ijk} are sufficient statistics of the data for the model $\mathbf{m}$. In addition, we obtain the marginal likelihood (derived in Cooper and Herskovits, 1992):

$$p(D \mid \mathbf{m}) = \prod_{i=1}^{n} \prod_{j=1}^{q_i} \frac{\Gamma(\alpha_{ij})}{\Gamma(\alpha_{ij} + N_{ij})} \cdot \prod_{k=1}^{r_i} \frac{\Gamma(\alpha_{ijk} + N_{ijk})}{\Gamma(\alpha_{ijk})} \tag{11}$$

where

$$\alpha_{ij} = \sum\nolimits_{k=1}^{r_i} \alpha_{ijk} \text{ and } N_{ij} = \sum\nolimits_{k=1}^{r_i} N_{ijk}$$

We then use equation 1 and equation 11 to compute the posterior probabilities $p(\mathbf{m} \mid D)$.

As a simple illustration of these ideas, suppose our hypothesis of interest is the outcome of $\mathbf{X}_{N+1}$, the next case to be seen after D. Also suppose that, for each possible outcome $\mathbf{x}_{N+1}$ of $\mathbf{X}_{N+1}$, the value of X_i is x_i^k and the configuration of $\mathbf{Pa}_i$ is $\mathbf{pa}_i^j$, where k and j depend on i. To compute $p(\mathbf{x}_{N+1} \mid D)$, we first average over our uncertainty about the parameters. Using equations 4, 7, and 8, we obtain

$$p(\mathbf{x}_{N+1} \mid D, \mathbf{m}) = \int \left(\prod_{i=1}^{n} \theta_{ijk} \right) p(\boldsymbol{\theta}_m \mid D, \mathbf{m}) \, d\boldsymbol{\theta}_m$$

Because parameters remain independent given D, we get

$$p(\mathbf{x}_{N+1} \mid D, \mathbf{m}) = \prod_{i=1}^{n} \int \theta_{ijk} \, p(\boldsymbol{\theta}_{ij} \mid D, \mathbf{m}) \, d\boldsymbol{\theta}_{ij}$$

Because each integral in this product is the expectation of a Dirichlet distribution, we have

$$p(\mathbf{x}_{N+1} \mid D, \mathbf{m}) = \prod_{i=1}^{n} \frac{\alpha_{ijk} + N_{ijk}}{\alpha_{ij} + N_{ij}} \tag{12}$$

Finally, we average this expression for $p(\mathbf{x}_{N+1} \mid D, \mathbf{m})$ over the possible models using equation 5 to obtain $p(\mathbf{x}_{N+1} \mid D)$.

3. Model Selection and Search

The full Bayesian approach is often impractical, even under the simplifying assumptions that we have described. One computation bottleneck in the full Bayesian approach is averaging over all models in equation 4. If we consider causal models with n variables, the number of possible structure hypotheses is at least exponential in n. Consequently, in situations where we cannot exclude almost all of these hypotheses, the approach is intractable. Statisticians, who have been confronted by this problem for decades in the context of other types of models, use two approaches to address this problem: *model selection* and *selective model averaging*. The former approach is to select a "good" model (i.e., structure hypothesis) from among all possible models, and use that model as if it were the correct model. The latter approach is to select a manageable number of good models from among all possible models and pretend that these models are exhaustive. These related approaches raise several important questions. In particular, do these approaches yield accurate results when applied to causal structures? If so, how do we search for good models?

The question of accuracy is difficult to answer in theory. Nonetheless, several researchers have shown experimentally that the selection of a single model that is likely a posteriori often yields accurate predictions (Cooper and Herskovits 1992; Aliferis and Cooper 1994; Heckerman, Geiger, and Chickering 1995) and that selective model averaging using Monte-Carlo methods can sometimes be efficient and yield even better predictions (Herskovits 1991, Madigan et al. 1996).

Chickering (1996a) has shown that for certain classes of prior distributions the problem of finding the model with the highest posterior is NP-complete. However, a number of researchers have demonstrated that greedy search methods over a search space of DAGs works well. Also, constraint-based methods have been used as a first-step heuristic search for the most likely causal model (Singh and Valtorta 1993, Spirtes and Meek 1995). In addition, performing greedy searches in a space where Markov equivalent models (see the definition that follows) are represented by a single model has improved performance (Spirtes and Meek 1995, Chickering 1996b).

4. Priors

To compute the relative posterior probability of a model structure, we must assess the structure prior $p(\mathbf{m})$ and the parameter priors $p(\theta_m \mid \mathbf{m})$. Unfortunately, when many model structures are possible, these assessments will be intractable. Nonetheless, under certain assumptions, we can derive the structure and parameter priors for many model structures from a manageable number of direct assessments.

4.1 Priors for Model Parameters

First, let us consider the assessment of priors for the parameters of model structures. We consider the approach of Heckerman, Geiger, and Chickering (1995) who address the case where the local likelihoods are multinomial distributions and the assumption of parameter independence holds. Their approach is based on two key concepts: Markov equivalence and distribution equivalence. We say that two model structures for $\mathbf{X}$ are *Markov equivalent* if they represent the same set of conditional-independence assertions for $\mathbf{X}$ (Verma and Pearl 1990). For example, given $\mathbf{X} = \{X, Y, Z\}$, the model structures $X \to Y \to Z$, $X \leftarrow Y \to Z$, and $X \leftarrow Y \leftarrow Z$ represent only the independence assertion that X and Z are conditionally independent given Y. Consequently, these model structures are Markov equivalent. Another example of Markov equivalence is the set of complete model structures on $\mathbf{X}$; a *complete model* is one that has no missing edge and which encodes no assertion of conditional independence. When $\mathbf{X}$ contains n variables, there are $n!$ possible complete model structures; one model structure for each possible ordering of the variables. All complete model structures for $p(\mathbf{x})$ are Markov equivalent. In general, two model structures are Markov equivalent if and only if they have the same structure ignoring arc directions and the same v-structures (Verma and

Pearl 1990). A *v-structure* is an ordered tuple (X, Y, Z) such that there is an arc from X to Y and from Z to Y, but no arc between X and Z.

The concept of distribution equivalence is closely related to that of Markov equivalence. Suppose that all causal models for $\mathbf{X}$ under consideration have local likelihoods in the family $\mathscr{F}$. This is not a restriction, per se, because $\mathscr{F}$ can be a large family. We say that two model structures $\mathbf{m}_1$ and $\mathbf{m}_2$ for X are *distribution equivalent* with respect to (wrt) $\mathscr{F}$ if they represent the same joint probability distributions for X—that is, if, for every θ_{m1}, there exists a θ_{m2} such that $p(\mathbf{x} \mid \theta_{m1}, \mathbf{m}_1) = p(\mathbf{x} \mid \theta_{m2}, \mathbf{m}_2)$, and vice versa.

Distribution equivalence wrt some $\mathscr{F}$ implies Markov equivalence, but the converse does not hold. For example, when $\mathscr{F}$ is the family of generalized linear-regression models, the complete model structures for $n \geq 3$ variables do not represent the same sets of distributions. Nonetheless, there are families $\mathscr{F}$—for example, multinomial distributions and linear-regression models with Gaussian noise—where Markov equivalence implies distribution equivalence wrt $\mathscr{F}$ (Heckerman and Geiger 1996). The notion of distribution equivalence is important, because if two model structures $\mathbf{m}_1$ and $\mathbf{m}_2$ are distribution equivalent wrt to a given $\mathscr{F}$, then it is often reasonable to expect that data cannot help to discriminate them. That is, we expect $p(D \mid \mathbf{m}_1) = p(D \mid \mathbf{m}_2)$ for any data set D. Heckerman, Geiger, and Chickering (1995) call this property *likelihood equivalence*. Note that the constraint-based approach also does not discriminate among Markov equivalent structures.

Now let us return to the main issue of this section: the derivation of priors from a manageable number of assessments. Geiger and Heckerman (1995) show that the assumptions of parameter independence and likelihood equivalence imply that the parameters for any complete model structure $\mathbf{m}_c$ must have a Dirichlet distribution with constraints on the hyperparameters given by

$$\alpha_{ijk} = \alpha \; p\!\left(x_i^k, \mathbf{pa}_i^j \mid \mathbf{m}_c\right) \tag{13}$$

where α is the user's equivalent sample size,[2] and

$$p\!\left(x_i^k, \mathbf{pa}_i^j \mid \mathbf{m}_c\right)$$

is computed from the user's joint probability distribution $p(\mathbf{x} \mid \mathbf{m}_c)$. This result is rather remarkable, as the two assumptions leading to the constrained Dirichlet solution are qualitative.

To determine the priors for parameters of *incomplete* model structures, Heckerman, Geiger, and Chickering (1995) use the assumption of *parameter modularity*, which says that if X_i has the same parents in model structures $\mathbf{m}_1$ and $\mathbf{m}_2$, then

$$p\!\left(\theta_{ij} \mid \mathbf{m}_1\right) = p\!\left(\theta_{ij} \mid \mathbf{m}_2\right)$$

for $j = 1, \ldots, q_i$. They call this property parameter modularity, because it says that the distributions for parameters θ_{ij} depend only on the structure of the model that is local to variable X_i —namely, X_i and its parents.

Given the assumptions of parameter modularity and parameter independence, it is a simple matter to construct priors for the parameters of an arbitrary model structure given the priors on complete model structures. In particular, given parameter independence, we construct the priors for the parameters of each node separately. Furthermore, if node X_i has parents $\mathbf{Pa}_i$ in the given model structure, we identify a complete model structure where X_i has these parents and use equation 13 and parameter modularity to determine the priors for this node. The result is that all terms α_{ijk} for all model structures are determined by equation 13. Thus, from the assessments α and $p(\mathbf{x} \mid \mathbf{m}_c)$, we can derive the parameter priors for all possible model structures. We can assess $p(\mathbf{x} \mid \mathbf{m}_c)$ by constructing a causal model called a prior model that encodes this joint distribution. Heckerman, Geiger, and Chickering (1995) discuss the construction of this model.

4.2 Priors for Model Structures

Now, let us consider the assessment of priors on model structures. The simplest approach for assigning priors to model structures is to assume that every structure is equally likely. Of course, this assumption is typically inaccurate and used only for the sake of convenience. A simple refinement of this approach is to ask the user to exclude various structures (perhaps based on judgments of cause and effect), and then impose a uniform prior on the remaining structures. We illustrate this approach in section 7.

Buntine (1991) describes a set of assumptions that leads to a richer yet efficient approach for assigning priors. The first assumption is that the variables can be ordered (e.g., through a knowledge of time precedence). The second assumption is that the presence or absence of possible arcs are mutually independent. Given these assumptions, $n(n - 1)/2$ probability assessments (one for each possible arc in an ordering) determine the prior probability of every possible model structure. One extension to this approach is to allow for multiple possible orderings. One simplification is to assume that the probability that an arc is absent or present is independent of the specific arc in question. In this case, only one probability assessment is required.

An alternative approach, described by Heckerman, Geiger, and Chickering (1995) uses a prior model. The basic idea is to penalize the prior probability of any structure according to some measure of deviation between that structure and the prior model. Heckerman, Geiger, and Chickering (1995) suggest one reasonable measure of deviation.

Madigan and York(1995) give yet another approach that makes use of imaginary data from a domain expert. In their approach, a computer program helps the user create a hypothetical set of complete data. Then, using techniques such as those in section 2, they compute the posterior probabili-

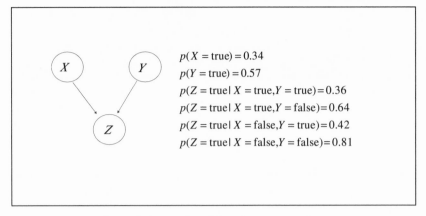

$$p(X = \text{true}) = 0.34$$
$$p(Y = \text{true}) = 0.57$$
$$p(Z = \text{true} \mid X = \text{true}, Y = \text{true}) = 0.36$$
$$p(Z = \text{true} \mid X = \text{true}, Y = \text{false}) = 0.64$$
$$p(Z = \text{true} \mid X = \text{false}, Y = \text{true}) = 0.42$$
$$p(Z = \text{true} \mid X = \text{false}, Y = \text{false}) = 0.81$$

Figure 1. A causal model used to generate data.

ties of model structures given this data, assuming the prior probabilities of structures are uniform. Finally, they use these posterior probabilities as priors for the analysis of the real data.

5. Example

In this section, we provide a simple example that applies Bayesian model averaging and Bayesian model selection to the problem of causal discovery. In addition, we compare these methods with a constraint-based approach.

Let us consider a simple domain containing three binary variables $X, Y,$ and Z. Let h denote the hypothesis that variable X causally influences variable Z. For brevity, we will sometimes state h as "X causes Z."

First, let us consider Bayesian model averaging. In this approach, we use equation 4 to compute the probability that h is true given data D. Because our models are causal, the expression $p(D \mid \mathbf{m})$ reduces to an index function that is true when $\mathbf{m}$ contains an arc from node X to node Z. Thus, the right-hand-side of equation 4 reduces to

$$\sum_{m''} P(\mathbf{m}'' \mid D)$$

where the sum is taken over all causal models $\mathbf{m}''$ that contain an arc from X to Z. For our three-variable domain, there are 25 possible causal models and, of these, there are eight models containing an arc from X to Z.

To compute $p(\mathbf{m} \mid D)$, we apply equation 1, where the sum over $\mathbf{m}'$ is taken over the twenty-five models just mentioned. We assume a uniform prior distribution over the twenty-five possible models, so that $p(\mathbf{m}') = 1/25$ for every $\mathbf{m}'$. We use equation 11 to compute the marginal likelihood $p(D \mid \mathbf{m})$. In applying equation 11, we use the prior given by $\alpha_{ijk} = 1/r_i q_i$, which we ob-

number of cases	sufficient statistics						
	$\bar{x}\,\bar{y}\,\bar{z}$	$\bar{x}\,\bar{y}\,z$	$\bar{x}\,y\,\bar{z}$	$\bar{x}\,y\,z$	$x\,\bar{y}\,\bar{z}$	$x\,\bar{y}\,z$	$x\,y\,\bar{z}$	$x\,y\,z$
150	5	36	38	15	7	16	23	10
250	10	60	51	27	15	25	41	21
500	23	121	103	67	19	44	79	44
1000	44	242	222	152	51	80	134	75
2000	88	476	431	311	105	180	264	145

Table 1. A summary of data used in the example.

number of cases	p ("X causes Z" $\mid D$)	output of Bayesian model selection	output of PC algorithm
150	0.036	X and Z unrelated	X and Z unrelated
250	0.123	X and Z unrelated	X causes Z
500	0.141	X causes Z or Z causes X	X and Z unrelated (with inconsistency)
1000	0.593	X causes Z	X causes Z
2000	0.926	X causes Z	X causes Z

Table 2. Bayesian model averaging, Bayesian model selection, and constraint-based results for an analysis of whether "X causes Z" given data summarized in table 1.

tain from equation 13 using a uniform distribution for $p(\mathbf{x} \mid \mathbf{m}_c)$ and an equivalent sample $\alpha = 1$. Because this equivalent sample size is small, the data strongly influences the posterior probabilities for h that we derive.

To generate data, we first selected the model structure $X \rightarrow Z \leftarrow Y$ and randomly sampled its probabilities from a uniform distribution. The resulting model is shown in figure 1. Next, we sampled data from the model according to its joint distribution. As we sampled the data, we kept a running total of the number cases seen in each possible configuration of $\{X, Y, Z\}$. These counts are sufficient statistics of the data for any causal model $\mathbf{m}$. These statistics are shown in table 1 for the first 150, 250, 500, 1,000, and 2,000 cases in the data set.

The second column in table 2 shows the results of applying equation 4 under the assumptions stated above for the first N cases in the data set. When $N = 0$, the data set is empty, in which case probability of hypothesis h is just the prior probability of "X causes Z": 8/25 = 0.32. Table 2 shows that as the number of cases in the database increases, the probability that "X causes Z" increases monotonically as the number of cases increases. Although not shown, the probability increases toward 1 as the number of cases increases beyond 2,000.

Column 3 in table 2 shows the results of applying Bayesian model selection. Here, we list the causal relationship(s) between X and Z found in the model or models with the highest posterior probability $p(\mathbf{m} \mid D)$. For example, when $N = 500$, there are three models that have the highest posterior probability. Two of the models have Z as a cause of X; and one has X as a cause of Z.

Column 4 in table 2 shows the results of applying the PC constraint-based causal discovery algorithm (Spirtes, Glymour, and Scheines 1993), which is part of the Tetrad II system (Scheines et al. 1994). PC is designed to discover causal relationships that are expressed using DAGs.[3] We applied PC using its default settings, which include a statistical significance level of 0.05. Note that, for $N = 500$, the PC algorithm detected an inconsistency. In particular, the independence tests yielded (1) X and Z are dependent, (2) Y and Z are dependent, (3) X and Y are independent given Z, and (4) X and Z are independent given Y. These relationships are not consistent with the assumption underlying the PC algorithm that the only independence facts found to hold in the sample are those entailed by the causal Markov condition applied to the generating model. In general, inconsistencies may arise due to the use of thresholds in the independence tests.

There are several weaknesses of the Bayesian-model-selection and constraint-based approaches illustrated by our results. One is that the output is categorical—there is no indication of the strength of the conclusion. Another is that the conclusions may be incorrect in that they disagree with the generative model. Model averaging (column 2) does not suffer from these weaknesses, because it indicates the strength of a causal hypothesis.

Although not illustrated here, another weakness of constraint-based approaches is that their output depends on the threshold used in independence tests. For causal conclusions to be correct asymptotically, the threshold must be adjusted as a function of sample size (N). In practice, however, it is unclear what this function should be.

Finally, we note that there are practical problems with model averaging. In particular, the domain can be so large that there are too many models over which to average. In such situations, the exact probabilities of causal hypotheses cannot be calculated. However, we can use selective model averaging to derive approximate posterior probabilities, and consequently give some indication of the strength of causal hypotheses.

6. Methods for Incomplete Data and Hidden Variables

Among the assumptions that we described in section 2, the one that is most often violated is the assumption that all variables are observed in every case. In this section, we examine Bayesian methods for relaxing this assumption.

An important distinction for this discussion is that of hidden versus observable variable. A *hidden variable* is one that is unknown in all cases. An *observable variable* is one that is known in some (but not necessarily all) of the cases. We note that constraint-based and Bayesian methods differ significantly in the way that they treat missing data. Whereas constraint-based methods typically throw out cases that contain an observable variable with a missing value, Bayesian methods do not.

Another important distinction concerning missing data is whether or not the absence of an observation is dependent on the actual states of the variables. For example, a missing datum in a drug study may indicate that a patient became too sick—perhaps because of the side effects of the drug—to continue in the study. In contrast, if a variable is hidden, then the absence of this data is independent of state. Although Bayesian methods and graphical models are suited to the analysis of both situations, methods for handling missing data where absence is independent of state are simpler than those where absence and state are dependent. Here, we concentrate on the simpler situation. Readers interested in the more complicated case should see Rubin (1978), Robins (1986), Cooper (1995), and Spirtes, Meek, and Richardson (1995).

Continuing with our example using discrete-multinomial likelihoods, suppose we observe a single incomplete case. Let $\mathbf{Y} \subset \mathbf{X}$ and $\mathbf{Z} = \mathbf{X} \setminus \mathbf{Y}$ denote the observed and unobserved variables in the case, respectively. Under the assumption of parameter independence, we can compute the posterior distribution of θ_{ij} for model structure $\mathbf{m}$ as follows:

$$p\left(\boldsymbol{\theta}_{ij} \mid \mathbf{y}, \mathbf{m}\right) = \sum_{\mathbf{z}} p(\mathbf{z} \mid \mathbf{y}, \mathbf{m}) \; p\left(\boldsymbol{\theta}_{ij} \mid \mathbf{y}, \mathbf{z}, \mathbf{m}\right)$$

$$= \left(1 - p\left(\mathbf{pa}_i^j \mid \mathbf{y}, \mathbf{m}\right)\right)\left\{p\left(\boldsymbol{\theta}_{ij} \mid \mathbf{m}\right)\right\} + \sum_{k=1}^{r_i} p\left(x_i^k, \mathbf{pa}_i^j \mid \mathbf{y}, \mathbf{m}\right) p\left(\boldsymbol{\theta}_{ij} \mid x_i^k, \mathbf{pa}_i^j, \mathbf{m}\right) \qquad (14)$$

(See Spiegelhalter and Lauritzen 1990 for a derivation.) Each term

$$p\left(\boldsymbol{\theta}_{ij} \mid x_i^k, \mathbf{pa}_i^j, \mathbf{m}\right)$$

in equation 14 is a Dirichlet distribution. Thus, unless both X_i and all the variables in $\mathbf{Pa}_i$ are observed in case $\mathbf{y}$, the posterior distribution of θ_{ij} will be a linear combination of Dirichlet distributions—that is, a Dirichlet mixture with mixing coefficients

$$\left(1 - p\left(\mathbf{pa}_i^j \mid \mathbf{y}, \mathbf{m}\right)\right) \text{ and } p\left(x_i^k, \mathbf{pa}_i^j \mid \mathbf{y}, \mathbf{m}\right), k = 1, \dots, r_i$$

When we observe a second incomplete case, some or all of the Dirichlet components in equation 14 will again split into Dirichlet mixtures. That is, the posterior distribution for θ_{ij} will become a mixture of Dirichlet mixtures. As we continue to observe incomplete cases, each missing values for $\mathbf{Z}$, the posterior distribution for θ_{ij} will contain a number of components that is exponential in the number of cases. In general, for any interesting set of local likelihoods and priors, the exact computation of the posterior distribution for θ_m will be intractable. Thus, we require an approximation for incomplete data.

6.1 Monte-Carlo Methods

One class of approximations is based on Monte-Carlo or sampling methods. These approximations can be extremely accurate, provided one is willing to wait long enough for the computations to converge. In this section, we discuss one of many Monte-Carlo methods known as Gibbs sampling, introduced by Geman and Geman (1984). Given variables $\mathbf{X} = \{X_1,\ldots, X_n\}$ with some joint distribution $p(\mathbf{x})$, we can use a Gibbs sampler to approximate the expectation of a function $f(\mathbf{x})$ with respect to $p(\mathbf{x})$ as follows. First, we choose an initial state for each of the variables in $\mathbf{X}$ somehow (e.g., at random). Next, we pick some variable X_i, unassign its current state, and compute its probability distribution given the states of the other $n - 1$ variables. Then, we sample a state for X_i based on this probability distribution and compute $f(\mathbf{x})$. Finally, we iterate the previous two steps, keeping track of the average value of $f(\mathbf{x})$. In the limit, as the number of cases approach infinity, this average is equal to $E_{p(\mathbf{x})}(f(\mathbf{x}))$ provided two conditions are met. First, the Gibbs sampler must be *irreducible*. That is, the probability distribution $p(\mathbf{x})$ must be such that we can eventually sample any possible configuration of $\mathbf{X}$ given any possible initial configuration of X. For example, if $p(\mathbf{x})$ contains no zero probabilities, then the Gibbs sampler will be irreducible. Second, each X_i must be chosen infinitely often. In practice, an algorithm for deterministically rotating through the variables is typically used. Introductions to Gibbs sampling and other Monte-Carlo methods—including methods for initialization and a discussion of convergence—are given by Neal (1993) and Madigan and York (1995).

To illustrate Gibbs sampling, let us approximate the probability density $p(\theta_m \mid D, \mathbf{m})$ for some particular configuration of θ_m, given an incomplete data set $D = \{\mathbf{y}_1,\ldots, \mathbf{y}_N\}$ and a causal model for discrete variables with independent Dirichlet priors. To approximate $p(\theta_m \mid D, \mathbf{m})$, we first initialize the states of the unobserved variables in each case somehow. As a result, we have a complete random sample D_c. Second, we choose some variable X_{il} (variable X_i in case l) that is not observed in the original random sample D, and reassign its state according to the probability distribution

$$p(x_{il}' \mid D_c \setminus x_{il}, \mathbf{m}) = \frac{p(x_{il}', D_c \setminus x_{il} \mid \mathbf{m})}{\sum_{x_{il}''} p(x_{il}'', D_c \setminus x_{il} \mid \mathbf{m})}$$

where $D_c \setminus x_{il}$ denotes the data set D_c with observation x_{il} removed, and the sum in the denominator runs over all states of variable X_{il}. As we have seen, the terms in the numerator and denominator can be computed efficiently (see equation 11). Third, we repeat this reassignment for all unobserved variables in D, producing a new complete random sample D_c'. Fourth, we compute the posterior density $p(\theta_m \mid D_c', \mathbf{m})$ as described in equations 9 and 10. Finally, we iterate the previous three steps, and use the average of $p(\theta_m \mid D_c', \mathbf{m})$ as our approximation.

Monte-Carlo approximations are also useful for computing the marginal likelihood given incomplete data. One Monte-Carlo approach, described by Chib (1995) and Raftery (1996), uses Bayes' theorem:

$$p(D \mid \mathbf{m}) = \frac{p(\theta_m \mid \mathbf{m}) p(D \mid \theta_m, \mathbf{m})}{p(\theta_m \mid D, \mathbf{m})}$$

For any configuration of θ_m, the prior term in the numerator can be evaluated directly. In addition, the likelihood term in the numerator can be computed using causal-model inference (Jensen, Lauritzen, and Oleson 1990). Finally, the posterior term in the denominator can be computed using Gibbs sampling, as we have just described. Other, more sophisticated Monte-Carlo methods are described by DiCiccio et al. (1995).

6.2 The Gaussian Approximation

Monte-Carlo methods yield accurate results, but they are often intractable—for example, when the sample size is large. Another approximation that is more efficient than Monte-Carlo methods and often accurate for relatively large samples is the *Gaussian approximation* (e.g., Kass, Tierney, and Kadane 1988, Kass and Raftery 1995). The idea behind this approximation is that, for large amounts of data, $p(\theta_m \mid D, \mathbf{m}) \propto p(D \mid \theta_m, \mathbf{m}) \cdot p(\theta_m \mid \mathbf{m})$ can often be approximated as a multivariate-Gaussian distribution. In particular, let

$$g(\theta_m) \equiv \log\left(p(D \mid \theta_m, \mathbf{m}) \cdot p(\theta_m \mid \mathbf{m})\right) \tag{16}$$

Also, define $\tilde{\theta}_m$ to be the configuration of θ_m that maximizes $g(\theta_m)$. This configuration also maximizes $p(\theta_m \mid D, \mathbf{m})$, and is known as the *maximum a posteriori* (MAP) configuration of θ_m. Using a second-degree Taylor polynomial of $g(\theta_m)$ about the $\tilde{\theta}_m$ to approximate $g(\theta_m)$, we obtain

$$g(\theta_m) \approx g(\tilde{\theta}_m) - \frac{1}{2}(\theta_m - \tilde{\theta}_m) A (\theta_m - \tilde{\theta}_m)^t \tag{17}$$

where $(\theta_m - \tilde{\theta}_m)^t$ is the transpose of row vector $(\theta_m - \tilde{\theta}_m)$, and A is the negative Hessian of $g(\theta_m)$ evaluated at $\tilde{\theta}_m$. Raising $g(\theta_m)$ to the power of e and using equation 16, we obtain

$$p(\theta_m \mid D, \mathbf{m}) \propto p(D \mid \theta_m, \mathbf{m}) \, p(\theta_m \mid \mathbf{m})$$

$$\approx p(D \mid \tilde{\theta}_m, \mathbf{m}) \, p(\tilde{\theta}_m \mid \mathbf{m}) \exp\left\{-\frac{1}{2}(\theta_m - \tilde{\theta}_m) A (\theta_m - \tilde{\theta}_m)^t\right\} \tag{18}$$

Hence, the approximation for $p(\theta_m \mid D, \mathbf{m})$ is Gaussian.

To compute the Gaussian approximation, we must compute $\tilde{\theta}_m$ as well as the negative Hessian of $g(\theta_m)$ evaluated at $\tilde{\theta}_m$. In the following section, we discuss methods for finding θ_m^-. Meng and Rubin (1991) describe a numerical technique for computing the second derivatives. Raftery (1995) shows how to approximate the Hessian using likelihood-ratio tests that are available in many statistical packages. Thiesson (1995) demonstrates that, for multinomial distributions, the second derivatives can be computed using causal-model inference.

Using the Gaussian approximation, we can also approximate the marginal likelihood. Substituting equation 18 into equation 3, integrating, and taking the logarithm of the result, we obtain the approximation:

$$\log p(D\,|\,\mathbf{m}) \approx \log p\big(D\,|\,\theta_m^-,\mathbf{m}\big) + \log p\big(\theta_m^-\,|\,\mathbf{m}\big) + \frac{d}{2}\,\log(2\pi) - \frac{1}{2}\log|A| \quad (19)$$

where d is the dimension of $g(\theta_m)$. For a causal model with multinomial distributions, this dimension is typically given by

$$\prod_{i=1}^{n} q_i(r_i - 1)$$

Sometimes, when there are hidden variables, this dimension is lower. See Geiger, Heckerman, and Meek (1996) for a discussion of this point. This approximation technique for integration is known as *Laplace's method,* and we refer to equation 19 as the *Laplace approximation.* Kass, Tierney, and Kadane (1988) have shown that, under certain regularity conditions, the relative error of this approximation is $O_p(1/N)$, where N is the number of cases in D. Thus, the Laplace approximation can be extremely accurate. For more detailed discussions of this approximation, see—for example—Kass, Tierney, and Kadane (1988) and Kass and Raftery (1995).

Although Laplace's approximation is efficient relative to Monte-Carlo approaches, the computation of $|A|$ is nevertheless intensive for large-dimension models. One simplification is to approximate $|A|$ using only the diagonal elements of the Hessian A. Although in so doing, we incorrectly impose independencies among the parameters, researchers have shown that the approximation can be accurate in some circumstances (see for example, Becker and Le Cun 1989, and Chickering and Heckerman 1997). Another efficient variant of Laplace's approximation is described by Cheeseman and Stutz (1995) and Chickering and Heckerman (1997).

We obtain a very efficient (but less accurate) approximation by retaining only those terms in equation 19 that increase with N: $\log p(D\,|\,\theta_m^-,\mathbf{m})$, which increases linearly with N, and $\log|A|$, which increases as $d\log N$. Also, for large N, θ_m^- can be approximated by $\hat{\theta}_m$, the maximum likelihood (ML) configuration of θ_m (see the following section). Thus, we obtain

$$\log p(D\,|\,\mathbf{m}) \approx \log p\big(D\,|\,\theta_m^-,\mathbf{m}\big) - \frac{d}{2}\,\log N \quad (20)$$

This approximation is called the *Bayesian information criterion* (BIC). Schwarz (1978) has shown that the relative error of this approximation is

$O_p(1)$ for a limited class of models. Haughton (1988) has extended this result to curved exponential models.

The BIC approximation is interesting in several respects. First, roughly speaking, it does not depend on the prior. Consequently, we can use the approximation without assessing a prior.[4] Second, the approximation is quite intuitive. Namely, it contains a term measuring how well the parameterized model predicts the data $(\log p(D \mid \hat{\theta}_m, \mathbf{m}))$ and a term that punishes the complexity of the model $(d/2 \, \log N)$. Third, the BIC approximation is exactly minus the minimum description length (MDL) criterion described by Rissanen (1987).

6.3 The MAP and ML Approximations and the EM Algorithm

As the sample size of the data increases, the Gaussian peak will become sharper, tending to a delta function at the MAP configuration $\tilde{\theta}_m$. In this limit, we can replace the integral over θ_m in equation 5 with $p(h \mid \tilde{\theta}_m, \mathbf{m})$. A further approximation is based on the observation that, as the sample size increases, the effect of the prior $p(\theta_m \mid \mathbf{m})$ diminishes. Thus, we can approximate $\tilde{\theta}_m$ by the maximum *maximum likelihood* configuration of θ_m:

$$\hat{\theta}_m = \underset{\theta_m}{\arg\max} \left\{ p(D \mid \theta_m, \mathbf{m}) \right\}$$

One class of techniques for finding an ML or MAP is gradient-based optimization. For example, we can use gradient ascent, where we follow the derivatives of $g(\theta_m)$ or the likelihood $p(D \mid \theta_m, \mathbf{m})$ to a local maximum. Russell et al. (1995) and Thiesson (1995) show how to compute the derivatives of the likelihood for a causal model with multinomial distributions. Buntine (1994) discusses the more general case where the likelihood comes from the exponential family. Of course, these gradient-based methods find only local maxima.

Another technique for finding a local ML or MAP is the expectation–maximization (EM) algorithm (Dempster, Laird, and Rubin 1977). To find a local MAP or ML, we begin by assigning a configuration to θ_m somehow (e.g., at random). Next, we compute the *expected* sufficient statistics for a complete data set, where expectation is taken with respect to the joint distribution for $\mathbf{X}$ conditioned on the assigned configuration of θ_m and the known data D. In our discrete example, we compute

$$E_{p(x \mid D, \theta_s, \mathbf{m})}\left(N_{ijk}\right) = \sum_{l=1}^{N} p\left(x_i^k, \mathbf{pa}_i^j \mid \mathbf{y}_l, \theta_m, \mathbf{m}\right) \tag{21}$$

where $\mathbf{y}_l$ is the possibly incomplete lth case in D. When X_i and all the variables in $\mathbf{Pa}_i$ are observed in case $\mathbf{x}_l$, the term for this case requires a trivial computation: it is either zero or one. Otherwise, we can use any causal-model inference algorithm to evaluate the term. This computation is called the *expectation step* of the EM algorithm.

Next, we use the expected sufficient statistics as if they were actual sufficient statistics from a complete random sample D_c. If we are doing an ML calculation, then we determine the configuration of θ_m that maximizes $p(D_c \mid \theta_m, \mathbf{m})$. In our discrete example, we have

$$\theta_{ijk} = \frac{E_{p(\mathbf{x} \mid D, \theta_s \mathbf{m})}\left(N_{ijk}\right)}{\sum_{k=1}^{r_i} E_{p(\mathbf{x} \mid D, \theta_s \mathbf{m})}\left(N_{ijk}\right)}$$

If we are doing a MAP calculation, then we determine the configuration of θ_m that maximizes $p(\theta_m \mid D_c, \mathbf{m})$. In our discrete example, we have[5]

$$\theta_{ijk} = \frac{\alpha_{ijk} + E_{p(\mathbf{x} \mid D, \theta_s \mathbf{m})}\left(N_{ijk}\right)}{\sum_{k=1}^{r_i}\left(\alpha_{ijk} + E_{p(\mathbf{x} \mid D, \theta_s, \mathbf{m})}\left(N_{ijk}\right)\right)}$$

This assignment is called the *maximization step* of the EM algorithm. Under certain regularity conditions, iteration of the expectation and maximization steps will converge to a local maximum. The EM algorithm is typically applied when sufficient statistics exist (i.e., when local likelihoods are in the exponential family), although generalizations of the EM algorithm have been used for more complicated local distributions (see for example McLachlan and Krishnan 1997).

7. A Case Study

To further illustrate the Bayesian approach and differences between it and the constraint-based approach, let us consider the following example. Sewell and Shah (1968) investigated factors that influence the intention of high school students to attend college. They measured the following variables for 10,318 Wisconsin high-school seniors: *Sex* (SEX): male, female; *Socioeconomic Status* (SES): low, lower middle, upper middle, high; *Intelligence Quotient* (IQ): low, lower middle, upper middle, high; *Parental Encouragement* (PE): low, high; and *College Plans* (CP): yes, no. Our goal here is to understand the causal relationships among these variables.

The data are described by the sufficient statistics in table 3. Each entry denotes the number of cases in which the five variables take on some particular configuration. The first entry corresponds to the configuration SEX=male, SES=low, IQ=low, PE=low, and CP=yes. The remaining entries correspond to configurations obtained by cycling through the states of each variable such that the last variable (CP) varies most quickly. Thus, for example, the upper (lower) half of the table corresponds to male (female) students.

First, let us analyze the data under the assumption that there are no hidden

4	349	13	64	9	207	33	72	12	126	38	54	10	67	49	43
2	232	27	84	7	201	64	95	12	115	93	92	17	79	119	59
8	166	47	91	6	120	74	110	17	92	148	100	6	42	198	73
4	48	39	57	5	47	123	90	9	41	224	65	8	17	414	54
5	454	9	44	5	312	14	47	8	216	20	35	13	96	28	24
11	285	29	61	19	236	47	88	12	164	62	85	15	113	72	50
7	163	36	72	13	193	75	90	12	174	91	100	20	81	142	77
6	50	36	58	5	70	110	76	12	48	230	81	13	49	360	98

Table 3. Sufficient statistics for the Sewall and Shah (1968) study.

variables. To generate priors for model parameters, we use the method described in section 4.1 with an equivalent sample size of 5 and a prior model where $p(\mathbf{x} \mid \mathbf{m}_c)$ is uniform. (The results are not sensitive to the choice of parameter priors. For example, none of the results reported in this section change qualitatively for equivalent sample sizes ranging from 3 to 40.) For structure priors, we assume that all model structures are equally likely, except, on the basis of prior causal knowledge about the domain, we exclude structures where SEX and/or SES have parents, and/or CP have children. Because the data set is complete, we use equation 11 to compute the posterior probabilities of model structures. The two most likely model structures found after an exhaustive search over all structures are shown in figure 2. Note that the most likely graph has a posterior probability that is extremely close to one so that model averaging is not necessary.

If we adopt the causal Markov condition and also assume that there are no hidden variables, then the arcs in both graphs can be interpreted causally. Some results are not surprising—for example the causal influence of socioeconomic status and IQ on college plans. Other results are more interesting. For example, from either graph we conclude that sex influences college plans only indirectly through parental influence. Also, the two graphs differ only by the orientation of the arc between PE and IQ. Either causal relationship is plausible.

We note that the second most likely graph was selected by Spirtes, Glymour, and Scheines (1993), who used the constraint-based PC algorithm with essentially identical assumptions. The only differences in the independence facts entailed by the most likely graph and the second-most likely graph are that the most likely graph entails that SEX and IQ are independent given SES and PE, whereas the second-most likely graph entails that SEX and IQ are marginally independent. Although both Bayesian and classical independence tests indicate that the conditional independence holds more strongly given the data, the PC algorithm chooses the second most likely graph be-

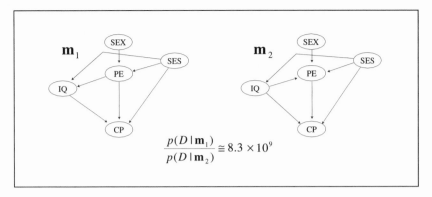

$$\frac{p(D \mid \mathbf{m}_1)}{p(D \mid \mathbf{m}_2)} \cong 8.3 \times 10^9$$

Figure 2. The a posteriori most likely model structures without hidden variables.

cause of its greedy nature. In particular, after the PC algorithm decides that SEX and IQ are marginally independent (at the threshold used by Spirtes, Glymour, and Scheines 1993), it never considers the independence of SEX and IQ given SES and PE.

Returning to our analysis, the most suspicious result is the suggestion that socioeconomic status has a direct influence on IQ. To question this result, let us consider new models obtained from the models in figure 2 by replacing this direct influence with a hidden variable pointing to both SES and IQ. Let us also consider models where (1) the hidden variable points to two or three of SES, IQ, and PE, (2) none, one, or both of the connections SES—PE and PE—IQ are removed, and (3) no variable has more than three parents. For each structure, we vary the number of states of the hidden variable from two to six.

We approximate the posterior probability of these models using the Cheeseman-Stutz (1995) variant of the Laplace approximation. To find the MAP $\tilde{\theta}_m$, we use the EM algorithm, taking the largest local maximum from among 100 runs with different random initializations of θ_m. The model with the highest posterior probability is shown in figure 3. This model is $2 \cdot 10^{10}$ times more likely than the best model containing no hidden variable. The next most likely model containing a hidden variable, which has one additional arc from the hidden variable to PE, is $5 \cdot 10^{-9}$ times less likely than the best model. Thus, if we again adopt the causal Markov condition and also assume that we have not omitted a reasonable model from consideration, then we have strong evidence that a hidden variable is influencing both socioeconomic status and IQ in this population—a sensible result. In particular, according to the probabilities in figure 3, both SES and IQ are more likely to be high when H takes on the value 1. This observation suggests that the hidden variable represents "parent quality."

It is possible for constraint-based methods which use independence con-

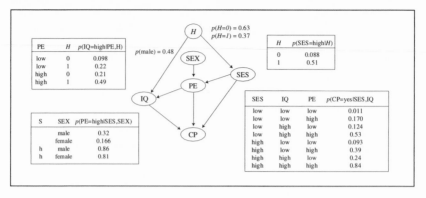

Figure 3. The a posteriori most likely model structure with a hidden variable. Probabilities shown are MAP values. Some probabilities are omitted for lack of space.

straints to discriminate between models with and without hidden variables and to indicate the presence of latent variables (see Spirtes, Glymour, and Scheines 1993). Constraint-based methods also use non-independence constraints—for example, tetrad constraints—to make additional discriminations. However, these methods cannot distinguish between the model in figure 3 and the most likely graph without hidden variables (the network on the left in figure 1). Conditional independence constraints alone cannot be used to distinguish the models, because the two graphs entail the same set of independence facts on the observable variables. Independence constraints in combination with known nonindependence constraints also fail to discriminate between the models. In addition, as this study illustrates, Bayesian methods can sometimes be used to determine the number of classes for a latent variable. A constraint-based method using only independence constraints can never determine the number of classes for a latent variable. We conjecture that any distinction among causal structures which can be made by constraint-based methods, even those not restricted to independence constraints, can be made using Bayesian methods. In addition, we conjecture that, asymptotically, when a constraint-based method chooses one model over another, the Bayesian approach will make the same choice, provided the causal Markov condition and the assumption of faithfulness hold.

8. Open Issues

The Bayesian framework gives us a conceptually simple framework for learning causal models. Nonetheless, the Bayesian solution often comes with a high computational cost. For example, when we learn causal models containing hidden variables, both the exact computation of marginal likelihood and model averaging or selection can be intractable. Although the approximations described in section 6 can be applied to address the difficulties associated with the computation of the marginal likelihood, model averaging and model selection remain difficult. The number of possible models with hidden variables is significantly larger than the number of possible DAGs over a fixed set of variables. Without constraining the set of possible models with hidden variables—for instance, by restricting the number of hidden variables—the number of possible models is infinite. On a positive note, Spirtes , Glymour, and Scheines (1993) have shown that constraint-based methods under suitable assumptions can sometimes indicate the existence of a hidden common cause between two variables. Thus, it may be possible to use the constraint-based methods to suggest an initial set of plausible models containing hidden variables that can then be subjected to a Bayesian analysis.

Another problem associated with learning causal models containing hidden variables is the assessment of parameter priors. The approach in section 4 can be applied in such situations, although the assessment of a joint distribution $p(\mathbf{x} \mid \mathbf{m}_c)$ in which $\mathbf{x}$ includes hidden variables can be difficult. Another approach may be to employ a property called strong likelihood equivalence (Heckerman 1995). According to this property, data should not help to discriminate among two models that are distribution equivalent with respect to the nonhidden variables. Heckerman (1995) showed that any method that uses this property will yield priors that differ from those obtained using a prior network.[6]

One possibility for avoiding this problem with hidden-variable models, when the sample size is sufficiently large, is to use BIClike approximations. Such approximations are commonly used (Crawford 1994, Raftery 1995). Nonetheless, the regularity conditions that guarantee $O_p(1)$ or better accuracy do not typically hold when choosing among causal models with hidden variables. Additional work is needed to obtain accurate approximations for the marginal likelihood of these models.

Even in models without hidden variables there are many interesting issues to be addressed. In this chapter we discuss only discrete variables having one type of local likelihood: the multinomial. Thiesson (1995) discusses a class of local likelihoods for discrete variables that use fewer parameters. Geiger and Heckerman (1994) and Buntine (1994) discuss simple linear local likelihoods for continuous nodes that have continuous and discrete variables. Buntine (1994) also discusses a general class of local likelihoods from the exponential family for nodes having no parents. Nonetheless, alternative likelihoods for discrete and continuous variables are desired. Local likelihoods with fewer parameters might allow for the selection of correct models with less data. In addition, local likelihoods that express more accurately the data–generating process would allow for easier interpretation of the resulting models.

Acknowledgments

We thank Max Chickering for implementing the software used in our analysis of the Sewall and Shah (1968) data.

Notes

1. Bernardo and Smith (1994) provide a summary of likelihoods from the exponential family and their conjugate priors.

2. Discussions of equivalent sample size can be found in Winkler (1967) and Heckerman, Geiger, and Chickering (1995).

3. The algorithm assumes that there are no hidden variables. See sections 6 and 7 for a discussion of hidden-variable models and methods for learning them.

4. One of the technical assumptions used to derive this approximation is that the prior is bounded and bounded away from zero around $\hat{\theta}_m$.

5. The MAP configuration θ_m^- depends on the coordinate system in which the parameter variables are expressed. The MAP given here corresponds to the canonical coordinate system for the multinomial distribution (see, e.g., Bernardo and Smith 1994, 199–202).

6. In particular, Heckerman (1995) showed that strong likelihood equivalence is not consistent with parameter independence and parameter modularity.

References

Aliferis, C., and Cooper, G. 1994. An Evaluation of an Algorithm for Inductive Learning of Bayesian Belief Networks Using Simulated Data Sets. In *Proceedings of the Tenth Conference on Uncertainty in Artificial Intelligence,* 8–14. San Francisco: Morgan Kaufmann.

Becker, S., and LeCun, Y. 1989. Improving the Convergence of Back-Propagation Learning with Second-Order Methods. In *Proceedings of the 1988 Connectionist Models Summer School,* 29–37. San Francisco: Morgan Kaufmann.

Bernardo, J., and Smith, A. 1994. *Bayesian Theory.* New York: Wiley.

Buntine, W. 1994. Operations for Learning with Graphical Models. *Journal of Artificial Intelligence Research* 2:159–225.

Buntine, W. 1991. Theory Refinement on Bayesian Networks. In *Proceedings of the Seventh Conference on Uncertainty in Artificial Intelligence,* 52–60. San Francisco: Morgan Kaufmann.

Cheeseman, P., and Stutz, J. 1995. Bayesian Classification (autoclass): Theory and Results. In *Advances in Knowledge Discovery and Data Mining,* eds. U. Fayyad, G. Piatesky-Shapiro, P. Smyth, and R. Uthurusamy, 153–180. Menlo Park, Calif.: AAAI Press.

Chib, S. 1995. Marginal Likelihood from the Gibbs Output. *Journal of the American Statistical Association* 90(432): 1313–1321.

Chickering, D. 1996a. Learning Bayesian Networks Is NP-Complete. In *Learning from Data,* eds. D. Fisher and H. Lenz, 121–130. New York: Springer-Verlag.

Chickering, D. 1996b. Learning Equivalence Classes of Bayesian-Network Structures. In *Proceedings of the Twelfth Conference on Uncertainty in Artificial Intelligence,* 87–89. San Francisco: Morgan Kaufmann.

Chickering, D., and Heckerman, D. 1997. Efficient Approximations for the Marginal Likelihood of Bayesian Networks with Hidden Variables. *Machine Learning* 29(43): 181–212.

Cooper, G. 1995. Causal Discovery from Data in the Presence of Selection Bias. Paper presented at the Fifth International Workshop on Artificial Intelligence and Statistics, Fort Lauderdale, Florida, Jan. 4–7.

Cooper, G., and Herskovits, E. 1992. A Bayesian Method for the Induction of Probabilistic Networks from Data. *Machine Learning* 9(4): 309–347.

Crawford, S. 1994. An Application of the Laplace Method to Finite-Mixture Distributions. *Journal of the American Statistical Association* 89(425): 259–267.

Dempster, A.; Laird, N.; and Rubin, D. 1977. Maximum Likelihood from Incomplete Data via the EM Algorithm. *Journal of the Royal Statistical Society* B39(1): 1–38.

DiCiccio, T.; Kass, R.; Raftery, A.; and Wasserman, L. 1995. Computing Bayes Factors by Combining Simulation and Asymptotic Approximations. Technical Report, 630, Department of Statistics, Carnegie Mellon University.

Geiger, D., and Heckerman, D. 1995. A Characterization of the Dirichlet Distribution Applicable to Learning Bayesian Networks. Technical Report MSR-TR-94-16, Microsoft Research, Redmond, Washington.

Geiger, D., and Heckerman, D. 1994. Learning Gaussian Networks. In *Proceedings of the Tenth Conference on Uncertainty in Artificial Intelligence,* 235–243. San Francisco: Morgan Kaufmann.

Geiger, D.; Heckerman, D.; and Meek, C. 1996. Asymptotic Model Selection for Directed Networks with Hidden Variables. In *Proceedings of the Twelfth Conference on Uncertainty in Artificial Intelligence,* 283–290. San Francisco: Morgan Kaufmann.

Geman, S., and Geman, D. 1984. Stochastic Relaxation, Gibbs Distributions, and the Bayesian Restoration of Images. *IEEE Transactions on Pattern Analysis and Machine Intelligence* 6(6): 721–742.

Haughton, D. 1988. On the Choice of a Model to Fit Data from an Exponential Family. *Annals of Statistics* 16(1): 342–355.

Heckerman, D. 1995. A Bayesian Approach for Learning Causal Networks. In *Proceedings of the Eleventh Conference on Uncertainty in Artificial Intelligence,* 285–295. San Francisco: Morgan Kaufmann.

Heckerman, D., and Geiger, D. 1996. Likelihoods and Priors for Bayesian Networks. Technical Report MSR-TR-95-54, Microsoft Research, Redmond, Washington.

Heckerman, D.; Geiger, D.; and Chickering, D. 1995. Learning Bayesian Networks: The Combination of Knowledge and Statistical Data. *Machine Learning* 20(3): 197–243.

Herskovits, E. 1991. Computer-Based Probabilistic Network Construction. Ph.D. dissertation, Medical Information Sciences, Stanford University.

Jensen, F.; Lauritzen, S.; and Olesen, K. 1990. Bayesian Updating in Recursive Graphical Models by Local Computations. *Computational Statisticals Quarterly* 4:269–282.

Kass, R., and Raftery, A. 1995. Bayes Factors. *Journal of the American Statistical Association* 90(430): 773–795.

Kass, R., and Wasserman, L. 1995. A Reference Bayesian Test for Nested Hypotheses and Its Relationship to the Schwarz Criterion. *Journal of the American Statistical Association* 90(431): 928–934.

Kass, R.; Tierney, L.; and Kadane, J. 1988. Asymptotics in Bayesian Computation. In *Bayesian Statistics 3,* eds. J. Bernardo, M. DeGroot, D. Lindley, and A. Smith, 261–278. Oxford, U.K.: Oxford University Press.

McLachlan, G., and Krishnan, T. 1997. *The EM Algorithm and Extensions.* New York: Wiley.

Madigan, D., and York, J. 1995. Bayesian Graphical Models for Discrete Data. *International Statistical Review* 63(2): 215–232.

Madigan, D.; Garvin, J.; and Raftery, A. 1995. Eliciting Prior Information to Enhance the Predictive Performance of Bayesian Graphical Models. *Communications in Statistics: Theory and Methods* 24(9): 2271–2292.

Madigan, D.; Raftery, A.; Volinsky, C.; and Hoeting, J. 1996. Bayesian Model Averaging. Paper presented at the AAAI Workshop on Integrating Multiple Learned Models for Improving and Scaling Machine Learning Algorithms, Portland, Oregon, August 4–8.

Meek, C. 1995. Strong Completeness and Faithfulness in Bayesian Networks. In *Proceedings of the Eleventh Conference on Uncertainty in Artificial Intelligence,* 411–418. San Francisco: Morgan Kaufmann.

Meng, X., and Rubin, D. 1991. Using EM to Obtain Asymptotic Variance-Covariance Matrices: The SEM Algorithm. *Journal of the American Statistical Association* 86(416): 899–909.

Neal, R. 1993. Probabilistic Inference Using Markov Chain Monte Carlo Methods. Technical Report, CRG-TR-93-1, Department of Computer Science, University of Toronto.

Raftery, A. 1996. Hypothesis Testing and Model Selection. In *Markov Chain Monte Carlo in Practice,* ed. W. R. Gilks, D. J. Spiegelhalter, and S. Richardson, 163–188. New York: Chapman and Hall.

Raftery, A. 1995. Bayesian Model Selection in Social Research. In *Sociological Methodology*, ed. P. Marsden. Cambridge, UK: Blackwells.

Rissanen, J. 1987. Stochastic Complexity (with Discussion). *Journal of the Royal Statistical Society* B49:223–239, 253–265.

Robins, J. 1986. A New Approach to Causal Interence in Mortality Studies with Sustained Exposure Results. *Mathematical Modeling* 7:1393–1512.

Rubin, D. 1978. Bayesian Inference for Causal Effects: The Role of Randomization. *Annals of Statistics* 6:34–58.

Russell, S.; Binder, J.; Koller, D.; and Kanazawa, K. 1995. Local Learning in Probabilistic Networks with Hidden Variables. In Proceedings of the Fourteenth International Joint Conference on Artificial Intelligence, 1146–1152. Menlo Park, Calif.: International Joint Conferences on Artificial Intelligence.

Scheines, R.; Spirtes, P.; Glymour, C.; and Meek, C. 1994. *TETRAD II: User's Manual.* Hillsdale, N.J.: Lawrence Erlbaum.

Schwarz, G. 1978. Estimating the Dimension of a Model. *Annals of Statistics* 6:461–464.

Sewell, W., and Shah, V. 1968. Social Class, Parental Encouragement, and Educational Aspirations. *American Journal of Sociology* 73(5): 559–572.

Singh, M., and Valtorta, M. 1993. An Algorithm for the Construction of Bayesian Network Structures from Data. In *Proceedings of the Ninth Conference on Uncertainty in Artificial Intelligence,* 259–265. San Francisco: Morgan Kaufmann.

Spiegelhalter, D., and Lauritzen, S. 1990. Sequential Updating of Conditional Probabilities on Directed Graphical Structures. *Networks* 20:579–605.

Spirtes, P., and Meek, C. 1995. Learning Bayesian Networks with Discrete Variables from Data, 294–299. In *Proceedings of the First International Conference on Knowledge Discovery and Data Mining.* Menlo Park, Calif.: AAAI Press.

Spirtes, P.; Glymour, C.; and Scheines, R. 1993. *Causation, Prediction, and Search.* New York: Springer-Verlag.

Spirtes, P.; Meek, C.; and Richardson, T. 1995. Causal Inference in the Presence of Latent Variables and Selection Bias. In *Proceedings of the Eleventh Conference on Uncertainty in Artificial Intelligence,* 499–506. San Francisco: Morgan Kaufmann.

Thiesson, B. 1995. Score and Information for Recursive Exponential Models with Incomplete Data. In *Proceedings of the Thirteenth Conference on Uncertainty in Artificial Intelligence,* 453–463. San Francisco: Morgan Kaufmann.

Verma, T., and Pearl, J. 1990. Equivalence and Synthesis of Causal Models. In *Proceedings of the Sixth Conference on Uncertainty in Artificial Intelligence,* 220–227. San Francisco: Morgan Kaufmann.

Winkler, R. 1967. The Assessment of Prior Distributions in Bayesian Analysis. *Journal of the American Statistical Association* 62:776–800.

CHAPTER FIVE

Truth Is Among the Best Explanations: Finding Causal Explanations of Conditional Independence and Dependence

*Richard Scheines, Peter Spirtes, Clark Glymour,
Christopher Meek and Thomas Richardson*

1. Background

In applied sciences statistical models typically have a double role, to specify both a family of probability distributions and a set of explanatory relationships, usually causal relationships. Scientific inquiry aims to select a model or models that usefully approximate correct explanatory and distributional relationships, and to estimate the parameters of such models. Estimation theory sets a standard for model specification. Statistical theory has developed and investigated a wealth of procedures for estimating features of probability disttributions. Asymptotic properties and expected values of estimators are investigated mathematically; small sample properties may be the subject of mathematical investigation, as well, but they are also studied extensively through simulation. Of course, the proofs that an estimator has one or another virtue are never free of assumptions, for example, assumptions about the distribution family and the sampling distribution. In contrast, while search procedures for models abound—factor analysis, multiple regression, many kinds of stepwise regression, modification indices, etc.—they almost never come with proofs relevant to the explanatory adequacy of the models the procedures produce, and thorough simulation studies of the error probabilities of search procedures are almost as rare. An odd doublethink results: the estimation of parameters and the testing of hypotheses about their values is examined with great rigor; the selection of the models in which those parameters occur is not.

The rigor that statistics has brought to the development and evaluation of algorithms for parameter estimation can and should be applied to algorithms for model specification. In a model specification problem a class of models is searched and various models assessed. Our concern is with structuring such searches so that, insofar as possible, there are guarantees of reliability analogous to those available for parameter estimators. We do not propose to replace well-founded theoretical sources of model specification with automatic procedures. Where theory and domain knowledge provide justified constraints on model specification, those constraints should be used, and one of the important desiderata for model search procedures is that they make use of whatever domain knowledge is available. But rarely, if ever, is social scientific theory and background knowledge sufficiently well confirmed and sufficiently strong to entail a unique model specification. There are typically many theoretically plausible alternatives to a given model, some of which support wholly different causal conclusions and thus lead to different conclusions about which policies should be adopted.

As with parameter estimation, the results we will present here do not free one from having to make assumptions; instead, they make rigorous and explicit what can and cannot be learned about the world if one is willing to make certain assumptions and not others. If, for example, one is willing to assume that causal relations are approximately linear and additive, that there is no feedback, that error terms are independent and identically distributed and uncorrelated, and that the causal independence and faithfulness assumptions (explained in detail in sections 3.1 and 3.2) are satisfied, then quite a lot can be learned about the causal structure underlying one's data. If one is only willing to make weaker assumptions, then less can be learned, although what can be learned may still be useful. Our aim is to make precise exactly what can and cannot be learned in each context. As with proofs of properties of estimators, the results are mathematical, not moral: they do not say what assumptions ought to be made.

Most of the results and procedures we will describe are very general and apply to models of categorical as well as continuous data. Because most of the applications described later in this book use linear models, we will illustrate general representations, their implications, and search procedures with linear structural equation models (hereafter, SEMs) (Bollen 1989; James, Mulaik, and Brett 1982). SEMs include linear regression models (Weisberg 1985), path analytic models (Wright 1934), factor analytic models (Lawley and Maxwell 1971), panel models (Blalock 1985; Wheaton et al. 1977), si-

$$X_1 = \varepsilon_1$$
$$X_2 = \beta_1 X_1 + \varepsilon_2$$
$$X_3 = \beta_2 X_2 + \varepsilon_3$$

Figure 1. Structural equations for SEMs S_1 and S_2.

multaneous equation models (Goldberger and Duncan 1973), MIMIC models (Bye, Gallicchio, and Dykacz 1985), and multiple indicator models (Sullivan and Feldman 1979). But we will also briefly describe how the representations and search procedures over them are applied in the case of categorical variables, ordered variables with a finite number of values, and combinations of both continuous and discretely valued variables.

1.1. Structural Equation Models and Directed Graphs

The variables in a SEM can be divided into two sets, the error variables and the substantive variables. Corresponding to each substantive variable X_i is a linear equation with X_i on the left hand side of the equation, and the direct causes of X_i plus the error term ε_i on the right hand side of the equation. Since we have no interest in first moments, without loss of generality each variable can be expressed as a deviation from its mean.

Consider, for example, two SEMs S_1 and S_2 over $\mathbf{X} = \{X_1, X_2, X_3\}$, where in both SEMs X_1 is a direct cause of X_2 and X_2 is a direct cause of X_3. The structural equations[1] in figure 1 are common to both S_1 and S_2.

In these equations, β_1 and β_2 are free parameters ranging over real values, and ε_1, ε_2 and ε_3 are unmeasured random variables called error terms. Suppose that ε_1, ε_2 and ε_3 are distributed as multivariate normal. In S_1 we will assume that the correlation between each pair of distinct error terms is fixed at zero. The free parameters of S_1 are $\theta = \langle \beta, \mathbf{P} \rangle$, where β is the set of linear coefficients $\{\beta_1, \beta_2\}$ and $\mathbf{P}$ is the set of variances of the error terms. We will use $\Sigma_{S1}(\theta_1)$ to denote the covariance matrix parameterized by the vector θ_1 for model S_1, and occasionally leave out the model subscript if the context makes it clear which model is being referred to. If all the pairs of error terms in a SEM S are uncorrelated, we say S is a SEM with *uncorrelated errors*.

Let S_2 contain the same structural equations as S_1, but in S_2 allow the errors between X_2 and X_3 to be correlated, i.e., make the correlation between the errors of X_2 and X_3 a free parameter, instead of fixing it at zero, as in S_1.

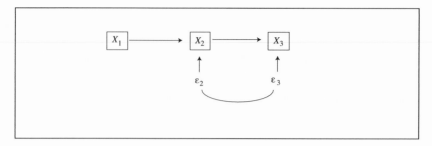

Figure 2. SEM S2 with correlated errors.

In S_2 the free parameters are $\theta = <\beta, P'>$, where β is the set of linear coefficients $\{\beta_1, \beta_2\}$ and P' is the set of variances of the error terms and the correlation between ε_2 and ε_3. If any of the correlations between error terms in a SEM are not fixed at zero, we will call it a SEM with *correlated errors*.[2]

It is possible to associate with each SEM with uncorrelated errors a directed graph that represents the causal structure of the model and the form of the linear equations. For example, the directed graph associated with the substantive variables in S_1 is $X_1 \to X_2 \to X_3$, because X_1 is the only substantive variable that occurs on the right hand side of the equation for X_2, and X_2 is the only substantive variable that appears on the right hand side of the equation for X_3. We generally do not include error terms in our path diagrams of SEMs unless the errors are correlated. We enclose measured variables in boxes, latent variables in circles, and leave error variables unenclosed.

The typical path diagram that would be given for S_2 is shown in figure 2. This is not strictly a directed graph because of the curved line between error terms ε_2 and ε_3, which indicates that ε_2 and ε_3 are correlated. It is generally accepted that correlation is to be explained by some form of causal connection. Accordingly, if ε_2 and ε_3 are correlated we will assume that either ε_2 causes ε_3, ε_3 causes ε_2, some latent variable causes both ε_2 and ε_3, or some combination of these. In other words, curved lines are an ambiguous representation of a causal connection. In section 3.1, for each SEM S with correlated errors we will show how to construct a directed acyclic graph G with latent variables that represents important causal and statistical features of S. Finally, a directed graph is *acyclic* if it contains no directed path from a variable back to itself. A SEM is said to be *recursive* (an RSEM) if its directed graph is acyclic.

1.2 Causal Structure: Predicting the Effects of Manipulations

A theory of interventions for linear models was given in Strotz and Wold (1960). Robins (1986) made important advances on the problem of predicting the effects of interventions in models with latent variables. A general theory of representing interventions in causal systems (not limited to RSEMs) in a graphical framework, and of predicting the effects of interventions for a partially specified model is presented in chapter 7 of Spirtes, Glymour, and Scheines (1993). An early version of that theory is presented in chapter 2 of this book. Examples of making predictions from a partially specified model will be presented in section 5. Pearl (1995) gives a more general solution of the problem of predicting the effects of interventions in models; that solution is presented and extended in chapter 3 of this book.

1.3 Parameter Estimation and SEM Specification

Ideally, there are at least four properties that an estimation procedure should have. The first property is *identification*. An estimation procedure should be able to determine whether or not a parameter is identifiable, i.e. determine whether or not there is a unique estimate that satisfies the given constraints. The second property is *consistency*. If a parameter is identified, it should be the case that as the sample size grows without limit, the probability approaches one that the difference between the true value and the estimated value approaches zero. The third property is *error probabilities*. The sampling distribution of the estimator should be known. The fourth property an estimation procedure should have is *practical reliability*. The estimation procedure should be reliable on samples of realistic size, and relatively robust against small violations of the operative assumptions.

We will examine each of these desiderata in more detail and point out analogies (and some disanalogies) between parameter estimation and model specification procedures. To see how the analogy extends to model specification procedures, we will consider for the sake of concreteness properties of the PC algorithm, which is a model specification search procedure implemented in the Build module of Tetrad II (described in section 5.1.1). For the points we make in this section, it is not necessary to know the details of the PC algorithm. The only features relevant to this section are that it takes as input (1) a sample covariance matrix (under the assumption of multivariate normality) and (2) background knowledge, and it outputs a graphical object called a *pattern* that represents a class of RSEMs without latent variables or correlated errors that are statistically equivalent (in a sense we make precise in section 4 below). Again, for concreteness, we will use maximum likelihood (ML) estimation and the algorithms that implement it as the example of a parameter estimator.

1.3.1 Identifiability

If there is a unique ML estimate of a parameter in a SEM, then the parameter is said to be identifiable. When a parameter is not identifiable, it has more than one value for which the likelihood of the data is maximal given the model. Although many special cases have been solved (e.g., see Becker, Merckens, and Wansbeek 1994), necessary and sufficient conditions for SEM parameter identifiability are not known.

In the case of SEM specification procedures there is a problem analogous to parameter nonidentifiability. There are many pairs of RSEMs R_1 and R_2 that have the same set of measured variables, and no latent variables or correlated errors, that are *covariance equivalent* in the following sense: for every parameterization θ_i of R_1 there is a parameterization θ_j of R_2 such that $\Sigma_{R1}(\theta_i) = \Sigma_{R2}(\theta_j)$, and vice versa. When R_1 and R_2 have no latent variables or correlated errors, then covariance equivalence has the following consequence: for any covariance matrix over the measured variables, if R_1 and R_2 are both parameterized by the respective ML estimates of their free parameters $\Sigma_{R1}(\theta_{ML})$ and $\Sigma_{R2}(\theta_{ML})$, then the p-values of the χ^2 likelihood ratio test for R_1 and R_2 will be identical. Thus the data cannot help us distinguish between R_1 and R_2. This is a kind of "causal underidentification."

The slogan that "correlation is not causation" expresses the idea that from data including only the existence of a single significant correlation between variables A and B, the causal structure governing A and B is underidentified. That is, a correlation between two variables A and B could be produced by A causing B, B causing A, a latent variable that causes both A and B, or some combination of these. But just as a single example of an underidentified SEM does not show that parameters are always underidentified, or that parameter estimation is always impossible or useless, the existence of a single example of covariance equivalent SEMs does not show that specification search for SEMs is always impossible or useless.

For some SEMs, certain parameters may be identifiable while others are not. Similarly, certain features of an RSEM R might be common to every R' that is covariance equivalent to R. We will show examples in which a covariance equivalence class of RSEMs *all* share the feature that some variable A is a (possibly indirect) cause of B; we will show other examples in which *none* of the members of a covariance equivalence class is (even indirectly) a cause of B. As explained in detail in section 4, for various special cases, necessary and sufficient, or necessary conditions for various kinds of statistical equivalence, are known. Because of the problem of covariance equivalence, the output of our algorithms will generally not be a single RSEM. Instead the output will be an object that represents a *class* of RSEMs consistent with the assumptions made and which marks those features shared by all of the members of the RSEMs' output.

By outputting a representation of covariance equivalence class of RSEMs, rather than a single SEM, the PC algorithm addresses the problem that there may be many different structural equation models that are compatible with background knowledge and fit the data equally well (as measured by a p-value, for example). However, it may be the case that there are SEMs which are not covariance equivalent, but nonetheless fit the data *almost* equally well; ideally an algorithm should output all such models, rather than simply choose the best. This problem could be addressed by outputting multiple patterns, rather than a single pattern. Devising an algorithm (or modifying the PC algorithm) to output representations of all models that fit the data well and are compatible with background knowledge is an important area of future research.

1.3.2 Consistency and Correctness

A SEM parameter estimation algorithm takes as input a sample covariance matrix S and distributional assumptions about the population from which S was drawn, and produces as output an estimate θ_{est} of the population parameters θ_{pop}. If the measured variables are indeed multivariate normal, and the specified model holds in the population, then asymptotically, as the sample size goes to infinity, the sampling distribution of θ_{ML} goes to $N(\theta_{pop}, J^{-1}(\theta))$, where $J(\theta)$ is the Fisher information matrix (cf. Tanner 1993, p. 16). So θ_{ML} is a *consistent* estimator in the sense that as the sample size grows without bound the difference between θ_{pop} and θ_{ML} will, with probability 1, converge to zero.

The PC algorithm takes as input a sample covariance matrix S, the assumption that S is drawn from a multivariate normal population described by an RSEM R_{pop} with no latent variables or correlated errors, and produces as output a *pattern* which represents a class of RSEMs that are covariance equivalent to R_{pop} (see section 4).[3] Let M_{PC} be the pattern output by the PC algorithm, and M_{pop} be the pattern that represents the class of RSEMs covariance equivalent to R_{pop}. Since there is no obvious metric to express the difference between M_{PC} and M_{pop}, we will not follow the analogy with parameter estimation and say that the PC algorithm is consistent. We can, however, state and prove a closely related property which we call correctness. The PC algorithm is *correct* in the following sense: if the causal independence, faithfulness and distributional assumptions are satisfied, then, as the sample grows without bound, the probability that $M_{PC} = M_{pop}$ converges to one.[4]

1.3.3 Sampling Distribution

In a SEM, to estimate the sampling distribution of θ_{ML} on finite samples, we have two choices. First, if the sample size is reasonably large we can use θ_{ML} as an estimate of θ_{pop}, and then use the asymptotic theory described above $(\theta_{ML} \sim N(\theta_{pop}, J^{-1}(\theta)))$ as an estimate of the sampling distribution of θ_{ML}. Second, we can approximate the sampling distribution of θ_{ML} empirically by Monte Carlo techniques (Boomsma 1982). We can do this by assuming $\Sigma(\theta_{ML}) = \Sigma(\theta_{pop})$. We can then repeatedly sample from $\Sigma(\theta_{pop})$, and calculate the *ML* estimate for each sample (figure 3). Although for small N the sam-

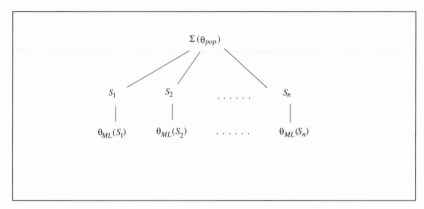

Figure 3. Monte Carlo approximation of the sampling distribution for θ_{ML}.

pling distribution of θ_{ML} is not multivariate normal (Boomsma 1982), it can be still be usefully summarized by the standard deviation (standard errors) and the mean.

On samples from a given model with specified parameters, the sampling distribution of M_{PC} is well defined. However, M_{PC} is not a vector of real valued parameters as θ_{ML} is, but rather a graphical object (see section 5.1.1) that represents an equivalence class of RSEMs. Hence M_{PC} is a categorical variable with no meaningful ordering of the categories. Thus the variance and mean are not very useful summaries of features of the distribution. We do not know how to calculate an analytic approximation of the sampling distribution for M_{PC} on finite samples. But we can apply empirical techniques parallel to those mentioned above for *ML* parameter estimation. To approximate the sampling distribution for M_{PC} on finite samples, consider figure 4, which is analogous to figure 3.

A slight disanalogy occurs in estimating $\Sigma(\theta_{pop})$. In the maximum likelihood setting, $\Sigma(\theta_{ML})$ is used as an estimate of $\Sigma(\theta_{pop})$. To obtain $\Sigma(\theta_{ML})$ from our sample **S** and M_{PC}, we can pick an arbitrary member M_i of the equivalence class of RSEMs represented by M_{PC} and then calculate θ_{ML} for M_i and **S**. (The resulting covariance matrix $\Sigma_{Mi}(\theta_{ML})$ is the same regardless of which member M_i of M_{PC} we choose.) We can then use $\Sigma_{Mi}(\theta_{ML})$ as an estimate of $\Sigma(\theta_{pop})$.

1.3.4 Practical Reliability

Finally, we want to know if the estimation procedure is reliable in practice. θ_{ML} has, by definition, the property that there is no $\theta_i \neq \theta_{ML}$ s.t. $p(\mathbf{S} \mid \theta_i) > p(\mathbf{S} \mid \theta_{ML})$. On samples of realistic size, however, iterative procedures that search the parameter space such as those implemented in LISREL (Jöreskog and Sörbom 1993) and EQS (Bentler 1995) cannot guarantee that they will find θ_{ML}. They must begin, for example, from some starting point in the parameter

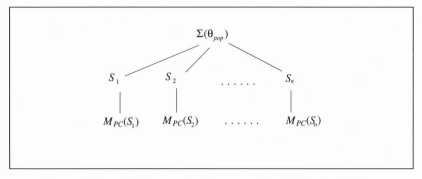

Figure 4. Monte Carlo approximation to sampling distribution for M_{PC}.

space and hill climb, and the likelihood surface might have local maxima (Scheines, Hoijtink, and Boomsma 1995). We can investigate the practical reliability of an ML estimation procedure at a given sample size by first, drawing an RSEM R from a distribution over RSEMs, second, drawing a parameterization θ_i from a distribution over the parameters of R to give a population $\Sigma_R(\theta_i)$, and third, drawing a sample $\mathbf{S}$ from $\Sigma_R(\theta_i)$. We can then use $\mathbf{S}$ as the input to the implemented estimator E, finally comparing $\Sigma_R(\theta_E)$ to $\Sigma_R(\theta_i)$ or just θ_E to θ_i.

We can investigate the reliability of model specification algorithms in an analogous way. The PC algorithm performs statistical tests of vanishing partial correlations, and if it cannot reject the null hypothesis at a significance level set by the user, then the procedure accepts the null hypothesis. If the null hypothesis is wrongly accepted or rejected, the output of the procedure can be incorrect. On finite samples, the reliability of the model specification algorithms depends upon the power of the statistical tests, the significance level used in the tests, the distribution over the models, and the parameters of the models.

In Spirtes, Glymour, and Scheines (1993), and in Scheines et al. (1994), we report on systematic Monte Carlo simulation studies to approximate features of the sampling distribution over the PC algorithm (and a variety of our other RSEM specification algorithm) by first drawing an RSEM R from a distribution over RSEMs; second drawing a parameterization θ_i from a distribution over the parameters for R; third drawing a sample $\mathbf{S}$ from the multivariate normal population $\Sigma_R(\theta_i)$, and then using $\mathbf{S}$ as input to the PC algorithm. Finally, we compare M_{PC} to M_{pop}.

These tests indicate that the PC algorithm is reliable with respect to determining which variables are adjacent in the population causal graph as long as the sample sizes are on the order of 500 and the population RSEM is not highly interconnected (i.e., that not everything is either a cause or an effect of everything else). For example, at sample size 500 for sparsely connected

RSEMs with 50 variables, the PC algorithm incorrectly hypothesized an adjacency less than once in 1,000 times such a mistake was possible, and incorrectly omitted an adjacency approximately 10 percent of the time, with the accuracy improving as the sample size grows (see page 155 of Spirtes et. al. 1993). We should note, however, that these simulation tests satisfied all the distributional assumptions underlying the algorithm and did not allow parameter values close to 0. We have not yet systematically explored the effect of small violations of these or other assumptions.

1.4 Difficulty of Search

In practice, model specification problems are very difficult for (at least) the following reasons:

- Data sets may fail to record variables (confounders) that produce associations among recorded variables.
- When no limitation is placed on the number of "latent variables," the number of alternative structures may be literally infinite.
- Many distinct models may produce the same or nearly the same distributions of recorded variables.
- Natural and social populations may be mixtures of structures with different causal graphs.
- Values of quantities recorded for some units in a data set may be missing for other units.
- There may be "selection bias"—that is, a measured variable may be causally connected to whether an individual is or is not included in the sample.
- The causal structure may involve feedback loops.
- The functional relations between causes and their effects may be continuous but nonlinear.
- Actual distributions may not be closely approximated by any well known probability distributions.

In the last fifteen years a movement in computer science and statistics has made theoretical progress on a number of these issues,[5] progress that has led to computer–based methods to aid in model specification.

1.5 Search Procedures

Two approaches to RSEM specification have been pursued in the statistics and computer science literature. The first focuses on searching for the RSEM or RSEMs that maximize some score.[6] The second approach focuses on searching for the RSEMs that satisfy a set of constraints judged to hold in the population (e.g., Spirtes, Glymour, and Scheines 1993). (See Richardson 1996 for a correct algorithm for searching for nonrecursive SEMs without latent variables.) Searches based on maximizing a score have been developed for RSEMs with no latent variables (e.g., Geiger and Heckerman 1994; Cooper and Herskovits 1992); typically they are either stepwise forward (they add edges), stepwise backward (they take away edges), or some combination of stepwise forward and backward. Most regression searches are of this type, although they are restricted to searching a very restricted class of RSEMs. The "modification index" searches based on the Lagrange multiplier statistic (Bentler 1986; Kaplan 1989 1990; Jöreskog and Sörbom 1993; Sörbom 1989) in LISREL and EQS are restricted versions of this strategy. They typically begin with a given SEM M and perform a stepwise forward search (EQS can also perform a stepwise backward search).

One difficulty with searches that maximize a score is that no proofs of correctness are yet available. A more difficult problem is that there are as of now no feasible score-maximization searches that include SEMs with latent variables. The modification index searches cannot suggest adding or removing a latent variable, for example. Also, these searches output a single SEM, rather than an equivalence class of SEMs. Another search strategy based upon maximizing a score is to search not RSEMs themselves, but covariance equivalence classes of RSEMs (Spirtes and Meek 1995).

In contrast to a score maximization search, a constraint search uses some testing procedure for conditional independence, vanishing partial correlations, vanishing tetrad differences, or other constraints on the covariance matrix. One advantage of this kind of search is that there are provably correct search algorithms for certain classes of RSEMs. For example, we will later discuss correct algorithms for multivariate normal RSEMs even when the population RSEM may contain latent variables (Spirtes, Glymour, and Scheines 1993).

In order to understand model specification search procedures based on constraints, one must first understand how SEMs entail constraints on the covariance matrix. Various equivalence relations between SEMs also need to be explained. We turn to those topics in the next sections.

2. Constraints Entailed by SEMs

We use two kinds of correlation constraints in our searches: zero partial correlation constraints, and vanishing tetrad constraints.

2.1 Zero Partial Correlation Constraints

In a SEM some partial correlations may be equal to zero for *all* values of the model's free parameters (for which the partial correlation is defined). (See Blalock 1962; Kiiveri and Speed 1982). In this case we will say that the SEM *entails* that the partial correlation is zero.[7] For example, in SEM S_1 (figure 1), where all of the error terms are uncorrelated, $\rho_{X1X3 \cdot X3} = 0$ for all values of the free parameters of S_1.

Judea Pearl (1988) discovered a fast procedure that can be used to decide, for any partial correlation $\rho_{A,B,C}$ and any RSEM with uncorrelated errors, whether the RSEM entails that $\rho_{A,B,C}$ is zero. Pearl defined a relation called *d-separation* that can hold between three disjoint sets of vertices in a directed acyclic graph. A simple consequence of theorems proved by Pearl, Geiger, and Verma shows that in an RSEM R with uncorrelated errors a partial correlation $\rho_{A,B,C}$ is entailed to be zero if and only if $\{A\}$ and $\{B\}$ are *d*-separated by C in the directed graph associated with R (Pearl 1988). Spirtes (1995) showed that these connections between graphical structure and vanishing partial correlations hold as well for nonrecursive SEMs, i.e. in a SEM with uncorrelated errors a partial correlation $\rho_{A,B,C}$ is entailed to be zero if and only if $\{A\}$ and $\{B\}$ are d-separated given C. (The if part of the theorem was shown independently in Koster (1994).

There is also a way to decide which partial correlations are entailed to be zero by a SEM with correlated errors, such as S_2 (figure 2). This is done by first creating a directed graph G with latent variables and then applying d-separation to G to determine if a zero partial correlation is entailed. The directed graph G (with latent variables but without correlated errors) that we associate with a SEM S with correlated errors is created in the following way. Start with the usual graphical representation of S that contains undirected lines connecting correlated errors (e.g. SEM S_2 in figure 2). For each pair of correlated error terms ε_i and ε_j, introduce a new latent variable T_{ij} and edges from T_{ij} to X_i and X_j. Finally replace ε_i and ε_j with uncorrelated errors ε_i' and ε_j'. When this process is applied to SEM S_2, the result is shown in figure 5.

In a SEM like S_2, with correlated errors, one can decide whether $\rho_{X1X3 \cdot X3}$ is entailed to be zero by determining whether $\{X_1\}$ and $\{X_3\}$ are *d*-separated given $\{X_2\}$ in the graph in figure 5. In this way the problem of determining whether a SEM with correlated errors entails a zero partial correlation is reduced to the already solved problem of determining whether a SEM without correlated errors entails a zero partial correlation. In general if S is a SEM with correlated errors and G is the latent variable graph with uncorrelated errors associated with S, it is *not* the case that for every linear parameterization θ_1 of S there is a linear parameterization θ_2 of G such that $\Sigma_S(\theta_1) = \Sigma_G(\theta_2)$. We are making the weaker claim that *d*-separation applied to G correctly describes which zero partial correlations are entailed by S. For the proof, see Spirtes et al. 1996.

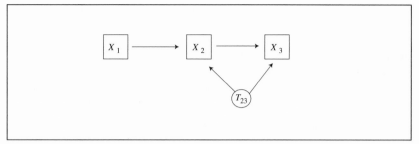

Figure 5. SEM S_2' Correlated errors in S_2 replaced by latent common cause.

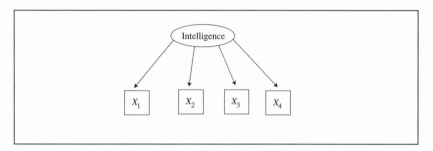

Figure 6. Factor model of intelligence.

2.2.Vanishing Tetrad Constraints

In SEMs containing latent variables, zero partial correlation constraints among the measured covariances Σ are often uninformative. For example, consider figure 6 in which Intelligence is a latent variable. The only correlations entailed to be zero by this SEM are those that are partialed on at least Intelligence. Since intelligence is unmeasured, however, our data will only include partial correlations among the measured variables $\mathbf{X} = \{X_1, X_2, X_3, X_4\}$, and there is no partial correlation involving only variables in $\mathbf{X}$ that is entailed to be zero by this SEM.

The vanishing tetrad difference (Spearman 1904), however, can provide extra information about the specification of this model. A tetrad difference involves two products of correlations, each of which involve the same four variables but in different permutations. In the SEM of figure 6 there are three tetrad differences among the measured correlations that are entailed to vanish for all values of the free parameters (for which the correlations are defined):

$$\rho_{X1,X2}\,\rho_{X3,X4} - \rho_{X1,X3}\,\rho_{X2,X4}$$
$$\rho_{X1,X2}\,\rho_{X3,X4} - \rho_{X1,X4}\,\rho_{X2,X3}$$
$$\rho_{X1,X3}\,\rho_{X2,X4} - \rho_{X1,X4}\,\rho_{X2,X3}$$

If a SEM S entails that $\rho_{X1,X2}\,\rho_{X3,X4} - \rho_{X1,X3}\,\rho_{X2,X4} = 0$ for all values of its free parameters we say that S *entails* the vanishing tetrad difference. The tetrad differences that are entailed to vanish by a SEM without correlated errors are also completely determined by the directed graph associated with the SEM. The graphical characterization is given by the tetrad representation theorem (Spirtes 1989; Spirtes, Glymour, and Scheines 1993; Shafer, Kogan, and Spirtes 1993), which leads to a general procedure for computing the vanishing tetrad differences entailed by a SEM, implemented in the tetrads module of the Tetrad II program (Scheines, Spirtes, Glymour and Meek 1994). Bollen and Ting (1993) discuss the advantages of using vanishing tetrad differences in SEM analysis; e.g. they can be used to compare underidentified SEMs.

3. Assumptions Relating Probability to Causal Relations

In this section, we discuss two assumptions relating probabillity to causal relations: the causal independence assumption and the faithfulness assumption.

3.1 The Causal Independence Assumption

Our most fundamental assumption relating causality and probability is the following:

> *Causal Independence Assumption:* If A does not cause B, and B does not cause A, and there is no third variable which causes both A and B, then A and B are independent.

This assumption provides a bridge between statistical facts and causal features of the process that underlies the data. It is an assumption, and does not always hold; for example when the values of two variables both influence whether a unit is in a sample, the units may be associated (no matter how large the sample) even if there is no causal connection of any kind between them.

In certain cases the assumption allows us to draw a *causal* conclusion from *statistical* data and lies at the foundation of the theory of randomized experiments. If the value of A is randomized, the experimenter knows that the randomizing device is the sole cause of A. Hence the experimenter knows B did not cause A, and that there is no other variable which causes both A and B. This leaves only two alternatives: either A causes B or it does not. If A and B are correlated in the experimental population, the experimenter concludes that A does cause B, which is an application of the causal independence assumption.

The causal independence assumption entails that if two error terms are correlated, such as ε_2 and ε_3 in S_2 (see figure 2), then there is at least one la-

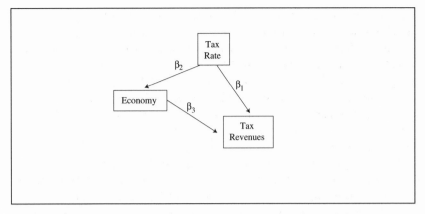

Figure 7. Distribution is unfaithful to SEM when $\beta_1 = -(\beta_2\beta_3)$.

tent common cause of the explicitly modeled variables associated with these errors, i.e., X_2 and X_3.

3.2. The Faithfulness Assumption

In addition to the zero partial correlations and vanishing tetrad differences that are entailed for *all* values of the free parameters of a SEM, there may be zero partial correlations or vanishing tetrad differences that hold only for *particular* values of the free parameters of a SEM. For example, suppose figure 7 is the directed graph of a SEM that describes the relations among the tax rate, the economy, and tax revenues.

In this case there are no vanishing partial correlation constraints entailed for all values of the free parameters. But if $\beta_1 = -(\beta_2\beta_3)$, then tax rate and tax revenues are uncorrelated. The SEM postulates a direct effect of tax rate on revenue (β_1) and an indirect effect through the economy ($\beta_2\beta_3$). The parameter constraint indicates that these effects *exactly* offset each other, leaving no total effect whatsoever. In such a case we say that the population is *unfaithful* to the SEM that generated it. A distribution is *faithful* to SEM M (or its corresponding directed graph) if each partial correlation that is zero in the distribution is entailed to be zero by M, and each tetrad difference that is zero in the distribution is entailed to be zero by M.

Faithfulness assumption: If the directed graph associated with a SEM M correctly describes the causal structure in the population, then each partial correlation and each tetrad difference that is zero in $\Sigma_M(\theta_{pop})$ is entailed to be zero by M.

The faithfulness assumption is a kind of simplicity assumption. If a distribution P is faithful to an RSEM R_1 without latent variables or correlated errors, and P also results from a parameterization of another RSEM R_2 to which P is not faithful, then R_1 has fewer free parameters than R_2.

The faithfulness assumption limits the SEMs considered to those in which population constraints are entailed by structure, not by particular values of the parameters. If one assumes faithfulness, then if A and B are *not* d-separated given C, then $\rho_{A,B,C} \neq 0$ (because it is not entailed to equal zero for all values of the free parameters). Faithfulness should not be assumed when there are deterministic relationships among the substantive variables, or equality constraints upon free parameters, since either of these can lead to violations of the assumption. Some form of the assumption of faithfulness is used in every science, and amounts to no more than the belief that an improbable and unstable cancellation of parameters does not hide real causal influences. When a theory cannot explain an empirical regularity save by invoking a special parameterization, most scientists are uneasy with the theory and look for an alternative.

It is also possible to give a personalist Bayesian argument for assuming faithfulness. For any SEM with free parameters, the set of parameterizations of the SEM that lead to violations of faithfulness are Lebesque measure zero. Hence any Bayesian whose prior over the parameters is absolutely continuous with Lebesque measure assigns a zero prior probability to violations of faithfulness. Of course, this argument is not relevant to those Bayesians who place a prior over the parameters that is not absolutely continuous with Lebesgue measure and assign a nonzero probability to violations of faithfulness. All of the algorithms we have developed assume faithfulness, and from here on we use it as a working assumption.

The faithfulness assumption is necessary to guarantee the correctness of the model specification algorithms used in Tetrad II. It does *not* guarantee that on samples of finite size the model specification algorithms are reliable.[8]

4. SEM Equivalence

Two SEMs S_1 and S_2 with the same substantive variables (or their respective directed graphs) are *covariance equivalent* if for every parameterization θ_i of S_1 with covariance matrix $\Sigma_{S1}(\theta_i)$ there is a parameterization θ_j of S_2 with covariance matrix $\Sigma_{S2}(\theta_j)$ such that $\Sigma_{S1}(\theta_i) = \Sigma_{S2}(\theta_j)$, and vice versa. Two SEMs with the same substantive variables (or their respective directed graphs) are *partial correlation equivalent* if they entail the same set of zero partial correlations among the substantive variables.

If two SEMs contain latent variables, and the same set of measured variables V, we may be interested if they are equivalent on the measured vari-

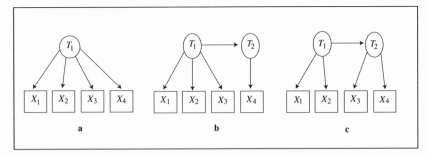

Figure 8. Three SEMs.

ables. Two SEMs S_1 and S_2 (or their respective directed graphs) are *covariance equivalent over a set of measured variables* V if for every parameterization θ_i of S_1 with covariance matrix $\Sigma_{S1}(\theta_i)$ there is a parameterization θ_j of S_2 with covariance matrix $\Sigma_{S2}(\theta_j)$ such that the margin of $\Sigma_{S1}(\theta_i)$ over V = the margin of $\Sigma_{S2}(\theta_j)$ over V, and vice versa. Two SEMs are *partial correlation equivalent over a set of measured vertices* V if they entail the same set of zero partial correlations among variables in V.

We illustrate the difference between equivalence and equivalence over a set V with the models in figure 8. Models *a* and *b* do not share the same set of substantive variables, so they are not covariance or partial correlation equivalent. Models *b* and *c* share the same substantive variables, but are not covariance equivalent or partial correlation equivalent because, for example, model *c* entails $\rho_{X2,X3.T2} = 0$ while model *b* does not. For V = $\{X_1, X_2, X_3, X_4\}$, however, the situation is quite different. All three models are partial correlation equivalent over V, and models *a* and *b* are covariance equivalent over V. Models *b* and *c* are not covariance equivalent over V because, for example, model *b* entails that $\rho_{X1,X2} \rho_{X3,X4} = \rho_{X1,X3} \rho_{X2,X4}$ while model *c* does not. The next four subsections will outline what is known about these various kinds of equivalence in both recursive and nonrecursive SEMs.

4.1 Covariance and Partial Correlation Equivalence in Recursive SEMs

In this section we consider equivalence over RSEMs with no correlated errors. For two such RSEMs, covariance equivalence holds if and only if zero partial correlation equivalence holds (Spirtes, Glymour, and Scheines 1993). In RSEMs, only two concepts need to be defined to graphically characterize covariance (or partial correlation) equivalence: *adjacency* and *unshielded collider*. Two variables X and Y are adjacent in a directed graph G just in case $X \to Y$ is in G, or $Y \to X$ is in G.

A triple of variables <X,Z,Y> is a *collider* in G just in case $X \to Z \leftarrow Y$ is in G, and Z is an *unshielded collider* between X and Y just in case <X,Z,Y> is

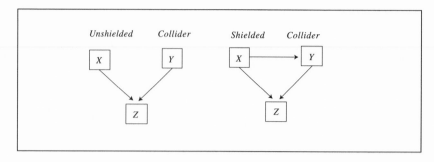

Figure 9.

a collider and X and Y are not adjacent (figure 9). The first theorem stated below is a simple consequence of a theorem proved in Verma and Pearl (1990), and in Frydenberg (1990).

RSEM partial correlation equivalence theorem. Two RSEMs with the same variables and no correlated errors are partial correlation equivalent if and only if their respective directed graphs have the same adjacencies and the same unshielded colliders.

RSEM covariance equivalence theorem: Two RSEMs with the same variables and no correlated errors are covariance equivalent if and only if their respective directed graphs have the same adjacencies and the same unshielded colliders.

By the first theorem, if two RSEMs with the same variables and no correlated errors have the same adjacencies and unshielded colliders, then they are partial correlation equivalent. It is easy to show that for any RSEM M without correlated errors or latents, and any correlation matrix C which satisfies the partial correlation constraints entailed by M, there is a θ such that $\Sigma_M(\theta)$ $= C$. Hence two RSEMs that are partial correlation equivalent are also covariance equivalent. (A complete proof is given in Spirtes, Richardson, and Meek [1997]).

4.2 Covariance and Partial Correlation Equivalence
Over the Measured Variables in RSEMs

We now consider the case where there may be latent variables and/or correlated errors, and the question is whether two SEMs are covariance equivalent or partial correlation equivalent over a set of measured variables **V**. Since an RSEM with correlated errors is partial correlation equivalent to another RSEM with a latent variable but no correlated errors, the problem of deciding partial correlation equivalence over the measured variables when there are correlated errors reduces to the problem of deciding partial correlation

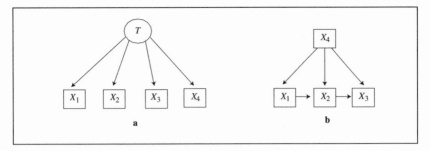

Figure 10. Two graphs that are partial correlation equivalent over $\{X_1, X_2, X_3, X_4\}$, but not covariance equivalent over $\{X_1, X2, X_3, X_4\}$.

equivalence over the measured variables when there are no correlated errors.

Covariance equivalence over the measured variables entails partial correlation equivalence over the measured variables, but the converse does not hold. Consider the directed graphs a and b in figure 10, where the set of measured variables $\mathbf{V} = \{X_1, X_2, X_3, X_4\}$ and the errors are uncorrelated. Although these graphs are partial correlation equivalent over $\mathbf{V}$ (neither entails any partial correlations among the measured variables), they are not covariance equivalent over $\mathbf{V}$, since model *a* but not model *b* entails that

$$\rho_{X1,X2}\,\rho_{X3,X4} = \rho_{X1,X3}\,\rho_{X2,X4} = \rho_{X1,X4}\,\rho_{X2,X3}$$

Spirtes, Meek, and Richardson (1995) have given a polynomial (in the number of variables in the two RSEMs) time algorithm for deciding when two RSEMs with uncorrelated errors are partial correlation equivalent over the measured variables. The algorithm is too complex to present here, but some examples of partial correlation equivalence are given in section 5.1. A feasible algorithm for deciding covariance equivalence over a set of measured variables is not known.

4.3. Covariance and Partial Correlation Equivalence in Nonrecursive SEMs

Assuming uncorrelated errors, Richardson (1994 1995) has given an algorithm for deciding when two nonrecursive SEMs are partial correlation equivalent that is polynomial in the number of variables in the two SEMs. Partial correlation equivalence does not entail covariance equivalence in this case.

One noteworthy corollary of Richardson's theorem is that for every SEM with a directed cycle, there is another partial correlation equivalent SEM with a cycle reversed in direction. And while partial correlation equivalent RSEMs without correlated errors always have the same adjacencies, partial correlation equivalent SEMs without correlated errors can have directed cyclic graphs with different adjacencies. For example, the two SEMs in figure 11 are partial correlation equivalent but do not have the same adjacencies.

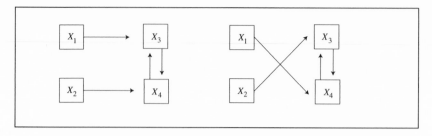

Figure 11. Partial correlation equivalent cyclic SEMs.

4.4. Covariance and Partial Correlation Equivalence over the Measured Variables in Nonrecursive SEMs

No feasible general algorithm for deciding either partial correlation or covariance equivalence over a set of measured variables is known for nonrecursive SEMs when the measured variables are a proper subset of the substantive variables in the SEM.

5. Search Algorithms in Tetrad II

In this section we describe some of the constraint based, provably correct (in
the large sample limit) search procedures that we have implemented in
Tetrad II. Our approach is to design algorithms that search for all RSEMs
consistent with background knowledge that entail constraints on the covariance matrix that are judged to hold in the population. Depending on the type
of background knowledge, and what kind of RSEM is sought, we use either
vanishing partial correlation constraints or vanishing tetrad constraints. Because in many cases the number of possible constraints is too large to examine exhaustively, some of the algorithms we describe make sequential decisions about constraints and thus test only a subset of the possible constraints
during the search process. These sequential procedures are still correct in the
sense we defined in section 1.3.2, but might not be optimal on realistic samples because mistakes about constraints made early in the sequence can rami-
fy into mistakes made later.

5.1 The Build Algorithm

The build module[9] of Tetrad II takes as input (1) sample data (either raw or as
a covariance matrix) and (2) background knowledge that constrains RSEM
specification, and gives as output (1) a representation of the partial correlation equivalence class of RSEMs that is consistent with the background

knowledge and (2) a set of features that this class of RSEMs has in common.

Build performs statistical tests of hypotheses that specific partial correlations vanish in the population, and if it cannot reject the null hypothesis at a significance level set by the user, then the procedure accepts the null hypothesis (see the appendix in Scheines et al. 1994). Because Build uses only information about which partial correlations are zero, it cannot distinguish between any members of a partial correlation equivalence class; hence its output is a representation of a partial correlation equivalence class of RSEMs consistent with background knowledge. In order to achieve enough efficiency to be practical for large numbers of variables (up to 100), the algorithms in Build use the results of tests of lower order partial correlation (i.e., correlations conditional on small sets of variables) to restrict the tests it needs to perform on partial correlations of higher order.

The algorithms are correct in the sense of section 1.3.2. The background knowledge a user enters may include assumptions about (1) whether the population RSEM contains correlated errors, or latent common causes; (2) time order among the variables; (3) known causal relationships among the variables; and (4) causal relationships among the variables known not to hold.

5.1.1 Build for RSEMs Without Correlated Errors or Latent Common Causes

If you assume that the generating RSEM contains no latent common causes, then Build runs the PC algorithm, which is documented and traced in Spirtes, Glymour, and Scheines (1993) and Scheines et. al (1994). The output of the PC algorithm is a *pattern* (Verma and Pearl 1990,) which is a compact representation of a partial correlation (and covariance) equivalence class of RSEMs without correlated errors or latent common causes. A pattern contains a mixture of directed and undirected edges. If a pattern contains an edge $A \rightarrow B$, then the directed graph of *every* RSEM represented by the pattern contains the edge $A \rightarrow B$. If a pattern contains an edge $A \!-\! B$ then A and B are adjacent in the directed graph of *every* RSEM represented by the pattern, but the graphs of some RSEMs represented by the pattern may contain the edge $A \rightarrow B$, and others may contain the edge $A \leftarrow B$. If a pattern contains no adjacency between A and B, then in every RSEM represented by the pattern, A and B are not adjacent.

Suppose we measure only two variables A and B and find that they are significantly correlated. There are two RSEMs without correlated errors or latent variables containing just A and B that are compatible with A and B being correlated in the population: $A \rightarrow B$, and $A \leftarrow B$. The output of Build in this case is the pattern $A \!-\! B$, which represents the two RSEMs in this equivalence class. This illustrates the slogan "correlation is not causation," because the statistical information is not sufficient to predict the results of an ideal intervention on A or B.

In this example the output of Build is not useful for predicting the effects

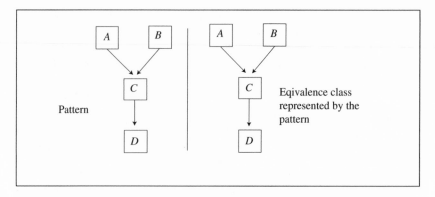

Figure 12. The output of Build can provide more useful causal knowledge.

of ideal interventions. The next example shows how the output of Build can in some cases provide more useful causal knowledge. Suppose that for four measured variables, A, B, C, and D, from sample data we conclude that in the population, $\rho_{A,B} = 0$, $\rho_{A,D,C} = 0$, and $\rho_{B,D,C} = 0$, but that no other partial correlations (other than those entailed by those listed) vanish. In that case the output of Build is the pattern in figure 12, which represents an equivalence class of RSEMs with only one member, also shown in figure 12.[10]

In this case, the output of Build is sufficient to predict the results of ideally intervening on A, B, C, or D. Of course, the assumption of no correlated errors or latent variables is a very strong one, and in the next section we consider what happens when it is abandoned.

5.1.2 Build for RSEMs with Correlated Errors

If you allow that the RSEM that generated the data might have correlated errors or latent common causes, then Build runs the FCI algorithm, which is documented in chapter 6 of Spirtes, Glymour, and Scheines (1993). The output of the FCI algorithm is a *partial ancestor graph* (PAG).[11] A is an *ancestor* of B in a directed graph when there is a directed path from A to B. Just as patterns represent features common to a partial correlation equivalence class of RSEMs without latent variables, PAGs represent features common to a set of RSEMs that are partial correlation equivalent over the measured variables. (In this section, for the sake of brevity, we will refer to the PAG simply as an equivalence class.) We will illustrate with the two examples from the previous section.

Again, suppose we measure two variables, A and B, and find that they have a significant correlation and conclude that they are correlated in the population. The output of Build in this case is the partial ancestor graph shown in figure 13. Because we have placed no limit on the number of distinct latent variables, the equivalence class represented by the output is actu-

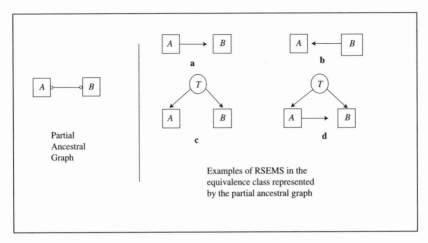

Partial
Ancestral
Graph

Examples of RSEMS in the
equivalence class represented
by the partial ancestral graph

Figure 13. A simple PAG and its equivalence class.

ally infinite, and we have shown only a few members of the equivalence class in figure 13. The presence of an *"o"* at both ends of an edge in a PAG makes no claim about the ancestor relationship common to every member of the equivalence class. Note that in some of the RSEMs represented by the PAG (e.g. figure 13a and d), *A* is an ancestor of *B,* and in others (e.g. figure 13b and c) it is not. Similarly, in some of the members of the equivalence class (e.g. figure 13b) *B* is an ancestor of *A,* and in others (e.g. figure 13a, c, and d) it is not. Thus this PAG shows us that we cannot predict the results of ideally intervening to change either *A* or *B* from this data without further background knowledge.

Whereas the pattern *A — B* informed us that either *A* is a cause of *B* or *B* is a cause of *A,* the PAG *A* o—o *B* informs us that either *A* is a cause of *B, B* is a cause of *A,* there is a latent common cause, or there is some combination of these causal connections responsible for the correlation. The next example shows how PAGs output by Build can be used to predict the effects of some ideal interventions. Consider the example from figure 12 again, where there are four measured variables *A, B, C,* and *D,* and we conclude from the data that in the population $\rho_{A,B} = 0$, $\rho_{A,D,C} = 0$, and $\rho_{B,D,C} = 0$, but that no other partial correlations vanish. Assuming that correlated errors might exist in the generating RSEM, the output of Build is the PAG in the left hand side of figure 14.

A and *C* are adjacent in the PAG because the correlation of *A* and *C* conditional on every subset of the measured variables does not vanish (i.e. $\rho_{A,C}$, $\rho_{A,C.B}$, $\rho_{A,C.D}$, $\rho_{A,C.BD}$ do not vanish.) The *"o"* at the *A* end of the edge between *A* and *C* entails neither that *A* is an ancestor of *B* in every member of the equivalence class nor that *A* is not an ancestor of *B* in every member of

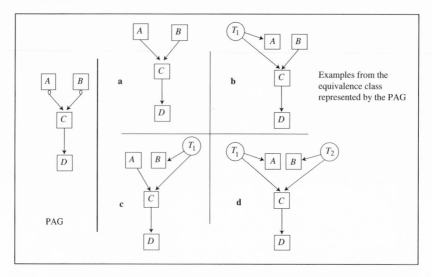

Figure 14. A more complicated PAG and its equivalence class.

the equivalence class. The ">" at the *C* end of the edge between *A* and *C* in the PAG means that *C* is not an ancestor of *A* in any RSEM in the partial correlation equivalence class. Similarly, *C* is not an ancestor of *B*, and *D* is not an ancestor of *C* in any RSEM in the partial correlation equivalence class. Finally, a "—" at the *C* end of the edge between *C* and *D* means that *C* *is* an ancestor of *D* in every RSEM in the equivalence class.

From this PAG we can make predictions about the effects of some ideal interventions, but not others. For example, it is not possible to determine if an ideal intervention on *A* will affect *C*, because in some members of the equivalence class *A* is a cause of *C*, and in others it is not. On the other hand, it is possible to determine that an ideal intervention on *C* will affect *D*, because *C* is a cause of *D* in every RSEM in the equivalence class. (Given the distributional assumption, it is also possible to determine the size of the effect that an ideal intervention on *C* will have on D. See chapter 7 of Spirtes, Glymour, and Scheines [1993].)

The partial correlation equivalence class in figure 14, which includes RSEMs with latent variables, is much larger (in fact it is infinite) than the partial correlation equivalence class in figure 12, which does not include models with latent variables. This in turn means that the conclusions that we can draw are weaker than if we assume that the generating RSEM has no correlated errors or latent common causes. For example, with this assumption we can conclude that *A* is a cause of *C*; without it we cannot. With the assumption we can estimate the size of the effect that an ideal intervention on *A* will have on *C*; without it we cannot. While the conclusions that can be drawn even without the assumption of no latent variables are weaker than when the assumption is made, they are not trivial. Asymptotically, we can reliably conclude that C is a cause of D, and we can estimate the size of the effect an ideal intervention on C will have on D.

It should also be noted that even though in general not all of the members of the partial correlation equivalence class are covariance equivalent, this does not affect the reliability of the conclusions. It simply means that there may be stronger conclusions that could be drawn if we used more information than simply which partial correlations vanish.

Finally, we note that there are examples in which there is no RSEM without latent variables that is compatible with a correlation matrix, but there are RSEMs with latent variables that are. Suppose that we measure A, B, C, and D and from the data conclude that in the population, $\rho_{A,C} = 0$, $\rho_{A,D} = 0$, and $\rho_{B,D} = 0$, but that no other partial correlations (other than those entailed by these three) vanish. In that case the output of Build is $A \; o{\rightarrow} \; B \leftrightarrow C \leftarrow o \; D$. The double headed arrow between B and C means that in every member of the equivalence class represented by the PAG B is not an ancestor of C and C is not an ancestor of B. This is only possible in an RSEM with a latent variable causing both B and C, so every member of the equivalence class contains a latent variable.

5.1.3 What Can Go Wrong

In general, the correctness of Build's output depends upon several factors:
(1) The correctness of the background knowledge input to the algorithm. (2) Whether the recursiveness condition holds, i.e., that there are no feedback loops. (3) Whether the causal independence assumption holds. (4) Whether the faithfulness assumption holds. (5) Whether the distributional assumptions made by the statistical tests hold. (6) The power of the statistical tests against alternatives. (7) The significance level used in the statistical tests.

In the case of Build under the assumption of no latent variables, it is not difficult to take the output pattern which represents a partial correlation equivalence class (and a covariance equivalence class) of RSEMs and use it to find a single RSEM in the equivalence class. A sketch of this process is described in the Tetrad II manual and can be automated (Meek 1995). Once this is done, the user can estimate and test the selected RSEM using such programs as EQS, or LISREL. (All RSEMs in the partial correlation equivalence class parameterized by their respective ML parameter estimates have the same p-value.) In addition, the user can approximate the sampling distribution using the method described in section 1.3.3. The user should keep in mind, however, that the sampling distribution of the output may show that even when the RSEMs suggested by Tetrad II fit the data very well, it is possible that there are other RSEMs that will also fit the data well and are equally compatible with background knowledge, particularly when the sample size is small. This suggests that further research on the search is needed, and that Build might be improved by outputting multiple patterns—something which can be done in a limited way in the present implementation by varying the significance level used in the procedure. Also, at large sample sizes, even slight deviations from normality or linearity can lead to the rejection of an otherwise correct RSEM. Finally, if a model produced by search is tested on the data used to find the model specification, the p-value of the test is not a measure of the error probability of the model specification procedure. For a discussion of the meaning of such p-values, see Glymour et al. (1987). Where possible, models generated from one sample should be cross-validated on others.

In the case of Build under the assumption of latent variables, more research is needed to find out how to construct (efficiently) from the PAG which represents the entire partial correlation equivalence class a single, representative RSEM. In this case the output partial correlation equivalence class is not a covariance equivalence class, so that different RSEMs represented by the output can have different p-values when parameterized by their ML parameter estimates. More research is needed on estimating and testing the output of Build under the assumption of latent variables. Spirtes, Glymour, and Scheines (1993) describes some algorithms that can be used for predicting the effects of some policy interventions from a given PAG.

The Build procedures can all be applied to variables taking a finite number of values. The Tetrad II program tests for independence and conditional independence among such variables assuming a multinomial distribution. In principle, the same techniques can be extended to mixed systems of variables, in which discrete variables are multinomial and continuous variables are conditionally Gaussian.

5.2 Specification Search for Latent Variable RSEMs: Purify and MIMbuild

In many applications of structural equation modeling, the focus of interest is the causal relationships among latent variables. In many such cases the latent variables are measured with multiple indicators, and the output of Build on data for these indicators is correct but uninformative; the correct RSEM entails no zero partial correlation constraints on the indicators alone and the output of Build on the indicators is completely connected and completely undirected, whether it is a pattern or a PAG. In these cases the Purify and MIMbuild modules of Tetrad II can help in RSEM specification. Purify helps locate unidimensional measurement models (Anderson, Gerbing, and Hunter 1987; Anderson and Gerbing 1988; Scheines 1993). The basic idea of unidimensionality is that each indicator measures exactly one latent and all error terms are uncorrelated (the exact definition is more complicated). Finding a unidimensional measurement model is one way in which the correlations

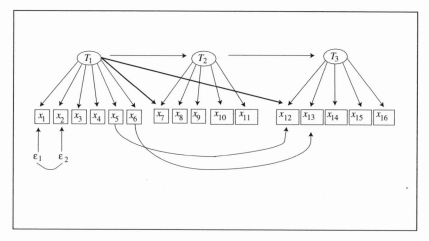

Figure 15. Population RSEM.

among the latent variables may be estimated consistently. Also, given a uni-dimensional measurement model, the MIMbuild module uses vanishing tetrad constraints to search the space of structural models, i.e., RSEM models containing only the latent variables.

5.2.1 Purify

We make our explanation of both Purify and MIMbuild concrete by accompanying it with an example taken from the user's manual to Tetrad II (Scheines et al. 1994, chapter 9). The example shows how Purify can aid in finding a unidimensional measurement model and why it is important to do so. The population RSEM is shown in figure 15. Our data for the example consist of the correlations among the X variables in a pseudorandom multi-variate normal sample drawn from a random parameterization of this RSEM ($N = 2,000$).

Suppose our interest is in the causal relationships between the three latent variables T_1, T_2, and T_3. The part of the RSEM specifying the relationships between the latent variables is called the structural model; the rest is called the measurement model. In this case the population structural model is shown in figure 16, and the population measurement model is shown in figure 17.

One approach to this problem is to use background knowledge to build a measurement model for each latent variable and then perform a specification search for the structural model constrained by background knowledge and aided by a computer, e.g., the Search module of Tetrad II, or the modification indices of LISREL, or the Lagrange multiplier statistic of EQS. There are several problems with this approach. First, while background knowledge may

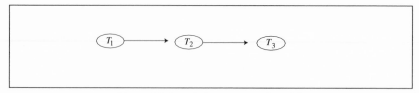

Figure 16. Population structural model.

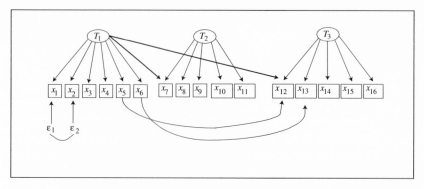

Figure 17. Population measurement model.

often be sufficient to construct part of the population measurement model (i.e., we may know which of the latent variables each indicator variable is a measure of), background knowledge is seldom detailed enough to completely specify the full population measurement model (e.g., an indicator may be a measure of several latent variables, or indicator variables may have correlated errors). This means that the specification search must also seek to correct the hypothesized measurement model, as well as discover the structural model. Because there are often a large number of indicator variables, this search space is astronomically large. Moreover, a search that at each step chooses to add the edge (free the parameter) that will most improve the fit can easily go wrong for several reasons. First, it may be that freeing a number of different parameters improves the fit to the same degree, so there is no way to choose which parameter to free at that point in the search. In addition, there may be pairs of parameters which if freed will greatly improve the overall fit, even though freeing either parameter by itself does not improve the fit much. Also, when the initial RSEM to be modified is far from the population RSEM, the parameter estimates may be far from their population values, which can affect the estimates of the Lagrange multipliers, or may prevent the estimation algorithms from converging at all.

The Purify module represents a different approach to the problem that is a provably correct[12] algorithm for finding unidimensional measurement models (Scheines 1993). Instead of searching for parameters to free, i.e., edges to

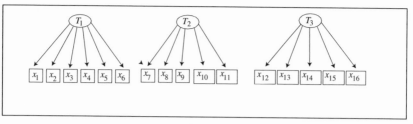

Figure 18. Hypothesized measurement model.

add, Purify searches for a submodel of the originally specified measurement model that contains a subset of the indicators originally specified, but that is correctly specified as unidimensional. Such a submodel can be used to find consistent estimates of the correlations between the latent variables and thus aid in the search for structural models.[13]

For example, the measurement model in figure 17 is not unidimensional because of the edges and correlated errors that are in boldface. But note that the population model does contain a unidimensional submodel, shown in figure 19, which is obtained by simply removing X_1, X_7, X_{12}, and X_{13} from the model.

Purify searches for unidimensional submodels in the following way. First we suppose that we are given as input a hypothetical measurement model which is unidimensional, for example, the measurement model shown in figure 18. We assume the input measurement model is a submodel of the population measurement model, that is, every edge specified in the input measurement model exists in the population measurement model. However, we do not assume that the input measurement model is complete; the population measurement model may be nonunidimensional because a single indicator may be caused by multiple latents, cause other indicators, or have correlated errors with other variables.

Given this input, if the population measurement model is unidimensional, it entails a characteristic set of vanishing tetrad differences, *regardless of the population structural model* (Scheines 1993). For example, if the population measurement model is unidimensional, and X_1, X_2, and X_3 measure a single latent, then $\rho_{X1,X2} \rho_{X3,X4} - \rho_{X1,X3} \rho_{X2,X4}$ is entailed to be zero regardless of the population structural model. This means that Purify can test whether the specified measurement model is truly unidimensional without knowing the structural model. If the characteristic set of vanishing tetrad differences entailed by a unidimensional measurement model is judged to hold in the population, Purify concludes that the measurement model specified is truly unidimensional and halts. If the population measurement model is the one in figure 17, some of the tetrad differences entailed by the initially specified model in figure 18, e.g., $\rho_{X1,X2} \rho_{X3,X4} - \rho_{X1,X3} \rho_{X2,X4}$, are not entailed to vanish, and with a representative sample Purify will conclude that the population measurement model

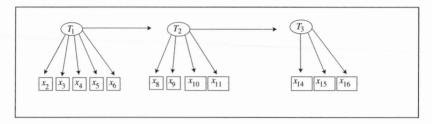

Figure 19. Model with correctly specified unidimensional measurement model.

among the given set of indicator variables is not unidimensional. Purify then begins to search for a submodel that is unidimensional by sequentially eliminating indicators. In general, searching all subsets of the given measured indicators for a set of indicators that form a unidimensional measurement model would take too long, due to the enormous number of subsets. But by examining *which* vanishing tetrad differences do not hold in the population, the algorithm can greatly narrow the search, making it feasible to handle initially specified measurement models with more than 50 measured variables in minutes. In this case on simulated data it correctly removes X_1, X_7, X_{12}, and X_{13} from the measurement model, leaving a set of indicators that have a measurement model correctly specified as unidimensional.

5.2.2 MIMbuild

In many studies the theoretical question addressed cannot be reduced to the significance of a single parameter in an otherwise reliably specified model. There might be many latent variables, and the problem of finding a reasonable structural model is then difficult. With just four latent variables there are well over 700 structural models with no correlated errors. Even with substantial background knowledge, this is a large space to search. With eight latent variables the space is astronomical. Several strategies for automatic structural model search are possible. One might begin with a null structural model and do a Lagrange multiplier search limited to structural parameters. To the best of our knowledge no one has studied the behavior of this strategy. One might estimate the correlations among the latent variables and then apply Build to the latents as if they were measured. In our experience, this works well in simulation studies at moderate to large sample sizes, but we do not know how to properly adjust the sample size when testing for vanishing partial correlations among latents that are being treated "as if" they are measured. A third alternative takes further advantage of the vanishing tetrad difference constraint.

We have already seen that if the population measurement model is unidimensional, a SEM entails a characteristic set of vanishing tetrad differences, regardless of what the population structural model may be. But if the measurement model is unidimensional, there are other tetrad differences which are entailed to vanish for some structural models, but are not entailed to vanish for other structural models. These constraints are extremely easy to compute and test, and the tests are not susceptible to specification error in other parts of the structural model (Scheines 1993). For example, in the model in figure 19 (where the population measurement model is unidimensional), all three tetrad constraints involving one indicator from T_1, two from T_2, and one from T_3 are entailed by the model if and only if there is no edge between T_1 and T_3. The MIMbuild algorithm uses tests of vanishing tetrad differences to construct a set of structural models that entail vanishing partial correlations among latent variables judged to hold in the population.

The set of structural models that MIMbuild outputs entail the same set of unconditional correlations and partial correlations with only one variable in the conditioning set. Because it can output models which are not fully partial correlation equivalent or covariance equivalent, MIMbuild represents only a partial solution to the RSEM structural model specification problem. A "?" is attached to those parts of MIMbuild's output that might change if second order or higher partial correlations among latent variables could be tested.

6. Applications

In this section we will illustrate the application of the search procedures to three data sets, two published and one simulated. In the case of the empirical examples we do not mean to endorse the assumptions made by the researchers who used the data sets, or the scales they constructed. In the first case our intent is to show how the search procedures implemented in Tetrad II can be used to find plausible alternatives to a published model. The existence of these alternatives weakens the evidential support for conclusions published, but it is not our intent to claim that the alternatives found by Tetrad II are correct. In the second case we ran the Purify and Search procedures on a published data set with the same results as those published, and in the third case we show how the procedures perform on a very large search space. Other applications can be found in Scheines et al. (1994), and in Spirtes, Glymour, and Scheines (1993), and in later chapters in this book.

6.1 Finding Alternative Models

Before giving a proposed hypothesis any great credence, good scientific practice ought to try to articulate and investigate every serious alternative. A frequent objection to causal models in any discipline is that they are arbitrarily selected without any sound arguments that would exclude alternative explanations of data. That some cherished causal model cannot be rejected statistically is little reason to believe its causal claims: There might be alternatives that also cannot be rejected statistically, but that make contrary causal claims. Published studies may be defective in their general distributional assumptions, in their data collection procedures, or in their assumptions about what is influencing what. Here is an illustration of how Tetrad II is meant to be used to help search for and articulate alternative causal explanations under varying background assumptions. In a study published in the *American Sociological Review*, Timberlake and Williams (1984) claimed that foreign investment in third world or "peripheral" nations causes the exclusion of various groups from the political process. In other words, foreign investment inhibits democracy. Their empirical case for this claim rests on fitting a linear regression. They develop measures of political exclusion (PO), foreign investment penetration (FI), economic development (EN), and civil liberties (CV) (measured on an ordered scale from 1 to 7, with lower values indicating *greater* civil liberties.) We show the correlations given by Timberlake and Williams for these variables on 72 "noncore" countries in table 1.

An apparent embarrassment to their claim is that political exclusion is negatively correlated with foreign investment; further, foreign investment is negatively correlated with the civil liberties scale (and hence because of their reverse ordering of the civil liberties scale, *positively* correlated with civil liberties). To defeat this objection, Timberlake and Williams regress PO on the other variables on the assumption that the coefficient relating FI to PO is a measure of FI's causal influence on PO that is superior to their simple correlation. A regression on the correlations above yields the following:

$$PO = .227*FI - .176*EN + .880*CV + \varepsilon$$
$$(.058) \qquad (.059) \qquad (.060)$$
$$3.941 \qquad -2.985 \qquad 14.604$$

You can see that the crucial coefficient is positive and highly significant. Timberlake and Williams took this as evidence to support the claim that foreign investment causes more political exclusion. They do not explicitly consider any alternative models.

However, a regression model is only one among many that might describe the relations among these four variables. To search for alternatives, we again use Tetrad II's Build module, again without considering whether the linearity and normality assumptions are warranted.[14] Without assuming that all common causes are included in the variables measured, and using a significance level (α) of .05 for its statistical hypothesis tests, Build's output is the PAG in figure 20.

Because this structure entails that foreign investment (FI) and political exclusion (PO) are uncorrelated, we increase α to .15, at which point Build produces the PAG in figure 21.

Because all of the connections in the PAG involving FI have arrowheads

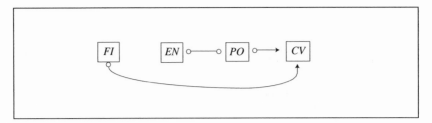

Figure 20. Build output at $\alpha = .05$.

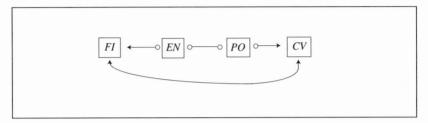

Figure 21. Build output at $\alpha = .15$.

directed into FI, these data indicate that foreign investment is not a cause of any of the other variables. A large number of causal models are members of the equivalence class represented by the output in figure 21. The model in figure 22 is one of the simplest in this class, and is plausible besides.

This model asserts that EN (a measure of economic development) causes both the level of foreign investment and the level of political exclusion. Political exclusion causes the lack of civil liberties, and there is some unmeasured common cause connecting foreign investment and civil liberties (or in other terms, that their errors are correlated). Estimating this model with EQS yields a $\chi^2 = .136$ with two degrees of freedom, with $p(\chi^2) = .934$. We give the coefficients with their standard errors and t-statistics in figure 23.

The signs of the coefficients suggest that the relation between FI and PO is negative and mediated by a common cause, contrary in two ways to Timberlake and Williams' hypothesis. We do not mean to suggest that this analysis shows our alternative to be correct. At this small a sample size statistical tests have little power against alternatives, so it is difficult to statistically distinguish between two models even when they are not statistically equivalent. Our point is to show how the Build module can be used to search for plausible alternatives to a given model.

6.2 Specifying Measurement Models of Political Democracy

Bollen (1980) studied whether a number of measures of political democracy

PO	FI	EN	CV
1.000			
-0.175	1.000		
-0.480	0.330	1.000	
0.868	-0.391	-0.430	1.000

Table 1. Political repression data (n = 72).

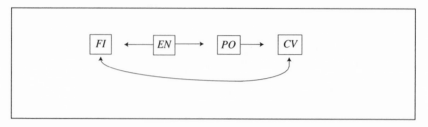

Figure 22. An alternative to Timberlake and William's model.

were unidimensional indicators of a common feature of societies. Bollen used the following measures:

PF   press freedom
FG   freedom of group opposition
GS   government sanctions
FE   fairness of elections
ES   executive selection
LS   legislature selection

He considered the unidimensional factor model specified in figure 24, where it is understood that for each of the measured variables there is an error term.

Bollen estimated this model with LISREL and found that the data reject it.[15] Instead of attempting to locate and discard the impure indicators, Bollen elaborated his original model by correlating error terms (figure 25). When estimated with EQS, this model has a χ^2 of 6.009 based on six degrees of freedom, with $p(\chi^2) = 0.42218$. The search module of Tetrad II, which uses vanishing tetrad differences to search for elaborations of an initial model, arrives at a set of factor models which contains Bollen's model and others.

Although Bollen's final measurement model of democracy fits the data well, it is not unidimensional. To find a unidimensional submodel, we can run Purify on Bollen's original model (figure 24) and data. Giving the initial model and the measured covariances to Purify, FG and LS are identified as

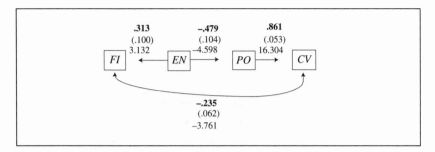

Figure 23. Estimated alternative model.

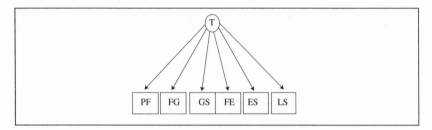

Figure 24. Initial measurement model of political democracy.

impure indicators and discarded, resulting in the measurement model we picture in figure 26.

Estimating the resulting unidimensional measurement model (figure 26) with EQS yields a $\chi^2 = 1.687$ based on two degrees of freedom, with $p(\chi^2) = 0.43013$.

6.3. A Large Search Space: The Alarm Network

By interviewing several medical experts, Beinlich et al. (1990) developed a large causal model of the probabilistic relations in emergency medicine (figure 27).[16] Using the directed graph associated with this model (figure 27), called the ALARM network, linear coefficients with values between .1 and .9 were randomly assigned to each directed edge in the graph. Using a standard joint normal distribution (mean 0, variance 1) on the exogenous variables, three sets of simulated data were generated, each with a sample size of 2,000. The covariance matrix and sample size were given to the Tetrad II program. No information about the orientation of the variables was given to the program. With thirty-seven variables, the space of possible models is astronomical,[17] yet the program almost instantly returns a pattern on a modern PC. In each trial the output pattern omitted two edges in the ALARM network; in one of the cases it also added one edge that was not present in the ALARM network.

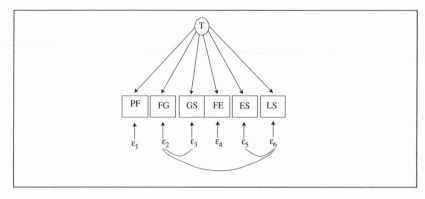

Figure 25. Bollen's respecification of the measurement model.

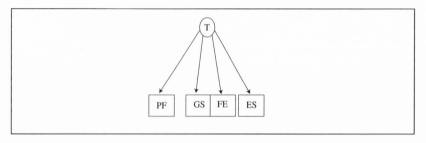

Figure 26. Submodel found by purify.

7. Conclusion

The work we have described is based on assumptions that are implicit, and sometimes explicit, throughout scientific practice. The causal independence assumption, for example, posits a relation between the absence of causal connection and statistical independence that is fundamental to experimental design; the faithfulness assumption states a preference for explanation by structure over explanation by coincidence that, in various forms, is used in every science. Consequences of these assumptions were worked out for special cases by many social scientists such as Simon (1954), Blalock (1962) and Costner (1971).

The methods we have described are incomplete, and there is a great deal of research that remains to be done and that should lead to improved modeling. Important outstanding problems include improving the reliability of model search through better statistical and algorithmic procedures, deriving computationally tractable algorithms for testing covariance equivalence of linear, latent variable models, finding correct methods for clustering measured variables that share a latent common cause, completing and imple-

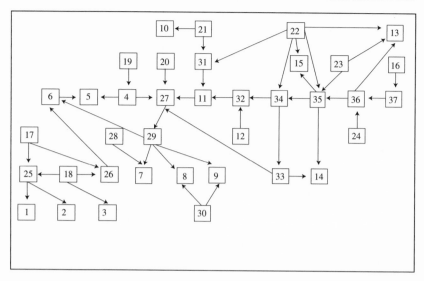

Figure 27. The ALARM network.

menting known algorithms for predicting the outcomes of interventions from partial causal and distributional specifications, implementing searches for nonrecursive models, and much more.

Notes

1. We realize that it is slightly unconventional to write the trivial equation for the exogenous variable X_1 in terms of its error, but this serves to give the error terms a unified and special status as providing all the exogenous source of stochastic variation for the system.

2. We do not consider SEMs with other sorts of constraints on the parameters, e.g., equality constraints.

3. In some cases the input to the PC algorithm is not consistent with the assumptions made. In these cases it is possible that the output of the PC algorithm is not strictly a pattern.

4. The PC algorithm performs a series of statistical tests of zero partial correlations; the asymptotic results assume that we systematically lower the significance level as the sample size increases, in order to decrease the probabilities of both type I and type II errors to zero.

5. Some of this literature is published in the annual proceedings of the conferences on Uncertainty in Artificial Intelligence, Knowledge Discovery in Data Bases, and the bi-annual conference on Artificial Intelligence and Statistics. Examples of important papers in this tradition include those by Buntine (1991); Cooper and Herskovits (1992); Geiger (1990); Geiger and Heckerman (1991, 1994); Geiger, Verma, and Pearl (1990); Hand (1993); Lauritzen et al. (1990); Lauritzen and Wermuth (1984);

Pearl (1988); Pearl and Dechter (1989); Pearl and Verma (1991); Robins (1986); and Spiegelhalter (1986).

6. For example, the Bayesian Information Criterion (Raftery 1993), or the posterior probability, (Geiger and Heckerman 1994).

7. Correlations and partial correlations are zero exactly when the corresponding covariances and partial covariances are zero. While there may be important different statistical properties of partial correlations and partial covariances, they are not germane to the discussion of the constraints entailed by a SEM.

8. One issue that would be interesting to investigate is how to characterize the sorts of priors over models that make the use of the faithfulness assumption in finite samples a reasonable approximation to Bayesian inference.

9. The Build module is documented in Scheines et al. (1994) and its algorithms described in detail in Spirtes, Glymour, and Scheines (1993).

10. See Scheines, et al. (1994) for an example in which the equivalence class is larger.

11. In fact the output is described in Spirtes, Glymour, and Scheines (1993) and Scheines et al. (1994) as a POIPG, or partially oriented inducing path graph. POIPGs can, without loss of generality, be interpreted much more naturally as PAGs. In cases where the input is not consistent with the assumptions made, the output may not be a POIPG.

12. Purify is a correct search procedure in the following sense: Given that there are correctly specified unidimensional submodels of the initially specified measurement model with at least three indicators for each latent, then as the sample grows without bound and the significance level is adjusted properly, the probability that Purify will find one of the unidimensional submodels converges to one.

13. This two–stage search process was also suggested by Anderson and Gerbing (1988).

14. Because our aim is to illustrate the use of Tetrad II in finding alterantives to a given model, the correctness of the distribution and linearity assumptions made by Timberlake and Williams is not at issue. We note, however, that we were unable to reproduce their correlation matrix from the sources they cite.

15. EQS yields a $\chi^2 = 42.076$ based on 9 degrees of freedom, with $p(\chi^2) < 0.001$.

16. Beinlich's network was over discrete variables, and we have run Build on a discrete version of this network with results similar to those we report here for a SEM interpretation of the structure. For the labeling in this graph see Spirtes, Glymour, and Scheines (1993).

17. With 37 variables there are 666 pairs of variables. Assuming that each pair $<X,Y>$ has either (1) no edge between therm, or (2) an edge from X to Y, or (3) an edge from Y to X, the number of possible models is 3^{666}. The actual number to search is smaller, because some of these models will contain cycles, but the space remaining is still far too big to search by evaluating each member.

References

Anderson, J., and Gerbing, D. 1988. Structural Equation Modeling in Practice: A Review and Recommended Two-Step Approach. *Psychological Bulletin* 103(3): 411–423.

Anderson, J.; Gerbing, D.; and Hunter, J. 1987. On the Assessment of Unidimensional Measurement: Internal and External Consistency and Overall Consistency Criteria. *Journal of Marketing Research* 24:432–437.

Becker, P.; Merckens, A.; and Wansbeek, T. 1994. *Identification, Equivalent Models, and Computer Algebra*. San Diego, Calif.: Academic.

Beinlich, I.; Suermondt, H.; Chavez, R.; and Cooper, G. 1990. The ALARM Monitoring System: A Case Study with Two Probabilistic Inference Techniques for Belief Networks. In *Proceedings of the Second European Conference on Artificial Intelligence in Medicine,* 247–256. London: Chapman and Hall.

Bentler, P. 1995. EQS: *Structural Equations Program Manual*. Encino, Calif.: Multivariate Software, Inc.

Bentler, P. 1986. Lagrange Multiplier and Wald Tests for EQS and EQS/PC. BMDP Statistical Software, Los Angeles, California.

Blalock, H., ed. 1985. *Causal Models in Panel and Experimental Designs*. New York: Aldine Publishing Company.

Blalock, H. 1962. Four-Variable Causal Models and Partial Correlations. *American Journal of Sociology* 68(2): 182–194.

Bollen, K. 1990. Outlier Screening and a Distribution-Free Test for Vanishing Tetrads. *Sociological Methods and Research* 19(1):80–92.

Bollen, K. 1989. *Structural Equations with Latent Variables*. New York: Wiley.

Bollen, K. 1980. Issues in the Comparative Measurement of Political Democracy. *American Sociological Review* 45(3): 370–390.

Bollen, K., and Long, J. 1993. *Testing Structural Equation Models*. Newbury Park, Calif.: Sage.

Bollen, K., and Ting, K. 1993. Confirmatory Tetrad Analysis. In *Sociological Methodology, 23,* 147–175. Oxford: Blackwell.

Boomsma, A. 1982. The Robustness of LISREL against Small Sample Sizes in Factor Analysis Models. In *Systems under Indirect Observation: Causality, Structure, Prediction, Part I*, eds. K. G. Joreskog and H. Wold, 149–173. Amsterdam, The Netherlands: North Holland.

Buntine, W. 1991. Theory Refinement on Bayesian Networks. Paper Presented at the AAAI-91 Knowledge Discovery in Data Bases Workshop, Anaheim, Calif., July.

Bye, B.; Gallicchio, S.; and Dykacz, J. 1985. Multiple-Indicator, Multiple-Cause Models for a Single Latent Variable with Ordinal Indicators. *Sociological Methods and Research* 13(4): 487–509.

Callahan, J., and Sorensen, S. 1992. Using Tetrad II as an Automated Exploratory Tool. *Social Science Computer Review* 10(3): 329–336.

Cheeseman, P., and Oldford, R. 1994. *Selecting Models from Data.*

Lecture Notes in Statistics 89. New York: Springer-Verlag.

Cooper, G., and Herskovits, E. 1992. A Bayesian Method for the Induction of Probabilistic Networks from Data. *Machine Learning* 9:308–347.

Cooper, G.; Aliferis, C.; Ambrosino, R.; Aronis, J.; Buchanan, B.; Caruana, R.; Fine, M.; Glymour, C.; Gordon, G.; Hanusa, B.; Janosky, J.; Meek, C.; Mitchell, T.; Richardson, T.; and Spirtes, P. 1995. An Evaluation of Machine-Learning Methods for Predicting Pneumonia Mortality. Technical Report, CMU-PHIL-66, Dept. of Philosophy, Carnegie Mellon University.

Costner, H. 1971. Theory, Deduction and Rules of Correspondence. In *Causal Models in the Social Sciences*, ed. H. Blalock, 299–319. Chicago: Aldine Publishing Company.

Druzdzel, M., and Glymour, C. 1994. Application of the Tetrad II Program to the Study of Student Retention in U.S. Colleges. In Knowledge Discovery in Databases, ed. U. Fayyad and R. Uthurusamy. Tech Rep. WS-94-03, American Association for Artificial Intelligence, Menlo Park, Calif.

Frydenberg, M. 1990. The Chain Graph Markov Property. *Scandinavian Journal of Statistics* 17(4): 333–353.

Geiger, D. 1990. Graphoids: A Qualitative Framework for Probabilistic Inference. Ph.D. dissertation, Dept. of Computer Science, University of California, Los Angeles, Calif.

Geiger, D., and Heckerman, D. 1994. Learning Gaussian Networks. Technical Report, MSR-TR-94-10, Microsoft Corp., Redmond, Wash.

Geiger, D., and Heckerman, D. 1991. Advances in Probabilistic Reasoning. In *Proceedings of the Seventh Conference on Uncertainty in AI*, ed. B. D'Ambrosio. San Francisco, Calif.: Morgan Kaufmann.

Geiger, D.; Verma, T.; and Pearl, J. 1990. Identifying Independence in Bayesian Networks. *Networks* 20:507–533.

Glymour, C.; Scheines, R.; Spirtes, P.; and Kelly, K. 1987. *Discovering Causal Structure*. San Diego, Calif.: Academic.

Goldberger, A., and Duncan, O., eds. 1973. *Structural Equation Models in the Social Sciences*. New York: Seminar.

Hand, D. 1993. *Artificial Intelligence Frontiers in Statistics: AI and Statistics III*. New York: Chapman and Hall.

Hausman, D. 1984. Causal Priority. *Nous* 18:261–279.

James, L.; Mulaik, S.; and Brett, J. 1982. *Causal Analysis: Assumptions, Models, and Data*. Beverly Hills, Calif.: Sage.

Jöreskog, K., and Sörbom, J. 1993. *LISREL 8: User's Reference Guide*. Hillsdale, N.J.: Lawrence Erlbaum.

Kaplan, D. 1990. Evaluating and Modifying Covariance Structure Models: A Review and Recommendation. *Multivariate Behavioral Research* 25(2): 137–155.

Kaplan, D. 1989. Model Modification in Covariance Structure Analysis: Application of the Expected Parameter Change Statistic. *Multivariate Behavioral Research* 24(3): 285–305.

Kaplan, D. 1988. The Impact of Specification Error on the Estimation, Testing, and Improvement of Structural Equation Models. *Multivariate Behavioral Research* 23(1): 69–86.

Kiiveri, H., and Speed, T. 1982. Structural Analysis of Multivariate Data: A Review. In *Sociological Methodology*, ed. S. Leinhardt, 209–289. San Francisco, Calif.: Jossey-Bass.

Koster, J. T. A. 1994. Markov Properties of Non-Recursive Causal Models. *Annals of Statistics* 24(5): 2148–2177.

Lauritzen, S., and Wermuth, N. 1984. Graphical Models for Associations between

Variables, Some of Which Are Qualitative and Some Quantitative. *Annals of Statistics* 17(1): 31–57.

Lauritzen, S.; Dawid, P.; Larsen, B.; and Leimer, H. 1990. Independence Properties of Directed Markov Fields. *Networks* 20(5): 491–505.

Lawley, D., and Maxwell, A. 1971. *Factor Analysis as a Statistical Method*. London: Butterworth.

Lee, S. 1987. *Model Equivalence in Covariance Structure Modeling*. Ph.D. diss., Department of Psychology, Ohio State University.

Luijben, T.; Boomsma, A.; and Molenaar, I. 1986. Modification of Factor Analysis Models in Covariance Structure Analysis. A Monte Carlo study. In *On Model Uncertainty and Its Statistical Implications, ed.* T. Dijkstra, 70–101. *Lecture Notes in Economics and Mathematical Systems 307*. Berlin: Springer-Verlag.

MacCallum, R. 1986. Specification Searches in Covariance Structure Modeling. *Psychological Bulletin* 100(1): 107–120.

Meek, C. 1995. Causal Inference and Causal Explanation with Background Knowledge. In *Proceedings of the Eleventh Conference on Uncertainty in Artificial Intelligence*, eds. P. Besnard and S. Hanks, 403–410. San Francisco, Calif.: Morgan Kaufmann.

Pearl, J. 1995. Causal Diagrams for Empirical Research. *Biometrika* 82(4): 669–709.

Pearl, J. 1988. *Probabilistic Reasoning in Intelligent Systems*. San Francisco, Calif.: Morgan Kaufmann.

Pearl, J., and Dechter, R. 1989. Learning Structure from Data: A Survey. Paper presented at the Second Annual Workshop on Computational Learning Theory (COLT '89), University of Calif., Santa Cruz, Calif., 31 July–2 Aug.

Pearl, J., and Verma, T. 1991. A Theory of Inferred Causation. In *Principles of Knowledge Representation and Reasoning: Proceedings of the Second International Conference,* 441–452. San Francisco, Calif.: Morgan Kaufmann.

Raftery, A. E. 1993. Bayesian Model Selection in Structural Equation Models. In *Testing Structural Equation Models,* eds. K. A. Bollen and J. S. Long, 163–180. Newbury Park, Calif.: Sage.

Richardson, T. 1996. Discovering Cyclic Causal Structure. Technical Report, CMU-PHIL-68, Department of Philosophy, Carnegie Mellon University.

Richardson, T. 1995. A Polynomial-Time Algorithm for Deciding Markov Equivalence of Directed Cyclic Graphical Models. Technical Report, CMU-PHIL-63, Department of Philosophy, Carnegie Mellon University.

Richardson, T. 1994. *Properties of Cyclic Graphical Models*. Master's thesis, Department of Philosophy, Carnegie Mellon University.

Robins, J. 1986. A New Approach to Causal Inference in Mortality Studies with Sustained Exposure Periods—Application to Control of the Healthy Worker Survivor Effect. *Mathematical Modeling* 7: 1393–1512.

Saris, W.; Satorra, A.; and Sorbom, D. 1987. The Detection and Correction of Specification Errors in Structural Equation Models. In *Sociological Methodology,* ed. C. Clogg, 105–129. San Francisco, Calif.: Jossey-Bass.

Scheines, R. 1994. Inferring Causal Structure among Unmeasured Variables. In *Selecting Models from Data: AI and Statistics IV,* eds. P. Chessman and R. W. Oldford, 197–204. New York: Springer-Verlag.

Scheines, R. 1993. Unidimensional Linear Latent Variable Models. Technical Report, CMU-PHIL-39, Dept. of Philosophy, Carnegie Mellon University, Pittsburgh, Penn.

Scheines, R.; Hoijtink, H.; and Boomsma, A. 1995. Bayesian Estimation and Testing of Structural Equation Models. Technical Report, CMU-PHIL-66, Department of Philosophy, Carnegie Mellon University.

Scheines, R.; Spirtes, P.; Glymour, C.; and Meek, C. 1994. *TETRAD II: User's Manual.* Hillsdale, N.J.: Lawrence Erlbaum.

Shafer, G.; Kogan, A.; and Spirtes, P. 1993. Generalization of the Tetrad Representation Theorem. GSM Working Paper, 93-36, Graduate School of Management, Rutgers University.

Shipley, B. 1997. A Quantitative Interspecific Model of Functional Coordination Involving Foliar Nitrogen, Stomatal Regulation, and Photosynthetic Capacity in a Wetland Flora. *American Naturalist* 149(6)(June): 1113–1138.

Shipley, B. 1995. Structured Interspecific Determinants of Specific Leaf Area in 34 Species of Hebaceous Angiosperms. *Functional Econology* 9(1): 312–319.

Simon, H. 1954. Spurious Correlation: A Causal Interpretation. *Journal of the American Statistical Association* 49:467–479.

Simon, H. 1953. Causal Ordering and Identifiability. In *Studies in Econometric Methods*, eds. W. Hood and T. Koopmans, 49–74. New York: Wiley.

Sörbom, D. 1989. Model Modification. *Psychometrika* 54:371–384.

Spearman, C. 1904. General Intelligence Objectively Determined and Measured. *American Journal of Psychology* 15:201–293.

Spiegelhalter, D. 1986. Probabilistic Reasoning in Predictive Expert Systems. In *Uncertainty in Artificial Intelligence*, eds. K. Kanal and J. Lemmer. Amsterdam, The Netherlands: North-Holland.

Spirtes, P. 1995. Directed Cyclic Graphical Representation of Feedback Models. In *Proceedings of the Eleventh Conference on Uncertainty in Artificial Intelligence*, eds. P. Besnard and S. Hanks, 491–498. San Francisco, Calif.: Morgan Kaufmann.

Spirtes, P. 1994a. Conditional Independence in Directed Cyclic Graphical Models for Feedback. Technical Report, CMU-PHIL-54, Department of Philosophy, Carnegie Mellon University.

Spirtes, P. 1994b. Discovering Causal Relations among Latent Variables in Recursive Structural Equation Models. Technical Report, CMU-PHIL-69, Department of Philosophy, Carnegie Mellon University.

Spirtes, P. 1989. A Necessary and Sufficient Condition for Conditional Independencies to Imply a Vanishing Tetrad Difference. Technical Report, CMU-LCL-89-3, Laboratory for Computational Linguistics, Carnegie Mellon University.

Spirtes, P., and Meek, C. 1995. Learning Bayesian Networks with Discrete Variables from Data. In *Proceedings of the First International Conference on Knowledge Discovery and Data Mining*, eds. U. M. Fayyad and R. Uthurusamy, 294–299. Menlo Park, Calif.: AAAI Press.

Spirtes, P.; Glymour, C.; and Scheines, R. 1993. *Causation, Prediction, and Search.* Lecture Notes in Statistics 81. New York: Springer-Verlag.

Spirtes, P.; Meek, C.; and Richardson, T. 1995. Causal Inference in the Presence of Latent Variables and Selection Bias. In *Proceedings of the Eleventh Conference on Uncertainty in Artificial Intelligence*, eds. P. Besnard and S. Hanks, 499–506. San

Francisco, Calif.: Morgan Kaufmann.

Spirtes, P.; Richardson, T.; and Meek, C. 1997. The Dimensionality of Mixed Ancestral Graphs. Technical Report, CMU-83-Phil, Department of Philosophy, Carnegie Mellon University, Pittsburgh, Penn.

Spirtes, P.; Scheines, R.; and Glymour, C. 1990. Simulation Studies of the Reliability of Computer Aided Specification Using the Tetrad II, EQS, and LISREL Programs. *Sociological Methods and Research* 19(1): 3–66.

Spirtes, P.; Richardson, T.; Meek, C.; Scheines, R.; and Glymour, C. 1996. Using d-Separation to Calculate Zero Partial Correlations in Linear Models with Correlated Errors. Technical Report, CMU-PHIL-72, Department of Philosophy, Carnegie Mellon University, Pittsburgh, Penn.

Strotz, R., and Wold, H. 1960. Recursive versus Nonrecursive Systems: An Attempt at Synthesis. *Econometrica* 28(2): 417–427.

Sullivan, J., and Ferldman, S. 1979. *Multiple Indicators: An Introduction*. Beverly Hills, Calif.: Sage.

Tanner, M. A. 1993. *Tools for Statistical Inference: Methods for the Exploration of Posterior Distributions and Likelihood Functions*. 2d ed. New York: Springer-Verlag.

Timberlake, M., and Williams, K. 1984. Dependence, Political Exclusion, and Government Repression: Some Cross-National Evidence. *American Sociological Review* 49(1): 141–146.

Verma, T., and Pearl, J. 1990. Equivalence and Synthesis of Causal Models. In Proceedings of the Sixth Conference on Uncertainty in AI, 220–227. Mountain View, Calif.: Association for Uncertainty in AI.

Waldemark, J., and Norqvist, P. 1995. In-Flight Calibration of Satellite Ion Composition Data Using Artificial Intelligence Methods. Unpublished manuscript, Department of Applied Physics and Electronics, Umea University.

Weisberg, S. 1985. *Applied Linear Regression*. 2d. ed. New York: Wiley.

Wheaton, B.; Muthen, B.; Alwin, D.; and Summers, G. 1977. Assessing Reliability and Stability in Panel Models. *Sociological Methodology 1977*, ed. D. Heise. San Francisco, Calif.: Jossey-Bass.

Wright, S. 1934. The Method of Path Coefficients. *Annals of Mathematics and Statistics* 5(1): 161–215.

CHAPTER SIX

An Algorithm for Causal Inference in the Presence of Latent Variables and Selection Bias

Peter Spirtes, Christopher Meek, and Thomas Richardson

1. Introduction

Whenever the use of nonexperimental data for discovering causal relations or predicting the outcomes of experiments or interventions is contemplated, two difficulties are routinely faced. One is the problem of latent variables, or confounders: factors influencing two or more measured variables may not themselves have been measured or recorded. The other is the problem of sample selection bias: values of the variables or features under study may themselves influence whether a unit is included in the data sample.

Latent variables produce an association between measured variables that is not due to the influence of any measured variable on any other. It is well known that where unrecognized latent common causes occur, regression methods, for example, no matter whether linear or nonlinear, give incorrect estimates of influence. When two or more variables under study both influence membership in a sample or inclusion in a database, an association between the variables occurs in the sample that is not due to any influence of a measured variable on other measured variables, nor to an unmeasured common cause.

Difficult as these problems are separately, they can both occur in the same sample or database, as in the following example. Suppose a survey of college students is done to determine whether there is a link between *intelligence* and *sex drive*. Let *student status* be a binary variable that takes on the value 1 when someone is a college student. Suppose *age* causes *sex drive*, and *age* and *intelligence* also causes *student status*. Hence whether or not one is in the sample is influenced by the two variables in the study, and there may be a statistical dependency between *intelligence* and *sex drive* in the sample even when no such dependency exists in the population. (This example will be discussed in more detail in section 2. Here *age* is obviously a proxy for a combination of physical and mental states associated with age.) The combination of a latent variable (*age*) and a selection variable (*student status*) would produce a dependency which (naively interpreted) would make it appear as if there is a causal connection of some kind between *intelligence* and *sex drive*, even though none exists.

A reasonable attitude toward most uncontrolled convenience samples (and a lot of "experimental" samples as well) is that they may be liable to both difficulties. For that reason many statistical writers have implicitly or explicitly concluded that reliable causal and predictive inference is impossible in such cases, no matter whether by human or by machine. We think it is more fruitful to consider whether, under conditions only slightly stronger than those used for causal inference from experimentally controlled data, causal inferences can sometimes reliably be made. This chapter uses Bayesian network models for that investigation. Bayesian networks, or directed acyclic graph (DAG) models have proved very useful in representing both causal and statistical hypotheses. The nodes of the graph represent vertices, directed edges represent direct influences, and the topology of the graph encodes statistical constraints. We will consider features of such models that can be determined from data under assumptions that are related to those routinely applied in experimental situations as follows.

First is the Markov condition for DAGs interpreted as causal hypotheses. An instance of the causal Markov assumption is the foundation of the theory of randomized experiments. It is also the foundation for the practice of constructing Bayesian networks to be used for diagnosis or classification by eliciting *causal* relations from experts.

Second is an assumption that the population selected by sampling criteria has the same causal structure (although because of sample selection bias not necessarily the same statistical properties) as the population about which causal inferences are to be made. This assumption, which we call the population inference assumption is of course essential whenever experimental results on a sample are used to guide policy on a larger population.

Third is a version of the causal faithfulness assumption, which says essentially that observed independence and conditional independence relations are due to the topology of the causal graph rather than to special parameter values. The assumption is used, implicitly or in other terms through the behavioral sciences, for example in econometrics to test "exogeneity". See Epstein (1987).

To deal with the problems raised by latent variables and selection bias, we will use *partial ancestor graphs* (or PAGs) to represent a class of DAGs. For a DAG *G* which may have both latent and selection variables, the PAG that represents *G* contains information about both the conditional independencies entailed by *G*, and partial information about the ancestor relations in *G*. We will briefly describe how PAGs can be used to search for latent variable DAG models, to perform efficient classifications, and to predict the effects of interventions in causal systems. There are several advantages of the PAGs representation. First, the space of PAGs is smaller than the space of DAGs they represent, making search over PAGs more feasible than a search over DAGs. For a given set of measured variables, the set of PAGs is finite, whereas the set of DAGs that contain the measured variables but may also contain latent variables is infinite. Second, in some cases where large sample (or even population) data would not discriminate between different DAGs, the same data would select a single PAG, which could be used to answer some (but not all) questions about the effects of intervening upon an existing causal structure. Third, quite apart from any causal interpretation of PAGs, in some cases there is a PAG that is a more parsimonious representation of a distribution than any DAG containing the same variables. Hence a PAG may be used to obtain unbiased estimates of population parameters that have lower variance than estimates obtained from any DAG without latent variables.

Using PAGs, we characterize the causal information that can (and in some cases cannot) be obtained from independence and conditional independence relations in a population subject to both sample selection bias and latent variables. Given an oracle (such as a family of statistical tests) for judging population conditional independence relations among a set of recorded variables, we provide an asymptotically reliable algorithm for constructing PAGs, under the set of assumptions described above (and described again more precisely in sections 3.1 and 3.2). The algorithm is exponential in the worst case, but feasible for sparse graphs with up to 100 variables. We will also describe the results of a simulation study on the reliability of the algorithm.

2. Representation of Selection Bias

We distinguish two different reasons why a sample distribution may differ from the population distribution from which it is drawn. The first is simply the familiar phenomenon of *sampling variability:* the frequency distribution of a finite random sample of variables in a set **V** does not in general perfectly represent the probability distribution over **V** from which the sample is drawn.

The second reason is that causal relationships between variables in **V**, on the one hand, and the mechanism by which individuals in the sample are selected from a population, on the other hand, may lead to differences between the expected parameter values in a sample and the population parameter values. In this case we will say that the differences are due to *selection bias*. Sampling bias tends to be remedied by drawing larger samples; selection bias does not.

We will not consider the problems of sample bias in this chapter (except in the simulation studies); we will always assume that we are dealing with an idealized selected subpopulation of infinite size, but one which may be selection biased.

For the purposes of representing selection bias, following Cooper (1995) we assume that for each *measured* random variable A, there is a binary random variable S_A that is equal to one if the value of A has been recorded, and is equal to zero otherwise. (We will say that a variable is measured if its value is recorded for any member of the sample.) If **V** is a set of variables, we will always suppose that **V** can be partitioned into three sets: the set **O** (standing for observed) of measured variables, the set **S** (standing for selection) of selection variables for **O**, and the remaining variables **L** (standing for latent). Although this representation allows for the possibility that some units have missing values for some variables and not others, the algorithms for causal inference that we will describe assume that we are using only the data for the subset of the sample in which all of the units have no missing data for any of the measured variables (i.e. **S** = 1). Since in some circumstances this reduces the usable sample dramatically (or even to zero), it would obviously be desirable to make use of the full sample; how to do this is an open research problem.

In the marginal distribution over a subset **X** of **O** in a selected subpopulation, the set of selection variables **S** has been conditioned on, since its value is always equal to 1 in the selected subpopulation. Hence for disjoint subsets **X**, **Y**, and **Z** of **O**, we will assume that we cannot determine whether $\mathbf{X} \perp\!\!\!\perp \mathbf{Z} \mid \mathbf{Y}$, but that we can determine whether $\mathbf{X} \perp\!\!\!\perp \mathbf{Z} \mid (\mathbf{Y} \cup (\mathbf{S} = 1))$. ($\mathbf{X} \perp\!\!\!\perp \mathbf{Z} \mid \mathbf{Y}$ means **X** is independent of **Z** given all values of **Y**. If **Y** is empty, we simply write $\mathbf{X} \perp\!\!\!\perp \mathbf{Z}$. If the only member of **X** is X, then we write $X \perp\!\!\!\perp \mathbf{Z} \mid \mathbf{Y}$ instead of $\{X\} \perp\!\!\!\perp \mathbf{Z} \mid \mathbf{Y}$. $\mathbf{X} \perp\!\!\!\perp \mathbf{Z} \mid (\mathbf{Y} \cup (\mathbf{S} = 1))$ means **X** is independent of **Z** given all values of **Y**, and the value **S** = 1.) There may be cases in which all of the variables in **S** always take on the same value; this corresponds to the case where there are no missing values in the sample. In such cases we will represent the selection with a single variable S.

The three causal DAGs for a given population shown in figure 1 illustrate a number of different ways in which selection variables can be related to nonselection variables. The causal DAG in (a) would occur, for example, if the members of the population whose X values were recorded and the mem-

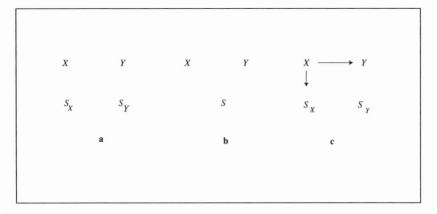

Figure 1. Three examples of selection variables.

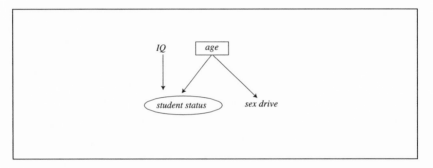

Figure 2. Selection bias makes IQ and sex drive dependant.

bers of the population whose Y values were recorded were randomly selected by flips of a pair of independent coins. The DAG in (b) would occur if the flip of a single coin was used to choose units which would have both their X and Y values recorded (i.e. $S_X = S_Y$ and there are no missing values in the sample). The DAG in (c) would occur if, for example, X is years of education, and people with higher X values respond to a questionnaire about their education—and thus appear in the sample—more often than people with lower X values. We do not preclude the possibility that a variable Y can be cause of S_X for some variable $X \neq Y$, nor do we preclude the possibility that S_X can be a cause as well as an effect, respectively, of one or more different variables. (In [c] a variable is enclosed in a rectangle when it is unmeasured, and enclosed in an oval when it is a selection variable.)

The causal DAG that represents the intelligence and sex drive example described in section 1 is shown in figure 2.

The causal inferences that we make rest on three different assumptions. The causal Markov and causal faithfulness assumptions are described in chapter 2. The population inference assumption described below is the third assumption we make that guarantees the asymptotic correctness of the causal inference procedures described in the following sections.

Consider the case where one is interested in causal inferences about the whole population from the selected subpopulation. The notion of a causal graph, as we have defined it, is relative to a set of variables and a population. Hence the causal graph of the whole population and the causal graph of the selected subpopulation can conceivably be different. For example, if a drug has an effect on people with black hair, but no effect on people with brown hair, then there is an edge from drug to outcome in the first subpopulation, but not in the second. Because of this, in order to draw causal conclusions about either the whole population or the unselected subpopulation (e.g. the black–haired subpopulation) from the causal graph of the selected subpopulation (e.g. the brown–haired subpopulation), we will make the following assumption:

> *Population inference assumption:* If **V** is a causally sufficient set of variables, then the causal DAG relative to **V** in the population is identical with the causal DAGs relative to **V** in the selected subpopulation and the unselected subpopulation.

This is the sort of assumption that is routinely made when, for example, the results of drug trials conducted in Cleveland are generalized to the rest of the country. Of course, there may be examples where the assumption is less plausible. For example, a drug may have no effect on outcome in men, but have an effect on women.

There are some subtleties about the application of these assumptions to different sets of variables and different populations which are explained in more detail in the proofs in section 8, but are not needed in order to understand the rest of the chapter.

3. Using Partial Ancestral Graphs

Let us consider several different sets of conditional independence and dependence relations, and what they can tell us about the causal DAGs that generated them, under a variety of different assumptions.

Given a causal graph G over a set of variables **V**, we will say there is no selection bias if and only if for any three disjoint sets of variables **X**, **Y**, and **Z** included in **V** \ **S**, G entails $\mathbf{X} \perp\!\!\!\perp \mathbf{Z} \mid (\mathbf{Y} \cup (\mathbf{S} = 1))$ if and only if G entails $\mathbf{X} \perp\!\!\!\perp \mathbf{Z} \mid \mathbf{Y}$.[1] This happens, for example, when the variables in **S** are causally unconnected to any other variables in **V**. (Note that this does not in general entail that the *distributions* in the selected subpopulation and the population are the same; it just entails that the same conditional independence relations holds in both.) In that case, when we depict a DAG in a figure we will omit the variables in **S** and edges that have an endpoint in **S**.

For a given DAG G, and a partition of the variable set **V** of G into observed (**O**), selection (**S**), and latent (**L**) variables, we will write $G(\mathbf{O}, \mathbf{S}, \mathbf{L})$. We assume that the only conditional independence relations that can be tested are those among variables in **O** conditional on any subset of **O** when **S** = 1; we will call this the set of *observable* conditional independence relations. If **X**, **Y**, and **Z** are included in **O**, and $\mathbf{X} \perp\!\!\!\perp \mathbf{Z} \mid (\mathbf{Y} \cup (\mathbf{S} = 1))$, then we say it is an *observed* conditional independence relation. Let **Cond** be a set of conditional independence relations among the variables in **O**. A DAG $G(\mathbf{O}, \mathbf{S}, \mathbf{L})$ is in **O-Equiv(Cond)** just when $G(\mathbf{O}, \mathbf{S}, \mathbf{L})$ entails that $\mathbf{X} \perp\!\!\!\perp \mathbf{Z} \mid (\mathbf{Y} \cup (\mathbf{S} = 1))$ if and only if $\mathbf{X} \perp\!\!\!\perp \mathbf{Z} \mid \mathbf{Y}$ is in **Cond**. If $G'(\mathbf{O}, \mathbf{S}', \mathbf{L}')$ entails that $\mathbf{X} \perp\!\!\!\perp \mathbf{Z} \mid (\mathbf{Y} \cup (\mathbf{S}' = 1))$ if and only if $G(\mathbf{O}, \mathbf{S}, \mathbf{L})$ entails that $\mathbf{X} \perp\!\!\!\perp \mathbf{Z} \mid (\mathbf{Y} \cup (\mathbf{S} = 1))$, then $G'(\mathbf{O}, \mathbf{S}', \mathbf{L}')$ is in **O-Equiv(G)**.

Imagine now that a researcher does not know the correct causal DAG, but can determine whether an observed conditional independence relation is in **Cond**, perhaps by performing statistical tests of conditional independence on the selected subpopulation. (As we will see later, because many of the conditional independencies in **Cond** entail other members of **Cond**, only a small fraction of the membership of **Cond** actually need be tested.) From this information alone, and the causal Markov assumption, the causal faithfulness assumption, and the population inference assumption, the most he or she could conclude is that the true causal DAG is some member of **O-Equiv(Cond)**. This information by itself is not very interesting, unless the members of **O-Equiv(Cond)** all share some important features. The examples below show that sometimes the members of **O-Equiv(Cond)** do share important features.

Our strategy for finding PAGs even when there may be latent variables or selection bias is a generalization of the strategy without selection bias described in Spirtes, Glymour, and Scheines 1993. A is an *ancestor* of B in DAG G when there is a directed path from A to B, or $A = B$. We will construct from **Cond** a graphical object called a *partial ancestral graph* (PAG)[2], using the causal Markov, causal faithfulness, and population inference assumptions. The PAG represents information about which variables are or are not ancestors of other variables in all of the DAGs in **O-Equiv(Cond)**. If A is an ancestor of B in all DAGs in **O-Equiv(Cond)**, then although from **Cond** we cannot tell exactly which DAG in **O-Equiv(Cond)** is the true causal DAG because we know that all of the DAGs in **O-Equiv(Cond)** contain a directed path from A to B, we can reliably conclude that in the true causal DAG, A is a (possibly indirect) cause of B. This strategy is represented schematically in figure 3. In the following examples we will apply this strategy to particular sets of observed conditional independence relations. We will also show what features of DAGs can be reliably inferred and what features cannot.

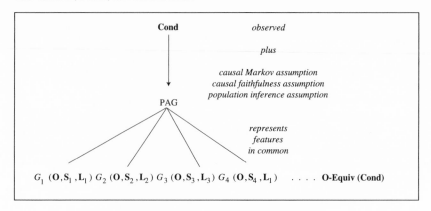

Figure 3. PAG represents **O-Equiv(Cond)**.

The formal definition of a PAG is given below. There are three kinds of endpoints an edge in a PAG can have "-" or "o" or ">." These can be combined to form the following four kinds of edges: $A \rightarrow B$, $A \leftrightarrow B$, $A \circ\!\!\rightarrow B$, or $A \circ\!\!-\!\!\circ B$. Let "*" be a metasymbol that stands for any of the three kinds of endpoints. More formally:

A PAG π *represents* a DAG $G(\mathbf{O}, \mathbf{L}, \mathbf{S})$ if and only if:

1. The set of variables in π is $\mathbf{O}$.
2. If there is any edge between A and B in π, it is one of the following kinds: $A \rightarrow B$, $A \circ\!\!\rightarrow B$, $A \circ\!\!-\!\!\circ B$, or $A \leftrightarrow B$.
3. There is at most one edge between any pair of vertices in π.
4. A and B are adjacent in π if and only if for every subset $\mathbf{Z}$ of $\mathbf{O}\backslash\{A, B\}$, G does not entail that A and B are independent conditional on $\mathbf{Z} \cup \mathbf{S}$.
5. An edge between A and B in π is oriented as $A \rightarrow B$ only if A is an ancestor of B but not $\mathbf{S}$ in every DAG in **O-Equiv**(G).
6. An edge between A and B in π is oriented as $A *\!\!\rightarrow B$ only if B is not an ancestor of A or $\mathbf{S}$ in every DAG in **O-Equiv**(G).
7. $A *\!\!\!-\!\!\!\!\underline{* B*}\!\!-\!\!* C$ in π only if in every DAG in **O-Equiv**(G) either B is an ancestor of C, or A, or $\mathbf{S}$. (Whenever A and B are adjacent, and B and C are adjacent, and A and C are not adjacent, and the edges in the PAG are not both into B, i.e., the PAG does not contain $A *\!\!\rightarrow B \leftarrow\!\!* C$, then the underlining of B should be assumed to be present, although we do not explicitly put the underlining in π.)

(If a PAG π represents a DAG G, we also say π is a PAG of G and G is a DAG with PAG π.)

An "o" on the end of an edge places no restriction on the ancestor relationships. Note that more than one PAG can represent a DAG $G(\mathbf{O}, \mathbf{L}, \mathbf{S})$. Two

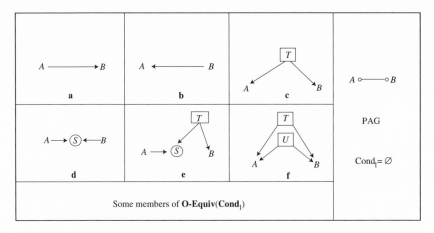

Figure 4. Some DAGs in **O-Equiv(Cond$_1$)**.

such PAGs π_1 and π_2 that represent $G(\mathbf{O}, \mathbf{L}, \mathbf{S})$ have the same adjacencies, but are differently oriented in the sense that π_1 may contain a, "o" where π_2 contains a ">" or a "–" or vice-versa. Examples of PAGs are shown in the following subsections.

3.1 A Simple Example

We will start out with a very simple example, in which the set of observed conditional independence relations is not very informative. (For simplicity, in all of the following examples we assume that all of the variables in **S** take on the same value, and hence can be represented by a single variable *S*.) For example, suppose first that the set **Cond$_1$** of observed conditional independence relations is empty, i.e. **Cond$_1$** = ∅. We now want to find out what DAGs are in **O-Equiv(Cond$_1$)**. Let **V** be a set of causally sufficient variables. Suppose that we assume or know from background knowledge that **O** = {*A, B*} is causally sufficient and there is no selection bias. (In general it is not possible to test these assumptions from observational data alone.) Under these assumptions there are exactly two DAGs that entail **Cond$_1$**, labeled (a) and (b) in figure 4. In general, when there are no latent variables and no selection bias, there is an edge between *A* and *B* if and only if for any subset **X** of **O**\{*A, B*}, $G(\mathbf{O}, \mathbf{S}, \mathbf{L})$ entails that *A* and *B* are dependent given **X**.

Now suppose that there are latent variables but no selection bias, and that the set of measured variables **O** = {*A, B*}. Then, if we do not limit the number of latent variables in a DAG, there are an infinite number of DAGs that entail **Cond$_1$**, many of which do not contain an edge between *A* and *B*. Two such DAGs are shown in figure 4c and f. (Latent variables in **L** are represented by variables in boxes.) The examples in figure 4c and f show that when

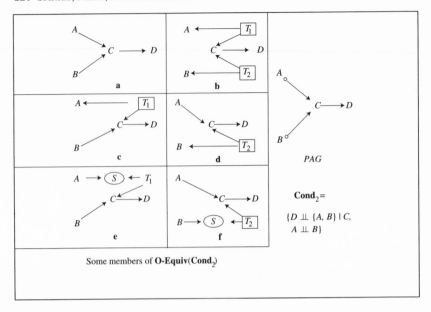

Figure 5. Some DAGs in **O-Equiv(Cond$_2$)**.

there are latent variables it is not the case that there is an edge between A and B if for all subsets $\mathbf{X}$ of $\mathbf{O}\backslash\{A, B\}$, $G(\mathbf{O}, \mathbf{S}, \mathbf{L})$ entails that A and B are dependent given $\mathbf{X}$. (Recall that if there is no selection bias, then A and B are dependent given $\mathbf{X} \cup (\mathbf{S} = 1)$ if and only if A and B are dependent given $\mathbf{X}$.)

Finally, let us consider the case where there are latent variables and selection bias. Examples of DAGs in **O-Equiv(Cond$_1$)** with selection bias are shown in figure 4d and e.

The DAGs in **O-Equiv(Cond$_1$)** seem to have little in common, particularly when there is the possibility of both latent variables and selection bias. While there are a great variety of DAGs in **O-Equiv(Cond$_1$)**, it is not the case that every DAG is in **O-Equiv(Cond$_1$)**. For example, a DAG $G(\mathbf{O}, \mathbf{S}, \mathbf{L})$ with no edges at all is not in **O-Equiv(Cond$_1$)**.

If **Cond$_1$** is observed, it is not possible to determine anything about the ancestor relationships between A and B in the causal DAG describing the population. We represent this information in a partial ancestral graph with the edge $A \circ\!\!-\!\!\circ B$. The "o" on each end of the edge means that the PAG does not specify whether or not A is an ancestor of B, or B is an ancestor of A. (Since there are DAGs in **O-Equiv(Cond$_1$)** in which A is an ancestor of B, and others in which B is an ancestor of A, every PAG which represents **O-Equiv(Cond$_1$)** has an "o" on each end of the edge between A and B.)

3.2 Another Example

Let $\mathbf{O} = \{A, B, C, D\}$ and $\mathbf{Cond}_2 = \{D \perp\!\!\!\perp \{A, B\} \mid C, A \perp\!\!\!\perp B\}$ and all of the other conditional independence relations entailed by these. Once again the simplest case is when it is assumed that there are no latent variables and no selection bias. In that case the only DAG that entails $\mathbf{Cond}_2$ is figure 5a.

Now suppose that we consider DAGs with latent variables so $\mathbf{V} \neq \mathbf{O}$, but no selection bias. In that case if there is no upper limit to the number of latent variables allowed, then there are an infinite number of DAGs in $\mathbf{O\text{-}Equiv(Cond}_2)$, several of which are shown in figure 5 b, c, and d.

Suppose that we now consider DAGs with selection bias. Figure 5e and 5f show some examples of DAGs that are in $\mathbf{O\text{-}Equiv(Cond}_2)$ that have selection bias and latent variables.

Is there anything that all of the DAGs in figure 5 have in common? In all of the DAGs in $\mathbf{O\text{-}Equiv(Cond}_2)$, there is a subset $\mathbf{Z}$ of $\mathbf{O}$ such that for each of the pairs $<A, D>$, $<B, D>$, and $<A, B>$, the pair is independent conditional on $\mathbf{Z} \cup \{S\}$. This is represented in the PAG by the lack of edges between A and D, between B and D, and between A and B. Moreover, in some of the DAGs in figure 5, A is an ancestor of C, while in others it is not. Note that in none of them is C an ancestor of A or any member of $\mathbf{S}$. It can be shown that in none of the DAGs in $\mathbf{O\text{-}Equiv(Cond}_2)$ is C an ancestor of A or of any member of $\mathbf{S}$. In the PAG representing $\mathbf{O\text{-}Equiv(Cond}_2)$, we represent this by $A \, o \!\!\rightarrow C$.

The "o" on the A end of the $A \, o \!\!\rightarrow C$ edge means the PAG does not say whether or not A is an ancestor of C; and the ">" on the C end of the edge means that C is not an ancestor of A or any member of $\mathbf{S}$ in *all* of the DAGs in $\mathbf{O\text{-}Equiv(Cond}_2)$. It is also the case that in all of the DAGs in figure 5, C is an ancestor of D but not of any member of $\mathbf{S}$, and D is not an ancestor of C or any member of $\mathbf{S}$. It can be shown that in all of the DAGs in $\mathbf{O\text{-}Equiv(Cond}_2)$ C is an ancestor of D but not of any member of $\mathbf{S}$ and D is not an ancestor of C or any member of $\mathbf{S}$. These facts are represented in the PAG by the edge between C and D having a ">" at the D end and a "–" at the C end.

There is an important distinction between the conditional distribution of D on $C = c$, and the distribution that results when C is forced (by intervening on the structure) to have the value c. The latter quantity depends upon the causal relations between C and D. If C is a cause of D, then forcing the value c on C will in general have an effect on the value of D, while if C is an effect of D, then forcing a value of c on C will not have an effect on the value of D. See Spirtes, Glymour, and Scheines (1993) and Pearl (1995) for details. In this particular case, it is possible to make both qualitative and quantitative predictions about the effects on the value of D of interventions that set the value of C from the PAG and the measured conditional distribution of D on $C = c$. This is because every DAG in $\mathbf{O\text{-}Equiv(Cond}_2)$ makes the same

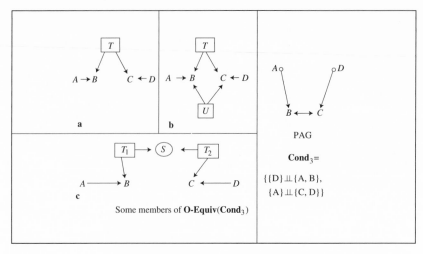

Figure 6. Some DAGs in **O-Equiv(Cond₃)**.

quantitative prediction about the effects of intervening to set the value of C to c. The details of the algorithm for making this prediction are given in Spirtes, Glymour and Scheines (1993). In this case we can determine that the only source of dependency between C and D are directed paths from C to D, so if $P(D \mid C = c)$ is the conditional distribution of D on C in the population, and C is forced to have the value c, then the new distribution of D will be $P(D \mid C = c)$.

3.3 Final Example

Finally, consider an example in which $\mathbf{Cond}_3 = \{D \perp\!\!\!\perp \{A, B\}, A \perp\!\!\!\perp \{C, D\}\}$. There is no DAG in **O-Equiv(Cond₃)** in which both $\mathbf{V} = \mathbf{O}$ and there is no selection bias. Hence we can conclude that the DAG that entails **Cond₃** either contains a latent variable or there is selection bias or both. Figure 6a and b are examples of DAGs with latent variables that entail **Cond₃**. Note that in each of them, there is a latent cause of B and C, B is not an ancestor of C or any member of **S**, and C is not an ancestor of B or any member of **S**. As long as there is no selection bias, these properties can be shown to hold of any DAG in **O-Equiv(Cond₃)**.

Suppose now that we also consider DAGs with selection bias. Figure 6c is an example of a DAG with selection bias that entails **Cond₃**. Note that figure 6c does not contain a latent common cause of C and B. However, in each of the DAGs in figure 5, B is not an ancestor of C or any member of **S**, and C is not an ancestor of B or any member of **S**; these properties can be shown to hold of any DAG in **O-Equiv(Cond₃)**, even when there are latent variables and selection bias. Hence in the PAG we have an edge $B \leftrightarrow C$. Thus, if the conditional independence relations in $\textbf{Cond}_3$ are ever observed, it can be reliably concluded that even though there may be latent variables and selection bias, regardless of the causal connections of the latent variables and selection variables to other variables, in the causal DAG that generated $\textbf{Cond}_3$, B is not a direct or indirect cause of C and C is not a direct or indirect cause of B.

Suppose $P(\textbf{O})$ is a distribution that has just the conditional independence relations in $\textbf{Cond}_3$. In the linear case the PAG in figure 6 can be parameterized in such a way that it represents $P(\textbf{O})$, and is more parsimonious (its parameterization is lower dimensional) than any DAG that contains just the variables in $\textbf{O}$ and represents $P(\textbf{O})$. For example in the linear case, the PAG can be given a complete orientation with all "o" ends removed, and interpreted as a linear structural equation model with correlated errors. See Spirtes, et al. 1996 for details. The parameterizations of other families of distributions have not yet been worked out in detail, although it is clear how to assign a reasonable score to such models.) Hence the PAG can be used to find an unbiased estimator of the population parameters that has lower variance than any unbiased estimator based on a DAG with the same set of variables. Even if one is not interested in predicting the effects of interventions, but merely seeks to find a parsimonious representation of a distribution in order to classify or diagnose members of a population, the PAG in figure 6 has advantages over any DAG with the same variables.

4. Summary of PAG Theorems

Note that it follows from the definition of a PAG and the assumed acyclicity of the directed graphs that there are no edges $A \,\text{—}\, B$ in a PAG, and no directed cycles in a PAG. (PAGs can also be used to represent directed cyclic graphs. See Richardson 1996.)

Informally, a directed path in a PAG is a path that contains only "$\rightarrow$" edges pointing in the same direction.

Theorem 1. If π is a partial ancestral graph, and there is a directed path U from A to B in π, then in every DAG $G(\textbf{O}, \textbf{S}, \textbf{L})$ with PAG π, there is a directed path from A to B, and A is not an ancestor of $\textbf{S}$.

(This follows directly from the definition of an "$\rightarrow$" edge in a PAG.)

A semidirected path from A to B in a partial ancestral graph π is an undirected path U from A to B in which no edge contains an arrowhead pointing toward A, (i.e., there is no arrowhead at A on U, and if X and Y are adjacent on the path, and X is between A and Y on the path, then there is no arrowhead at the X end of the edge between X and Y). Theorems 4, 5, and 6 give information about what variables appear on causal paths between a pair of variables A and B, i.e. information about how those paths could be blocked.

Theorem 2. If π is a partial ancestral graph, and there is no semidirected path from A to B in π that contains a member of $\mathbf{C}$, then every directed path from A to B in every DAG $G(\mathbf{O}, \mathbf{S}, \mathbf{L})$ with PAG π that contains a member of $\mathbf{C}$ also contains a member of $\mathbf{S}$.

Theorem 3. If π is a partial ancestral graph of DAG $G(\mathbf{O}, \mathbf{S}, \mathbf{L})$, and there is no semidirected path from A to B in π, then every directed path from A to B in every DAG $G(\mathbf{O}, \mathbf{S}, \mathbf{L})$ with PAG π contains a member of $\mathbf{S}$.

Theorem 4. If π is a partial ancestral graph, and every semidirected path from A to B contains some member of $\mathbf{C}$ in π, then every directed path from A to B in every DAG $G(\mathbf{O}, \mathbf{S}, \mathbf{L})$ with PAG π contains a member of $\mathbf{S} \cup \mathbf{C}$.

5. An Algorithm for Constructing PAGs

We have seen that a PAG contains valuable information about the causal relationships between variables; it also represents conditional independence relations in the margin and can be used for classification. However, the number of observable conditional independence relations grows exponentially with the number of members of $\mathbf{O}$. In addition, some of the independence relations are conditional on large sets of variables, and often these cannot be reliably tested on reasonable sample sizes. Is it feasible to construct a PAG from data?

The fast causal inference (FCI) algorithm constructs PAGs that are correct even when selection bias may be present (under the causal Markov assumption, the causal faithfulness assumption, the population inference assumption, and the assumption that conditional independence relations can be reliably tested). The description in Spirtes, Glymour, and Scheines (1993) did not allow the possibility of selection bias. If the possibility of selection bias is allowed, the algorithm described there gives the correct output (called a POIPG in Spirtes, Glymour, and Scheines [1993]), but the conclusions that one can draw from the PAG are the slightly different ones described in section IV, rather than those described in Spirtes, Glymour, and Scheines (1993). Since the algorithm decides which conditional independence tests to perform, we will assume that for each $\mathbf{X}$, $\mathbf{Y}$, and $\mathbf{Z}$ included in $\mathbf{O}$, the algorithm has some method for reliably determining if $\mathbf{X}$ is independent of $\mathbf{Y}$ given $\mathbf{Z} \cup (\mathbf{S} = 1)$ in the distribution $P(\mathbf{V})$; we will call this method an *oracle* for $P(\mathbf{V})$ over $\mathbf{O}$ given $\mathbf{S} = 1$. In practice, the oracle can be a statistical test of conditional independence (which is of course not completely reliable on finite sample sizes.)

Theorem 5. If $P(\mathbf{V})$ is faithful to $G_1(\mathbf{O}, \mathbf{S}_1, \mathbf{L}_1)$, and the input to the FCI algorithm is an oracle for $P(V)$ over $\mathbf{O}$ given $\mathbf{S} = 1$, the output is a PAG of $G_1(\mathbf{O}, \mathbf{S}_1, \mathbf{L}_1)$.

Even if one drops the assumptions relating causal DAGs to probability distributions, then the output PAG is still a parsimonious representation of the marginal of the distribution.

In the worst case the number of times the FCI algorithm consults the oracle is exponential in the number of variables (as is any correct algorithm whose output is a function of the answers of a conditional independence oracle). Even when the maximum number of vertices any given vertex is adjacent to is held fixed, in the worse case the algorithm is exponential in the number of variables. In light of this the title "Fast Causal Inference Algorithm" is perhaps somewhat over-optimistic; however, on simulated data it can often be run on up to 100 variables provided the true graph is sparse. This is because it is (usually) not necessary to examine the entire set of observable conditional independence relations; many conditional independence relations are entailed by other conditional independence relations. The FCI algorithm relies on this fact to test a relatively small set of conditional independence relations, and test independence relations conditional on as few variables as possible.

The FCI algorithm can be divided into two parts. First the adjacencies in the PAG are found, and then the edges are oriented. First we will describe how the adjacencies are found.

5.1 The Fast Causal Inference—Adjacencies Algorithm

The details of the adjacency phase of the FCI algorithm are stated at the end of this section. Here we will give an informal description and motivation for the steps of the algorithm.

There is a very simple, but slow and unreliable way of determining when two variables in a PAG are adjacent. Start off with a complete undirected graph. By definition, two variables A and B in a PAG for $G(\mathbf{O}, \mathbf{L}, \mathbf{S})$ are adjacent if and only if there is no subset $\mathbf{Z}$ of $\mathbf{O}\backslash\{A, B\}$ such that A and B are entailed to be independent given $\mathbf{Z} \cup \mathbf{S}$. So, for each pair of variables A and B, and each subset $\mathbf{Z}$ of $\mathbf{O}\backslash\{A, B\}$ one could simply ask the oracle if A and B are entailed to be independent given $\mathbf{Z} \cup \mathbf{S}$. The edge between A and B is removed if and only if the oracle answers yes to any of these questions. The problems with this algorithm are that the number of questions asked of the oracle grows exponentially with the number of variables in $\mathbf{O}$, and in prac-

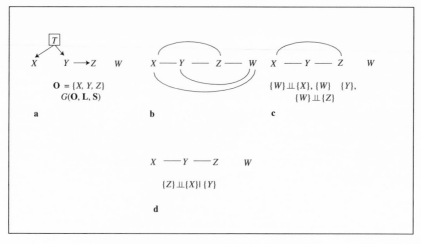

Figure 7. Example of steps of the FCI algorithm.

tice, the oracle is unreliable if the number of variables in **Z** is large. Clearly it is desirable to ask as few questions of the oracle as possible, and to ask questions in which **Z** is as small as possible.

Since when the algorithm asks an oracle a question, it is trying to limit the size of the conditioning sets, it makes sense to first ask the oracle about independencies conditional on the empty set, then independencies conditional on sets with one variable, then independencies conditional on sets with two variables, etc. However, this still leads to asking unnecessary questions of the oracle.

The strategy that the FCI algorithm adopts for avoiding asking such unnecessary questions of the oracle is based on the following idea. Suppose the original unknown graph is $G(\mathbf{O}, \mathbf{L}, \mathbf{S})$ in figure 7a, where for purposes of illustration there is no selection bias, so we do not need to condition on **S**. If we applied the strategy described above, we would first create the complete undirected graph shown in figure 7b. After we asked the oracle if W is independent of X, Y, and Z (in each case receiving the answer "yes"), we would obtain the result shown in figure 7c. At this point, although the graph created is not a PAG for $G(\mathbf{O}, \mathbf{L}, \mathbf{S})$ (because it contains the wrong adjacencies), and we have very incomplete information about $G(\mathbf{O}, \mathbf{L}, \mathbf{S})$, it is easy to show that W does not lie on any path between X and Z in $G(\mathbf{O}, \mathbf{L}, \mathbf{S})$. Hence if X and Z are independent conditional on any subset of $\mathbf{O} \backslash \{A, B\}$ that contains W, they are also independent given some other subset of $\mathbf{O} \backslash \{A, B\}$ that does not contain W. So there is never any need to ever ask the oracle if X and Z are independent given any subset containing W. For example, the algorithm never asks whether X and Z are independent given W. This reduces the number of questions asked of the oracle, and limits the size of the conditioning sets.

The adjacency phase of the FCI algorithm, which is stated at the end of this section, contains four steps, A, B, C and D. Step A of the algorithm simply creates a complete undirected graph. In step B, in searching for a subset $\mathbf{Z}$ of $\mathbf{O} \backslash \{A, B\}$ such that A and B are independent conditional on $\mathbf{Z} \cup \mathbf{S}$, the algorithm restricts the search to subsets of variables that are adjacent to A in the undirected graph it has constructed thus far, or subsets of variables adjacent to B. If there were no latent variables or selection bias in G, no more questions would need to be asked of the oracle in order to determine the correct set of adjacencies in the PAG. Unfortunately, if there are latent variables or selection bias, some further questions are needed. This is done in step D of the FCI algorithm.

Consider the DAG $G(\mathbf{O}, \mathbf{L}, \mathbf{S})$ shown in figure 8a. The PAG for $G(\mathbf{O}, \mathbf{L}, \mathbf{S})$ is shown in figure 9b. In the PAG, X_3 is not adjacent to either X_1 or X_5. However, in $G(\mathbf{O}, \mathbf{L}, \mathbf{S})$, the only subset $\mathbf{Z}$ of $\mathbf{O}$ such that X_1 and X_5 are independent, conditional on $\mathbf{Z} \cup \mathbf{S}$ contains X_3. Hence we need to consider asking independence questions conditional on sets of variables that contain variables not adjacent to either X_1 or X_5. The algorithm constructs a set of variables called **Possible-D-Sep**(A, B, π), which is a function of A, B, and the graphical object π constructed by the algorithm thus far which has the following property: if A and B are independent conditional on any subset of $\mathbf{O} \backslash \{A, B\} \cup \mathbf{S}$, then they are independent given some subset of **Possible-D-Sep**(A, B, π) or **Possible-D-Sep**(B, A, π).

A, B, and C form a *triangle* in a graph or a PAG if and only if A and B are adjacent, B and C are adjacent, and A and C are adjacent. V is in **Possible-D-Sep**(A, B, π) in π if and only if there is an undirected path U between A and B in π such that for every subpath $X \ast\!\!-\!\!\ast Y \ast\!\!-\!\!\ast Z$ of U either Y is a collider on the subpath, or X, Y, and Z form a triangle in π. In figure 8 (f), **Possible-D-Sep**$(X_1, X_5, \pi) =$ **Possible-D-Sep**$(X_5, X_1, \pi) = \{X_2, X_3, X_4\}$. Thus in step D of the algorithm, the only independence questions that are asked of the oracle for a given pair of variables A and B are conditional on subsets of **Possible-D-Sep**(A, B, π) or **Possible-D-Sep**(B, A, π).

The construction of **Possible-D-Sep**(A, B, π) requires some limited orientation information about the edges in the PAG. Step C performs some orientation of the PAG, so that the membership of **Possible-D-Sep**(A, B, π) can be calculated in step D. The orientation principles used in step C are essentially the same as those used in step F of the orientation phase of the algorithm. Step F will be discussed in the next section, so we will not discuss step C here.

When the algorithm removes an edge between A and B, it does so because it has found some subset $\mathbf{Z}$ of $\mathbf{O} \backslash \{A, B\}$ such that A and B are independent conditional on $\mathbf{Z} \cup \mathbf{S}$. The subset $\mathbf{Z}$ is recorded in **Sepset**(A, B) and **Sepset**(B, A). This information is used later in the orientation phase of the algorithm. Because each edge is removed at most once, **Sepset**(A, B) contains

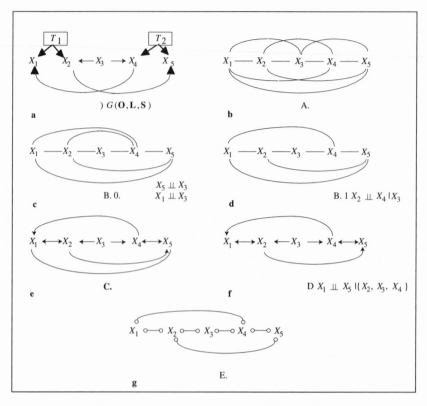

Figure 8. Example of application of FCI algorithm.

at most one subset of $\mathbf{O}\backslash\{A,\ B\}$. In the algorithm, **Adjacencies**$(Q,\ X)$ is the set of vertices that are adjacent to X in graph Q. **Adjacencies**$(Q,\ X)$ changes as the algorithm progresses, because the algorithm removes edges from Q. (However, **Possible-D-Sep** is calculated only once, and remains fixed, even as the graph changes.)

5.1.1 Fast Causal Inference Algorithm—Adjacencies

A. Form the complete undirected graph Q on the vertex set **V**.

B. $n = 0$.

repeat

   repeat

   select an ordered pair of variables X and Y that are adjacent in Q such that **Adjacencies**$(Q, X)\backslash\{Y\}$ contains at least n members,

   repeat

      select a subset **T** of **Adjacencies**$(Q, X)\backslash\{Y\}$ with n members, and if X and Y are independent given $\mathbf{T} \cup \mathbf{S}$, delete the edge between X and Y from Q and record **T** in **Sepset**(X, Y) and **Sepset**(Y, X)

until all subsets of **Adjacencies**$(Q, X) \backslash \{Y\}$ of size n have been checked for independence given $\mathbf{T} \cup \mathbf{S}$ or there is no edge between X and Y;

until all ordered pairs of adjacent variables X and Y such that **Adjacencies**$(Q, X) \backslash \{Y\}$ has at least n members have been selected;

$n = n + 1$;

until for each ordered pair of adjacent vertices X, Y, **Adjacencies**$(Q, X) \backslash \{Y\}$ has fewer than n members.

C. Let π_0 be the undirected graph resulting from step B. For each triple of vertices A, B, C such that the pair A, B and the pair B, C are each adjacent in π_0 but the pair A, C are not adjacent in π_0, orient $A \ast\!\!-\!\!B\!-\!\!\ast C$ as $A \ast\!\!\rightarrow B \leftarrow\!\ast C$ if and only if B is not in **Sepset**(A, C).

D. Let π_1 be the undirected graph resulting from step C. For each pair of variables A and B adjacent in π_1, if there is a subset **T** of **Possible-D-SEP**$(A, B, \pi_1) \backslash \{A, B\}$ or of **Possible-D-SEP**$(B, A, \pi_1) \backslash \{A, B\}$ such that A and B are independent conditional on $\mathbf{T} \cup \mathbf{S}$, remove the edge between A and B from π_1 and record **T** in **Sepset**(A, B) and **Sepset**(B, A).

E. Orient each edge as "o—o". Call this graph π_2.

Figure 8 illustrates the application of the adjacency phase of the FCI algorithm to DAG $G(\mathbf{O}, \mathbf{L}, \mathbf{S})$. We show only those steps which make changes to the PAG being created.

5.2 The Fast Causal Inference—Orientations Algorithm

The details of the orientation phase of the algorithm are stated at the end of this section. Step F states that for each triple of vertices A, B, C such that the pair A, B and the pair B, C are each adjacent in π_2 but the pair A, C are not adjacent in π_2, orient $A \ast\!\!-\!\!\ast B \ast\!\!-\!\!\ast C$ as $A \ast\!\!\rightarrow B \leftarrow\!\ast C$ if and only if B is not in **Sepset**(A, C). The intuition behind rule F is the following. It is easy to see if a DAG G with a set of variables $\mathbf{V}$ contains $A \rightarrow B \leftarrow C$, and A and C are not adjacent, then the path between A and C entails that A and C are dependent given every subset of $\mathbf{V} \backslash \{A, C\}$ that contains B. Alternatively, if G contains $A \rightarrow B \rightarrow C$, $A \leftarrow B \leftarrow C$, or $A \leftarrow B \rightarrow C$, and A and C are not adjacent, then A and C are entailed to be dependent given any subset of $\mathbf{V} \backslash \{A, C\}$ that does not contain B. This property generalizes to PAGs as well. Hence, if a PAG contains $A \ast\!\!-\!\!\ast B \ast\!\!-\!\!\ast C$ and A and C are not adjacent in the PAG, a PAG can be oriented as $A \ast\!\!\rightarrow B \leftarrow\!\ast C$ if and only if **Sepset**(A, C) does not contain B. (In the version of the algorithm that we implemented for the simulation studies in this chapter, we have actually replaced step F by a more complicated step which is more reliable on small samples.)

The proofs of correctness of the orientation rules in step G of the algorithm are all inductive arguments that show that the $n+1^{st}$ application of an orientation rule is correct if the first n applications of the orientation rules are correct.

G(i) states that if there is a directed path from A to B, and an edge A *—* B, orient A *—* B as A *$\rightarrow$ B. This is correct because if there is a directed path from A to B in π_2, and π_2 has been oriented correctly thus far, then A is an ancestor of B in every member of the O-equivalence class of $G(\mathbf{O}, \mathbf{S}, \mathbf{L})$. Because each member of the O-equivalence class of $G(\mathbf{O}, \mathbf{S}, \mathbf{L})$ is acyclic, it follows that B is not an ancestor of A in any member of the O-equivalence class of $G(\mathbf{O}, \mathbf{S}, \mathbf{L})$. Hence the edge can be oriented as A *$\rightarrow$ B. (In the version of the algorithm that we implemented for the simulation studies in this chapter, we have actually deleted step G(i) because although theoretically correct, it is expensive to calculate and leads to errors on small samples.)

G(ii) states that if P *$\rightarrow$ $\underline{M}$ *—* R then orient as P *$\rightarrow$ $M \rightarrow R$. The underlining means that M is an ancestor of either P or R or $\mathbf{S}$ in every member of the O-equivalence class of $G(\mathbf{O}, \mathbf{S}, \mathbf{L})$. P *$\rightarrow$ M means that in no member of the O-equivalence class of $G(\mathbf{O}, \mathbf{S}, \mathbf{L})$ is M an ancestor of P or $\mathbf{S}$. It follows that M is an ancestor of R in every member of the O-equivalence class of $G(\mathbf{O}, \mathbf{S}, \mathbf{L})$. Hence the edge can be oriented as $M \rightarrow R$.

G(iii) states that if B is a collider along $<A, B, C>$ (i.e. A *$\rightarrow$ $B \leftarrow$* C) in π_2, D is adjacent to A, B, and C, and D is in **Sepset**(A, C), then orient B *—* D as $B \leftarrow$* D. Suppose that D is in **Sepset**(A, C). Because the PAG contains orientation information about every member of the O-equivalence class of $G(\mathbf{O}, \mathbf{S}, \mathbf{L})$, in some cases it is possible to show from even a partially oriented PAG that X and Y are entailed to be dependent conditional on $\mathbf{Z}$ in every member of the O-equivalence class of $G(\mathbf{O}, \mathbf{S}, \mathbf{L})$. Suppose that there were some member $G'(\mathbf{O}, \mathbf{S}', \mathbf{L}')$ of the O-equivalence class of $G(\mathbf{O}, \mathbf{S}, \mathbf{L})$ in which B was an ancestor of D. It can be proved that in that DAG, A and C are entailed to be dependent conditional on any set containing D; but this is a contradiction because D is in **Sepset**(A, C), and A and C are entailed to be independent given **Sepset**(A, C) in every member of the O-equivalence class of $G(\mathbf{O}, \mathbf{S}, \mathbf{L})$. Hence B is not an ancestor of D in any member of the O-equivalence class of $G(\mathbf{O}, \mathbf{S}, \mathbf{L})$.

Rule G(iv) states that if $B \leftarrow$*C, $B \rightarrow D$, and D o—* C, then orient as $D \leftarrow$* C. By hypothesis, B is not an ancestor of C, but is an ancestor of D. Hence D is not an ancestor of C.

Rule G(v) is somewhat complicated, and not often applied, so the reader may wish to skip the following discussion of it. G(v) uses definite discriminating paths to orient edges in the PAG. The concept of a definite discriminating path is illustrated in figure 9 and defined more formally in the following paragraphs.

Consider the graph shown in figure 9. All of the orientations shown can be

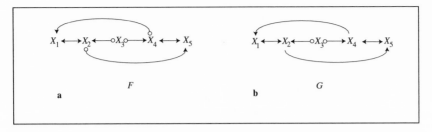

Figure 9. Example of orientation part of FCI algorithm.

derived without using step G(v) of the FCI algorithm. It can be proved that in every member $G'(\mathbf{O}, \mathbf{S'}, \mathbf{L'})$ of the **O**-equivalence class of $G(\mathbf{O}, \mathbf{S}, \mathbf{L})$, if $G'(\mathbf{O}, \mathbf{S'}, \mathbf{L'})$ entails that A and C are entailed to be independent conditional on $\mathbf{Z} \cup \mathbf{S'}$, and $G'(\mathbf{O}, \mathbf{S'}, \mathbf{L'})$ does not entail that A and C are independent conditional on any proper subset of $\mathbf{Z} \cup \mathbf{S'}$, then **Sepset**$(A, C)$ contains B if and only if the edges between B and C and B and D do not collide at B. This orientation rule, when applied repeatedly, can lead to "long distance" orientations, i.e., a conditional independence relation between A and C can orient edges into B, even though the shortest path from A to B is arbitrarily long. The sorts of paths that have to exist in order to perform this "long distance" orientation are called definite discriminating paths. (In a partial ancestral graph π, U is a *definite discriminating path for B* if and only if U is an undirected path between X and Y, B is the predecessor of Y on U, $B \neq X$, every vertex on U except for the endpoints and possibly B is a collider on U, for every vertex V on U except for the endpoints there is an edge $V \to Y$, and X and Y are not adjacent.) An example of a definite discriminating path is given in figure 9.

5.2.1 Fast Causal Inference Algorithm—Orientations

F. For each triple of vertices A, B, C such that the pair A, B and the pair B, C are each adjacent in π_2 but the pair A, C are not adjacent in π_2, orient $A *\!\!-\!\!* B *\!\!-\!\!* C$ as $A *\!\!\to B \leftarrow\!\!* C$ if and only if B is not in **Sepset**(A, C).

G. repeat

(i) If there is a directed path from A to B, and an edge $A *\!\!-\!\!* B$, orient $A *\!\!-\!\!* B$ as $A *\!\!\to B$,

(ii) else if $P *\!\!\to \underline{M} *\!\!-\!\!* R$ then orient as $P *\!\!\to M \to R$,

(iii) else if B is a collider along $<A, B, C>$ in π_2, A is not adjacent to C, D is adjacent to A, B, and C, and D is a noncollider along $<A, D, C>$, then orient $B *\!\!-\!\!* D$ as $B \leftarrow * D$,

(iv) else if $B \leftarrow *C$, $B \to D$, and $D \,o\!\!-\!\!* C$, orient as $D \leftarrow * C$;

(v) If U is a definite discriminating path between A and C for B in π_2, D is adjacent to C on U, and D, B, and C form a triangle, then if

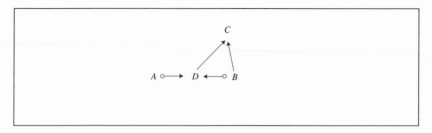

Figure 10. <A, D,B,C> is a definite discriminating path for B.

B is in **Sepset**(A, C) mark B as a noncollider on subpath $D *\!\!-\!\!* B$ $*\!\!-\!\!* C$, else orient $D *\!\!-\!\!* B *\!\!-\!\!* C$ as $D *\!\!\to B \leftarrow\!* C$

until no more edges can be oriented.

Figure 10 shows the application of the orientation part of the FCI algorithm to the example begun in figure 8.

We do not know whether the orientation rules of the FCI algorithm are complete in the sense that if any edge A o—* B occurs in the output, then in some member of the set of DAGs represented by the PAG, A is an ancestor of B, and in some other member of the set of DAGs represented by the PAG A is not an ancestor of B. However, we have proved that the FCI algorithm provides enough orientations so that any two DAGs represented by the output are in the same **O-equivalence** class. See Spirtes and Verma (1992) and Spirtes and Richardson (1997) for details.

6. Simulation Study

We ran some preliminary simulation studies of the FCI algorithm that were intended to show how making various variables latent or selection variables would change what information could theoretically be inferred from population information and how much sample bias would affect the actual performance of the algorithm.

We used 10, 000 cases generated pseudo-randomly by Cooper (1992) from the Alarm network, shown in figure 11. The ALARM network was developed to model an emergency medical system (Beinlich et al. 1989). The 37 variables are all discrete, taking 2, 3 or 4 distinct values. There are 46 edges in the DAG. In most instances a directed arrow indicates that one variable is regarded as a cause of another. The physicians who built the network also assigned it a probability distribution: each variable V is given a probability distribution conditional on each vector of values of the variables having edges directed into V. This data has been used to test several different discovery algorithms (e.g. Spirtes, Glymour, and Scheines 1993, Cooper and Herskovits

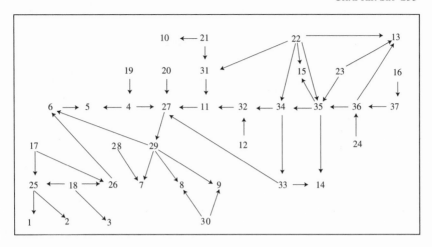

Figure 11. The Alarm network.

1992, Chickering 1994.) The interpretation of the variables is not relevant to the study described here.

We scored the PAG's output by the algorithm in the following way. For each ordered pair of variables *A* and *B* the PAG either entails nothing about whether *A* is an ancestor of *B*, or it entails that *A* is an ancestor of *B*, or it entails that *A* is not an ancestor of *B*. We count the number of ordered pairs for which the output PAG entails that *A* is an ancestor of *B*, the percentage of times the entailment is correct, the number of ordered pairs for which the output PAG entails that *A* not is an ancestor of *B*, and the percentage of times the entailment is correct. For purposes of comparison, we note that in the Alarm DAG there are 122 ordered pairs of distinct variables <*A, B*> such that *A* is an ancestor of *B* (18.32% of the ordered pairs), and 544 ordered pairs of distinct variables <*A, B*> such that *A* is not an ancestor of *B* (81.68% of the ordered pairs.) Of course, making a variable or variables latent and conditioning on a value of a selection variable will reduce the number of ancestor pairs.

We ran the algorithm on 6 different versions of the Alarm network, variously obtained by treating some of the Alarm variables as latent, and by selecting on values of some of the Alarm variables. The results are shown in table 1. A variable *A* is made latent by simply removing all of its values from the original data set. A variable *B* is made a selection variable by choosing a subpopulation which all share the same *B* value. Because conditioning on a *B* value reduces the sample size, we chose by hand selection variable values that did not reduce the sample size too much. In no case was the sample size reduced below 6000. We ran the algorithm with no latent variables or selection variables, with variable 29 made latent (abbreviated 29L in table 1), with

		Results of Simulation Studies		
Model	Number of Ancestor Relations Predicted	% Ancestor Relations Predicted Correct	Number of Non-Ancestor Relations Predicted	% Non-Ancestor Relations Predicted Correct
Alarm	62	100.00	1088	96.97
29L	21	100.00	1119	90.80
29L, 22L	25	100.00	1059	91.60
29L, 8S	43	97.67	1082	92.05
29L, 1S	31	83.87	1117	86.75
29L, 22L, 4L, 8S, 1S	23	86.96	861	91.52

Table 1. Results of running the FCI algorithm on six versions of the Alarm network.

variables 29 and 22 made latent, with variable 29 latent and 8 a selection variable (abbreviated 8S in table 1), with 29 latent and 1 a selection variable, and with 29, 22, and 4 latent and 8 and 1 as selection variables.

Often, when the output PAG incorrectly states that *A* is *not* an ancestor of *B*, the mistake would produce only small errors in predicting the effects on *B* of intervening on *A*, because the influence of *A* on *B* is very weak. For example, in the last simulation test we did, the output PAG incorrectly stated that 32 is not an ancestor of 6. However, 6 and 32 are almost independent; they pass a test of independence at the .01 significance level. So for the purposes of predicting the effects of intervention, this particular error is not important. However, we have not yet systematically calculated how important the errors that the algorithm makes are for prediction.

7. Future Work

The FCI algorithm could be improved in several ways. First, when the results of the statistical tests that it performs conflict in the sense that they are not compatible with any DAG, it could make more intelligent compromises based on what the preponderance of the evidence is. Second, there has been some progress recently in heuristic greedy DAG searches based upon maximizing some model score such as the posterior probability of the minimum description length (Cooper and Herskovits [1992], Heckerman, Geiger, and Chickering [1994], Chickering, Geiger, and Heckerman [1994]). Combining an independence test algorithm for DAG search (essentially a special case of FCI) and greedy DAG searches based upon maximizing a score has proved successful in simulation studies (Spirtes and Meek [1995], Singh and Valorta

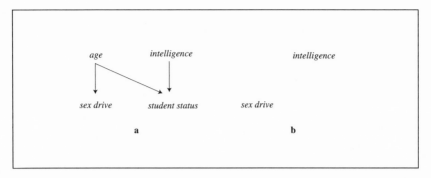

*Figure 12. (a) Causal DAG for **V** in Pop and Pop′.*
*(b) Causal DAG for **V′** in Pop and Pop′.*

[1993]). An analogous strategy might improve the accuracy of the FCI algorithm, although the task of calculating scores for a PAG faces a number of obstacles. We intend to test the FCI algorithm on a wider variety of DAGs, and empirical examples.

8. Proofs and Assumptions

In this section we describe some subtleties in the application of the Population inference assumption.

8.1 The Assumptions

The causal Markov assumption does not hold for every set of variables, nor for every subpopulation. Consider the following example. Suppose that the DAG in figure 12a is an accurate description of the causal relations in a population *Pop* for the set of variables **V** = {*age, intelligence, sex drive, student status*}and the causal Markov assumption and the causal faithfulness assumption hold in *Pop* for **V**.

Let **V′** = {*intelligence, sex drive*}. The causal DAGs for the sets of variables **V** and **V′** are shown in figure 12a and b respectively.

There is no edge between *intelligence* and *sex drive* in figure 12b because *intelligence* is not a cause of *sex drive* and *sex drive* is not a cause of *intelligence*. Note that although figure 12a and b are different DAGs, the causal facts represented in figure 12b are a subset of the causal facts represented in figure12a.

It follows from the causal Markov assumption and the causal faithfulness assumption for **V** in *Pop*, that *sex drive* and *intelligence* are dependent in the subpopulation *Pop'* of college students. (Causal faithfulness entails that *sex drive* and *intelligence* are dependent conditional on some value of *student status*, and because student status is binary, it follows that *sex drive* and *intelligence* are dependent on both values of *student status*).

The causal Markov assumption is not true in *Pop'* for **V'**, because *sex drive* and *intelligence* are dependent in the subpopulation *Pop'* of college students; i.e., they are not independent given the parents in figure 12b of sex drive or of intelligence (i.e. not independent given the empty set). Indeed because the causal Markov and causal faithfulness assumptions hold in *Pop* for **V**, the causal Markov assumption is *entailed* to fail in *Pop'* for **V'**.

As a consequence, in general we will *not* assume for the set of measured variables and the subpopulation from which the sample was drawn that the causal Markov and causal faithfulness assumptions hold. Rather we will assume, as in this example, that there is a larger set of variables that includes the measured variables, and a larger population that includes the subpopulation from which the sample was drawn such that (1) the causal DAG in the expanded set of variables for the expanded population satisfies the causal Markov and causal faithfulness assumptions; and (2) the causal structure in the subpopulation is the same as the causal structure in the expanded population.

In general, there will be more than one way of expanding the set of variables and the population so that the conditions described above are satisfied; corresponding to these different sets of variables and populations will be different causal DAGs. (For example, instead of adding just *age* and *student status* to **V'**, we could add *age* , *student status*, and some irrelevant variable such as *eye color*, with no edges between *eye color* and any of the other variables.) This does not matter, because the conclusions that we will draw will be true of *all* of the causal DAGs that satisfy the conditions we have laid down.

The assumptions that (1) the $S = 1$ subpopulation from which the sample is drawn is part of a population *Pop* in which the causal Markov and causal faithfulness assumptions hold for some causally sufficient set of variables V and (2) the causal structures relative to V in *Pop* and the $S = 1$ subpopulation are the same, are sufficient (but not necessary) conditions for the following assumption:

8.1.1 Selection Bias Causal Assumption

For each set of variables **O**, and each population *Pop* such that **S** = 1, there is a causally sufficient set of variables **V** such that $O \cup S \subseteq V$ and for all **A**, **B**, $C \subseteq O$, $A \perp\!\!\!\perp B \mid (C \cup (S = 1))$ in *Pop* if and only if the causal DAG *G* relative to **V** in *Pop* entails that $A \perp\!\!\!\perp B \mid (C \cup (S = 1))$ in *Pop*.

The selection bias causal assumption is sufficient for the asymptotic correctness of the methods of inference described in this chapter.

8.2 Proofs

In this section we will prove all of the theorems in the main body of the chapter. In order to simplify the proofs, the theorems are not proved in the order they were stated.

In the usual graph theoretic definition, a graph is an ordered pair <V, E> where **V** is a set of vertices, and **E** is a set of edges. The members of **E** are pairs of vertices (an ordered pair in a directed graph and an unordered pair in an undirected graph). For example, the edge $A \rightarrow B$ is represented by the ordered pair <A, B>. In directed graphs the ordering of the pair of vertices representing an edge in effect marks an arrowhead at one end of the edge. For our purposes we need to represent a larger variety of marks attached to the ends of undirected edges. In general, we allow that the end of an edge can be marked "out of" by "–" or can be marked "into" with ">" or can be marked with an "o."

In order to specify completely the type of an edge, therefore, we need to specify the variables and *marks* at each end. For example, the left end of "$A \text{ o} \rightarrow B$" can be represented as the ordered pair $[A, \text{o}]^3$, and the right end can be represented as the ordered pair $[B, >]$. We will also call $[A, \text{o}]$ the A end of the edge between A and B. The first member of the ordered pair is called an endpoint of an edge, e.g. in $[A, \text{o}]$ the endpoint is A. The entire edge consists of a set of ordered pairs that represent both of the endpoints, e.g. $\{[A, \text{o}], [B, >]\}$. The edge $\{[B, >], [A, \text{o}]\}$ is the same as $\{[A, \text{o}], [B, >]\}$ since it doesn't matter which end of the edge is listed first.

Note that a directed edge such as $A \rightarrow B$ has a mark "–"at the A end.

We say a *graph* is an ordered triple <V, M, E> where **V** is a nonempty set of vertices, **M** is a nonempty set of marks, and **E** is a set of sets of ordered pairs of the form $\{[V_1, M_1], [V_2, M_2]\}$, where V_1 and V_2 are in **V**, $V_1 \neq V_2$, and M_1 and M_2 are in **M**. If $G = $ <V, M, E> we say that G is *over* **V**.

We distinguish the following kinds of edges. An edge $\{[A, -], [B, >]\}$ is a directed edge from A to B, and is written $A \rightarrow B$ or $B \leftarrow A$. An edge $\{[A, -], [B, -]\}$ is an undirected edge between A and B, and is written $A - B$. An edge $\{[A, >], [B, >]\}$ is a bidirected edge between A and B, and is written $A \leftrightarrow B$. An edge $\{[A, \text{o}], [B, >]\}$ is a partially directed edge from A to B and is written $A \text{ o} \rightarrow B$ or $A \leftarrow\text{o} B$. An edge $\{[A, \text{o}], [B, \text{o}]\}$ is a nondirected edge between A and B and is written $A \text{ o—o } B$. Two vertices V_1 and V_2 are adjacent in a graph G if and only if there is a pair $\{[V_1, M_1], [V_2, M_2]\}$ in **E**. Vertices X, Y, and Z are in a *triangle* in graph G if and only if A and B are adjacent, B and C are adjacent, and A and C are adjacent.

For a directed edge $A \rightarrow B$, A is the *tail* of the edge and B is the *head;* the edge is *out of* A and *into* B, and A is *parent* of B and B is a *child* of A. A sequence of edges $<E_1, ..., E_n>$ in G is an *undirected path* if and only if there exists a sequence of vertices $<V_1, ..., V_{n+1}>$ such that for $1 \leq i \leq n$, E_i has endpoints V_i and V_{i+1}, and $E_i \neq E_{i+1}$. An empty sequence of edges with an associated sequence of vertices $<V_1>$ is an *empty path* between V_1 and V_1. A path U is *acyclic* if no vertex appears more than once in the corresponding sequence of vertices. We will assume that an undirected path is acyclic unless specifically mentioned otherwise. A sequence of edges $<E_1, ..., E_n>$ in G is a *directed path D from* V_1 to V_{n+1} if and only if there exists a sequence of vertices $<V_1, ..., V_{n+1}>$ such that for $1 \leq i \leq n$, there is a directed edge $V_i \rightarrow V_{i+1}$ on D. If there is an acyclic directed path from A to B or $B = A$ then A is an *ancestor* of B, and B is a *descendant* of A. If $\mathbf{Z}$ is a set of variables, A is an *ancestor* of $\mathbf{Z}$ if and only if it is an ancestor of a member of $\mathbf{Z}$, and similarly for *descendant*. If $\mathbf{X}$ is a set of vertices in directed acyclic graph $G(\mathbf{O}, \mathbf{S}, \mathbf{L})$, let **Ancestors**$(G, \mathbf{X})$ be the set of all ancestors of members of $\mathbf{X}$ in $G(\mathbf{O}, \mathbf{S}, \mathbf{L})$. (If the context makes clear which graph is being referred to, we will simply write **Ancestors**$(\mathbf{X})$.)

In a *directed graph*, all of the edges are directed edges. A directed graph is *acyclic* if and only if it contains no directed cyclic paths. A vertex V is a *collider* on an undirected path U if and only if U contains a pair of distinct edges adjacent on the path and into V. The *orientation* of an acyclic undirected path between A and B is the set consisting of the A end of the edge on U that contains A, and the B end of the edge on U that contains B.

If U is an undirected path that is a sequence of edges $<E_1, ..., E_n>$, and U' is a subsequence of the edges in U that is also an undirected path, then U' is a *subpath* of U. Note that if U is a cyclic undirected path and U contains edges $E_i = X \rightarrow Y$ and $E_j = Y \rightarrow Z$ that are not adjacent on U, then a subpath U' may leave out all of the edges between E_i and E_j. If U is acyclic, then there for any two vertices on U there is a unique subpath of U between the two vertices. If U is an acyclic undirected path between X and Y, and U contains distinct vertices A and B, then $U(A, B)$ is the unique subpath of U between A and B.

For three disjoint sets of variables $\mathbf{A}$, $\mathbf{B}$, and $\mathbf{C}$, $\mathbf{A}$ is *d-separated* from $\mathbf{B}$ given $\mathbf{C}$ in DAG G, if and only if there is an undirected path from some member of $\mathbf{A}$ to a member of $\mathbf{B}$ such that every collider on that path is either in $\mathbf{C}$ or has a descendant in $\mathbf{C}$, and every noncollider on the path is not in $\mathbf{C}$. For three disjoint sets of variables $\mathbf{A}$, $\mathbf{B}$, **and** $\mathbf{C}$, $\mathbf{A}$ is *d-connected* to $\mathbf{B}$ given $\mathbf{C}$ in DAG G if and only if $\mathbf{A}$ is not *d*-separated from $\mathbf{B}$ given $\mathbf{C}$. Geiger, Pearl, and Verma have shown that G entails $\mathbf{A}$ is independent of $\mathbf{B}$ given $\mathbf{C}$ if and only if $\mathbf{A}$ is *d*-separated from $\mathbf{B}$ given $\mathbf{C}$ in G. See Pearl (1988).

LEMMA 1. In a directed acyclic graph G over V, if X and Y are not in $\mathbf{Z}$, and there is a sequence H of distinct vertices in V from X to Y, and there is a set $\mathbf{T}$ of undirected paths such that

1. for each pair of adjacent vertices V and W in H, there is a unique

undirected path in **T** that *d*-connects *V* and *W* given **Z**\{*V*, *W*}, and

2. if a vertex *Q* in *H* is in **Z**, then the paths in **T** that contain *Q* as an endpoint collide at *Q*, and

3. if for three vertices *V*, *W*, *Q* occurring in that order in *H,* the *d*-connecting paths in **T** between *V* and *W*, and *W* and *Q* collide at *W,* then *W* has a descendant in **Z**,

then there is a path *U* in *G* that *d*-connects *X* and *Y* given **Z**. In addition, if all of the edges in all of the paths in **T** that contain *X* are into (out of) *X* then *U* is into (out of) *X*, and similarly for *Y*.

Proof. Let *U'* be the concatenation of all of the paths in **T** in the order of the sequence *H*. *U'* may not be an acyclic undirected path, because it may contain some vertices more than once. Let *U* be the result of removing all of the cycles from *U'*. If each edge in *U'* that contains *X* is into (out of) *X*, then *U* is into (out of) *X*, because each edge in *U* is an edge in *U'*. Similarly, if each edge in *U'* that contains *Y* is into (out of) *Y*, then *U* is into (out of) *Y*, because each edge in *U* is an edge in *U'*. We will prove that *U d*-connects *X* and *Y* given **Z**.

We will call an edge in *U* containing a given vertex *V* an *endpoint edge* if *V* is in the sequence *H* and the edge containing *V* occurs on the path in *T* between *V* and its predecessor or successor in *H*; otherwise the edge is an internal edge.

First we prove that every member *R* of **Z** that is on *U* is a collider on *U*. If there is an endpoint edge containing *R* on *U* then it is into *R* because by assumption the paths in **T** containing *R* collide at *R*. If an edge on *U* is an internal edge with endpoint *R,* then it is into *R* because it is an edge on a path that *d*-connects two variables *A* and *B* not equal to *R* given **Z**\{*A, B*}, and *R* is in **Z**. All of the edges on paths in **T** are into *R*, and hence the subset of those edges that occur on *U* are into *R*.

Next we show that every collider *R* on *U* has a descendant in **Z**. *R* is not equal to either of the endpoints *X* or *Y*, because the endpoints of a path are not colliders along the path. If *R* is a collider on any of the paths in **T** then *R* has a descendant in **Z** because it is an edge on a path that *d*-connects two variables *A* and *B* not equal to *R* given **Z**\{*A, B*}. If *R* is a collider on two endpoint edges then it has a descendant in **Z** by hypothesis. Suppose then that *R* is not a collider on the path in **T** between *A* and *B*, and not a collider on the path in **T** between *C* and *D*, but after cycles have been removed from *U'*, *R* is a collider on *U*. In that case *U'* contains an undirected cycle containing *R*. Because *G* is acyclic, the undirected cycle contains a collider. Hence *R* has a descendant that is a collider on *U'*. Each collider on *U'* has a descendant in **Z**. Hence *R* has a descendant in **Z**. Q.E.D.

LEMMA 2. If *G* is a directed acyclic graph, *R* is *d*-connected to *Y* given **Z** by undirected path U, and W and X are distinct vertices on U not in $\mathbf{Z}$, then $U(W, X)$ d-connects W and X given $\mathbf{Z}$.

Proof. Suppose G is a directed acyclic graph, R is d-connected to Y given $\mathbf{Z}$ by undirected path U, and W and X are distinct vertices on U not in $\mathbf{Z}$. Each noncollider on $U(W, X)$ except for the endpoints is a noncollider on U, and hence not in $\mathbf{Z}$. Every collider on $U(W, X)$ has a descendant in $\mathbf{Z}$ because each collider on $U(W, X)$ is a collider on U, which d-connects R and Y given $\mathbf{Z}$. It follows that $U(W, X)$ d-connects W and X given $\mathbf{Z} = \mathbf{Z}\backslash\{W, X\}$. Q.E.D.

LEMMA 3. If G is a directed acyclic graph, R is d-connected to Y given $\mathbf{Z}$ by undirected path U, there is a directed path D from R to X that does not contain any member of $\mathbf{Z}$, and X is not on U, then X is d-connected to Y given $\mathbf{Z}$ by a path U' that is into X. If D does not contain Y, then U' is into Y if and only if U is into Y.

Proof. Let D be a directed path from R to X that does not contain any member of $\mathbf{Z}$, and U an undirected path that d-connects R and Y given $\mathbf{Z}$ and does not contain X. Let Q be the point of intersection of D and U that is closest to Y on U. Q is not in $\mathbf{Z}$ because it is on D.

If D does contain Y, then $Y = Q$, and $D(Y, X)$ is a path into X that d-connects X and Y given $\mathbf{Z}$ because it contains no colliders and no members of $\mathbf{Z}$.

If D does not contain Y then $Q \neq Y$. $X \neq Q$ because X is not on U and Q is. By lemma 2, $U(Q, Y)$ d-connects Q and Y given $\mathbf{Z}\backslash\{Q, Y\} = \mathbf{Z}$. Also, $D(Q, X)$ d-connects Q and X given $\mathbf{Z}\backslash\{Q, X\} = \mathbf{Z}$. $D(Q, X)$ is out of Q, and Q is not in $\mathbf{Z}$. By lemma 1 there is a path U' that d-connects X and Y given $\mathbf{Z}$ that is into X. If Y is not on D, then all of the edges containing Y in U' are on $U(Q, Y)$, and hence by lemma 1 U' is into Y if and only if U is. Q.E.D.

U is an *inducing path* between A and B in DAG $G(\mathbf{O}, \mathbf{S}, \mathbf{L})$ relative to $\mathbf{O}$ given $\mathbf{S}$ if and only if there is an acyclic undirected path from A to B such that every collider on U has a descendant in $\{A, B\} \cup \mathbf{S}$, and no noncollider on U is in $\mathbf{O} \cup \mathbf{S}$. For example, all of the paths between A and B in figure 4 are inducing paths relative to $\mathbf{O}$ given $\mathbf{S}$. The following theorems generalize Verma and Pearl (1990).

LEMMA 4. In directed graph $G(\mathbf{O}, \mathbf{S}, \mathbf{L})$, if there is an inducing path between A and B that is out of A and into B, then for any subset $\mathbf{Z}$ of $\mathbf{O}\backslash\{A, B\}$ there is an undirected path C that d-connects A and B given $\mathbf{Z} \cup \mathbf{S}$ that is out of A and into B.

Proof. Let U be an inducing path between A and B that is out of A and into B. Every member of $\mathbf{O} \cup \mathbf{S}$ on U except for the endpoints is a collider, and every collider is an ancestor of either A or B or a member of $\mathbf{S}$.

If every collider on U has a descendant in $\mathbf{Z} \cup \mathbf{S}$, then let $C = U$. C d-connects A and B given $\mathbf{Z} \cup \mathbf{S}$ because every collider has a descendant in $\mathbf{Z} \cup \mathbf{S}$, and no noncollider is in $\mathbf{Z} \cup \mathbf{S}$. C is out of A and into B.

Suppose that not every collider on U has a descendant in $\mathbf{Z} \cup \mathbf{S}$. Let R be the collider on U closest to A that does not have a descendant in $\mathbf{Z} \cup \mathbf{S}$, and W be the collider on U closest to A. $R \neq A$ and $R \neq B$ because A and B are not colliders on U.

Suppose first that $R = W$. R is not in $\mathbf{Z} \cup \mathbf{S}$ because R has no descendant in $\mathbf{Z} \cup \mathbf{S}$. There is a directed path from R to B that does not contain A, because otherwise there is a cycle in $G(\mathbf{O}, \mathbf{S}, \mathbf{L})$. B is not on $U(A, R)$. $U(A, R)$ d-connects A and R given $\mathbf{Z} \cup \mathbf{S}$, and is out of A. By lemma 3 there is a d-connecting path C between A and B given $\mathbf{Z} \cup \mathbf{S}$ that is out of A and into B.

Suppose then that $R \neq W$. Because U is out of A, W is a descendant of A. W has a descendant in $\mathbf{Z} \cup \mathbf{S}$ by definition of R. It follows that every collider on U that is an ancestor of A has a descendant in $\mathbf{Z} \cup \mathbf{S}$. Hence R is an ancestor of B, and not of A. B is not on $U(A, R)$. $U(A, R)$ d-connects A and R given $\mathbf{Z} \cup \mathbf{S}$ and is out of A. By hypothesis, there is a directed path D from R to B that does not contain A or any member of $\mathbf{Z} \cup \mathbf{S}$. By lemma 3, there is a path that d-connects A and B given $\mathbf{Z} \cup \mathbf{S}$ that is out of A and into B. Q.E.D.

LEMMA 5. If $G(\mathbf{O}, \mathbf{S}, \mathbf{L})$ is a directed acyclic graph, and there is an inducing path U between A and B that is into A and into B, then for every subset $\mathbf{Z}$ of $\mathbf{O} \backslash \{A, B\}$ there is an undirected path C that d-connects A and B given $\mathbf{Z} \cup \mathbf{S}$ that is into A and into B.

Proof. If every collider on U has a descendant in $\mathbf{Z} \cup \mathbf{S}$, then U is a d-connecting path between A and B given $\mathbf{Z} \cup \mathbf{S}$ that is into A and into B. Suppose then that there is a collider that does not have a descendant in $\mathbf{Z} \cup \mathbf{S}$. Let W be the collider on U closest to A that does not have a descendant in $\mathbf{Z} \cup \mathbf{S}$. Suppose first that W is the source of a directed path D to B that does not contain A. B is not on $U(A, W)$. $U(A, W)$ is a path that d-connects A and W given $\mathbf{Z} \cup \mathbf{S}$, and is into A. By lemma 3, there is an undirected path C that d-connects A and B given $\mathbf{Z} \cup \mathbf{S}$ and is into A and into B. Similarly, if R is the closest collider to B on U that does not have a descendant in $\mathbf{Z} \cup \mathbf{S}$, and R is the source of a directed path D to A that does not contain B, then by lemma 3, A and B are d-connected given $\mathbf{Z} \cup \mathbf{S}$ by an undirected path into A and into B.

Suppose then that the collider W on U closest to A that does not have a descendant in $\mathbf{Z} \cup \mathbf{S}$ is not the source of a directed path to B that does not contain A, and that the collider R on U closest to B that does not have a descendant in $\mathbf{Z} \cup \mathbf{S}$ is not the source of a directed path to A that does not contain B. The subpath of U from W to A does not contain B or a member of $\mathbf{Z} \cup \mathbf{S}$, and the subpath of U from R to B does not contain A or a member of $\mathbf{Z} \cup \mathbf{S}$. It follows that there exist two colliders E and F on U such that there is a directed path from E to A that does not contain B, there is a directed path from F to B that does not contain A, F is between E and B, and every collider between E and F is an ancestor of a member of $\mathbf{Z} \cup \mathbf{S}$. $U(E, F)$ d-connects E and F given $(\mathbf{Z} \cup \mathbf{S}) \backslash \{E, F\}$ because no member of $\mathbf{O} \cup \mathbf{S}$ is a noncollider on

$U(E, F)$ except for the endpoints, and every collider on $U(E, F)$ has a descendant in $\mathbf{Z} \cup \mathbf{S}$. The directed path from E to A d-connects E and A given $(\mathbf{Z} \cup \mathbf{S})\backslash\{E, A\}$ and the directed path from F to B d-connects F and B given $(\mathbf{Z} \cup \mathbf{S})\backslash\{F, B\}$. By lemma 1 there is an undirected path that d-connects A and B given $\mathbf{Z} \cup \mathbf{S}$ that is into A and into B. Q.E.D.

LEMMA 6. If $G(\mathbf{O}, \mathbf{S}, \mathbf{L})$ is a directed acyclic graph and U is an inducing path out of both A and B then every collider on U is an ancestor of a member of $\mathbf{S}$.

Proof. Let W be the collider on U closest to A and let R be the collider on U closest to B. Since U is out of A and $G(\mathbf{O}, \mathbf{S}, \mathbf{L})$ is acyclic, W is not an ancestor of A. Similarly, R is not an ancestor of B. Let Q be the collider on U closest to A that is not an ancestor of a member of $\mathbf{S}$. Since Q is not an ancestor of $\mathbf{S}$, it follows that Q is an ancestor of A or B, and hence is an ancestor of W or R.

Suppose, for a contradiction, that $W = Q$. Hence Q is an ancestor of B. $Q \neq R$ since R is not an ancestor of B. R is not an ancestor of A, since otherwise there would be a cycle in $G(\mathbf{O}, \mathbf{S}, \mathbf{L})$. Thus R is an ancestor of a member of $\mathbf{S}$ and Q is an ancestor of a member of $\mathbf{S}$. This is a contradiction. The argument for $R = Q$ is similar.

Suppose that $W \neq Q$ and $R \neq Q$. Because $G(\mathbf{O}, \mathbf{S}, \mathbf{L})$ is acyclic, either W or R is an ancestor of $\mathbf{S}$. Without loss of generality, suppose that W is an ancestor of $\mathbf{S}$. If R is an ancestor of A, then R is an ancestor of $\mathbf{S}$ since A is an ancestor of W. If R is not an ancestor of A, then R is an ancestor of a member of $\mathbf{S}$ from the definition of inducing path. In either case R is an ancestor of $\mathbf{S}$. Since W and R are ancestors of $\mathbf{S}$, A and B are ancestors of $\mathbf{S}$ and therefore Q is an ancestor of $\mathbf{S}$. Q.E.D.

LEMMA 7. If $G(\mathbf{O}, \mathbf{S}, \mathbf{L})$ is a directed acyclic graph over $\mathbf{V}$, and there is an inducing path U between A and B that is out of A and out of B, then for every subset $\mathbf{Z}$ of $\mathbf{O}\backslash\{A, B\}$ there is an undirected path C that d-connects A and B given $\mathbf{Z} \cup \mathbf{S}$ that is out of A and out of B.

Proof. Let U be an inducing path out of both A and B. By lemma 6 every collider on U has a descendant in $\mathbf{Z} \cup \mathbf{S}$. Thus U d-connects A and B given $\mathbf{Z} \cup \mathbf{S}$ and is out of both endpoints. Q.E.D.

LEMMA 8. If $G(\mathbf{O}, \mathbf{S}, \mathbf{L})$ is a directed acyclic graph over $\mathbf{V}$ and an undirected path U in G d-connects A and B, given $((\mathbf{Ancestors}(G, \{A, B\} \cup \mathbf{S}) \cap \mathbf{O}) \cup \mathbf{S})\backslash\{A, B\}$ then U is an inducing path between A and B.

Proof. If there is a path U that d-connects A and B given $((\mathbf{Ancestors}(G, \{A, B\} \cup \mathbf{S}) \cap \mathbf{O}) \cup \mathbf{S})\backslash\{A, B\}$ then every collider on U is an ancestor of a vertex in $((\mathbf{Ancestors}(G, \{A, B\} \cup \mathbf{S}) \cap \mathbf{O}) \cup \mathbf{S})\backslash\{A, B\}$ and hence has a descendant in $\{A, B\} \cup \mathbf{S}$. Every vertex on U is an ancestor of either A or B or a collider on U, and hence every vertex on U is an ancestor of A or B or $\mathbf{S}$.

If U d-connects A and B given $((\mathbf{Ancestors}(G, \{A, B\} \cup \mathbf{S}) \cap \mathbf{O}) \cup \mathbf{S})\backslash\{A, B\}$, then every member of $((\mathbf{Ancestors}(G, \{A, B\} \cup \mathbf{S}) \cap \mathbf{O}) \cup \mathbf{S})\backslash\{A, B\}$ that is on U, except for the endpoints, is a collider. Since every vertex on U is in $\mathbf{Ancestors}(G, \{A, B\} \cup \mathbf{S})$, every member of $\mathbf{O}$ that is on U, except for the endpoints, is a collider. Every member of $\mathbf{S}$ on U is a collider. Hence U is an inducing path between A and B. Q.E.D.

LEMMA 9. $G(\mathbf{O}, \mathbf{S}, \mathbf{L}))$ entails that for all subsets $\mathbf{X}$ of $\mathbf{O}$, A is dependent on B given $(\mathbf{X} \cup \mathbf{S})\backslash\{A, B\}$ if and only if there is an inducing path between A and B.

Proof. This follows from lemma 4, lemma 5, lemma 7, and lemma 8 Q.E.D.

If $G(\mathbf{O}, \mathbf{S}, \mathbf{L})$ is a directed acyclic graph, and in $G(\mathbf{O}, \mathbf{S}, \mathbf{L})$ there is a sequence of distinct vertices M (each of which is in $\mathbf{O}$) starting with A and ending with C and a set of paths F such that for every pair of vertices I and J adjacent in M in that order there is exactly one inducing path W between I and J in F, and if $J \neq C$ then W is into J, and if $I \neq A$, then W is into I, and if I and J are ancestors of $\{A, C\} \cup \mathbf{S}$, then F is an *inducing sequence* between A and C.

LEMMA 10. If $G(\mathbf{O}, \mathbf{S}, \mathbf{L})$ is a directed acyclic graph and there is an inducing sequence F between A and C in $G(\mathbf{O}, \mathbf{S}, \mathbf{L})$, then in $G(\mathbf{O}, \mathbf{S}, \mathbf{L})$ a subpath of the concatenation of the paths in F is an inducing path T between A and C such that if the path in F between A and its successor in M is into A then U is into A, and if the path in F between C and its predecessor in M is into C then U is into C.

Proof. Suppose that in $G(\mathbf{O}, \mathbf{S}, \mathbf{L})$ there is a sequence M of vertices in $\mathbf{O}$ starting with A and ending with C, and a set of paths F such that for every pair of vertices I and J adjacent in M there is exactly one inducing path W between I and J, and if $J \neq C$ then W is into J, and if $I \neq A$ then W is into A, and I and J are ancestors of either A or C or $\mathbf{S}$. Let T' be the concatenation of the paths in F. T' may not be an acyclic undirected path because it might contain undirected cycles. Let T be an acyclic undirected subpath of T' between A and C. We will now show that except for the endpoints, every vertex in $\mathbf{O} \cup \mathbf{S}$ on T is a collider, and every collider on T is an ancestor of $\{A, C\} \cup \mathbf{S}$.

If V is a vertex in $\mathbf{O} \cup \mathbf{S}$ that is on T but that is not equal to A or C, every edge on every path in F is into V. Hence, every edge on T that contains V is into V because the edges on T are a subset of the edges on inducing paths in F.

Let R and H be the endpoints of a path W in F. We will now show that every vertex on W is an ancestor of $\{A, C\} \cup \mathbf{S}$. By hypothesis, R is an ancestor of $\{A, C\} \cup \mathbf{S}$, and H is an ancestor of $\{A, C\} \cup \mathbf{S}$. Because W is an inducing path, every collider on W is an ancestor of $\{R, H\} \cup \mathbf{S}$, and hence an ancestor of $\{A, C\} \cup \mathbf{S}$. Every noncollider on W is an ancestor of R or H, or an ancestor of a collider on W. Hence every vertex on W is an ancestor of $\{A, C\}$

∪ **S**. It follows that every collider on T is an ancestor of $\{A, C\} \cup \mathbf{S}$, because the vertices on T are a subset of the vertices on paths in T'.

By definition, T is an inducing path between A and C. Suppose the path in F between A and its successor is into A. If the edge on T with endpoint A is on the path in F on which A is an endpoint, then T is into A because by hypothesis that inducing path is into A. If the edge on T with endpoint A is on an inducing path in which A is not an endpoint of the path, then T is into A because A is in **O**, and hence a collider on every inducing path for which it is not an endpoint. Similarly, T is into C if in F the path between C and its predecessor is into C. Q.E.D.

LEMMA 11. If $G(\mathbf{O}, \mathbf{S}, \mathbf{L})$ is a directed acyclic graph, A and B are in O, and $G(\mathbf{O}, \mathbf{S}, \mathbf{L})$ contains an inducing path U between A and B that is out of A and into B, and A is not an ancestor of **S**, then there is a directed path from A to B in $G(\mathbf{O}, \mathbf{S}, \mathbf{L})$.

Proof. Suppose that A is not an ancestor of **S**, and U is an inducing path between A and B that is out of A and into B. If U does not contain a collider, then U is a directed path from A to B. If U does contain a collider, let D be the first collider after A. By definition of inducing path, there is either a directed path from D to B, D to a member of **S**, or D to A. There is no path from D to A because there is no cycle in $G(\mathbf{O}, \mathbf{S}, \mathbf{L})$. There is no directed path from D to a member of **S**, because A is an ancestor of D, but not an ancestor of a member of **S**. Hence there is a directed path from D to B. Because U is out of A, and D is the first collider after A, there is a directed path from A to D. Hence there is a directed path from A to B. Q.E.D.

$V \in$ **D-SEP**(A, B) in DAG $G(\mathbf{O}, \mathbf{S}, \mathbf{L})$ if and only if there is a sequence of vertices $U \equiv \langle A...V \rangle$ in $\mathbf{O} \cap$ **Ancestors**$(\{A, B\} \cup \mathbf{S})$ such that (1) there is an inducing path between every consecutive pair of vertices on U and (2) with the exception of the endpoints every vertex on U is not an ancestor of the vertices preceding or succeeding it in the sequence U nor an ancestor of **S**.

LEMMA 12. In DAG $G(\mathbf{O}, \mathbf{S}, \mathbf{L})$, if there is some subset $\mathbf{W} \subseteq \mathbf{O}\backslash\{A, B\}$ such that A and B are d-separated by $\mathbf{W} \cup \mathbf{S}$, then A and B are d-separated given **D-SEP**$(A, B) \cup \mathbf{S}$.

Proof. Suppose there is some subset $\mathbf{W} \subseteq \mathbf{O}\backslash\{A, B\}$ such that A and B are d-separated by $\mathbf{W} \cup \mathbf{S}$, but A and B are d-connected given **D-SEP**$(A, B) \cup \mathbf{S}$. Let $P \equiv \langle A, ...B \rangle$ be a path d-connecting A and B given **D-SEP**$(A, B) \cup \mathbf{S}$.

If every vertex in **O** on P occurs as a collider, then every observed vertex on P is an ancestor of A or B or **S** (since **D-SEP**$(A, B) \cup \mathbf{S} \subseteq$ **Ancestors**$(\{A, B\} \cup \mathbf{S})$). Hence in this case P constitutes an inducing path between A and B, and so there is no subset $\mathbf{W} \subseteq \mathbf{O}\backslash\{A, B\}$ such that A and B are d-separated by some $\mathbf{W} \cup \mathbf{S}$.

Hence there is some vertex $O \in \mathbf{O}$, such that O is a noncollider on P. Suppose without loss that O is the first such vertex on P. We will now show that $O \in$ **D-SEP**$(A, B) \cup$ **S**.

Consider the subpath $P(A, O)$. Let $<C_1, \ldots C_m>$ denote the (possibly empty) sequence of colliders on $P(A, O)$, which are ancestors of **D-SEP**(A, B), but not ancestors of **S**. Hence there is a directed path (possibly of length 0) from $C_i \rightarrow \ldots \rightarrow D_i$, where $D_i \in$ **D-SEP**(A, B). Let F_i be the first measured vertex on the path $C_i \rightarrow \ldots \rightarrow D_i$; such an F_i is guaranteed to exist since $D_i \in$ **O**.

We will now show that there is an inducing path between F_i and F_{i+1}. It follows that no F_i is an ancestor of **S**, because no C_i is an ancestor of **S**. Consider the path Q_i formed by concatenating the directed path $F_i \leftarrow \ldots \leftarrow C_i$, the subpath $P(C_i, C_{i+1})$, and the directed path $C_{i+1} \rightarrow \ldots F_{i+1}$. It follows from the construction, that with the exception of F_i and F_{i+1} the only measured vertices on Q_i are on $P(C_i, C_{i+1})$. Moreover, since O is the first noncollider on P that is in **O**, every measured vertex on $P(C_i, C_{i+1})$ is a collider. Hence by construction of the sequence $<C_1, \ldots C_m>$, every measured vertex on $P(C_i, C_{i+1})$ is an ancestor of **S**. Hence Q_i is an inducing path.

Similarly, by concatenating the path $P(A, C_1)$ and the path $C_1 \rightarrow \ldots \rightarrow F_1$, and by concatenating the path $F_m \leftarrow \ldots \leftarrow C_m$ and $P(C_m, O)$, we may form inducing paths Q_0 and Q_m between A and F_1, and between F_m and O respectively.

Note that all of the inducing path Q_k that we have constructed are into the F_i vertices. The sequence $R \equiv <A \equiv F_0, F_1, \ldots F_m, F_{m+1} \equiv O>$ thus consists of a sequence each of which is an ancestor of A or B or **S**, and such that each consecutive pair in the sequence is connected by an inducing path. Hence this sequence satisfies the first condition necessary to show that $O \in$ **D-SEP**(A, B).

We now construct a subsequence of $T \equiv <A \equiv F_{\alpha(0)}, F_{\alpha(1)} \ldots F_{\alpha(t)} \equiv O>$ satisfying property (ii) as follows:

1. Let $\alpha(0) = 0$, so $F_{\alpha(0)} \equiv F_0 \equiv A$.
2. Let $\alpha(1)$ be the largest η such that there is an inducing path between $F_{\alpha(0)}$ and F_η which is into F_η if there is such an inducing path, else let $F_{\alpha(1)} \equiv O$.
3. Let $\alpha(k+1)$ be the largest $\eta > k$ such that there is an inducing path between $F_{\alpha(k)}$ and F_η which is into $F_{\alpha(k)}$ and, if $\eta < m+1$, into F_η.
4. If $\alpha(k) = m+1$ then stop.

(Note that at each stage in the construction, so long as $\alpha(k) < m+1$, there is guaranteed to be some η such that there is an inducing path between $F_{\alpha(k)}$ and F_η which is into $F_{\alpha(k)}$ and, if $\eta < m+1$, into F_η, since, for $i > 0$ there is an inducing path between F_i and F_{i+1}, which is into F_i, and for $i+1 < m+1$, into F_{i+1}.)

We will now show that for $i \neq 0$, and $i \neq m+1$, $F_{\alpha(i)}$ is not an ancestor of $F_{\alpha(i-1)}$ or $F_{\alpha(i+1)}$. Suppose that $F_{\alpha(i)}$ is an ancestor of $F_{\alpha(i-1)}$ or $F_{\alpha(i+1)}$. By construction there is an inducing path between $F_{\alpha(i)}$ and $F_{\alpha(i-1)}$ which is into

$F_{\alpha(i)}$; likewise there is an inducing path between $F_{\alpha(i)}$ and $F_{\alpha(i+1)}$ which is into $F_{\alpha(i)}$. Hence if $F_{\alpha(i)}$ is an ancestor of $F_{\alpha(i-1)}$ or $F_{\alpha(i+1)}$ then there is an inducing path between $F_{\alpha(i-1)}$ and $F_{\alpha(i+1)}$ which is into both $F_{\alpha(i-1)}$ and $F_{\alpha(i+1)}$ (unless $F_{\alpha(i-1)}$ or $F_{\alpha(i+1)}$ is an endpoint). But in that case $\alpha(i)$ is not the largest η such that there is an inducing path between $F_{\alpha(i-1)}$ and F_η which is into $F_{\alpha(i-1)}$ and, if $\eta < m+1$, into F_η. This is a contradiction. Q.E.D.

LEMMA 13. If π_0 is the partially oriented graph constructed in step C of the Fast Causal Inference Algorithm for $G(\mathbf{O}, \mathbf{S}, \mathbf{L})$, A and B are in $\mathbf{O}$, and A is not an ancestor of B in G, then every vertex in **D-SEP**(A, B) in $G(\mathbf{O}, \mathbf{S}, \mathbf{L})$ is in **Possible-D-SEP**(A, B, π_0).

Proof. Suppose that A is not an ancestor of B. If V is in **D-SEP**(A, B), in $G(\mathbf{O}, \mathbf{S}, \mathbf{L})$, there is a sequence of vertices $U \equiv <A...V>$ in $\mathbf{O} \cap$ **Ancestors**$(\{A, B\} \cup \mathbf{S})$, an inducing path between every consecutive pair of vertices on U with the exception of the endpoints, and every vertex on U is not an ancestor of the vertices preceding or succeeding it in the sequence U. The proof is by induction on the length of U. If the length of U is 1, **Possible-D-SEP**(A, B, π_0) contains V because it contains all edges adjacent to A in π_0. Suppose that, for each vertex V that is in **D-SEP**(A, B) because of a sequence U of no more than length n, V is in **Possible-D-SEP**(A, B, π_0). Let W be a vertex in **D-SEP**(A, B) because of a sequence U of length $n + 1$, and X is the predecessor of W in U, and Y is the predecessor of X in U. If there is an inducing path between W and Y, then W is in **Possible-D-SEP**(A, B, π_0) since W, X, and Y form a triangle. Suppose there is no inducing path between W and Y. It then follows that X is not an ancestor of Y or W, and so the inducing path between W and X is into X. Similarly, the inducing path between Y and X is into X. Hence X is not in any set that d-separates Y and W. Y and W are d-separated given a subset of $\mathbf{O}\setminus\{W, Y\}$ because there is no inducing path between them. Hence, step C of the FCI algorithm orients both the edge between W and X and the edge between Y and X into X. It follows that W is in **Possible-D-SEP**(A, B, π_0). Q.E.D.

Because π_0 contains more edges than the output PAG, the orientations in π may not be correct for the two following reasons. First, an edge that is in π_0, but not in the output PAG, may hide some collider along a path. Second, a vertex may be oriented as a collider in π_0, but not in the output PAG, because of a "collision" involving an edge in π that does not occur in the output PAG. However, either of these mistakes in orientation in π simply makes **Possible-D-SEP**(A, B, π) larger, and so it still includes **D-SEP**(A, B, G).

LEMMA 14. Suppose that in a graph $G(\mathbf{O}, \mathbf{S}, \mathbf{L})$, $X, Y, Z \in \mathbf{O}$, and Y is not an ancestor of X or Z or $\mathbf{S}$. If there is a set $\mathbf{Q} \subseteq \mathbf{O}$ containing Y such that for every subset $\mathbf{T} \subseteq \mathbf{Q}\setminus\{Y\}$, X and Z are d-connected given $\mathbf{T} \cup \mathbf{S}$, then X and Z are d-connected given $\mathbf{Q} \cup \mathbf{S}$.

Proof: Let $\mathbf{T}^* = ($**Ancestors**$(\{X, Z\} \cup \mathbf{S})) \cap \mathbf{Q}$. Now $\mathbf{T}^* \subseteq \mathbf{Q}$, but since, by hypothesis, $Y \notin$ **Ancestors**$(\{X, Z\} \cup \mathbf{S})$, it follows that $\mathbf{T}^* \subseteq \mathbf{Q}\backslash\{Y\}$. Hence, again, by hypothesis, there is a path P d-connecting X and Z given $\mathbf{T}^* \cup \mathbf{S}$. By the definition of a d-connecting path, every vertex on P is either an ancestor of X or Z, or $\mathbf{T}^* \cup \mathbf{S}$. Since $\mathbf{T}^* \subseteq ($**Ancestors**$(\{X, Z\} \cup \mathbf{S})) \cap \mathbf{Q}$, it follows that every vertex on P is in **Ancestors**$(\{X, Z\} \cup \mathbf{S})$. Since no vertex in $\mathbf{Q}\backslash\mathbf{T}^*$ is in **Ancestors**$(\{X, Z\} \cup \mathbf{S})$, it follows that no vertex in $\mathbf{Q}\backslash\mathbf{T}^*$ lies on P. But since $\mathbf{T}^* \cup \mathbf{S} \subseteq \mathbf{Q} \cup \mathbf{S}$, the only way in which P could fail to d-connect X and Z given $\mathbf{Q} \cup \mathbf{S}$ would be if some vertex in $(\mathbf{Q} \cup \mathbf{S})\backslash(\mathbf{T}^* \cup \mathbf{S}) = \mathbf{Q}\backslash\mathbf{T}^*$ lay on the path. Hence P still d-connects X and Z given $\mathbf{Q} \cup \mathbf{S}$. Q.E.D.

In a graph $G(\mathbf{O}, \mathbf{S}, \mathbf{L})$ if X and Z are d-separated given $\mathbf{Q} \cup \mathbf{S}$, $(\{X, Z\} \cup \mathbf{Q} \subseteq \mathbf{O})$, and for any proper subset $\mathbf{T} \subset \mathbf{Q}$, X and Z are d-connected given $\mathbf{T} \cup \mathbf{S}$, then $\mathbf{Q}$ is a *minimal d-separating set* for X and Z in $G(\mathbf{O}, \mathbf{S}, \mathbf{L})$.

COROLLARY. If Y is in a minimal d-separating set for X and Z in $G(\mathbf{O}, \mathbf{S}, \mathbf{L})$, then Y is an ancestor of X or Z or $\mathbf{S}$ in $G(\mathbf{O}, \mathbf{S}, \mathbf{L})$.

Proof: Suppose for a contradiction that there was a minimal d-separating set $\mathbf{Q}$ for X and Z, which contained some vertex $Y \notin$ **Ancestors**$(\{X, Z\} \cup \mathbf{S})$. It would then follow from lemma 14 and the definition of a minimal d-separating set that X and Z were d-connected given $\mathbf{Q} \cup \mathbf{S}$, which is a contradiction. Q.E.D.

THEOREM 5. If $P(V)$ is faithful to $G_1(\mathbf{O}, \mathbf{S}_1, \mathbf{L}_1)$, and the input to the FCI algorithm is an oracle for $P(V)$ over $\mathbf{O}$ given $\mathbf{S} = 1$, the output is a PAG of $G_1(\mathbf{O}, \mathbf{S}_1, \mathbf{L}_1)$.

Proof. The adjacencies are correct by lemma 12 and lemma 13. We will now show that the orientations are correct. The proof is by induction on the number of applications of orientation rules in the repeat loop of the fast causal inference algorithm. Let the object constructed by the algorithm after the nth iteration of the repeat loop be π'_n (Note that according to the notation of the algorithm, $\pi'_0 = \pi_2$.) Note that each set **Sepset**(A, C) is a minimal d-connecting set, because if there were any subset $\mathbf{X}$ of **Sepset**(A, C) such that $\mathbf{X} \cup \mathbf{S}$ d-separated A and C, then the algorithm would have found $\mathbf{X}$ at an earlier stage and made **Sepset**(A, C) equal to $\mathbf{X}$.

Base Case: Suppose that the only orientation rule that has been applied is that if $A *\!\!-\!\!* B *\!\!-\!\!* C$ in π'_0, but A and C are not adjacent in π'_0, $A *\!\!-\!\!* B *\!\!-\!\!* C$ is oriented as $A *\!\!\rightarrow B \leftarrow\!\!* C$ if B is not a member of **Sepset**(A, C) and as $A *\!\!-\!\!* B *\!\!-\!\!* C$ if B is a member of **Sepset**(A, C). Suppose first that B is not in **Sepset**(A, C), and that contrary to the hypothesis B is an ancestor of A or C or $\mathbf{S}$. If $G(\mathbf{O}, \mathbf{S}, \mathbf{L})$ is an arbitrary member of **O-Equiv**$(G_1(\mathbf{O}, \mathbf{S}_1, \mathbf{L}_1))$, there is an inducing path between A and B and an inducing path between B and C. Hence there is a path U_1 that d-connects A and B given **Sepset**$(A, C) \cup \mathbf{S}$ and a path U_2 that d-connects B and C given **Sepset**$(A, C) \cup \mathbf{S}$. If U_1 and U_2 do not collide at B then, by lemma 1, A and C are d-connected given

Sepset(*A*, *C*) ∪ **S**, which is a contradiction. If *U*1 and *U*$_2$ do collide at *B*, and *B* is an ancestor of **S**, then, by lemma 1, *A* and *C* are *d*-connected given **Sepset**(*A*, *C*) ∪ **S**, which is a contradiction. If *B* is an ancestor of *A* or *C* but not of **S**, then either there is a directed path *D*$_1$ from *B* to *A* that does not contain *C* or **S**, or there is a directed path *D*$_2$ from *B* to *C* that does not contain *A* or **S**. Suppose without loss of generality that the latter is the case. It follows that *D*$_2$ *d*-connects *B* and *C* given **Sepset**(*A*, *C*)\{*C*} ∪ **S** and is out of *B*. It follows by lemma 1 that *A* and *C* are *d*-connected given **Sepset**(*A*, *C*) ∪ **S**, which is a contradiction.

Suppose next that *B* is in **Sepset**(*A*, *C*), but that *B* is not an ancestor of *A* or *C* or **S**. It follows from lemma 11 that the inducing paths in *G*(**O**, **S**, **L**) are both into *B*. It follows from lemma 1 that *A* and *C* are *d*-connected given **Sepset**(*A*, *C*) ∪ **S**, which is a contradiction. Hence, *B* is an ancestor of *A* or *C* or of **S**.

Induction Case: Suppose π'_n is a partial ancestral graph of *G*(**O**, **S**, **L**). We will now show that π'_{n+1} is a partial ancestral graph of *G*(**O**, **S**, **L**).

Case 1: There is a directed path *D* from *A* to *B* and an edge *A* *—* *B* in π'_n, so *A* *—* *B* is oriented as *A* *→ B*. By the induction hypothesis, there is a directed path from *A* to *B* in *G*(**O**, **S**, **L**). Hence *B* is not an ancestor of *A* in *G*(**O**, **S**, **L**).

Case 2: If *B* is a collider along <*A*, *B*, *C*> in π_2, *A* is not adjacent to *C*, *D* is adjacent to *A*, *B*, and *C*, and *D* is a noncollider along <*A*, *D*, *C*>, then orient *B* *—* *D* as *B* ← * *D*. Because *D* is a noncollider along <*A*, *D*, *C*>, *D* is an ancestor of *A* or *C* or **S**. If *B* is an ancestor of *D*, then *B* is an ancestor of *A* or *C* or **S**. But because *B* is a collider along <*A*, *B*, *C*>, it is not an ancestor of *A* or *C* or **S**. Hence *B* is not an ancestor of *D*.

Case 3: If *P* *→ M *—* R* then the orientation is changed to *P* *→ M → R*. By the induction hypothesis, if *P* *→ M *—* R* in π'_n, then in *G*(**O**, **S**, **L**) *M* is an ancestor of either *P* or *R* or **S**. Because *P* *→ M* in π'_n, *M* is not an ancestor of *P* or **S**. Hence *M* is an ancestor of *R*.

Case 4: If *B* ← * *C*, *B* → *D*, and *D* o—* *C*, then orient as *D* ←* *C*. By the induction hypothesis, *B* is not an ancestor of *C*, but is an ancestor of *D*. Hence *D* is not an ancestor of *C*.

Case 5: If *U* is a definite discriminating path between *A* and *C* for *B* in π'_n and *D* is adjacent to *B* on *U*, and *D*, *B*, and *C* form a triangle, then if *B* is in **Sepset**(*A*, *C*) mark *B* as a noncollider on subpath *D* *—* *B* *—* *C* else orient *D* *—* *B* *—* *C* as *D* *→ B* ← * *C*.

There are two cases. First suppose that *B* is in **Sepset**(*A*, *C*). Suppose, contrary to the hypothesis that *B* is not an ancestor of *C* or *D* or **S** in *G*(**O**, **S**, **L**). Because **Sepset**(*A*, *C*) is a minimal *d*-connecting set and *B* is in **Sepset**(*A*, *C*), then *B* is an ancestor of *A* or *C* or **S**. Because it is not an ancestor of *C* or **S** it is an ancestor of *A*. Because there are inducing paths between *B* and *C*, and *B* and D in $G(\mathbf{O}, \mathbf{S}, \mathbf{L})$, but B is not an ancestor of C or D or $\mathbf{S}$, it follows from lemma 11 that the inducing paths between D and B, and between B and C, are both into B. The directed edge from each vertex X_i on U (except for A) to C in π', entails that X_i is an ancestor of C but not of $\mathbf{S}$ in $G(\mathbf{O}, \mathbf{S}, \mathbf{L})$. So the inducing path in $G(\mathbf{O}, \mathbf{S}, \mathbf{L})$ corresponding to a bi-directed edge between X_i and X_{i+1} on U is into X_i and X_{i+1}. Hence in $G(\mathbf{O}, \mathbf{S}, \mathbf{L})$ there is an inducing sequence between A and C. Hence, by lemma 10 in $G(\mathbf{O}, \mathbf{S}, \mathbf{L})$ there is an inducing path between A and C, which is a contradiction.

Suppose next that B is not in **Sepset**(A, C). First we will show that every vertex along U except for the endpoints is an ancestor of **Sepset**(A, C) in $G(\mathbf{O}, \mathbf{S}, \mathbf{L})$. Suppose, contrary to the hypothesis that some vertex on U is not an ancestor of **Sepset**(A, C), and let W be the closest such vertex on U to B. It follows that in $G(\mathbf{O}, \mathbf{S}, \mathbf{L})$ there is a sequence of vertices $<A, X_1, ..., X_n, W>$ such that each pair of vertices X_i and X_{i+1} that are adjacent in the sequence are d-connected given **Sepset**$(A, C)\backslash\{X_i, X_{i+1}\}$ (because of the existence of the inducing path into X_i and X_{i+1}), and if a pair of paths d-connects X_{i-1} and X_i, and X_i and X_{i+1} respectively, they collide at X_i. By hypothesis, in $G(\mathbf{O}, \mathbf{S}, \mathbf{L})$ X_i is an ancestor of **Sepset**(A, C) and W is an ancestor of C but not of **Sepset**(A, C). It follows there is a path D from W to C that d-connects W and C given **Sepset**(A, C) in $G(\mathbf{O}, \mathbf{S}, \mathbf{L})$. By lemma 1 it follows that A and C are d-connected given **Sepset**(A, C) in $G(\mathbf{O}, \mathbf{S}, \mathbf{L})$, which is a contradiction.

Since every vertex along U except for the endpoints is an ancestor of **Sepset**(A, C) in $G(\mathbf{O}, \mathbf{S}, \mathbf{L})$, it follows that there is a sequence of vertices $<A, X_1, ..., X_n, B>$ such that each pair of vertices X_i and X_{i+1} that are adjacent in the sequence are d-connected given **Sepset**$(A, C)\backslash\{X_i, X_{i+1}\}$, and if a pair of paths d-connects X_{i-1} and X_i, and X_i and X_{i+1} respectively, they collide at X_i. Since each of the X_i has a descendant in **Sepset**(A, C) in $G(\mathbf{O}, \mathbf{S}, \mathbf{L})$, A and B are d-connected given **Sepset**(A, C) in $G(\mathbf{O}, \mathbf{S}, \mathbf{L})$

Suppose, contrary to the claim, that B is an ancestor of C. There are two cases. If B is an ancestor of **Sepset**(A, C), then in $G(\mathbf{O}, \mathbf{S}, \mathbf{L})$ A and B are d-connected given **Sepset**(A, C), and B and C are d-connected given **Sepset**(A, C), and B is an ancestor of **Sepset**(A, C) but not in **Sepset**(A, C). It follows from lemma 1 that A and C are d-connected given **Sepset**(A, C), which is a contradiction. If in $G(\mathbf{O}, \mathbf{S}, \mathbf{L})$ B is not an ancestor of **Sepset**(A, C) but is an ancestor of C, then in $G(\mathbf{O}, \mathbf{S}, \mathbf{L})$ there is a directed path D from B to C that contains no member of **Sepset**(A, C). By lemma 1 it follows that A and C are d-connected given **Sepset**(A, C) in $G(\mathbf{O}, \mathbf{S}, \mathbf{L})$, which is a contradiction. It follows that B is not an ancestor of C. Because in $G(\mathbf{O}, \mathbf{S}, \mathbf{L})$ B is not an ancestor of C, but by hypothesis, D is an ancestor of C, B is not an ancestor of D. Q.E.D.

THEOREM 1. If π is a partial ancestral graph, and there is a directed path U from A to B in π, then in every DAG $G(\mathbf{O}, \mathbf{S}, \mathbf{L})$ with PAG π, there is a directed path from A to B and A is not an ancestor of $\mathbf{S}$.

Proof. By Theorem 5, for each directed edge between M and N in U there is a directed path from M to N in $G(\mathbf{O}, \mathbf{S}, \mathbf{L})$ and M is not an ancestor of $\mathbf{S}$. The concatenation of the directed paths in $G(\mathbf{O}, \mathbf{S}, \mathbf{L})$ contains a subpath that is a directed path from A to B in $G(\mathbf{O}, \mathbf{S}, \mathbf{L})$. Because there is a directed edge between A and its successor on U, A is not an ancestor of $\mathbf{S}$. Q.E.D.

A *semidirected path from A to B* in partial ancestral graph π is an undirected path U from A to B in which no edge contains an arrowhead pointing towards A; that is, there is no arrowhead at A on U, and if X and Y are adjacent on the path, and X is between A and Y on the path, then there is no arrowhead at the X end of the edge between X and Y.

LEMMA 15. If π is a partial ancestral graph of directed acyclic graph $G(\mathbf{O}, \mathbf{S}, \mathbf{L})$, there is a directed path D from A to B in $G(\mathbf{O}, \mathbf{S}, \mathbf{L})$ that does not contain any member of $\mathbf{S}$, and $\mathbf{C}$ is the set of vertices in $\mathbf{O}$ on D, then there is a semidirected path from A to B in π that contains just the members of $\mathbf{C}$.

Proof. Suppose there is a directed path D from A to B in $G(\mathbf{O}, \mathbf{S}, \mathbf{L})$ that does not contain any member of $\mathbf{S}$. Let $\mathbf{C}$ be the set of vertices in $\mathbf{O}$ on D, and D' in π be the sequence of edges between vertices in $\mathbf{O}$ along D in the order in which they occur on D. Let X and Y be any pair of vertices adjacent on D' for which X is between A and Y or $X = A$. Because X is an ancestor of Y in $G(\mathbf{O}, \mathbf{S}, \mathbf{L})$, the edge in π between X and Y has either an "o" or "–" at the X end of the edge. Hence D' is a semidirected path from A to B in π that contains the members of $\mathbf{C}$.

THEOREM 2. If π is a partial ancestral graph, and there is no semidirected path from A to B in π that contains a member of $\mathbf{C}$, then every directed path from A to B in every DAG $G(\mathbf{O}, \mathbf{S}, \mathbf{L})$ with PAG π that contains a member of $\mathbf{C}$ also contains a member of $\mathbf{S}$.

Proof. This follows from lemma 15. Q.E.D.

THEOREM 3. If π is a partial ancestral graph of DAG $G(\mathbf{O}, \mathbf{S}, \mathbf{L})$ and there is no semidirected path from A to B in π, then every directed path from A to B in every DAG $G(\mathbf{O}, \mathbf{S}, \mathbf{L})$ with PAG π contains a member of $\mathbf{S}$.

Proof. By lemma 15, if there is a directed path from A to B in $G(\mathbf{O}, \mathbf{S}, \mathbf{L})$ that contains no member of $\mathbf{S}$, there is a semidirected path from A to B in π. Q.E.D.

THEOREM 4. If π is a partial ancestral graph and every semidirected path from A to B contains some member of $\mathbf{C}$ in π, then every directed path from A to B in every DAG $G(\mathbf{O}, \mathbf{S}, \mathbf{L})$ with PAG π contains a member of $\mathbf{S} \cup \mathbf{C}$.

Proof. Suppose that U is a directed path in $G(\mathbf{O}, \mathbf{S}, \mathbf{L})$ from A to B that does not contain a member of **C** or **S**. Then by lemma 15 there is a semidirected path from *A* to *B* in π that does not contain any member of **C**. Q.E.D.

Acknowledgements

We wish to thank Clark Glymour and Greg Cooper for many helpful conversations. This research was supported in part by ONR contract Grant #: N00014-93-1-0568

Notes

1. For those readers familiar with *d*-separation, a graph *G* entails that **X** is independent of **Y** conditional on **Z** if and only if **X** is *d*-separated from **Y** given **Z** in *G*. See chapter 2.

2. A similar object was called a partially oriented inducing path graph (POIPG) in Spirtes, Glymour, and Scheines 1993. Wermuth, Cox, and Pearl (1994) introduced summary graphs, which represent the results of marginalizing and conditionalizing on the variables in a graph. Unlike summary graphs, PAGs represent a kind of equivalence class of graphs whose variables have been marginalized and conditionalized.

3. It is customary to represent the ordered pair *A*, *B* with angle brackets as <*A*, *B*>, but for endpoints of an edge we use square brackets so that the angle brackets will not be misread as arrowheads.

References

Beinlich, I.; Suermondt, H.; Chavez, R.; and Cooper, G. 1989. The ALARM Monitoring System: A Case Study with Two Probabilistic Inference Techniques for Belief Networks. Paper presented at the Second European Conference on Artificial Intelligence in Medicine, London, U.K., 15–17 August.

Bollen, K. 1989. *Structural Equations with Latent Variables*. New York: Wiley.

Chickering, D.; Geiger, D.; and Heckerman, D. 1994. Learning Bayesian Networks: Search Methods and Experimental Results. Presented at the Fifth International Workshop on Artificial Intelligence and Statistics, 5–7 January, Fort Lauderdale, Florida.

Cooper, G. 1995. Causal Discovery from Data in the Presence of Selection Bias. In Preliminary papers of the Fifth International Workshop on Artificial Intelligence and Statistics, 5–7 January, Fort Lauderdale, Florida.

Cooper, G., and Herskovits, E. 1992. A Bayesian Method for the Induction of Probabilistic Networks from Data. *Machine Learning* 9(4): 309–347.

Epstein, R. 1987. *A History of Econometrics*. New York: North-Holland.

Heckerman, D.; Geiger, D.; and Chickering, D. 1994. Learning Bayesian Networks: The Combination of Knowledge and Statistical Data. In *Proceedings of the Tenth Conference on Uncertainty in Artificial Intelligence*, 293–302. San Francisco, Calif.: Morgan Kaufmann.

Lauritzen, S.; Dawid, P.; Larsen, B.; and Leimer, H. 1990. Independence Properties of Directed Markov Fields. *Networks* 20(5): 491–505.

Meek, C. 1995. Strong Completeness and Faithfulness in Bayesian Networks. In *Un-

certainty in Artificial Intelligence: Proceedings of the Eleventh Conference, 411–413. San Francisco, Calif.: Morgan Kaufmann.

Pearl, J. 1995. Causal Diagrams for Empirical Research. *Biometrika* 82(3): 669–710.

Pearl, J. 1988. *Probabilistic Reasoning in Intelligent Systems.* San Francisco, Calif.: Morgan Kaufmann.

Richardson, T. 1996. A Discovery Algorithm for Directed Cyclic Graphs. In *Proceedings of the Twelfth Conference on Uncertainty in Artificial Intelligence,* eds. E. Horvitz and F. Jensen, 451–461. San Francisco, Calif.: Morgan Kaufmann.

Singh, M., and Valtorta, M. 1993. An Algorithm for the Construction of Bayesian Network Structures from Data. In *Proceedings of the Ninth Conference on Uncertainty in Artificial Intelligence,* 259–265. San Francisco, Calif.: Morgan Kaufmann.

Spirtes, P. 1994. Building Causal Graphs from Statistical Data in the Presence of Latent Variables. In *Logic, Methodology, and Philosophy of Science IX,* ed. D. Prawitz, B. Skyrms, and D. Westerstahl, 813–829. Amsterdam: Elsevier.

Spirtes, P., and Meek, C. 1995. Learning Bayesian Networks with Discrete Variables from Data. In *Proceedings of the First International Conference on Knowledge Discovery and Data Mining,* ed. by Usama M. Fayyad and Ramasamy Uthurusamy, 294–299. Menlo Park, Calif.: AAAI Press.

Spirtes, P., and Verma, T. 1992. Equivalence of Causal Models with Latent Variables, Technical Report, Phil-33, Department of Philosophy, Carnegie Mellon University.

Spirtes, P.; Glymour, C.; and Scheines, R. 1993. *Causation, Prediction, and Search.* Lecture Notes in Statistics 81. New York: Springer-Verlag.

Spirtes, P.; Glymour, C.; and Scheines, R. 1991. An Algorithm for Fast Recovery of Sparse Causal Graphs. *Social Science Computer Review* 9(1): 62–72.

Spirtes, P.; Glymour, C.; and Scheines, R. 1990. Causality from Probability. Paper presented at the Advanced Computing for the Social Sciences Conference, Williamsburg, Virginia, April 10–12.

Spirtes, P.; Richardson, T.; Meek, C.; Scheines, R.; and Glymour, C. 1996. Using D-Separation to Calculate Zero Partial Correlations in Linear Models with Correlated Errors, Technical Report, Phil-72, Department of Philosophy, Carnegie Mellon University.

Verma, T., and Pearl, J. 1991. Equivalence and Synthesis of Causal Models. Technical Report, R-150, Cognitive Systems Laboratory, University of California at Los Angeles.

Verma, T., and Pearl, J. 1990. Equivalence and Synthesis of Causal Models. In Proceedings of the Sixth Conference on Uncertainty in AI, 220–227. Mountain View, Calif.: Association for Uncertainty in AI.

Wermuth, N.; Cox, D.; and Pearl, J. 1994. Explanations for Multivariate Structures Derived from Univariate Recursive Regressions, Report, 94-1, Dept. of Statistics, University of Mainz.

Wright, S. 1934. The Method of Path Coefficients. *Annals of Mathematical Statistics.* 5(3): 161–215.

CHAPTER SEVEN

Automated Discovery of Linear Feedback Models

Thomas Richardson and Peter Spirtes

1. Introduction

The introduction of statistical models represented by directed acyclic graphs (DAGs) has proved fruitful in the construction of expert systems, in allowing efficient updating algorithms that take advantage of conditional independence relations (Pearl 1988, Lauritzen and Spiegelhalter 1988) and in inferring causal structure from conditional independence relations (Spirtes and Glymour 1991; Spirtes, Glymour, and Scheines 1993; Pearl and Verma 1991; Cooper and Herskovits 1992). As a framework for representing the combination of causal and statistical hypotheses, DAG models have shed light on a number of issues in statistics ranging from Simpson's Paradox to experimental design (Spirtes, Glymour, and Scheines 1993). The relations of DAGs with statistical constraints, and the equivalence and distinguishability properties of DAG models, are now well understood, and their characterization and computation involve three properties connecting graphical structure and probability distributions: (1) a local directed Markov property, (2) a global directed Markov property, and (3) factorizations of joint densities according to the structure of a graph (Lauritzen et al. 1990).

Recursive structural equation models are one kind of DAG model. However, nonrecursive structural equation models are not DAG models and are instead naturally represented by directed *cyclic* graphs in which a finite series of edges representing influence leads from a vertex representing a variable back to that same vertex. Such graphs have been used to model feedback systems in electrical engineering (Mason 1953, 1956) and to represent economic processes (Haavelmo 1943, Strotz and Wold 1960, Goldberger 1964). In contrast to the acyclic case, almost nothing general is known about how directed cyclic graphs (DCGs) represent conditional independence constraints, or about their equivalence or identifiability properties, or about characterizing classes of DCGs from conditional independence relations or other statistical constraints. This chapter addresses all of these issues. The issues turn on how the relations among properties (1), (2) and (3) essential to the acyclic case generalize—or fail to generalize—to directed cyclic graphs and associated families of distributions. It will be shown that when DCGs are interpreted by analogy with DAGs as representing functional dependencies with independently distributed noises or "error variables, " the equivalence of the fundamental global and local Markov conditions characteristic of DAGs no longer holds, even in linear systems. For linear systems associated with DCGs with independent errors or noises, a characterization of conditional independence constraints is obtained, and it is shown that the result generalizes in a natural way to systems in which the error variables or noises are statistically dependent.

We also present a correct polynomial time (on sparse graphs) discovery algorithm for linear cyclic models that contain no latent variables. This algorithm outputs a representation of a class of nonrecursive linear structural equation models given observational data as input. Under the assumption that all conditional independencies found in the observational data are true for structural reasons rather than because of particular parameter values, the algorithm discovers causal features of the structure which generated the data. (Discovery algorithms for directed acyclic graphs based upon similar assumptions are described in Spirtes, Glymour, and Scheines 1993, and Pearl and Verma 1991.) The remainder of this chapter is organized as follows: Section 2 defines relevant mathematical ideas and gives some necessary technical results on DAGs and DCGs. Section 3 obtains results for nonrecursive linear structural equations models. Section 4 describes a discovery algorithm. Section 5 describes some open research problems. All proofs are in Section 6.

2. Directed Graphs and Probability Distributions

A *directed graph* (DG) is an ordered pair of a finite set of vertices $\mathbf{V}$ and a set of directed edges $\mathbf{E}$. (We place sets of variables in boldface.) A directed edge from A to B is an ordered pair of distinct vertices $<A, B>$ in $\mathbf{V}$ (depicted as $A \rightarrow B$) in which A is the *tail* of the edge and B is the *head;* the edge is *out of* A and *into* B, and A is a *parent* of B and B is a *child* of A; also A and B are *adjacent.* A sequence of edges $<E_1, ..., E_n>$ in a directed graph G is an *undi-*

rected path if and only if there exists a sequence of vertices $<V_1, ..., V_{n+1}>$ such that for $1 \le i \le n$ either $<V_i, V_{i+1}> = E_i$ or $<V_{i+1}, V_i> = E_i$ and $E_i \ne E_{i+1}$. A sequence of edges $<E_1, ..., E_n>$ in a directed graph G is a *directed path* if and only if there exists a sequence of vertices $<V_1, ..., V_{n+1}>$ such that for $1 \le i \le n$ $<V_i, V_{i+1}> = E_i$. A (directed or undirected) path U is *acyclic* if no vertex occurring on an edge in the path occurs more than once. If there is an acyclic directed path from A to B or $B = A$ then A is an *ancestor* of B, and B is a *descendant* of A. The set of ancestors of A in G is denoted by **An**(A), the descendants of A, by **Descendants**(A); and the parents of A, by **Parents**(A). Note that $A \in$ **Descendants**(A), and $A \in$ **An**(A). A directed graph is *acyclic* if and only if it contains no directed cyclic paths.[1]

A directed acyclic graph (DAG) G with a set of vertices **V** can be given two distinct interpretations. On the one hand, such graphs can be used to represent causal relations between variables, where an edge from A to B in G means that A is a direct cause of B relative to **V**. A *causal graph* is a DAG given such an interpretation. Here we take the concept of "direct cause relative to a set of variables" to be primitive. There is a large body of philosophical literature that attempts to define various causal relations (see e.g. Sosa 1975). However, for the theorems in this chapter, such definitions are not needed. The key assumptions we make are the ones *relating* causal relations to probability distributions, and these are stated and justified in section 4.

On the other hand, a DAG with a set of vertices **V** can also represent a set of probability measures over **V** (where the members of **V** are both the vertices of the graph and random variables). Following the terminology of Lauritzen et al. (1990), we can say that a probability measure over a set of variables **V** satisfies the *local directed Markov property* for a directed acyclic graph (or DAG) G with vertices **V** if and only if for every W in **V**, W is independent of **V**\(**Descendants**(W) $\cup$ **Parents**(W)) given **Parents**(W). (Note that the vertices do not merely *index* the random variables; rather the random variables are the vertices of the graph. A vertex is its own ancestor and descendant, although not its own parent or child.) A DAG G *represents* the set of probability measures which satisfy the local directed Markov property for G.

The use of DAGs to simultaneously represent a set of causal hypotheses and a family of probability distributions extends back to the path diagrams introduced by Sewall Wright (1934). Variants of probabilistic DAG models were introduced in the 1980s in Wermuth (1980), Wermuth and Lauritzen (1983), Kiiveri, Speed, and Carlin (1984), Kiiveri and Speed (1982), and Pearl (1988). In section 4 we will present assumptions which link the two interpretations of directed graphs.

Pearl (1988) defines a global directed Markov property that has been shown to be equivalent to the local directed Markov property for DAGs, and can be used to calculate the consequences of the local directed Markov property. (See e.g. Lauritzen et al. 1990.[2]) Several preliminary notions are required. Vertex

X is a *collider* on an undirected path U in directed graph G if and only if there are two consecutive edges on U directed into X (e.g. $A \rightarrow X \leftarrow B$). Every other vertex on U is a *noncollider* on U. In a directed graph G, if X and Y are not in $\mathbf{Z}$, then an undirected path U *d-connects* X and Y given $\mathbf{Z}$ if and only if every collider on U has a descendant in $\mathbf{Z}$, and no noncollider on U is in $\mathbf{Z}$. For three disjoint sets $\mathbf{X}$, $\mathbf{Y}$, and $\mathbf{Z}$, $\mathbf{X}$ and $\mathbf{Y}$ are *d-connected* given $\mathbf{Z}$ in G if and only if there is a path U that *d*-connects some X in $\mathbf{X}$ to some Y in $\mathbf{Y}$ given $\mathbf{Z}$. For three disjoint sets $\mathbf{X}$, $\mathbf{Y}$, and $\mathbf{Z}$, $\mathbf{X}$ and $\mathbf{Y}$ are *d-separated* given $\mathbf{Z}$ in G if and only if $\mathbf{X}$ is not *d*-connected to $\mathbf{Y}$ given $\mathbf{Z}$. A probability distribution P satisfies the global directed Markov property for directed graph G if and only if for any three disjoint sets of variables $\mathbf{X}$, $\mathbf{Y}$, and $\mathbf{Z}$, if $\mathbf{X}$ is *d*-separated from $\mathbf{Y}$ given $\mathbf{Z}$ in G, then $\mathbf{X}$ is independent of $\mathbf{Y}$ given $\mathbf{Z}$ in P.

The following theorems relate the global directed Markov property to factorizations of a density function. Denote a density function over $\mathbf{V}$ by $f(\mathbf{V})$, where for any subset $\mathbf{X}$ of $\mathbf{V}$, $f(\mathbf{X})$ denotes the marginal density of $f(\mathbf{V})$. If $f(\mathbf{V})$ is the density function for a probability measure over a set of variables $\mathbf{V}$ and $\mathbf{An}(\mathbf{X})$ is the set of ancestors of members of $\mathbf{X}$ in directed graph G, say that $f(\mathbf{V})$ *factors according to directed graph* G with vertices $\mathbf{V}$ if and only if for every subset $\mathbf{X}$ of $\mathbf{V}$,

$$f(\mathbf{An}(\mathbf{X})) = \prod_{V \in \mathbf{An}(X)} g_V(V, \mathbf{Parents}(V))$$

where each g_V is a nonnegative function.

The following result was proved in Lauritzen et al. (1990). (A more precise description of the weak assumptions that need to be made about the underlying probability spaces and densitites is given there.)

THEOREM 1. If $\mathbf{V}$ is a set of random variables with a probability measure P that has a density function $f(\mathbf{V})$, then $f(\mathbf{V})$ factors according to DAG G if and only if P satisfies the global directed Markov property for G.

As in the case of acyclic graphs, the existence of a factorization according to a cyclic directed graph G does entail that a measure satisfies the global directed Markov property for G. The proof given in Lauritzen et al. (1990) for the acyclic case carries over essentially unchanged to the cyclic case. (Lauritzen et al. use a different definition of *d*-separation that is equivalent to Pearl's in both the cyclic and the acyclic case.)

THEOREM 2. If $\mathbf{V}$ is a set of random variables with a probability measure P that has a density function $f(\mathbf{V})$ and $f(\mathbf{V})$ factors according to directed (cyclic or acyclic) graph G, then P satisfies the global directed Markov property for G.

However, unlike the case of acyclic graphs, if a probability measure over a set of variables $\mathbf{V}$ satisfies the global directed Markov property for cyclic graph G and has a density function $f(\mathbf{V})$, it does not follow that $f(\mathbf{V})$ factors according to G, even if $f(\mathbf{V})$ is positive. (We thank an anonymous referee for pointing this fact out.)

3. Nonrecursive Linear Structural Equation Models

The problem considered in this section is to investigate the generalization of the Markov properties to linear, nonrecursive structural equation models. First we must relate the social scientific terminology to graphical representations, and clarify the questions.

The variables in a structural equation model (SEM) can be divided into two sets, the "error" variables and the "substantive" variables. Corresponding to each substantive variable X_i is an equation expressing X_i as a *linear* function of the direct causes of X_i plus a unique error variable ε_i where the linear coefficient of each variable that is not an error variable is a *free* parameter. (We will not consider nonlinear models in this chapter. For a discussion of nonlinear cyclic models see Spirtes [1995], Pearl and Dechter [1996].) Since we have no interest in first moments, without loss of generality each variable can be expressed as a deviation from its mean.

Consider, for example, two SEMs S_1 and S_2 over $\mathbf{X} = \{X_1, X_2, X_3\}$, where in both SEMs X_1 is a direct cause of X_2 and X_2 is a direct cause of X_3. The structural equations[3] in figure 1 are common to both S_1 and S_2 where β_{21} and β_{32} are free parameters ranging over real values, and ε_1, ε_2 and ε_3 are error variables. In addition suppose that ε_1, ε_2 and ε_3 are distributed as multivariate normal. In S_1 we will assume that the correlation between each pair of distinct error variables is fixed at zero. The free parameters of S_1 are $\theta_1 = <\beta$, $\mathbf{P}>$, where β is the set of linear coefficients $\{\beta_{21}, \beta_{32}\}$ and $\mathbf{P}$ is the set of variances of the error variables. We will use $\Sigma_{S_1}(\theta_1)$ to denote the covariance matrix parameterized by the vector θ_1 for model S_1, and occasionally leave out the model subscript if the context makes it clear which model is being referred to. If all the pairs of error variables in a SEM S are uncorrelated, we say S is a SEM with *uncorrelated errors*.

S_2 contains the same structural equations as S_1, but in S_2 we will allow the errors between X_2 and X_3 to be correlated; i.e., we make the correlation between the errors of X_2 and X_3 a free parameter, instead of fixing it at zero, as in S_1. In S_2 the free parameters are $\theta_2 = <\beta$, $\mathbf{P}'>$, where β is the set of linear coefficients $\{\beta_{21}, \beta_{32}\}$ and $\mathbf{P}'$ is the set of variances of the error variables and the correlation between ε_2 and ε_3. If the correlations between any of the error variables in a SEM are not fixed at zero, we will call it a SEM with *correlated errors*.[4]

If the coefficients in the linear equations are such that the substantive variables are a unique linear function of the error variables alone, the set of equa-

$$X_1 = \varepsilon_1$$

$$X_2 = \beta_{21} X_1 + \varepsilon_2$$

$$X_3 = \beta_{32} X_2 + \varepsilon_3$$

Figure 1. Structural equations for SEMs S_1 and S_2.

tions is said to have a *reduced form*. A linear SEM with a reduced form also determines a joint distribution over the substantive variables. We will consider only linear SEMs which have coefficients for which there is a reduced form, all variances and partial variances among the substantive variables are finite and positive, and all partial correlations among the substantive variables are well defined.

It is possible to associate with each SEM with uncorrelated errors a directed graph that represents the causal structure of the model and the form of the linear equations. For example, the directed graph associated with the substantive variables in S_1 is $X_1 \rightarrow X_2 \rightarrow X_3$, because X_1 is the only substantive variable that occurs on the right hand side of the equation for X_2, and X_2 is the only substantive variable that appears on the right hand side of the equation for X_3. We generally do not include error variables in the causal graph associated with a SEM unless the errors are correlated. When the distinction is relevant to the discussion, we enclose measured variables in boxes, latent variables in circles, and leave error variables unenclosed.

The typical path diagram that would be given for S_2 is shown in figure 2. This is not strictly a directed graph because of the curved line between error variables ε_2 and ε_3, which indicates that ε_2 and ε_3 are correlated. It is generally accepted that correlation is to be explained by some form of causal connection. Accordingly if ε_2 and ε_3 are correlated we will assume that either ε_2 causes ε_3, ε_3 causes ε_2, some latent variable causes both ε_2 and ε_3, or some combination of these. In other words, curved lines are an ambiguous representation of a causal connection.

A SEM is said to be *recursive* (an RSEM) if its directed graph is acyclic; otherwise it is *nonrecursive*.[5]

A SEM containing disjoint sets of variables **X**, **Y**, and **Z** *linearly entails* that **X** is independent of **Y** given **Z** if and only if **X** is independent of **Y** given **Z** for all values of free parameters in the SEM. A DG G containing disjoint sets of variables **X**, **Y**, and **Z** *linearly entails* that **X** is independent of **Y** given **Z** if and only if the SEM with DG G and no correlated errors linearly entails that **X** is independent of **Y** given **Z**. Similarly we may say that a SEM containing X, Y, and **Z**, where $X \neq Y$ and X and Y are not in **Z**, *linearly entails*

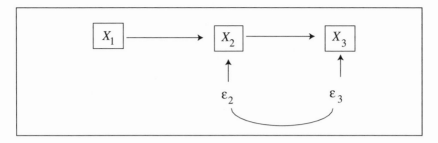

Figure 2. SEM S_2 with correlated errors.

that $\rho_{XY.\mathbf{Z}}= 0$, if and only if $\rho_{XY.\mathbf{Z}}= 0$ for all values of free parameters in the SEM (where $\rho_{XY.\mathbf{Z}}$ is the partial correlation of X and Y given $\mathbf{Z}$). DG G *linearly entails* that $\rho_{XY.\mathbf{Z}}= 0$ if and only if the SEM with DG G and no correlated errors linearly entails $\rho_{XY.\mathbf{Z}}= 0$. It follows from Kiiveri and Speed (1982) that if the error variables are jointly independent, then any distribution that forms a linear, recursive SEM with a directed acyclic graph G satisfies the local directed Markov property for G. One can therefore apply d-separation to the DAG in a linear, recursive SEM to compute the conditional independencies and zero partial correlations it linearly entails. The d-separation relation provides a polynomial (in the number of vertices) time algorithm for deciding whether a given conditional independence relation or vanishing partial correlation is linearly entailed by a SEM with a given DAG.

Linear *nonrecursive* structural equation models are commonly used in the econometrics literature to represent feedback processes that have reached equilibrium.[6] Corresponding to a set of nonrecursive linear equations is a cyclic graph, as figure 3 (adapted from Whittaker [1990]) illustrates.

Theorem 3 and Theorem 4, from Spirtes (1995), state that the set of conditional independence relations (and hence zero partial correlations) linearly entailed by a SEM correspond to the d-separation relations in the associated directed graph, even in the case of cyclic graphs. (Theorem 3 was independently proved by J. Koster: see Koster 1996.)

THEOREM 3. The probability measure P over the substantive variables of a linear SEM L (recursive or nonrecursive) with jointly independent error variables satisfies the global directed Markov property for the directed (cyclic or acyclic) graph G of L; i.e., if $\mathbf{X}$, $\mathbf{Y}$, and $\mathbf{Z}$ are disjoint sets of variables in G and $\mathbf{X}$ is d-separated from $\mathbf{Y}$ given $\mathbf{Z}$ in G, then $\mathbf{X}$ and $\mathbf{Y}$ are independent given $\mathbf{Z}$ in P.

THEOREM 4. In a linear SEM L with jointly independent error variables and directed (cyclic or acyclic) graph G containing disjoint sets of variables $\mathbf{X}$, $\mathbf{Y}$ and $\mathbf{Z}$, if $\mathbf{X}$ is not d-separated from $\mathbf{Y}$ given $\mathbf{Z}$ in G, then L

$$X_1 = \varepsilon_{X_1}$$

$$X_2 = \varepsilon_{X_2}$$

$$X_3 = \beta_{31} X_1 + \beta_{34} X_4 + \varepsilon_{X_3}$$

$$X_4 = \beta_{42} X_2 + \beta_{43} X_3 + \varepsilon_{X_4}$$

ε_{X_1}, ε_{X_2}, ε_{X_3}, ε_{X_4} are jointly independent and normally distributed

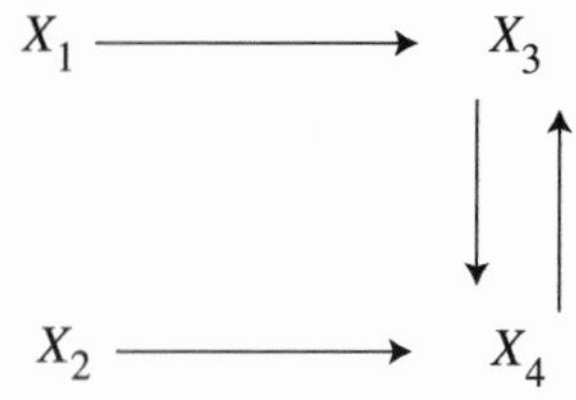

Figure 3. Example of a nonrecursive SEM.

does not linearly entail that **X** is independent of **Y** given **Z**.

Applying theorem 3 and theorem 4 to a linear SEM with the directed graph in figure 3, the conditional independence relations linearly entailed are: X_1 is independent of X_2; X_1 is independent of X_2 given X_3 and X_4. It is easy to see from theorem 3 and theorem 4 that in a linear SEM L with jointly independent error variables and (cyclic or acyclic) directed graph G containing substantive variables X, Y and **Z**, where $X \neq Y$ and **Z** does not contain X or Y, X is d-separated from Y given **Z** in G if and only if L linearly entails that $\rho_{XY.\mathbf{Z}} = 0$ (even if the error terms are not normally distributed).

As in the acyclic case, d-separation provides a polynomial time procedure for deciding whether a linear SEM with a cyclic graph linearly entails a conditional independence or vanishing partial correlation.

In DAGs the global directed Markov property entails the local directed Markov property, because a variable V is d-separated from its nonparental nondescendants given its parents. However, this is not always the case in cyclic graphs. For example, in figure 3, X_4 is not d-separated from its nonparental nondescendant X_1 given its parents X_2 and X_3, so the local directed Markov property does not hold.[7]

There is also a way to decide which partial correlations are entailed to be zero by a SEM with correlated errors, such as S_2 (figure 2). This is done by first creating a directed graph G with latent variables but no correlated errors, and then applying d-separation to G to determine if a zero partial correlation is entailed. The latent variable directed graph G (without correlated errors) that we will associate with a SEM S with correlated errors is created in the following way. Start with the usual graphical representation of S, that contains undirected lines connecting correlated errors (e.g. SEM S_2 in figure 2). For each pair of error variables ε_i and ε_j connected by an undirected edge, introduce a new latent variable T_{ij}, and edges from T_{ij} to X_i and X_j. Finally remove all of the error variables from the graph. When this process is applied to SEM S_2, the result is shown in figure 4.

In a SEM such as S_2, with correlated errors, one can decide whether $\rho_{X_1 X_3 \cdot X_2}$ is entailed to be zero by determining whether $\{X_1\}$ and $\{X_3\}$ are d-separated given $\{X_2\}$ in the directed graph in figure 4. In this way the problem of determining whether a SEM with correlated errors entails a zero partial correlation is reduced to the already solved problem of determining whether a SEM without correlated errors entails a zero partial correlation. (In general if S is a SEM with correlated errors, and S' is the SEM with uncorrelated errors and the latent variable directed graph associated with S, it is *not* the case that for every instantiation θ_1 of the free parameters of S there is an instantiation θ_2 of the free parameters of S' such that $\Sigma_S(\theta_1) = \Sigma_{S'}(\theta_2)$. We are making the weaker claim that d-separation applied to G correctly describes which zero partial correlations are linearly entailed by S. See Spirtes et al. [1996.])

4. The Discovery Problem

Suppose that we are given data sampled from a population whose causal structure is correctly described by some linear nonrecursive structural equation model **M**. Is it possible to discover the causal graph of **M** from the data, or at least recover some features of the causal graph from the data? In Spirtes, Meek, and Richardson (1995) the problem of discovering features of the causal graph is considered under the assumption that it is acyclic, but that there may be latent common causes (i.e., there may be unmeasured variables that are the direct cause of at least two measured variables.) Here we will consider the problem of discovering features of the causal graph under the assumption that it may be cyclic, but there are no latent common causes. Future research is needed on the problem of discovering the causal graph when it may be cyclic *and* there may be latent common causes. Likewise we do not consider the problem of causal discovery when the data is generated by a nonlinear, nonrecursive structural equation model (see Spirtes 1995, Pearl and Dechter 1996).

In order to make inferences about causal relations from a sample distribution it is necessary to introduce some axioms that link probability distribu-

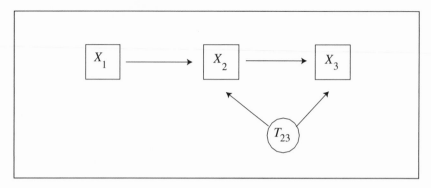

*Figure 4. SEM S_2': Correlated errors in S_2
replaced by latent common cause.*

tions to causal relations. The two assumptions that we will make are the
causal independence and causal faithfulness assumptions, described in the
next two subsections.

4.1 The Causal Independence Assumption

The most fundamental assumption relating causality and probability that we
will make is the following:

Causal Independence Assumption

If A does not cause B, and B does not cause A, and there is no third variable that causes both A and B, then A and B are independent.

This assumption allows us to draw a *causal* conclusion from *statistical* data
and lies at the foundation of the theory of randomized experiments. If the value of A is randomized, the experimenter knows that the randomizing device is
the sole cause of A. Hence the experimenter knows B did not cause A, and that
there is no third variable which causes both A and B. This leaves only two alternatives: either A causes B or A and B are independent. If A and B are dependent in the experimental population, the experimenter concludes that A
does cause B, which is an application of the causal independence assumption.

The causal independence assumption entails that if two error variables,
such as ε_2 and ε_3 in figure 2, are correlated there is a latent common cause of
X_2 and X_3 responsible for the correlation. In other words, when X_2 and X_3
have correlated errors, we assume that the distribution over X_2 and X_3 is the
marginal of some other distribution including a finite number of latent causes
of X_2 and X_3 in which the error variables are uncorrelated. Since we are making the assumption that there are no latent common causes, it follows that the
error variables of the causal graph are uncorrelated. The correctness of the *d*-
separation criterion for deciding which partial correlations are linearly en-

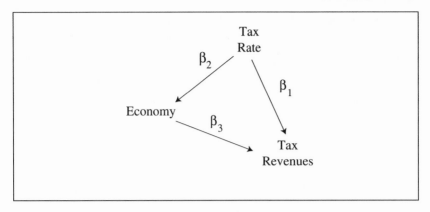

Figure 5. Economic model.

tailed to be zero by a SEM with an associated directed graph G then follows from theorem 3 and theorem 4.

4.2 The Faithfulness Assumption

In addition to the zero partial correlations that are entailed for *all* values of the free parameters of a SEM with a given directed graph, there may be zero partial correlations that hold only for some *particular* assignments of values to the parameters. For example, suppose figure 5 is the directed graph of a SEM that describes the relations among tax rate, the economy, and tax revenues, where β_1, β_2 and β_3 are free parameters.

In this case there are no vanishing partial correlation constraints entailed for all values of the free parameters. But if in the population $\beta_1 = - (\beta_2 \cdot \beta_3)$, then tax rate and tax revenues are uncorrelated. The SEM postulates a direct effect of tax rate on revenue (β_1), and an indirect effect through the economy ($\beta_2 \cdot \beta_3$). The parameter constraint indicates that these effects *exactly* offset each other in the population, leaving no total effect whatsoever. In such a case we say that the distribution is *unfaithful* to the directed graph of the causal structure that generated it. A distribution is *faithful* to a directed graph G if each vanishing partial correlation in the distribution is linearly entailed by G (i.e., entailed for all values of the free parameters of the SEM with directed graph G and no correlated errors).

Causal Faithfulness Assumption

If the directed graph associated with a SEM M correctly describes the causal structure in the population, and θ_{pop} are the population parameter values, then if $\rho_{XZ.Y} = 0$ in $\Sigma_M(\theta_{pop})$, M linearly entails that $\rho_{XZ.Y} = 0$.

The faithfulness assumption limits the SEMs considered to those in which population constraints are entailed by structure, not by particular values of the parameters. If one assumes faithfulness, then if A and B are *not* d-separated given $\mathbf{C}$, then $\rho_{AB\cdot\mathbf{C}} \neq 0$ (because it is not linearly entailed to equal zero). Faithfulness should not be assumed when there are deterministic relationships among variables, or equality constraints upon free parameters, since either of these can lead to violations of the assumption. Some form of the assumption of faithfulness is used in every science, and amounts to no more than the belief that an improbable and unstable cancellation of parameters does not hide real causal influences. When a theory cannot explain an empirical regularity save by invoking a special parameterization, most scientists are uneasy with the theory and look for an alternative.

It is also possible to give a personal Bayesian argument for assuming faithfulness. For any directed graph, the set of linear parameterizations of the directed graph that lead to violations of linear faithfulness are Lebesgue measure zero. Hence any Bayesian whose prior over the parameters is absolutely continuous with Lebesgue measure assigns a zero prior probability to violations of faithfulness. Of course, this argument is not relevant to those Bayesians who place a prior over the parameters that is not absolutely continuous with Lebesgue measure and assigns a nonzero probability to violations of faithfulness.

The assumption of faithfulness guarantees the asymptotic correctness of the cyclic causal discovery (CCD) algorithm described in section 4.4. It does *not* guarantee that on samples of finite size this algorithm is reliable.

Given the causal independence assumption, an assumption of no latent variables, a linearity assumption, and the causal faithfulness assumption, it follows that in a distribution P generated by a causal structure represented by a directed graph G, $\rho_{XY\cdot\mathbf{Z}} = 0$ if and only if X is d-separated from Y given $\mathbf{Z}$ in G. So if we can perform statistical tests of zero partial correlations, then we can use that information to draw conclusions about the d-separation relations in G and then to reconstruct as much information about G as possible. Henceforth we will speak of reconstructing features of G from d-separation relations and from zero partial correlations interchangeably, since given our assumptions, these are equivalent. We assume that the discovery algorithm has access to a *d-separation oracle* that correctly answers questions about d-separation relations in G. In practice, of course, the oracle is some kind of statistical test of the hypothesis that a particular partial correlation is zero in a population that satisfies the global Markov and faithfulness properties for G. (The algorithm is correct for any distribution for which a d-separation oracle is available, but because in the case where the functional relations between variables are nonlinear and the system is nonrecursive, d-separation is not a sufficient condition for conditional independence, the only case we know of in which such an oracle is available is the linear case.)

Of course the number of distinct d-separation relations grows exponentially with the number of variables in the directed graph. Therefore it is important to discover the features of G from a subset of the set of all d-separation relations. The CCD algorithm that we describe below chooses the subset of d-separation relations that it needs to reconstruct features of G as it goes along.

4.3 Output Representation—Partial Ancestral Graphs (PAGs)

In general, it is not possible to reconstruct a unique directed graph G given information only about its d-separation relations, because there may be more than one directed graph in which exactly the same set of d-separation relations hold. Two directed graphs G, G^* are said to be *d-separation equivalent* if the same set of d-separation relations holds in both directed graphs. The set of directed graphs d-separation equivalent to a given directed graph G is denoted by **Equiv**(G). (Note that there is a stronger sense of equivalence, which we will call linear statistical equivalence, between two directed graphs G and G' which holds when for every instantiation θ_1 of the free parameters of SEM S with directed graph G and no correlated errors, there is an instantiation θ_2 of the free parameters of SEM S' with directed graph G' and no correlated errors, such that $\Sigma_S(\theta_1) = \Sigma_{S'}(\theta_2)$, and vice versa. In the acyclic case it is known that d-separation equivalence implies linear statistical equivalence, but it is known that this is not so for cyclic graphs.)

The members of **Equiv**(G) always have certain features in common. We now introduce the formalism with which we will represent features common to all directed graphs in **Equiv**(G) for some fixed G. A partial ancestral graph (PAG) is an extended graph consisting of a set of vertices **V** and a set of edges between vertices where there may be the following kinds of edges: $A \leftrightarrow B$, $A \circ\!\!-\!\!\circ B$, $A - B$, $A \circ\!\!\rightarrow B$, $A \leftarrow\!\!\circ B$, $A \rightarrow B$, $A \leftarrow B$, $A \circ\!\!- B$, and $A -\!\!\circ B$ (The $A \leftrightarrow B$, $A \leftarrow\!\!\circ B$, and $A \circ\!\!\rightarrow B$ edges appear only in PAGs for directed graphs with latent variables. Because in this chapter we are considering only directed graphs without latent variables, none of these types of edge occur in the PAGs we consider here.) We say that the A endpoint of an $A \rightarrow B$, $A - B$, or $A -\!\!\circ B$ edge is "–"; the A endpoint of an $A \leftrightarrow B$, $A \leftarrow\!\!\circ B$, or $A \leftarrow B$ edge is "<"; and we say the A endpoint of an $A \circ\!\!-\!\!\circ B$, $A \circ\!\!\rightarrow B$, or $A \circ\!\!- B$ edge is "o". The conventions for the B endpoints are analogous. In addition, pairs of edge endpoints may be connected by underlining or dotted underlining ($\rightarrow \underline{X} \leftarrow$ and $\rightarrow \underline{X} \leftarrow$). A partial ancestral graph for G contains partial information about the ancestor relations in G, namely only those ancestor relations common to all members of **Equiv**(G). In the following definition, which provides a semantics for PAGs we use "*" as a meta-symbol indicating the presence of any one of {o, –, >}, i.e., $A -\!\!* B$ represents any of the following edges: $A -\!\!\circ B$, or $A - B$, or $A \rightarrow B$.

Partial Ancestral Graphs (PAGs)[8]

Ψ is a PAG for directed graph G with vertex set $\mathbf{V}$ if and only if

(1) There is an edge between A and B in Ψ if and only if A and B are d-connected in G given any subset $\mathbf{W} \subseteq \mathbf{V}\backslash\{A, B\}$.

(2) If there is an edge in Ψ out of A (not necessarily into B), i.e., A—∗ B, then A is an ancestor of B in every directed graph in $\mathbf{Equiv}(G)$.

(3) If there is an edge in Ψ into B, i.e., $A*{\rightarrow}B$, then in every directed graph in $\mathbf{Equiv}(G)$, B is *not* an ancestor of A.

(4) If there is an underlining $A*$—$*\underline{B}*$—$*C$ in Ψ then B is an ancestor of (at least one of) A or C in every directed graph in $\mathbf{Equiv}(G)$.

(5) If there is an edge from A into B and from C into B, $(A \rightarrow B{\leftarrow} C)$, then the arrowheads at B are joined by dotted underlining $(A \rightarrow B{\leftarrow}C)$ only if in every directed graph in $\mathbf{Equiv}(G)$ B is not a descendant of a common child of A and C.

(6) Any edge endpoint not marked in one of the above ways is left with a small circle thus: ∘—∗.

Two vertices, X and Y, in a directed cyclic graph G are *p-adjacent* if there is an edge between them, $X*$—$*Y$, in any (hence every) PAG for G. It follows directly from the definitions that a pair of vertices X, Y are p-adjacent in G if and only if X and Y are d-connected given every subset of the other vertices in G.

Observe that condition (1) in the definition of the PAG differs from the other five conditions in providing necessary *and* sufficient conditions on $\mathbf{Equiv}(G)$ for a given symbol, in this case an edge, to appear in a PAG. The other five conditions merely state necessary conditions. For this reason there are in fact many different PAGs for a directed graph G. Although they all have the same p-adjacencies, the edges may be of different types. Some of the PAGs provide more information than others about causal structure; e.g., they have fewer "o's" at the ends of edges.[9]

If Ψ is a PAG for directed graph G, we also say that Ψ *represents* G. Since every clause in the definition refers only to $\mathbf{Equiv}(G)$, it follows that if Ψ is a PAG for directed graph G, and $G^* \in \mathbf{Equiv}(G)$, then Ψ is also a PAG for G^*. This is not surprising since, as the output of the discovery algorithm we present below, the PAG is designed to represent features common to all directed graphs in the d-separation equivalence class. However, some PAGs may represent directed graphs from different d-separation equivalence classes. This leaves open the possibility that an algorithm might output the same PAG given directed graphs from different d-separation classes as input. However, any PAG output by the discovery algorithm we present provides sufficient information to ensure that the algorithm never outputs the same PAG given oracles for two directed graphs unless those directed graphs are d-separation equivalent. Hence the algorithm provides a 1-1 mapping from d-separation equivalence classes into PAGs.

The set of features described by a PAG is rich enough to enable us to distinguish between any two d-separation equivalence classes, i.e., there is some set of features common to all directed graphs in one d-separation equivalence class that is not true of all directed graphs in another d-separation equivalence class, and this difference can be expressed by a difference in the PAGs representing those d-separation equivalence classes.

Example

Suppose G is the graph in figure 6. In this case it can be shown that **Equiv**(G) contains (only) the two directed graphs shown in figure 7.

The PAG which the CCD algorithm outputs given as input an oracle for deciding conditional independence facts in G, is given in figure 8. Observe that the PAG tells us the following facts about **Equiv**(G):[10]

(a) X is an ancestor of Y, and Y is an ancestor of X in every directed graph in **Equiv**(G).

(b) In no directed graph in **Equiv**(G) is X or Y an ancestor of A or B.

(c) In every directed graph in **Equiv**(G) both A and B are ancestors of X and Y.

Note that not every edge in the PAG appears in every directed graph in **Equiv**(G). This is because an edge in the PAG indicates only that the two variables connected by the edge are d-connected given any subset of the other variables. In fact it is possible to show something stronger, namely that if there is an edge between two vertices in a PAG, then there is some directed graph represented by the PAG in which that edge is present.[11]

This example is atypical in that the PAG given by the algorithm contains no "o" endpoints; however it shows how much information a PAG may provide. Notice that the graphs in figure 9 are also PAGs for G, although they are less informative.

The CCD algorithm we describe does not always give the most informative PAG for a given directed graph G in that there may be features common to all directed graphs in the d-separation equivalence class which are not captured by the PAG that the algorithm outputs. In this sense the algorithm is not complete. However, the algorithm is *d-separation complete* in the sense that if the d-separation oracles for two different directed graphs cause the algorithm to produce the same PAG as output, then the two directed graphs are d-separation equivalent.

The following definition is required to state the algorithm. For graph Ψ, **Adjacencies**(Ψ, X) is a function giving the set of variables Y s.t. there is an edge $X*\!\!-\!\!*Y$ in Ψ.[12] Ψ is a dynamic object in the algorithm that changes as the algorithm progresses, and hence **Adjacencies**(Ψ, X) also changes as the

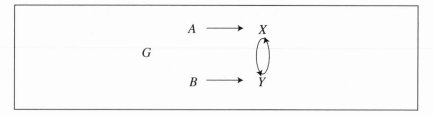

Figure 6. A directed cyclic graph.

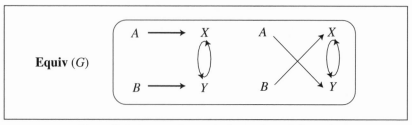

Figure 7. A d-separation equivalence class of directed cyclic graphs, containing the graph in figure 6.

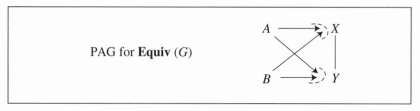

Figure 8. PAG for the d-separation equivalence class in figure 7.

algorithm progresses. A trace of the algorithm on a simple example is given in section 4.8.

4.4 The Cyclic Causal Discovery (CCD) Algorithm

The overall strategy for discovery is shown in figure 10. Note that once the following algorithm adds a "–," ">," or "<" endpoint to an edge it never removes or changes it; similarly once it adds underlining (dotted or not) it never removes it or changes it. For each pair of variables X and Y the set **Sepset**<X, Y> is assigned a value at most once by the algorithm. For some pairs of variables the algorithm does not assign a value to **Sepset**<X, Y>, but in those cases, the values are not needed by the algorithm. Similar remarks hold for **SupSepset**<X, Y, Z>. The algorithm correctly creates PAGs for acyclic as well as cyclic graphs.

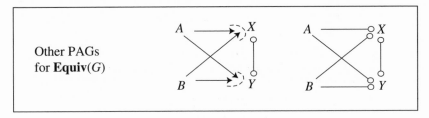

Figure 9. Other PAGs for the d-separation equivalence class in figure 7.

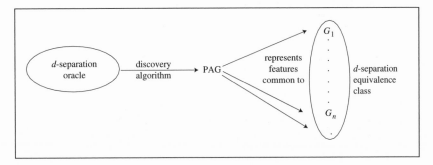

Figure 10. Strategy employed by the CCD algorithm.

CCD Algorithm

Input: An oracle for answering questions of the form: "Is X d-separated from Y given set $\mathbf{Z}$, $(X, Y \notin \mathbf{Z})$ in directed graph G?"

Output: A PAG for G.

Step A a) Form the complete graph Ψ, such that between every pair of variables A and B there is an edge $A\circ\!\!-\!\!\circ B$ in Ψ.

　　b) $n = 0$.

　　　repeat

　　　　repeat

　　　　　　select an ordered pair of variables X and Y such that there is an edge $X\circ\!\!-\!\!\circ Y$ in Ψ and the number of vertices in **Adjacencies**$(\Psi, X)\backslash\{Y\}$ is greater than or equal to n;

　　　　　　repeat

　　　　　　　select a subset $\mathbf{S}$ of **Adjacencies**$(\Psi, X)\backslash\{Y\}$ with n vertices;

　　　　　　　if X and Y are d-separated given $\mathbf{S}$ delete edge $X\circ\!\!-\!\!\circ Y$ from Ψ and set **Sepset**$<X, Y> = \mathbf{S}$ and **Sepset**$<Y, X> = \mathbf{S}$;

　　　　　　until every subset $\mathbf{S}$ of **Adjacencies**$(\Psi, X)\backslash\{Y\}$ with n vertices has been selected or some subset $\mathbf{S}$ has been found for which X and Y are d-separated given $\mathbf{S}$;

　　　　until all ordered pairs of vertices X, Y such that $X\circ\!\!-\!\!\circ Y$ in Ψ and

Adjacencies(Ψ, X)\\{Y} has greater than or equal to n vertices have been selected;

$n = n + 1$;

until for each ordered pair of vertices X, Y, such that X∘–∘Y in Ψ, **Adjacencies**(Ψ, X)\\{Y} has less than n vertices.

Step B. For each triple of vertices A, B, C such that the pair A, B and the pair B, C are each adjacent in Ψ but the pair A, C are not adjacent in Ψ, then:

(1) orient $A*$—$*B*$—$*C$ as $A{\rightarrow}B{\leftarrow}C$ if and only if $B \notin$ **Sepset**<A, C>;
(2) orient $A*$—$*B*$—$*C$ as $A*$—$\underline{*B*}$—$*C$ if and only if $B \in$ **Sepset**<A, C>.

Step C. For each triple of vertices <A, X, Y> in Ψ such that
(a) A is not adjacent to X and A is not adjacent to Y in Ψ,
(b) X and Y are adjacent, i.e., $X*$—$*Y$, in Ψ, and
(c) $X \notin$ **Sepset**<A, Y>
if A and X are d-connected given **Sepset**<A, Y> then orient X ∘–∘ Y or X ∘— Y as $X{\leftarrow}Y$

Step D. For each vertex V in Ψ form the following set: $X \in$ **Local**(Ψ, V) if and only if X is p-adjacent to V in Ψ, or there is some vertex Y such that $X{\rightarrow}Y{\leftarrow}V$ in Ψ. (Local(Ψ, V) is calculated once for each vertex V and does not change as the algorithm progresses.)

$m = 1$.

repeat

repeat

select a pair of vertices {A, C} and a third vertex B s.t. A and C are not adjacent, $A{\rightarrow}B{\leftarrow}C$, in Ψ, and
Local(Ψ, A)\ (**Sepset**<A, C> $\cup$ {B, C})
has greater than or equal to m vertices.

repeat

select a set $\mathbf{T} \subseteq$ **Local**(Ψ, A)\(**Sepset**<A, C> $\cup$ {B, C}) with m vertices; if A and C are d-separated given $\mathbf{T} \cup$ **Sepset**<A, C> $\cup$ {B}
then orient the triple $A{\rightarrow}B{\leftarrow}C$ as $A{\rightarrow}B{\leftarrow}C$, and record $\mathbf{T} \cup$ **Sepset**<A, C> $\cup$ {B} in **SupSepset**<A, B, C> and **SupSepset**<C, B, A>.

until every subset $\mathbf{T} \subseteq$ **Local**(Ψ, A)\(**Sepset**<A, C> $\cup$ {B, C}) with m vertices has been selected or a d-separating set for A and C has been recorded in **SupSepset**<A, B, C> and **SupSepset**<C, B, A>.

until all triples such that $A{\rightarrow}B{\leftarrow}C$, (i.e., not $A{\rightarrow}\underline{B}{\leftarrow}C$), A and C are not adjacent in Ψ, and
Local(Ψ, A)\(**Sepset**<A, C> $\cup$ {B, C})

have greater than or equal to m vertices, have been selected.
$m = m + 1$.
until each ordered triple $<A, B, C>$ such that $A \rightarrow B \leftarrow C$ but A and C are not adjacent in Ψ, is such that
Local$(\Psi, A)\backslash(\textbf{Sepset}<A, C> \cup \{B, C\})$
has fewer than m vertices.

Step E. If there is a quadruple $<A, B, C, D>$ of distinct vertices such that
(1) $A \rightarrow B \leftarrow C$ in Ψ
(2) $A \rightarrow D \leftarrow C$ or $A \rightarrow D \leftarrow C$ in Ψ
(3) B and D are adjacent in Ψ
then orient $B \circ\!\!-\!\!\circ D$ or $B -\!\!\circ D$ as $B \rightarrow D$ in Ψ if D is not in
SupSepset$<A, B, C>$
else orient $B *\!\!-\!\!\circ D$ as $B *\!\!-\!\! D$ in Ψ if D is in **SupSepset**$<A, B, C>$.

Step F. For each quadruple $<A, B, C, D>$ of distinct vertices such that
(1) $A \rightarrow B \leftarrow C$ in Ψ
(2) D is not adjacent to both A and C in Ψ
(3) B and D are adjacent in Ψ
if A and C are a pair of vertices d-connected given
SupSepset$<A, B, C> \cup \{D\}$, then orient the edge
$B \circ\!\!-\!\!\circ D$ or $B -\!\!\circ D$ as $B \rightarrow D$ in Ψ.

Notes Concerning the Operation of the CCD Algorithm:

(Step A) The search in step A looks for d-separating sets for pairs of vertices X, Y in G. If such a set is found, then it is recorded in **Sepset**$<X, Y>$ and **Sepset**$<Y, X>$, after which the edge between X and Y in Ψ is deleted. It can be shown (see proof of theorem 5) that if X and Y are not p-adjacent in G, then step A is guaranteed to find a set which d-separates X and Y. Consequently at the end of step A there is an edge between a pair of vertices V and W in Ψ if and only if V and W are p-adjacent in G. Further, since all edges in Ψ at this stage have the form $\circ\!\!-\!\!\circ$, at this point Ψ is a PAG for G, though not a very informative one.

Step A always tests every subset of a given set before testing that set itself. It can be shown (see lemma 6, corollary 2) that as a consequence, every vertex in **Sepset**$<X, Y>$ is an ancestor of either X or Y in every directed graph in **Equiv**(G). Observe that **Sepset**$<X, Y>$ is set at most once: the algorithm removes the edge between X and Y in Ψ, as soon as a d-separating set for X and Y is found, and only attempts to find such a d-separating set if there is still an edge between X and Y in Ψ. Note that although no explicit order is given for considering pairs of vertices X, Y, the result of step A will be the same for any such ordering (see the note following lemma 5).

(Step B) In this step each triple of vertices $<A, B, C>$ in Ψ, such that there is an edge between A and B, and B and C, but there is no edge between A and C, is either oriented as $A{\rightarrow}B{\leftarrow}C$ or as $A*\!\!-\!\!\underline{*B*}\!\!-\!\!*C$. The orientation rule makes use of the property (mentioned above) that every vertex in **Sepset**$<A$, $C>$ is an ancestor of A or C. The rule also uses the fact that if A and B, and B and C are p-adjacent, but A and C are not p-adjacent, and B is an ancestor of A or C, then B occurs in every set which d-separates A and C (See lemma 7). Note that the premise in step B that there is no edge between A and C in Ψ ensures that **Sepset**$<A$, $C>$ exists and has been set in step A. The proof of correctness for the algorithm implicitly shows that this rule can never lead to contradictory conclusions (e.g. a graph containing $A{\rightarrow}\underline{B}{\leftarrow}C$) as long as the d-separation oracle gives correct answers about d-separation in directed graph G.)

(Step C) This step performs additional orientations in Ψ. The rule applies to certain triples of vertices $<A, X, Y>$ where X and Y are p-adjacent but A is not p-adjacent to X or Y. The rule infers from the existence of a d-connecting path from A to X given **Sepset**$<A, Y>$, ($X \notin$ **Sepset**$<A, Y>$) and the absence of a d-connecting path from A to Y given **Sepset**$<A, Y>$, that X is not an ancestor of Y. The inference is based on the idea that if X were an ancestor of Y then the d-connecting path between A and X could be "extended" to a d-connecting path between A and Y, given **Sepset**$<A, Y>$. Note again that the condition that there is no edge between A and Y ensures that **Sepset**$<A, Y>$ has been set in step A.

(Step D) In this step, the algorithm considers each triple $<A, B, C>$, which at this point is oriented as $A{\rightarrow}B{\leftarrow}C$ in Ψ and attempts to find a set **Z** which d-separates A and C, but contains $\{B\} \cup$ **Sepset**$<A, C>$. If such a set is found, then it is recorded in **SupSepset**$<A, B, C>$ and **SupSepset**$<C, B, A>$, and dotted underlining is added, linking the arrowheads at B thus: $A{\rightarrow}\underset{....}{B}{\leftarrow}C$.

Since step D looks for the smallest superset of $\{B\} \cup$ **Sepset**$<A, C>$, it can be proved (see corollary 3) that every vertex in **SupSepset**$<A, B, C>$ is an ancestor of A, B or C in every directed graph in **Equiv**(G). (This makes use of the analogous property, mentioned above, that **Sepset**$<A, C> \subset$ **An**$(\{A, C\})$ in every directed graph in **Equiv**(G).)

Note that step D looks for **SupSepset**$<A, B, C>$ only if $A{\rightarrow}B{\leftarrow}C$ in Ψ, A and C are not p-adjacent, and there is no underlining at B joining the arrowheads on these edges. Since underlining is added at B if a set which satisfies the conditions on **SupSepset**$<A, B, C>$ is found, it follows that **SupSepset**$<A, B, C>$ is set at most once by the algorithm.

(Step E and Step F) These last two sections make additional inferences concerning ancestor relations by examining **SupSepset**$<A, B, C>$. Both rules make use of the fact that **SupSepset**$<A, B, C> \subset$ **An**$(\{A, B, C\})$ as mentioned above. Note that antecedent (1) in step E and step F ensures that **SupSepset**<*A, B, C*> exists and has been set by step D of the algorithm.

4.5 Propagation Rules

There are many inferences that are validated by the semantics of a PAG, without referring to the *d*-separation oracle. For example the following inference rule:

$$A \circ {\rightarrow} \underline{B} \circ {-} \circ C \Rightarrow A \circ {\rightarrow} \underline{B} {-} \circ C$$

The underlining at *B* asserts that *B* is an ancestor of *A* or *C*, while the arrowhead at *B* on the *A→B* edge asserts that *B* is not an ancestor of *A;* hence *B* is an ancestor of *C*. We shall call such inferences *propagation* rules, since they "propagate" information that is already present in the PAG. The CCD algorithm as it stands includes almost no such propagation rules.[13] The development of a complete set of such propagation rules is an area for future research.

It will follow from the completeness theorem (theorem 6) that all of the structural information about the directed graph that can ever be obtained from the oracle can be obtained by applying propagation rules (which do not require further oracle consultation) to the output of the CCD algorithm. If any of the steps of the algorithm were omitted, this would no longer be the case: in certain cases further consultation of the *d*-separation oracle would be needed in order to find the most informative PAG, i.e., the PAG in which there are the smallest number of "o" endpoints.

4.6 Soundness

THEOREM 5. (soundness) Given as input an oracle for *d*-separation relations in the (cyclic or acyclic) directed graph *G*, the output of the CCD algorithm is a PAG Ψ for *G*.

Theorem 5 is proved by showing that each section of the algorithm makes correct inferences about the structure of *G* from the answers of the *d*-separation oracle for *G*.

In practice, an approximation to a *d*-separation oracle can be implemented as a statistical test that the corresponding partial correlation vanishes. As the sample size increases without limit, if the significance level of the statistical test is systematically lowered, then the probabilities of both type I and type II error for the test approach zero, so that the statistical test is correct with probability one. Of course, this does not guarantee that the CCD algorithm as implemented is reliable on realistic sample sizes. The reliability of the algorithm depends upon the following factors:

1. Whether the causal independence assumption holds (i.e., there are no latent variables).

2. Whether the causal faithfulness assumption holds.

3. Whether the distributional assumptions made by the statistical tests hold.

4. The power of the statistical tests against alternatives.

5. The significance level used in the statistical tests.

In the future, we will test the sensitivity of the algorithm to these factors on simulated data.

4.7 Completeness

The statement of the algorithm in section 4.4 does not specify completely an order in which sets are to be tested in step A and step D: it is only required that no set may be tested until all of the sets of smaller cardinality have been tried, but the order in which sets of the same cardinality are to be tested is un-specified.

If such an order is specified and the process of selecting sets is deterministic, then it follows that given oracles for two d-separation equivalent directed graphs G_1 and G_2, the algorithm will generate the same PAG. This is because, relative to a fixed order of selecting subsets, the output is determined entirely by the responses of the oracle, and for d-separation equivalent directed graphs the oracle, by definition, will give the same responses.

However, this leaves open the possibility that different orderings of the oracle consultations might generate different PAGs, given the same directed graph (or d-separation equivalent directed graphs) as input. In fact this may occur in certain circumstances: selecting sets in a different order may result in a different PAG as output. It can in fact be shown that the operation of sections step A, step B, step D and step E will be unaffected by the order in which subsets of the same cardinality are selected. However, step C and step F may orient more edges under some orderings than others.[14]

In spite of this it is still the case that if, given oracles for two directed graphs, the CCD algorithm produces the same PAG as output then the directed graphs are d-separation equivalent. This remains true even if the PAGs were generated by different implementations of the algorithm, which selected subsets differently:[15]

THEOREM 6. (d-separation completeness). If the CCD algorithm, when given as input d-separation oracles for the directed graphs G_1, G_2 produces as output PAGs Ψ_1, Ψ_2 respectively, then Ψ_1 is identical to Ψ_2 only if G_1 and G_2 are d-separation equivalent, i.e., $G_2 \in \mathbf{Equiv}(G_1)$ and vice versa.

The proof is based on the characterization of d-separation equivalence in Richardson (1994b, 1997).

As argued above, relative to a fixed, deterministic method for selecting subsets, the converse to theorem 6 also holds: Oracles for d-separation equiv-

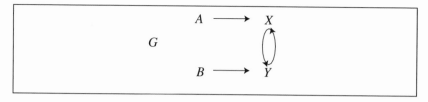

Figure 11. A directed cyclic graph.

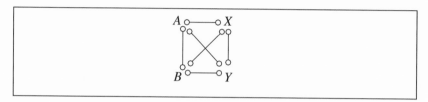

Figure 12. Ψ at the start of the CCD algorithm.

alent directed graphs will produce the same PAG as output from the algorithm. Hence the CCD algorithm, together with a fixed method of selecting sets, will produce the same PAG as output if and only if given oracles for *d*-separation equivalent directed graphs as input.

4.8 Trace of CCD Algorithm

This section illustrates the operation of the algorithm given as input a *d*-separation oracle for the directed graph in figure 11. The state of Ψ at the start of the algorithm is shown in figure 12.

Step A

Since A and B are *d*-separated given the empty set, the algorithm removes the edge between A and B and records **Sepset**<A, B> = **Sepset**<B, A> = $\varnothing$. This is the only pair of vertices that are *d*-separated given a subset of the other variables. Hence after step A, Ψ, which is now a PAG for G, is given in figure 13.

Step B

Since $X \notin$ **Sepset**<A, B> and $Y \notin$ **Sepset**<A, B>, A∘–∘X∘–∘B and A∘–∘Y∘–∘B are oriented respectively as $A{\rightarrow}X{\leftarrow}B$ and $A{\rightarrow}Y{\leftarrow}B$. The state of Ψ at the end of step B is shown in figure 14.

Step C

No orientations are performed in this case.

Step D

Since A and B are *d*-separated given $\{X, Y\}$, the algorithm records
SupSepset<A, X, B> = **SupSepset**<A, Y, B> = $\{X, Y\}$,

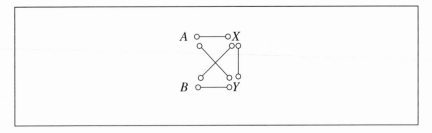

Figure 13. Ψ after step A of the CCD algorithm.

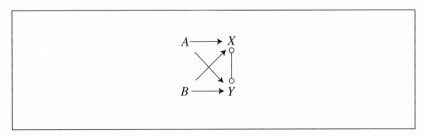

Figure 14. Ψ after step B of the CCD algorithm.

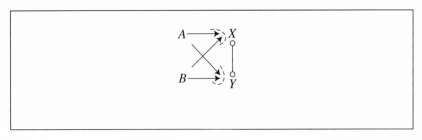

Figure 15. Ψ after step D of the CCD algorithm.

and it orients $A\rightarrow X\leftarrow B$ as $A\rightarrow\underset{\cdot\cdot\cdot\cdot\cdot}{X}\leftarrow B$, and $A\rightarrow Y\leftarrow B$ as $A\rightarrow\underset{\cdot\cdot\cdot\cdot\cdot}{Y}\leftarrow B$. The state of PAG Ψ after step D is shown in figure 15.

Step E

The quadruple $<A, B, X, Y>$ is such that (1) $A\rightarrow\underset{\cdot\cdot\cdot\cdot\cdot}{X}\leftarrow B$, (2) $A\rightarrow\underset{\cdot\cdot\cdot\cdot\cdot}{Y}\leftarrow B$, (3) X and Y are p-adjacent; thus it satisfies the conditions in step E. Since

$Y \in$ **SupSepset**$<A, X, B>$,

the edge $Y \circ\!\!-\!\!\circ X$ is oriented as $Y\!-\!\circ X$. Since $X \in$ **SupSepset**$<A, Y, B>$, this edge is further oriented as $Y\!-\!X$.

Step F

No orientations are performed in this case; hence the PAG that is output is as shown in figure 16.

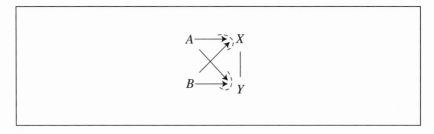

Figure 16. Ψ after completion of CCD algorithm.

4.9 Complexity of CCD Algorithm

Let $\text{MaxDegree}(G) = \underset{Y \in \mathbf{V}}{\text{Max}} |\{X \mid Y \leftarrow X, \text{ or } X \leftarrow Y \text{ in } G\}|,$

and $\text{MaxAdj}(G) = \underset{Y \in \mathbf{V}}{\text{Max}} |\{X \mid Y \text{ is } p\text{-adjacent to } Y \text{ in } G\}|$

The number of d-separation tests performed by ¶A of the CCD algorithm will, in a worst case, be bounded as follows:

$$\begin{matrix} \text{Total number of} \\ \text{oracle consultations in } \text{¶A} \end{matrix} \leq 2 \cdot \binom{n}{2} \sum_{i=0}^{k} \binom{n-2}{i} \leq \frac{(k+1)n^2(n-2)^{k+1}}{k!}$$

where n = number of vertices in G, and $k = \text{MaxAdj}(G)$. Since $\text{MaxAdj}(G) \leq (\text{MaxDegree}(G))^2$, with $\text{MaxDegree}(G) = r$ this step is

$$O\left(n^{r^2+3}\right).$$

It should be stressed that even as a worst case complexity bound, this is a very loose one; the bound presumes that there is a directed graph in which for every pair of vertices (X, Y) not p-adjacent in the directed graph, X and Y are only d-separated given all vertices adjacent to X or all vertices adjacent to Y.

Step B performs no additional tests of d-separation.

Step C performs at most one d-separation test for each triple satisfying the conditions given. Thus this step is $O(n^3)$.

In a worst case the number of tests of d-separation that step D performs is bounded by

$$\begin{matrix} \text{Total number of} \\ \text{oracle consultations in } \text{¶D} \end{matrix} \leq \binom{n}{3} \sum_{i=0}^{m} \binom{n-3}{i} \leq \frac{(m+1)n^3(n-3)^{m+1}}{m!}$$

where

$$m = \underset{Y \in \mathbf{V}}{\text{Max}} |\{X \mid X \in \text{Local}(\Psi, Y)\}$$

in step D. Since $m \leq (\text{MaxDegree}(G))^2$, this step is

$$O\left(n^{r^2+4}\right).$$

Again this is a loose bound.

Step E performs no tests of d-separation, while step F performs at most one test for each quadruple satisfying the conditions. Hence this step is $O(n^4)$, (though in many directed graphs there may be very few quadruples satisfying all four conditions). Thus overall the algorithm is of complexity

$$O\left(n^{r^2+4}\right).$$

5. Conclusion

These results raise a number of interesting questions whose answers may be of practical importance. Are there other parameterizations of directed cyclic graphs which entail the global Markov condition? Richardson (1996) gives a polynomial time algorithm for deciding whether two directed cyclic graphs are d-separation equivalent, based on the characterization of d-separation equivalence stated in the cyclic equivalence theorem. Spirtes and Verma (1992) and Spirtes and Richardson (1997) give polynomial time algorithms for deciding whether two directed acyclic graphs with latent variables are d-separation equivalent over the subset of measured variables. Is there a polynomial algorithm for determining when two arbitrary directed graphs (cyclic or acyclic) have the same set of d-separation relations over a common subset of variables **O**? As we have seen there are correct, polynomial time algorithms for inferring features of sparse directed graphs (cyclic or acyclic) from a probability distribution when there are no latent common causes. There are similarly correct, but not polynomial time, algorithms for inferring features of directed acyclic graphs from a probability distribution even when there may be latent common causes (see Spirtes and Verma 1992; Spirtes, Glymour and Scheines 1993; Spirtes, Meek, and Richardson 1995; and Pearl and Verma 1991). Are there comparable algorithms for inferring features of directed graphs (cyclic or acyclic) from a probability distribution even when there may be latent common causes?

6. Proofs

Some of the proofs are simplified by using a graphical relation (which we will call "Lauritzen d-separation") shown in Lauritzen et al. (1990) to be equivalent to Pearl's d-separation relation defined in section 2. Several preliminary definitions are needed to define Lauritzen d-separation. An *undirected graph* is an ordered pair of a finite set of vertices **V** and a set of undirected edges **E**. An undirected edge between A and B is an unordered pair of distinct vertices $\{A, B\}$ in **V**. A sequence of edges $<E_1, ..., E_n>$ in an undirected graph H is an *undirected path* if and only if there exists a sequence of vertices $<V_1, ..., V_{n+1}>$ such that for $1 \leq i \leq n$ $\{V_i, V_{i+1}\} = E_i$ and $E_i \neq E_{i+1}$.

Let $G(\mathbf{X})$ be the "induced" directed subgraph of directed graph G that contains only vertices in $\mathbf{X}$, with an edge from A to B in $G(\mathbf{X})$ if and only if there is an edge from A to B in G. Moral(G) *moralizes* a directed graph G if and only if Moral(G) is an undirected graph with the same vertices as G, and a pair of vertices X and Y are adjacent in Moral(G) if and only if either X and Y are adjacent in G or they have a common child in G. In an undirected graph H, if $\mathbf{X}$, $\mathbf{Y}$, and $\mathbf{Z}$ are disjoint sets of vertices, then $\mathbf{X}$ is *separated* from $\mathbf{Y}$ given $\mathbf{Z}$ if and only if every undirected path between a member of $\mathbf{X}$ and a member of $\mathbf{Y}$ contains a member of $\mathbf{Z}$. If $\mathbf{X}$, $\mathbf{Y}$ and $\mathbf{Z}$ are disjoint sets of variables, $\mathbf{X}$ and $\mathbf{Y}$ are *Lauritzen d-separated* given $\mathbf{Z}$ in a directed graph G just when $\mathbf{X}$ and $\mathbf{Y}$ are separated given $\mathbf{Z}$ in Moral$(G(\mathbf{An}(\mathbf{X} \cup \mathbf{Y} \cup \mathbf{Z})))$.

Since some of the vertices in the proofs are defined as satisfying certain properties in the graph, if A and B are vertices, we write $A \equiv B$ when A and B are different names for the same vertex. If there is an undirected path U containing vertices A and B in directed graph G and there is only one subpath of U between A and B, then $U(A, B)$ is the subpath of U between A and B.

6.1 Proof of Theorem 3

The following two lemmas are used in the proof of theorem 3.

LEMMA 1. In a directed graph G with vertices $\mathbf{V}$, if $\mathbf{X}$, $\mathbf{Y}$, and $\mathbf{Z}$ are disjoint subsets of $\mathbf{V}$, and $\mathbf{X}$ is d-connected to $\mathbf{Y}$ given $\mathbf{Z}$ in G, then $\mathbf{X}$ is d-connected to $\mathbf{Y}$ given $\mathbf{Z}$ in an acyclic directed subgraph of G.

Proof. Suppose that P^* is an undirected path, possibly cyclic, that d-connects a pair of vertices $X \in \mathbf{X}$ and $Y \in \mathbf{Y}$ given $\mathbf{Z}$. We will first show that there is an acyclic undirected path that d-connects X and Y given $\mathbf{Z}$. Let P be an acyclic subpath formed by removing all cycles from P^*.

If a vertex W is a noncollider on P then there is an edge on $P*$ that is out of W (since the edges on P are a subset of those on $P*$). Thus W occurred as a noncollider on $P*$; hence $W \notin \mathbf{Z}$.

Recall that every vertex W on a d-connecting path $P*$ is an ancestor of $\mathbf{Z}$ or the endpoints, X or Y; further, if W is not an ancestor of $\mathbf{Z}$, then either the subpath of $P*$ between X and W takes the form $X \leftarrow \ldots \leftarrow W$, or the subpath between W and Y takes the form $W \rightarrow \ldots \rightarrow Y$. If W is a collider on P then there is a least one edge occurring on $P*$ between X and W which is into W, i.e., $X \ldots \rightarrow W$, and there is at least one edge occurring on $P*$ between W and Y, which is also into W, i.e., $W \leftarrow \ldots Y$. It then follows that the subpaths of $P*$ between X and W, or W and Y are not directed paths into the endpoints; hence W is an ancestor of $\mathbf{Z}$, so P d-connects X and Y given $\mathbf{Z}$.

If C is a collider on P, then let *length*$(C, \mathbf{Z})$ be 0 if C is a member of $\mathbf{Z}$; otherwise it is the length of a shortest directed path from C to a member of $\mathbf{Z}$. Let *size*(P) equal the number of colliders on P plus the sum over all col-

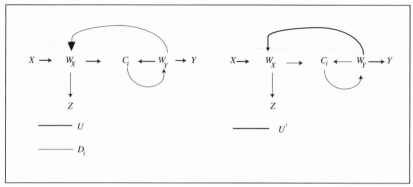

Figure 17. If a shortest directed path D_i from a collider C_i on U to a vertex $Z \in \mathbf{Z}$ intersects U then U is not a minimal d-connecting path.

liders C on P of *length(C, $\mathbf{Z}$)*. U is a *minimal acyclic d-connecting path* between X and Y given $\mathbf{Z}$, if U d-connects X and Y given $\mathbf{Z}$ and there is no other acyclic path U' that d-connects X and Y given $\mathbf{Z}$ such that *size(U')* < *size(U)*. If there is a path that d-connects X and Y given $\mathbf{Z}$, there is at least one minimal acyclic d-connecting path between X and Y given $\mathbf{Z}$.

Let U be a minimal acyclic d-connecting path between X and Y given $\mathbf{Z}$. First we will show that no shortest acyclic directed path D_i from a collider C_i on U to a member of $\mathbf{Z}$ intersects U except at C_i by showing that if such a point of intersection exists then U is not minimal, contrary to our assumption. See figure 17.

Form the path U' in the following way. If D_i intersects U at a vertex other than C_i then let W_X be the vertex closest to X on U that is on both D_i and U, and W_Y be the vertex closest to Y on U that is on both D_i and U. Suppose without loss of generality that W_X is after W_Y on D_i. Let U' be the concatenation of $U(X, W_X)$, $D_i(W_Y, W_X)$, and $U(W_Y, Y)$. It is now easy to show that U' d-connects X and Y given $\mathbf{Z}$, and *size(U')* < *size(U)* because U' contains no more colliders than U and a shortest directed path from W_X to a member of $\mathbf{Z}$ is shorter than D_i. Hence U is not minimal, contrary to the assumption.

Next, we will show that if U is minimal, then it does not contain a pair of colliders C and D such that a shortest directed path from C to a member of $\mathbf{Z}$ intersects a shortest path from D to a member of $\mathbf{Z}$. Suppose this is false. See figure 18.

Let D_1 be a shortest directed acyclic path from C to a member of Z that intersects D_2, a shortest directed acyclic path from D to a member of Z. Let the vertex on D_1 closest to C that is also on D_2 be R. Let U' be the concatenation of $U(X, C)$, $D_1(C, R)$, $D_2(D, R)$, and $U(Y, D)$. It is now easy to show that U' d-connects X and Y given Z and *size(U')* < *size(U)* because C and D are not colliders on U', the only collider on U' that may not be on U is R, and the

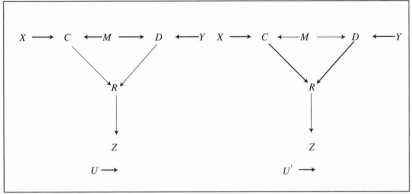

Figure 18. If C and D are colliders on U and a shortest
*directed path from C to a vertex in **Z** intersects a shortest directed*
*path from D to a vertex in **Z** then U is not a minimal d-connecting path.*

length of a shortest path from R to a member of Z is less than the length of a shortest path from D to a member of Z. Hence U is not minimal, contrary to the assumption.

For each collider C on a minimal path U that d-connects X and Y given **Z**, a shortest directed path from C to a member of **Z** does not intersect U except at C, and does not intersect a shortest directed path from any other collider D to a member of **Z**. It follows that the directed subgraph consisting of U and a shortest directed acyclic path from each collider on U to a member of **Z** is acyclic. Q.E.D.

LEMMA 2 (Lauritzen et al. 1990): In a directed (cyclic or acyclic) graph G, disjoint sets of variables **X**, **Y** and **Z**, **X** and **Y** are Pearl d-connected given **Z** if and only if **X** and **Y** are Lauritzen d-connected given **Z**.

Lauritzen et al., originally proved this for the acyclic case, but the proof goes over essentially unchanged to the cyclic case.[16] Since Lauritzen d-separation and Pearl d-separation are equivalent, henceforth we will simply refer to "d-separation" when the context makes clear which definition is being used.

THEOREM 3. The probability measure P over the substantive variables of a linear SEM L (recursive or nonrecursive) with jointly independent error variables satisfies the global directed Markov property for the directed (cyclic or acyclic) graph G of L; i.e., if **X**, **Y**, and **Z** are disjoint sets of variables in G and **X** is d-separated from **Y** given **Z** in G, then **X** and **Y** are independent given **Z** in P.

Proof. Let $\mathbf{Err}(\mathbf{X})$ be the set of error variables corresponding to a set of substantive variables **X**. In order to distinguish the density function for **V** from the density function for the error variables, we will use $f_{\mathbf{V}}$ to represent the density function (including marginal densities) for the former and $f_{\mathbf{Err}}$ to represent the density function of the latter. If $\mathbf{V}$ is the set of variables in G, then by hypothesis,

$$f_{\mathbf{Err}}(\mathbf{Err}(\mathbf{V})) = \prod_{\varepsilon \in \mathbf{Err}(\mathbf{V})} f_{\mathbf{Err}}(\varepsilon)$$

.

It is possible to integrate out the error variables not in $\mathbf{Err}(\mathbf{An}(\mathbf{X}))$ and obtain

$$f_{\mathbf{Err}}(\mathbf{Err}(\mathbf{An}(\mathbf{X}))) = \prod_{\varepsilon \in \mathbf{Err}(\mathbf{An}(\mathbf{X}))} f_{\mathbf{Err}}(\varepsilon)$$

.

Because for each variable X in $\mathbf{V}$, X is a linear function of its parents in G plus a unique error variable ε_X, it follows that ε_X is a linear function g_X of X and the parents of X in G. Hence $\mathbf{Err}(\mathbf{An}(\mathbf{X}))$ is a function of $\mathbf{An}(\mathbf{X})$. Following Haavelmo (1943) it is possible to derive the density function for the set of variables $\mathbf{An}(\mathbf{X})$ by replacing each ε_X in $f_{\mathbf{Err}}(\varepsilon_X)$ by $g_X(X, \mathbf{Parents}(X))$ and multiplying by the absolute value of the Jacobian:

$$f_{\mathbf{V}}(\mathbf{An}(\mathbf{X})) = \prod_{X \in \mathbf{An}(\mathbf{X})} f_{\mathbf{Err}}(g_X(X, \mathbf{Parents}(X))) \times |J|$$

where J is the Jacobian of the transformation. Because the transformation is linear, the Jacobian is a constant. All of the terms in the multiplication are nonnegative because they are either a density function or a positive constant. It follows from theorem 2 that if $\mathbf{X}$ and $\mathbf{Y}$ are d-separated given $\mathbf{Z}$ then $\mathbf{X}$ and $\mathbf{Y}$ are independent given $\mathbf{Z}$. Q.E.D.

6.2. Proof of Theorem 4

THEOREM 4. In a linear SEM L with jointly independent error variables and directed (cyclic or acyclic) graph G containing disjoint sets of variables $\mathbf{X}$, $\mathbf{Y}$ and $\mathbf{Z}$, if $\mathbf{X}$ is not d-separated from $\mathbf{Y}$ given $\mathbf{Z}$ in G then L does not linearly entail that $\mathbf{X}$ is independent of $\mathbf{Y}$ given $\mathbf{Z}$.

Proof. Suppose that $\mathbf{X}$ is not d-separated from $\mathbf{Y}$ given $\mathbf{Z}$. By lemma 1, if $\mathbf{X}$ is not d-separated from $\mathbf{Y}$ given $\mathbf{Z}$ in a cyclic directed graph G, then there is some acyclic directed subgraph G' of G in which $\mathbf{X}$ is not d-separated from $\mathbf{Y}$ given $\mathbf{Z}$. Geiger and Pearl (1988) have shown that if $\mathbf{X}$ is not d-separated from $\mathbf{Y}$ given $\mathbf{Z}$ in a directed acyclic graph, then there is some distribution represented by the directed acyclic graph in which $\mathbf{X}$ is not independent of $\mathbf{Y}$ given $\mathbf{Z}$, and it has been shown (Spirtes, Glymour and Scheines 1993) that there is in particular an instantiation of a linear parameterization of a SEM with directed graph G and no correlated errors in which $\mathbf{X}$ is not independent of $\mathbf{Y}$ given $\mathbf{Z}$. If P satisfies the global directed Markov property for G' it also satisfies it for G because every d-connecting path in G' is a d-connecting path in G. Hence there is a distribution represented by G in which $\mathbf{X}$ is not independent of $\mathbf{Y}$ given $\mathbf{Z}$. Q.E.D.

6.3 Proof of Theorem 5

THEOREM 5 (SOUNDNESS). Given as input an oracle for testing d-separation relations in the directed (cyclic or acyclic) graph G, then the output is a PAG Ψ for G.

Proof. The proof proceeds by showing that each section of the CCD algorithm makes correct inferences from the answers given by the d-separation oracle for G, to the structure of G (and hence any directed graph in **Equiv**(G)).

6.3.1 Step A

LEMMA 3. Let G be a directed graph with vertex set **V**, and $X, Y \in$ **V**. The following are equivalent:

(a) $\exists \mathbf{Z} \subseteq \mathbf{V} \backslash \{X, Y\}$ such that X and Y are d-separated given **Z**; i.e., X and Y are not p-adjacent.

(b) $\{X, Y\}$ is not an edge in Moral($G(\mathbf{An}(\{X, Y\}))$).

(c) None of the following conditions hold in G:

    (1) X is a parent of Y

    (2) Y is a parent of X

    (3) X and Y have a common child C that is an ancestor of X or Y.

Proof: (a)$\Rightarrow$(b) Observe that Moral($G(\mathbf{An}(\{X, Y\}))$) is a subgraph of Moral($G(\mathbf{An}(\{X, Y\} \cup \mathbf{Z}))$). The hypothesis implies that $\{X, Y\}$ is not an edge in Moral($G(\mathbf{An}(\{X, Y \cup \mathbf{Z}\}))$). Hence it is also not an edge in Moral($G(\mathbf{An}(\{X, Y\}))$).

(b)$\Leftrightarrow$(c) By definition of the operation of graph moralization on $G(\mathbf{An}(\{X, Y\}))$: there is an edge between X and Y in Moral($G(\mathbf{An}(\{X, Y\}))$) if and only if either there is an edge between X and Y in $G(\mathbf{An}(\{X, Y\}))$ and thus in G, i.e., (1) or (2) holds, or X and Y have a common child C in $G(\mathbf{An}(\{X, Y\}))$, in which case (3) holds.

(c)$\Rightarrow$(a) Take $\mathbf{Z} = \mathbf{An}(\{X, Y\}) \backslash \{X, Y\}$. By definition, every vertex in Moral($G(\mathbf{An}(\{X, Y\}))$) is an ancestor of X or Y. Since (c)$\Rightarrow$(b) there is no edge between X and Y in Moral($G(\mathbf{An}(\{X, Y\}))$). Thus there is a vertex in **Z** lying on every path from X to Y in

Moral($G(\mathbf{An}(\{X, Y\}))$) $\equiv$ Moral($G(\mathbf{An}(\mathbf{Z} \cup \{X, Y\}))$).

Hence X and Y are d-separated given **Z**. Q.E.D.

COROLLARY 1. In directed graph G, if X and Y are p-adjacent then either X is an ancestor of Y, or Y is an ancestor of X (or both).

Proof: This follows immediately from the previous lemma: if X and Y are p-adjacent then either (1) X is a parent of Y, (2) Y is a parent of X, or (3) X and Y have a common child C that is an ancestor of X or Y (or some combination). Q.E.D.

LEMMA 4. In directed graph G, if X and Y are not p-adjacent, then X and

Y are d-separated given

$$T_{X;Y} = \{V|\ V \text{ is adjacent to } X \text{ in Moral}(G(\mathbf{An}(\{X,\ Y\})))\ \}.$$

Further, either $T_{X;Y} \subseteq \{V \mid V \text{ is } p\text{-adjacent to } X \text{ in } G\}$ or X is an ancestor of Y in G.

Proof: Since X and Y are not p-adjacent it follows from lemma 3 that there is no edge between X and Y in Moral$(G(\mathbf{An}(\{X,\ Y\})))$. Hence every path from X to Y in Moral$(G(\mathbf{An}(\{X,\ Y\})))$ contains at least two edges. Hence the vertex closest to X on any path is in $T_{X;Y}$. So X and Y are d-separated given $T_{X;Y}$.

We now show that either $T_{X;Y} \subseteq \{V \mid V \text{ is } p\text{-adjacent to } X \text{ in } G\}$ or X is an ancestor of Y in G. By the definition of graph moralization, in G every vertex in $T_{X;Y}$ is either (a) a parent of X, (b) a child of X, or (c) a parent V of some vertex C, where C is also a child of X and an ancestor of X or Y. Any vertex in the first two categories is clearly p-adjacent to X. If C is an ancestor of X, then V is p-adjacent to X. If C is an ancestor of Y, then X is an ancestor of Y. Q.E.D.

LEMMA 5. In a directed graph G, if A and B are not p-adjacent then A and B are d-separated either by a set of vertices all of which are p-adjacent to A, or by a set of vertices all of which are p-adjacent to B.

Proof. Let $T_{A;B}$, and $T_{B;A}$ be defined as in lemma 4. It follows from this lemma that A and B are d-separated given $T_{A;B}$ and A and B are d-separated given $T_{B;A}$. There are three cases to consider:

CASE 1. A is not an ancestor of B.

From lemma 4, since A is not an ancestor of B,

$$T_{A;B} \subseteq \{V \mid V\ p\text{-adjacent to } A\}.$$

CASE 2. B is not an ancestor of A. Symmetrical to case 1.

CASE 3. B is an ancestor of A, and A is an ancestor of B. Any vertex V in $T_{A;B}$ is either a child of A, a parent of A, or a parent of some vertex C, which is also a child of A and an ancestor of A or B. Clearly vertices in the first two categories are p-adjacent to A; as before, vertices in the last category are p-adjacent to A if C is an ancestor of A. Since C is an ancestor of A or B, and B is an ancestor of A, consequently C is an ancestor of A. (Note that in this case every vertex in $T_{B;A}$ is also p-adjacent to B.) Q.E.D.

Suppose that the input to the algorithm is a d-separation oracle for a directed graph G. To find a set which d-separates some pair of variables A and B in G, the algorithm tests subsets of **Adjacencies** (Ψ, A) and subsets of **Adjacencies** (Ψ, B) to see if they d-separate A and B. Since the vertices which are p-adjacent to A in G are at all times a subset of **Adjacencies** (Ψ, A),[17] and likewise the vertices p-adjacent to B are always a subset of **Adjacencies** (Ψ, B), it follows from lemma 5 that step A is guaranteed to find a set which d-separates

A and *B*, if any set *d*-separates *A* and *B* in *G*. Clearly the order in which subsets of **Adjacencies** (Ψ, *A*) and **Adjacencies** (Ψ, *B*) of a fixed cardinality are tested in step A will not affect whether or not a *d*-separating set for a given pair of variables is found: the above argument shows that the search in step A is guaranteed to find some *d*-separating set for *A* and *B* if such exists, i.e., *A* and *B* are not *p*-adjacent. (Similarly, the order in which pairs of vertices *A*, *B* s.t. *A* ∘─∘ *B* in Ψ are considered in step A will not affect whether a *d*-separating set is found.) However, *which d*-separating set the search finds first may be influenced by the ordering of the tests in step A.[18]

6.3.2 Step B

The next lemma and corollaries give an important property of *d*-separating sets that are found through a search which never tests a set unless it has already tested every proper subset of that set (as in step A of the CCD algorithm).

LEMMA 6. Suppose that in a directed graph *G*, *Y* is not an ancestor of *X* or *Z* or **R**. If there is a set **S**, such that **R** ⊂ **S**, *Y* ∈ **S**, and for every set **T** s.t. **R** ⊆ **T** ⊆ **S**\{*Y*}, *X* and *Z* are *d*-connected given **T** in *G*, then **S** *d*-connects *X* and *Z* in *G*.

Proof. Let $\mathbf{T}^* = \mathbf{An}(\{X, Z\} \cup \mathbf{R}) \cap \mathbf{S}$. Since by assumption $Y \notin \mathbf{An}(\{X, Z\} \cup \mathbf{R})$, $Y \notin \mathbf{T}^*$. Now, $\mathbf{R} \subseteq \mathbf{T}^*$, and $\mathbf{T}^* \subseteq \mathbf{S}\backslash\{Y\}$, so by hypothesis there is a *d*-connecting path, *P*, between *X* and *Z*, conditional on $\mathbf{T}^*$. By the definition of a *d*-connecting path, every vertex on *P* is either an ancestor of one of the endpoints, or $\mathbf{T}^*$. Moreover, by definition, every vertex in $\mathbf{T}^*$ is an ancestor of *X* or *Z* or **R**. Thus every vertex on the path *P* is an ancestor of *X* or *Z* or **R**. Since neither *Y* nor any vertex in $\mathbf{S}\backslash\mathbf{T}^*$ is an ancestor of *X* or *Z* or **R**, it follows that no vertex in $\mathbf{S}\backslash\mathbf{T}^*$ lies on *P*. Since $\mathbf{T}^* \subset \mathbf{S}$ the only way in which *P* could fail to *d*-connect *X* and *Z* given **S** would be if some vertex in $\mathbf{S}\backslash\mathbf{T}^*$ lay on the path. Hence *P* still *d*-connects *X* and *Z* given **S**. Q.E.D.

In a directed graph *G*, if *X* and *Y* are *d*-separated given **S**, and are *d*-connected given any proper subset of **S**, then **S** is a *minimal d-separating* set for *X* and *Y* in *G*.

The following corollaries are useful:

COROLLARY 2. In a directed graph *G*, if **S** is a minimal *d*-separating set for *X* and *Y*, then any vertex in **S** is an ancestor of *X* or *Y* in *G*.

Proof. The corollary follows immediately from lemma 6, with **R** = ∅ via contraposition. Q.E.D.

COROLLARY 3. In a directed graph *G* containing vertices *X*, *Y*, and set **R** (*X*, *Y* ∉ **R**), if **S** is a set s.t. **R** ⊂ **S** and **S** *d*-separates *X* and *Y*, but there is no subset **Q** ⊂ **S** s.t. **R** ⊂ **Q**, and **Q** *d*-separates *X* and *Y*, then any vertex in **S** is an ancestor of *X, Y* or **R** in *G*.

Proof. Follows immediately from lemma 6, via contraposition. Q.E.D.

Corollary 2 shows that orientation rule step B(2) is correct. If *A* and *B*, and *B* and *C* are *p*-adjacent, but **Sepset**<*A, C*> contains *B*, then we know from the search procedure that *A* and *C* are not *d*-separated given any proper subset of **Sepset**<*A, C*>. It follows that *B* is an ancestor of *A* or *C*. Hence *A*∗──∗*B*∗──∗*C* should be oriented as *A*∗──*∗B*∗──∗*C* in the PAG.

The following lemma shows the correctness of the orientation rule step B(1):

LEMMA 7. In a directed graph *G*, if *A* and *B* are *p*-adjacent, *B* and *C* are *p*-adjacent, and *B* is an ancestor of *A* or *C*, then *A* and *C* are *d*-connected given any set **S**, s.t. *A, B, C* ∉ **S**.

Proof. Since *A* and *B*, and *B* and *C* are *p*-adjacent in *G* it follows from Lemma 3 that {*A, B*} and {*B, C*} are edges in Moral(*G*(**An**({*A, B*}))) and Moral(*G*(**An**({*B, C*}))) respectively; hence also in Moral(*G*(**An**({*A, B, C*} ∪ **S**))). If *B* ∈ **An**({*A, C*}), then **An**({*A, B, C*} ∪ **S**) = **An**({*A, C*} ∪ **S**); hence {*A, B*} and {*B, C*} are edges in Moral(*G*(**An**({*A, C*} ∪ **S**))). If B ∉ **S** then *A*──*B*──*C* is a path circumventing **S** in Moral(*G*(**An**({*A, C*} ∪ **S**))); hence *A* and *C* are *d*-connected given **S**. Q.E.D.

It follows by contraposition that if *A* and *B* are *p*-adjacent, *B* and *C* are *p*-adjacent, *A* and *C* are *d*-separated given **Sepset**<*A, C*>, and B ∉ **Sepset**<*A, C*>, then *B* is not an ancestor of *A* or *C*; hence *A*∗──∗*B*──∗*C* should be oriented as *A*∗→*B*←∗*C* in the PAG. It then follows from corollary 1 that *A* is an ancestor of *B*, and *C* is an ancestor of *B*; hence these edges are correctly oriented as *A*→*B*←*C*.

6.3.3 Step C

LEMMA 8. In a directed graph *G*, suppose *X* is an ancestor of *Y*. If there is a set **S** such that *A* and *Y* are *d*-separated given **S**, *X* and *Y* are *d*-connected given **S**, and *X* ∉ **S**, then *A* and *X* are *d*-separated given **S**.

Proof. Suppose for a contradiction that *A* and *X* are *d*-connected given **S**. In that case there is a path *P* between *A* and *X* in Moral(*G*(**An**({*A, X*} ∪ **S**))) on which there is no vertex in **S**. Since by hypothesis *X* and *Y* are *d*-connected given **S**, there is a path *Q* between *X* and *Y* in Moral(*G*(**An**({*X, Y*} ∪ **S**))) on which there is no vertex in **S**. Since {*X, Y*} ∪ **S** and {*A, X*} ∪ **S** are subsets of {*A, X, Y*} ∪ **S,** path *P* and path *Q* exist in Moral(*G*(**An**({*A, X, Y*} ∪ **S**))). Since *X* is an ancestor of *Y*, **An**({*A, X, Y*} ∪ **S**) = **An**({*A, Y*} ∪ **S**). Thus *P* and *Q* exist in Moral(*G*(**An**({*A, Y*} ∪ **S**))). Since *P* and *Q* intersect at least once (at *X*) and do not contain any vertices in **S**, it follows that there is a path *R* from *A* to *Y* in Moral(*G*(**An**({*A, Y*} ∪ **S**))), which also does not contain any vertices in **S**. But this is a contradiction. Q.E.D.

LEMMA 9. Let A, X and Y be three vertices in a directed graph G, such that X and Y are p-adjacent. If there is a set $\mathbf{S}$ such that:

(1) $X \notin \mathbf{S}$,

(2) A and Y are d-separated given $\mathbf{S}$, and

(3) A and X are d-connected given $\mathbf{S}$, then X is not an ancestor of Y.

Proof. Suppose that there is such a set $\mathbf{S}$. If X and Y are p-adjacent, then X and Y are d-connected by every subset of the other variables. In particular X and Y are d-connected given $\mathbf{S}$. Since $\mathbf{S}$ d-separates A and Y but d-connects A and X, it follows from lemma 8 by contraposition that X is not an ancestor of Y. Q.E.D.

Step C simply applies lemma 9. Suppose that $<A, X, Y>$ is a triple such that:

(1) A is not p-adjacent to X or Y,

(2) X and Y are p-adjacent in Ψ, and

(3) $X \notin$ **Sepset**$<A, Y>$.

Suppose further that A and X are d-connected given **Sepset**$<A, Y>$. Since $X \notin$ **Sepset**$<A, Y>$, setting $\mathbf{S} =$ **Sepset**$<A, Y>$, we can apply lemma 9 to orient $X \circ\!\!-\!\!\circ Y$ or $X \circ\!\!- Y$ as $X \leftarrow\!\!* Y$. It then follows by corollary 1 that Y is an ancestor of X; hence the edge is oriented as $X \leftarrow Y$.

It is a feature of this orientation rule that X and Y may be arbitrarily far from A. Rules of this type are needed by a cyclic discovery algorithm, because, as was shown in Richardson (1994), two cyclic directed graphs may agree "locally" on d-separation relations, but disagree on some d-separation relation between distant variables.[19]

We state without proof the following lemma, used subsequently in the proof, which is an easy generalization of lemma 3.3.1 in Spirtes, Glymour, and Scheines (1993). The lemma states conditions under which a set of "short" d-connecting paths may be put together to form a single d-connecting path.

LEMMA 10 (Richardson 1994). In a directed (cyclic or acyclic) graph G over a set of vertices $\mathbf{V}$, if the following conditions hold:

(a) R is a sequence of vertices in $\mathbf{V}$ from A to B, $R \equiv <A \equiv X_0, ..., X_{n+1} \equiv B>$, such that $\forall i$, $0 \leq i \leq n$, $X_i \neq X_{i+1}$ (the X_i are only *pairwise distinct*, i.e., not necessarily distinct),

(b) $\mathbf{Z} \subseteq \mathbf{V}\backslash\{A, B\}$,

(c) $\mathbf{T}$ is a set of undirected paths such that

(1) for each pair of consecutive vertices in R, X_i and X_{i+1}, there is a unique undirected path in $\mathbf{T}$ that d-connects X_i and X_{i+1} given $\mathbf{Z}\backslash\{X_i, X_{i+1}\}$,

(2) if some vertex X_k in R is in $\mathbf{Z}$, then the paths in $\mathbf{T}$ that contain X_k as an endpoint collide at X_k, (i.e., all such paths are directed into X_k)

(3) if for three vertices X_{k-1}, X_k, X_{k+1} occurring in R, the d-connecting paths in **T** between X_{k-1} and X_k, and X_k and X_{k+1}, collide at X_k then X_k has a descendant in **Z**,

then there is a path U in G that d-connects $A \equiv X_0$ and $B \equiv X_{n+1}$ given **Z** that contains only edges occurring in **T**.

6.3.4 Step D

This section searches to find "extra" d-separating sets for triples oriented as $X{\rightarrow}Y{\leftarrow}Z$ by step B (where X and Z are not p-adjacent). In the acyclic case, a triple of vertices $X*{-}*Y*{-}*Z$, where X and Y are p-adjacent, Y and Z are p-adjacent, but X and Z are not p-adjacent, either has the property that every d-separating set for X and Z contains Y, or that every d-separating set for X and Z does not contain Y. However, in the cyclic case it is possible for X and Z to be d-separated by one set containing Y, and one set not containing Y. We already know from lemma 7 that if X and Z are d-separated by some set which does not contain Y, then Y is not an ancestor of X or Z. What can we infer if, in addition, X and Z are also d-separated by a set which contains Y? This is answered by the next lemma and corollary.

LEMMA 11. In a directed graph G, if Y is a descendant of a common child of X and Z, then X and Z are d-connected by any set containing Y.

Proof. Suppose that Y is a descendant of a common child C of X and Z. Then the path $X{\rightarrow}C{\leftarrow}Z$ d-connects X and Z given any set containing Y. Q.E.D.

COROLLARY 4. In a directed graph G, with vertices X, Y and Z, if there is some set **S** such that $Y \in$ **S**, and X and Z are d-separated given **S**, then Y is not a descendant of a common child of X and Z.

LEMMA 12. In a directed graph G, if X and Z are not p-adjacent, and Y is not a descendant of a common child of X and Z, then X and Z are d-separated by the set **T**, defined as follows:
T $= \{V \mid V$ is adjacent to X in Moral$(G(\mathbf{An}(\{X, Y, Z\})))\}$.
Further, if X and Y are p-adjacent then $Y \in$ **T**.

Proof: Since X and Z are not p-adjacent, it follows by lemma 3 that X and Z are not adjacent in Moral$(G(\mathbf{An}(\{X, Z\})))$. As Y is not a descendant of a common child of X and Z, it then follows that X and Z are not adjacent in Moral$(G(\mathbf{An}(\{X, Y, Z\})))$. Hence $Z \notin$ **T** and every path from X to Z in Moral$(G(\mathbf{An}(\{X, Y, Z\})))$ contains some vertex in **T**. Thus X and Z are d-separated given **T**. If X and Y are p-adjacent in G, then Y is adjacent to X in Moral$(G(\mathbf{An}(X, Y)))$, and therefore in Moral$(G(\mathbf{An}(\{X, Y, Z\})))$. Thus $Y \in$ **T**. Q.E.D.

COROLLARY 5: In a directed graph G, if $<X, Y, Z>$ is a triple such that X

and Z are d-connected given any set containing Y and d-separated by some set not containing Y, then Y is a descendant of a common child of X and Z.

LEMMA 13. In directed graph G, if X and Z are d-separated by some set $\mathbf{R}$, then for all sets $\mathbf{Q} \subseteq \mathbf{An}(\mathbf{R} \cup \{X, Z\})\backslash\{X, Z\}$, X and Z are d-separated by $\mathbf{R} \cup \mathbf{Q}$.

Proof. If $\mathbf{Q} \subseteq \mathbf{An}(\mathbf{R} \cup \{X, Z\})\backslash\{X, Z\}$ then $\mathbf{An}(\mathbf{R} \cup \{X, Z\}) = \mathbf{An}(\mathbf{R} \cup \mathbf{Q} \cup \{X, Z\})$. It follows that $\mathrm{Moral}(G(\mathbf{An}(\mathbf{R} \cup \{X, Z\}))) = \mathrm{Moral}(G(\mathbf{An}(\mathbf{R} \cup \mathbf{Q} \cup \{X, Z\})))$. The result then follows via the (Lauritzen) definition of d-connection. Q.E.D.

The search in step D considers in turn each triple $A \rightarrow B \leftarrow C$ in Ψ, A and C not p-adjacent, and attempts to find a set $\mathbf{R}$ which is a subset of $\mathbf{Local}(\Psi, A)\backslash\{B, C\}$ such that A and C are d-separated given $\mathbf{R} \cup \{B\} \cup \mathbf{Sepset}{<}A, C{>}$. It follows from lemma 11 that if there is some set which d-separates A and C and contains B, then B is not a descendant of a common child of A and C. It then follows from lemma 12 that in this case there is some subset, the set $\mathbf{T}$ given in the lemma, which contains B, d-separates A and C and in which every vertex is either a parent of A, a child of A, or a parent of a child of A and so $\mathbf{T} \subseteq \mathbf{Local}(\Psi, X)$. Since $\mathbf{Sepset}{<}A, C{>}$ is a minimal d-separating set for A and C, it follows that $\mathbf{Sepset}{<}A, C{>} \subseteq \mathbf{An}(\{A, C\})\backslash\{A, C\}$ ($\subseteq \mathbf{An}(\mathbf{T} \cup \{A, C\})$). Hence by lemma 13, $\mathbf{T} \cup \mathbf{Sepset}{<}A, C{>}$ also d-separates A and C.

The reader may wonder why step D tests sets of the form $\mathbf{T} \cup \mathbf{Sepset}{<}A, C{>}$, (where $\mathbf{T} \subseteq \mathbf{Local}(\Psi, A)$), instead of just testing sets of the form $\mathbf{T} \subseteq \mathbf{Local}(\Psi, A)$); lemma 12 shows that a search of the latter kind would succeed in finding a d-separating set for A and C which contained B. The answer is that from lemma 13 we know that any set $\mathbf{T} \subseteq \mathbf{Local}(\Psi, A)$ which d-separates A and C is such that $\mathbf{T} \cup \mathbf{Sepset}{<}A, C{>}$ also d-separates A and C, but the reverse is not true. In particular the smallest set $\mathbf{T}$ such that $\mathbf{T} \cup \mathbf{Sepset}{<}A, C{>}$ d-separates A and C may be considerably smaller than the smallest set $\mathbf{T}$ which d-separates A and C alone; hence the search is significantly faster.[20]

We require one more lemma to explain why we initialize $m = 1$, and do not test $\mathbf{T} = \varnothing$.

LEMMA 14. In a directed graph G, if X and Y are p-adjacent, Y and Z are p-adjacent, X and Z are not p-adjacent, Y is not an ancestor of X or Z, and $\mathbf{S}$ is a minimal d-separating set for X and Z, then X and Z are d-connected given $\mathbf{S} \cup \{Y\}$.

Proof. According to lemma 3, if X and Y are p-adjacent then either $X \rightarrow Y$, $Y \rightarrow X$ or $X \rightarrow C \leftarrow Y$, where C is an ancestor of X or Y. Thus under the hypothesis that Y is not an ancestor of X, it follows that X is an ancestor of Y. Moreover, it follows that there is a directed path P from X to Y on which every vertex except X is a descendant of Y, and hence on which every vertex except X is not an ancestor of X or Z. (In the case $X{\to}Y$, the last assertion is trivial. In the other case it merely states a property of the path $X{\to}C{\to}...Y$, where C is a common child of X and Y.) Likewise there is a path Q from Z to Y on which every vertex except Z is not an ancestor of X or Z.

If **S** is a minimal d-separating set for X and Z, then every vertex in **S** is an ancestor of X or Z (and X, $Z \notin$ **S**). Hence no vertex on P or Q is in **S**. It follows that P d-connects X and Y given **S**, and Q d-connects Y and Z given **S**. It then follows from lemma 10 that these paths can be combined to form a single path which d-connects X and Z given $\mathbf{S} \cup \{Y\}$. Q.E.D.

This completes the proof that step D of the algorithm will succeed in finding a set which d-separates A and C, and contains B, for each triple $A{\to}B{\leftarrow}C$ in the PAG, if any such set exists. A number of the subsequent proofs make use of the following consequence: For *every* triple A, B, C such that Ψ contains $A{\to}B{\leftarrow}C$, A and C are not p-adjacent in Ψ, and B is not a descendant of a common child of A and C, step D orients $A{\to}B{\leftarrow}C$ as $A{\to}B{\leftarrow}C$.

6.3.5 Step E

The following lemma provides the justification of step E where $A{\to}B{\leftarrow}C$, $A{\to}D{\leftarrow}C$, and D is not in **SupSepset**$<A, B, C>$, in which case $B \circ\!\!-\!\!\circ D$ or $B -\!\!\circ$ D is oriented as $B{\to}D$.

LEMMA 15. If in a PAG Ψ for G, $X{\to}V{\leftarrow}Z$, $X{\to}W{\leftarrow}Z$, X and Z are not p-adjacent, and W is an ancestor of V in G, then any set **S** such that $V \in$ **S**, and X and Z are d-separated by **S**, also contains W.

Proof. Suppose there were some d-separating set **S** for X and Z which contained V and did not contain W. Then, since W is an ancestor of V and $V \in$ **S**, but $W \notin$ **S**, it follows by lemma 10 that we could put together a d-connecting path from X to W given **S** and from W to Z given **S** to form a new d-connecting path from X to Z given **S** (irrespective of whether or not these paths collide at W). Such d-connecting paths between X and W, and between W and Z exist (by lemma 3) since X is p-adjacent to W and W is p-adjacent to Z. This is a contradiction. Q.E.D.

In the case in which $A{\to}B{\leftarrow}C$, $A{\to}D{\leftarrow}C$, and D is in **SupSepset**$<A, B, C>$ the algorithm orients $B*\!\!-\!\!\circ D$ as $B*\!\!-\!\!D$, the inference can be justified as follows. If D is in **SupSepset**$<A, B, C>$ then it follows from corollary 3, and the fact that step **D** looks for the smallest superset of $\{B\} \cup$ **Sepset**$<A, C>$ which d-separates A and C, that D is an ancestor of $\{B\} \cup$ **Sepset**$<A, C>$. Since **Sepset**$<A, C>$ is a minimal d-separating set for A and C, every vertex in **Sepset**$<A, C>$ is an ancestor of A or C. Thus if D is in **SupSepset**$<A, B, C>$, D is an ancestor of A, C or B. However, since there are arrowheads at D on the edges from A to D, and C to D in Ψ, it follows that D is not an ancestor of A or C; hence D is an ancestor of B. Thus it is correct to orient B *–∘ D as $B*$—D.

In the case in which $A{\rightarrow}D{\leftarrow}C$ in Ψ, (A and C are not p-adjacent and there is no dotted underlining $A{\rightarrow}\underset{...}{D}{\leftarrow}C$), it does not matter whether D is in **SupSepset**<A, B, C> or not. A and C are d-connected by any set **S** that contains D but does not contain A or C (because of the lack of underlining in the edge pair $A{\rightarrow} D {\leftarrow}C$). It follows from lemma 12 by contraposition that D is a descendant of a common child of A and C. Moreover since A and C are d-separated by some set containing B (because of the underlining in the edge pair $A{\rightarrow}\underset{...}{B}{\leftarrow}C$), B is not a descendant of a common child of A and C. Hence B is not a descendant of D, and so by corollary 1, B is an ancestor of D. Thus in the case where $A{\rightarrow}\underset{...}{B}{\leftarrow}C$, $A{\rightarrow}D{\leftarrow}C$, and B and D are p-adjacent in Ψ, B ∘–∘ D or B –∘ D should be oriented as $B{\rightarrow}D$.

6.3.6 Step F

A and C are d-separated by **SupSepset**<A, B, C>, and $B \in$ **SupSepset**<A, B, C>. By lemma 13, if D is an ancestor of B, then A and C are d-separated by **SupSepset**<A, B, C> $\cup$ $\{D\}$. Hence by contraposition, if A and C are d-connected given **SupSepset**<A, B, C> $\cup$ $\{D\}$ then D is not an ancestor of B. (In fact, it follows that D is not an ancestor of A, B or C.) Since D is not an ancestor of B, but B and D are p-adjacent, it follows by corollary 1 that B is an ancestor of D. Thus B ∘–∘ D or B –∘ D should be oriented as $B{\rightarrow}D$ in Ψ.

This completes the proof of the correctness of the CCD algorithm. Q.E.D.

6.4. Proof of Theorem 6

In order to prove the d-separation completeness of the CCD algorithm, all that is required is to show that whenever the first input to the CCD algorithm is a d-separation oracle for G_1 that results in output Ψ_1, and the second input to the CCD algorithm is a d-separation oracle for G_2 that results in output Ψ_2, and Ψ_1 and Ψ_2 are identical, then G_1 and G_2 are d-separation equivalent. We shall do this by proving that when d-separation oracles for G_1 and G_2 are used as input to the CCD algorithm and produce the same PAG as output, then G_1 and G_2 satisfy the five conditions of the cyclic equivalence theorem CET(I)-(V) (given below) with respect to one another. It has already been shown in Richardson(1994, 1997) that two directed graphs G_1 and G_2 are d-separation equivalent to one another if and only if they satisfy these 5 conditions. These conditions lead directly to a polynomial-time ($O(n^9)) \equiv O(n^3 e^4)$) algorithm for determining whether or not two directed cyclic graphs are d-separation equivalent. See Richardson (1994, 1996, 1997).

Before stating the cyclic equivalence theorem, we require a number of extra definitions. In a directed graph G, call a triple of vertices <A, B, C> an *unshielded triple* if A and B are p-adjacent, B and C are p-adjacent, but A and C are not p-adjacent.

Call an unshielded triple a *conductor* if B is an ancestor of A or C; otherwise, if B is not an ancestor of A or C, call it a *nonconductor.* (Note that it follows from corollary 1 that if $<A, B, C>$ is a nonconductor, then A and C are ancestors of B.) Call a nonconductor *perfect* if B is a descendant of a common child of A and C; otherwise call it *imperfect.*

If $<X_0, X_1, ..., X_{n+1}>$ is a sequence of distinct vertices s.t. $\forall i \ 0 \le i \le n$, X_i and X_{i+1} are p-adjacent then we will refer to $<X_0, X_1, ..., X_{n+1}>$ as an *itinerary.*

If $<X_0, ..., X_{n+1}> \ (n \ge 2)$ is an itinerary such that:

1. $\forall t \ 1 \le t \le n$, $<X_{t-1}, X_t, X_{t+1}>$ is a conductor,

2. $\forall k \ 1 \le k \le n$, X_{k-1} is an ancestor of X_k, and X_{k+1} is an ancestor of X_k, and

3. X_1 is *not* an ancestor of X_0, and X_n is *not* an ancestor of X_{n+1},

then $<X_0, X_1, X_2>$ and $<X_{n-1}, X_n, X_{n+1}>$ are *mutually exclusive (m.e.) conductors on the itinerary* $<X_0, ..., X_{n+1}>$.[21]

If $<X_0, ..., X_{n+1}>$ is an itinerary such that $\forall i, j \ (0 \le i, j \le n+1)$, X_i and X_j are p-adjacent if and only if $|i - j| = 1$, then we say that $<X_0, ..., X_{n+1}>$ is an *uncovered itinerary;* i.e., an itinerary is uncovered if the only vertices on the itinerary which are p-adjacent to other vertices on the itinerary are those that occur consecutively on the itinerary.

CYCLIC EQUIVALENCE THEOREM, (Richardson 1994). Directed graphs G_1 and G_2 are d-separation equivalent if and only if the following five conditions hold:

CET(I) G_1 and G_2 have the same p-adjacencies,

CET(II) G_1 and G_2 have (a) the same conductors and (b) the same perfect nonconductors,

CET(III) For all triples $<A, B, C>$ and $<X, Y, Z>$, $<A, B, C>$ and $<X, Y, Z>$ are m.e. conductors on some uncovered itinerary $P \equiv <A, B, C, ..., X, Y, Z>$ in G_1 if and only if $<A, B, C>$ and $<X, Y, Z>$ are m.e. conductors on some uncovered itinerary $Q \equiv <A, B, C, ..., X, Y, Z>$ in G_2,

CET(IV) If $<A, X, B>$ and $<A, Y, B>$ are imperfect nonconductors (in G_1 and G_2), then X is an ancestor of Y in G_1 if and only if X is an ancestor of Y in G_2,

CET(V) If $<A, B, C>$ and $<X, Y, Z>$ are mutually exclusive conductors on some uncovered itinerary $\mathbf{P} \equiv <A, B, C, ..., X, Y, Z>$ and $<A, M, Z>$ is an imperfect nonconductor (in G_1 and G_2), then M is a descendant of B in G_1 iff M is a descendant of B in G_2.

LEMMA 16. Given a sequence of vertices $<X_0, ..., X_{n+1}>$ in a directed graph G having the properties that $\forall k, \ 0 \le k \le n$, X_k is an ancestor of

X_{k+1}, and X_k is p-adjacent to X_{k+1} there is a subsequence of the X_i's, which we label the Y_j's, having the following properties:

(a) $X_0 \equiv Y_0$

(b) $\forall j$, Y_j is an ancestor of Y_{j+1}

(c) $\forall j, k$ $(0 \leq j, k \leq n+1)$ Y_j and Y_k are p-adjacent in G if and only if $|j-k| = 1$; i.e., the only Y_k's which are p-adjacent are those that occur consecutively.

Proof. The Y_k's can be constructed as follows:

Let $Y_0 \equiv X_0$.

If $Y_k \equiv X_\alpha^{22}$ then let $Y_{k+1} \equiv X_\eta$ where η is the greatest $h > \alpha$ s.t. X_h is p-adjacent to X_α.

Property (a) is immediate from the construction. Property (b) follows from the transitivity of the ancestor relation and the fact that the Y_k's are a subsequence of the X_i's. It is also clear from the construction that if $k = j + 1$, then Y_j and Y_k are p-adjacent. Moreover, if $Y_j \equiv X_\alpha$ and $Y_k \equiv X_\beta$ are p-adjacent, and $j < k$, then it follows again from the construction that if $Y_{j+1} \equiv X_\gamma$, then $\beta \leq \gamma$, so $k \leq j+1$. (This is because the Y_k's are a subsequence of the X_i's.) Hence $k = j + 1$ and $Y_{j+1} \equiv Y_k$. Q.E.D.

LEMMA 17. Let G_1 and G_2 be two directed graphs satisfying CET(I)–(III). Suppose there is a sequence of vertices $<D_1, ..., D_n>$ in G_1 having the property that D_k is an ancestor of D_{k+1} and D_k and D_{k+1} are p-adjacent $(1 \leq k < n)$. Let D_0 be a vertex distinct from $D_1, ..., D_n$, s.t. D_0 is p-adjacent to D_1 in G_1 and G_2, D_0 is not p-adjacent to $D_2, ..., D_n$ in G_1 or G_2 and D_0 is not a descendant of D_1 in G_1 or G_2. It then follows that D_1 is an ancestor of D_n in G_2.

Proof. It follows from lemma 16 that in G_1 there is a subsequence $<D_{\alpha(0)} \equiv D_0, D_{\alpha(1)}, D_{\alpha(2)}, ..., D_{\alpha(m)} \equiv D_n>$ such that the only p-adjacent vertices are those that occur consecutively, and each vertex is an ancestor of the next vertex in the sequence. Since G_1 and G_2 satisfy CET(I), they have the same p-adjacencies; hence also in G_2 the only vertices in the subsequence that are p-adjacent are those that occur consecutively. Moreover, since, by hypothesis, D_0 is not p-adjacent to $D_2, ..., D_n$ in G_1 or G_2 it follows that $D_{\alpha(1)} \equiv D_1$ and $m \geq 2$.

Suppose, for a contradiction, that some vertex $D_{\alpha(k-1)}$ is not an ancestor of its successor $D_{\alpha(k)}$ in the corresponding sequence in G_2. Let r be the smallest k $(1 < k \leq m)$ such that $D_{\alpha(k-1)}$ is not an ancestor of $D_{\alpha(k)}$ in G_2. Let s be the greatest j $(1 < j \leq r - 1)$ such that $D_{\alpha(j)}$ is not an ancestor of $D_{\alpha(j-1)}$ in G_2. (Such a j exists since $D_{\alpha(1)} \equiv D_1$ and $D_{\alpha(0)} \equiv D_0$ is not a descendant of D_1.)

There are now two cases: $s = r - 1$ or $s < r - 1$.

If $s = r - 1$, then the unshielded triple $<D_{\alpha(s-1)}, D_{\alpha(s)} \equiv D_{\alpha(r-1)}, D_{\alpha(r)}>$ is a nonconductor in G_2, since $D_{\alpha(s)} \equiv D_{\alpha(r-1)}$ is not an ancestor of $D_{\alpha(s-1)}$ or

$D_{\alpha(r)}$. But in G_1, by hypothesis, $D_{\alpha(r-1)}$ is an ancestor of $D_{\alpha(r)}$; hence $<D_{\alpha(s-1)}, D_{\alpha(s)} \equiv D_{\alpha(r-1)}, D_{\alpha(r)}>$ is a conductor in G_2. But this is a contradiction since G_1 and G_2 have the same conductors by CET(IIa).

If $s < r - 1$, then it follows that $<D_{\alpha(s-1)}, D_{\alpha(s)}, D_{\alpha(s+1)}>$ and $<D_{\alpha(r-2)}, D_{\alpha(r-1)}, D_{\alpha(r)}>$ are mutually exclusive conductors on the uncovered itinerary $<D_{\alpha(s-1)}, ..., D_{\alpha(r)}>$ in G_2. But these two triples are not mutually exclusive in G_1 since $D_{\alpha(r-1)}$ is an ancestor of $D_{\alpha(r)}$ in G_1; hence G_1 and G_2 fail to satisfy CET(III), which is a contradiction. Q.E.D.

THEOREM 6 (d-separation completeness). If the CCD algorithm, when given as input d-separation oracles for the directed graphs G_1, G_2 produces as output PAGs Ψ_1, Ψ_2 respectively, then Ψ_1 is identical to Ψ_2 only if G_1 and G_2 are d-separation equivalent, i.e., $G_2 \in$ **Equiv**(G_1) and vice versa.

Proof. We will show that if two directed graphs G_1 and G_2 are *not d*-separation equivalent, then the PAGs output by the CCD algorithm, given d-separation oracles for G_1 and G_2 as input, would differ in some respect.

It follows from the cyclic equivalence theorem that if G_1 and G_2 are not d-separation equivalent, then they fail to satisfy one or more of the five conditions CET(I)-(V).

Case 1. G_1 and G_2 fail to satisfy CET(I). In this case the two directed graphs have different p-adjacencies. It has already been established (theorem 5) that the CCD algorithm outputs a PAG. It follows from clause (i) of the definition that G_1 and G_2 have different p-adjacencies if and only if the corresponding PAGs, Ψ_1 and Ψ_2, possess different adjacencies.

Case 2. G_1 and G_2 fail to satisfy CET(IIa). We assume that G_1 and G_2 satisfy CET(I). In this case the two directed graphs have different conductors and hence different nonconductors. Thus we may assume, without loss of generality, that there is some unshielded triple of vertices $<X, Y, Z>$ such that in G_1, Y is an ancestor of X or Z, while Y is not an ancestor of either X or Z in G_2.

If Y is an ancestor of X or Z, then it follows from lemma 7 that every set which d-separates X and Z contains Y. Hence $Y \in$ **Sepset**$<X, Z>$ in G_1. It then follows from step B(2) that in Ψ_1, $X*\text{--}*Y*\text{--}*Z$.

If Y is not an ancestor of X or Z in G_2, then Y is not in any minimal d-separating set for X and Z. In particular $Y \notin$ **Sepset**$<X, Z>$ for G_2. Again it follows from the correctness of the algorithm that $<X, Y, Z>$ is oriented as $X \rightarrow Y \leftarrow Z$ or $X \rightarrow Y \leftarrow Z$ in Ψ_2. Thus Ψ_1 and Ψ_2 are different.

Case 3. G_1 and G_2 fail to satisfy CET(IIb). We assume that G_1 and G_2 satisfy CET(I) and CET(IIa). In this case the two directed graphs have different imperfect nonconductors; i.e., there is some triple $<X, Y, Z>$ such that it forms a nonconductor in both G_1 and G_2, but in one directed graph Y is a descendant of a common child of X and Z, while in the other directed graph it is not. Let us assume that Y is a descendant of a common child of X and Z in G_1, while in G_2 it is not.

It follows from lemma 11 that in G_1, X and Z are d-connected given any subset containing Y. In this case the search in CCD step D will fail to find any set **SupSepset**$<X, Y, Z>$. Hence $<X, Y, Z>$ will be oriented as $X \rightarrow Y \leftarrow Z$ (i.e., without dotted underlining) in Ψ_1.

If Y is not a descendant of a common child of X and Z in G_2, then it follows from lemma 12 and lemma 13 that there is some subset **T** of **Local**(Ψ_2, X), such that X and Z are d-separated given $\mathbf{T} \cup \{Y\} \cup$ **Sepset**$<X, Z>$. Step D is guaranteed to find such a set **T**, and hence $<X, Y, Z>$ will be oriented as $X \rightarrow Y \leftarrow Z$ in Ψ_2. Since no subsequent orientation rule removes or adds dotted underlining, it follows that Ψ_1 and Ψ_2 are different.

Case 4. G_1 and G_2 fail to satisfy CET(III). We assume that G_1 and G_2 satisfy CET(I), CET(IIa), and CET(IIb). In this case the two directed graphs have the same p-adjacencies, and the same conductors, and perfect nonconductors. However, the two directed graphs have different mutually exclusive conductors. Hence in both G_1 and G_2 there is an uncovered itinerary $<X_0, ..., X_{n+1}>$ such that every triple $<X_{k-1}, X_k, X_{k+1}>$ $(1 \leq k \leq n)$ on this itinerary is a conductor, but in one directed graph $<X_0, X_1, X_2>$ and $<X_{n-1}, X_n, X_{n+1}>$ are mutually exclusive; hence X_1 is not an ancestor of X_0, and X_n is not an ancestor of X_{n+1}, while in the other they are not mutually exclusive. Let us suppose without loss of generality that $<X_0, X_1, X_2>$ and $<X_{n-1}, X_n, X_{n+1}>$ are mutually exclusive in G_1, while in G_2 they are not, and that no pair of mutually exclusive conductors on a shorter uncovered itinerary have this property.

From the definition of a pair of m.e. conductors, it follows that in G_1 the vertices $X_1, ..., X_n$ inclusive, are *not* ancestors of X_0 or X_{n+1}. Hence $\{X_1, ..., X_n\}$ $\cap$ **Sepset**$<X_0, X_{n+1}> = \varnothing$, since **Sepset**$<X_0, X_{n+1}>$ is minimal, and so is a subset of **An**$(\{X_0, X_{n+1}\})$. (Here, **Sepset**$<X_0, X_{n+1}>$ is calculated for G_1.) For the same reason Descendants$(\{X_1, ..., X_n\}) \cap$ **Sepset**$<X_0, X_{n+1}> = \varnothing$. It follows from the definition of a pair of m.e. conductors on an itinerary that X_k is an ancestor of X_{k+1} $(1 \leq k < n)$; thus there is a directed path $P_k \equiv X_k \rightarrow ... \rightarrow X_{k+1}$ in G_1. Since no descendant of $X_1, ..., X_n$ is in **Sepset**$<X_0, X_{n+1}>$, each of the directed paths P_k d-connects each vertex X_k to its successor X_{k+1} $(1 \leq k < n)$, conditional on **Sepset**$<X_0, X_{n+1}>$. In addition, since X_0 and X_1 are p-adjacent there is some path Q d-connecting X_0 and X_1 given **Sepset**$<X_0, X_{n+1}>$. Since each P_i is out of X_i (i.e., the path goes $X_i \rightarrow ... \rightarrow X_{i+i}$), by applying lemma 10, with $\mathbf{T} = \{Q, P_1, ..., P_n\}$, $R = <X_0, ..., X_n>$, and $\mathbf{S} =$ **Sepset**$<X_0, X_{n+1}>$, it follows that we can form a path d-connecting X_0 and X_n given **Sepset**$<X_0, X_{n+1}>$. A symmetric argument shows that X_1 and X_{n+1} are also d-connected given **Sepset**$<X_0, X_{n+1}>$. It then follows that the edges $X_0 * \!\!-\!\! * X_1$ and $X_n * \!\!-\!\! * X_{n+1}$ are oriented as $X_0 \rightarrow X_1$ and $X_n \leftarrow X_{n+1}$ in Ψ_1 by step C of the CCD algorithm (unless they have already been oriented this way in a previous stage of the algorithm). Thus again, by the correctness of the algorithm these arrowheads will be present in Ψ_1. (Subsequent stages of the algorithm only add "–" and ">" endpoints, not "o" endpoints. If either of the arrowheads, ">," at X_1 or X_n were replaced with a "–," the algorithm would be incorrect. The same is true if either of the tails "–" at X_0 or X_{n+1} were replaced with a ">.")

Since by hypothesis, the uncovered itinerary $<X_0, \ldots, X_{n+1}>$ is composed only of conductors, no two of which are mutually exclusive in G_2, it follows that either X_1 is an ancestor of X_0, or X_n is an ancestor of X_{n+1} in G_2. It then follows from the correctness of the orientation rules in the CCD algorithm that the pair of edges X_0*—$*X_1$ and X_n*—$*X_{n+1}$ will not both be oriented as $X_0*\to X_1$ and $X_n\leftarrow*X_{n+1}$ in Ψ_2. Thus Ψ_1 and Ψ_2 will once again be different.

Case 5. G_1 and G_2 fail to satisfy either CET(IV) or CET(V). We assume that G_1 and G_2 satisfy CET(I)–(III).[23] If G_1 and G_2 fail to satisfy either CET(IV) or CET(V), then in either case we have the following situation: there is some sequence of vertices in G_1 and G_2, $<X_0, X_1, \ldots, X_n, X_{n+1}, V>$,[24] satisfying the following:

(a) $\forall i, j\ (0 \le i, j \le n+1)$ X_i and X_j are p-adjacent if and only if $|i - j| = 1$,

(b) X_1 is not an ancestor of X_0, and X_n is not an ancestor of X_{n+1},

(c) $\forall k,\ 1 \le k \le n,\ X_{k-1}$, and X_{k+1} are ancestors of X_k,

(d) $<X_0, V, X_{n+1}>$ is an imperfect nonconductor, and

(e) in one directed graph V is a descendant of X_1, while in the other directed graph V is not a descendant of X_1.

As explained in case 3, condition (d) implies that in both Ψ_1 and Ψ_2, $X_0\to V\leftarrow X_{n+1}$.

Let us suppose without loss of generality that V is a descendant of X_1 in G_1, and V is not a descendant of X_1 in G_2. As in previous cases it is sufficient to show that if Ψ_1 and Ψ_2 are CCD PAGs corresponding to G_1 and G_2 respectively, then Ψ_1 and Ψ_2 are different. We may suppose, again without loss of generality, that V is the closest such vertex to any $X_k\ (1 \le k \le n)$ in G_1; more precisely a shortest directed path $P \equiv X_k\to\ldots\to V$ in G_1 contains at most the same number of vertices as a shortest directed path in G_1 from any X_k $(1\le k \le n)$ to some other vertex V' satisfying the conditions on V.

Claim: Let W be the first vertex on P which is p-adjacent to V (both in G_1 and G_2 since by CET(I) G_1 and G_2 have the same p-adjacencies). We will show that the assumption that V is the closest such vertex to any X_k (in G_1) together with the assumption that G_1 and G_2 satisfy CET(I)-(III) implies that W is a descendant of X_1 in G_2. We prove this by showing that every vertex in the directed subpath $P(X_k, W) \equiv X_k\to\ldots W$ in G_1 is also a descendant of X_1 in G_2.

Proof of Claim: By induction on the vertices occurring on the path $P(X_k, W)$.

Base Case: X_k. By hypothesis X_k is a descendant of X_1 in both G_1 and G_2.

Induction Case: Consider Y_r, where $P(X_k, W) \equiv X_k \to Y_1 \to \ldots \to Y_r \to \ldots Y_t \equiv W$. By the induction hypothesis, for $s < r$, Y_s is a descendant of X_1 in G_2. Now there are two subcases to consider:

Subcase 1: Not both X_0 and X_{n+1} are p-adjacent to Y_r. Suppose without loss of generality that X_0 is not p-adjacent to Y_r. Since in G_1 there is a directed path $X_0 \to \ldots X_k \to Y_1 \to \ldots Y_r$, by lemma 16 it then follows that there is some subsequence of this sequence of vertices, $Q \equiv \langle X_0, \ldots, Y_r \rangle$, such that consecutive vertices in Q are p-adjacent, but only these vertices are p-adjacent. Moreover, since X_0 is not p-adjacent to Y_r, this sequence of vertices is of length greater than 2, i.e., $Q \equiv \langle X_0, D \ldots Y_r \rangle$ where D is the first vertex in the subsequence after X_0; hence either $D \equiv X_\kappa$ ($1 \leq \kappa \leq k$) or $D \equiv Y_\mu$, ($1 \leq \mu < r$). Since in either case D is a descendant of X_1 in both G_1 and G_2, (either by the induction hypothesis or by the hypothesis of case 5), but X_0 is not a descendant of X_1 in G_1 or G_2 it follows that D is not an ancestor of X_0 in G_1 or G_2. Hence we may apply lemma 17 to Q to deduce that Y_r is a descendant of D in G_2. Hence Y_r is a descendant of X_1 in G_2 since X_1 is an ancestor of D.

Subcase 2: Both X_0 and X_{n+1} are p-adjacent to Y_r. First note that in G_1 the vertex Y_r is a descendant of X_k, and X_k is not an ancestor of X_0 or X_{n+1}. It follows that Y_r is not an ancestor of X_0 or X_{n+1} in G_1. Moreover, since X_0 and X_{n+1} are not p-adjacent, $\langle X_0, Y_r, X_{n+1} \rangle$ forms a nonconductor in G_1. Hence $\langle X_0, Y_r, X_{n+1} \rangle$ forms a nonconductor in G_2, since by hypothesis G_1 and G_2 satisfy CET(IIa). So Y_r is not an ancestor of X_0 or X_{n+1} in G_1 or G_2. Further, since Y_r is an ancestor of V in G_1 and V is not a descendant of a common child of X_0 and X_{n+1} in G_1, it follows that Y_r is not a descendant of a common child of X_0 and X_{n+1} in G_1. Thus $\langle X_0, Y_r, X_{n+1} \rangle$ forms an imperfect nonconductor in G_1. Since G_1 and G_2 satisfy CET(I), CET(IIa), and CET(IIb), $\langle X_0, Y_r, X_{n+1} \rangle$ forms an imperfect nonconductor in G_2. Now, if Y_r were not a descendant of X_1 in G_2, then Y_r would satisfy the conditions on V, yet be closer to X_k than V (Y_r occurs before V on a shortest directed path from X_k to V in G_1). This is a contradiction; hence Y_r is a descendant of X_1 in G_2.

This completes the proof of the claim. We now show that Ψ_1 and Ψ_2 are different.

Consider the edge $W*\!-\!*V$ in Ψ_1. In G_1, W is an ancestor of V; hence it follows from the correctness of the algorithm that in Ψ_1 this edge is oriented as $W\circ\!-\!*V$ or $W\!-\!\!*V$. In G_2, however, since X_1 is not an ancestor of V, but, as we have just shown X_1 is an ancestor of W, it follows that W is not an ancestor of V. Further, since W is a descendant of X_1 and so also of X_n, it follows from (b) that W is not an ancestor of X_0 or X_{n+1}. There are now two cases to consider:

Subcase 1: W is p-adjacent to both X_0 and X_{n+1}. Since W is not an ancestor of X_0 or X_{n+1} in G_1 or G_2, $\langle X_0, W, X_{n+1} \rangle$ is a nonconductor in both G_1 and G_2. Further, since $X_0 \to V \leftarrow X_{n+1}$ in Ψ_1 (and Ψ_2), and W is an ancestor of V in

G_1, it follows that W is not a descendant of a common child of X_0 and X_{n+1} in G_1. Thus $X_0 \rightarrow W \leftarrow X_{n+1}$ in Ψ_1 and hence, by CET(II), also in Ψ_2. **SupSepset**$<X_0, V, X_{n+1}>$ is the smallest set containing **Sepset**$<X_0, X_{n+1}> \cup \{V\}$ which d-separates X_0 and X_{n+1}. It follows from corollary 3 that **SupSepset**$<X_0, V, X_{n+1}> \subseteq$ **An**(**Sepset**$<X_0, X_{n+1}> \cup \{X_0, X_{n+1}, V\})$. Since **Sepset**$<X_0, X_{n+1}> \subseteq$ **An**$(\{X_0, X_{n+1}\})$, therefore **SupSepset**$<X_0, V, X_{n+1}> \subseteq$ **An**$(\{X_0, X_{n+1}, V\})$. We have already shown that W is not an ancestor of X_0, X_{n+1}, or V in G_2. Hence in step D of the algorithm given a d-separation oracle for G_2 as input $W \notin$ **SupSepset**$<X_0, V, X_{n+1}>$. Thus step E of the CCD algorithm will orient an edge $W \circ\!\!-\!\!\circ V$ or $W \circ\!\!- V$ in Ψ_2 as $W \leftarrow V$ (unless they have already been oriented this way in a previous stage of the algorithm). Thus Ψ_1 and Ψ_2 are not the same.

Subcase 2: W is not p-adjacent to both X_0 and X_{n+1}.

Claim: X_0 and X_{n+1} are d-connected given **SupSepset**$<X_0, V, X_{n+1}> \cup \{W\}$ *in G_2.*

Proof. Since in both G_1 and G_2, X_0 is p-adjacent to X_1, but X_1 is not an ancestor of X_0, it follows from corollary 1 that X_0 is an ancestor of X_1. Hence in both G_1 and G_2 there is a directed path P_0 from X_0 to X_1 on which every vertex except for X_0 is a descendant of X_1. (In the case $X_0 \rightarrow X_1$, the last assertion is trivial. In the other case it merely states a property of the path $X_0 \rightarrow C \rightarrow \ldots X_1$, where C is a common child of X_0 and X_1.) Since W is a descendant of X_1, it follows that there is a directed path P_1 from X_1 to W. Concatenating P_0 and P_1, we construct a directed path P^* from X_0 to W on which every vertex except X_0 is a descendant of X_1. Since X_1 is not an ancestor of X_0, X_{n+1} or V in G_2, it follows that no vertex on P^*, except X_0, is an ancestor of X_0, X_{n+1} or V in G_2. Similarly we can construct a path from Q^* from X_{n+1} to W on which no vertex, except X_{n+1}, is an ancestor of X_0, X_{n+1} or V in G_2.

Since, by corollary 3, every vertex in **SupSepset**$<X_0, V, X_{n+1}>$ is an ancestor of X_0, X_{n+1} or **Sepset**$<X_0, X_{n+1}> \cup \{V\}$, it follows as before that every vertex in **SupSepset**$<X_0, V, X_{n+1}>$ is an ancestor of X_0, X_{n+1} or V in G_2. (Here **SupSepset** $<X_0, V, X_{n+1}>$ is calculated for G_2.) Thus no vertex in **SupSepset**$<X_0, V, X_{n+1}>$ lies on P^* or Q^* ($X_0, X_{n+1} \notin$ **SupSepset**$<X_0, V, X_{n+1}>$ by definition). It now follows by lemma 10 that we can concatenate P^* and Q^* to form a path R which d-connects X_0 and X_{n+1} given **SupSepset**$<X_0, V, X_{n+1}> \cup \{W\}$ in G_2.

Since W is not p-adjacent to both X_0 and X_{n+1}, it follows directly from the existence of R in G_2 that step F of the CCD algorithm will orient the edge $W \circ\!\!-\!\!\circ V$ or $W \circ\!\!- V$ as $W \leftarrow V$ in Ψ_2 (unless they have already been oriented this way in a previous stage of the algorithm). Hence Ψ_1 and Ψ_2 are different.

Since cases 1-5 exhaust the possible ways in which G_1 and G_2 may fail to satisfy CET(I)-(V), this completes the proof. Q.E.D.

Acknowledgements

Research for this chapter was supported by the National Science Foundation through grant 9102169 and the Navy Personnel Research and Development Center and the Office of Naval Research through contract number N00014-93-1-0568. We are indebted to Clark Glymour, Richard Scheines, Christopher Meek, and Marek Druzdel for helpful conversations. We also wish to thank anonymous referees for helpful comments, corrections, simplifications, and clarifications.

Notes

1. An undirected path is often defined as a sequence of vertices rather than a sequence of edges. The two definitions are essentially equivalent for acyclic directed graphs, because a pair of vertices can be identified with a unique edge in the graph. However, a cyclic graph may contain more than one edge between a pair of vertices. In that case, it is no longer possible to identify a pair of vertices with a unique edge.

2. However, in section 3 we show that the local and global directed Markov properties are not equivalent for cyclic directed graphs.

3. We realize that it is slightly unconventional to write the trivial equation for the exogenous variable X_1 in terms of its error, but this serves to give the error variables a unified and special status as providing all the exogenous sources of variation for the system.

4. We do not consider SEMs with other sorts of constraints on the parameters, e.g., equality constraints.

5. Note that this use of cyclic directed graphs to represent feedback processes represents an extension of the causal interpretation of directed graphs.

6. Cox and Wermuth (1993), Wermuth (1992), Wermuth and Lauritzen (1990) and (indirectly) Frydenberg (1990) consider a class of linear models they call *block recursive*. The block recursive models overlap the class of SEMs, but they are neither properly included in that class, nor properly include it. Frydenberg (1990) presents necessary and sufficient conditions for the equivalence of two block recursive models. The graphs of SEMs without correlated errors are a subclass of the reciprocal graphs introduced in Koster (1996).

7. We are indebted to C. Glymour for pointing out that the local Markov condition fails in Whittaker's model. Indeed, there is *no* acyclic graph (even with additional variables) that linearly entails all and only the conditional independence relations linearly entailed by figure 3, although the directed cyclic graph of figure 3 is equivalent to one in which the edges from X_1 to X_3 and X_2 to X_4 are replaced, respectively, by edges from X_1 to X_4 and from X_2 to X_3.

8. The extended graphs which we introduce here—partial ancestral graphs—use a superset of the set of symbols used by partially oriented inducing path graphs (POIPGs) described in Spirtes, Glymour, and Scheines (1993) but the *graphical* interpretation of the orientations given to edges is different. However, Spirtes, Meek, and Richardson show in chapter 6 of this book that a POIPG can be interpreted directly as a PAG. A direct corollary is that PAGs can be used to represent the d-separation equivalence class for directed *acyclic* graphs with *latent* variables. It is an open question whether or not the set of symbols is sufficiently rich to allow us to represent d-separation classes of cyclic graphs with latent variables.

9. If one PAG for a graph G has a ">" at the end of an edge, then every other PAG for

the same graph either has a ">" or a "o" in that location. Similarly if one PAG for a graph G has a "–" at the end of an edge, then every other PAG for the same graph either has a "–" or an "o" in that location.

10. This is not an exhaustive list. For example, the presence of the dotted line connecting the arrowheads on the $A \rightarrow X$, and $B \rightarrow X$ edges tells us that in no graph in **Equiv**(G) are both of these edges present. Likewise with the dotted line connecting the arrowheads of the $B \rightarrow Y$ and $A \rightarrow Y$ edges.

11. See footnote 9.

12. Here as elsewhere "*" is a meta-symbol indicating any of the three ends –, o, >.

13. In certain special instances, rules step C, step E, and step F may redundantly consult the d-separation oracle in the sense that the answer to the query could be inferred from orientations that are already present in the PAG. In such cases these rules behave as propagation rules. (We have not removed these redundant tests because, so far as we can see, this would involve a substantial increase in computational complexity.)

14. If Ψ_1 and Ψ_2 are different PAGs for the same graph resulting from different implementations, then any edge endpoint oriented with a "–" or a ">" in Ψ_1 but with a "o" in Ψ_2 could also be oriented in Ψ_2 by applying a propagation rule (see section 4.5) to Ψ_2 (and vice versa).

15. This is not in conflict with the statement that different implementations may produce different PAGs. (See previous footnote.)

16. The proof in Lauritzen et al. (1990) is incomplete since the construction does not consider the possibility that the path formed may intersect itself; however the lacuna is not difficult to fill.

17. This is because if a pair of vertices X, Y are p-adjacent in G, then no set is found which d-separates them, and hence the edge between X and Y in Ψ is never deleted.

18. In this regard, note that there may be vertices in **Sepset**<A, B> that are not p-adjacent to A or B. This is because although, in searching for **Sepset**<A, B> only subsets of **Adjacencies** (Ψ, A) and **Adjacencies**(Ψ, B) are tested, there may be vertices which are in these sets on account of edges in Ψ that have yet to be deleted at that point in the search, i.e., vertices which are not p-adjacent to A or B.

19. Whether or not such rules will ever be used on real data, in which "distant" variables are generally found to be independent by statistical tests is another question.

20. In some cases the cardinality of the smallest set ($\mathbf{T} \cup$ **Sepset**<A, C>) may be greater than the cardinality of the smallest $\mathbf{T}$; but this is not true in general, and since we only intend to discover linear models, this is insignificant. (With discrete models conditioning on a large set of variables in a conditional independence test may reduce dramatically the power of the test.)

21. Note that a pair of m.e. conductors on an uncovered itinerary are a generalization of a nonconductor. In both cases there is a set of vertices "in the middle" that are not ancestors of the vertices at the "ends."

22. That is, the kth vertex in the sequence of Y vertices is the αth vertex in the sequence of X vertices.

23. The conditions under which CET(IV) or CET(V) fail are quite intricate precisely because the assumption that CET(I)-(III) are satisfied implies that the graphs agree in many respects.

24. In the case where CET(IV) fails $n = 1$, while if CET(V) fails $n > 1$.

References

Basmann, R. 1965. A Note on the Statistical Testability of "Explicit Causal Chains" against the Class of "Interdependent" Models. *Journal of the American Statistical Association* 60(312): 1080–1093.

Cooper, G., and Herskovits, E. 1992. A Bayesian Method for the Induction of Probabilistic Networks from Data. *Machine Learning* 9(4): 308–347.

Cox, D. R., and Wermuth, N. 1993. Linear Dependencies Represented by Chain Graphs. *Statistical Science* 8(3): 204–283.

Frydenberg, M. 1990. The Chain Graph Markov Property. *Scandinavian Journal of Statistics* 17(4): 333–353.

Geiger, D., and Pearl, J. 1988. Logical and Algorithmic Properties of Conditional Independence. Technical Report, R-97, Cognitive Systems Laboratory, University of California at Los Angeles.

Goldberger, A. S. 1964. *Econometric Theory.* New York: Wiley.

Haavelmo, T. 1943. The Statistical Implications of a System of Simultaneous Equations. *Econometrica* 11:1–12.

Kiiveri, H., and Speed, T. 1982. Structural Analysis of Multivariate Data: A Review. In *Sociological Methodology,* ed. S. Leinhardt, 209–289. San Francisco: Jossey-Bass.

Kiiveri, H.; Speed, T.; and Carlin, J. 1984. Recursive Causal Models. *Journal of the Australian Mathematical Society* Series A, 36(1): 30–52.

Koster, J. 1996. Markov Properties of Non-Recursive Causal Models. *Annals of Statistics* 24(5): 2148–2178.

Lauritzen, S., and Spiegelhalter, D. 1988. Local Computation with Probabilities in Graphical Structures and Their Applications to Expert Systems. *Journal of the Royal Statistical Society* B50(2): 157–224.

Lauritzen, S.; Dawid, A.; Larsen, B.; and Leimer, H. 1990. Independence Properties of Directed Markov Fields. *Networks* 20(5): 491–505.

Mason, S. 1956. Feedback Theory—Further Properties of Signal Flow Graphs. In *Proceedings of the Institute of Radio Engineers,* 44. New York: Institute of Radio Engineers.

Mason, S. 1953. Feedback Theory—Some Properties of Signal Flow Graphs. In *Proceedings of the Institute of Radio Engineers,* 41. New York: Institute of Radio Engineers.

Pearl, J. 1988. *Probabilistic Reasoning in Intelligent Systems.* San Francisco: Morgan Kaufmann.

Pearl, J., and Dechter, R. 1996. Identifying Independencies in Causal Graphs with Feedback. In *Uncertainty in Artificial Intelligence, Proceedings of the Twelfth Conference,* eds. E. Horvitz and F. Jensen, 420–426. San Francisco: Morgan Kaufmann.

Pearl, J., and Verma, T. 1991. A Theory of Inferred Causation. In *Principles of Knowledge Representation and Reasoning: Proceedings of the Second International Conference,* 441–452. San Francisco: Morgan Kaufmann.

Richardson, T. 1997. A Characterization of Markov Equivalence for Directed Cyclic Graphs. *International Journal for Approximate Reasoning* 17(2–3): 107–162.

Richardson, T. 1996. A Polynomial-Time Algorithm for Deciding Markov Equivalence of Directed Cyclic Graphical Models. In *Uncertainty in Artificial Intelligence, Proceedings of the Twelfth Conference,* eds. E. Horvitz and F. Jensen, 462–469. San Francisco: Morgan Kaufmann.

Richardson, T. 1994. Properties of Cyclic Graphical Models. M.S. thesis, Dept. of Philosophy, Carnegie Mellon University, Pittsburgh, Penn.

Sosa, E. 1975. *Causation and Conditionals.* London: Oxford University Press.

Spirtes, P. 1995. Directed Cyclic Graphical Representation of Feedback Models. In *Proceedings of the Eleventh Conference on Uncertainty in Artificial Intelligence,* eds. P. Besnard and S. Hanks, 491–498. San Francisco: Morgan Kaufmann.

Spirtes, P., and Richardson, T. 1997. A Polynomial Time Algorithm for Determining DAG Equivalence in the Presence of Latent Variables and Selection Bias. Paper presented at the Sixth International Workshop on Artificial Intelligence and Statistics, Ft. Lauderdale, Fla., 4–7 Jan.

Spirtes, P., and Verma, T. 1992. Equivalence of Causal Models with Latent Variables. Technical Report, CMU-PHIL-33, Department of Philosophy, Carnegie Mellon University, Pittsburgh, Penn.

Spirtes, P.; Glymour, C.; and Scheines, R. 1993. *Causation, Prediction, and Search.* Lecture Notes in Statistics 81. New York: Springer-Verlag.

Spirtes, P.; Meek, C.; and Richardson, T. 1995. Causal Inferences in the Presence of Latent Variables and Selection Bias. In *Proceedings of the Eleventh Conference on Uncertainty in Artificial Intelligence,* eds. P. Besnard and S. Hanks, 499–506. San Francisco: Morgan Kaufmann.

Spirtes, P.; Richardson, T.; Meek, C.; Scheines, R.; and Glymour, C. 1996. Using d-Separation to Calculate Zero Partial Correlations in Linear Models with Correlated Errors. Technical Report, CMU-Phil-72, Department of Philosophy, Carnegie Mellon University, Pittsburgh, Penn.

Strotz, R. H., and Wold, H. O. A. 1960. Recursive versus Nonrecursive Systems: An Attempt at Synthesis. *Econometrica* 28(2): 417–427.

Wermuth, N. 1992. On Block-Recursive Linear Regression Equations. *Revista Brasileira de Probabilidade e Estatistica* (with Discussion) 6:1–56.

Wermuth, N. 1980. Linear Recursive Equations, Covariance Selection, and Path Analysis. *Journal of the American Statistical Association* 75(372): 963–972.

Wermuth, N., and Lauritzen, S. 1990. On Substantive Research Hypotheses, Conditional Independence Graphs, and Graphical Chain Models. *Journal of the Royal Statistical Society* B52(1): 21–50.

Wermuth, N., and Lauritzen, S. 1983. Graphical and Recursive Models for Contingency Tables. *Biometrika* 72(3): 537–552.

Whittaker, J. 1990. *Graphical Models in Applied Multivariate Statistics.* New York: Wiley.

Wright, S. 1934. The Method of Path Coefficients. *Annals of Mathematical Statistics* 5(3): 161–215.

PART THREE

Controversy Over Search

Understanding cause and effect relationships has been one of the principal motivations for the historical development and application of the wealth of beautiful ideas in probability and statistics. At the same time, especially in the 20th century, many statisticians have been ill at ease with talk of cause and effect, and especially ill at ease with the very idea of causal inferences drawn from data without randomized treatments.

The use of directed graphical models to represent both causal and statistical relations, and algorithmic searches over that class of models, has come in for a lot of criticism from a few statisticians. Among the criticisms, many of which are misinformed or marginal or even disingenuous, the objections of Robins and Wasserman are notable for their relevance, clarity, and candor.

Robins and Wasserman focus their criticism on constraint-based search procedures, presumably because these procedures come with proofs of what is sometimes called "Fisher consistency," meaning they are guaranteed to give correct answers if given true population independencies and conditional independencies. A crude summary of their criticisms and of the responses by Glymour, Spirtes, and Richardson is this: Robins and Wasserman say for any sample size there exist prior probabilities for which, conditional on the data, a true hypothesis about causation has small probability; they show this by describing a procedure for revising priors as a function of sample size so that the truth is driven towards a zero posterior probability as the sample size increases without bound. Glymour, Spirtes, and Richardson reply that the revision procedure is un-Bayesian, and that the priors needed are unrealistic. Robins and Wasserman reply that epidemiologists in fact have such priors. Glymour, Spirtes, and Richardson reply that if epidemiologists really used such priors, then their methods would be unreliable.

The exchange is not entirely hostile, and interesting research issues emerge. They are addressed in a collaborative paper caused by this exchange: J. Robins, R. Scheines, P. Spirtes, and L. Wasserman, "The Limits of Causal Knowledge," Technical Report CMU-Phil-97, Department of Philosophy, Carnegie Mellon University, 1999.

CHAPTER EIGHT

On the Impossibility of Inferring Causation from Association without Background Knowledge

James M. Robins and Larry Wasserman

Spirtes, Glymour and Scheines, in their book *Causation, Prediction, and Search* (1993) and Pearl and Verma, in their paper "A Theory of Inferred Causation" (1991) make the startling claim that it is possible to infer causal relationships between two variables X and Y from associations found in observational (nonexperimental) data without substantive subject-matter-specific background knowledge. When causal relationships are represented by directed acyclic graphs (DAGs), Spirtes, Glymour, and Scheines argue that their claim follows, mathematically, from two reasonable assumptions: (1) the sample size is sufficiently large and (2) the distribution of the random variables is faithful to the causal graph. In particular, Spirtes, Glymour, and Scheines have shown that under their faithfulness assumption, there exist methods for identifying causal relationships which are asymptotically (in sample size) correct.

However, we shall show that Spirtes, Glymour, and Scheines's (1993) asymptotics implicitly assume that the probability of there being "no unmeasured common causes" of X and Y is positive and not small relative to sample size. We prove that, under an asymptotics for which the probability of "no unmeasured common causes" is small relative to sample size, causal relationships are nonidentifiable from the data alone, even when we assume distributions are faithful to the causal graph. We argue that, in observational epidemiologic, econometric, and social scientific studies, a formal asymptotic analysis that models the probability of "no unmeasured common causes" as small relative to sample size accurately reflects the beliefs of practicing professionals. We argue that these beliefs derive both from experience and from the fact that the world contains so many potential unmeasured common causes (i.e., confounders) that it is a priori highly unlikely that not a single one actually causes both X and Y. We conclude that, in observational studies, small causal effects can never be either reliably ruled in or ruled out; furthermore, one should not make the leap from even relatively large empirical associations to causation without substantive subject-matter-specific background information.

1. Introduction

Several authors have used directed acyclic graphs (DAGs) as a basis for inferring causal relationships from nonexperimental (i.e., observational) data. For example, Spirtes, Glymour and Scheines (1993) and Pearl (1995) show that many issues in causal inference can be illuminated using causal DAGs. In a causal DAG, the presence or absence of an arrow between two variables represents the presence or absence of a direct causal effect. Robins (1995, 1997) shows that these DAG models are isomorphic to a causal model of Robins (1986, 1987). In Robins's (1986, 1987) approach, the causal DAG is based on background information, such as time order and subject matter knowledge of potential confounding factors. The possibility that additional unsuspected unmeasured confounders may well exist is explored through sensitivity analysis (Robins 1997) and Robins, Rotnitzky, and Scharfstein (1999). In contrast, Spirtes, Glymour, and Scheines (1993) and Pearl and Verma (1991) go further and claim it is possible to deduce aspects of the DAG from the data in the absence of background information. That is, they claim that they can "deduce causation from associations" in the data without substantive subject matter knowledge. Spirtes, Glymour, and Scheines show that their methods for doing so are correct, asymptotically in sample size, assuming a condition called "faithfulness." Statisticians, philosophers and epidemiologists have been skeptical of such claims. Humphrey and Freedman (1996) and Freedman (1993), in extended critiques, attacked many of Spirtes, Glymour, and Scheines's arguments and assumptions, including both the faithfulness assumption itself and Spirtes, Glymour, and Scheines's treatment of unobserved potential common causes. Robins (1997, section 11) centered his critique around the possibility of unobserved potential confounders (i.e. common causes). But Spirtes, Glymour, and Scheines explicitly allow for unobserved confounders.

However, we will show that the Spirtes, Glymour, and Scheines asymptotic analysis implicitly assumes that the sample size is not only large, but is large relative to the number of potential confounders. As a consequence, Spirtes, Glymour, and Scheines's asymptotics also implicitly assumes that the probability that there exists "no unmeasured common causes (confounders)" is not small relative to sample size. We investigate the implica-

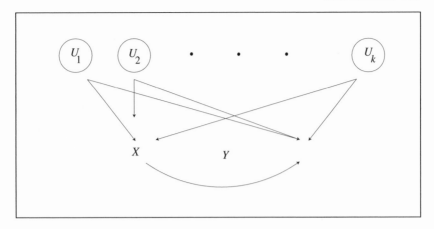

Figure 1. Directed acyclic graph for the first example.

tions of violations of this latter assumption. Specifically, we first carry out a formal analysis under an asymptotics for which the probability of "no un-measured common causes" is small relative to sample size. We perform this analysis from a Bayesian point of view because Bayesian reasoning is a co-herent and important normative approach to inference and decision making under uncertainty. The specific result we derive is that, under some mild re-strictions on our prior distributions, the Bayes factor for the presence of a causal relation is not consistent; i.e., the Bayes factor remains bounded away from 0 and infinity as sample size tends to infinity when the prior probability of no unmeasured confounders is small relative to sample size. Thus a causal hypothesis is not decidable, even asymptotically, based on data alone. A sim-ple formula emerges from our analysis that allows one to examine the sensi-tivity of causal inferences to the prior probability of "no unmeasured con-founders."

Finally we argue that in most epidemiologic, econometric, or social scien-tific studies, the beliefs of subject matter experts are accurately represented by an asymptotics that models the probability of "no unmeasured common causes" as small relative to sample size. In most observational studies, there will be measured as well as unmeasured potential confounders. Our results apply directly to this case by arguing conditionally within levels of the mea-sured potential confounding factors.

2. A Simple Causal Model

Let $(X, Y, U_1, \ldots, U_k)$ be random variables where X and Y are observed and $U_1, \ldots, U_k$ are unobserved. X is known to occur before Y and we are interested in the causal relationship between X and Y. The random variables $U_1, \ldots, U_k$ are potential confounders. They are to represent all potential confounders in the universe, so k might be very large. To begin, assume the variables have a joint normal distribution. (We will drop this assumption in section 4, but for now it simplifies the analysis.)

For simplicity, assume $U_i \sim N(0, 1)$, $i = 1, \ldots, k$ independently of each other and of X and Y. Furthermore, assume that

$$X = \sum_{i=1}^{k} \alpha_i U_i + \mu_x + \sigma_x \varepsilon_x \tag{1}$$

$$Y = \sum_{i=1}^{k} \beta_i U_i + \theta X + \mu_Y + \sigma_Y \varepsilon_Y \tag{2}$$

where ε_x and ε_Y are independent standard normals and Θ α_i, β_i, μ_x, μ_Y, σ_x, and σ_Y are parameters. The model is illustrated by the directed acyclic graph in figure 1. In the social science literature, our model would be referred to as a linear structural equations model (SEM) with latent variables U_i, $i = 1, \ldots, k$.

Let $s = (s_1, \ldots, s_k)$ denote a string of 0's and 1's and let

$$S = \left\{ s = \left(s_1, \ldots, s_k \right); s_i \in \{0, 1\}, i = 1, \ldots, k \right\}.$$

Let G_s denote the subgraph which contains only those confounders such that $s_i = 1$. Let G_s^* be the graph G_s with the arrow from X to Y removed. For example, $G_{(1,0,\ldots,0)}$ is the graph in which the only confounder is U_1. If the data were actually generated by graph $G_{(1,0,\ldots,0)}$ we say that, of the potential confounders $(U_1, \ldots, U_k)$, only U_1 is a (true) confounder.

Remark: Note that a graph G_s having an arrow from X to Y corresponds to $\theta \neq 0$ in equation (2). The graphs G_s^* correspond to $\theta = 0$. Similarly, the graph $G_{(1,0,\ldots,0)}$ in which the only confounder is U_1 corresponds to $\alpha_1 \beta_1 \neq 0$ and $\alpha_i \beta_i = 0$, $i = 2, \ldots, k$, in the SEM model equations (1-2). This reflects the fact that U_m is a confounder for (i.e., an unmeasured common cause of) X and Y if and only if $\alpha_m \beta_m \neq 0$.

Let G be all 2^k possible graphs with an arrow from X to Y; let G^* be all 2^k possible graphs without an arrow from X to Y; and let $\mathcal{H} = G \cup G^*$. Finally, let ψ_s be the parameters corresponding to a given graph G_s and similarly let ψ_s^* be the parameters corresponding to a given graph G_s^*.

The prior is defined as follows. Each graph $G \in \mathcal{H}$ has prior probability $1/2^{k+1}$. Let ψ denote the parameters in a subgraph G. We assume that the prior for ψ is absolutely continuous with respect to Lebesque measure with density $\pi(\psi)$, say. (This is equivalent to putting a single prior on the big graph which is a mixture of priors, each of which is singular and hence gives positive measure to certain confounders being absent.) Let A be the event "there is an arrow from X to Y" and let C_i be the event "U_i is a confounder." Then, a priori, (1) $P(A) = 1/2$, (2) $P(C_i) = 1/2$ and (3) the probability

$$P\left(C_1^c \cap \cdots \cap C_k^c\right)$$

of no (unmeasured) confounders is 2^{-k}. It is important to note that any given confounder has positive probability of being absent. Nonetheless, the probability that there exist no confounders is small. As discussed later, this seems to capture precisely the way most subject matter experts would treat an observational study.

Spirtes, Glymour, and Scheines require one further property called "faithfulness." This is a technical condition which asserts that, conditional on a graph G being the true graph generating the data, the underlying distribution possesses only those independences shared by all distributions whose densities can be factorized according to the graph. Informally, an unfaithfulness occurs if variables are independent, not by the absence of an arrow in the graph, but by a coincidental cancellation of parameter values. See Spirtes, Glymour, and Scheines (1993, page 35) for more details. Rather than saying that Spirtes, Glymour, and Scheines require faithfulness, a more accurate statement is this: in their asymptotic analysis, they exclude unfaithful distributions. Under any prior on the parameter space which parameterizes the set of distributions over the graph and which is absolutely continuous with respect to Lebesque measure, the unfaithful distributions are a set of measure 0. Thus, Spirtes, Glymour, and Scheines argue, and we agree, that ignoring these distributions is harmless. Our assumption that the priors $\pi_s(\bullet)$ and $\pi_s^*(\bullet)$ are smooth densities with respect to Lebesque measure respect Spirtes, Glymour, and Scheines's faithfulness condition since, a priori, $P(D) = 0$ where D is the event that unfaithfulness occurs. This follows since $P(D) = \Sigma_G P(D|G)P(G)$ and $P(D|G) = 0$ for all $G \in \mathcal{H}$.

Remark: Note that the event that the variable U_i is not a common cause of X and Y (i.e., the event $\alpha_i \beta_i = 0$) has positive prior probability even though the event $\alpha_i \beta_i = 0$ has Lebesgue measure zero. This prior represents beliefs implicitly held by Spirtes, Glymour, and Scheines (and with which we agree) that, for any given variable U_i, the probability that it does not cause both X and Y is nonzero.

3. Analysis Using Faithfulness

Spirtes, Glymour, and Scheines use the faithfulness assumption to deduce the absence of a causal relation as follows. (Pearl and Verma use a similar assumption called "stability.") Suppose that n is large and that, in this large sample, we discover that X and Y are independent (i.e., the sample correlation between X and Y is exactly zero). This observed independence is consistent with the graph G_0^* in which there are no confounders and there is no arrow from X to Y. In every other graph $G \in \mathcal{H}$, the only way to achieve independence of X and Y is to violate faithfulness. Thus, under the assumption of faithfulness and the assumption that the sample is large enough to reliably estimate lack of dependence between X and Y, we conclude that the only graph consistent with the data is G_0^*. We have deduced no causal relationship between X and Y and no confounders, simultaneously. We conclude that were Spirtes, Glymour, and Scheines's faithfulness analysis valid, we could infer no causation from no empirical association in the absence of any substantive subject-matter-specific background information and, indeed, even without knowledge of the real world variables represented by X and Y.

Remark: Of course, the event that the sample correlation between X and Y is precisely zero is an event that has probability zero when the data have been generated by any graph in $\mathcal{H}$ including G_0^*. Therefore, in practice, Spirtes, Glymour, and Scheines suggest that when the p-value for a test of the hypothesis that "the population correlation is zero" is sufficiently large (say, greater than .5) and the sample size n is large, one concludes that X and Y are independent and thus, by faithfulness, that graph G_0^* generated the data.

4. A Formal Asymptotic Analysis

The Spirtes, Glymour, and Scheines analysis assumes the sample size n is large but says nothing about the relative size of n and the number of potential confounders k. We will now carry out a formal Bayesian statistical analysis which takes the relative size into account. We are interested in the Bayes factor

$$B_n = \frac{P(A^c \mid Z^n)}{P(A \mid Z^n)} = \frac{\sum_{s \in S^*} m_s^*}{\sum_{s \in S} m_s} \tag{3}$$

where

$$m_s = \int L(\psi_s) \pi_s(\psi_s) d\psi_s$$

and $L(\psi_s)$ is the likelihood function for G_s, $Z^n = (Z_1, \ldots, Z_n)$ and $Z_i = (X_i, Y_i)$ are independent, identically distributed observations from the model. Similarly

$$m_s^* = \int L(\psi_s^*) \pi_s^*(\psi_s^*) d\psi_s^*$$

Bayes factors are discussed in Jeffreys (1961, chapter 3) and Kass and Raftery (1995). B_n has the formal interpretation as the posterior odds of the event A^c that X does not cause Y, since each graph has the same prior probability. Thus, if B_n is very large, we would infer that there is no causal rela-

tion. If B_n were near zero, we would infer a causal relation.
The observables (X, Y) are bivariate normal and

$$T = \left(\sum_i X_i, \sum_i Y_i, \sum_i X_i^2, \sum_i Y_i^2, \sum_i X_i Y_i \right)$$

is a five dimensional minimal sufficient statistic. Apart from G_0 and G_0^*, each graph contains more than five parameters. Graph G_0 contains exactly five parameters, i.e., $E(X)$, $E(Y)$, $var(X)$, $var(Y)$, $E(XY)$. Graph G_0^* contains only four parameters, since $E(XY) - E(X)E(Y)$ is zero.

Consider any graph except G_0^*. Reparameterize ψ as (υ, τ) where $\upsilon = h(\psi)$ is a five dimensional identified parameter and τ is such that reparameterization is smooth and 1-1. This leaves τ unidentified. Such a reparameterization is possible since we are dealing with an exponential family. One possible choice of υ is $\upsilon = (E(X), E(Y), E(X^2), E(Y^2), E(XY))$. Because (X, Y) is bivariate normal, the likelihood is a function of υ, $L(\upsilon, \tau) = L(\upsilon)$. For simplicity, in this section, assume that the marginal prior for υ is the same in each subgraph. A more realistic analysis which does not make this assumption is provided in section 6. For any subgraph except G_0^*, we have

$$m = \iint L(\upsilon, \tau) \pi(\upsilon, \tau) d\upsilon d\tau$$

$$= \iint L(\upsilon) \pi(\upsilon, \tau) d\upsilon d\tau$$

$$= \iint L(\upsilon) \pi(\upsilon) d\upsilon$$

$$= c_n, \text{say}.$$

However, m_0^* will typically not equal c_n since distributions for graph G_0^* have only four free parameters. It follows from equation 3 that

$$B_n = \frac{(2^k - 1)c_n + m_0^*}{2^k c_n} = 1 - 2^{-k} + B^* 2^{-k} \tag{4}$$

where $B^* = m_0^*/c_n$. Note that B^* is precisely the Bayes factor for comparing G_0^* versus G_0, i.e., for testing the presence or absence of an arrow from X to Y under the assumption of no confounders.

Now consider the limiting behavior of B_n. For this analysis we rely on well known results about the asymptotic behavior of likelihoods and integrated likelihoods (Kass, Tierney and Kadane 1990; Kass and Wasserman 1995; Haughton 1988). Generally, the behavior of Bayes factors may be summarized as follows; (details can be found in section 9). In comparing two models M_1 and M_2, where M_1 is nested in M_2, the following happens. If the true density p is such that $p \in M_2 \cap M_1^c$ then B_n tends to 0 exponentially quickly almost surely. If $p \in M_2 \cap M_1$ then B_n tends to infinity at rate $n^{d/2}$ where d is the difference in the dimensions of the two models. The latter case is an instance of Occam's razor in which the Bayes factor chooses the simpler model when both contain the true distribution.

Turning to our case, and applying the above reasoning to B^*, we see the following. Suppose the true model is any model other than G_0^*. Then B^* tends to 0 almost surely and hence $B_n \to 1\text{-}2^{-k}, \approx 1$. Thus, the posterior odds that X causes Y converges to the prior odds and thus the causal hypothesis cannot be decided.

If G_0^* were true—and this is the important case for it corresponds to the case in section 3—then B^* tends to infinity at $\sqrt{(n)}$, i.e., $1/B^* = Op(n^{-1/2})$. Indeed, as shown in section 9, even the maximum of B^* over all data configurations (which occurs when the sample correlation between X and Y is zero) only tends to infinity at rate $\sqrt{(n)}$.

Now, if k were fixed and n were allowed to grow, we could vindicate the Spirtes, Glymour, and Scheines faithfulness analysis that X does not cause Y since then B_n would tend to infinity in probability. But, even with n large, we might be concerned that k is large. Mathematically, we can capture this by allowing $k = k_n$ to grow with n. We do not mean that, literally, the number of confounders grows with sample size. Rather, we mean that in any asymptotic analysis we must ensure that we account for the fact k and n can simultaneously both be large. Spirtes, Glymour, and Scheines implicitly assume that $k_n = o(\log n)$. However, from equation 4 we see that if k_n is such that $k_n - (\log n)/(2 \log2) \to \infty$ as n goes to infinity, then $B_n \to 1$ (in probability). We have arrived at the following result.

THEOREM 1. If $k_n - (\log n)/(2 \log 2) \to \infty$ as $n \to \infty$ then, whatever model is true, $B_n \to 1$ in probability.

In words, if the number of confounders is large relative to the log sample size, the data alone cannot inform us about the causal hypothesis. In the model studied in this section, as the number of potential confounders k increases, the prior probability $1/2^k$ of no unmeasured confounders decreases. Thus we can recast theorem 1 as saying that when the prior probability of no unmeasured confounders is $o(n^{-1/2})$, the data alone will not allow us to infer that X does not cause Y. In section 6 we show, in a much more general setup, that magnitude of the prior probability of "no unmeasured confounders" relative to sample size is the crucial determinant of whether one can infer that X does not cause Y.

4.1 Spirtes, Glymour, and Scheines Faithfulness Analysis Revisited

When the prior probability of no unmeasured confounders is $o(n^{-1/2})$, and X and Y are uncorrelated in the data, the Spirtes, Glymour, and Scheines faithfulness analysis of section 3 leads to the inappropriate conclusion that, with near certainty, there is no arrow from X to Y. The error committed by the faithfulness analysis is to conclude that X and Y are truly independent if the sample correlation is zero and the sample size is large. To see why, it is convenient to first consider the case in which the prior probability of no unmeasured confounders is exactly zero as in Robins (1997). That is, we are certain that graphs G_0 and G_0^* do not generate the data. The appropriate inference to draw from the sample correlation between X and Y being zero is that, with high posterior probability, the true correlation coefficient between X and Y lies in a small interval around zero. Since, by faithfulness, among all the graphs in $\mathcal{H}$ only G_0^* is consistent with the correlation coefficient of zero, we further conclude that the true correlation lies in a small interval around zero, but (with posterior probability 1) is not zero itself. Thus, a posteriori, we would infer there exists a true nonzero correlation between X and Y. Since this correlation can be explained by the unmeasured confounders, whether or not there is an additional arrow from X to Y, we remain uncertain as to whether an arrow from X to Y indeed exists.

More specifically, if we modify our linear SEM example by setting the prior probability of the two graphs G_0 and G_0^* with no unmeasured confounders equal to zero and increase the prior probability of each of the other graphs to $1/(2^{k+1} - 2)$, we find that the posterior probability that X causes Y is exactly the prior probability (i.e., $B_n = 1$) for all data realizations without resorting to asymptotics.

Now suppose the prior probability that there are no unmeasured confounders is small relative to sample size, although nonzero. Then, with high posterior probability, the true correlation between X and Y will now lie in a small interval around zero that includes zero itself. However, we can infer that X does not cause Y only if our posterior probability is nearly one for the event that the true value of the correlation is zero and thus, by faithfulness, that graph G_0^* is the true graph. But, since the posterior probability of a zero true correlation is zero when, with certainty, there are no unmeasured confounders, this probability will not jump discontinuously to near 1 as we begin to increase (from zero) our prior probability of "no unmeasured confounders."

5. A More Complex Example

In the example in the previous section, Spirtes, Glymour, and Scheines's faithfulness analysis led to an inappropriate conclusion of the absence of a causal relationship. We now show that the reverse case can occur. Specifically, we show Spirtes, Glymour, and Scheines's faithfulness analysis can lead to an inappropriate conclusion that a causal relationship exists.

Consider the following "faithfulness analysis" discussed by Pearl and Verma (1991) and Spirtes, Glymour, and Scheines (1993). Let X, Y, and Z be

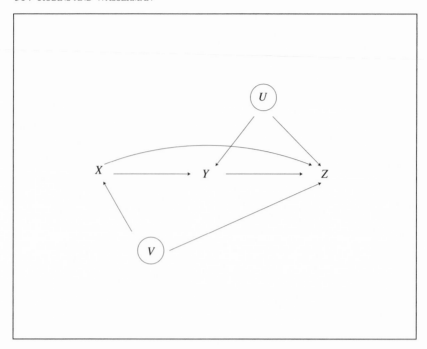

Figure 2. Directed acyclic graph for the second example.

time ordered and, let U represent all potential confounders between Y and Z and let V represent all potential confounders between X and Z; see figure 2. For compactness of notation, in figure 2, we have not split up these potential confounders into many different potential confounders as we did before. The question of interest is whether Y is a direct cause of Z.

Suppose we observe a very large i.i.d. sample $\{(X_i, Y_i, Z_i); i = 1,..., n\}$ from a trivariate normal. In the sample we find the following facts (with p-values in parentheses):

1. X and Z are dependent $(p < 10^{-6})$;
2. Y and Z are dependent $(p < 10^{-6})$;
3. X and Z are independent given Y $(p = 1.000)$.

Suppose now, following Spirtes, Glymour, and Scheines, we assume that facts 1 to 3 are also true in the population and we impose faithfulness. Then from fact 3 and the assumption of faithfulness, we deduce that the arrow from X to Z can be removed. We can now prove, by contradiction, that Y causes Z. Specifically, we shall prove that, if there were no arrow from Y to Z, and facts 1 to 3 held in the population, then the distribution of the data would be unfaithful to the graph in figure 2, which is not allowed.

Suppose then there is no arrow from Y to Z. If we remove U from the graph but leave V, we would deduce a dependence between X and Z given Y contradicting fact 3; thus U cannot be removed. Likewise, if we remove V from the graph but leave U, we would deduce a dependence between X and Z given Y contradicting fact 3; thus V cannot be removed. (These facts follow from well known properties of the multivariate normal distribution or, more simply, from the d-separation properties of DAGs; see Spirtes, Glymour, and Scheines [1993 page 36].) What happens if we leave both U and V? In that case, fact 3 cannot hold unless the parameters of the distribution of the graph cancel fortuitously to give fact 3. But this is precisely a violation of faithfulness and is not allowed. Hence, we must remove U and V from the graph. But with U and V removed, Y and Z are independent, violating fact 2. Thus, following Pearl and Verma (1991) and Spirtes, Glymour, and Scheines, we conclude that there must be an arrow from Y to Z (and furthermore, by faithfulness, that V and W are absent). We have deduced a causal relationship between Y and Z. Note that the logic leading to the deduction of a causal relationship between Y and Z continues to hold unchanged even if the sample correlation $\hat{\rho}$ between Y and Z is only 10^{-4}.

If we now expand U and V to show that each explicitly represents many potential confounders, then the Bayesian reasoning of section 4 can be used here too to show that (1) the analysis is undecidable (in the sense that the posterior odds that Y causes Z do not converge to zero or to infinity as n $\to \infty$) if the number of potential confounders is allowed to be large relative to n and thus the prior probability of "no unmeasured confounders" is small relative to sample size, but (2) if the number of potential confounders is small relative to n, then the Spirtes, Glymour, and Scheines faithful analysis is vindicated and we could conclude that Y causes Z even if the sample correlation $\hat{\rho}$ was but 10^{-4}. Again, when the prior probability of "no unmeasured confounders" is small relative to sample size, the error committed by the faithfulness analysis is to conclude that facts 1 to 3 hold in the population solely because they hold in the sample and the sample size is large.

6. Robustness to the Assumptions

In section 4, we have shown that, when the probability of there being "no unmeasured confounders" is small relative to sample size, the Spirtes, Glymour, and Scheines faithful analysis can lead to the unwarranted conclusion that X does not cause Y under our model. However, our model relied on three simplifying assumptions. These assumptions were (1) normality, (2) the same prior was used for the parameters v in each graph and (3) each subgraph was given equal prior probability; none of them are substantively entirely plausible. (As an example, suppose one believes that if X caused Y ($\theta \neq 0$), then most likely $\theta > 0$. In that case, one might expect that, in violation of (2), the prior probability that $cov(X, Y) > 0$ would be greater under model G_s with $\theta \neq 0$ than under model G_s^* with $\theta = 0$.) We will now show that dropping assumptions 1 to 3 does not materially change our conclusions.

Consider any fixed subgraph G. Let U denote all the unobserved random variables in this graph. Write the joint density as

$$f^G(x, y, u) = f_1^G(x, y) f_2^G(u \mid x, y)$$

We can think of the densities f_1 and f_2 themselves as parameters; this includes parametric and nonparametric approaches simultaneously. The pair (f_1, f_2) lie in a space of densities $\mathcal{F}$ equipped with an appropriate σ-field $\mathcal{B}$. Let π^G be the prior on this space. Now π^G induces a prior $\tilde{\pi}^G$ on f_1. Our previous assumption was that $\tilde{\pi}^G$ did not depend on G. Instead, we shall make a weaker assumption. Recall that $\mathcal{G}$ is the set of all subgraphs in which there is an arrow from X to Y and $\mathcal{G}^*$ is the set of all subgraphs in which there is not an arrow from X to Y. For convenience, let γ denote the prior for f_1 in the graph G_0.

Assumption. With the possible exception of the prior for the graph G_0^*, the priors $\tilde{\pi}^G$ are mutually absolutely continuous with respect to each other. Moreover, there exist constants, $0 < b < B < \infty$, independent of k, such that for each $G \in \mathcal{H} - \{ G_0^* \}$

$$b < \text{ess inf}_{f_1} \left| \frac{d\tilde{\pi}^G(f_1)}{d\gamma(f_1)} \right| < \text{ess sup}_{f_1} \left| \frac{d\tilde{\pi}^G(f_1)}{d\gamma(f_1)} \right| < B$$

(5)

where the essential infimum and supremum are with respect to γ.

The assumption merely asserts that the prior for f_1 over the various subgraphs cannot vary wildly. The reason for excluding G_0^* is that this graph imposes an independence not found in the other graphs and we can imagine using, therefore, a prior on a lower dimensional submanifold.

Another assumption we made was that each subgraph had equal prior probability. Instead, let each graph have nonzero prior probability p_G and let p_0^* denote the prior probability of G_0^*. Let $P(A) = \sum_{G \in \mathcal{G}} p_G$ be the prior probability of an arrow from X to Y.

Now the posterior odds that X does not cause Y is

$$B_n = \frac{\sum_{G \in \mathcal{G}^*} p_G m_G}{\sum_{G \in \mathcal{G}} p_G m_G}.$$

(6)

For any graph except G_0^* we have

$$m_G = \int \prod_i f_1(X_i, Y_i) d\pi^G(f_1, f_2)$$

$$= \int \prod_i f_1(X_i, Y_i) d\tilde{\pi}^G(f_1)$$

$$= \int \prod_i f_1(X_i, Y_i) \frac{d\tilde{\pi}^G}{d\gamma}(f_1) d\gamma(f_1).$$

By the assumption, it follows that $bc_n < m < Bc_n$, where c_n is m for the graph G_0. Using similar calculations as in section 4, we have the following result.

THEOREM 2. Under the given assumptions we have

$$c_1 + c_2 B^* \leq B_n \leq C_1 + C_2 B^*$$

where

$$c_1 = \frac{b(P(A^c) - p_0^*)}{BP(A)}, \; C_1 = \frac{B(P(A^c) - p_0^*)}{bP(A)},$$

$$c_2 = \frac{p_0^*}{bP(A)}, \; C_2 = \frac{p_0^*}{BP(A)}$$

and B^* is the Bayes factor for G_0^* versus G_0.

Without being more specific about the priors it is difficult to make precise statements about the asymptotic behavior of B^*. However, for every smooth parametric model, the best one can hope for is that B^* will increase at rate n^r for some r (usually $r = 1/2$); similar or slower behavior would be typical of a nonparametric model. Thus, as long as p_0^* is small relative to sample size (it was 2^{-k} in section 4), we are led again to the conclusion that B_n is asymptotically bounded away from 0 and infinity.

Specifically, we have the following result. Let N be the event that "there are no unmeasured confounders."

THEOREM 3. The posterior odds B_n that X does not cause Y is always bounded away from 0. Furthermore, if $B^* = O_P(n^r)$ and if $P(N) = o(n^{-r})$, then $B_n \to \psi$ in probability, where $0 < \psi < \infty$ and ψ depends on the prior odds that X does not cause Y.

We believe that our assumptions can be weakened further though we do not pursue the details here.

Remark: Theorem 2 notwithstanding, for certain priors, the data can greatly increase one's belief that X causes Y. For example, suppose (1) there was a moderately strong empirical correlation between X and Y, say $\hat{\rho} = .3$, (2) the sample size n was very large, (3) the SEM model of equations (1)-(2) was true, and (4) one believed, based on substantive background knowledge, that (a) the prior probability that X caused Y was .5, (b) the net magnitude of confounding by the unmeasured factors U was small

318 ROBINS AND WASSERMAN

so that, if X did not cause Y ($\theta = 0$), the prior probability that the covariance ρ between X and Y exceeded .1 was quite small, and (c) there was a nonnegligible prior probability that the absolute value of θ was sufficiently large for ρ to exceed .3 even in the absence of unmeasured confounders. Then the posterior odds B_n that X does not cause Y would be small (although greater than c_1), and thus the data would have been quite informative as to the hypothesis that X causes Y.

7. Prior Beliefs

The authors and every other epidemiologist and statistician we know believe that, given any two variables X and Y, there almost always exist unmeasured confounders (i.e., common causes) linking the two variables. For example, early in their first epidemiology course, students are taught that no matter how extreme the p-value for a test of association, observational epidemiology is unable to either reliably rule in or rule out small causal effects. Only randomized trials can reliably detect such effects. These teachings imply that the subjective beliefs of epidemiologists hold that the prior probability that there are no unmeasured confounders is extremely small, if not zero (Robins, 1997, section 11). Otherwise, if sample size n were very large, then (a) as noted in the setting of section 4, when X and Y are uncorrelated in the data, we could reliably conclude that X does not cause Y and thus rule out even small causal effects, and (b) as noted in the setting of section 5, if (1) tests of the hypotheses that Z and Y and X and Z were independent, were rejected with extreme p-values (say, $p < 10^{-6}$), (2) the sample partial correlation between X and Z given Y was zero, and (3) the magnitude of the empirical correlation between Z and Y was small (say, $\hat{\rho} = 10^{-4}$), we could reliably conclude that Y has a small causal effect on Z.

It is our guess that these subjective beliefs of epidemiologists derive chiefly from two facts, one empirical and one philosophical. Empirically, in studies with large sample sizes, one typically observes highly statistically significant associations between variables which are firmly believed, on biological grounds, not to be causally associated. Philosophically, the universe contains so many unmeasured potential common causes that it is a priori highly unlikely that not a single one is an actual common cause.

In discussions with a number of economists and social scientists, it is our impression that they too believe that the probability that there are no unmeasured confounders is small if not precisely zero.

8. Practical and Philosophical Implications

We have shown that the Spirtes, Glymour, and Scheines faithful analysis can lead to inappropriate causal conclusions when the prior probability of there being "no unmeasured confounders" is small relative to sample size. Therefore, we would caution against relying on computer programs such as Spirtes, Glymour, and Scheines's Tetrad that use the "faithfulness" analysis of section 3 as a tool for searching epidemiologic data bases for causal associations. However, our argument against the use of the Spirtes, Glymour, and Scheines "faithfulness analysis" in analyzing epidemiologic data is not an argument against using a "faithfulness" analysis in analyzing data in simple stereotyped environments where the number of unmeasured potential confounders is known to be small. Thus in artificial intelligence programs designed to allow robots to learn from data obtained in a rather stereotyped environment, the use of a "faithfulness" analysis and thus of a Tetradlike program might be extremely useful. Furthermore, our argument is not inconsistent with Pearl and Verma's speculation that children might naturally employ an informal version of the faithfulness analysis of section 5 to learn simple causal relationships in settings where the number of alternative explanations entertained is not large. Rather, our argument against the use of a "faithfulness analysis" pertains to observational studies with moderate expected effect sizes and large numbers of potential confounding factors (such as studies of the effect of preschool Head Start programs on later high school performance or of alcohol consumption on coronary artery disease) that require large investments in study design, data collection, quality control, and data analysis (including investment in the graduate training of epidemiologists, statisticians, economists and sociologists).

We are not claiming that inferring causal relationships empirically is impossible. Randomized studies with complete compliance are a well-known example where reliable causal inference is possible. Indeed, well-supported causal inferences based on observational data are sometimes possible by (1) adjusting for or matching on measured confounders (Rubin 1974); (2) using subject matter knowledge based on experience and biology to argue, as in the remark of section 6, that the magnitude of confounding due to unmeasured factors is likely small relative to the size of the observed association; and (3) combining information from data obtained on different populations and from different types of studies, including laboratory and animal studies. The inference that cigarette smoking causes lung cancer is perhaps the best known such example. However, observational studies cannot reliably rule in or rule out small causal effects.

9. Asymptotic Behavior of Bayes Factors

We now examine the asymptotic behavior of B_n in the case in section 4. By Laplace's method,

$$c_n = L(\hat{v})\pi(\hat{v})(2\pi)^{5/2}\{\det(\sigma)\}^{1/2} n^{-5/2}\left(1 + O_p(n^{-1})\right)$$

$$m_0^* = L(\hat{v}^*)\pi(\hat{v}^*)(2\pi)^{4/2}\{\det(\sigma^*)\}^{1/2} n^{-4/2}\left(1 + O_p(n^{-1})\right)$$

where σ is the Fisher information (for a single observation) in G_0, σ^* is the Fisher information (for a single observation) in G_0^*, $\hat{v}$ is the maximum likelihood estimate in G_0 and $\hat{v}^*$ is the maximum likelihood estimate in G_0^*. The term m_0^*/c_n tends to infinity at rate $O_p(n^{1/2})$ if A is false and tends to 0 exponentially quickly if A is true. Since $L(\hat{v}^*)$ is less than or equal to $L(\hat{v})$ with equality if and only if the sample correlation is zero, m_0^*/c_n is maximized for data sets with zero sample correlation. Even for such data sets, m_0^*/c_n tends to infinity only at rate $O_p(n^{1/2})$.

Acknowledgments

We thank David Freedman and Judea Pearl for comments on an earlier draft of this paper. Robins's research was supported by NIH Grant AI32475. Wasserman's research was supported by NIH grant R01-CA54852 and NSF grants DMS-9303557 and DMS-9357646.

References

Freedman, D. 1993. From Association to Causation via Regression. Technical Report, 414, Department of Statistics, University of California at Berkeley.

Haughton, D. M. A. 1988. On the Choice of a Model to Fit Data from an Exponential Family. *The Annals of Statistics* 16(1): 342–355.

Humphreys, P., and Freedman, D. 1996. The Grand Leap. *British Journal for the Philosophy of Science* 47(1): 113–123.

Jeffreys, H. 1961. *Theory of Probability.* 3d ed. Oxford, U.K.: Oxford University Press.

Kass, R. E., and Raftery, A. 1995. Bayes Factors. *Journal of the American Statistical Association* 90(430): 773–795.

Kass, R., and Wasserman, L. 1995. A Reference Bayesian Test for Nested Hypotheses with Large Samples. *Journal of the American Statistical Association* 90(431): 928–934.

Kass, R. E.; Tierney, L.; and Kadane, J. 1990. The Validity of Posterior Asymptotic Expansions Based on Laplace's Method. In *Bayesian and Likelihood Methods in Statistics and Econometrics*, eds. S. Geisser, J. S. Hodges, S. J. Press, and A. Zellner, 473–488. New York: North Holland.

Pearl, J. 1995. Causal Diagrams for Empirical Research. *Biometrika* 82(4): 669–709.

Pearl, J., and Verma, T. 1991. A Theory of Inferred Causation. In *Principles of Knowledge Representation and Reasoning: Proceedings of the Second International Conference,* eds. J. A. Allen, R. Fikes, and E. Sandewall, 441–452. San Francisco, Calif.: Morgan Kaufmann Publishers.

Robins, J. M. 1997. Causal Inference from Complex Longitudinal Data. In *Latent Variable Modeling and Applications to Causality: Lecture Notes in Statistics 20,* ed. M. Berkane, 69–177. Berlin: Springer-Verlag.

Robins, J. M. 1995. Discussion of "Causal Diagrams for Empirical Research" by J. Pearl. *Biometrika* 82(4): 695–698.

Robins, J. M. 1987. Addendum to "A New Approach to Causal Inference in Mortality Studies with Sustained Exposure Periods Application to Control of the Healthy Worker Survivor Effect." *Computers and Mathematics with Applications* 14(9-12): 923–945.

Robins, J. M. 1986. A New Approach to Causal Inference in Mortality Studies with Sustained Exposure Periods Application to Control of the Healthy Worker Survivor Effect. *Mathematical Modeling* 7: 1393–1512.

Robins, J. M.; Rotnitszky, A.; and Scharfstein, D. 1999. Sensitivity Analysis for Selection Bias and Unmeasured Confounding in Missing Data and Causal Inference Models. In *Statistical Models in Epidemiology: The Environment and Clinical Trials,* ed. E. Halloran and D. Berry. Berlin: Springer-Verlag.

Rubin, D. B. 1974. Estimating Causal Effects of Treatments in Randomized and Nonrandomized Studies. *Journal of Educational Psychology* 66(5): 688–701.

Spirtes, P.; Glymour, C.; and Scheines, R. 1993. *Causation, Prediction, and Search.* New York: Springer-Verlag.

CHAPTER NINE

On the Possibility of Inferring Causation from Association without Background Knowledge

Clark Glymour, Peter Spirtes, and Thomas Richardson

1. Introduction

The distinctive power of the Tetrad II program (Spirtes, Glymour, and Scheines 1993, Scheines et al. 1994), comes from its capacity, in certain circumstances, to determine that two variables, say X and Y, do not have a common cause and that any association between them is due to the influence of X on Y or of Y on X. When other parts of the procedure, or prior knowledge, say for example, that Y does not cause X, the search procedure concludes that X causes Y. Robins and Wasserman (1996) question the possibility of reliably making such inferences without background knowledge.

Consider the two hypotheses "X causes Y" and "X does not cause Y." Robins and Wasserman (1996) concede that priors that do not assign either of these hypotheses a zero probability will, in some circumstances, lead the Tetrad II inference procedures to give correct information with probability one in the large sample limit. But concession is not their point. They prove that with a prior probability that is adjusted with sample size, the Tetrad II procedures do not converge to the truth in the large sample limit. Specifically, they consider (1) a rule that associates a prior distribution over the hypotheses "X causes Y" and "X does not cause Y" with the number of potential confounders, and (2) a rule that associates the number of potential confounders with a sample size. With their rules, they show that in the large sample limit the Tetrad II inference procedures cannot learn that there is no direct causal connection between X and Y, in the sense that the Bayes factor approaches neither zero nor infinity as the sample size increases without bound. (They are implicitly using a zero-one loss function that assigns complete failure to the Tetrad II inference procedures if it concludes that "X causes Y" regardless of the weakness of the causal connection.)

Robins and Wasserman's rule for associating a prior distribution over the hypotheses "X causes Y" and "X does not cause Y" with the sample size is not to be taken literally; i.e. they are not advocating that an investigator's prior does or should change with sample size. What they do claim is this: for those who believe that there are a large number of confounders of almost everything, the alternative limiting analysis in which the prior does change with sample size may be more informative about their beliefs about the behavior of the Tetrad II procedures in empirical applications to large samples. In other words, one should have so much prior confidence that a sample of thousands will be confounded that, no matter what the data, the posterior probability that X does not cause Y will be less than 1/2.

Robins and Wasserman's main nontechnical conclusion is that under plausible and widely used priors, and under a (presumably) interesting and widely used zero-one loss function, their limiting analysis casts doubt upon whether the Tetrad II inference procedures are reliable, even at large but realistic sample sizes. The questions then become (1) how plausible such priors are upon reflection, and (2) whether such a prior and loss function are actually used.

2. The Robins-Wasserman Prior

There are a number of ways in which one could argue for a prior which assigns a low probability to the hypothesis of no confounding. One could argue that given any set of variables, the correct causal graph is always complete, because a missing edge corresponds to a causal influence of exactly zero, which has Lebesque measure zero. However, Robins and Wasserman do not adopt this prior and instead argue that even if one is willing to grant a high prior to the correct causal graph not being complete, there is still reason to adopt a prior which assigns a very low probability to the hypothesis of no confounding.

Robins and Wasserman point out that, given their prior, in the large sample limit the probability of the hypothesis that A is a cause of B is bounded away from zero, regardless of whether that hypothesis is true, or whether the contrary hypothesis that A does not cause B is true. That is correct, but is somewhat irrelevant to the conclusions drawn from the Tetrad II procedures in the case Robins and Wasserman consider, involving only two variables. The

Tetrad II procedures would never infer, from two variables only, that A is a cause of B. It would either infer that A and B were not causally connected (i.e. given the time order, that A did not cause B and there were no unmeasured confounders of A and B), or it would infer that A and B are causally connected: that is, either one influences the other *or* there is a third common cause of both A and B. If the latter hypothesis is true, then the Bayes factor for the two hypotheses approaches zero exponentially quickly almost surely, and the Tetrad II procedures succeed. In the rest of this section, we will concentrate on the case where A and B are not causally connected.

The details of the Robins and Wasserman prior are obtained by a counting argument. Given two variables A and B whose time order is known, with k potential, distinct confounders, there are $2^k - 1$ distinct graphs with confounders when A causes B, and $2^k - 1$ distinct graphs with confounders when A does not cause B. In contrast, there is just one graph without confounders when A causes B, and one graph without confounders when A does not cause B. Hence Robins and Wasserman assign a probability of $1/2^{k+1}$ to the hypothesis of no confounding, and a probability of $1 - 1/2^{k+1}$ to the hypothesis of confounding. Thus even if the probability of any particular model of confounding is low, the probability of some confounding is very high if k is large. Robins and Wasserman first consider the case where the variables are normally distributed, each graph has the same prior over the identified parameters (except for the graph where A and B are causally unconnected), and each graph is given the same prior probability. None of these assumptions is essential to their analysis, but because they make the analysis easier, this is the case we will discuss. The arguments we will give are also relevant to the case where the assumptions are dropped. Given these assumptions, they prove the following theorem, where k_n is the number of potential confounders associated with sample size n, and B_n is the Bayes factor of the no confounding model versus the confounding model at sample size n:

> If $k_n - \log(n)/(2\log 2) \to \infty$ as $n \to \infty$ then, whatever model
> is true, $B_n \to 1$ in probability.

The Robins-Wassermann prior has a number of counter-intuitive features. The two most important concerns are how it individuates confounders, and how it individuates models. In an asymptotic analysis, as $k_n - \log(n)/(2\log 2) \to \infty$, it is clear that one cannot ordinarily have an actual list of potential confounders; all that one has is a number of potential confounders. According to the way Robins and Wasserman count graphs, there are k_n graphs with one actual confounder. If one had a list of actual confounders, this would be the right way to individuate the graphs they are considering. For example, if genetics is a possible confounder of smoking and lung cancer, and atmospheric pollution is a possible confounder of smoking and lung cancer, then the hypothesis that genetics is the only confounder of smoking and lung cancer is clearly different from the hypothesis that atmospheric pollution is the only confounder of smoking and lung cancer. These are two empirically different hypotheses making two quite distinct claims. But if one is given only the number of possible confounders (2 in this instance) and two names, U_1 and U_2, which are not attached to particular random variables, then in what sense is the hypothesis that U_1 is the only confounder of lung cancer and smoking different from the hypothesis that U_2 is the only confounder of lung cancer and smoking? The two graphs associated with these hypotheses are just relabelings of each other, and the relabelings don't change the hypothesis since the names were not associated with particular random variables to begin with. The theory should simply be interpreted as asserting "There is one actual confounder of smoking and lung cancer." Given this interpretation, there are not k_n different graphs with one actual confounder, but there is one graph with one potential confounder. If graphs are counted in this way, then for k_n potential confounders, there are k_n+1 different graphs, each receiving probability $1/(k_n+1)$. If this is the case, then in order for B_n not to approach infinity as n approaches infinity, $k_n - (n-1)^{1/2} \rightarrow \infty$ as $n \rightarrow \infty$.

In addition to the problem of individuating different models with the same number of potential confounders, there is the problem of individuating and counting confounders, when the confounders are unspecified. In terms of the probability distributions that can be represented, any distribution that can be represented by a graph with n latent binary variables can also be represented by a graph with one latent variable with 2^n states. In a linear model, any distribution that can be represented with n confounders of a pair of variables can also be represented by a single confounder of the pair of variables. It is not clear why, when the variables are unspecified, the larger count of potential confounders is correct, as the Robins-Wasserman analysis requires.

Another feature of the Robins-Wasserman prior that can be questioned is that (as they point out) it assigns a probability of 1/2 to each potential confounder actually being a confounder. If the probability of each potential confounder actually being a confounder is $(1/2)^m$ for some integer m greater than 1, then even if one used their count of the number of graphs with potential confounders, k_n would have to grow more quickly than $\log(n)/(2\log 2)$ in order for B_n not to approach infinity.

The Robins-Wasserman prior also assumes that whether each potential confounder is an actual confounder is independent of whether other potential confounders are actually confounders. A reason for doubting this is illustrated in figure 1. Consider the two graphs in figure 1, where U_1 and U_2 are confounders of X and Y. In figure 1a, U_2 is a direct cause of X and Y. In figure 1b, U_2 is a direct cause of Y, but is only an indirect cause of X (via U_1.) In the former case we say that U_2 is a *direct confounder* of X and Y (relative to U_1, U_2), and in the latter case we say that U_2 is an *indirect con-*

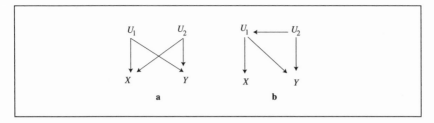

Figure 1. A reason to doubt the Robins-Wasserman prior assumption.

founder of X and Y (relative to U_1, U_2).

Note that when U_2 is an indirect confounder of X and Y, it can be a confounder of X and Y only when some other variable is also a confounder of X and Y. Now, suppose that there are k possible confounders of X and Y, but U_1 is the only possible direct confounder of X and Y. In that case, if U_1 is not a confounder of X and Y, then there are no confounders of X and Y. It follows that if each graph is equally probable, then the probability of no confounding is 1/2. So to get the Robins-Wasserman prior it is not enough to suppose that there are k possible confounders; one must make the stronger assumption that there are k possible *direct* confounders.

Finally, note that Robins and Wasserman implicitly assume that for a system of m measured variables, the probability that U_i is a confounder of A_1 and A_2 is independent of whether U_j is a confounder of A_3 and A_4. This cannot be the case, however, if each measured variable is a potential confounder of each other pair of measured variables. Assuming acyclicity, it is not possible for A_3 to be an actual confounder of A_1 and A_2, and for A_2 to be an actual confounder of A_1 and A_3. For example, if A_1, A_2, and A_3 are all measured, and for each pair of variables A_i and A_j the only potential confounder is A_k ($k \neq i$, $k \neq j$), then each pair of variables has a potential confounder. However, only one pair of variables can be confounded at a time.

3. Are the Robins-Wasserman Prior and Loss Function Actually Used?

Does anyone actually hold the combination of priors and loss function that Robins and Wasserman use in their analysis? This is a somewhat difficult question to answer, because almost always no formal Bayesian analysis of a problem in the social sciences or in epidemiology is given. First, using the Robins and Wasserman rules for associating priors with the number of possible confounders, note the following priors associated with the following numbers of potential confounders: if there are 10 potential confounders of X and Y, the prior probability of there being no confounders between X and Y is .00098; with 20 it is .00000095; with 30 it is .00000000093; and with 40 it is .00000000000091. That is, given 40 potential confounders, their prior assigns less than one chance in a trillion that there is no confounding of X and Y.

Robins and Wasserman argue that the behavior of epidemiologists indicates that they believe that the prior probability of no confounding is quite low. Epidemiologists do not accept that at large sample sizes, if X and Y are uncorrelated that we can reliably conclude that X does not cause Y and rule out even small causal effects. But of course at large sample sizes, the sample correlation is never exactly zero. If the sample correlation is not exactly zero, then one would have to do a statistical test to determine if the effect is zero. But it is well known that at very large sample sizes the results of statistical tests are extremely sensitive to a host of factors, including minor violations of the distributional assumptions, outliers, rounding error, measurement errors, etc. Moreover, no matter how large the sample size, the power of a statistical test against an alternative that is sufficiently close to the null hypothesis is low. Thus there is good reason to question the results of these tests even if one grants that the prior probability of no confounding is not tiny, especially if the alternative hypothesis is that the causal effect is very small.

Robins and Wasserman offer a second argument that epidemiologists assign a tiny prior probability to the hypothesis of no confounding. Consider the following possible evidence one might gather: the hypotheses that Z and Y, and X and Z are independent are rejected with extreme p-values (say $p < 10^{-6}$), the sample partial correlation between X and Z given Y is zero, and the magnitude of the empirical correlation between Z and Y is small (e.g. on the order of 10^{-4}.) Robins and Wasserman point out that epidemiologists would not accept this as conclusive evidence that Y has a small causal effect on Z. They conclude that this shows that epidemiologists assign a tiny prior probability to the hypothesis of no confounding. But the same arguments we made in the previous paragraph also apply here. In addition, the test of whether or not the direct effect of X on Z is zero in this case becomes a test of whether the correlation between X and Z given Y is zero. If the standardized linear coefficient of the direct effect of X on Z is r, and the correlation between Z and Y is small, the correlation between X and Z given Y is less than r. Hence, the power of a test that the direct causal effect of X on Z is zero against the alternative hypothesis that the direct causal effect of X on Z is small, is quite low.

We believe that, contrary to Robins and Wasserman's claims, the combination of priors and loss function that Robins and Wasserman use in their analysis is not compatible with the inferences that epidemiologists and social scientists are actually willing to make.

For example, according to Robins and Wasserman, inferring the presence or absence of causal relationships from nonexperimental data is possible, using the technique of adjusting for or matching on measured confounders (suggested by Rubin [1974], among others), or combining information from data obtained on different populations and from different types of studies. It is difficult to see how either of these methods could be reliable, unless Robins and Wasserman's prior is being implicitly denied.

Suppose that it is granted that the Robins-Wasserman prior accurately reflects the situation in observational studies, and that given a sample of size n, there will in general be at least $\sqrt{(n)}$-many confounding variables. At least in the case of discrete variables it would then appear impossible *in principle* to estimate the size of a treatment effect, by controlling for sufficiently many confounding variables. To simplify matters let us suppose that all variables, including confounders, are binary. In order to make any inference concerning the treatment effect, in the absence of confounders, we must have a sample of a certain size, say n_0. However in the Robins-Wasserman world, there will then be approximately $\sqrt{(n_0)}$ confounders associated with this sample. This will mean that our state space increases by a factor of $2\sqrt{(n_0)}$. Thus in order to assess the dependence between treatment and outcome, conditional upon these confounding variables, we will require a sample that is considerably larger, say of size n_1, for otherwise our data will be too sparse for us to make a reliable inference. (If we cannot assume that the confounders are independent, then $\mathbf{n_1}$ might need to be on the order of $2\sqrt{(n_0)}$ times as large as n_0, but this is inessential for the argument here; requiring a sample twice as large would be quite sufficient) However, once again, associated with the larger sample that we now require will be an increased number of confounders, and so on. We are caught in a vicious circle: to control for more confounders we require more data, owing to the increased state-space, but more data in turn is associated with more confounders.

Thus the method of adjusting for measured confounders is not reasonable given the Robins-Wasserman prior. Of course one could argue that one is only interested in the question of the approximate size of the causal effect (i.e. a different loss function based on how far off the predicted causal effect is from the actual causal effect), and Rubin's method is reasonable as long as the prior that there is no *strong* unmeasured confounder is near one. But an analogous defense of the Tetrad II procedures could be made.

Another technique that seems to be incompatible with the Robins-Wasserman prior, is the Wu-Hausman test of exogeneity. This test is equivalent to a test of independence, and as a test of exogeneity, is subject to failure due to violations of faithfulness (Davidson 1993). It is nevertheless widely used in econometrics.

It is less clear what prior is implicit in the example of the "smoking causes lung cancer" inference, if only because the actual method used to draw this conclusion is much less clear. Of course, laboratory and animal studies were used, but we are concerned here with the use of the statistical evidence relating human smoking to lung cancer. One type of evidence that has been marshaled for the conclusion that smoking causes lung cancer is that the association between smoking and lung cancer remains strong, even after controlling for a variety of measured possible confounders. But it is difficult to see what could justify this reasoning unless one believed that one had measured a significant proportion of the potential confounders. If there are 1000, or 10,000, or 100,000 possible confounders, but one has measured only 50 or 100 of them, it is hard to see why a strong association controlling for the measured confounders should be taken as evidence that smoking causes lung cancer. And if a strong association controlling for the measured confounders should be taken as evidence that smoking causes lung cancer, then (assuming coherence) not having a strong association controlling for the measured confounders should be taken as evidence that smoking is not a cause of lung cancer. Again, one could argue that one is only interested in the question of the approximate size of the causal effect, and the method is reasonable as long as the prior that there is no *strong* unmeasured confounder is near one; but again one could make the same argument for the Tetrad II procedures. Alternatively, one could argue that a strong association controlling for the measured confounders is not considered conclusive evidence that smoking causes lung cancer, but is instead interpreted as supportive. It is only conjunction with all of the other evidence (such as laboratory and animal studies) that the conclusion is considered conclusive. Again, however, one could make the same argument for the Tetrad II procedures. They should not be considered as conclusive evidence in favor of the hypothesis, but as one type of evidence that should be taken into account.

Robins and Wasserman remark that their result shows the implausibility of detecting very weak causal influences from nonexperimental data. We agree with their conclusion; but we think these procedures still play an important role in detecting larger causal influences. We further agree that it would be very useful to have studies that examine the sensitivity of the output of the Tetrad II procedures to different assumptions and different priors, using as a measure of success the difference between the predicted and the actual causal influences. So, in conclusion, we think Robins and Wasserman have identified an interesting research issue, but have described only implausible priors, not congruent with practice, under which automated search procedures cannot succeed.

References

Davidson, R., and Mackinnon, J. 1993. *Estimation and Inference in Econometrics.* Oxford, U.K.: Oxford University Press.

Epstein, R. L. 1987. *A History of Econometrics.* Amsterdam, The Netherlands: North-Holland.

Engle, R.; Hendry, D.; and Richard, J. F. 1983. Exogeneity. *Econometrica* 51(4): 277–304.

Hausman, J. A. 1978. Specification Tests in Econometrics. *Econometrica* 46(1): 1251–1271.

Robins, J., and Wasserman, L. 1996. On the Possibility of Inferring Causation from Association without Background Knowledge. Technical Report, 649, Department of Statistics, Carnegie Mellon University, Pittsburgh, Penn.

Rubin, D. 1974. Estimating Causal Effects of Treatments in Randomized and Nonrandomized Studies. *Journal of Educational Psychology* 66(2): 688–701.

Scheines, R.; Spirtes, P.; Glymour, C.; and Meek, C. 1994. *Tetrad II: Tools for Causal Modeling*. Hillsdale, N.J.: Lawrence Erlbaum.

Spirtes, P.; Glymour, C.; and Scheines, R. 1993. *Causation, Prediction, and Search*. Lecture Notes in Statistics 81. New York: Springer-Verlag.

Wu, D.-M. 1973. Alternative Tests of Independence between Stochastic Regressors and Disturbances. *Econometrica* 41(3): 733–750.

CHAPTER TEN

Rejoinder to Glymour and Spirtes

James M. Robins and Larry Wasserman

1. Introduction

The opening sentence to the abstract of our paper is the statement that Spirtes, Glymour, and Scheines and Pearl and Verma make the startling claim that it is possible to infer causal relationships between two variables X and Y from associations found in observational data without substantive subject-matter–specific background knowledge. Such a claim seemed, on its face, specious to us and to other epidemiologists, statisticians, and social scientists we polled.

What was fascinating to us was (1) that Spirtes, Glymour, and Scheines and Pearl and Verma proved, given their causal framework (i.e., in the absence of selection bias, the observed distributions of a set of variables is the marginal of a distribution faithful to some causally sufficient DAG) that, without substantive subject matter knowledge, there exist methods for discovering causal structure from observational data which are asymptotically correct, and (2) that we did not find their causal framework or their faithfulness assumption to be unreasonable.

However, we then recognized that implicit in their asymptotics was the assumption that the prior probability of there being no unmeasured confounders was positive and not small in relation to sample size. We proved that without this additional assumption, Spirtes, Glymour, and Scheines's and Pearl and Verma's methods cannot be reliably used to infer causal structure from observational data. Having read Glymour, Spirtes, and Richardson's reply, we continue to believe that essentially any pair of variables is dependent due to unmeasured confounders. Indeed, as we argued in the chapter, we believe the following proposition (which we also believe is well accepted by practicing epidemiologists, statisticians, and social scientists): due to residual unmeasured confounding, essentially any two causally unconnected variables will be found to have a highly statistically significant association in most very large observational studies. Glymour, Spirtes, and Richardson argue in their section 3 that we offered no convincing evidence that practicing epidemiologists endorsed this proposition. However, we will show below that the Glymour, Spirtes, and Richardson's argument is flawed.

In section 3 of their reply, Glymour, Spirtes, and Richardson concede one of our main points: in observational studies, small causal effects cannot be reliably ruled in nor ruled out, no matter how large the study size. In the final sections of our rejoinder, we give our view on the possible implications of this concession as to the reliability of causal searches based on the Tetrad program.

2. The Loss Function

We now turn to a detailed consideration of Glymour, Spirtes, and Richardson's argument in their reply. At the end of their section 1, Glymour, Spirtes, and Richardson raised two questions: (1) how plausible our priors are upon reflection, and (2) whether such priors and loss functions are actually used in practice. We agree these are critical questions to which we now give answers.

To begin, our decision to focus on the zero-one loss function (i.e., whether a variable was or was not the cause of another variable) rather than the magnitude of any causal effect was not because we think the zero-one loss function to be the most relevant—we don't; rather, it is because Spirtes, Glymour, and Scheines and Pearl and Verma themselves emphasize the zero-one loss functions, it being implicit whenever they say they can reliably determine causal structure. Indeed, nowhere in Spirtes, Glymour, and Scheines or Pearl and Verma is there, as far as we know, any extended discussion of the fact that we emphasized in our chapter: small causal effects cannot be reliably ruled out or ruled in based on observational data, no matter how large the sample size.

The impact of this point is ameliorated to some extent by the fact that, for policy purposes, the loss associated with misidentifying small causal effects is usually less than that associated with misidentifying large causal effects. However, the scale on which the loss associated with misidentifying a causal effect is measured for policy purposes may differ from the scale on which identification of causal effects can be reliably determined, as the following discussion illustrates.

In epidemiology, it is commonly argued that one of the main criteria for determining the likelihood of an association as a causal association is its magnitude (Hill 1951). However, as stressed by Robins et al. (1985), for a dichotomous outcome, this magnitude is to be measured on a ratio (i.e., relative) scale, not on a difference (i.e., absolute) scale.

As an example, given sufficiently large studies so that sampling variability does not dominate uncertainty, a tenfold increase in the risk of soft tissue sarcoma associated with an occupational exposure *A* is more likely to be causal than a twenty percent increase in the risk of coronary heart disease associated with an exposure *B,* all else being equal. This statement reflects both the fact that it is harder to imagine that bias due to unmeasured common causes, measurement error, and selection bias could easily explain a risk ratio of eleven than a risk ratio of 1.2 .

Yet the public health benefits of preventing exposure to a causal agent are properly measured on a difference rather than ratio scale. Specifically, because the background rate of coronary heart disease is so many times greater than the background rate of soft tissue sarcoma, the number of excess deaths associated with a true twenty percent increase in coronary heart disease mortality due to agent *B* would exceed by seven-fold the excess deaths associated with a true tenfold increase in the risk of soft tissue sarcoma. It follows that any method that will allow us to reliably determine from observational data whether an increase in coronary heart disease of twenty percent was likely to be causal would be invaluable. The Tetrad project, as described in Spirtes, Glymour, and Scheines (1993), would seem to offer such promise. However, for the reasons we discuss in our chapter, we are skeptical. We believe that no purely statistical methods can ever help us to determine whether small relative increases in risk are causal.

3. Plausibility of Priors

We turn now to consider the plausibility of our priors. In section 2, Glymour, Spirtes, and Richardson criticize the prior we worked with in section 2. As we stress in the chapter, this prior is not meant to represent the actual subjective beliefs of anyone. It was chosen for only one purpose: to make the formal Bayesian calculations we propose transparent and explicit. Glymour, Spirtes, and Richardson state that their comments also are relevant to the realistic priors of our section 6. We disagree with this claim. We regard Glymour, Spirtes, and Richardson's section 2 largely as an attack on our highly unrealistic prior of section 2, rather than on the realistic priors discussed in our section 6. It will be helpful here if we here restate our main conclusions concerning the realistic priors of our section 6.

Let *n* be the sample size and *P* (*N*) be the prior probability of the event *N* that there are no unmeasured common causes of X and Y where X is known to be temporally prior to Y. Then under the minimal assumptions on our prior described in our section 6, our theorem 3 can be restated as follows.

If the probability of there being no unmeasured common causes is small relative to sample size [specifically, $P(N) = o(n^{-1/2})$], then, even when X and Y are exactly uncorrelated in the data, the posterior odds that X does not cause Y converges as $n \to \infty$ to a number ψ that depends on the prior odds that X does not cause Y and ψ is bounded away from zero in infinity. As a consequence, the causal relationship that X does not cause Y cannot be determined by the data alone, no matter how large the sample size, even assuming faithfulness.

Thus, in view of our theorem 3, and as Glymour, Spirtes, and Richardson recognize in their section 3, the important question is not how reasonable is our simplistic prior of section 2 but rather (1) do practicing epidemiologists, statisticians, and social scientists have prior beliefs satisfying $P(N) = o(n^{-1/2})$, and (2) should they still hold these beliefs after reading the discussion in Glymour, Spirtes, and Richardson?

To determine the beliefs of practicing professionals, we asked six epidemiologists at Harvard and UCLA the following question. Consider twenty large epidemiologic studies (say, with sample size 240,000 or greater). Consider any dichotomous exposure X and any dichotomous outcome Y which you believe are not causally connected and that have been measured in each of the twenty studies. Suppose further the prevalence of each variable is approximately 50 percent. What is your best guess as to the fraction of the twenty studies in which the empirical odds ratio for the two variables OR_{XY} will lie outside of the interval (.98, 1.02)?

Of the epidemiologists queried, the mean was 90 percent with a minimum of 75 percent. Since the empirical odds ratio lying outside of this interval implies that the p-value for the usual χ^2 test of independence is less than .02, we conclude that these epidemiologists believe that with high probability, any two variables will be correlated in large observational studies.

Furthermore, the mean fell only to 85 percent when we further told the epidemiologists that known confounding factors had been adjusted for. In addition, all of the epidemiologists agreed with the statement that, even when the odds ratio was contained in the interval (.98, 1.02), this fact should not be taken as strong evidence that X and Y are uncorrelated, because there may be inadequate power to detect small but nonzero correlations at the $p < .02$ level.

When questioned further as to whether such associations were due to confounding, selection bias, or both, most epidemiologists chose the combination of the two. However, it is easy to show that the arguments in section 6 of our chapter go through unchanged if we consider $P(N)$ as the prior probability of the event that there is neither confounding by unmeasured common causes nor selection bias (i.e., due to conditioning on a common effect of X

and Y). Henceforth, as is common in epidemiology, we shall say that such noncausal associations between X and Y are due to unmeasured confounding (regardless of whether this confounding is due to an unmeasured common cause or to conditioning on a common effect).

We conclude that the above small poll is consistent with our statement that practicing epidemiologists believe the proposition that, due to unmeasured confounding, with probability nearly 1, two causally unconnected variables X and Y will be associated in the population.

How is it that Glymour, Spirtes, and Richardson argue that we offer no convincing evidence that epidemiologists believe this proposition? We believe their argument derives from a misreading of our chapter. (The way the chapter was written partly invited such a misreading.) In our section 7 on prior beliefs, it is in the second paragraph that we discuss where beliefs in the above proposition derive from. Unfortunately, Glymour, Spirtes, and Richardson attack the arguments we make in the first paragraph of section 7, which were meant to be only subsidiary to the central arguments given in the second paragraph.

Specifically, in the first paragraph of section 7, we state that subjective beliefs of epidemiologists hold that the prior probability of no unmeasured confounders is extremely small, if not zero, for otherwise, if the sample size n were large, then when X and Y are uncorrelated in the data, we could reliably conclude that X does not cause Y and thus rule out the small causal effects. Glymour, Spirtes, and Richardson argue, not without some merit, that in this setting epidemiologists may be unwilling to conclude that X and Y are truly uncorrelated because the power of the tests may be poor due to various forms of measurement error, i.e., outliers, rounding error, etc. (Since many analysts know to use robust nonparametric tests—such as the Wilcoxon test—we do not believe minor violations of distributional assumptions should be the issue.)

Suppose Glymour, Spirtes, and Richardson are correct here. Then, on the one hand, this poor power will, as we have argued, lead to incorrect inferences based on a faithfulness analysis as implemented in Tetrad. On the other hand and even more importantly, as discussed just above and in the second paragraph of our section 7, the main reason that epidemiologists believe that essentially any two variables will be correlated is because of the highly statistically significant associations that are the rule in large observational studies. Indeed, the ubiquity of such statistically significant empirical associations even in the presence of the random (nondifferential) measurement error argued by Glymour, Spirtes, and Richardson is strong evidence for, not against, the proposition that essentially any two variables are correlated.

We now consider the question whether after reading Glymour, Spirtes, and Richardson's reply, practicing epidemiologists should continue to believe that essentially any two variables are correlated due to residual unmeasured confounders. We believe the answer is yes. However, in their section 2, Glymour, Spirtes, and Richardson make a philosophical argument against the following philosophical claim which we make in the second paragraph of our section 7: Given any two variables X and Y, the universe contains so many unmeasured potential common causes that it is a priori highly unlikely that not a single one is an actual common cause. We were not persuaded by their philosophical argument against this claim. More importantly, however, even had we been sympathetic to their argument, we would reject its conclusion when confronted with the empirical evidence that in most large observational studies, most variables are highly statistically significantly associated.

4. Conclusions Re: Detection of Small Effects

In our chapter, we demonstrated that if the prior probability is near one that any two variables are correlated due to unmeasured confounding, then small causal effects can neither be ruled in nor ruled out based on observational data. In their concluding paragraph, Glymour, Spirtes, and Richardson agree that small effects cannot be either ruled in or out (although, as discussed in detail above, they apparently disagree with the logic by which we reach this conclusion). Glymour, Spirtes, and Richardson go on to conclude that it would be useful to have studies which examine the sensitivity of the output of Tetrad to different assumptions and priors, using as a measure of success the difference between the predicted and actual causal influences. We agree that such studies are necessary to begin to validate the usefulness of Tetrad, since, up to the present, the only justification offered for reliance on Tetrad is asymptotic under the disputed assumption that the probability of there being no unmeasured confounders is not small in relation to sample size. As evidence of our enthusiasm for sensitivity studies, we are collaborating with Glymour, Spirtes, and Richardson and their coworkers in the design of these studies. However, until such sensitivity studies have been conducted, we believe that inferences made by the Tetrad program should be viewed with great skepticism.

5. Comparison of Tetrad and Standard Adjustment Re: Detection of Large Effects

In this section, we compare, by means of examples, standard adjustment with Tetrad as tools for detecting moderate to large causal effects. We believe that familiarity with these examples will help a user to critically interpret the output of Tetrad. The following two paradigmatic examples make us leery about the use of Tetrad to help detect even large causal effects. As our first paradigmatic example, consider a nonexperimental study of the effect of a new surgical procedure Y on a life-threatening illness Z. Often associations (even adjusted for measured variables) will be large in such studies (especially when they are conducted by the surgeon who developed and believes in the new procedure), even though later randomized trials prove that the surgical procedure has no beneficial effect. The reason for this is that surgeons tend to operate on healthier patients. In a standard (non-Tetrad) analysis, one would adjust for measured presurgical indicators of health status. However, even were a large adjusted apparent beneficial effect for the surgical procedure found in the data, these results would be treated with skepticism since, unlike the cigarette smoking example of our chapter, our prior probability of there being no strong unmeasured confounders would not be small, since surgeons often can recognize good operative candidates based on subtle clues not recorded in the medical chart. Only randomized experiments would be conclusive.

However, suppose now that our surgeon had access to Tetrad and he used the fast causal inference (FCI) algorithm, assuming (correctly) no selection bias and imposing the constraints implied by our knowledge of the temporal ordering of the variables. The FCI algorithm would then search and, if it found some pretreatment variable X such as ethnicity, socioeconomic status, etc., that was correlated with having the operation Y and surgical success Z but not significantly associated with surgical success conditional on Y (as described in our section 5), it would conclude that the operation was causally beneficial. However, while under Spirtes, Glymour, and Scheines's asymptotics this should not occur, we would not be surprised if such occurrences were common due to poor power and the large number of covariates X. The surgeon would then have Tetrad's support for his treatment being beneficial and might then argue that conducting the randomized trial (which would establish the uselessness of his treatment) was now unethical. It is precisely because, in contrast to standard adjustment methods, Tetrad appears (we believe inappropriately) to be able to rule out the hypothesis of no unmeasured confounders in examples like these, that we are wary about its use.

Note in contrast to Glymour, Spirtes, and Richardson's implication in their reply, the standard adjustment approach and the Tetrad approach are not roughly comparable when the goal is to detect rather large causal effects. In fact, the basic semantics of the two approaches differ. Specifically, the standard adjustment point of view simply says that if there are no strong unmeasured confounders, then strong associations are causal; it does not presume to infer from the data that there are indeed no strong unmeasured confounders. The standard approach can be usefully generalized by incorporating sensitivity analyses that indicate how one's inferences should change under different assumptions about the magnitude of unmeasured confounding (Robins 1997),still, without attempting to infer the true magnitude of residual confounders from the data. Analyses of nonexperimental data with Tetrad to determine the frequency of disagreement with subsequent randomized trial data would be an important test of the Tetrad program and one we understand Glymour, Spirtes, and Richardson and coworkers hope to conduct.

As our second paradigmatic example, consider now the obverse of the previous example. Suppose now Y is cigarette smoking, Z is lung cancer, and data are again available on many variables X that precede Y and Z such as ethnicity or socioeconomic status. Suppose a cigarette company hopes to show that cigarette smoking Y does not cause lung cancer Z despite their very large and striking association. To do so, they use the FCI algorithm in Tetrad to discover a variable X which is associated with lung cancer Z conditional on Y but is marginally independent of Z. Then, by faithfulness and the fact that Y is prior to Z, the Tetrad program will report that it has discovered (1) that Y is not a cause of Z and (2) that the strong empirical association between Y and Z was entirely attributable to one or more strong unmeasured common causes. Now if in fact Y does cause Z, Spirtes, Glymour, and Scheines's asymptotics imply that the above scenario should not occur. However, again we would not be surprised if it did occur due to poor power and the large number of potential covariates X. Again, in this example, the standard adjustment approach and the Tetrad approach are not roughly comparable.

Now one response that an advocate of Tetrad might have to the above examples is that they are unsurprising. For, after all, Tetrad, in contrast to a standard analysis, is trying to do more – it is trying to discover causal structure. Hence, since it risks taking a position on causal structure, it, of course, risks being wrong (particularly in the face of a multiple testing problem presented by having many covariates X). We agree there can be no "risk free" way to search for causal structure. However, since we have no way in general to validate whether taking such risks leads to benefit or harm on average, it seems inappropriate to advocate for Tetrad.

In the next two paragraphs, we shall show that, when our goal is to detect large causal effects when there are no strong unmeasured confounders, there are other paradigmatic settings in which the two approaches are comparable. However, they are often comparable in the sense that Tetrad reduces to and thus adds nothing to the standard adjustment approach.

As our next paradigmatic example, again suppose that X is temporally prior to Y and the magnitude of the $X - Y$ association in the data is small or nonexistent (irrespective of whether the p-value for a test of independence between X and Y is or is not extreme). Then, from the standard adjustment point of view, if we are essentially certain there are no strong unmeasured confounders, we conclude that the magnitude of the causal effect of X and Y

must be small, regardless of whether a test for the independence of X and Y does or does not reject. This reflects the fact that if the causal effect were large, then the lack of a strong $X - Y$ association would require a strong unmeasured confounder. It follows in this setting that it is irrelevant to test for independence between X and Y. However, such a test is the sine qua non of the Tetrad procedure. That is, it is what defines the Tetrad procedure as possibly different from the standard approach.

As our next paradigmatic example, consider again the setting of section 5 where X, Y, and Z are temporally ordered, all correlated, and the magnitude of the $Y - Z$ association controlling for X is small. Then, under the assumption of no strong unmeasured confounders, the standard adjustment approach would declare that the magnitude of the causal effect of Y on Z is small, regardless of whether a statistical test for the independence of X and Z given Y does or does not reject. Thus, performing such a test (which is the sine qua non of a Tetrad analysis) adds nothing to our causal conclusions. In this same setting, suppose now that the conditional association between Y and Z given X were large. Then a standard adjustment approach, under the assumption of no strong unmeasured confounders, would conclude that Y is an important cause of Z, irrespective of whether or not a test for conditional independence between X and Z given Y rejects. Thus again, Tetrad has nothing additional to offer.

As an example where Glymour, Spirtes, and Richardson might still argue that Tetrad might be useful even under the assumption of no strong unmeasured confounders, consider the setting described in the last paragraph but now assume that $X = (X_1,...,X_n)$ is highly multivariate with n components. To further simplify the problem, suppose that we know that there are no unmeasured confounders. Since X is highly multivariate, standard regression techniques are unsuitable because of huge standard errors. In this setting, Tetrad could be used to try to determine that certain subsets of the covariates in X are not confounders and thus can be eliminated by conducting preliminary tests of (1) unconditional independence between various components of X and/or (2) conditional independence between components of X and Z given Y. However, a preliminary test approach to the control of confounding has a long history in statistics and is widely viewed as an inadequate approach, as it does not approximate a Bayes approach except for certain specific priors. Further, even for those priors, it is not Bayes, since preliminary test estimators are not admissible. These issues are well discussed for the normal model by Leamer (1978). Thus, it is not clear that Tetrad will be useful for model selection, even in a setting in which there are no unmeasured confounders and we are interested in large causal effects.

In summary, as we have urged, Glymour, Spirtes, and Richardson have abandoned justifying the use of Tetrad based on an asymptotics that assumes the probability of no unmeasured confounders is not small in comparison to sample size and have accepted our argument that small causal effects cannot be ruled in or ruled out from observational data. Given these admissions, it seems that a great deal of work will be necessary to justify, if possible, the usefulness of Tetrad as a reliable search engine for causal effects. We would guess that if such a justification can be formulated, it will be in association with a highly modified and more cautious Tetrad algorithm.

References

Hill, A. B. 1951. *Principles of Medical Statistics, 9th Edition.* New York: Oxford University Press.

Leamer, E. 1978, *Specification Searches.* New York: John Wiley & Sons.

Robins, J. M. 1997. Causal Inference from Complex Longitudinal Data. In *Latent Variable Modeling and Applications to Causality. Lecture Notes in Statistics (120),* ed. M. Berkane, 69-117. Berlin: Springer-Verlag.

Robins, J. M., Landrigan P. J., Robins T. G., and Fine L. J. 1985. Decision-Making under Uncertainty in the Setting of Environmental Health Regulations. *Journal of Public Health Policy,* 6(3): 322-328.

Spirtes, P.; Glymour, C.; and Scheines, R. 1993. *Causation, Prediction, and Search* New York: Springer-Verlag.

CHAPTER ELEVEN

Response to Rejoinder

Clark Glymour, Peter Spirtes, Thomas Richardson

Robins and Wasserman agree with us that under a plausible set of assumptions, Tetrad II is an asymptotically correct procedure for inferring causal structure from observational data. We agree with Robins and Wasserman that on realistic sample sizes and data sets, if a zero-one loss function is used, no causal inference procedure that fails to employ very strong domain specific background knowledge is likely to be both correct and useful if variables of interest have many observed causes, or if influences are weak. Other loss functions, which emphasize the difference between the probabilities predicted from interventions and the actual probabilities upon interventions, are arguably more useful. We agree that the use of a sequence of statistical tests of conditional independence raise significant worries about the low power of the tests, particularly when there are a large number of covariates (as indicated by the remarks in causation, prediction, and search that it would be desirable to output a set of PAGs, rather than a single pattern, because the data might not be able to strongly discriminate among different PAGs). This seems to us to leave several interesting questions to be resolved: Assuming a non zero-one loss function, can the worries about the low power of the tests and large numbers of covariates be addressed by modifications to the Tetrad II procedures (or some other procedure entirely)? And what sorts of priors are needed in order to make the success of such procedures probable on realistic sample sizes? Robins and Wasserman note that the conclusions that epidemiologists draw from observational data rest on the assumption that "there are no strong unmeasured confounders" of the putative cause and its effect. The first point to notice is the somewhat ambiguous phrasing of "no strong unmeasured confounders." Given the kinds of priors that Robins and Wasserman describe, it is quite possible to have "no strong unmeasured confounders" while still having strong confounding (from the combination of many small confounders). Epidemiologists seem actually to make the stronger assumption that there is no strong unmeasured confounding.

What sort of background knowledge could one have which would reasonably support the conclusion that there is no strong unmeasured confounding? In physics, one might believe as much about the motions of the planets because one is very familiar with all the kinds of forces typically operating in such a situation and how those forces are generated This is in short contrast to the situation in epidemiology where a myriad of different factors, varying from disease to disease, are the operative causes, and the ability to predict who will contract a given disease is quite poor. If the conclusions of epidemiology rest on what Robins and Wasserman consider to be an untestable substantive assumption, then this certainly puts all causal conclusions from observational studies on extremely shaky ground. So any reliable method that can make weaker assumptions would be valuable. One way of addressing the worries about low power and large numbers of covariates, as well as the problem of sequential testing of conditional independence relations and the possible low power of such tests, is to assign a score (such as the Bayes Information Criterion [BIC]) to a (d-separation) equivalence class of causal models (see Spirtes and Richardson [1997]). In this way, instead of dealing with a sequence of tests, there is a sense in which all of the conditional independence relations are simultaneously tested. Under the procedures we have described, if model $M1$ were created by removing an edge from model $M2$ because of a statistical test of conditional independence, the search would output model $M1$, with nothing in the output to indicate whether the test had high or low power. In the modified procedures we have devised, a BIC score would be calculated for both $M1$ and $M2$, and if the difference in the scores was small (as would be the case if the test of conditional independence which caused the edge to be removed from $M2$ had low power) both of the models and their respective scores would be output. On the other hand, if the test of conditional independence had high power, then the difference in BIC score between the two models would be large, and only $M1$ would be output. In addition, because there is a whole family of BIClike scores which are consistent, but assign different penalties to the complexity of a model, it would be possible to have the user put a kind of quasi-prior down on simplicity by adjusting the penalty term.

Even with the suggested modifications to Tetrad, it is still the case that the sorts of priors that would support the conclusions the program draws would incorporate acceptance of a kind of faithfulness asumption. Is this assumption reasonable? It will help to distinguish between several different versions of the causal faithfulness assumption.

We and Robins and Wasserman agree on a principle that we will call the population causal faithfulness assumption: If X and Y are independent conditional on Z, then X and Y are not directly causally connected except through Z (i.e., X does not cause Y directly, Y does not cause X directly, and no third variable outside of Z causes both X and Y directly). If one wishes to draw exact causal inferences from finite samples, a different assumption is needed. Call it the *sample causal faithfulness assumption:* in a large sample, if X and Y are almost independent conditional on Z, that is evidence that X and Y are not directly causally connected except through Z. Robins and Wasserman have presented a prior in which the sample causal faithfulness assumption is false. We have already given our comments on their prior.

The sample causal faithfulness assumption is certainly used in our search procedures; however, in many practical situations a still weaker principle will suffice for causal inference. For that reason, we will turn to an assumption that is relevant when the difference between no direct causal relation and a very weak direct causal relation is not important. For those situations, the relevant inference principle may be called the *weak sample causal faithfulness assumption:* in a large sample, if X and Y are almost independent conditional on Z, that is evidence that X and Y are at most weakly directly causally connected except through Z.

Should the weak sample causal faithfulness assumption be accepted? If one is a Bayesian, the answer obviously depends upon what prior one holds. Is the weak sample causal faithfulness assumption accepted by epidemiologists? Note that both the Robins-Wasserman prior, and their claim that epidemiologists place a very high prior on every population correlation being non-zero, while incompatible with the sample causal faithfulness assumption, are perfectly compatible with the weak sample causal faithfulness assumption. Anyone who accepts that an almost zero correlation between X and Y in a large sample (even if the correlation is statistically significant) is at least prima facie evidence for a weak direct causal connection between X and Y thereby accepts an instance of the weak sample causal faithfulness assumption. In addition, anyone who accepts that a small (but perhaps statistically significant) coefficient for a variable X in a regression (linear, logistic, or other kind) is at least prima facie evidence for a weak direct causal connection between X and the outcome variable, also uses an instance of the weak sample causal faithfulness assumption.

Acknowledgement

Research for this paper was supported by grants DMS-9704573 and BES-940239.

Part Four

Estimating Causal Effects

Parameter estimation in causal models has extra dimensions absent in parameter estimation in purely probabilistic models. In addition to estimating parameters that specify a probability distribution over the variables, causal models present the problem of estimating parameters that specify the probability distributions that will result from various possible interventions.

Especially in econometrics, but also in other subjects, parameter estimation is beset by varieties of the identification problem; for example, for many models there may exist no unique maximum likelihood estimate of a parameter, either because no such estimate exists or because many do. Recent simulation algorithms for computing posterior probabilities offer an interesting path to estimating parameters in under identified models: prior probabilities are imposed on the parameters and then, through simulation, good approximations to posterior probabilities are computed.

The three chapters in this section explore alternative approaches to these parameter estimation problems, including the Bayesian approach. They are illustrated by applications to interesting—and in the case of Scheines's chapter, historically very important—data sets.

CHAPTER TWELVE

Testing and Estimation of Direct Effects by Reparameterizing Directed Acyclic Graphs with Structural Nested Models

James M. Robins

The standard way to parameterize the distributions represented by a directed acyclic graph is to insert a parametric family for the conditional distribution of each random variable given its parents. In this chapter, I show that when the goal is to test for or estimate the direct effect of a treatment, this natural parameterization has serious deficiencies. Furthermore, in most settings, the no direct-effect null hypothesis does not entail any conditional independence restrictions and thus cannot be tested using computer programs designed to search for conditional independencies in the data. By reparameterizing the graph using direct-effect structural nested models, these problems can be overcome. A direct-effect structural nested model is a causal model for the direct effect of a final brief blip of treatment on the outcome of interest.

1. Introduction

Consider a set of random variables $V = (X_1, ..., X_M)$ whose joint density $f(v)$ is represented by a directed acyclic graph (DAG) G. If Pa_m represents the parents of X_m, then the density factorizes as

$$f(v) = \prod_{m=1}^{M} f(x_m \mid pa_m). \tag{1}$$

In practice, in order to estimate $f(v)$ from independent realizations V_i, $i = 1, ..., n$, obtained on n study subjects, one often needs to assume some particular parametric form for each $f(x_m \mid pa_m)$. Thus one writes

$$f(v) = \prod_{n=1}^{M} f\left(x_m \mid pa_m; \, \theta_m\right)$$

where θ_m is an element of the parameter space θ_m, an open subset of a finite dimensional Euclidean space. For example, suppose the parent of X_2 is X_1. Then $p(x_2 \mid pa_2; \, \theta_2)$ might be $N(\beta_0 + \beta_1 x_1, \, \sigma^2)$ so that $\theta_2 = (\beta_0, \beta_1, \sigma)$. In general, if one inserts a parametric family $f(x_m \mid pa_m; \, \theta_m)$ into the right-hand side of each term of equation 1 and the θ_m are variation independent, we call this a standard parameterization of the DAG. This seems to be the usual way of using DAGs in practice. The parameters θ_m are said to be variation independent if the joint parameter space for $\theta = (\theta_1', \ldots, \theta_M')'$ is the product space $\theta_1 \times \theta_2 \times \ldots \times \theta_M$.

As natural as it seems to parameterize a DAG in this way, there are problems with the standard parameterization when one's goal is to test for or estimate the direct effect of a treatment or control variable. This has been noted by Robins (1986, 1997). The next section gives a simple example that illustrates the problem. In this simple example, the goal is to test for and estimate the direct effect of an AIDS drug, prophylaxis therapy (A_P), on serum HIV RNA levels (Y) among AIDS patients, many of whom also receive a second active AIDS therapy, AZT (A_Z).

Briefly put, the problem is this: Suppose the DAG G represents treatments and covariates in a longitudinal study. Further suppose that the partial ordering of the variables in V entailed by the DAG G is consistent with the temporal ordering of the variables. The goal is to test for a direct effect of A_P treatment on the outcome Y when A_Z is held fixed. In certain settings, such as a sequential randomized trial, the null hypothesis of "no direct treatment effect," although identifiable based on the observed data, cannot be tested simply by testing for the presence or absence of arrows in the DAG G as one might expect. These conditions, far from being pathological, are indeed likely to hold in most real examples. Fortunately, the direct-effect null hypothesis can be tested by examining a particular integral called the "G-computation algorithm functional." The null is true if this integral satisfies a certain complex condition. Indeed, this complex condition does not entail any conditional independence restrictions on the joint distribution of the observed variables and thus cannot be tested using programs such as Tetrad (Spirtes, Glymour, and Scheines 1993) that test for conditional independencies (Robins 1986; Verma and Pearl 1991; Spirtes, Glymour, and Scheines 1993). Furthermore, theorem 2 proves that there is an additional complication. Specifically, common choices for the parametric families in a standard parameterization often lead to joint densities such that the integral can never satisfy the required condition; as a consequence, in large samples, the null hypothesis of no direct treatment effect, even when true, will be falsely rejected regardless of the data. These problems are exacerbated in high dimensional problems. In summary, currently available methods cannot be used to test for direct treatment effects.

I propose a new class of tests, the direct-effect g-tests, of the hypothesis of no direct effect of a (possibly time-varying sequential) treatment A_P on an outcome Y when a second treatment A_Z is held fixed. A direct-effect g-test reweights the g-null test (Robins 1986) of conditional independence of A_P and Y by the inverse of the probability of receiving treatment A_Z. When the direct-effect g-test rejects, it is of interest to estimate the magnitude of the effect of A_P on Y when treatment A_Z is held fixed at a specified value a_Z. In order to do so, I introduce the class of direct-effect structural nested models (SNMs). A direct-effect SNM models the effect of a final brief blip of treatment with A_P at time t on Y when A_Z is set to a_Z. Direct-effect SNMs offer a unified approach to testing for and estimation of direct effects. This unified approach uses a class of robust semiparametric tests and estimators, the direct-effect g-tests and estimators, for the parameter ψ of a direct-effect SNM. These tests and estimators are semiparametric in the sense that they only require that one specify a parametric model for the probability of treatment with A_P and A_Z given their parents on the DAG.

In contrast to this approach, in the graphical modeling literature, the usual approach to estimation is to (1) specify a fully parametric model for the distribution of the DAG and (2) then estimate parameters of interest either by maximum likelihood or Bayesian methods. In this spirit, I describe a complete reparameterization of the distribution of the DAG with a direct-effect structural nested model for the effect of A_P on Y with A_Z set to a_Z as one component. A second component of the reparameterization is a marginal structural model (Robins 1999, 1998) for the effect of A_Z on Y when A_P is withheld. This reparameterization allows a fully parametric likelihood or Bayesian approach to testing for and estimation of direct effects. I compare the strengths and weaknesses of the semiparametric approach with this fully parametric approach and ultimately recommend a mixed approach that combines the best aspects of both.

I study two different direct-effect structural nested models, direct-effect structural nested mean models (SNMMs) and direct-effect structural nested distribution models (SNDMs). The SNMMs model the direct effect of a treatment A_P on the mean of the outcome Y, whereas the SNDMs model the direct effect of A_P on the entire distribution of Y. SNDMs are only appropriate if the outcome Y is continuous, whereas SNMMs can be used to analyze both discrete and continuous responses. The direct-effect SNMs differ from the standard SNMs discussed in Robins (1989, 1993, 1995, 1997) and Robins and Wasserman (1997). I introduce direct-effect SNMs because, as shown by Robins and Wasserman (1997), the standard SNDMs are not adequate to test for and/or estimate direct effects except in special cases. Specifically, in section 12, I show that the standard SNDMs are adequate to test for and estimate the direct effect of A_P when A_Z is held fixed only if the magnitude of the effect of A_Z on Y is not modified by pretreatment covariates.

Finally, I note that the direct-effect SNMs introduced in this chapter differ from the direct-effect SNMs introduced in appendix 3 of Robins (1997). I recommend that an analyst use the direct-effect SNMs of this chapter rather than those of Robins (1997), because the direct-effect SNMs introduced here, in contrast to those of Robins (1997), admit robust semiparametric direct-effect g-tests and estimates. However, the direct-effect SNMs introduced here are intrinsically asymmetric, in that, in contrast to the models in Robins (1997), a single model cannot be used to simultaneously test for a direct effect of A_P fixing A_Z and for a direct effect of A_Z fixing A_P.

1.1 An Example

To illustrate the problem at hand, consider the generic example of a sequential randomized clinical trial (figure 1) depicted by DAG 1a in which data have been collected on variables $V = (A_0, A_1, L, Y)$ on each of n AIDS patients. The continuous variable A_0 represents the dose in milligrams of prophylaxis therapy for PCP (AIDS pneumonia) received by AIDS patients at time t_0; the continuous variable A_1 represents the dose in milligrams of AZT received at time t_1; the dichotomous variable L records whether a patient developed PCP in the interval from t_0 to t_1; the continuous variable Y represents a subject's HIV viral load measured at end-of-follow-up; and the hidden (unmeasured) variable U denotes a patient's underlying immune function at the beginning of the study. U is a measure of a patient's underlying health status.

The prophylaxis therapy dose A_0 was assigned at random to subjects at time t_0 so, by design, $A_0 \perp\!\!\!\perp U$. AZT treatment A_1 was randomly assigned at time t_1 with randomization probabilities that depend on the observed past (A_0, L), so, by design $U \perp\!\!\!\perp A_1 \mid A_0, L$. For simplicity, I shall assume that no other unmeasured common causes (confounders) exist. That is, each arrow in DAG 1a represents the direct causal effect of a parent on its child, as in Pearl and Verma (1991) or Spirtes, Glymour, and Scheines (1993). Note DAG 1a is not complete because of three missing arrows: the arrows from U to A_0 and A_1 and the arrow from L to Y. The arrows from U are missing by design. The missing arrow from L to Y represents a priori biological knowledge that L has no effect on HIV viral load Y. (The missing arrow from L to Y is not essential to what follows and is assumed to simplify the exposition.) Hence, by the Markov properties of a DAG, we know that $L \perp\!\!\!\perp Y \mid A_0, A_1, U$. It is known that A_0 causes PCP, so $A_0 \not\!\perp\!\!\!\perp L$. It is also known that the unmeasured variable U has a direct effect on L and Y, i.e., U causes both PCP and an elevated HIV RNA. Finally, we suppose it is known that AZT has a direct effect on the outcome Y. That is, there is an arrow from A_1 to Y and so $A_1 \not\!\perp\!\!\!\perp Y \mid L, A_0, U$.

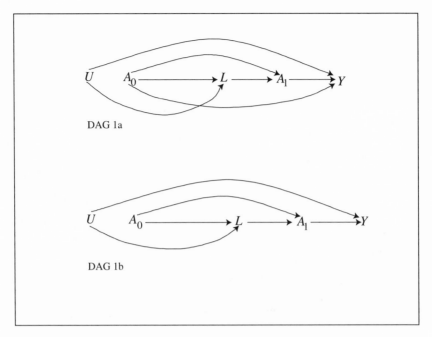

Figure 1. Generic example of a sequential randomized clinical trial.

1.2 Representing the Direct-Effect Null Hypothesis

Suppose the trial data have been collected in order to test the null hypothesis that prophylaxis therapy A_0 has no direct effect on viral load Y. This "no-direct-effect null" hypothesis is the hypothesis that the arrow from A_0 to Y in DAG 1a is missing, which would imply that the true causal graph generating the data was DAG 1b. The alternative to this null hypothesis is that the true causal graph generating the data is graph 1a.

Following Pearl and Verma (1991) and Spirtes, Glymour, and Scheines (1993), we assume the joint distribution of (V, U) is faithful to the true graph where $V = (A_0, A_1, L, Y)$. That is, if B, C, and D are distinct (possibly empty) subsets of the variables in (V, U), then B is independent of C given D if and only if B is d-separated from C given D on the true causal graph generating the data. It follows that the "no-direct-effect null hypothesis" of DAG 1b is true if and only if $A_0 \perp\!\!\!\perp Y \mid A_1, L, U$. Indeed, since we have assumed no arrows from L to Y, $A_0 \perp\!\!\!\perp Y \mid A_1, L, U$ *is* equivalent to the hypothesis $A_0 \perp\!\!\!\perp Y \mid A_1, U$. The question is: can we still characterize the null hypothesis even if U is not observed? The answer is yes, according to the following theorem.

THEOREM 1.1. Suppose the distribution of (V, U) is faithful to either DAG 1a or 1b, one of which generated the data. Then, the direct-effect

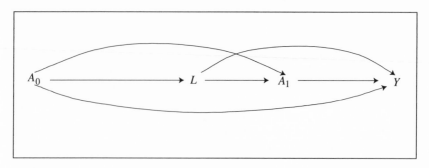

Figure 2. DAG 2.

null hypothesis $A_0 \perp\!\!\!\perp Y \mid A_1$, U holds (i.e., DAG 1b generated the data) if and only if

$$\sum_{\ell=0}^{1} f(y \mid a_0, a_1, \ell) f(\ell \mid a_0) \text{ does not depend on } a_0. \tag{2}$$

Thus, even though U is unobserved, we can still tell if the null holds by checking equation 2, which only involves the observables.

Remark. Even without imposing faithfulness, $A_0 \coprod Y \mid A_1$, U implies equation 2, although the converse is no longer true. Note

$$\sum_{\ell=0}^{1} f(y \mid a_0, a_1, \ell) f(\ell \mid a_0)$$

is the marginal density of Y in the manipulated subgraph (Spirtes, Glymour, and Scheines 1993) of the complete DAG (figure 2) for the observed data V = (A_0, A_1, L, Y) in which arrows into A_0 and A_1 have been removed and (A_0, A_1) set to (a_0, a_1). Robins (1986) refers to this marginal density as the *g-computational algorithm formula* for the effect of (A_0, A_1) on Y. Because U has no arrows into A_0 or A_1, theorem 1.1 is a special case of theorem F.3 of Robins (1986). See also Pearl and Robins (1995).

By the *d*-separation criterion applied to DAG 1a and 1b, we see that if either of DAGs 1a or 1b generated the data, then the joint distribution of V is represented by the complete DAG 2 without missing arrows. The additional restriction (equation 2) that distinguishes the no-direct-effect hypothesis of DAG 1b from DAG 1a is not representable by removing arrows from DAG 2. This is an important observation because a common way of testing the direct-effect null hypothesis is to test for the absence of an arrow from A_0 to Y and to test $A_0 \coprod Y \mid L, A_1$; I call this the "naive test." This test is incorrect. Specifically, if the no-direct-effect hypothesis of DAG 1b is correct and the distribution of V, U is faithful, then $A_0 \coprod Y \mid L, A_1$ will be false, and the naive test will falsely reject the no direct-effect null hypothesis with probability converging to one in large samples.

Thus, testing the null hypothesis of no direct effect of prophylaxis therapy

A_0 cannot be accomplished by testing for the presence or absence of arrows on DAG 2. This is because the arrows of the marginal DAG 2 do not have a causal interpretation (even though the arrows on the underlying causal DAG do have a causal interpretation). Indeed, by applying the d-separation criteria to DAG 1b, we discover that DAG 1b does not entail any conditional independence restrictions among the observed variables V. Thus, the direct-effect null hypothesis of DAG 1b cannot be distinguished from the alternative DAG 1a by a search program such as Tetrad that uses conditional independence relations among the observed variables V to distinguish between underlying causal graphs (Robins 1986; Verma and Pearl 1991; Spirtes, Glymour, and Scheines 1993, page 193). One solution to this problem is to test equation 2 directly. With standard parameterizations, this approach will also fail, as the next section shows. In section 2, I derive an appropriate alternative test of equation 2, the direct-effect g-test.

1.3 The Problem with Standard Parameterizations

We saw that to test the null hypothesis, it does not suffice to test whether the arrow in DAG 2 from A_0 to Y is broken. Rather, we need to test equation 2. I now show that such a test will falsely reject if one uses a standard parameterization. To test the null hypothesis (equation 2), the standard approach is to first specify parametric models for the conditional distribution of each parent given its children in the complete DAG 2 representing the observed data.

Hence let $\{f(y \mid a_0, a_1, \ell; \theta); \theta \in \Theta \subset R^q\}$ and $\{f(\ell \mid a_0; \gamma); \gamma \in \Gamma \subset R^p\}$ denote parametric models for the unknown densities $f(y \mid a_0, a_1, \ell)$ and $f(\ell \mid a_0)$. Of course, we cannot guarantee these models are correctly specified. We say the model $f(y \mid a_0, a_1, \ell; \theta)$ is correctly specified if there exists $\theta_0 \in \Theta$ such that $f(y \mid a_0, a_1, \ell; \theta_0)$ is equal to the true (but unknown) density $f(y \mid a_0, a_1, \ell)$ generating the data. Results in this section require the concept of linear faithfulness. The distribution of (V, U) is linearly faithful to the true causal graph generating the data, if for any disjoint (possibly empty) subsets B, C, and D of the variables in (V, U), B is d-separated from C given D on the graph if and only if the partial correlation matrix $r_{BC.D}$ between B and C given D is the zero matrix. If (V, U) is jointly normal, linear faithfulness and faithfulness are equivalent. For (V, U) nonnormal, neither implies the other. However, the argument that the distribution of (V, U) should be linearly faithful to the generating causal DAG is essentially identical to the argument that the distribution should be faithful to the generating causal DAG given by Spirtes, Glymour, and Scheines (1993) and Pearl and Verma (1991).

To see why standard parameterizations may not work, consider a specific example. Recall that Y is continuous and that L is binary. Commonly used models in these cases are normal linear regression models and logistic regression models. Thus suppose that we adopt the following models:

$$Y \mid a_0, a_1, \ell; \theta, \sigma^2 \sim N(\theta_0 + \theta_1 a_0 + \theta_2 \ell + \theta_3 a_1, \sigma^2) \tag{3}$$

and

$$f(\ell = 1 \mid a_0; \gamma) = expit(\gamma_0 + \gamma_1 a_0) \tag{4}$$

where $expit(b) = e^b / (1 + e^b)$ and $N(\mu, \sigma^2)$ denotes a normal distribution with mean μ and variance σ^2. I now prove the following results.

LEMMA 1.1. If the no-direct-effect null hypothesis represented by DAG 1b is true and the distribution of (V, U) is either faithful or linearly faithful to DAG 1b, then equation 3 and/or equation 4 is guaranteed to be misspecified; that is, the set of distributions $\mathcal{F}_{par}$ for V satisfying equations 3–4 is disjoint from the set $\mathcal{F}_{mar}$ of distributions that are marginals of distributions for (V, U) that are either faithful or linearly faithful to DAG 1b.

Since equation 3 and/or equation 4 are guaranteed to be misspecified under the no-direct-effect null hypothesis, one might expect that tests of the null assuming equations 3–4 will perform poorly. This expectation is borne out by the following theorem.

THEOREM 1.2. Suppose (1) the data analyst tests the no-direct-effect null hypothesis using the parametric models (equations 3 and 4) fit by the method of maximum likelihood, (2) the no-direct-effect null hypothesis represented by DAG 1b is true, (3) the distribution of (V, U) is linearly faithful to DAG 1b. Then, with probability converging to 1, the no-direct-effect null hypothesis (equation 2) will be falsely rejected.

Theorem 1.2 implies that if we use the parametric models (equations 3 and 4), then in large samples we will reject the no-direct-effect null hypothesis, even when true, for nearly all data sets (i.e., with probability approaching 1). That is, by specifying equations 3 and 4, we will have essentially rejected the no direct effect null hypothesis, when true, even before seeing the data!

Proof of theorem 1.2 and lemma 1.1. The following proof of theorem 1.2 also proves lemma 1.1. Note equation 2 implies that

$$b(a_0, a_1) \equiv \sum_{\ell=0}^{1} E[Y \mid \ell, a_0, a_1] f(\ell \mid a_0) \tag{5}$$

does not depend on a_0. Now, under equations 3 and 4, the maximum likelihood estimator of $b(a_0, a_1)$ is

$$b(a_0, a_1; \hat{\theta}, \hat{\gamma}) = \hat{\theta}_0 + \hat{\theta}_1 a_0 + \hat{\theta}_3 a_1 + \left\{ \hat{\theta}_2 e^{\hat{\gamma}_0 + \hat{\gamma}_1 a_0} \right\} / \left\{ 1 + e^{\hat{\gamma}_0 + \hat{\gamma}_1 a_0} \right\}$$

where the maximum likelihood estimators $\hat{\theta}, \hat{\gamma}$ satisfy the normal and logistic score equations $\sum_{i=1}^{n}(Y_i - \hat{\theta} Z_i) Z_i = 0$ and $0 = \sum_{i=1}^{n}\{L_i - expit(\hat{\gamma}_0 + \hat{\gamma}_1 A_{0i})\}$ $(1, A_{0i})'$ where $Z_i = (1, A_{0i}, L_i, A_{1i})'$, $\theta' = (\theta_0, \theta_1, \theta_2, \theta_3)$, and $\gamma' = (\gamma_0, \gamma_1)$. Further, the probability limits θ^* and γ^* of $\hat{\theta}$ and $\hat{\gamma}$ satisfy $E[\{Y_i - \theta^* Z_i\} Z_i] = 0$ and $E[\{L_i - expit(\gamma_0^* + \gamma_1^* A_{0i})\}(1, A_{0i})'] = 0$, where the expectations are with respect to the true distribution generating the data regardless of whether equations 3 and 4 are correctly specified. The MLE $b(a_0, a_1; \hat{\theta}, \hat{\gamma})$ converges in probability to $b(a_0, a_1, \theta^*, \gamma^*)$. It follows that an analyst using equations 3 and 4 fit by maximum likelihood will reject equation 2 with probability approaching 1 as $n \to \infty$ if $b(a_0, a_1; \theta^*, \gamma^*)$ depends on a_0. I now prove such a dependence by contradiction.

It is clear that $b(a_0, a_1; \theta^*, \gamma^*)$ does not depend on a_0 if and only if either (1) $\theta_1^* = \theta_2^* = 0$, or (2) $\theta_1^* = \gamma_1^* = 0$. However, it follows from standard least squares theory that point 1 is true if and only if the partial correlations between Y and A_0 and between Y and L given A_1 are both zero. But this contradicts the assumption that the distribution of (V, U) is linearly faithful to DAG 1b since both Y and L and Y and A_0 are not d-separated conditional on A_1. Similarly, if point 2 is true, then $\gamma_1^* = 0$. But an easy calculation shows that $\gamma_1^* = 0$ if and only if $cov(L, A_0) = 0$. However, $cov(L, A_0) = 0$ contradicts the linear faithfulness assumption since L and A_0 are not d-separated on DAG 1b. The argument in this last paragraph also proves lemma 1.1.

Remark. One might conjecture that the problem could be solved by adding a small number of interaction terms to the model. However, using reasoning like that above, one can show that this is not the case.

2. The Direct-Effect *g*-Null Test

An appropriate approach to testing the direct-effect null hypothesis is based on the following theorem, which is a special case of theorem 5.1 below. We assume $f(a_1 \mid L, A_0) > 0$ with probability one for all a_1 in the support of A_1.

THEOREM 2.1 (direct effect *g*-null theorem). Equation 2 is true if and only if for any function $t(\cdot, \cdot)$

$E[t(Y, A_1) / f(A_1 \mid L, A_0) \mid A_0]$ does not depend on A_0 w.p.1   (6)

whenever the expectation is finite. Here w.p.1 means "with probability 1."

Proof. By Fubini's theorem, the expectation in equation 6 can be written

$$\int \left\{ \int t(y, a_1) \left[\sum_{\ell=0}^{1} f(y \mid \ell, a_1, A_0) f(\ell \mid A_0) \right] dy \right\} da_1 .$$

Comparing the expression in brackets with equation 2 and recalling that $t(y, a_1)$ is arbitrary proves the theorem.

Theorems 2.1 and 1.1 together then have the following corollary.

COROLLARY 2.1. Under the suppositions of theorem 1.1, the direct effect null hypothesis

$$A_0 \coprod Y \mid A_1, \ U \quad \text{i.e.,} \quad f(y \mid a_0, a_1, u) = f(y \mid a_1, u) \tag{7}$$

is true if and only if equation 6 is true.

Remark. The theorem and corollary remain true if we restrict attention to the set of functions $t(y, a_1)$ that factor as

$$t(y, a_1) = t_1(y) t_2(a_1) \ . \tag{8}$$

Indeed, they remain true if we, in addition, require $t_2(a_1)$ to be a density, i.e.,

$$1 = \int t_2(a_1) \, da_1 \ . \tag{9}$$

Because of the fundamental importance of corollary 2.1, I reprove the corollary with $t(y, a_1)$ satisfying equations 8 and 9 using a proof that should be particularly helpful to readers familiar with testing hypotheses about DAGs using d-separation and conditional independence.

Alternative proof of corollary 2.1. Let DAG 1a* and DAG 1b* be "manipulated subgraphs" of DAGs 1a and 1b in which all arrows into A_1 have been removed and equip DAG 1a* with the density $f^*(v, u) = f(u) f(a_0) f(\ell \mid a_0, u)$ $t_2(a_1) f(y \mid a_0, a_1, u)$ where $t_2(a_1)$ is the new marginal density for the now parentless variable A_1 and the remaining factors in $f^*(v, u)$ are the same as in the density $f(v, u)$ of the true causal DAG 1a. Suppose, for the moment, that DAG 1a* or 1b* generated the data with density $f^*(v, u)$. If the null hypothesis (equation 7) is true, then there is no arrow from A_0 to Y and DAG 1b* generated the data. By d-separation applied to DAG 1b*, the null hypothesis (equation 7) now implies the conditional independence restriction that $A_0 \coprod Y$ under $f^*(v, u)$. Given faithfulness, the converse also is true. Now it is well known that $A_0 \coprod Y$ under $f^*(v, u)$ if and only if for all functions $t_1(y)$

$$E^* [t_1(Y) \mid A_0] \text{ does not depend on } A_0 \text{ w.p.1} \tag{10}$$

where $E^*(\bullet)$ denotes expectations with respect to $f^*(v, u)$ and $E(\bullet)$ denotes expectations with respect to the true density $f(v, u)$. Since the direct-effect null hypothesis (equation 7) is the same under $f^*(v, u)$ as under $f(v, u)$, corollary 2.1 will be proved if the following can be established.

LEMMA 2.1. Equation 10 is true if and only if equation 6 is true for $t(y, a_1)$ satisfying equations 8 and 9.

Proof of lemma. Writing out equation 10 explicitly, one obtains

$$\sum_{\ell=0}^{1} \iint t_1(y) f(y \mid a_1, A_0, \ell) t_2(a_1) f(\ell \mid A_0) \, dy \, da_1$$

does not depend on A_0 w.p.1. \hfill (11)

Now, upon multiplying the integrand in equation 11 by $1 = f(a_1 \mid \ell, A_0) / f(a_1 \mid \ell, A_0)$, equation 10 may be rewritten as

$$\sum_{\ell=0}^{1} \iint \left\{ t_1(y) \, t_2(a_1) / f(a_1 \mid \ell_1, A_0) \right\} f(y \mid a_1, A_0, \ell_0) \, f(a_1 \mid \ell, A_0) \, f(\ell \mid A_0) \, dy \, da_1$$

(12)

which is precisely equation 6.

The direct-effect g-null theorem implies that any test of the conditional independence of Y and A_0 (linear in Y) that one would have used to test the direct-effect null hypothesis had A_1 been parentless can still be used to test the null hypothesis when A_1 has parents L and A_0 provided, when calculating the test statistic, Y is replaced by $\mathcal{W} = Y \, t_2(A_1) / f(A_1 \mid L, A_0)$ or, even more generally, by $t(A_1, Y) / f(A_1 \mid L, A_0)$ where $t_2(A_1)$ and $t(A_1, Y)$ are arbitrary functions chosen by the data analyst. This prescription can be followed in a sequential randomized trial where $f(A_1 \mid L, A_0)$ is known by design. In observational studies, $f(A_1 \mid L, A_0)$ will have to be estimated from the data in a preliminary step. I suspect that, after having estimated $f(A_1 \mid L, A_0)$ in a preliminary step, causal search programs such as Tetrad can be modified to allow the analyst to test for direct effects.

As an example, suppose, by design, $A_0 \sim N(\pi_1, 1)$ and $A_1 \mid A_0, L \sim N(\pi_2(A_0, L), 1)$. If we define $U = \{f(A_1 \mid L, A_0)\}^{-1} \, t(Y, A_1) \{A_0 - E(A_0)\}$ where $t(\bullet, \bullet)$ is chosen by the data analyst, then, by the direct-effect g-null theorem, $\sum_{i=1}^{n} U_i$ is a sum of independent and identically distributed random variables that have mean zero under the direct-effect null (equation 2). Therefore, provided U has a finite variance,

$$\chi \equiv \frac{\sum_i U_i}{\left\{ \sum_i U_i^2 \right\}^{\frac{1}{2}}}$$

is asymptotically distributed $N(0, 1)$ under the direct-effect null. Thus the test that rejects when $|\chi| > 1.96$ is an asymptotically .05-level test of this null hypothesis. As discussed later, the power of the test will depend on the choice of the function $t(y, a_1)$. As noted above, a simple alternative to this test is simply to test whether $\mathcal{W}$ and A_0 are correlated using standard software.

Remark. Note if A_1 is discrete, we can choose $t_2(A_1) \equiv 1$. However, if A_1 is continuous, as in our example, $\mathcal{W}$ may not have a finite expectation or variance if $t_2(A_1) \equiv 1$ (since $E(\mathcal{W}) = \int t_2(a_1) \, q(a_1) \, da_1$ with $q(a_1) \equiv \sum_{\ell=0}^{1} \iint y \, f[y \mid \ell, a_0, a_1] \, f(\ell \mid a_0) \, f(a_0) \, dy \, da_0$); in that case, $t_2(A_1)$ needs to be chosen to downweight the tails of $\mathcal{W}$'s distribution so that the expectation and variance of $\mathcal{W}$ will be finite.

There are some important caveats an analyst needs to be aware of. First, the direct effect g-null hypothesis (equation 2) does not imply that $\mathcal{W} \equiv Y t_2(A_1) / f(A_1 \mid L, A_0)$ is independent of A_0. If it were, then for any function $g(\bullet)$, $E[g(\mathcal{W}) \mid A_0]$ would not depend on A_0, which will not be true in general, because $f(A_1 \mid L, A_0)$ may be "bound up" in the possibly nonlinear function $g(\bullet)$. There is also a lack of symmetry, which is not seen with conditional independence. Specifically, the direct-effect g-null hypothesis (equation 2) does imply that $\mathcal{W}$ and A_0 are uncorrelated. However, it does not imply that Y and $\mathcal{W}^* \equiv A_0 t_2(A_1) / f(A_1 \mid L, A_0)$ are uncorrelated, since $E(Y) \, E(\mathcal{W}^*) = E(Y)[\int t_2(a_1) \, da_1] \, E(A_0)$ while $E[Y\mathcal{W}^*] = E[\mathcal{W}A_0] = E[\mathcal{W}]$ $E[A_0] = \{\Sigma_{\ell=0}^1 \int E[Y \mid A_0, a_1, \ell] f(\ell \mid A_0) t_2(a_1)(da_1\} \, E(A_0)$ where, under the direct-effect g-null hypothesis (equation 2), the expression in set braces is a constant independent of A_0.

In observational studies, the densities $f(a_1 \mid a_0, \ell)$ and $f(a_0)$ will not be known and thus $f(a_1 \mid a_0, \ell)$ and $E(A_0)$ will need to be estimated from the observed data V_i, $i = 1, \ldots, n$. As an example, suppose we assume $f(a_0)$ and $f(a_1 \mid \ell, a_0)$ lie in parametric families $\{f(a_0; \alpha^{(0)}); \alpha^{(0)} \in \alpha^{(0)}\}$ and $\{f(a_1 \mid \ell, a_0; \alpha^{(1)}); \alpha^{(1)} \in \alpha^{(1)}\}$. The maximum likelihood estimator $\hat{\alpha} = (\hat{\alpha}^{(0)}, \hat{\alpha}^{(1)})'$ maximizes the likelihood $\mathcal{L}(\alpha) = \prod_{i=1}^{n} f(A_{0i}; \alpha^{(0)}) f(A_{1i} \mid L_i, A_{0i}; \alpha^{(1)})$. Now define $\hat{\chi} \equiv \Sigma_i U_i(\hat{\alpha}) / \hat{v}^{1/2}$ where $\hat{U} \equiv U(\hat{\alpha}) = t(Y, A_1) \{A_0 - E_{\hat{\alpha}^{(0)}} [A_0]\}/ f(A_1 \mid L, A_0; \hat{\alpha}^{(1)})$ and the correction term $\widehat{(corr)} = \hat{\Gamma} \, \hat{I}^{-1} \, \hat{\Gamma}'$ in the estimated variance

$$\hat{v} \equiv \sum_i \hat{U}_i^2 - \widehat{(corr)}$$

accounts for the estimation of the unknown α. Here $\hat{I}$ is the 2×2 matrix of second partial derivatives of log $\mathcal{L}(\alpha)$ evaluated at $\hat{\alpha}$ and $\hat{\Gamma} = \Sigma_i \partial U_i(\hat{\alpha})/ \partial \alpha$. $\hat{\chi}$ remains asymptotically $N(0, 1)$ under the direct-effect null hypothesis (equation 2) provided the models for $f(a_0)$ and $f(a_1 \mid \ell, a_0)$ are correctly specified. In contrast, the p-value outputted by an off-the-shelf software program testing the independence of $\mathcal{W}$ and A_0 will be greater than the true p-value when $f(A_1 \mid L, A_0)$ has been estimated (i.e., the test is conservative), although an appropriate p-value can be simply computed. (In this simple example, it would have been appropriate and simpler to have estimated $E(A_0)$ by $\Sigma_i A_{0i}/n$.)

In contrast to the disturbing results summarized in lemma 1.1, any parametric models for A_0 and $A_1 \mid A_0, L$ are compatible with the direct-effect null hypothesis (equation 2). That is, there exist joint distributions for V under which these parametric models are correctly specified and the direct-effect null hypothesis (equation 2) holds.

We now have valid tests for the no-direct-effect null hypothesis of no effect of prophylaxis therapy A_0 on Y when A_1 is fixed (set) to any particular value a_1, but ultimately we want more. In particular, we would like to estimate the size of the direct effect. To discuss this, we first need to generalize the simple example and then precisely define the direct effect. I do this in sections 3 to 5. Then I introduce direct-effect structural nested models, which provide a unified approach to estimation of and testing for direct effects while avoiding both the problems of standardly parameterized DAGs and of search programs such as Tetrad that rely on conditional independences.

3. The *G*-Computation Algorithm Formula

Let G be a directed acyclic graph with a vertex set of random variables $V = (V_1, \ldots, V_M)$ with associated distribution function $F(v)$ and density function $f(v)$ with respect to the dominating measure μ. Here μ is the product measure of Lebesgue and counting measure corresponding to the continuous and discrete components of V. By the defining Markov property of DAGs, the density of V can be factored

$$\prod_{j=1}^{M} f\left(v_j \mid pa_j\right)$$

where pa_j are realizations of the parents Pa_j of V_j on G. Our results will not require that G has any missing arrows; that is, G may be taken to be complete.

We assume V is partitioned into disjoint sets A, L, and Y where the univariate outcome variable Y is the variable in V with the latest temporal occurrence, $A = \{A_0, \ldots, A_K\}$ are temporally ordered treatments or control variables given at times $t_0, \ldots, t_K$ and $L = \{L_0, L_1, \ldots, L_K\}$ are other response variables. The response variables in L_m are temporally subsequent to A_{m-1} and prior to A_m. As will be clear below, both A_m and L_m may consist of more than one variable. Now for any variable Z, let $\mathscr{Z}$ be the support (i.e., the possible realizations) of Z. For any $z_0, \ldots, z_m$, define $\bar{z}_m = (z_0, \ldots, z_m)$. By convention $\bar{z}_{-1} \equiv z_{-1} \equiv 0$. Now define a treatment regime or plan g to be a collection of $K + 1$ functions $g = \{g_0, \ldots, g_K\}$ where $g_m : \mathscr{L}_m \to \mathscr{A}_m$ maps outcome histories $\bar{\ell}_m \in \mathscr{L}_m$ into a treatment $g_m(\bar{\ell}_m) \in \mathscr{A}_m$. If $g_m(\bar{\ell}_m)$ is a constant, say a_m^*, not depending on $\bar{\ell}_m$ for each m, we say regime g is nondynamic and write $g = \bar{a}^*$, $\bar{a}^* \equiv (a_0^*, \ldots, a_K^*)$. Otherwise, g is dynamic. We let $\mathscr{G}$ be the set of all regimes g.

Associated with each regime g is the "manipulated" graph G_g and distribution $F_g(v)$ with density $f_g(v)$ (Spirtes, Glymour, and Scheines 1993). Given the regime $g = (g_0, g_1, \ldots, g_K)$ and the joint density

$$f(v) = f(\ell_0) f(a_0 \mid \ell_0) f(\ell_1 \mid a_0, \ell_0) f(a_1 \mid \ell_1, a_0, \ell_0) \ldots f(y \mid \bar{\ell}_K, \bar{a}_K) \quad (13)$$

$f_g(v)$ is the density $f(v)$ except that in the factorization (equation 13), $f(a_0 \mid \ell_0)$ is replaced by a degenerate distribution at $a_0 = g_0(\ell_0)$, $f(a_1 \mid \ell_1, a_0, \ell_0)$ is replaced by a degenerate distribution at $a_1 = g_1(\ell_0, \ell_1)$, and, in general, $f(a_k \mid \bar{\ell}_k, \bar{a}_{k-1})$ is replaced by a degenerate distribution at $a_k = g_k(\bar{\ell}_k)$.

In the following, let $g(\bar{\ell}_k) \equiv (g_0(\bar{\ell}_0), \ldots, g_k(\bar{\ell}_k))$ and $g_k(\bar{\ell}_k)$ denote realizations of $\bar{A}_k$ and A_k, respectively. Then the marginal density $f_g(y)$ of Y under the distribution $F_g(\cdot)$ is

$$f_g(y) = \int f_g\left(y, \bar{\ell}_K\right) d\mu\left(\bar{\ell}_K\right) \equiv \int \ldots \int f\left(y \mid \bar{\ell}_K, g(\bar{\ell}_K)\right) \prod_{j=0}^{K} f\left(\ell_j \mid \bar{\ell}_{j-1}, g(\bar{\ell}_{j-1})\right) d\mu\left(\ell_j\right).$$

Similarly, the marginal distribution function of Y under $F_g(\cdot)$ is

$$F_g(y) = \int \ldots \int pr\left[Y < y \mid \bar{\ell}_K, g(\bar{l}_K)\right] \prod_{j=0}^{K} f\left(\bar{\ell}_j \mid \bar{\ell}_{j-1}, g(\bar{\ell}_{j-1})\right) d\mu\left(\ell_j\right). \tag{14}$$

Robins (1986) referred to equation 14 as the G-computation algorithm formula or functional for the effect of regime g on outcome Y. Throughout we assume that for each $g \in \mathcal{G}$, $f(\bar{\ell}_k, g(\bar{\ell}_k)) \neq 0$ implies $f(a \mid \bar{\ell}_k, g(\bar{\ell}_k)) \neq 0$ for all a in the support of A_k so that the right-hand side of equation 14 is well-defined. For A_k continuous, this positivity assumption needs to be slightly modified to properly account for measure theoretic difficulties (Gill and Robins 1997), due to the existence of different versions of conditional distributions. Robins (1986) and Pearl and Robins (1995) give sufficient conditions under which equation 14 has a causal interpretation as the distribution of Y that would be observed if all subjects were treated with (i.e., forced to follow) plan g. A sufficient condition, exemplified by DAG 1a, is the following.

G-*identifiability.* Any hidden variable U that is an ancestor of A_k on the causally sufficient graph generating the data is, for each k, d-separated from A_k conditional on the past $(\bar{L}_k, \bar{A}_{k-1})$.

G-identifiability will hold in any sequential randomized trial and is assumed to hold throughout the remainder of the chapter.

Informally, G-identifiability will be true if all determinants of the outcome Y that are used by patients and physicians to determine the dosage of treatment at each time k are recorded in $(\bar{L}_k, \bar{A}_{k-1})$. It is a primary goal of epidemiologists conducting observational studies to collect data on a sufficient number of covariates in $\bar{L}_k$ to ensure that G-identifiability will hold, at least approximately. However, the assumption of G-identifiability cannot be subjected to an empirical test. G-identifiability is equivalent to the assumption of sequential randomization or, equivalently, of no unmeasured confounders as used in the counterfactual approach to causal inference (Robins 1997).

It should be noted that the approach to causal inference used in this chapter based on causally sufficient DAGs with hidden variables is mathematically equivalent to the approach based on counterfactuals (Robins 1995, 1997, Pearl 1995).

From this point on, the chapter is solely concerned with estimation of and tests concerning the functionals $F_g(y)$. As $F_g(y)$ is a function of the joint distribution of the observed data V, a reader skeptical about causal language and inference is free to regard the remainder of this chapter as simply an exposition as to how one might model and estimate the functionals $F_g(y)$, putting aside why and when one might be interested in these particular functionals.

4. The Direct-Effect "*g*"-Null Hypothesis

In settings where the treatments $\overline{A} \equiv \overline{A}_K = (A_0, \ldots, A_K)$ represent a single type of treatment given at different times, an important first question is whether the "*g*"-null hypothesis of no effect of treatment on Y is true, i.e., whether

$$F_{g_1}(y) = F_{g_2}(y) \text{ for all } y \text{ and all } g_1, g_2 \in \mathcal{G} \qquad (15)$$

Equation 15 is a hypothesis about the distribution of the observable V whether or not the *g*-identifiability assumption holds. When *g*-identifiability holds, equation 15 implies that the distribution of Y will be the same under any choice of regime g, and thus it does not matter whether the treatments A_k are given or withheld at each occasion k. When *g*-identifiability holds, I also refer to equation 15 as the *g*-null hypothesis, the removal of " " from around g indicating that equation 15 now has a causal interpretation.

This chapter will not be concerned with the "*g*"-null hypothesis (equation 15). Rather, I suppose that (1) treatment $A_m = (A_{Pm}, A_{Zm})$ at time t_m comprises two different treatments A_{Pm} and A_{Zm} (e.g., prophylaxis therapy and AZT treatment) and (2) the treatment A_{Zm} is known to affect the outcome Y. The hypothetical trial in section 1.1 is the special case in which $K = 1$, $L_0 \equiv 0$, $L_1 \equiv L$, $A_0 = (A_{P0}, A_{Z0})$ with $A_{Z0} \equiv 0$ for all subjects and $A_1 = (A_{P1}, A_{Z1})$ with $A_{P1} \equiv 0$ for all subjects since no subject received AZT therapy at t_0 or prophylaxis therapy at t_1. In such settings, an important first question is whether there is a direct effect of the treatment $\overline{A}_{PK} \equiv (A_{P0}, \ldots, A_{PK})$ on the outcome Y when the treatment $\overline{A}_{ZK}$ is set to any history $\overline{a}_{ZK}$.

Notational convention. I introduce the convention that the subscripts (k, ℓ, j) generally subscript the times at which treatments are given and the lack of a subscript indicates time t_K. Furthermore, the subscript i will be reserved to index study subjects $i = 1, \ldots, n$. Thus, for example, $\overline{A}_{Zi} \equiv \overline{A}_{ZKi}$ is the AZT history through t_K of subject i. Finally, as above, I will often suppress the subscript i and write $\overline{A}_{Zi}$ as $\overline{A}_Z$. I also introduce the notational convention that for any random variable Z_k, both Z_{-1} and $\overline{Z}_{-1}$ are identically zero.

To formalize the no-direct-effect null hypothesis, let $g_P \equiv (g_{P0}, \ldots, g_{PK})$ be a collection of functions where $g_{Pm} : \mathcal{L}_m \to \mathcal{A}_{Pm}$. Let $\mathcal{G}_P$ be the set of all g_P. Then, for history $\overline{a}_Z \in \mathcal{\overline{A}}_Z$, let $g = (g_P, \overline{a}_Z)$ be the treatment regime or plan given by $g_m(\overline{\ell}_m) = \{g_{Pm}(\overline{\ell}_m), a_{Zm}\}$. Then, given *g*-identifiability, $F_{(g_P, \overline{a}_Z)}(y)$ is the distribution of Y that would be observed if $\overline{A}_Z$ was set to $\overline{a}_Z$ and the treatments $\overline{A}_P$ were assigned, possibly dynamically, according to the plan g_P. If g_P is the nondynamic regime $\overline{a}_P$, we write $F_{\overline{a}_P, \overline{a}_Z}(y)$.

DEFINITION. The direct-effect "*g*"-null hypothesis of no direct effect of $\overline{A}_P$ controlling for $\overline{A}_Z$ is the hypothesis

$$F_{g_{P1}, \overline{a}_Z}(y) = F_{g_{P2}, \overline{a}_Z}(y) \qquad (16)$$

for all $\bar{a}_Z$ and $g_{P1}, g_{P2} \in \mathcal{G}_P$.

Remark. Given the *g*-identifiability assumption of section 3, the hypothesis that, on the causally sufficient graph underlying the DAG G, all directed paths from any variable A_{Pm} to Y include some A_{Zk} implies the direct-effect "*g*"-null hypothesis (equation 16). Under a faithfulness assumption, the converse is also true.

An alternative characterization of the direct effect "*g*"-null hypothesis in terms of the conditional distributions $F_g(y \mid \bar{\ell}_k)$ for nondynamic regimes g is provided in the following lemma whose proof is left to the reader.

LEMMA 4.1. The direct effect "*g*"-null hypothesis (equation 16) is true if and only if

$$F_{\bar{a}_P, \bar{a}_Z}(y \mid \bar{\ell}_k) \text{ does not depend on } \underline{a}_{Pk} \equiv (a_{Pk}, \dots, a_{PK}) \tag{17}$$

for all $\bar{a}_P, \bar{a}_Z, y,$ and $\bar{\ell}_k.$

Note $F_g(y \mid \bar{\ell}_k)$ is given by equation 14 except with the product taken from $k + 1$ to K rather than from 0 to K. If we apply this lemma to the simple example in section 1, we recover equation 2. That is, the direct-effect "*g*"-null hypothesis for the observed data $V = (A_0, A_1, L, Y)$ of section 1 is precisely equation 2.

4.1 Failure of the Usual Parameterization for Testing the Direct-Effect "*g*"-Null Hypothesis

In section 1, we saw that it was difficult to test the direct effect "*g*"-null hypothesis (equation 17) using the usual parameterization of a DAG. These problems are exacerbated in the general case. Indeed, there are several difficulties. First, even if the densities appearing in the *G*-computation formula (equation 14) were known for each $g \in \mathcal{G}$, since $F_g(y)$ is a high-dimensional integral, in general, it cannot be analytically evaluated for any g and, thus, must be evaluated by a Monte Carlo integral approximation—the Monte Carlo *G*-computation algorithm (Robins 1987, 1989). Second, even if $F_g(y)$ could be well-approximated for each regime g, the cardinality of the set $\mathcal{G}$ is enormous (growing at faster than an exponential rate in K [Robins 1989]). Thus it would be computationally infeasible to evaluate $F_g(y)$ for all g necessary to determine whether the direct-effect "*g*"-null hypothesis held.

However, as we saw in section 1, the most fundamental difficulty with the usual parameterization of a DAG in terms of the densities $f(v_j \mid pa_j)$ is that if we use standard parametric models for $f(v_j \mid pa_j)$, (1) there is no parameter, say ψ, which takes the value zero if and only if the direct-effect "*g*"-null hypothesis is true, and (2) the direct-effect "*g*"-null hypothesis, even when true, may, with probability approaching 1, be rejected in large samples.

5. Direct-Effect *g*-Null Tests

As in the special case discussed in section 1, an appropriate approach to testing the direct-effect "*g*"-null hypothesis is based on the following theorem, which is a corollary of theorems 10.1 and 10.2 below. However, since theorem 5.1 is perhaps the key result of this chapter, I provide an independent proof in section 5.2 below. This proof contains many of the important ideas of this chapter. The proof is similar to the alternative proof of corollary 2.1 above, except it avoids appealing to an underlying causally sufficient graph generating the data.

For any variable $\overline{X} = \overline{X}_K$, let $\underline{X}_m \equiv (X_m, ..., X_K)$ and let $W_m = \prod_{k=m}^K f(A_{Zk} | \overline{A}_{k-1}, \overline{L}_k)$. By convention $W_{K+1} \equiv 1$.

THEOREM 5.1 (direct-effect "*g*"-null theorem). The direct-effect "*g*"-null hypothesis (equation 17) is true if and only if for each m, $m = 0, ..., K$, and each function $T_m = t_m(Y, \underline{A}_{Z(m+1)})$,

$$E[T_m / W_{m+1} | \overline{A}_m, \overline{L}_m] \text{ does not depend on } A_{Pm} \text{ w.p.1} \qquad (18)$$

whenever the expectation is finite.

We can use equation 18 to construct tests of the direct-effect "*g*"-null hypothesis. I first provide, in theorem 5.2 below, a quite general approach to testing equation 18. I then suggest a practical approach that allows the analyst to test equation 18 using easily available off-the-shelf software.

General approach to testing. First consider a sequential randomized trial where $f(A_m | \overline{A}_{m-1}, \overline{L}_m)$ and thus $f[A_{Pm} | A_{Zm}, \overline{A}_{m-1}, \overline{L}_m]$, $f[A_{Zm} | \overline{A}_{m-1}, \overline{L}_m]$ and W_{m+1} are known. Let $T_m^*(A_{Pm}, Y) \equiv t_m^*(A_{Pm}, Y, \underline{A}_{Zm}, \overline{A}_{m-1}, \overline{L}_m)$ be a function chosen by the data analyst. Now define $U_m = \{T_m^*(A_{Pm}, Y) - \int T_m^*(a_{Pm}, Y) \, dF [a_{Pm} | A_{Zm}, \overline{A}_{m-1}, \overline{L}_m]\} / W_{m+1}$ and let $U_\bullet = \sum_{m=0}^K U_m$. Then, by the direct-effect "*g*"-null theorem, we obtain the following result.

THEOREM 5.2. If the direct-effect "*g*"-null hypothesis (equation 17) is true and $var(U_\bullet) < \infty$, then $E(U_\bullet) = 0$ and $\chi \equiv \sum_i U_{\bullet i} / [\sum_i U_{\bullet i}^2]^{1/2}$ converges to a $N(0, 1)$ random variable.

It follows from theorem 5.2 that the so-called direct-effect *g*-test that rejects when $|\chi| > 1.96$ is an asymptotically .05-level test of equation 17. The power of the test depends on the choice of the function t_m^*, as discussed later. The test given in section 2 is the special case of the test χ with $K = 1$, $A_{Z1} \equiv A_1$, $A_{P0} \equiv A_0$, $T_0^*(A_{P0}, Y) \equiv t(A_1, Y) A_0$ and $T_1^*(A_{P1}, Y) \equiv 0$.

In an observational study, we would (1) specify a parametric model

$$f(A_k | \overline{A}_{k-1}, \overline{L}_k; \alpha)$$

for the now unknown densities $f[A_k | \overline{A}_{k-1}, \overline{L}_k]$, then (2) replace the unknown densities in the definition of W_{m+1} and U_m by their maximum likelihood estimates obtained by maximizing the likelihood $\mathcal{L}(\alpha) = \prod_{i=1}^n \prod_{m=0}^K$

$f(A_{ki} \mid \overline{A}_{(k-1)i}, \overline{L}_{ki}; \alpha)$ over α, and (3) redefine $\hat{\chi} = \Sigma_i U_{\bullet i}(\hat{\alpha}) / \hat{\upsilon}$, where $U_{\bullet i} \equiv U_{\bullet i}(\alpha_0)$ and the variance estimator $\hat{\upsilon}$ appropriately adjusts for estimation of α. Specifically, $\hat{\upsilon} = \Sigma_i \hat{D}_i(0) \hat{D}_i'(0)$ where $\hat{D}_i(0)$ is defined following equation 33.

5.1 Practical Approach to Testing

I describe a practical approach to testing (equation 18) that only requires access to easily available off-the-shelf software. Further, the approach has the advantage that we only need to correctly specify a model for the conditional mean of A_{Pm} given A_{Zm}, $\overline{A}_{m-1}$, $\overline{L}_{m-1}$ rather than a model for the entire conditional distribution. I describe the approach in several steps.

Step 1. Specify a parametric model $f(A_{Zk} \mid \overline{A}_{k-1}, \overline{L}_k; \alpha^{(1)})$ and calculate the MLE $\hat{\alpha}^{(1)}$ that maximizes $\prod_i \prod_{k=0}^{K} f(A_{Zki} \mid \overline{A}_{(k-1)i}, \overline{L}_{ki}, \alpha^{(1)})$ and let $W_{mi}(\hat{\alpha}^{(1)})$ denote W_{mi} evaluated under the density indexed by $\hat{\alpha}^{(1)}$.

Step 2. For $m = 0, \ldots, K$, specify a model for the conditional mean of A_{Pm} depending on a parameter vector $\alpha^{(0)}$

$$E\left[A_{Pm} \mid A_{Zm} \overline{A}_{m-1}, \overline{L}_m\right] = d\left(\alpha^{(0)'} \mathcal{Q}_m\right), \tag{19}$$

where $\mathcal{Q}_m$ is a known vector function of A_{Zm}, $\overline{A}_{m-1}$, $\overline{L}_m$ and $d(\bullet)$ is a known link function. For example, if A_{Pm} is dichotomous, we might choose $d(x) = \{1 + \exp(-x)\}^{-1}$. If A_{Pm} is continuous, we might choose $d(x) = x$.

Step 3. Compute an α-level test of the hypothesis that $\theta = 0$ in the extended model that adds the term $\theta \mathcal{Q}_m^* = \theta q_m^*(Y, A_{Zm}, \overline{A}_{m-1}, \overline{L}_m, A_{Z(m+1)}) / W_{m+1}(\hat{\alpha}^{(1)})$ to the $\alpha^{(0)'} \mathcal{Q}_m$ in equation 19, where (1) $q_m^*(\bullet)$ is a known function chosen by the data analyst, (2) in testing $\theta = 0$, we treat the $\mathcal{Q}_m^*$ as "fixed covariates" and (3) we use off-the-shelf generalized estimating equation (GEE) software for "clustered" data available in S+ or SAS that regards the $A_{P0}, \ldots, A_{PK}$ on each subject as correlated (i.e., clustered). Often the software will ask the user to specify a so-called working covariance matrix; one can specify the independence covariance matrix.

It can be shown that, if our model for $f(A_{Zk} \mid \overline{A}_{k-1}, \overline{L}_{k-1})$ and equation 19 are correctly specified, then under direct-effect null hypothesis (equation 18), in large samples, the rejection rate of the α-level test in step 3 will be less than or equal to α. That is, the test is "conservative." The reason that the test may reject, even in large samples, at a rate less than its nominal α-level is that the variance computed by the off-the-shelf software programs does not adjust for the effect of estimating $\alpha^{(1)}$ (although it does correctly adjust for the effect of estimating $\alpha^{(0)}$).

All the above tests are referred to as direct-effect g-tests. A direct-effect g-test is a semiparametric test since it only requires we specify a model for $f(A_m \mid \overline{L}_m, \overline{A}_{m-1})$ rather than for the entire joint distribution of the observed data $V = (Y, \overline{L}, \overline{A})$. In an observational study, the g-test is only guaranteed to reject at a rate no greater than its nominal level if the model for $f(A_m \mid \overline{A}_{m-1}, \overline{L}_m)$ is correct. Again, however, in contrast to the disturbing results of lemma 1.1, any model for $f(A_m \mid \overline{L}_m, \overline{A}_{m-1})$ will be compatible with the direct-effect g-null hypothesis (equation 17).

5.2 Proof of Theorem 5.1

First, some definitions. Let DAG G^* be the manipulated subgraph of DAG G in which all arrows into each A_{Zk} have been removed except those from A_{Z0}, ..., $A_{Z(k-1)}$ and equip G^* with the density

$$f^*(v) = t_2(\overline{a}_Z) f\left(y \mid \overline{a}_K, \overline{\ell}_K\right) \prod_{m=0}^{K} f\left(a_{Pm} \mid a_{Zm}, \overline{a}_{m-1}, \overline{\ell}_{m-1}\right) f\left(\ell_m \mid \overline{\ell}_{m-1}, \overline{a}_{m-1}\right)$$

where $t_2(\overline{a}_Z)$ is the new marginal density for the "composite" parentless variable $\overline{A}_Z = (A_{Z0}, ..., A_{ZK})$. The remaining factors are as in the density $f(v)$ of the true DAG G. Asterisks will refer to the DAG G^* and its associated density $f^*(v)$. I now outline the proof.

In the proof of a preliminary lemma, I show that the direct-effect null hypothesis (equation 17) is identical under G^* and G. However, when, as in G^*, $\overline{A}_Z$ is exogenous (parentless), testing for no direct effect of A_P is equivalent for testing for no overall effect of A_P. From my previous work (Robins 1986), it is known how to test for no overall effect. Finally, I show that any test under G^* implies that a corresponding test under G is obtained by reweighting the test statistic by the inverse probability of treatment with $\overline{A}_Z$, i.e., by the W_m's.

LEMMA 5.1. The direct-effect "g"-null hypothesis (equation 16) holds (under $f(v)$) if and only if

$$A_{Pm} \coprod^* \left(Y, \underline{A}_{Z(m+1)}\right) \mid \overline{L}_m, A_{Zm}, \overline{A}_{m-1} \tag{20}$$

where the $\coprod^*$ means independence under the law $f^*(v)$.

Proof. Since $F_{(g_P, \overline{a}_Z)}(y)$ does not depend on the densities $f(a_{Zm} \mid \overline{a}_{m-1}, \overline{\ell}_{m-1})$ modified in $f^*(v)$, we have

$$F^*_{(g_P, \overline{a}_Z)}(y) = F_{(g_P, \overline{a}_Z)}(y) \ . \tag{21}$$

Thus, equation 16 also represents the direct-effect "g"-null hypothesis under DAG G^*. However, because the composite variable $\overline{A}_Z$ is exogenous on DAG G^*, the distribution, under $f^*(v)$, of Y when $\overline{A}_P$ follows plan g_P and $\overline{A}_Z$ is set to plan $\overline{a}_Z$ equals the conditional distribution, given $\overline{A}_Z = \overline{a}_Z$, of Y when $\overline{A}_P$ is set to g_P. That is, by direct calculation,

$$f^*_{(g_P, \overline{a}_Z)}(y) = f^*_{g_P}\left(y \mid \overline{A}_Z = \overline{a}_Z\right) \tag{22}$$

where, by definition, $f^*{}_{gP}(v)$ is the density obtained by replacing in $f^*(v)$ the density $f(a_{Pm} \mid a_{Zm}, \bar{a}_{m-1}, \bar{\ell}_m)$ by a degenerate distribution at $a_{Pm} = g_{Pm}(\bar{\ell}_m)$ for $m = 0, \ldots, K$. Note, and this is why we introduced DAG G^*, equation 22 is false for DAG G. It follows from equation 22 that the direct-effect null hypothesis (equation 16) can be rewritten as

$$F^*_{g_{P1}}\left(y \mid \overline{A}_Z = \bar{a}_Z\right) = F^*_{g_{P2}}\left(y \mid \overline{A}_Z = \bar{a}_Z\right) \text{ for all } g_{P1}, g_{P2} \in \mathcal{G}_P \text{ and all } \bar{a}_Z \quad (23)$$

However, it is easy to show (Robins 1987) that equation 23 is equal to the "g"-null hypothesis of no overall effect of $\overline{A}_P$ on Y.

$$F^*_{g_{P1}}(y) = F^*_{g_{P2}}(y) \text{ for all } g_{P1}, g_{P2} \in \mathcal{G}_P . \quad (24)$$

The g-null theorem of Robins (1986) states that equation 24 is equivalent to

$$A_{Pm} \coprod {}^* Y \mid \overline{L}_m, \overline{A}_{P(m-1)}, \overline{A}_Z . \quad (25)$$

However, by d-separation on DAG G^*, we know

$$\underline{A}_{Z(m+1)} \coprod {}^*\left(\overline{L}_m, \overline{A}_{Pm}\right) \mid \overline{A}_{Zm} .$$

Hence, on DAG G^*, equation 25 is true if and only if equation 20 is true, proving the lemma.

Proof of theorem 5.1. It is well known that equation 20 is true if and only if for all functions $h_m(Y, \underline{A}_{Z(m+1)})$

$$E^*\left[h_m\left(Y, \underline{A}_{Z(m+1)}\right) \mid \overline{A}_m = \bar{a}_m, \overline{L}_m = \bar{\ell}_m\right] \text{ does not depend on } a_{Pm} \text{ w.p.1} \quad (26)$$

whenever the expectation is finite. Writing equation 26 out explicitly, we have

$$\iiint E\left[h_m\left(Y, \underline{a}_{Z(m+1)}\right) \mid \bar{a}_K, \bar{\ell}_K\right]$$
$$\left\{\prod_{k=m+1}^{K} dF\left[\ell_k \mid \bar{\ell}_{k-1}, \bar{a}_{(k-1)}\right] dF\left[a_{Pk} \mid a_{Zk}, \bar{a}_{(k-1)}, \bar{\ell}_k\right] t_2\left(a_{Zk} \mid \bar{a}_{Z(k-1)}\right) d\mu(a_{Zk})\right\} . \quad (27)$$

Multiplying the integral in equation 27 by

$$1 = \frac{\prod_{k=m+1}^{K} f\left(a_{Zk} \mid \bar{\ell}_k, \bar{a}_{k-1}\right)}{\prod_{k=m+1}^{K} f\left(a_{Zk} \mid \bar{\ell}_k, \bar{a}_{k-1}\right)},$$

we obtain

$$\iiint E\left[\frac{h_m\left(Y, \underline{a}_{Z(m+1)}\right)\prod_{k=m+1}^{K} t_2\left(a_{Zk} \mid \bar{a}_{Z(K-1)}\right)}{\left\{\prod_{k=m+1}^{K} f\left(a_{Zk} \mid \bar{\ell}_k, \bar{a}_{k-1}\right)\right\}} \middle| \bar{a}_K, \bar{\ell}_K\right] dF\left(\bar{\ell}_K, \bar{a}_K \mid \bar{a}_m, \bar{\ell}_m\right) ,$$

which equals

$$E\left[T_m \mid W_{m+1} \mid \overline{A}_m = \overline{a}_m, \overline{L}_m = \overline{\ell}_m\right] \text{ with } T_m \equiv h_m\left(Y, \underline{A}_{Z(m+1)}\right) \prod_{k=m+1}^{K} t_2\left(A_{Zk} \mid \overline{A}_{Z(k-1)}\right).$$

Since h_m was arbitrary, T_m is arbitrary as well. This proves the theorem.

6. Direct-Effect "g"-Null Mean Hypothesis

Now I would like to estimate various "direct-effect" contrasts of interest, such as the difference in the distribution functions $F_{(gP1,\overline{a}_Z)}(y) - F_{(gP2,\overline{a}_Z)}(y)$ for regimes g_{P1}, g_{P2}, and $\overline{a}_Z$ of interest. Often, rather than focusing on the contrasts between entire distribution functions, one may be most concerned with its estimating the effect of treatment with $\overline{A}_P$ on the *mean* of Y when $\overline{A}_Z$ is set to some value $\overline{a}_Z$ of interest. That is, we are interested both in the contrast

$$E_{(gP1,\overline{a}_Z)}(Y) - (E_{(gP2,\overline{a}_Z)}(Y) \tag{28}$$

where $E_g(Y) \equiv \int y dF_g(y)$ and in the following direct-effect "g"-null mean hypothesis.

DEFINITION. The direct-effect "g"-null mean hypothesis of no direct effect of $\overline{A}_P$ controlling for $\overline{A}_Z$ is the hypothesis

$$E_{(gP1,\overline{a}_Z)}(Y) = E_{(gP2,\overline{a}_Z)}(Y) \tag{29}$$

for all $\overline{a}_Z$, g_{P1}, g_{P2}.

Note that the direct-effect "g"-null hypothesis (equation 16) implies the direct-effect "g"-null mean hypothesis (equation 29) but the converse is false since treatment with $\overline{A}_P$ could affect the distribution of Y without affecting its mean. Similar to lemma 4.1, we have:

LEMMA. Equation 29 is true if and only if

$$E_{\overline{a}}(Y \mid \overline{\ell}_m) \text{ does not depend on } \underline{a}_{Pm} \tag{30}$$

for all $\overline{a} \equiv (\overline{a}_P, \overline{a}_Z)$, $\overline{\ell}_m$.

A further equivalent characterization is given in the following.

THEOREM 6.1 (direct-effect "g"-null mean theorem). Equation 29 is true if and only if for each m and each function $T_m = Yt_m(\underline{A}_{Z(m+1)}, \overline{A}_m, \overline{L}_m)$ linear in Y, $E[T_m \mid W_{m+1} \mid \overline{A}_m, \overline{L}_m]$ does not depend on A_{Pm}, whenever the expectation exists.

Proof Sketch. The proof is analogous to that given in section 5.2, except that the "g"-null mean hypothesis

$$E^*_{gP1}(Y) = E^*_{gP2}(Y) \tag{31}$$

of G^* is equivalent to the hypothesis $E^*[Y \mid \overline{A}_m, \overline{L}_m, \overline{A}_Z]$ does not depend on

A_{Pm} for each m (Robins 1994, 1997), which replaces equation 25 in the proof. Theorem 6.1 is also a direct corollary of theorems 7.1 and 8.1, which follow.

It follows that the asymptotic α-level test that rejects whenever the direct-effect g-test statistic χ of theorem 5.2 exceeds 1.96 in absolute value is an asymptotic α-level test of the direct-effect g-null mean hypothesis (equation 29) provided $T^*_m(A_{Pm}, Y) \equiv T^*_{m1}(A_{Pm}) Y + T^*_{m2}(A_{Pm})$ used in the definition of χ is linear in Y. Similarly, the off-the-shelf test of section 5.1 can be used, provided we choose q^*_m linear in Y.

I shall now develop a unified approach to testing the direct-effect g-null mean hypothesis (equation 29) and estimating the contrast (equation 28) based on semiparametric g-estimation of direct-effect structural nested mean models (SNMMs). I will then turn to development of a unified approach to testing the direct-effect "g"-null hypothesis (equation 17) and estimating distributional contrasts based on g-estimation of direct-effect structural nested distribution models (SNDMs).

I consider direct-effect structural nested mean models (SNMMs) in addition to direct-effect structural nested distribution models (SNDMs), because (1) the former are conceptually much easier to understand than the latter, (2) SNDMs are defined only for continuous Y whereas SNMMs allow Y to be continuous or discrete, (3) the direct-effect "g"-null mean hypothesis (equation 29) may be of greater subject matter interest than the direct-effect "g"-null hypothesis (equation 16), and (4) mean contrasts are much easier to compute than distributional contrasts.

7. A New Characterization of the Direct-Effect "g"-Null Mean Hypothesis

The first step in defining direct-effect SNMMs is yet another new characterization of the direct-effect "g"-null mean hypothesis (equation 29). Given any treatment history $\bar{a} = (\bar{a}_P, \bar{a}_Z)$ in obvious notation, adopt the convention that the treatment history that (1) agrees with $\bar{a}_Z$ through t_K for $\bar{A}_Z$ and (2) agrees with $\bar{a}_P$ through t_m and is zero thereafter for $\bar{A}_P$ will be denoted $(\bar{a}_{Pm}, \bar{a}_Z)$ or $(\{\bar{a}_{Pm}, 0\}, \bar{a}_Z)$. Denote $E_g(Y \mid \bar{\ell}_m)$ by $b(\bar{\ell}_m, g)$ and $E_g(Y)$ by $b(g)$. Write $b(\bar{\ell}_m, g = (\bar{a}))$ as $b(\bar{\ell}_m, \bar{a}) = b(\bar{\ell}_m, \bar{a}_{Pm}, \bar{a}_Z)$ when $\bar{a} = (\bar{a}_{Pm}, \bar{a}_Z)$. Then define the "blip function"

$$\gamma(\bar{\ell}_m, \bar{a}_{Pm}, \bar{a}_Z) \equiv b(\bar{\ell}_m, \bar{a}_{Pm}, \bar{a}_Z) - b(\bar{\ell}_m, \bar{a}_{P(m-1)}, \bar{a}_Z) .$$

Given the g-identifiability assumption, $\gamma(\bar{\ell}_m, \bar{a}_{Pm}, \bar{a}_Z)$ is the direct effect on the mean of Y of one final blip of A_{Pm} treatment of magnitude a_{Pm} at time t_m among subjects with history $(\bar{a}_{(m-1)}, \bar{\ell}_m)$ when treatment $\bar{A}_Z$ is set to $\bar{a}_Z$. In particular, note the "blip" function satisfies

$$\gamma(\bar{\ell}_m, \bar{a}_{Pm}, \bar{a}_Z) = 0 \text{ if } a_{Pm} = 0 \tag{32}$$

My interest in this function is based on the following theorem.

THEOREM 7.1. $\gamma(\bar{\ell}_m, \bar{a}_{Pm}, \bar{a}_Z) = 0$ for all y, m, $\bar{a}_{Pm}$, $\bar{a}_Z$ if and only if the direct-effect "g"-null mean hypothesis (equation 29) holds.

The theorem is a corollary of theorem 8.6, which follows. It also follows by noting that the direct-effect "g"-null mean hypothesis (equation 29) holds for DAG G if and only if the overall "g"-null mean hypothesis (equation 31) holds for DAG G^*. This later hypothesis holds if and only if $\gamma(\bar{\ell}_m, \bar{a}_{Pm}, \bar{a}_Z) \equiv 0$ by results in Robins (1994, 1997).

8. Direct-Effect SNMMs

In view of theorem 7.1, my approach will be to construct a parametric model for $\gamma(\bar{\ell}_m, \bar{a}_{Pm}, \bar{a}_Z)$ depending on a parameter ψ such that $\gamma(\bar{\ell}_m, \bar{a}_{Pm}, \bar{a}_Z) \equiv 0$ if and only if the true value ψ_0 of the parameter is zero.

Definition. The distribution F of the observables V follows a direct-effect pseudostructural nested mean model for the effect of $\bar{A}_P$ controlling for $\bar{A}_Z$ if $\gamma(\bar{\ell}_m, \bar{a}_{Pm}, \bar{a}_Z) = \gamma(\bar{\ell}_m, \bar{a}_{Pm}, \bar{a}_Z, \psi_0)$ where $\gamma(\bar{\ell}_m, \bar{a}_{Pm}, \bar{a}_Z, \psi)$ is a known function depending on a finite dimensional parameter ψ and $\gamma(\bar{\ell}_m, \bar{a}_{Pm}, \bar{a}_Z, \psi) = 0$ if $a_{Pm} = 0$ or $\psi = 0$, so $\psi_0 = 0$ represents the direct-effect "g"-null hypothesis (equation 29). As just one example, consider the model $\gamma(\bar{\ell}_m, \bar{a}_{Pm}, \bar{a}_Z, \psi) = \psi_1 a_{Pm} + \psi_2 a_{Pm} a_{P(m-1)} + \psi_3 a_{Pm} \ell^*_{m-1} + \psi_4 a_{Pm} a_{ZK}$ where ℓ^*_m is a given univariate function of $\bar{\ell}_m$. When g-identifiability holds, we also refer to $\gamma(\bar{\ell}_m, \bar{a}_{Pm}, \bar{a}_Z, \psi)$ as a direct-effect SNMM, the removal of "pseudo" reflecting the fact that $\gamma(\bar{\ell}_m, \bar{a}_{Pm}, \bar{a}_Z)$ now has a causal interpretation.

I now consider testing and estimation of ψ_0 in the semiparametric model (a) characterized by the restrictions that the law of V follows the direct-effect pseudo-SNMM $\gamma(\bar{\ell}_m, \bar{a}_{Pm}, \bar{a}_Z, \psi)$, and as in a sequential randomized trial, $f(a_m \mid \bar{a}_{m-1}, \bar{\ell}_m)$ is known. This model is referred to as semiparametric since it parameterizes some but not all of the joint distribution of V. My fundamental tool is the following theorem. For any function $\gamma^*(\bar{\ell}_m, \bar{a}_{Pm}, \bar{a}_Z)$ satisfying $\gamma^*(\bar{\ell}_m, \bar{a}_{Pm}, \bar{a}_Z) = 0$ if $a_{Pm} = 0$, define $H(\gamma^*) \equiv Y - \sum_{m=0}^{K} \gamma^*(\bar{L}_m, \bar{A}_{Pm}, \bar{A}_Z)$. The following theorem gives a useful characterization of the true blip function $\gamma(\bar{L}_m, \bar{A}_{Pm}, \bar{A}_Z)$.

THEOREM 8.1. $\gamma^*(\bar{L}_m, \bar{A}_{Pm}, \bar{A}_Z) = \gamma(\bar{L}_m, \bar{A}_{Pm}, \bar{A}_Z)$ w.p.1 if and only if for each $m = 0, \ldots, K$ and any function $t_m(\bullet)$

$$E[t_m(\underline{A}_{Z(m+1)}) H(\gamma^*) / W_{m+1} \mid \bar{A}_m, \bar{L}_m] \text{ does not depend on } A_{Pm} \text{ w.p.1.}$$

Proof. A direct proof is given in section 14. Here I sketch an alternative proof. On DAG G^*, we know by results of Robins (1994, 1997) on overall effects that $\gamma(\overline{L}_m, \overline{A}_{Pm}, \overline{A}_Z)$ is uniquely characterized by $E\,[H(\gamma) \mid \overline{A}_{Pm}, \overline{L}_m, \overline{A}_Z]$ does not depend on A_{Pm}. We use this to replace equation 25 and proceed analogously to the proof of theorem 5.1.

Remark. Note that theorem 6.1 is a direct corollary of theorems 7.1 and 8.1. We can use theorem 8.1 to construct semiparametric direct-effect g-tests and g-estimates for ψ_0. In a parallel to section 5, I first provide in theorem 8.2, which follows, a quite general approach to testing and estimation. I then suggest a practical approach that allows the analyst to use easily available off-the-shelf software.

8.1 General Approach to Testing and Estimation

To describe the asymptotic properties of the estimators introduced in this section, it will be useful to define an asymptotically linear estimator. An estimator $\hat{\psi}$ of ψ_0 is asymptotically linear with influence function B if

$$n^{\frac{1}{2}}(\hat{\psi} - \psi_0) = n^{-\frac{1}{2}}\sum_{i=1}^n B_i + o_p(1) \ ,$$

where $E(B) = 0$, $E(B'B) < \infty$, and $o_p(1)$ represents a random variable converging to zero in probability. Thus, an asymptotically linear estimator is asymptotically equivalent to the sum of independent and identically distributed random variables B_i. It follows, therefore, that if $\hat{\psi}$ is asymptotically linear, then, by the central limit theorem and Slutzky's theorem, $n^{1/2}(\hat{\psi} - \psi_0)$ is asymptotically normal with mean zero and variance $E\,[BB']$. Nearly all commonly encountered estimators are asymptotically linear. For example, the maximum likelihood estimator and most Bayes estimators of the parameter vector indexing a parametric model will be asymptotically linear with influence function equal to the inverse of the expected information matrix multiplied by the score vector (i.e., the derivative of the log likelihood contribution of a single subject with respect to the parameter). Two asymptotically linear estimators, $\hat{\psi}^{(1)}$ and $\hat{\psi}^{(2)}$ with the same influence function B are asymptotically equivalent in the sense that $n^{1/2}(\hat{\psi}^{(1)} - \hat{\psi}^{(2)})$ goes to zero in probability.

It will also be useful to define a regular estimator: a regular estimator is one whose convergence to its limiting distribution is locally uniform (Bickel et al. 1993). Regularity is a technical condition that prohibits super-efficient estimators. Thus, when we say the maximum likelihood estimator or a Bayes estimator is efficient, we mean it is efficient within the class of regular estimators. Thus, an estimator being regular, asymptotically linear (RAL) is a highly desirable property. With this background, we are ready to describe our general approach to testing and estimation.

Let $T_m^*(A_{Pm}, y) = T_{m1}^*(A_{Pm})\,y + T_{m2}^*(A_{Pm})$ where, for $j = 1, 2$, $T_{mj}^*(A_{Pm}) =$

$t^*_{mj}(A_{Pm}, \underline{A}_{Zm}, \overline{A}_{m-1}, \overline{L}_m)$. Write $H(\psi) = Y - \sum_{m=0}^{K} \gamma(\overline{L}_m, \overline{A}_{Pm}, \overline{A}_Z, \psi)$ and let $U_m(\psi, t^*) = W_{m+1}^{-1} \{T^*_m(A_{Pm}, H(\psi)) - \int T^*_m(a_{Pm}, H(\psi)) \, dF\,[a_{Pm} \mid A_{Zm}, \overline{A}_{m-1}, \overline{L}_m]\}$ and $U_.(\psi) \equiv U_.(\psi, t^*) \equiv \sum_{m=0}^{K} U_m(\psi, t^*)$, where t^* is the collection of functions $\{t^*_{mj}(\bullet); m = 0, ..., K, j = 0, 1\}$ chosen by the investigator. Also given functions $r_m(A_{Zm}, \overline{A}_{m-1}, \overline{L}_{m-1})$ chosen by the investigator, let $R_. = \sum_{m=0}^{K} R_m$, where $R_m = r_m(A_{Zm}, \overline{A}_{m-1}, \overline{L}_{m-1}) - \int r_m(a_{Zm}, \overline{A}_{m-1}, \overline{L}_{m-1}) \, dF\,(a_{Zm} \mid \overline{A}_{m-1}, \overline{L}_{m-1})$ and define $U^*_.(\psi) \equiv U^*_.(\psi, t^*, r) = U_.(\psi, t^*) - R_.$. In the following theorem, the functions t^*_{mj} and r_m are vector valued of the dimension of ψ.

THEOREM 8.2. If $var\,\{U^*_.(\psi_0, t^*, r)\}$ is finite, then (i) $E\,[U^*_.(\psi_0)] = 0$, and if ψ is one-dimensional,

$$\chi(\psi_0) \equiv \frac{\sum_i U^*_{.i}(\psi_0)}{\left[\sum_i U^*_{.i}(\psi_0)^2\right]^{\frac{1}{2}}}$$

converges to a $N(0, 1)$ random variable. Further, under standard regularity conditions, with probability approaching 1, the unique solution $\hat{\psi} \equiv \hat{\psi}\,(t^*, r)$ to $0 = \sum_i U^*_{.i}\,(\psi, t^*, r) = 0$ is a regular asymptotically linear (RAL) estimator of ψ_0 with influence function

$$-\left\{E\left[\frac{\partial U^*_.\,(\psi_0, t^*, r)}{\partial \psi}\right]\right\}^{-1} U^*_.\,(\psi_0, t^*, r) \,.$$

Remark. The test statistic χ discussed in the paragraph following theorem 6.1 is a special case of $\chi(\psi_0)$ with $\psi_0 = 0$ and $R_. \equiv 0$.

Elsewhere I prove there further exists t^*_{eff} and r_{eff} such that $\hat{\psi}\,(t^*_{eff}, r_{eff})$ is the most efficient possible estimator of ψ_0 under the restrictions imposed by our semiparametric model (a). That is, the asymptotic variance of $\hat{\psi}\,(t^*_{eff}, r_{eff})$ attains the semiparametric variance bound for the model. In particular, this implies that when ψ_0 is one-dimensional, the direct-effect g-test based on $\chi \equiv \chi\,(0)$ of the null hypothesis $\psi_0 = 0$ that uses t^*_{eff} and r_{eff} is locally most powerful among all regular asymptotic α-level tests (Robins and Rotnitzky 1992) of the direct-effect "g"-null mean hypothesis (equation 29) under the sole restriction that, as in a sequential randomized trial, the densities $f(a_m \mid \overline{a}_{m-1}, \overline{\ell}_{m-1})$ are known. We introduced the additional term $R_.$ in $U^*_.(\psi)$ to be able to characterize the most efficient semiparametric procedure; the choice $R_. \equiv 0$ of section 6 is inefficient.

In observational studies, we can replace the unknown density

$$f(A_m \mid \overline{L}_m, \overline{A}_{m-1})$$

by maximum likelihood estimates under a parametric model $f\,[A_m \mid \overline{L}_m, \overline{A}_{m-1}; \alpha]$. Let $U^*_.(\psi, \alpha) = U^*_.(\psi, t^*, r, \alpha)$ and $\hat{\psi}\,(\alpha) \equiv \hat{\psi}\,(t^*, r, \alpha)$ be $U^*_.(\psi, t^*, r)$ and $\hat{\psi}\,(t^*, r)$ with $f\,[A_m \mid \overline{L}_m, \overline{A}_{m-1}]$ replaced by $f\,[A_m \mid \overline{L}_m, \overline{A}_{m-1}; \alpha]$. Then if the parametric model $f\,[A_m \mid \overline{L}_m, \overline{A}_{m-1}; \alpha]$ is correctly specified, the estimator

$\hat{\psi}\,(t^*,\,r,\,\hat{\alpha})$ with $\hat{\alpha}$ the maximum likelihood estimator of α will be RAL with influence function $D = D(\psi_0) \equiv \Gamma^{-1}(\psi_0)\,D^*(\psi_0)$ where

$$\Gamma(\psi_0) \equiv -E\,[\partial U^*_\bullet(\psi_0,\,t^*,\,r)\,/\,\partial\psi]$$

and $D^*(\psi_0) \equiv U^*(\psi_0,\,t^*,\,r) - E\,[U^*(\psi_0,\,t^*,\,r)\,S'_\alpha]\,[E(S_\alpha S'_\alpha)]^{-1}\,S_\alpha,\ S_\alpha \equiv S_\alpha(\alpha_0)$ and $S_\alpha(\alpha)$ is the score for α (i.e., the derivative of the log-likelihood w.r.t α for a single subject). Furthermore, the asymptotic variance of $\hat{\psi}\ (t^*,\,r,\,\hat{\alpha})$ will be less than or equal to that of $\hat{\psi}\ (t^*,\,r)$. In particular, $\hat{\psi}\ (t^*_{eff},\,r_{eff})$ and $\hat{\psi}\ (t^*_{eff},\ r_{eff},\,\hat{\alpha})$ will have the same efficient variance. A consistent estimator of the asymptotic variance of $n^{1/2}\{\hat{\psi}(t,\,r,\,\hat{\alpha}) - \psi_0\}$ is

$$n^{-1}\sum_i \hat{D}_i(\hat{\psi})\hat{D}_i(\hat{\psi})' \tag{33}$$

where $\hat{D}(\psi) = \hat{\Gamma}^{-1}(\psi)\,\hat{D}^*(\psi)$ and $\hat{\Gamma}(\psi)$ and $\hat{D}^*(\psi)$ are the estimators of $\Gamma(\psi)$ and $D^*(\psi)$ obtained by replacing α by $\hat{\alpha}$ and expectations by sample averages over the n study subjects. Similarly, with ψ one-dimensional, if $\psi = \psi_0$

$$\hat{\chi}(\psi) \equiv \frac{\sum_i U^*_{\bullet i}(\psi,\,\hat{\alpha})}{\left\{\sum_i \hat{D}_i^{*2}(\psi)\right\}^{\frac{1}{2}}} \tag{34}$$

converges to a $N(0,\,1)$ random variable.

A practical approach to testing and estimation. A conservative α-level test of the hypothesis $\psi = \psi_0$ can be obtained using off-the-shelf software by following the practical testing algorithm of section 5.1, except in step 3 I replace $\mathcal{Q}^*_m$ by $\mathcal{Q}^*_m(\psi) = q^*_m\,[H(\psi),\,A_{Zm},\,\overline{A}_{m-1},\,\overline{L}_m,\,\underline{A}_{Z(m+1)}]$ with q^*_m linear in its first argument and treat $\mathcal{Q}^*_m(\psi)$ as a fixed covariate in the testing procedure. A RAL estimator $\tilde{\psi}$ of ψ_0 is then obtained as the value of ψ that makes this test statistic precisely zero. A conservative 95% confidence interval (i.e., an interval that is guaranteed in large samples to cover ψ_0 at least 95% of the time) can be obtained as the set of ψ for which the conservative .05-level test of $\psi = \psi_0$ of step 3 fails to reject.

I refer to all the above estimators as direct-effect g-estimators. It will also be pedagogically useful to reconsider the simple toy example of section 2 with $K = 1$, $A_{P0} \equiv A_0$, $A_{Z0} \equiv 0$, $A_{P1} \equiv 0$, $A_{Z1} \equiv A_1$, $L_0 \equiv 0$, $L_1 \equiv L$, $W_1 = f(A_1 \mid L, A_0)$, and $H(\psi) = Y - \psi A_0$. Then a test of the hypothesis $\psi = \psi_0$ is obtained by using standard software to test whether the variable $\mathcal{W}(\psi) \equiv H(\psi)\,t_2(A_1)\,/\,W_1$ is correlated with A_0 where $t_2(A_1)$ is chosen by the data analyst. Furthermore, an RAL estimator $\hat{\psi}$ of ψ_0 is obtained by estimating the linear regression model $Y_i = \beta + \psi A_{0i} + \varepsilon_i$ by weighted least squares with subject i receiving the weight $t_2(A_{1i})\,/\,W_{1i}$. Note that no tests and estimators quite this simple are available in the more complex settings discussed above.

It can be shown that consideration of the abstract estimating functions

$U^*_\bullet(\psi)$ is completely general in the sense that any other estimator $\tilde\psi$ of ψ_0, such as the off-the-shelf g-estimator, is asymptotically equivalent to an estimator $\hat\psi(t^*, r)$ for some choice of the functions t^* and r. That is, $\tilde\psi$ and $\hat\psi(t^*, r)$ have the same influence function and thus $n^{1/2}\{\tilde\psi - \hat\psi(t^*, r)\}$ converges in probability to zero.

Estimation of contrasts. When $\psi_0 \neq 0$, knowledge of ψ_0 alone will not allow one to calculate the mean contrasts $b(g_{P1}, \overline{a}_Z) - b(g_{P2}, \overline{a}_Z)$ with the following exception. Suppose that we were interested in contrasts between the nondynamic regimes $g_{P1} \equiv \overline{a}_P^{(1)}$ and $g_{P2} \equiv \overline{a}_P^{(2)}$ and

$$\gamma(\overline{\ell}_m, \overline{a}_{Pm}, \overline{a}_Z) \equiv \gamma(\overline{a}_{Pm}, \overline{a}_Z) \tag{35}$$

does not depend on $\overline{\ell}_m$ for each m. Define $b(\overline{a}_Z) \equiv b(0, \overline{a}_Z)$ to be $b(g)$ for $g = (\overline{a}_P, \overline{a}_Z)$ with $\overline{a}_P$ identically zero. Note $b(\overline{a}_Z) - b(\overline{a}_Z \equiv 0)$ is, under g-identifiability, the effect of treatment with $\overline{A}_Z = \overline{a}_Z$ on the mean of Y when treatment with $\overline{A}_P$ is withheld. It follows from theorem 8.3 below that $b(\overline{a}_P, \overline{a}_Z) - b(\overline{a}_Z)$ is $\sum_{m=0}^K \gamma(\overline{a}_{Pm}, \overline{a}_Z)$, which is only a function of the parameter ψ_0 of a correctly specified direct-effect SNMM $\gamma(\overline{a}_{Pm}, \overline{a}_Z, \psi)$.

Suppose, however, we wish to estimate the ratio

$$\frac{b\left(\overline{a}_P^{(1)}, \overline{a}_Z\right)}{b\left(\overline{a}_P^{(2)}, \overline{a}_Z\right)}$$

rather than the difference. The following theorem, which is a corollary to theorem 8.6 below, indicates that in order to do so, we also need an estimate of $b(\overline{a}_Z)$.

THEOREM 8.3. If equation 35 is true, $b(\overline{a}_P, \overline{a}_Z) = \sum_{m=0}^K \gamma(\overline{a}_{Pm}, \overline{a}_Z) + b(\overline{a}_Z)$.

With this motivation, the next goal will be to estimate $b(\overline{a}_Z)$. To do so, we modify the previous semiparametric model (a) to the more restrictive semiparametric model (b), which contains the additional assumption that $b(\overline{a}_Z) = b(\overline{a}_Z; \theta_0)$ where $b(\overline{a}_Z; \theta)$ is a known function of a finite dimensional parameter θ. The model $b(\overline{a}_Z; \theta)$ is a marginal structural model for the effect of $\overline{A}_Z$ on the mean of Y when $\overline{A}_P$ is set to zero (Robins 1999, 1998). The key tool in constructing an estimator for θ in this model is the following characterization of $b(\overline{a}_Z)$.

THEOREM 8.4. Let $\sigma(\gamma, b^*) = H(\gamma) - b^*(\overline{A}_Z)$. Then $b^*(\overline{A}_Z) = b(\overline{A}_Z)$ w. p. 1 if and only if, for all functions $t(\overline{a}_Z)$, $E[\sigma(\gamma, b^*)\,t(\overline{A}_Z)\,/\,W] = 0$, whenever the expectation is finite and $W \equiv W_0$.

Proof. A direct proof is given in section 14. Alternately by Robins (1994, 1997), $E^*[H(\gamma) \mid \overline{A}_Z] = b(\overline{A}_Z)$ on G^*, and thus we can use the proof methods of section 5.2.

Theorem 8.4 suggests the following estimation procedure for θ_0. Define

$\sigma(\psi, \theta) = H(\psi) - b(\overline{A}_Z; \theta)$. Let $S(\theta, \psi) \equiv S(\theta, \psi, t) \equiv \sigma(\psi, \theta) t(A_Z) / W$ where $t(A_Z)$ is now a vector-valued function of the dimension of θ chosen by the data analyst. Let $\hat{\theta} \equiv \hat{\theta}(\hat{\psi}) \equiv \hat{\theta}(\hat{\psi}, t)$ solve $0 = \Sigma_i S_i(\theta, \hat{\psi}, t)$ where $\hat{\psi} = \hat{\psi}(t^*, r)$ is the estimator of ψ_0 defined previously. Then since theorem 8.4 implies $E[S(\theta_0, \psi_0, t)] = 0$ under the more restrictive semiparametric model (b), we obtain the following theorem.

THEOREM 8.5. Given semiparametric model (b), under standard regularity conditions, $\hat{\rho}' = (\hat{\psi}', \hat{\theta}')$ is a RAL estimator of $\rho_0' = (\psi_0', \theta_0')$ with influence function $-\{E[\partial S^*(\rho_0) / \partial \rho]\}^{-1} S^*(\rho_0)$ where $S^*(\rho) = (U(\psi)', S(\theta, \psi)')'$.

Remark. Note that $\hat{\psi} \equiv \hat{\psi}(t^*_{eff}, r_{eff})$, although efficient in semiparametric model (a), will in general not be an efficient estimator of ψ_0 in the more restrictive semiparametric model (b). To see why, consider the extreme case where θ_0 was known a priori. Then, since for any function $t(\overline{A}_Z)$ of the dimension of ψ, $E[S(\theta_0, \psi_0, t)] = 0$ under the semiparametric model (b), we can use this fact to obtain an estimator, say $\tilde{\psi}(t^*, r, t)$, that is more efficient than $\hat{\psi}(t^*, r)$. Unfortunately, the estimator $\tilde{\psi}(t^*, r, t)$, in contrast to $\hat{\psi}(t^*, r)$, will be inconsistent for ψ_0 if the semiparametric model (b) is false due to the model $b(\overline{a}_Z; \theta)$ being misspecified. It follows that due to this possible misspecification, using $\tilde{\psi}(t^*, r, t)$ can lead us to falsely conclude that there exists a direct effect of $\overline{A}_P$ on the mean of Y (i.e., $\psi_0 \neq 0$) even in a sequential randomized experiment with known randomization probabilities. This error is avoided by basing inference on the less efficient estimator $\hat{\psi}(t^*, r)$.

Further contrasts. Suppose our goal is to estimate the contrast $b(g_{P1}, \overline{a}_Z) - b(g_{P2}, a_Z)$ and either equation 35 is false or g_{P1} and/or g_{P2} is a dynamic regime. According to the following theorem, it is then unnecessary to estimate $b(\overline{a}_Z)$, but we must now estimate the densities $f(\ell_m \mid \overline{\ell}_{m-1}, \overline{a}_{m-1})$. Furthermore, if we wish to estimate the ratio of the means rather than the difference, we must also estimate $b(\overline{a}_Z)$.

THEOREM 8.6. $b(g_P, \overline{a}_Z) \equiv b(\overline{a}_Z) +$
$$\iint \sum_{m=0}^{K} \gamma[\overline{\ell}_m, g_P(\overline{\ell}_m), \overline{a}_Z] \prod_{m=0}^{K} dF[\ell_m \mid \overline{\ell}_{m-1}, g_P(\overline{\ell}_{m-1}), \overline{a}_{Z(m-1)}] . \quad (36)$$

Proof. Robins (1994, 1997) shows $E^*_{gP}[Y \mid \overline{A}_Z = \overline{a}_Z]$ is given by equation 36 under G^*. However, as in section 5.2, by $\overline{A}_Z$ exogenous on G^*, $E^*_{gP}[Y \mid \overline{A}_Z = \overline{a}_Z] = E^*_{(gP,\overline{a}_Z)}(Y) \equiv b^*(g_P, \overline{a}_Z)$. However, all functionals in equation 36 are common to $f(v)$ and $f^*(v)$, so equation 36 must also equal $b(g_P, \overline{a}_Z)$. A quite different alternative proof is provided in section 9.

To estimate $b(g_P, \overline{a}_Z)$, we use our previous estimates $(\hat{\psi}, \hat{\theta})$. Estimates of $f(\ell_m \mid \overline{\ell}_{m-1}, \overline{a}_{m-1})$ that converge at rate $n^{1/2}$ can be obtained by specifying a parametric model $f(\ell_m \mid \overline{\ell}_{m-1}, \overline{a}_{m-1}; \eta)$ and then estimating η by $\hat{\eta}$ that maximizes $\prod_{i=1}^{n} \prod_{m=0}^{K} f(L_{mi} \mid \overline{L}_{(m-1), i}, \overline{A}_{(m-1), i}; \eta)$. The integral in equation 36 can be easily evaluated by Monte Carlo integration.

9. A Nonstandard Parameterization and Parametric Likelihood-Based Inference

In sections 7 and 8, I discussed inference for the direct effect of $\overline{A}_p$ on Y based on the semiparametric estimation of SNMMs. In contrast to our approach, in the graphical modeling literature, the usual approach to estimating a functional $q(F)$ [such as $b(g_p, \overline{a}_Z)$] of the joint distribution $F(v)$ of the observed data $V = (Y, \overline{L}, \overline{A})$ is to specify a fully parametric model for $F(v)$ depending on a finite dimensional parameter ρ. Then one estimates ρ and the functional $q(\rho)$ by maximum likelihood. Alternatively, one can give ρ a prior distribution and estimate the functional $q(\rho)$ by its posterior mean or median. Keeping with this spirit, I describe a reparameterization of the joint distribution of V in terms of the functions $\gamma(\overline{\ell}_m, \overline{a}_{Pm}, \overline{a}_Z)$ and $b(\overline{a}_Z)$ that will allow a fully parametric likelihood or Bayesian approach to testing the direct-effect "g"-null mean hypothesis (equation 29) and estimating the functionals $b(g_p, \overline{a}_Z)$. Such an approach is an alternative to the semiparametric methods described previously. To describe this approach, I need to define $v(\overline{\ell}_m, \overline{a}_{P(m-1)}, \overline{a}_Z) \equiv b(\overline{\ell}_m, \overline{a}_{P(m-1)}, \overline{a}_Z) - b(\overline{\ell}_{m-1}, \overline{a}_{P(m-1)}, \overline{a}_Z)$. Since, by definition, $b(\overline{\ell}_{m-1}, \overline{a}_{P(m-1)}, \overline{a}_Z) = \int b(\overline{\ell}_m, \overline{a}_{P(m-1)}, \overline{a}_Z) \, dF[\ell_m \mid \overline{\ell}_{m-1}, \overline{a}_{m-1}]$, we have

$$\int v(\overline{\ell}_m, \overline{a}_{P(m-1)}, \overline{a}_Z) \, dF[\ell_m \mid \overline{\ell}_{m-1}, \overline{a}_{m-1}] = 0 \ . \tag{37}$$

Write

$$\varepsilon = Y - E[Y \mid \overline{L}_K, \overline{A}_K] \equiv Y - b(\overline{L}_K, \overline{A}_K) \tag{38}$$

so

$$E[\varepsilon \mid \overline{L}_K, \overline{A}_K] = 0 \ . \tag{39}$$

Having defined ε, I next note that we have, from their definitions, that

$$b(\overline{\ell}_K, \overline{a}_K) = \sum_{m=0}^{K} \gamma(\overline{\ell}_m, \overline{a}_{Pm}, \overline{a}_Z) + v(\overline{\ell}_m, \overline{a}_{P(m-1)}, \overline{a}_Z) + b(\overline{a}_Z) \ . \tag{40}$$

Finally, we need the fact that equation 37 implies there exists a unique function $v^*(\overline{\ell}_m, \overline{a}_{P(m-1)}, \overline{a}_Z)$ satisfying the standardization condition

$$v^*(\overline{\ell}_m, \overline{a}_{P(m-1)}, \overline{a}_Z) = 0 \text{ if } \ell_m = 0 \tag{41}$$

such that

$$v(\overline{\ell}_m, \overline{a}_{P(m-1)}, \overline{a}_Z) =$$
$$v^*(\overline{\ell}_m, \overline{a}_{P(m-1)}, \overline{a}_Z) - \int v^*(\overline{\ell}_m, \overline{a}_{P(m-1)}, \overline{a}_Z) \, dF(\ell_m \mid \overline{\ell}_{m-1}, \overline{a}_{m-1}) \ . \tag{42}$$

Specifically, equations 41 and 42 imply

$$v^*(\overline{\ell}_m, \overline{a}_{P(m-1)}, \overline{a}_Z) = v(\overline{\ell}_m, \overline{a}_{P(m-1)}, \overline{a}_Z) - v(\{\overline{\ell}_{m-1}, \ell_m = 0\}, \overline{a}_{P(m-1)}, \overline{a}_Z) . \tag{43}$$

Combining equations 38, 40, and 42, we obtain

$$Y = \varepsilon + \sum_{m=0}^{K} \gamma\left(\bar{L}_m, \bar{A}_{Pm}, \bar{A}_Z\right) + b\left(\bar{A}_Z\right) +$$

$$\sum_{m=0}^{K} \left\{ v^*\left(\bar{L}_m, \bar{A}_{P(m-1)}, \bar{A}_Z\right) - \int v^*\left(\bar{L}_m, \bar{A}_{P(m-1)}, \bar{A}_Z\right) dF\left(L_m \mid \bar{L}_{m-1}, \bar{A}_{m-1}\right) \right\}.$$

(44)

Thus, the density of $f(v)$ factors as follows.

$$f(V) \equiv f\left(Y, \bar{L}_K, \bar{A}_K\right)$$

$$= f\left(\varepsilon \mid \bar{L}_K, \bar{A}_K\right) \prod_{m=0}^{K} f\left[L_m \mid \bar{L}_{m-1}, \bar{A}_{m-1}\right] f\left[A_m \mid \bar{L}_{m-1}, \bar{A}_{m-1}\right]$$

(45)

where ε is defined in terms of $(Y, \bar{L}_K, \bar{A}_K)$ by equation 44. Thus we have reparameterized the density $f(V)$ in terms of (1) the function $\gamma(\bar{\ell}_m, \bar{a}_{Pm}, \bar{a}_Z)$ satisfying equation 32, (2) the functions $v^*(\bar{\ell}_m, \bar{a}_{P(m-1)}, \bar{a}_Z)$ satisfying equation
41, (3) the functions $b(\bar{a}_Z)$, (4) the density of $\varepsilon \mid \bar{\ell}_K, \bar{a}_K$ subject to equation
39, (5) the densities $f(\ell_m \mid \bar{\ell}_{m-1}, \bar{a}_{m-1})$, and (6) the densities $f(a_m \mid \bar{\ell}_m, \bar{a}_{m-1})$.
We are now in a position to provide an alternative proof of theorem 8.6 that
demonstrates the usefulness of the decomposition (equation 44).

Alternative proof of theorem 8.6. Note from its definition in section 3, $f_g(v)$
is given by equations 44 and 45 except with the law of A_m given $\bar{L}_m, \bar{A}_{m-1}$
putting all its mass on $A_m = g_m(\bar{L}_m)$. Since $b(g_P, \bar{a}_Z) \equiv \int y dF_g(y)$ for $g = (g_P, \bar{a}_Z)$,
theorem 8.6 follows from equations 44 and 45 and the fact that, by equation 39
and 37, the terms in equation 44 in ε and v^* have mean zero both under $f(v)$
and $f_g(v)$.

If the support of Y is the whole real line, the reparameterization (1) – (6) is
unrestricted in the sense that given any functions and densities satisfying (1) –
(6), we can use the densities (4) – (6) to generate random variables $(\varepsilon, \bar{L}_K, \bar{A}_K)$
and then use the functions (1) – (3) to generate Y via equation 44. The result-
ing $V = (Y, \bar{L}, \bar{A})$ has a density $f(v)$ satisfying equation 45 with the functions
(1) – (3) the appropriate functionals of $f(v)$.

Remark A. Note, to obtain an unrestricted parameterization, it is essential
to replace $v(\bar{\ell}_m, \bar{a}_{P(m-1)}, \bar{a}_Z)$ by $v^*(\bar{\ell}_m, \bar{a}_{P(m-1)}, \bar{a}_Z)$ since arbitrary functions
$v(\bar{\ell}_m, \bar{a}_{P(m-1)}, \bar{a}_Z)$ and densities $f(\ell_m \mid \ell_{m-1}, \bar{a}_{m-1})$ will fail to satisfy equation
37. To be more precise, each possible density $f(v)$ of the data is generated by
one and only one collection of functions (1) – (6). However, if, in generating
data, we modify (1) – (6) by replacing $v^*(\bar{\ell}_m, \bar{a}_{P(m-1)}, \bar{a}_Z)$ by an unrestricted
function $v(\bar{\ell}_m, \bar{a}_{P(m-1)}, \bar{a}_Z)$ and then replace the terms in set braces in equation 44 by this $v(\bar{\ell}_m, \bar{a}_{P(m-1)}, \bar{a}_Z)$, then each density $f(v)$ is generated by
many different collections of the modified functions and densities (1) – (6).
Now consider a particular density $\mathring{f}(v)$ and its implied functions $\mathring{\gamma}, \mathring{b}, \mathring{v}$, and
densities $\mathring{f}(\varepsilon \mid \bar{\ell}_K, \bar{a}_K), \mathring{f}(\ell_m \mid \bar{\ell}_{m-1}, \bar{a}_{m-1}), \mathring{f}(a_m \mid \bar{\ell}_m, \bar{a}_{m-1})$. In particular, the
function $\mathring{v}$ satisfies equation 37 under $\mathring{f}(v)$. Then $\mathring{f}(v)$ is the image of many
different modified collections (1) – (6), precisely one of which has the func-

tions γ, b, v and densities (4) – (6) equal to those implied by $\mathring{f}(v)$—the collection for which v and density $f(\ell_m \mid \bar{\ell}_{m-1}, \bar{a}_{m-1})$ satisfy equation 37. We now consider conceptually quite distinct further restrictions on (1) – (6) induced by Y having a restricted sample space.

If, as discussed further below, the mean of Y is restricted (e.g., Y has bounded support), then the representation of $F(v)$ in terms of the densities and (unmodified) functions (1) – (6) still holds except that the reparameterization is no longer unrestricted. These densities and functions must satisfy additional side constraints. For example, if Y is a nonnegative random variable, a direct-effect SNMM fails to automatically impose the constraint that $E_g(Y) \equiv b(g)$ is positive. If the mean Y can take any nonnegative value (e.g., Y is a Poisson or overdispersed Poisson random variable), we can automatically impose this restriction by modeling $\ell n\{b(\bar{\ell}_m, \bar{a}_{Pm}, \bar{a}_Z) / b(\bar{\ell}_m, \bar{a}_{P(m-1)}, \bar{a}_Z)\}$ by $\gamma(\bar{\ell}_m, \bar{a}_{Pm}, \bar{a}_Z, \psi)$, which we refer to as a direct-effect multiplicative SNMM model. Although I do not investigate this possibility further, the relationship between direct-effect SNMMs and direct-effect multiplicative SNMMs is similar to that between standard SNMMs and standard multiplicative SNMMs discussed in Robins (1994, 1997) and Robins, Rotnitzky, and Scharfstein (1999). Neither direct-effect SNMMs nor direct-effect multiplicative SNMMs automatically impose the true restriction $0 \leq E_g(Y) \leq 1$ when Y is a Bernoulli random variable. Direct-effect logistic SNMMs that model $\ell ogit$ $\{b(\bar{\ell}_m, \bar{a}_{Pm}, \bar{a}_Z)\} - \ell ogit \{b(\bar{\ell}_m, \bar{a}_{P(m-1)}, \bar{a}_Z)\}$ by $\gamma(\bar{\ell}_m, \bar{a}_{Pm}, \bar{a}_Z, \psi)$ naturally impose this restriction but do not admit simple semiparametric estimators of ψ even when $f(a_m \mid \bar{\ell}_m, \bar{a}_{m-1})$ is known. This is because all influence functions for ψ depend on a high-dimensional smooth, i.e., a conditional expectation that is left unrestricted by the model.

9.1 A Fully Parametric Model

It follows from equation 45 that if we specify a direct-effect SNMM

$$\gamma(\bar{\ell}_m, \bar{a}_{Pm}, \bar{a}_Z, \psi)$$

and parametric models

$$b(\bar{a}_Z, \theta), f(\varepsilon \mid \bar{\ell}_K, \bar{a}_K; \eta_1), f(\ell_m \mid \bar{\ell}_{m-1}; \bar{a}_{m-1}; \eta_3), v^*(\bar{\ell}_m, \bar{a}_{P(m-1)}, \bar{a}_Z; \eta_2),$$

and $f(a_m \mid \bar{\ell}_m, \bar{a}_{m-1}, \alpha)$ subject to the restrictions

$$\int \varepsilon dF\left[\varepsilon \mid \bar{\ell}_K, \bar{a}_K; \eta_1\right] = 0$$

$$(46)$$

and

$$v^*(\bar{\ell}_m, \bar{a}_{P(m-1)}, \bar{a}_Z; \eta_2) = 0 \text{ if } \ell_m = 0 \tag{47}$$

the contribution to the likelihood for a single subject can be written

$$f(V;\rho) \equiv$$

$$f\left[Y \mid \overline{L}_K, \overline{A}_K; \psi, \theta, \eta\right] \prod_{m=0}^{K} f\left(A_m \mid \overline{L}_m, \overline{A}_{m-1}; \alpha\right) f\left(L_m \mid \overline{L}_{m-1}, \overline{A}_{m-1}; \eta_3\right) \tag{48}$$

with $\eta = (\eta_1', \eta_2', \eta_3')'$, $\rho \equiv (\psi', \theta', \eta', \alpha')'$,

$$f\left[Y \mid \overline{L}_K, \overline{A}_K; \psi, \theta, \eta\right] \equiv f\left[\varepsilon(\psi, \theta, \eta_2, \eta_3) \mid \overline{L}_K, \overline{A}_K; \eta_1\right], \tag{49}$$

$$\varepsilon(\psi, \theta, \eta_2, \eta_3) = \sigma(\psi, \theta) - \left\{ \sum_{m=0}^{K} v^*\left(\overline{L}_m, \overline{A}_{P(m-1)}, \overline{A}_Z; \eta_2\right)\right.$$

$$\left. - \int v^*\left(\overline{L}_m, \overline{A}_{P(m-1)}, \overline{A}_Z; \eta_2\right) dF\left(L_m \mid \overline{A}_{m-1}, \overline{L}_{m-1}; \eta_3\right)\right\} \tag{50}$$

where, again,

$$\sigma(\psi, \theta) \equiv H(\psi) - b\left(\overline{A}_Z; \theta\right), H(\psi) \equiv Y - \sum_{m=0}^{K} \gamma\left(\overline{L}_m, \overline{A}_{Pm}, \overline{A}_Z; \psi\right).$$

Note that $f(V; \rho)$ is a nonstandard parameterization of the DAG G since, for example, the parameter η_3 occurs both in $f(Y \mid \overline{L}_k, \overline{A}_K; \psi, \theta, \eta)$ and in $f\left[L_m \mid \overline{A}_{m-1}, \overline{L}_{m-1}; \eta_3\right]$. If $E\left(Y \mid \overline{L}_K, \overline{A}_K\right)$ can take any value in $(-\infty, \infty)$ the above parametrization, although nonstandard, is unrestricted and so can be chosen variation independent in the sense that the parameter space for $\rho' \equiv (\psi', \theta', \eta', \alpha')$ is the product of the parameter spaces for $\psi', \theta', \eta_1', \eta_2', \eta_3',$ and α'. If $E\left(Y \mid \overline{L}_K, \overline{A}_K\right)$ can only take any value in $(0, \infty)$, it is necessary to use multiplicative SNMMs to obtain an unrestricted parametrization that can be chosen variation independent. If $E\left(Y \mid \overline{L}_K, \overline{A}_K\right)$ can only take any value in $(0,1)$, it is necessary to use logistic SNMMs to obtain an unrestricted parametrization that can be chosen variation independent.

9.2 Estimation

We assume we have an unrestricted variation-independent parametrization. Let $\hat{\rho}_{MLE}$ maximize the likelihood $\prod_{i=1}^{n} f(V_i; \rho)$. Due to the fact that α only occurs in the terms $f(A_m \mid \overline{A}_{m-1}, \overline{L}_m; \alpha)$, the maximum likelihood estimators $(\hat{\psi}_{MLE}, \hat{\theta}_{MLE}, \hat{\eta}_{MLE})$ of (ψ, θ, η) are the same whether $f(A_m \mid \overline{A}_{m-1}, \overline{L}_m)$ is known (as in a sequential randomized trial), follows a parametric model depending on α, or is completely unknown. On the other hand, our semi-parametric g-estimator $\hat{\psi}$ of ψ_0 required that we either know (as in a sequential randomized trial) or model $f(A_m \mid \overline{A}_{m-1}, \overline{L}_m)$, but allowed us to leave (1) $f\left[\varepsilon \mid \overline{L}_K, \overline{A}_K\right]$, (2) $f(\overline{\ell}_m \mid \overline{\ell}_{m-1}, \overline{a}_{m-1})$, (3) $v^*(\overline{\ell}_m, \overline{a}_{P(m-1)}, \overline{a}_Z)$, and (4) $b(\overline{a}_Z)$ completely unrestricted. In contrast, to compute $\hat{\psi}_{MLE}$, we need to model the densities and functions (1) – (4), but the densities $f(A_m \mid \overline{A}_{m-1}, \overline{L}_m)$ can be left completely unrestricted.

If all models are correctly specified, $\hat{\psi}_{MLE}$ will be more efficient than even our most efficient g-estimator $\hat{\psi}(t^*_{eff}, r_{eff})$. Unfortunately, $\hat{\psi}_{MLE}$ will be inconsistent for ψ_0 if any of the models for the densities and functions (1) – (4) are misspecified. (However, in contrast with a standard parameterization, there will always exist a joint distribution for V compatible with $f(V; \rho)$ for which the direct-effect "g"-null mean hypothesis is true. Indeed, it will be true for any distribution $f(V; \rho)$ with $\psi = 0$.) As discussed previously, the g-estimator $\hat{\psi}$ will be consistent if, as in a randomized trial, $f(a_m \mid \bar{a}_{m-1}, \bar{\ell}_m)$ is known. In an observational study, it will be inconsistent if the model for these densities is misspecified. However, since (1) I believe it is much more feasible to specify a realistic model for $f(a_m \mid \bar{a}_{m-1}, \bar{\ell}_m)$ than to specify parametric models for the densities and functions (1) – (4) mentioned previously, and (2) I do not wish to conclude that $\bar{A}_p$ has a direct effect when in truth it does not (i.e., $\psi_0 = 0$), I prefer, in the interest of robustness, a g-estimator $\hat{\psi}$ to either the MLE $\hat{\psi}_{MLE}$ or a Bayes estimator $\hat{\psi}_B$ (which is asymptotically equivalent to $\hat{\psi}_{MLE}$). I also prefer the g-estimate $\hat{\psi}$ to $\hat{\psi}_{MLE}$ because of computational convenience, since the likelihood $\prod_{i=1}^{n} f(V_i; \rho)$ can be quite difficult to maximize.

Remark B. The greatest computational difficulty in maximizing $\prod_{i=1}^{n} f(V_i; \rho)$ will be due to the terms in set braces in equation 50. Therefore, we might consider modifying the likelihood by replacing the terms set in braces in equation 50 by a model $v(\bar{\ell}_m, \bar{a}_{P(m-1)}, \bar{A}_Z; \eta_2)$ for $v(\bar{\ell}_m, \bar{a}_{P(m-1)}, \bar{A}_Z)$ and maximize the modified likelihood subject to the equality constraint

$$0 = \int v\left(\bar{L}_m, \bar{A}_{P(m-1)}, \bar{A}_Z; \eta_2\right) dF\left(L_m \mid \bar{L}_{m-1}, \bar{A}_{m-1}; \eta_3\right) \tag{51}$$

as required by equation 37. Unfortunately, this may create difficulties similar to those found in lemma 1.1 and theorem 1.2. Often the only parameter values (η_2, η_3) for which equation 51 holds will be (η_2^*, η_3) such that $v(\bar{\ell}_m, \bar{a}_{P(m-1)}, \bar{A}_Z; \eta_2^*) \equiv 0$, which is a strong restriction we would not wish to impose (since it implies that L_m is not a predictor of Y). Suppose therefore we choose to maximize the modified likelihood without imposing the constraint (equation 51).

This implies that we are using the modified parameterization (1) – (6) described in remark A of section 9. Hence the parameter ρ is no longer guaranteed to be identified, since many modified collections of functions (1) – (6) imply the same distribution $f(v)$. However, if the parameter ρ is of small or moderate dimension, ρ will usually be identified. That is, the statement $f(V; \rho_1) = f(V; \rho_2)$ w.p.1 will be false for all ρ_1, ρ_2 in the parameter space. Assuming identification, let ρ^* be the probability limit of $\hat{\rho}$. Suppose, as will surely be the case, equation 51 fails under ρ^*. Then even if (1) the model is correctly specified so that $f(V; \rho^*)$ actually generated the data and (2) $\hat{\psi}_{MLE}$ converges to $\psi^* = 0$, we cannot conclude that the direct-effect "g"-null mean hypothesis (equation 29) is true. To see why, adopt the notation of remark A of section 9 and write $\hat{f}(v) \equiv f(v; \rho^*)$ to represent the distribution generating the data with associated blip function $\overset{\circ}{\gamma}(\bar{\ell}_m, \bar{a}_{Pm}, \bar{a}_Z)$. As discussed in remark A, (1) the function $\overset{\circ}{\gamma}(\bar{\ell}_m, \bar{a}_{Pm}, \bar{a}_Z)$ will differ from the function $\gamma(\bar{\ell}_m, \bar{a}_{Pm}, \bar{a}_Z; \psi^*)$ = 0 when equation 51 fails at ρ^* and (2) the direct-effect "g"-null hypothesis is the hypothesis that $\overset{\circ}{\gamma}(\bar{\ell}_m, \bar{a}_{Pm}, \bar{a}_Z) = 0$. Thus, unconstrained maximization of the modified likelihood is to be avoided.

9.3 Contrasts Revisited

As noted above, to estimate $b(g_P^{(1)}, \bar{a}_Z) - b(g_P^{(2)}, \bar{a}_Z)$, we must specify and estimate models for $\gamma(\bar{\ell}_m, \bar{a}_{Pm}, \bar{a}_Z)$ and $f(\ell_m \mid \bar{\ell}_{m-1}, \bar{a}_{m-1})$. To estimate ratio contrasts between these means, we must estimate the functional $b(\bar{a}_Z)$ as well. Finally, suppose we wish to estimate the contrasts between distribution functions corresponding to the regimes $(g_P^{(1)}, \bar{a}_Z)$ and $(g_P^{(2)}, \bar{a}_Z)$. To do so we must specify and estimate a parametric model for $v^*(\bar{\ell}_m, \bar{a}_{P(m-1)}, \bar{a}_Z)$, in which case we will have estimated enough of the joint distribution $F(v)$ of the observables that we can compute an estimate of the distribution function $F_g(y)$ for any regime g.

One relatively robust approach would be to calculate a g-estimate $\hat{\psi}$ for the parameter ψ_0 of an SNMM and then maximize the likelihood $\prod_i f(V_i; \rho)$ of a fully parametric model over (θ, η) with ψ held fixed at $\hat{\psi}$. Then, our estimation of the distribution function $F_g(y)$ will remain consistent with our earlier semiparametric g-test. In particular, in a sequential randomized trial with $f(a_m \mid \bar{a}_{m-1}, \bar{\ell}_{m-1})$ known, the actual rejection rate of the direct-effect "g"-null mean hypothesis will equal the nominal level. Indeed, because robustness in this sense is ensured, one might even be willing, as an approximation, to maximize the modified likelihood of remark B of section 9.2 without imposing the constraint (equation 51).

10. Direct-Effect Structural Nested Distribution Models

In this section, I describe the class of direct-effect structural nested distribution models (SNDMs) for a continuous outcome Y. I purposely reuse (through redefinition) much of the notation introduced in the section on SNMMs in order that the connection between SNDMs and SNMMs be as clear as possible.

10.1 A New Characterization of the Direct-Effect "g"-Null Hypothesis

The first step in constructing a direct-effect SNDM is a new characterization of the direct-effect "g"-null hypothesis (equation 17). We assume the conditional distribution of Y given $(\bar{\ell}_m, \bar{a}_m)$ has a continuous positive density with respect to Lebesgue measure. The quantile-quantile function $\gamma(y) = F_1^{-1}\{F_2(y)\}$ mapping quantiles of $F_2(y)$ into quantiles of $F_1(y)$ is the unique function such that if Y_1 and Y_2 are distributed $F_1(y)$ and $F_2(y)$, then $\gamma(Y_2)$ is distributed $F_1(y)$.

Let $\gamma(y, \bar{\ell}_m, \bar{a}_{Pm}, \bar{a}_Z)$ be the quantile-quantile function mapping quantiles of

$$F_{g=(\bar{a}_{Pm}, \bar{a}_Z)}\left(y \mid \bar{\ell}_m\right)$$

into quantiles of

$$F_{g=(\bar{a}_{P(m-1)}, \bar{a}_Z)}\left(y \mid \bar{\ell}_m\right) .$$

It follows from its definition as a quantile-quantile function that:
(a) $\gamma(y, \bar{\ell}_m, \bar{a}_{Pm}, \bar{a}_Z) = y$ if $a_{Pm} = 0$,
(b) $\gamma(y, \bar{\ell}_m, \bar{a}_{Pm}, \bar{a}_Z)$ is increasing in y, and
(c) the derivative of $\gamma(y, \bar{\ell}_m, \bar{a}_{Pm}, \bar{a}_Z)$ w.r.t. y is continuous. Examples of such functions are

$$\gamma(y, \bar{\ell}_m, \bar{a}_{Pm}, \bar{a}_Z) = y + 2a_{Pm} + 3a_{Pm}a_{P(m-1)} + 4a_{Pm}\ell_m^* + 5a_{Pm}a_{ZK} \qquad (52)$$

$$\gamma(y, \bar{\ell}_m, \bar{a}_{Pm}, \bar{a}_Z) = y \exp\{2a_{Pm} + 3a_{Pm}a_{P(m-1)} + 4a_{Pm}\ell_m^* + 5a_{Pm}a_{ZK}\} \qquad (53)$$

where ℓ_m^* is a given univariate function of $\bar{\ell}_m$. Given the g-identifiability assumption, $\gamma(\bar{\ell}_m, \bar{a}_{Pm}, \bar{a}_Z)$ is the direct effect on the quantiles of the distribution of Y of one final blip of A_{Pm} treatment of magnitude a_{Pm} at time t_m among subjects with history $(\bar{a}_{(m-1)}, \bar{\ell}_m)$ when treatment $\bar{A}_Z$ is set to $\bar{a}_Z$. Our interest in $\gamma(y, \bar{\ell}_m, \bar{a}_{Pm}, \bar{a}_Z)$ is based on the following theorem.

THEOREM 10.1. $\gamma(y, \bar{\ell}_m, \bar{a}_{Pm}, \bar{a}_Z) = y$ for all $y, m, \bar{\ell}_m, \bar{a}_{Pm}, \bar{a}_Z$ if and only if the direct-effect "g"-null hypothesis (equation 17) holds.

Proof. By Robins (1989, 1997) and Robins and Wasserman (1997), $\gamma(y, \bar{\ell}_m, \bar{a}_{Pm}, \bar{a}_Z) = y$ if and only if the (overall) "g"-null hypothesis (equation 24) holds on DAG G^*, which (by the arguments in the proof of lemma 5.1) is true if and only if equation 17 holds on DAG G.

10.2 Direct-Effect Structural Nested Distribution Models

In view of theorem 10.1, my approach will be to construct a parametric model for $\gamma(y, \bar{\ell}_m, \bar{a}_{Pm}, \bar{a}_Z)$ depending on a parameter ψ such that $\gamma(y, \bar{\ell}_m, \bar{a}_{Pm}, \bar{a}_Z) = y$ if and only if the true value ψ_0 of the parameter is 0.

Definition. The distribution F of V follows a direct-effect pseudostructural nested distribution model $\gamma(y, \bar{\ell}_m, \bar{a}_{Pm}, \bar{a}_Z, \psi)$ if $\gamma(y, \bar{\ell}_m, \bar{a}_{Pm}, \bar{a}_Z) = \gamma(y, \bar{\ell}_m, \bar{a}_{Pm}, \bar{a}_Z, \psi_0)$ where (1) $\gamma(y, \bar{\ell}_m, \bar{a}_{Pm}, \bar{a}_Z, \psi)$ is a known function, (2) ψ_0 is a finite vector of unknown parameters to be estimated, (3) for each value of ψ, $\gamma(y, \bar{\ell}_m, \bar{a}_{Pm}, \bar{a}_Z, \psi)$ satisfies conditions (a) to (c) that were satisfied by $\gamma(y, \bar{\ell}_m, \bar{a}_{Pm}, \bar{a}_Z)$, (4) $\partial\gamma(y, \bar{\ell}_m, \bar{a}_{Pm}, \bar{a}_Z, \psi) / \partial \psi$ and $\partial^2\gamma(y, \bar{\ell}_m, \bar{a}_{Pm}, \bar{a}_Z, \psi) / \partial\psi\partial y$ are continuous in ψ, and (5) $\gamma(y, \bar{\ell}_m, \bar{a}_{Pm}, \bar{a}_Z, \psi) = y$ if and only if $\psi = 0$ so that $\psi_0 = 0$ represents the direct-effect "g-"null hypothesis.

An example of an appropriate function $\gamma(y, \bar{\ell}_m, \bar{a}_{Pm}, \bar{a}_Z, \psi)$ can be obtained from equations 52 and 53 by replacing the quantities 2, 3, 4, and 5 with the components of $\psi = (\psi_1, \psi_2, \psi_3, \psi_4)$. We call models for $\gamma(y, \bar{\ell}_m, \bar{a}_{Pm}, \bar{a}_Z)$

pseudo-structural because they are models for the distribution F of the observables V regardless of whether this distribution has a structural (i.e., causal) interpretation (as it would in a sequential randomized trial or, more generally, whenever the assumption of g-identifiability holds). When $\gamma(y, \bar{\ell}_m, \bar{a}_{Pm}, \bar{a}_Z)$ does have a causal interpretation as well, the models are referred to as direct-effect SNDMs.

10.3 Semiparametric Estimation

I now consider testing and estimation of ψ_0 in the (redefined) semiparametric model (a), characterized by (1) the direct-effect SNDM $\gamma(y, \bar{\ell}_m, \bar{a}_{Pm}, \bar{a}_Z, \psi)$ and (2) the densities $f(a_m \mid \bar{a}_{m-1}, \bar{\ell}_m)$ are known. Our fundamental tool is the following theorem. For any function $\gamma^*(y, \bar{\ell}_m, \bar{a}_{Pm}, \bar{a}_Z)$ satisfying conditions (a) to (c), satisfied by $\gamma(y, \bar{\ell}_m, \bar{a}_{Pm}, \bar{a}_Z)$, I recursively redefine the following random variables: $H_K(\gamma^*) = \gamma^*(Y, \bar{L}_K, \bar{A}_{PK}, \bar{A}_Z)$, $H_m(\gamma^*) = \gamma^*(H_{m+1}(\gamma^*), \bar{L}_m, \bar{A}_{Pm}, \bar{A}_Z)$, and set $H(\gamma^*) \equiv H_0(\gamma^*)$. The following theorem, proved in section 14.2, characterizes the true quantile-quantile function $\gamma(y, \bar{\ell}_m, \bar{a}_{Pm}, \bar{a}_Z)$.

THEOREM 10.2. $\gamma^*(Y, \bar{L}_m, \bar{A}_{Pm}, \bar{A}_Z) = \gamma(Y, \bar{L}_m, \bar{A}_{Pm}, \bar{A}_Z)$ w.p.1 if and only if for $m = 0, ..., K$ and any functions $t_m(\cdot, \cdot)$,

$E\left[t_m(\underline{A}_{Z(m+1)}, H(\gamma^*)) / W_{m+1} \mid \bar{A}_m, \bar{L}_m\right]$ does not depend on A_{Pm} w.p.1.

Proof. A direct proof is given in section 14. Alternatively, by Robins (1989, 1997) and Robins and Wasserman (1997), the function γ is uniquely characterized on DAG G^* by $H(\gamma) \coprod {}^* A_{Pm} \mid \bar{A}_{P(m-1)}, \bar{L}_m, \bar{A}_Z$, which can be used in place of equation 25 and the proof strategy of section 5.2 adopted.

Given an SNDM, define $H(\psi)$ to be $H(\gamma^*)$ with γ^* the function

$$\gamma(y, \bar{\ell}_m, \bar{a}_{Pm}, \bar{a}_Z, \psi).$$

We can then construct direct-effect g-tests and g-estimates for ψ_0 analogous to those in section 8 since theorem 8.2 remains true with the functions $T_m^*(A_{Pm}, y)$ now arbitrary functions of Y rather than only linear functions. Again there exists a t_{eff}^* and r_{eff} such that the asymptotic variance of $\hat{\psi}(t_{eff}^*, r_{eff})$ attains the semiparametric efficiency bound for ψ_0 in the semiparametric model (a). Generalizations to observational studies with unknown $f(A_m \mid \bar{L}_m, \bar{A}_{m-1})$ are as described following theorem 8.2. Further, the practical tests and estimators of section 8 are available without requiring the functions q_m^* to be linear in their first argument.

10.4 Estimation of Some Contrasts

In this section, it will be convenient to adopt the following notation. Write $F_{g_P, \bar{a}_Z}(y \mid \bar{\ell}_m)$ as $b(y, \bar{\ell}_m, g_P, \bar{a}_Z)$, $F_{g_P, \bar{a}_Z}(y)$ as $b(y, g_P, \bar{a}_Z)$. When g_P is the $\bar{A}_P$-regime $(\bar{a}_{Pm}, 0)$, we write $b(y, \bar{\ell}_m, g_P, \bar{a}_Z)$ as $b(y, \bar{\ell}_m, \bar{a}_{Pm}, \bar{a}_Z)$ and

$b(y, g_P, \bar{a}_Z)$ as $b(y, \bar{a}_{P_m}, \bar{a}_Z)$. Finally, for the $\bar{A}_P$-regime that is identically zero, we write $b(y, g_P, \bar{a}_Z)$ as $b(y, 0, \bar{a}_Z) \equiv b(y, \bar{a}_Z)$. In this section, I propose methods to estimate some contrasts $b(y, g_P^{(1)}, \bar{a}_Z) - b(y, g_P^{(2)}, \bar{a}_Z)$. To do so, we shall estimate the quantile-quantile function $\tau(y, \bar{a}_Z)$ that maps quantiles of $b(y, \bar{a}_Z) \equiv b(y, 0, \bar{a}_Z)$ into those of $b(y, 0) \equiv b(y, 0, 0)$, i.e., $b(y, 0, \bar{a}_Z) \equiv b\{\tau(y, \bar{a}_Z), 0, 0\}$. Note that $\tau(y, \bar{a}_Z)$ is increasing in y and $\tau(y, \bar{a}_Z) = y$ if $\bar{a}_Z \equiv 0$. To estimate $\tau(y, \bar{a}_Z)$ we replace the semiparametric model (a) with the semiparametric model (b), which imposes the additional restriction that $\tau(y, \bar{a}_Z) = \tau(y, \bar{a}_Z; \theta_0)$ where $\tau(y, \bar{a}_Z; \theta)$ is a known increasing function of y satisfying $\tau(y, \bar{a}_Z, \theta) = y$ if $\bar{a}_Z \equiv 0$ or $\theta = 0$. Thus $\theta_0 = 0$ reflects the hypothesis $b(y, 0, \bar{a}_Z) = b(y, 0, 0)$ of no effect of treatment $\bar{A}_Z$ on the marginal distribution of Y when treatment with $\bar{A}_P$ is withheld. The model $\tau(\bar{y}, \bar{a}_Z; \theta)$ is a marginal structural transformation model in the sense of Robins (1998, 1999) for the effect of $\bar{A}_Z$ on Y when treatment with $\bar{A}_P$ is withheld. Any other marginal structural model for $b(y, \bar{a}_Z)$ could have been used. I chose the transformation model because of its relationship to the ordinary structural nested models discussed in section 12. The fundamental tool in constructing an estimate for θ is the following characterization of $\tau(y, \bar{a}_Z)$. Let $\tau^*(y, \bar{a}_Z)$ be any increasing function of y satisfying $\tau^*(y, \bar{a}_Z) = 0$ if $\bar{a}_Z = 0$.

Define $\sigma(\tau^*) \equiv \sigma(\gamma, \tau^*) \equiv \tau^* \{H(\gamma), \bar{A}_Z\}$. Given any function $t(\bullet,\bullet)$ and density $t_2(\bar{a}_Z)$ for $\bar{A}_Z$, i.e.,

$$\int t_2(\bar{a}_Z) d\mu(\bar{a}_Z) = 1 , \tag{54}$$

let

$$c_1(\bar{a}_Z) = E\left[\frac{t\{\sigma(\tau^*), \bar{a}_Z\} t_2(\bar{A}_Z)}{W} \right]$$

and

$$c_2(y) = E\left[\frac{t\{y, \bar{A}_Z\}}{W} \right]$$

with $W = W_0$.

THEOREM 10.3. The following are equivalent. (1) $\tau^*(y, \bar{A}_Z) = \tau(y, \bar{A}_Z)$ w.p.1., (2) for any function $t(\bullet, \bullet)$ and density $t_2(a_Z)$

$$E\left\{ W^{-1}\left[t\{\sigma(\tau^*), \bar{A}_Z\} - c_1(\bar{A}_Z) \right] \right\} = 0 \tag{55}$$

whenever the expectation is finite.
(3) for any $t(\bullet,\bullet)$ and density $t_2(\bar{a}_Z)$

$$E\left\{ W^{-1}\left[t\{\sigma(\tau^*), \bar{A}_Z\} - t_2(\bar{A}_Z) c_2\{\sigma(\tau^*)\} \right] \right\} = 0 \tag{56}$$

whenever the expectation is finite.

Proofs of theorems 10.3 to 10.5 are given at the end of this section.

Remark. The theorem is false if $t_2(\bar{a}_Z)$ is not a density.

Given a g-estimate $\hat{\psi}$ of ψ_0, equation 55 suggests the following estimator $\hat{\theta}^{(1)}$ of θ_0. Define $\sigma(\psi, \theta) = \tau\{H(\psi), \bar{A}_Z; \theta\}$ and let

$$\hat{S}_1(\theta, \psi) \equiv \hat{S}_1(\theta, \psi, t, t_2) =$$

$$W^{-1}\left[t\{\sigma(\psi, \theta), \bar{A}_Z\} - n^{-1}\sum_{i=1}^{n} t_2(\bar{A}_{Zi}) t\{\sigma_i(\psi, \theta), \bar{A}_Z\} / W_i \right],$$

where $t_2(\bar{a}_Z)$ satisfies equation 54. Let $\hat{\theta}^{(1)} = \hat{\theta}^{(1)}(\hat{\psi}) \equiv \hat{\theta}^{(1)}(\hat{\psi}, t, t_2)$ solve $0 = \sum_{i=1}^{n} \hat{S}_{1i}(\theta, \hat{\psi}, t, t_2)$.

Similarly, equation 56 suggests the following alternative estimator $\hat{\theta}^{(2)}$. Let

$$\hat{S}_2(\theta, \psi) = \hat{S}_2(\theta, \psi, t, t_2) =$$

$$W^{-1}\left[t\{\sigma(\psi, \theta), \bar{A}_Z\} - t_2(\bar{A}_Z)\left[n^{-1}\sum_{i=1}^{n} t\{\sigma(\psi, \theta), \bar{A}_{Zi}\} / W_i \right] \right]$$

and let

$$\hat{\theta}^{(2)} = \hat{\theta}^{(2)}(\hat{\psi}) \equiv \hat{\theta}^{(2)}(\hat{\psi}, t, t_2)$$

solve

$$0 = \sum_{i=1}^{n} \hat{S}_{2i}(\theta, \hat{\psi}, t, t_2) .$$

Then, under regularity conditions, by theorem 10.3, $\hat{\theta}^{(1)}$ and $\hat{\theta}^{(2)}$ will be RAL estimators of θ_0.

Given RAL estimators $\hat{\theta}$ and $\hat{\psi}$ of θ_0 and ψ_0, we can use the following theorem to estimate the distribution $b(y, 0) \equiv b(y, 0, 0)$ of Y had all subjects remained untreated with either treatment.

THEOREM 10.4. For any function $t(\bar{a}_Z)$, not necessarily a density,

$$E[W^{-1} t(\bar{A}_Z) \{I[\sigma(\tau) \leq y] - b(y, 0, 0)\}] = 0 \tag{57}$$

whenever the expectation is finite where, for any event Z, $I(Z) = 1$ if Z is true and 0 otherwise.

Theorem 10.4 implies that, having chosen $t(\bar{a}_Z)$ to ensure integrability, if $\bar{A}_Z$ is continuous, the estimator

$$\hat{b}(y, 0, 0) = b(y, 0, 0; \hat{\psi}, \hat{\theta}) \equiv \frac{\sum_i W_i^{-1} t(\bar{A}_{Zi}) I[\sigma_i(\hat{\psi}, \hat{\theta}) \leq y]}{\sum_i W_i^{-1} t(\bar{A}_{Zi})}$$

solving

$$\sum_i W_i^{-1} t(\bar{A}_{Zi}) \left\{ I[\sigma_i(\hat{\psi}, \hat{\theta}) \leq y] - b(y, 0, 0) \right\} = 0$$

will be a RAL estimator of $b(y, 0, 0)$. Thus $\hat{b}(y, 0, 0)$ is discrete with support at the $\sigma_i(\hat{\psi}, \hat{\theta})$ with density

$$\hat{f}_{0,0}(y) = \frac{\sum_i W_i^{-1} t(\bar{A}_{Zi}) I\{\sigma_i(\hat{\psi}, \hat{\theta}) = y\}}{\sum_i W_i^{-1} t(\bar{A}_{Zi})} \; .$$

(58)

Furthermore, we can use the following theorem to estimate the nondynamic contrast

$$b\left(y, \bar{a}_P^{(1)}, \bar{a}_Z\right) - b\left(y, \bar{a}_P^{(2)}, \bar{a}_Z\right)$$

whenever, for $m = 0, \ldots, K$,

$$\gamma(y, \bar{\ell}_m, \bar{a}_{Pm}, \bar{a}_Z) = \gamma(y, \bar{a}_{Pm}, \bar{a}_Z) \text{ does not depend on } \bar{\ell}_m.$$

(59)

First we need to develop some additional notation. Let $h(y, \bar{\ell}, \bar{a})$ be the function such that

$$H \equiv H(\gamma) = h(Y, \bar{L}, \bar{A}) \; .$$

(60)

This function is increasing in y and satisfies $h(y, \bar{\ell}, \bar{a}) = h(y, \bar{a})$ if equation 59 is true. For any function $q(y, \bullet, \bullet)$ increasing in y, I define $q^{-1}(y, \bullet, \bullet)$ to be the function satisfying $q^{-1}(u, \bullet, \bullet) = y$ if $q(y, \bullet, \bullet) = u$.

THEOREM 10.5. If equation 59 holds, then for any regime $\bar{a} = (\bar{a}_P, \bar{a}_Z)$

$$b(y, \bar{a}_P, \bar{a}_Z) = pr\left[h^{-1}\{\tau^{-1}(X, \bar{a}_Z), \bar{a}\} < y\right]$$

where X is a random variable with distribution $b(y, 0, 0)$.

Thus to estimate $b(y, \bar{a}_P, \bar{a}_Z)$ under equation 59, we compute

$$pr\left[h^{-1}\left\{\tau^{-1}\left(X, \bar{a}_Z; \hat{\theta}\right), \bar{a}, \hat{\psi}\right\} < y\right]$$

with X drawn from the density $\hat{f}_{0,0}(y)$ of equation 58, where $h^{-1}(\bullet, \bullet, \psi)$ is the function $h^{-1}(\bullet, \bullet)$ based on the blip function $\gamma(y, \bar{\ell}_m, \bar{a}_{Pm}, \bar{a}_Z, \psi) = \gamma(y, \bar{a}_{Pm}, \bar{a}_Z, \psi)$. We obtain

$$b\left(y, \bar{a}_P, \bar{a}_Z; \hat{\psi}, \hat{\theta}\right)$$

$$= \frac{\sum_i I\left[h^{-1}\left\{\tau^{-1}\left(\sigma_i(\hat{\psi}, \hat{\theta}), \bar{a}_Z; \hat{\theta}\right), \bar{a}, \hat{\psi}\right\} < y\right] W_i^{-1} t(\bar{A}_{Zi})}{\sum_i W_i^{-1} t(\bar{A}_{Zi})} \; .$$

When either equation 59 is false or g_P is a dynamic regime, it is much more difficult to obtain an estimator of $b(y, g_P, \bar{a}_Z)$ that is consistent with our direct-effect SNDM. I return to this issue in section 11.

Proof of theorem 10.3. A direct proof is given in section 14. Here is an alternative proof. Under DAG G^*, $pr^*[H(\gamma) < y \mid \bar{A}_Z] = b(y, 0, \bar{A}_Z)$ by results in Robins (1989, 1997) on estimation of the overall effect of $\bar{A}_P$ on G^*. Furthermore, these results imply that $\tau(\bullet, \bullet)$ is the unique function such that

$$\sigma \equiv \tau\{H(\gamma), \overline{A}_Z\} \amalg * \overline{A}_Z . \tag{61}$$

However, equation 61 is equivalent to

$$E^*[q(\sigma, \overline{a}_Z) - c_2(\sigma)] = 0 \tag{62}$$

for all $q(\bullet, \bullet)$ where $\sigma \equiv \sigma(\tau) \equiv \sigma(\gamma, \tau)$ and $c_2(y) \equiv E^*\{q(y, \overline{A}_Z)\}$. However, for any random variable N,

$$E^*(N) = E[Nt_2(\overline{A}_Z) / W], \tag{63}$$

where $t_2(\overline{a}_Z)$ is the density of $\overline{A}_Z$ on G^*. Invoking equation 63 and defining $t(\sigma, \overline{a}_Z) \equiv q(\sigma, \overline{a}_Z) \, t_2(\overline{a}_Z)$, we find that equation 62 is equivalent to equation 56 with $\sigma(\tau^*) \equiv \sigma$.

On the other hand, equation 61 is also equivalent to

$$E^*[q(\sigma, \overline{A}_Z) - c_1^*(\overline{A}_Z)] = 0 \tag{64}$$

for all $q(\bullet, \bullet)$ where $c_1^*(\overline{a}_Z) = E^*[q(\sigma, \overline{a}_Z)]$. Using equation 63 and putting $t(\sigma, \overline{a}_Z) = t_2(\overline{a}_Z) \, q(\sigma, \overline{a}_Z)$ and noting $t_2(\overline{a}_Z) \, c_1^*(\overline{a}_Z) = E^*[t_2(\overline{a}_Z) \, q(\sigma, \overline{a}_Z)] = c_1(\overline{a}_Z)$, we can conclude that equation 64 is equivalent to equation 55 with $\sigma(\tau^*) = \sigma$.

Proof of theorem 10.4. Under DAG G^*, it follows from Robins (1989, 1997) and equation 61 that $\sigma = \sigma(\gamma, \tau)$ has distribution $b(y, 0, 0)$. Hence, $E^*[I\{\sigma < y\} - b(y, 0, 0)] = 0$. Invoking equation 63 completes the proof. An alternative direct proof is given in section 14.

Proof of theorem 10.5. This is an immediate consequence of the definitions of $\tau(y, \overline{a}_Z)$, $\gamma(y, \overline{\ell}_m, \overline{a}_{Pm}, \overline{a}_Z)$, and $h(y, \overline{\ell}_K, \overline{a}_K)$.

11. Parametric Likelihood-Based Inference for Direct-Effect SNDMs

I now describe a reparameterization of the distribution of V in terms of the functions

$$\gamma(y, \overline{\ell}_m, \overline{a}_{Pm}, \overline{a}_Z) \text{ and } \tau(y, \overline{a}_Z)$$

that will allow a fully parametric likelihood or Bayesian approach to testing the direct-effect "g"-null hypothesis and estimating the functionals $b(y, g_P, \overline{a}_Z)$. To describe this approach, I first define $v(y, \overline{\ell}_m, \overline{a}_{P(m-1)}, \overline{a}_Z)$ by

$$b(y, \overline{\ell}_m, \overline{a}_{P(m-1)}, \overline{a}_Z) = b\{v(y, \overline{\ell}_m, \overline{a}_{P(m-1)}, \overline{a}_Z), \overline{\ell}_{m-1}, \overline{a}_{P(m-1)}, \overline{a}_Z\} . \tag{65}$$

That is, $v(y, \overline{\ell}_m, \overline{a}_{P(m-1)}, \overline{a}_Z)$ is the unique function mapping quantiles of $F_{\overline{a}}(y \mid \overline{\ell}_m)$ into quantiles of

$$F_{\overline{a}}\left(y \mid \overline{\ell}_{m-1}\right) \text{ with } \overline{a} = \left\{\left(\overline{a}_{P(m-1)}, 0\right), \overline{a}_Z\right\} .$$

Thus, since by definition,

$$\int b\left(y, \overline{\ell}_m, \overline{a}_{P(m-1)}, \overline{a}_Z\right) dF\left(\ell_m \mid \overline{\ell}_{m-1}, \overline{a}_{m-1}\right) = b\left(y, \overline{\ell}_{m-1}, \overline{a}_{P(m-1)}, \overline{a}_Z\right)$$

it follows that

$$\int b\left[v\{y, \overline{\ell}_m, \overline{a}_{P(m-1)}, \overline{a}_Z\}, \overline{\ell}_{m-1}, \overline{a}_{P(m-1)}, \overline{a}_Z\right] dF\left[\ell_m \mid \overline{\ell}_{m-1}, \overline{a}_{P(m-1)}, \overline{a}_{Z(m-1)}\right]$$

$$= b\left(y, \overline{\ell}_{m-1}, \overline{a}_{P(m-1)}, \overline{a}_Z\right) \tag{66}$$

Now we recursively define the random variables $\mathcal{H}_K$, $\mathcal{M}_K$, $\mathcal{H}_{K-1}$, $\mathcal{M}_{K-1}$, ..., $\mathcal{H}_0$, $\mathcal{M}_0$ by $\mathcal{H}_K = \gamma(Y, \overline{L}_K, \overline{A}_{PK}, \overline{A}_Z)$, $\mathcal{M}_k = v(\mathcal{H}_k, \overline{L}_k, \overline{A}_{P(k-1)}, \overline{A}_Z)$, $\mathcal{H}_k = \gamma(\mathcal{M}_{k+1}, \overline{L}_k, \overline{A}_{Pk}, \overline{A}_Z)$. Finally, define $\varepsilon \equiv \tau(\mathcal{M}_0, \overline{A}_Z)$. We also write $\varepsilon = d[Y, \overline{L}_K, \overline{A}_K]$ to emphasize that ε is a function $d(\cdot, \cdot, \cdot)$ of the data $(Y, \overline{L}_K, \overline{A}_K)$ that is increasing in Y. Thus we can write $Y = d^{-1}(\varepsilon, \overline{L}_K, \overline{A}_K)$. I prove the following in section 14.

THEOREM 11.1. (1)

$$pr[\mathcal{H}_m > y \mid \overline{L}, \overline{A}] = b(y, \overline{L}_m, \overline{A}_{P(m-1)}, \overline{A}_Z) \tag{67}$$

so that

$$\mathcal{H}_m \coprod (\underline{A}_{Pm}, \underline{L}_{m+1}) \mid \overline{L}_m, \overline{A}_Z, \overline{A}_{P(m-1)} \; ; \tag{68}$$

$$(2)\; pr[\mathcal{M}_m > y \mid \overline{L}, \overline{A}] = b(y, \overline{L}_{m-1}, \overline{A}_{P(m-1)}, \overline{A}_Z) \tag{69}$$

so

$$\mathcal{M}_m \coprod (\underline{L}_m, \underline{A}_{Pm}) \mid \overline{L}_{m-1}, \overline{A}_{P(m-1)}, \overline{A}_Z \; ; \tag{70}$$

$$(3)\; pr[\varepsilon > y \mid \overline{L}, \overline{A}] = b(y, 0, 0) \tag{71}$$

so

$$\varepsilon \coprod (\overline{L}, \overline{A}) \; . \tag{72}$$

Remark. $H_m \equiv H_m(\gamma)$ and $\sigma \equiv \sigma(\gamma, \tau)$, in contrast to $\mathcal{H}_m$ and ε, are not conditionally independent of any components of $(\overline{L}, \overline{A})$ given any other components. In particular

$$H_m \coprod A_{Pm} \mid \overline{L}_m, \overline{A}_{P(m-1)}, \overline{A}_Z \tag{73}$$

is false (although true on DAG G^*) for, were it true, the inverse weight W_{m+1} would not be necessary in equation 18 or in the expectation in theorem 10.2. Similarly, if σ were independent of $\overline{A}_Z$, the inverse weight W would not be necessary in equations 55 and 56 of theorem 10.3.

Theorem 11.1 implies that the density $f(V)$ factors as follows.

$$f(V) \equiv f\left(Y, \overline{L}_K, \overline{A}_K\right) \equiv \left\{\frac{\partial \varepsilon}{\partial Y}\right\} f(\varepsilon) \prod_{m=0}^{K} f\left[L_m \mid \overline{L}_{m-1}, \overline{A}_{m-1}\right] f\left[A_m \mid \overline{L}_m, \overline{A}_{m-1}\right] \tag{74}$$

where $\partial \varepsilon / \partial Y \equiv \partial d(Y, \overline{L}_K, \overline{A}_K) / \partial Y \equiv \{\partial d^{-1}(\varepsilon, \overline{L}_K, \overline{A}_K) / \partial \varepsilon\}^{-1}$. Thus we have reparameterized $f(V)$ in terms of the functions (1) $\gamma(y, \overline{\ell}_m, \overline{a}_{Pm}, \overline{a}_Z)$, (2)

$\tau(y, \overline{a}_Z)$, (3) $v(y, \overline{\ell}_m, \overline{a}_{P(m-1)}, \overline{a}_Z)$ satisfying equation 66, (4) the density $f(\varepsilon)$ of ε, (5) the densities $f(\overline{\ell}_m \mid \overline{\ell}_{m-1}, \overline{a}_{m-1})$, and (6) the densities $f(a_m \mid \overline{\ell}_m, \overline{a}_{m-1})$.

However, this reparameterization is not unrestricted since the constraint equation 66 will not hold for arbitrary densities $f(\overline{\ell}_m \mid \overline{\ell}_{m-1}, \overline{a}_{m-1})$ and functions $v(y, \overline{\ell}_m, \overline{a}_{P(m-1)}, \overline{a}_Z)$. An unrestricted parameterization is necessary in order to allow unconstrained likelihood-based inferences, and, more importantly, to avoid difficulties analogous to those discussed in remark B of section 9.2. Therefore, we replace in the parameterization the functions $v(y, \overline{\ell}_m, \overline{a}_{P(m-1)}, \overline{a}_Z)$ by the hazard ratio $v^*(y, \overline{\ell}_m, \overline{a}_{P(m-1)}, \overline{a}_Z)$, where

$$v^*(y, \overline{\ell}_m, \overline{a}_{P(m-1)}, \overline{a}_Z)$$
$$= \lambda(y, \overline{\ell}_m, \overline{a}_{P(m-1)}, \overline{a}_Z) / \lambda(y, \{\overline{\ell}_{m-1}, \ell_m = 0\}, \overline{a}_{P(m-1)}, \overline{a}_Z) \qquad (75)$$

so that

$$v^*(y, \overline{\ell}_m, \overline{a}_{P(m-1)}, \overline{a}_Z) = 1 \text{ if } \ell_m = 0$$
$$\text{and } v^*(y, \overline{\ell}_m, \overline{a}_{P(m-1)}, \overline{a}_Z) \text{ is nonnegative}. \qquad (76)$$

Here $\lambda(y, \overline{\ell}_m, \overline{a}_{P(m-1)}, \overline{a}_Z) \equiv -\partial\{\ell n [1 - b(y, \overline{\ell}_m, \overline{a}_{P(m-1)}, \overline{a}_Z)]\} / \partial y$. It may appear from equation 75 that in addition to the function v^* our parameterization also depends on the hazard function $\lambda(y, \{\overline{\ell}_{m-1}, \ell_m = 0\}, \overline{a}_{P(m-1)}, \overline{a}_Z)$. However, $\lambda(y, \{\overline{\ell}_{m-1}, \ell_m = 0\}, \overline{a}_{P(m-1)}, \overline{a}_Z)$ is completely determined (and thus not part of the parameterization) by $F_\varepsilon(y)$, $\tau(y, \overline{a}_Z)$, $\gamma(y, \overline{\ell}_m, \overline{a}_{Pm}, \overline{a}_Z)$, $f(\overline{\ell}_m \mid \overline{\ell}_{m-1}, \overline{a}_{m-1})$ and $v^*(y, \overline{\ell}_m, \overline{a}_{P(m-1)}, \overline{a}_Z)$.

Specifically, the $\lambda(y, \{\overline{\ell}_{m-1}, \ell_m = 0\}, \overline{a}_{P(m-1)}, \overline{a}_Z)$ are obtained recursively from these other functions and densities as follows. First, $b(y, 0, \overline{a}_Z) \equiv b(y, \overline{\ell}_{-1}, \overline{a}_{-1}, \overline{a}_Z)$ is given by $b(\tau^{-1}(y, \overline{a}_Z), 0, 0) \equiv F_\varepsilon(\tau^{-1}(y, \overline{a}_Z))$, where the convention $\overline{z}_{-1} \equiv 0$ is used. Now for $m = 0, \ldots, K - 1$, given

$$b(y, \overline{\ell}_{m-1}, \overline{a}_{P(m-1)}, \overline{a}_Z),$$

it follows from Robins, Rotnitzky, and Scharfstein (1999, section 8.7a) that $\lambda(y, \{\overline{\ell}_{m-1}, \ell_m = 0\}, \overline{a}_{P(m-1)}, \overline{a}_Z)$ is the unique solution $r(y, \overline{\ell}_{m-1}, \overline{a}_{P(m-1)}, \overline{a}_Z)$ to the Volterralike integral equation

$$r\left(y, \overline{\ell}_{m-1}, \overline{a}_{P(m-1)}, \overline{a}_Z\right) =$$

$$\frac{\partial\left\{b\left(y, \overline{\ell}_{m-1}, \overline{a}_{P(m-1)}, \overline{a}_Z\right)\right\} / \partial y}{\left\{\int \exp\left[-\int_{-\infty}^{y} v^*\left(u, \overline{\ell}_m, \overline{a}_{P(m-1)}, \overline{a}_Z\right) r\left(u, \overline{\ell}_{m-1}, \overline{a}_{P(m-1)}, \overline{a}_Z\right) du\right] \times v^*\left(y, \overline{\ell}_m, \overline{a}_{P(m-1)}, \overline{a}_Z\right) dF\left(\overline{\ell}_m \mid \overline{\ell}_{m-1}, \overline{a}_{m-1}\right)\right\}}$$

Thus

$$b\left(y, \bar{\ell}_m, \bar{a}_{P(m-1)}, \bar{a}_Z\right)$$

$$= 1 - \exp\left[-\int_{-\infty}^{y} v*\left(u, \bar{\ell}_m, \bar{a}_{P(m-1)}, \bar{a}_Z\right) \lambda\left(u, \{\bar{\ell}_{m-1}\, \ell_m = 0\}, \bar{a}_{P(m-1)}, \bar{a}_Z\right)\right] du$$

Further $v(y, \bar{\ell}_m, \bar{a}_{P(m-1)}, \bar{a}_Z)$ can now be obtained by equation 65. Finally, $b(y, \bar{\ell}_m, \bar{a}_{Pm}, \bar{a}_Z) = b\{\gamma(y, \bar{\ell}_m, \bar{a}_{Pm}, \bar{a}_Z), \bar{\ell}_m, \bar{a}_{P(m-1)}, \bar{a}_Z\}$. We are thus now in a position to repeat the recursion with m substituted for $m - 1$.

It follows from the factorization (equation 74) that if we specify a direct-effect SNDM $\gamma(y, \bar{\ell}_m, \bar{a}_{Pm}, \bar{a}_Z, \psi)$ and parametric models $\tau(y, \bar{a}_Z; \theta), f(\varepsilon; \eta_1),$ $f(\ell_m \mid \bar{\ell}_{m-1}, \bar{a}_{m-1}; \eta_3), v*(y, \bar{\ell}_m, \bar{a}_{P(m-1)}, \bar{a}_Z; \eta_2)$ and $f(a_m \mid \bar{\ell}_m, \bar{a}_{m-1}; \alpha)$ subject to the restrictions $\tau(y, \bar{a}_Z; \theta) = y$ if $\bar{a}_Z \equiv 0$ and the nonnegative function $v*(y, \bar{\ell}_m, \bar{a}_{P(m-1)}, \bar{a}_Z; \eta_2) = 1$ if $\bar{\ell}_m = 0$, then the contribution to the likelihood for a single subject can be written

$$f(V; \rho) =$$

$$\left\{\frac{\partial \varepsilon(\psi, \theta, \eta_2, \eta_3)}{\partial Y}\right\} f\left[\varepsilon(\psi, \theta, \eta_2, \eta_3); \eta_1\right] \prod_{m=0}^{K} f\left[A_m \mid \bar{L}_m, \bar{A}_{m-1}; \alpha\right] f\left[L_m \mid \bar{L}_{m-1}, \bar{A}_{m-1}; \eta_3\right].$$

The parameterization is nonstandard because the parameter η_3 occurs in two terms. Note that $\varepsilon(\psi, \theta, \eta_2, \eta_3)$ has no simple relationship to $\sigma(\psi, \theta)$ in contrast to what we found with SNMM models. The robustness properties of $\hat{\psi}_{MLE}$ are analogous to those described for direct-effect SNMM models. The parametrization is variation independent in the sense that any value of any parameter can occur with any value of any other parameter. However, the parametrization (equation 75) in terms of hazard ratios requires that the measure $b(y, \bar{\ell}_m, \bar{a}_{P(m-1)}, \bar{a}_Z)$ be absolutely continuous with respect to $b(y, \{\bar{\ell}_{m-1}, \ell_m = 0\}, \bar{a}_{P(m-1)}, \bar{a}_Z)$ for all ℓ_m, which we henceforth assume to be the case.

Remark. We could have tried to avoid the assumption of absolute continuity mentioned above by redefining the function $v*(y, \bar{\ell}_m, \bar{a}_{P(m-1)}, \bar{a}_Z)$ to be the unique function satisfying

$$v*(y, \bar{\ell}_m, \bar{a}_{P(m-1)}, \bar{a}_Z)$$
$$= v(y, \bar{\ell}_m, \bar{a}_{P(m-1)}, \bar{a}_Z) - v(y, \{\bar{\ell}_{m-1}, \ell_m = 0\}, \bar{a}_{P(m-1)}, \bar{a}_Z)$$

so that

$$v*(y, \bar{\ell}_m, \bar{a}_{P(m-1)}, \bar{a}_Z) = 0 \text{ if } \ell_m = 0.$$

It may appear that, in addition to the function $v*$, this alternative parametrization also depends on the function $v(y, \{\bar{\ell}_{m-1}, \ell_m = 0\}, \bar{a}_{P(m-1)}, \bar{a}_Z)$. However, it can be shown that $v(y, \{\bar{\ell}_{m-1}, \ell_m = 0\}, \bar{a}_{P(m-1)}, \bar{a}_Z)$ is completely determined (and thus not part of the parameterization) by the law $F_\varepsilon(y), \tau(y, \bar{a}_Z),$ $\gamma(y, \bar{\ell}_m, \bar{a}_{Pm}, \bar{a}_Z), f(\ell_m \mid \bar{\ell}_{m-1}, \bar{a}_{m-1})$ and $v*(y, \bar{\ell}_m, \bar{a}_{P(m-1)}, \bar{a}_Z)$. However, as discussed in Robins, Rotnitzky, and Scharfstein (1999, section 8.7a), this

alternative parametrization will not be unrestricted (i.e., variation indepen-
dent) if one allows $v^*(y, \bar{\ell}_m, \bar{a}_{P(m-1)}, \bar{a}_Z)$ to be nonmonotone in y. However,
nonmontonicity is required if all possible laws of the observed data are to
be represented by the parametrization.

The computational difficulty in computing $\hat{\rho}_{MLE}$ is much greater for direct-
effect SNDMs than for direct-effect SNMMs, since at each iteration
$\lambda(y,\{\bar{\ell}_{m-1}, \ell_m = 0\}, \bar{a}_{P(m-1)}, \bar{a}_Z)$ must be recursively computed by solving a series of Volterralike integral equations, as described above. With an estimator
of ρ in hand, we can estimate, through equation 74, the entire joint distribution $F(v)$ of the observables and thus $F_g(y)$ for any regime g. A robust and
computationally less demanding approach to estimating ρ than maximum
likelihood is to (1) calculate a g-estimate $\hat{\psi}$ of ψ_0, (2) compute $\hat{\theta} = \hat{\theta}(\hat{\psi})$ as described in section 10, (3) estimate $\hat{\eta}_3$ by maximizing

$$\prod_i \prod_{m=0}^{K} f\left(L_{mi} \mid \bar{L}_{(m-1)i}, \bar{A}_{(m-1)i}; \eta_3\right)$$

and (4) finally estimate η_1 and η_2 by maximizing

$$\prod_i f(V_i; \rho)$$

over (η_1, η_2) with (ψ, θ, η_3) fixed at $(\hat{\psi}, \hat{\theta}, \hat{\eta}_3)$. This guarantees the estimator
of $F_g(y)$ is consistent with the semiparametric g-test in section 3. However,
even this option may be computationally difficult because of the need to esti-
mate the $\lambda(y, \{\bar{\ell}_{m-1}, \ell_m = 0\}, \bar{a}_{P(m-1)}, \bar{a}_Z)$ at each iteration. In the next section, I discuss a different parameterization that will turn out to have difficul-
ties of its own but also, under further assumptions, much to recommend it.

12. An Alternative Approach to Estimation of Contrasts

Consider again estimation of $F_{g_P, \bar{a}_Z}(y) \equiv b(y, g_P, \bar{a}_Z)$. It follows from Robins
(1989, 1997) and Robins and Wasserman (1997) that, under the law $f^*(v)$ of
DAG G^* in section 5.1 with $\bar{A}_Z$ exogenous, $F_\sigma^*(y) = b(y, 0, 0)$, reflecting the
fact that $b(y, 0, 0) \equiv F^*_{(g_{P\equiv0}, \bar{a}_{Z\equiv0})}(y) = F^*_{g_{P\equiv0}}(y \mid \bar{A}_Z \equiv 0)$. Further, we obtain
independent realizations, say Y^*, from $F^*_{g_P}(y \mid \bar{a}_Z)$ by the following Monte
Carlo algorithm:

  Step 1. Draw σ from $b(y, 0, 0)$.
  Step 2. Draw L_0 from $f^*(\ell_0 \mid \bar{a}_Z, \sigma)$.
  Step 3. Recursively for $m = 1, \ldots, K$, draw L_m from
$f^*(\ell_m \mid \bar{L}_{m-1}, g_P(\bar{L}_{m-1}), \bar{a}_Z, \sigma)$.
  Step 4. Compute $Y^* = h^{-1}\{\tau^{-1}(\sigma, \bar{a}_Z), \bar{L}_K, g_P(\bar{L}_K), \bar{a}_Z\}$ where again
h^{-1} is the inverse function to $H = h(Y, \bar{L}_K, \bar{A}_{PK}, \bar{A}_{ZK})$ and is a functional
of $\gamma(y, \bar{\ell}_m, \bar{a}_{Pm}, \bar{a}_Z)$.

However, as shown in the proof of lemma 5.1, $F^*_{gP}(y \mid \bar{a}_Z) = F^*_{gP, \bar{a}_Z}(y) = F_{gP, \bar{a}_Z}(y)$, so we can in principle use the above algorithm to draw from our target distribution $F_{gP, \bar{a}_Z}(y)$ as follows. From a g-estimator $\hat{\psi}$, we obtain an estimate $h^{-1}(\cdot, \cdot, \cdot, \cdot, \hat{\psi})$ of $h^{-1}(\cdot, \cdot, \cdot, \cdot)$. From an estimator $\hat{\theta} = \hat{\theta}(\hat{\psi})$ of θ_0, we obtain an estimator $\tau^{-1}(\cdot, \cdot, \hat{\theta})$ of $\tau^{-1}(\cdot, \cdot)$. Further, from $(\hat{\theta}, \hat{\psi})$, we can draw from $b(y, 0, 0)$ using the estimated distribution $b(y, 0, 0; \hat{\theta}, \hat{\psi})$ with density $\hat{f}_{0,0}(y)$ given in equation 58. Hence to implement an estimated version of the algorithm, it only remains necessary to estimate

$$f^*(\ell_m \mid \bar{\ell}_{m-1}, \bar{a}_{P(m-1)}, \bar{a}_Z, \sigma) \ . \tag{77}$$

Suppose we could correctly specify a parametric model for equation 77 depending on a parameter η.

$$f(\ell_m \mid \bar{\ell}_{m-1}, \bar{a}_{P(m-1)}, \bar{a}_Z, \sigma, \eta) \ . \tag{78}$$

Then had the data been generated under G^*, the score $S(\eta) = \partial \ln f(L_m \mid \bar{L}_{m-1}, \bar{A}_{P(m-1)}, \bar{A}_Z, \sigma, \eta) / \partial \eta$ has mean zero under $f^*(v)$ at the true value of η. Equation 63 then implies

$$E[t_2(\bar{A}_Z) S(\eta) / W] = 0 \ . \tag{79}$$

Write $S(\eta) = S(\eta, \sigma)$ to emphasize the dependence of the score on σ. Then equation 79 suggests estimating η by $\hat{\eta}$ solving

$$0 = \sum_i t_2(\bar{A}_{Zi}) S_i \left(\eta, \sigma_i(\hat{\psi}, \hat{\theta}) \right) / W_i \ . \tag{80}$$

for some chosen $t_2(\bar{a}_Z)$. The solution $\hat{\eta}$ to equation 80 will be a RAL estimator of η if the models for (1) $\gamma(y, \bar{\ell}_m, \bar{a}_{Pm}, \bar{a}_Z)$, (2) $\tau(y, \bar{a}_Z)$, and (3) the density (equation 77) are correctly specified. However, except in the special case described later, it is unlikely that points 1 to 3 will all be correct, since a constraint must be satisfied. Specifically, as noted previously, by using d-separation on DAG G^*, we have

$$\underline{A}_{Zk} \coprod {}^* L_k \mid \bar{L}_{k-1}, \bar{A}_{k-1} \quad , \tag{81}$$

and further, by equation 61, on G^*, $\sigma \coprod {}^* \bar{A}_Z$. Also $\sigma \coprod {}^* A_{Pm} \mid \underline{A}_{Zm}, \bar{A}_{m-1}, \bar{L}_m$, since, by results in Robins (1997) for overall effects, $H \coprod {}^* A_{Pm} \mid \underline{A}_{Zm}, \bar{A}_{m-1}, \bar{L}_m$. These independencies imply that

$$\prod_{m=0}^{k} f^*\left(L_m \mid \bar{L}_{m-1}, \bar{A}_{m-1}\right) = \int \prod_{m=0}^{k} f^*\left(L_m \mid \bar{L}_{m-1}, \bar{A}_{m-1}, \underline{A}_{Zm}, \sigma\right) f^*(\sigma) d\sigma \tag{82}$$

for $k = 0, \dots, K$.

If we specify a model (equation 78) that imposes

$$\underline{A}_{Zm} \coprod {}^* L_m \mid \bar{L}_{m-1}, \bar{A}_{m-1}, \sigma \tag{83}$$

then equation 82 holds. However, equation 83 is a restriction on the allowable densities $f(v)$ for the data. If equation 83 is not true, it will be essentially impossible to specify a model (equation 78) such that, for some value of η_2, (1) equation 83 is false and (2) the constraint equation 82 holds. Hence when equation 83 is false, a parameterization in terms of (1) $F^*_\sigma(y) \equiv b\,(y, 0, 0)$, (2) the densities equation 77, and the functions (3) $\gamma(y, \bar{\ell}_m, \bar{a}_{Pm}, \bar{a}_Z)$ and (4) $\tau(y, \bar{a}_Z)$ that fails to impose equation 82 will suffer from the type of difficulties described in remark A of section 9. However, such a parameterization cannot be realized if equation 82 is imposed. Thus it becomes important to characterize equation 83 in some equivalent fashion with a clear causal interpretation, so that we can better judge when it is substantively reasonable to impose equation 83. I show that equation 83 can be characterized as a particular restriction on the functional form of a standard SNDM as studied in Robins (1997) and Robins and Wasserman (1997).

To characterize this restriction, recall the definition of a standard SNDM. Let $\dot{\gamma}(y, \bar{\ell}_m, \bar{a}_m)$ be the quantile-quantile function satisfying $b(y, \bar{\ell}_m, \bar{a}_m) = b[\dot{\gamma}(y, \bar{\ell}_m, \bar{a}_m), \bar{\ell}_m, \bar{a}_{m-1}]$ where $b(y, \bar{\ell}_m, \bar{a}_m) \equiv b\,(y, \bar{\ell}_m, \bar{a}_{Pm}, \bar{a}_{Zm})$ and $b\,(y, \bar{\ell}_m, \bar{a}_{Pk}, \bar{a}_{Zm}) \equiv F_g(y \mid \bar{\ell}_m)$ for the regime g that has (1) A_p history $\bar{a}_{Pk}$ through t_k and zero thereafter and (2) A_Z history $\bar{a}_{Zm}$ through t_m and zero thereafter. It follows that $\dot{\gamma}(y, \bar{\ell}_m, \bar{a}_m)$ is (1) increasing and continuously differentiable in y and (2) $\dot{\gamma}(y, \bar{\ell}_m, \bar{a}_m) = y$ if $a_m = 0$ (i.e., $a_{Pm} = a_{Zm} = 0$). Robins (1989, 1997) shows $\dot{\gamma}(y, \bar{\ell}_m, \bar{a}_m) \equiv y$ if and only if the "g"-null hypothesis (equation 15) holds. Now define $\dot{H} \equiv \dot{H}(\dot{\gamma}) \equiv \dot{H}_0(\dot{\gamma}) \equiv \dot{h}(y, \bar{L}_K, \bar{A}_K)$ recursively by $\dot{H}_{K+1}(\dot{\gamma}) \equiv Y$ and $\dot{H}_k(\dot{\gamma}) \equiv \dot{h}_k(Y, \bar{L}_K, \bar{A}_K) \equiv \dot{\gamma}[\dot{H}_{k+1}(\dot{\gamma}), \bar{L}_k, \bar{A}_k]$. Robins (1989, 1997) shows that

$$\dot{H} \coprod A_m \mid \bar{L}_m, \bar{A}_{m-1} \ . \tag{84}$$

Definition. The distribution $F(v)$ follows a standard SNDM $\dot{\gamma}(y, \bar{\ell}_m, \bar{a}_m, \delta)$ if $\dot{\gamma}(y, \bar{\ell}_m, \bar{a}_m) = \dot{\gamma}(y, \bar{\ell}_m, \bar{a}_m, \delta_0)$ and (1) $\dot{\gamma}(y, \bar{\ell}_m, a_m, \delta)$ satisfies points 1 to 2 above and $\dot{\gamma}(y, \bar{\ell}_m, \bar{a}_m, \delta) \equiv y$ if and only if $\delta = 0$, so $\delta_0 = 0$ represents the "g"-null hypothesis (equation 15). An example would be

$$\dot{\gamma}(y, \bar{\ell}_m, \bar{a}_m, \delta) = y + \delta_1 a_{Zm} a_{Z(m-1)} + \delta_2 a_{Zm} \ell^*_m + \delta_3 a_{Zm} a_{Pm} \ell^*_m$$
$$+ \delta_4 a_{Zm} a_{P(m-1)} + \delta_5 a_{Pm} + \delta_6 a_{Pm} a_{Z(m-1)} + \delta_7 a_{Pm} \ell^*_m\, a_{Z(m-1)}) \tag{85}$$

where $\delta = (\delta_1, \ldots, \delta_7)'$ and ℓ^*_m is a known function of $\bar{\ell}_m$. We need the following.

Definition. We say that $\dot{\gamma}(y, \bar{\ell}_m, \bar{a}_m)$ is A_P-direct-effect consistent if $\dot{\gamma}(y, \bar{\ell}_m, \bar{a}_m)$ is not a function of $\bar{\ell}_m$ when $a_{Pm} = 0$.

Example. Putting $a_{Pm} = 0$ in equation 85, we are left with the nonzero terms

$$\delta_1 a_{Zm} a_{Z(m-1)} + \delta_2 a_{Zm} \ell^*_m + \delta_4 a_{Zm} a_{P(m-1)}.$$

We thus deduce that $\dot{\gamma}(y, \bar{\ell}_m, \bar{a}_m)$ is A_P-direct-effect consistent if and only if the true value δ_{20} of δ_2 is zero. The importance of this definition is the following.

THEOREM 12.1. If $\dot{\gamma}(y, \bar{\ell}_m, \bar{a}_m)$ is A_P-direct-effect consistent, the direct-effect "g"-null hypothesis (equation 17) holds $\Leftrightarrow \dot{\gamma}(y, \bar{\ell}_m, \bar{a}_m)$ does not depend on $\bar{a}_{Pm} \Leftrightarrow \dot{\gamma}(y, \bar{\ell}_m, \bar{a}_m) = \dot{\gamma}(y, \bar{a}_{Zm})$ does not depend on $\bar{\ell}_m$ or $\bar{a}_{Pm}$.

Example. Suppose $\delta_{20} = 0$ in equation 85 so it is A_P-direct-effect consistent. Then the direct-effect "g"-null hypothesis holds $\Leftrightarrow \delta_{30} = \ldots = \delta_{70} = 0$. That is, $\dot{\gamma}(y, \bar{\ell}_m, \bar{a}_m, \delta_0) = \delta_{10} a_{Zm} a_{Z(m-1)}$. Note if $\delta_{20} \neq 0$ in equation 85, the direct-effect "g"-null hypothesis can be false even if $\delta_{30} = \ldots = \delta_{70} = 0$ since, for example, A_{P0} might affect ℓ_m^*, which then, in turn, affects Y via the interaction $a_{Zm}\ell_m^*$. Indeed, I developed the direct-effect SNDMs model precisely because, in the presence of terms such as $\delta_2 a_{Zm}\ell_m^*$, we are unable to use standard SNDMs to test the direct-effect "g"-null hypothesis. See Robins and Wasserman (1997, section 8.1) for further discussion. Before giving the main theorem, I give another condition equivalent to A_P-direct-effect consistency.

Definition. There is no $L - A_Z$ interaction if, for each m, the quantile-quantile function $\gamma_Z(y, \bar{\ell}_m, \bar{a}_{P(m-1)}, \bar{a}_{Zm})$ satisfying $b(y, \bar{\ell}_m, \bar{a}_{P(m-1)}, \bar{a}_{Zm}) = b\{\gamma_Z(y, \bar{\ell}_m, \bar{a}_{P(m-1)}, \bar{a}_{Zm}), \bar{\ell}_m, \bar{a}_{P(m-1)}, a_{Z(m-1)})\}$ does not depend on $\bar{\ell}_m$.

I am now ready to state the main theorem of this section, which gives alternative characterizations of equation 83.

THEOREM 12.2. The following are equivalent:
(1) Equation 83 holds.
(2) $\dot{\gamma}(y, \bar{\ell}_m, \bar{a}_m)$ is A_P-direct-effect consistent.
(3) There is no $L - A_Z$ interaction.
(4) $\sigma = \dot{H}$ w.p.1.
(5) $\sigma \perp\!\!\!\perp A_m \mid \bar{L}_m, \bar{A}_{m-1}$.
(6) $\sigma \perp\!\!\!\perp^* A_m \mid \bar{L}_m, \bar{A}_{m-1}$.

COROLLARY 12.1. Equation 83 implies $f^*(\bar{\ell}_m \mid \bar{\ell}_{m-1}, \bar{a}_{m-1}, \sigma)$ $= f(\bar{\ell}_m \mid \bar{\ell}_{m-1}, \bar{a}_{m-1}, \sigma)$ and $f(\sigma) = f^*(\sigma)$.

Theorem 12.2 indicates that weighting by W_m^{-1} is unnecessary when we impose equation 83. In particular, it follows from parts 4–5 of theorem 12.1 that (ψ, θ) can be estimated jointly by standard g-estimation of a standard SNDM as in Robins (1992, 1997). Further, by part 4 it follows that, given estimators $(\tilde{\psi}, \tilde{\theta})$, we can estimate the law $F_\sigma(y) = b(y, 0, 0)$ by $n^{-1} \Sigma_i I[\sigma_i(\tilde{\psi}, \tilde{\theta}) > y]$ as in Robins (1997). Finally, corollary 12.1 indicates that, given equation 83, the model (equation 78) can be fit by maximum likelihood without needing to reweight, since the model is also true for the density $f(\ell_m \mid \bar{\ell}_{m-1}, \bar{a}_{m-1}, \sigma)$. Note, however, that if one wanted an estimate of ψ_0 that would be consistent even under misspecification of the model $\tau(y, \bar{a}_Z; \theta)$, one would have to use the weighted g-estimator $\hat{\psi}$ of section 10, rather than the joint standard g-estimator of (ψ, θ) mentioned above.

The no $L - A_Z$ interaction characterization of equation 83 is probably the most easily interpreted characterization of equation 83 from a substantive point of view. In assessing the reasonableness of the no $L - A_Z$ interaction assumption, it is important to recognize that this absence of interaction is only on a particular scale, the quantile-quantile transformation scale as represented by the function $\gamma_Z (y, \bar{\ell}_m, a_{P(m-1)}, \bar{a}_{Zm})$ in the definition of no $L - A_Z$ interaction. The no $L - A_Z$ interaction assumption can be empirically tested by specifying a standard SNDM and testing for no A_P-direct-effect consistency. For example, given SNDM (equation 85), we would test the hypothesis $\delta_{20} = 0$ using a standard g-test as in Robins (1992, 1997).

13. Discussion

Following Robins (1999, 1998), I could have used direct-effect marginal structural models (MSMs) rather than direct-effect SNMs. A direct-effect marginal structural distribution model is a semiparametric model for $b(y, \bar{a}_P, \bar{a}_Z) = F_{\bar{a}_P, \bar{a}_Z}(y)$ depending on a finite dimensional parameter β_0 such that $\beta_0 = 0$ if and only if $F_{0, \bar{a}_Z}(y) = F_{\bar{a}_P, \bar{a}_Z}(y)$ for all $\bar{a}_P$. The direct-effect g-null hypothesis (equation 16) implies $\beta_0 = 0$ but the converse is false. An SNDM such as equation 85 with no $L - A_Z$ interaction (i.e. $\delta_{20} = 0$ apriori) is a direct effect marginal structural model, although the converse is false.

A direct-effect marginal structural mean model is a semiparametric model for $b(\bar{a}_P, \bar{a}_Z) = E_{\bar{a}_P, \bar{a}_Z}(Y)$ depending on a finite dimensional parameter β_0 such that $\beta_0 = 0$ if and only if $b(\bar{a}_P, \bar{a}_Z) = b(0, \bar{a}_Z)$ for all $\bar{a}_P$. The direct-effect g-null mean null hypothesis (equation 29) implies $\beta_0 = 0$ but the converse is false. Robins (1999, 1998) further discusses the advantages and disadvantages of marginal structural versus structural nested models.

14. Proofs

In this section, I provide proofs of theorems 8.1, 8.4, 10.2 to 10.4, 11.1 and 12.1.

14.1 Proof of Theorems 8.1 and 8.4

We need the following lemma. Let ε be as defined in equation 38.

LEMMA. For $j = -1, 0, \ldots, K$, and any function $t_j(\bullet)$

$$E[\varepsilon W_{j+1}^{-1} t_j (\underline{A}_{Z(j+1)}) \mid \bar{A}_j, \bar{L}_j] = 0 \tag{86}$$

$$E\left[b(\bar{A}_Z)W_{j+1}^{-1}t_j\left(\bar{A}_{Z(j+1)}\right) \mid \bar{A}_j, \bar{L}_j\right] = \iint b(\bar{A}_Z)t_j\left(\underline{A}_{Z(j+1)}\right) \prod_{k=j+1}^{K} d\mu\left(A_{Zk}\right) \tag{87}$$

$$E\left[v\left(\overline{L}_m,\overline{A}_{P(m-1)},\overline{A}_Z\right)W_{j+1}^{-1}t_j\left(\underline{A}_{Z(j+1)}\right)|\,\overline{A}_j,\overline{L}_j\right]=0 \text{ for } j<m\leq K \tag{88}$$

$$E\left[v\left(\overline{L}_m,\ \overline{A}_{P(m-1)}\overline{A}_Z\right)W_{j+1}^{-1}t_j\left(\underline{A}_{Z(j+1)}\right)|\,\overline{A}_j,\ \overline{L}_j\right]$$

$$=\iint v\left(\overline{L}_m,\ \overline{A}_{P(m-1)},\overline{A}_Z\right)t_j\left(\underline{A}_{Z(j+1)}\right)\prod_{k=j+1}^{K}d\mu(A_{Zk}),0\leq m<j\leq K\ . \tag{89}$$

Proof of lemma. Consider equation 88. By Fubini's theorem, the left-hand side of equation 88 is

$$\int\prod_{k=j+1}^{K}d\mu(A_{Zk})t_j\left(\underline{A}_{Z(j+1)}\right)$$

$$\left\{\iint\prod_{k=j+1}^{m-1}dF\left(A_{Pk}|\,\overline{A}_{k-1},A_{Zk}\right)dF\left(L_k|\,\overline{L}_{k-1},\overline{A}_{k-1}\right)\right.$$

$$\left.\left[\int v\left(\overline{L}_m,\overline{A}_{P(m-1)},\overline{A}_Z\right)dF\left(L_m|\,\overline{L}_{m-1},\overline{A}_{m-1}\right)\right]\right\}\ .$$

The term in the square brackets is zero by equation 37. Equations 86, 87, and 89 are established by similar calculations.

14.1.1 Proof of Theorem 8.1

$\Rightarrow$ Since the right-hand sides of equations 86–89 do not depend on A_j, the conclusion of the theorem follows from equations 38 and 40 when we set $m=j$.

$\Leftarrow$ Suppose $\gamma^*\ (\overline{L}_m,\ \overline{A}_{Pm},\ \overline{A}_Z)$ was a second function satisfying the premise of the theorem that differed from $\gamma(\overline{L}_m,\ \overline{A}_{Pm},\ \overline{A}_Z)$ on a set of positive probability. Let m^* be the largest value of m such that $\Delta\,(L_m,\overline{A}_{Pm},\overline{A}_Z)\equiv\gamma^*(\overline{L}_m,\overline{A}_{Pm},\overline{A}_Z)-\gamma(\overline{L}_m,\overline{A}_{Pm},\overline{A}_Z)$ is a function of A_{Pm} with positive probability. By the assumption that $\gamma^*(\overline{L}_m,\overline{A}_{Pm},\overline{A}_Z)=0$ if $A_{Pm}=0$, we are guaranteed that $m^*\geq 0$. It follows that the expectation in the theorem will be a function of A_{Pm^*} if and only if $\int d\mu\,(\underline{A}_{Z(m^*+1)})\,t\,\{\underline{A}_{Z(m^*+1)}\}\,\Delta\,(\overline{L}_{m^*},\overline{A}_{Pm^*},\overline{A}_Z)$ does not depend on A_{Pm^*}. But this clearly is false for a suitable choice of the function $t(\bullet)$.

14.1.2 Proof of Theorem 8.4

$\Rightarrow$We must show that

$$E\left[\sigma\,(\gamma,b)\,t(\overline{A}_Z)\,/\,W\right]\equiv E\left[\sigma\,(\gamma,b)\,t(\overline{A}_Z)\,/\,W_0\,|\,\overline{L}_{-1},\overline{A}_{-1}\,\right]=0\ . \tag{90}$$

But by equations 40 and 38,

$$\sigma(\gamma,b)\equiv H(\gamma)-b\left(\overline{A}_Z\right)=\varepsilon+\sum_{m=0}^{K}v\left(\overline{L}_m,\overline{A}_{P(m-1)},\overline{A}_Z\right)\ .$$

Equation 90 now follows from equations 86 and 88.

$\Leftarrow$ This can be proved analogously to theorem 8.1.

14.2 Proof of Theorems 10.2 to 10.4

Some preliminary results and definitions are required. First note for regime $g = \bar{a}$

$$f_{\bar{a}}\left(y \mid \bar{\ell}_m\right) = \int f_{\bar{a}}\left(y \mid \bar{\ell}_{m+1}\right) dF\left(\ell_{m+1} \mid \bar{L}_m = \bar{\ell}_m, \bar{A}_m = \bar{a}_m\right) . \tag{91}$$

Now let

$$f(y, \bar{\ell}_m, \bar{a}_{Pm}, \bar{a}_Z) \equiv \partial b\, (y, \bar{\ell}_m, \bar{a}_{Pm}, \bar{a}_Z) \,/\, \partial y \tag{92}$$

denote $f_g\left(y \mid \bar{\ell}_m\right)$ for $g = \bar{a}$, $\bar{a} = \{(\bar{a}_{Pm}, 0), \bar{a}_Z\}$. Also note that, from equation 92 and the definition of $\gamma(y, \bar{\ell}_m, \bar{a}_{Pm}, \bar{a}_Z)$, we have

$$f(u, \bar{\ell}_m, \bar{a}_{P(m-1)}, \bar{a}_Z)$$
$$= f\left[\gamma^{-1}\left(u, \bar{\ell}_m, \bar{a}_{Pm}, \bar{a}_Z\right), \bar{\ell}_m, \bar{a}_{Pm}, \bar{a}_Z\right] \partial \gamma^{-1}\left(u, \bar{\ell}_m, \bar{a}_{Pm}, \bar{a}_Z\right) / \partial u . \tag{93}$$

14.2.1 Proof of Theorem 10.2

$\Rightarrow$. I show by induction that, whenever the expectation is finite,

$$E\left[t\left(\bar{A}_Z, H_m, \bar{L}_m, \bar{A}_{P(m-1)}\right) / W_{m+1} \mid \bar{A}_m, \bar{L}_m\right]$$
$$= \int\left\{\int t\left(\bar{A}_Z, u, \bar{L}_m, \bar{A}_{P(m-1)}\right) f\left(u, \bar{L}_m, \bar{A}_{P(m-1)}, \bar{A}_Z\right) du\right\} du\left(\underline{A}_{Z(m+1)}\right) . \tag{94}$$

which is not a function of A_{Pm}. This proves the theorem, since $H \equiv H(\gamma)$ is a deterministic function of $H_m, \bar{A}_Z, \bar{L}_{m-1}, \bar{A}_{P(m-1)}$.

   Case 1. $m = K$: Equation 94 holds since (1) $H_K = \gamma(Y, \bar{\ell}_K, \bar{a}_{PK}, \bar{A}_Z)$ has density $f(u, \bar{L}_K, \bar{A}_{P(K-1)}, \bar{A}_Z)$ given $(\bar{A}_K, \bar{L}_K)$, and (2) $W_{K+1} \equiv 1$ and $A_{Z(K+1)} \equiv 0$ w.p.1. by convention.

   Case 2. Assume equation 94 is true with $m + 1$ replacing m. I show it as true for m. Now the left-hand side of equation 94 is

$$E\left\{q\left(\bar{A}_{m+1}, \bar{L}_{m+1}\right)\left\{f\left(A_{Z(m+1)} \mid \bar{A}_m, \bar{L}_m\right)\right\}^{-1} \mid \bar{A}_m, \bar{L}_m\right\} \tag{95}$$

with

$$q\left(\bar{A}_{m+1}, \bar{L}_{m+1}\right)$$
$$= E\left[W_{m+2}^{-1} t\left\{\bar{A}_Z, \gamma\left(H_{m+1}, \bar{L}_m, \bar{A}_{Pm}, \bar{A}_Z\right), \bar{L}_m, \bar{A}_{P(m-1)}\right\} \mid \bar{A}_{m+1}, \bar{L}_{m+1}\right] \tag{96}$$

where we have used the definition of H_m in terms of $H_{m\pm1}$. Now, by the induction hypothesis, $q(\bar{A}_{m+1}, \bar{L}_{m+1}) = \int d\mu\, (\underline{A}_{Z(m+2)})\, \{\int t\, [\bar{A}_Z, u, \bar{L}_m, \bar{A}_{P(m-1)}]$ $f(h, \bar{L}_{m+1}, \bar{A}_{Pm}, \bar{A}_Z)\, dh\}$ with $u \equiv \gamma(h, \bar{L}_m, \bar{A}_{Pm}, \bar{A}_Z)$, which is not a function of $A_{P(m+1)}$. Hence, equation 95 equals

$$\int d\mu\, \left(\underline{A}_{Z(m+1)}\right)\left\{t\left[\bar{A}_Z, u, \bar{L}_m, \bar{A}_{P(m-1)}\right]\left[\int f\left(h, \bar{L}_{m+1}, \bar{A}_{Pm}, \bar{A}_Z\right) dF\left(L_{m+1} \mid \bar{L}_m, \bar{A}_m\right)\right] dh\right\}$$
$$= \int d\mu\, \left(\underline{A}_{Z(m+1)}\right)\left\{\int t\left[\bar{A}_Z, u, \bar{L}_m, \bar{A}_{P(m-1)}\right] f\left(h, \bar{L}_m, \bar{A}_{Pm}, \bar{A}_Z\right) dh\right\} ,$$

by equation 91. I now change the variable of integration from h to u in this last expression to obtain,

$$\int d\mu\big(\underline{A}_{Z(m+1)}\big)\Big\{\int t\big(\bar{A}_Z, u, \bar{L}_m, \bar{A}_{P(m-1)}\big) f\big[\gamma^{-1}\big(u, \bar{L}_m, \bar{A}_{Pm}, \bar{A}_Z\big), \bar{L}_m, \bar{A}_{Pm}, \bar{A}_Z\big]$$
$$\left[\frac{\partial\gamma^{-1}\big(u, \bar{L}_m, \bar{A}_{Pm}, \bar{A}_Z\big)}{\partial u}\right] du\Big\} .$$

which is the right-hand side of equation 94 by equation 93.

$\Leftarrow$ The proof is analogous to that of theorem 8.1.

14.2.2 Proof of Theorem 10.3

$\Rightarrow$ It is straightforward to show that part 1 of the theorem implies parts 2 and 3 if we can show

$$E\left[\frac{t\big(\bar{A}_Z, \sigma\big)}{W}\right]$$
$$\equiv E\left[\frac{t\big\{\bar{A}_Z, \tau\big(H, \bar{A}_Z\big)\big\}}{W}\right]$$
$$= \int d\mu\big(\bar{A}_Z\big)\Big\{\int t\big(\bar{A}_Z, h\big)f(h, 0, 0)\, dh\Big\}$$

$$(97)$$

with $f(h, 0, 0) = \partial b(h, 0, 0)/\partial h$. Now the left-hand side of equation 97 is

$$E\Big[E\big\{t\big[\bar{A}_Z, \tau\big(H, \bar{A}_Z\big)\big]/W_1 \mid A_0, L_0\big\}\big\{f\big[A_{Z0}\mid L_0\big]\big\}^{-1}\Big]$$
$$= E\Big[\Big\{\int d\mu\big(\underline{A}_{Z1}\big)\int t\big[\bar{A}_Z, \tau\big(u, \bar{A}_Z\big)\big]f\big[u, L_0, 0, \bar{A}_Z\big]\, du\Big\}\big\{f\big[A_{Z0}\mid L_0\big]\big\}^{-1}\Big]$$

by equation 94,

$$= \int d\mu\big(\bar{A}_Z\big)\Big[\int t\big[\bar{A}_Z, \tau\big(u, \bar{A}_Z\big)\big]\Big\{\int f\big(u, L_0, 0, \bar{A}_Z\big)\, dF\big(L_0\big)\Big\}\, du\Big]$$
$$= \int d\mu\big(\bar{A}_Z\big)\Big[\int t\big[\bar{A}_Z, \tau\big(u, \bar{A}_Z\big)\big] f\big(u, 0, \bar{A}_Z\big)\, du\Big]$$

$$(98)$$

with $f(u, 0, \bar{A}_Z) = \partial b(u, 0, \bar{A}_Z)/\partial u$. But, by the change of variables $h = \tau(u, 0, \bar{A}_Z)$, equation 98 equals

$$\int d\mu\big(\bar{A}_Z\big)\Big[\int t\big(\bar{A}_Z, h\big) f\big\{\tau^{-1}\big(h, \bar{A}_Z\big), 0, \bar{A}_Z\big\}\big\{\partial\tau^{-1}\big(h, \bar{A}_Z\big)/\partial h\big\}\, dh\Big]$$
$$= \int d\mu\big(\bar{A}_Z\big)\Big[\int t\big(\bar{A}_Z, h\big) f\big(h, 0, 0\big)\, dh\Big]$$

by definition of $\tau(h, \bar{A}_Z)$. The other parts of the theorem I leave for the reader.

14.2.3 Proof of Theorem 10.4

Define $t(\bar{A}_Z, \sigma) \equiv t(\bar{A}_Z)[I(\sigma > y) - (b(y, 0, 0))]$. Then, by equation 97, we

have $E\left[W^{-1}t\left(\overline{A}_Z, \sigma\right)\right] = \int d\mu\left(\overline{A}_Z\right) t(\overline{A}_Z) \left[\int \{I[h > y] - b(y, 0, 0)\} f(h, 0, 0) \, dh\right]$
$= 0$, proving theorem 10.4.

14.3 Proof of Theorem 11.1

First note
$$pr\left[\mathcal{H}_K > y \mid \overline{L}, \overline{A}\right]$$
$$\equiv pr\left[Y > \gamma^{-1}\left(y, \overline{L}_K, \overline{A}_{PK}, \overline{A}_Z\right) \mid \overline{L}, \overline{A}\right]$$
$$= b\left[\gamma^{-1}\left(y, \overline{L}_K, \overline{A}_{PK}, \overline{A}_Z\right), \overline{L}_K, \overline{A}_{PK}, \overline{A}_Z\right]$$
$$= b\left[y, \overline{L}_K, \overline{A}_{P(K-1)}, \overline{A}_Z\right]$$

by definition of the function γ. The proof is now completed by induction using the following two lemmas.

LEMMA 14.1. If equation 67 is true, then equation 68 is true.

Proof. $pr[\mathcal{M}_m > y \mid \overline{L}, \overline{A}] \equiv pr[\mathcal{H}_m > v^{-1}(y, \overline{L}_m, \overline{A}_{P(m-1)}, \overline{A}_Z) \mid \overline{L}, \overline{A}] = b\{v^{-1}(y, \overline{L}_m, \overline{A}_{P(m-1)}, \overline{A}_Z), \overline{L}_m, \overline{A}_{P(m-1)}, \overline{A}_Z\} = b(y, \overline{L}_{m-1}, \overline{A}_{P(m-1)}, \overline{A}_Z)$ by definition of v.

LEMMA 14.2. If equation 68 is true with $m + 1$ replacing m, then equation 67 is true.

Proof. $pr[\mathcal{H}_m > y \mid \overline{L}, \overline{A}] \equiv pr[\mathcal{M}_{m+1} > \gamma^{-1}(y, \overline{L}_m, \overline{A}_{Pm}, \overline{A}_Z) \mid \overline{L}, \overline{A}]$
$= b[\gamma^{-1}(y, \overline{L}_m, \overline{A}_{Pm}, \overline{A}_Z), \overline{L}_m, \overline{A}_{Pm}, \overline{A}_Z] = b(y, \overline{L}_m, \overline{A}_{P(m-1)}, \overline{A}_Z)$ by definition of the function γ.

14.4 Proof of Theorem 12.1

Throughout, I use the convention that for any function $q(\bullet)$ with argument $\overline{a}_Z = \overline{a}_{ZK}$, $q(\overline{a}_{Zm})$ is $q(\overline{a}_Z)$ with $\overline{a}_Z = (\overline{a}_{Zm}, 0)$, and $q(0)$ has $\overline{a}_Z \equiv 0$. Analogous remarks hold for functions of $\overline{a}_P$.

I show $(1) \Rightarrow (6) \Rightarrow (5) \Rightarrow (4) \Rightarrow (2) \Leftrightarrow (3)$, $(3) \Rightarrow (4)$, and $(4) \Rightarrow (1)$.

$(1) \Rightarrow (6)$: I noted in section 12 that, whether or not equation 83 is imposed, $\sigma \coprod \, ^* \overline{A}_Z$ and $A_{Pm} \coprod \, ^* \sigma \mid \overline{L}_m, \overline{A}_{P(m-1)}, \overline{A}_Z$. Combining these restrictions with equation 83, we obtain the conditional independencies in part 6.

$(6) \Rightarrow (5)$: It is sufficient to show that
$$E[q(\sigma) \mid \overline{A}_m, \overline{L}_m] = E^* [q(\sigma) \mid \overline{L}_m, \overline{A}_m] \tag{99}$$
for any function $q(\bullet)$.

Proof by induction. In the proof I use the identity
$$E^*[q(\sigma) \mid \overline{L}_m, \overline{A}_m] = E[q(\sigma) t_2 (\underline{A}_{Z(m+1)}) \mid \overline{A}_{Zm} / W_{m+1} \mid \overline{L}_m, \overline{A}_m] \tag{100}$$
where $t_2 (\underline{A}_{Z(m+1)} \mid \overline{A}_{Zm})$ is the conditional density of $\underline{A}_{Z(m+1)}$ given $\overline{A}_{Zm}$ under $f^*(v)$.

Case 1. $m = K$: $E[q(\sigma) \mid \overline{A}_K, \overline{L}_K] = E^*[q(\sigma) \mid \overline{A}_K, \overline{L}_K]$ by equation 100.

Case 2. We assume equation 99 is true for $m + 1$ and will prove it true for m.

$$E[q(\sigma) \mid \overline{A}_m, \overline{L}_m]$$
$$= E[E\{q(\sigma) \mid \overline{A}_{m+1}, \overline{L}_{m+1}\} \mid \overline{A}_m, \overline{L}_m]$$
$$= E[E^*\{q(\sigma) \mid \overline{A}_m, \overline{L}_{m+1}\} \mid \overline{A}_m, \overline{L}_m]$$
$$= E^*[W_{m+1}\{t_2(\underline{A}_{Z(m+1)} \mid \overline{A}_{Zm})\}^{-1} E^*\{q(\sigma) \mid \overline{A}_m, \overline{L}_{m+1}\} \mid \overline{A}_m, \overline{L}_m]$$
$$= E^*[E^*\{q(\sigma) \mid \overline{A}_m, \overline{L}_{m+1}\} \mid \overline{A}_m, \overline{L}_m]$$
$$= E^*[q(\sigma) \mid \overline{A}_m, \overline{L}_m],$$

where the second inequality is by the induction hypothesis and $(\sigma, \underline{A}_{Z(m+1)})$ $\coprod^* A_{Pm} \mid \overline{L}_m, \overline{A}_{m-1}, A_{Zm}$, the third by equation 100, and the fourth by integration under $f^*(v)$.

$(5) \Rightarrow (4)$: We know from Robins (1989, 1995, 1997) and Robins and Wasserman (1997) that, given $f(v)$ there are unique densities (1) $f_{\dot{H}}(h)$, (2) $f(\ell_m \mid \overline{\ell}_{m-1}, \overline{a}_{m-1}, h)$, $f(a_m \mid \overline{\ell}_m, \overline{a}_{m-1})$ and unique functions $\dot{\gamma}(y, \overline{\ell}_m, \overline{a}_m)$ that have a continuous positive derivative with respect to y and satisfy $\dot{\gamma}(y, \overline{\ell}_m, \overline{a}_m) = 0$ if $a_m = 0$ such that

$$f(V) = \left\{\frac{\partial \dot{H}}{\partial Y}\right\} f(\dot{H}) \prod_{m=0}^{K} f(L_m \mid \overline{L}_{m-1}, \overline{A}_{m-1}, \dot{H}) f(A_m \mid \overline{A}_{m-1}, \overline{L}_m) \tag{101}$$

where $\dot{H} = \dot{h}(Y, \overline{L}_K, \overline{A}_K)$ is defined in terms of the $\dot{\gamma}(y, \overline{\ell}_m, \overline{a}_m)$ as in section 12. Hence, in view of (5), (4) follows if we can show that $\sigma \equiv \tau[h(Y, \overline{L}_K, \overline{A}_K), \overline{A}_Z]$ is equal to some function, say $h^*(Y, \overline{L}_K, \overline{A}_K)$, that is (1) recursively defined in terms of functions $\gamma^*(y, \overline{\ell}_m, \overline{a}_m)$ just as the function $\dot{h}$ was recursively defined in terms of the functions $\dot{\gamma}$ and (2) $\gamma^*(y, \overline{\ell}_m, \overline{a}_m)$ has a continuous positive derivative with respect to y and satisfies $\gamma^*(y, \overline{\ell}_m, \overline{a}_m) = 0$ if $a_m = 0$. To do so, let $h^{-1}(y, \overline{\ell}_K, \overline{a}_{Pm}, \overline{a}_{Zk})$ be shorthand for $h^{-1}(y, \overline{\ell}_K, (\overline{a}_{Pm}, 0), (\overline{a}_{Zk}, 0))$ and let $\tau^{-1}(y, \overline{a}_{Zm})$ be shorthand for $\tau^{-1}(y, (\overline{a}_{Zm}, 0))$. Note $h^{-1}(y, \overline{\ell}_K, \overline{a}_{Pm}, \overline{a}_{Zm}) \equiv h^{-1}(y, \overline{\ell}_m, \overline{a}_{Pm}, \overline{a}_{Zm})$ does not depend on ℓ_{m+1}, as is easily shown from its definition in terms of the $\gamma(y, \overline{\ell}_m, \overline{a}_{Pm}, \overline{a}_Z)$. Now define $\gamma^{*-1}(y, \ell_0, a_0) = h^{-1}\{\tau^{-1}(y, a_{Z0}), \ell_0, a_{P0}, a_{Z0}\}$ and define $\gamma^{*-1}(y, \overline{\ell}_m, \overline{a}_m)$ recursively by $\gamma^{*-1}(y, \overline{\ell}_m, \overline{a}_m) = h^{-1}\{\tau^{-1}[\gamma^*(y, \overline{\ell}_{m-1}, \overline{a}_{m-1}), \overline{a}_{Zm}], \overline{\ell}_m, \overline{a}_{Pm}, \overline{a}_{Zm}\}$, where $\gamma^*(y, \bullet)$ is the inverse function to $\gamma^{*-1}(y, \bullet)$. It is then straightforward to check that $\gamma^*(y, \overline{\ell}_m, \overline{a}_m)$ has a continuous positive derivative with respect to y and satisfies $\gamma^*(y, \overline{\ell}_m, \overline{a}_m) = 0$ if $a_m = 0$. Furthermore, one can check that $h^*(y, \overline{\ell}_K, \overline{a}_K)$ can be recursively obtained from the $\gamma^*(y, \overline{\ell}_m, \overline{a}_m)$ in the appropriate manner. This completes the proof.

$(4) \Rightarrow (2)$: It follows from the above proof that $(5) \Rightarrow (4)$ that when $a_{Pm} = 0$, $\dot{\gamma}^{-1}(y, \ell_0, a_0) = \tau^{-1}(y, a_{Z0})$ does not depend on ℓ_0, and that $\dot{\gamma}^{-1}(y, \overline{\ell}_m, \overline{a}_m) = \tau^{-1}[\dot{\gamma}(y, \overline{\ell}_{m-1}, \overline{a}_{m-1}), \overline{a}_{Zm}]$ does not depend on $\overline{\ell}_m$. Combining these results, we conclude that when $a_{Pm} = 0$, $\dot{\gamma}^{-1}(y, \overline{\ell}_m, \overline{a}_m)$ does not depend on $\overline{\ell}_m$, concluding the proof.

$(2) \Leftrightarrow (3)$: From their definitions, $\dot{\gamma}(y, \overline{\ell}_m, \overline{a}_m)$

$$= \gamma_Z \{ \gamma(y, \bar{\ell}_m, \bar{a}_{Pm}, \bar{a}_{Zm}), \bar{\ell}_m, \bar{a}_{P(m-1)}, \bar{a}_{Zm} \} \text{ so,}$$

when $a_{Pm} = 0$, $\dot{\gamma}(y, \bar{\ell}_m, \bar{a}_m) = \gamma_Z (y, \bar{\ell}_m, \bar{a}_{P(m-1)}, \bar{a}_{Zm})$.

(3) $\Rightarrow$ (4): We need to show that

$$\dot{h}(y, \bar{\ell}, \bar{a}) = \tau[h(y, \bar{\ell}, \bar{a}), \bar{a}_Z] \tag{102}$$

under the no $L - A_Z$ interaction assumption

$$\gamma_Z (y, \bar{\ell}_k, \bar{a}_{P(k-1)}, \bar{a}_{Zk}) = \gamma_Z(y, \bar{a}_{P(k-1)}, \bar{a}_{Zk}). \tag{103}$$

We require two preliminary lemmas.

LEMMA 14.3. Equation 103 implies, for $-1 \le k \le m$,

$$b(y, \bar{\ell}_k, \bar{a}_{P(m-1)}, \bar{a}_{Zm}) = b\{u, \bar{\ell}_k, \bar{a}_{P(m-1)}, \bar{a}_{Z(m-1)}\} \tag{104}$$

where $u \equiv \gamma_Z (y, \bar{a}_{P(m-1)}, \bar{a}_{Zm})$.

Proof of lemma 14.3. By definition of γ_Z, equation 104 holds for $k = m$. Hence it suffices to show that if equation 104 is true for k, it is true for $k - 1$. Now $b(y, \bar{\ell}_{k-1}, \bar{a}_{P(m-1)}, \bar{a}_{Zm}) \equiv \int b(y, \bar{\ell}_k, \bar{a}_{P(m-1)}, \bar{a}_{Zm}) \, dF(\ell_k \mid \bar{\ell}_{k-1}, \bar{a}_{k-1})$ $= \int b(u, \bar{\ell}_k, \bar{a}_{P(m-1)}, \bar{a}_{Z(m-1)}) \, dF(\ell_k \mid \bar{\ell}_{k-1}, \bar{a}_{k-1}) \equiv b(u, \bar{\ell}_{k-1}, \bar{a}_{P(m-1)}, \bar{a}_{Z(m-1)})$, where the second to last equality is by the induction hypothesis.

LEMMA 14.4. Equation 103 implies

$$\gamma_Z (u, 0, \bar{a}_{Zm}) = \gamma(u^*, \ell_0, a_{P0}, \bar{a}_{Z(m-1)}) \tag{105}$$

with $u \equiv \gamma(y, \ell_0, a_{P0}, \bar{a}_{Zm})$ and $u^* \equiv \gamma_Z (y, a_{P0}, \bar{a}_{Zm})$.

Proof. $b(y, \ell_0, a_{P0}, \bar{a}_{Zm}) = b[u^*, \ell_0, a_{P0}, \bar{a}_{Z(m-1)}] = b[\gamma(u^*, \ell_0, a_{P0}, \bar{a}_{Z(m-1)}), \ell_0, 0, \bar{a}_{Z(m-1)}]$ where the first equality is by lemma 14.3 with $\bar{a}_{P(m-1)} = (a_{P0}, 0)$ and the last equality is by definition of the direct-effect blip function γ. However, $b(y, \ell_0, a_{P0}, \bar{a}_{Zm}) = b[u, \ell_0, 0, \bar{a}_{Zm}] = b[\gamma_Z(u, 0, \bar{a}_{Zm}), \ell_0, 0, \bar{a}_{Z(m-1)}]$. Hence, since $b(y, \ell_0, 0, \bar{a}_{Z(m-1)})$ is monotone increasing in y, the lemma is proved.

Proof that equation 103 $\Rightarrow$ equation 102: I use induction on K.

Case 1. $K = 1$: Note $\dot{h}(s, \bar{\ell}_1, \bar{a}_1) = \gamma_Z (x^*, \ell_0, 0, a_{Z0})$ with $x^* = \gamma[u^*, \ell_0, a_{P0}, a_{Z0}]$ where $u^* = \gamma_Z (y, a_{P0}, a_{Z1})$ and $y = \gamma(s, \bar{\ell}_1, \bar{a}_{P1}, \bar{a}_{Z1})$. Similarly, $\tau[h(s, \bar{\ell}_1, \bar{a}_1), a_{Z1}] = \gamma_Z [x, \ell_0, 0, a_{Z0}]$ where $x = \gamma_Z [u, 0, \bar{a}_{Z1}]$, $u = \gamma(y, \ell_0, a_{P0}, \bar{a}_{Z1})$, and y is as defined above. Hence we must show that $x = x^*$, which is just equation 105 with $m = 1$.

Case 2. Assume the theorem is true for $K = K^*$. I now show it is true for $K = K^* + 1$. Given $(\bar{\ell}, \bar{a}) \equiv (\bar{\ell}_{K^*+1}, \bar{a}_{K^*+1})$, let $\gamma_m (y) \equiv \gamma(y, \bar{\ell}_m, \bar{a}_{Pm}, \bar{a}_Z)$ and $\gamma_{Zm}(y) \equiv \gamma_Z (y, 0, \bar{a}_{Zm})$. Then

$$\tau[h(y, \bar{\ell}, \bar{a}), \bar{a}_Z] = \gamma_{Z0} \circ \cdots \circ \gamma_{ZK^*} \circ \gamma_{Z(K^*+1)} \circ \gamma_0 \circ \cdots \circ \gamma_{K^*} \circ \gamma_{K^*+1} (y). \tag{106}$$

Equation 105 is now applied successively for $m = K^* + 1, K^*, \ldots, 1$ to obtain

$$\gamma_{Z0} \circ \cdots \circ \gamma_{Z(K^*+1)} \circ \gamma_0 (y) = \gamma_{Z0} \circ \gamma_{P0} \circ \gamma_{Z01} \circ \gamma_{Z02} \circ \cdots \circ \gamma_{Z0(K^*+1)} (y) \tag{107}$$

where $\gamma_{P0}(y) \equiv \gamma(y, \ell_0, a_{P0}, a_{Z0})$ and $\gamma_{Z0m}(y) \equiv \dot{\gamma}_Z(y, a_{P0}, \bar{a}_{Zm})$. Now since by their definitions, $\gamma_{Z0} \circ \gamma_{P0}(y) = \dot{\gamma}(y, \ell_0, a_0)$ and $h(y, \bar{\ell}, \bar{a}) = \dot{\gamma}[\dot{h}_1(y, \bar{\ell}, \bar{a}), \ell_0, a_0]$, the theorem is proved if we can show that

$$h_1(y, \bar{\ell}, \bar{a}) = \gamma_{Z01} \circ \cdots \circ \gamma_{Z0(K*+1)} \circ \gamma_1 \circ \cdots \circ \gamma_{K*+1}(y) . \tag{108}$$

However, treating (ℓ_0, a_0) as fixed, we find that equation 108 is true by the induction hypothesis since the right-hand side of equation 108 is $\tau \circ h$ for a study with $K = (K* + 1) - 1 = K*$.

(4) $\Rightarrow$ (1): This implication follows from a probability calculation on $G*$ using part 6.

Proof of corollary 12.1. Parts 5 and 6 of theorem 12.1 imply

$$f^*(v) = \left\{\frac{\partial\sigma}{\partial\gamma}\right\} f^*(\sigma) \prod_{m=0}^{K} f^*\left(\ell_m | \bar{\ell}_{m-1}, \bar{a}_{m-1}, \sigma\right) f^*\left(a_m | \bar{\ell}_m, \bar{a}_{m-1}\right)$$

and

$$f(v) = \left\{\frac{\partial\sigma}{\partial\gamma}\right\} f(\sigma) \prod_{m=0}^{K} f\left(\ell_m | \bar{\ell}_{m-1}, \bar{a}_{m-1}, \sigma\right) f\left(a_m | \bar{\ell}_m, \bar{a}_{m-1}\right) .$$

The corollary is now proved by noting that by the definition of $f^*(v)$,

$$f^*(v) / \prod_{m=0}^{K} f^*\left(a_m | \bar{\ell}_m, \bar{a}_{m-1}\right)$$

$$= f(v) / \prod_{m=0}^{K} f\left(a_m | \bar{\ell}_m, \bar{a}_{m-1}\right) .$$

Final Remark. It is interesting to note that in the context of an SNMM, the assumption of no $L - A_Z$ mean interaction, i.e., $\gamma_Z(\bar{\ell}_m, \bar{a}_{P(m-1)}, \bar{a}_{Zm}) \equiv b(\bar{\ell}_m, \bar{a}_{P(m-1)}, \bar{a}_{Zm}) - b(\bar{\ell}_m, \bar{a}_{P(m-1)}, \bar{a}_{Z(m-1)})$ does not depend on ℓ_m is true if and only if $v(\bar{\ell}_m, \bar{a}_{P(m-1)}, \bar{a}_Z)$ does not depend on $\underline{a}_{Zm}$. However, it is not true, in the setting of an SNDM, that the assumption (equation 103) of no $L - A_Z$ interaction either implies or is implied by the assumption that $v(y, \bar{\ell}_m, \bar{a}_{P(m-1)}, \bar{a}_Z)$ does not depend on $\underline{a}_{Zm}$ (unless the null hypothesis $\tau(y, \bar{a}_Z) \equiv y$ is also true). This reflects the fact that the scale in which the $L - A_Z$ interaction is measured by the function $v(y, \bar{\ell}_m, \bar{a}_{P(m-1)}, \bar{a}_Z)$ differs from the scale on which it is measured by $\gamma_Z(y, \bar{\ell}_m, \bar{a}_{P(m-1)}, \bar{a}_{Zm})$.

References

Gill, R., and Robins, J. M. 1997. From g-Computation to G-Computation. Unpublished manuscript.

Pearl, J. 1995. Causal Diagrams for Empirical Research. *Biometrika* 82(4): 669–690.

Pearl, J., and Robins, J. M. 1995. Probabilistic Evaluation of Sequential Plans from Causal Models with Hidden Variables. *Uncertainty in Artificial Intelligence 11,* eds. P. Besnard and S. Hanks, 444–453. San Francisco: Morgan Kaufmann Publishers.

Pearl, J., and Verma, T. 1991. A Theory of Inferred Causation. In *Principles of Knowledge Representation and Reasoning: Proceedings of the Second International Conference,* eds. J. A. Allen, R. Fikes, and E. Sandewall, 441–452. San Francisco: Morgan Kaufmann Publishers.

Robins, J. M. Forthcoming. Estimating the Causal Effect of a Time-Varying Treatment on Survival Using Structural Nested Failure Time Models. *Statistica Neederlandica.*

Robins, J. M. 1999. Marginal Structural Models versus Structural Nested Models as Tools for Causal Inference. In *Statistical Models in Epidemiology: The Environment and Clinical Trials,* ed. E. Halloran and D. Berry. New York: Springer-Verlag.

Robins, J. M. 1998. Marginal Structural Models. In *Proceedings of the American Statistical Association,* 1–10. Chicago: American Statistical Association.

Robins, J. M. 1997. Causal Inference from Complex Longitudinal Data. In *Latent Variable Modeling and Applications to Causality,* ed. M. Berkane, 69–117. Lecture Notes in Statistics 120. New York: Springer Verlag.

Robins, J. M. 1995. Discussion of Causal Diagrams for Empirical Research by J. Pearl. *Biometrika* 82(4): 695–698.

Robins, J. M. 1994. Correcting for Non-Compliance in Randomized Trials Using Structural Nested Mean Models. *Communications in Statistics* 23(8): 2379–2412.

Robins, J. M. 1993. Analytic Methods for Estimating HIV-Treatment and Cofactor Effects. In *Methodological Issues in AIDS Mental Health Research,* eds. D. G. Ostrow and R. C. Kessler, 213–290. New York: Plenum.

Robins, J. M. 1992. Estimation of the Time-Dependent Accelerated Failure Time Model in the Presence of Confounding Factors. *Biometrika* 79(2): 321–334.

Robins, J. M. 1989. The Analysis of Randomized and Non-Randomized AIDS Treatment Trials Using a New Approach to Causal Inference in Longitudinal Studies. In *Health Service Research Methodology: A Focus on AIDS,* eds. L. Sechrest, H. Freeman, and A. Mulley, 113-159. Washington, D.C.: U.S. Public Health Service, National Center for Health Services Research.

Robins, J. M. 1987. Addendum to "A New Approach to Causal Inference in Mortality Studies with Sustained Exposure Periods—Application to Control of the Healthy Worker Survivor Effect." *Computers and Mathematics with Applications* 14(9–12): 923–945.

Robins, J. M. 1986. A New Approach to Causal Inference in Mortality Studies with Sustained Exposure Periods—Application to Control of the Healthy Worker Survivor Effect. *Computers and Mathematics with Applications* 14: 923–945.

Robins, J. M., and Rotnitzky, A. 1992. Recovery of Information and Adjustment for Dependent Censoring Using Surrogate Markers. In *AIDS Epidemiology—Methodological Issues,* eds. N. Jewell, K. Dietz, and V. Farewell, 297–331. Boston, Mass.: Birkhäuser.

Robins, J. M., Rotnitzky, A., and Scharfstein, D. 1999. Sensitivity Analysis for Selection Bias and Unmeasured Confounding in Missing Data and Causal inference models. In *Statistical Models in Epidemiology: The Environment and Clinical Trials,* ed. E. Halloran and D. Berry. New York: Springer-Verlag.

Robins, J. M., and Wasserman, L. 1997. Estimation of Effects of Sequential Treatments by Reparameterizing Directed Acyclic Graphs. In *Proceedings of the Thirteenth Conference on Uncertainty in Artificial Intelligence,* ed. D. Geiger and P.

Shenoy, 409–418. San Francisco: Morgan Kaufmann.

Rosenbaum, P. R. 1984. Conditional Permutation Tests and the Propensity Score in Observational Studies. *Journal of the American Statistical Association* 79: 565–574.

Spirtes, P.; Glymour, C.; and Scheines, R. 1993. *Causation, Prediction, and Search.* New York: Springer-Verlag.

Verma, T., and Pearl, J. 1991. Equivalence and Synthesis of Causal Models. Technical Report, R-150, Cognitive Systems Laboratory, University of California, Los Angeles.

CHAPTER THIRTEEN

A Clinician's Tool for Analyzing Noncompliance

David Maxwell Chickering and Judea Pearl

1. Introduction

Standard clinical studies in the biological and medical sciences invariably invoke the instrument of randomized control; that is, subjects are assigned at random to various groups (or treatments or programs) and the mean differences between participants in different groups are regarded as measures of the efficacies of the associated programs. For example, to determine if a new drug is useful for treating some disease, subjects will be divided (at random) into a control group and a treatment group. The members of the control group are given a placebo and the members of the treatment group are given the drug in question. For each group, the clinician records the fraction of subjects that recover from the disease. By comparing these fractions the clinician can derive a quantitative measure of effectiveness of the drug for treating the disease. In particular, if f_c and f_t are the fractions of subjects that recovered from the control group and treatment group respectively, then the difference $E = f_t - f_c$ is an indication of the effectiveness of the drug.

The major source of difficulty in managing and analyzing such experiments has been subject noncompliance. For example, a subject in the treatment group may experience negative side effects and will stop taking the drug. Alternatively, if the experiment is testing a drug for a terminal disease, a subject suspecting that he is in the control group may obtain the drug from other sources. Imperfect compliance poses a problem because simply comparing the fractions as above may provide a misleading estimate for how effective the drug would be if applied uniformly to the population. For example, if those subjects who refused to take the drug are precisely those who would have responded adversely, the experiment might conclude that the drug is more effective than it actually is. It can be shown, in fact, that treatment effectiveness in such studies is *nonidentifiable*. That is, in the absence of additional modeling assumptions, treatment effectiveness cannot be estimated from the data without bias, even as the number of subjects in the experiment approaches infinity, and even when a record is available of the action and response of each subject (Pearl 1995a).

In a popular compromising approach to the problem of imperfect compliance, researchers perform an *intent-to-treat* analysis, in which the control and treatment group are compared without regard to whether the treatment was actually received[1]. The result of such an analysis is a measure of how well the treatment *assignment* affects the disease, as opposed to the desired measure of how well the treatment itself affects the disease. Estimates based on intent-to-treat analysis are valid only as long as the experimental conditions perfectly mimic the conditions prevailing in the eventual usage of the treatment. In particular, the experiment should mimic subjects' incentives for receiving each treatment. In situations where field incentives are more compelling than experimental incentives, as is usually the case when drugs receive the approval of a government agency, treatment effectiveness may vary significantly from assignment effectiveness. For example, imagine a study in which (a) the drug has an adverse effect on a large segment of the population and (b) only those members of the segment who drop from the treatment arm recover. The intent-to-treat analysis will attribute these cases of recovery to the drug since they are part of the treatment arm, when in reality these cases have recovered by avoiding the treatment (Pearl 1995b).

Another approach to the problem is to use a correction factor based on an "instrumental variables" formula (Angrist, Imbens, and Rubin 1996), according to which the intent-to-treat measure should be divided by the fraction of subjects who comply with the treatment assigned to them. Angrist, Imbens, and Rubin (1996) have shown that, under certain conditions, the corrected formula is valid for the subpopulation of "responsive" subjects, that is, subjects who would have changed treatment status if given a different assignment. Unfortunately, this subpopulation cannot be identified and, more seriously, it cannot serve as a basis for policies involving the entire population because it is instrument dependent—individuals who are responsive in the study may not remain responsive in the field, where the incentives for obtaining treatment differ from those used in the study. Using a graphical model with latent variables, Balke and Pearl (1994, 1997) derive bounds, rather than point estimates, for the treatment effect, while making no assumptions about the relationship between subjects' compliance and subjects' physical response to treatment. However, the derived bounds are "asymptotic," i.e., they ignore sampling variations by assuming that the proportions measured in the experiment are representative of the population as a whole, a condition that is valid only when the number of subjects is large. This large-sample assumption may be problematic when the study includes a relatively small number of subjects.

In this chapter we describe a system that provides an assessment of the actual treatment effect and is not limited to studies with large samples. The system uses the graphical model of Balke and Pearl (1994, 1997) to learn the treatment effect using Bayesian updating combined with Gibbs sampling. The system takes as input (1) the investigator's prior knowledge about subject compliance and response behaviors and (2) the observed data from the experiment, and outputs the posterior distribution of the treatment effect. The use of graphical models and Gibbs' methods for deriving posterior distributions in such models are both well known. The main contribution of this chapter is a description of how these techniques can be applied to the causal analysis of clinical trials, and a presentation of experimental results of a practical system applied to various simulated and real data. The basic idea of estimating causal effects using Bayesian analysis goes back to Rubin (1978), and was further used by Imbens and Rubin (1997) to estimate the correctional formula advocated by Angrist, Imbens, and Rubin (1996). In this work, we present an assessment of the average treatment effect using weaker assumptions that can be conveniently encoded in an intuitively appealing causal model.

The chapter is organized as follows: First, we introduce a graphical, causal model that represents a prototypical clinical trial with partial compliance, and define *treatment effect* in terms of the model. Next, we describe an equivalent graphical model, using potential-response variables (Balke and Pearl 1994), that allows the compliance and response behavior to be represented more efficiently. Next, we describe the general Bayesian-learning and Gibbs-sampling methods that were used to derive the posterior parameter densities in the graphical model. Finally, we describe experimental results obtained when our system is applied to various simulated and real data sets. We include results obtained when the system is modified to answer counterfactual queries about specific individuals, e.g., "what if Joe (who died with no treatment) had taken the treatment?"

2. The Graphical Model

Graphical models are convenient tools for representing causal and statistical assumptions about variables in a domain (Pearl 1995a). In this section, we describe the graphical model of figure 1, which is used to represent a prototypical clinical trial with partial compliance. We use Z, D, and Y to denote observed binary variables from the experiment, where Z represents the treat-

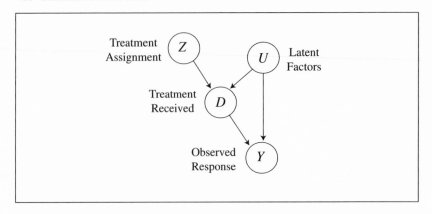

Figure 1: Graphical model for a prototypical clinical trial with partial compliance.

ment assignment, D represents the treatment received, and Y represents the observed outcome. To facilitate the notation, we let z, d, and y represent, respectively, the values taken by the variables Z, D, and Y, with the following interpretation: $z \in \{z_0, z_1\}$, z_1 asserts that the treatment has been assigned (z_0 its negation); $d \in \{d_0, d_1\}$, d_1 asserts that the treatment has been administered (d_0 its negation); and $y \in \{y_0, y_1\}$, y_1 asserts a positive observed response (y_0 its negation). We use U to denote all characteristics, both observed and unobserved, that influence the value of D and Y for the subjects. The domain of U is left unspecified, and in general will combine the spaces of several random variables, both discrete and continuous.

The graph of figure 1 represents the pair of structural equations

$d = g(z,u)$

$y = h(d, u)$ (1)

where g and h are arbitrary deterministic functions, and U is an arbitrary, unobserved random variable, independent of Z. The function g represents the process of treatment selection, while h represents the process of reacting to the treatment.

Let v_e denote the *physical probability* of the event $E = e$, or equivalently, the fraction of subjects in the population for which $E = e$. The graphical model explicitly represents two independence assumptions about the joint physical probability distribution $v_{z,d,y,u}$. First, the model asserts that the treatment assignment Z can influence Y only through the actual treatment D. That is, Z and Y are conditionally independent given D and U. Second, the model asserts that Z and U are marginally independent. This second independence is ensured through the randomization of Z, which rules out both (1) the existence of a common cause for both Z and U and (2) the possibility that U has causal influence on Z. The two independence assumptions together induce the following decomposition of the joint distribution:

$$v_{z,d,y,u} = v_z \, v_u \, v_{d|z,u} \, v_{y|d,u}$$

In addition to the independence assumptions, the graphical model also encodes causal assumptions (e.g., that Z does not effect Y directly) which permit one to predict how the joint probability will change in light of *exogenous* local interventions (Pearl 1995a). In particular, the absence of any direct link (or any spurious path) from Z to Y implies that $v_{y|d,u}$ is the same regardless if d is measured in an observational study or dictated by some (exogenous) public policy. Consequently, if we wish to predict the distribution of Y, under the new condition where the treatment $D = d$ is applied uniformly to the population, we should calculate $E_u[v_{y|d,u}]$, where E_u denotes the expectation with respect to v_u. Likewise, if we are interested in the average *change* in Y due to treatment, we use the *average causal effect*, denoted ACE($D \to Y$), as defined by Holland (1988):

$$\text{ACE}(D \to Y) = E_u[v_{y_1|d_1,u} - v_{y_1|d_0,u}] \tag{2}$$

Let $\mathcal{D}$ denote the observed collection of triples $\{z, d, y\}$, one for each subject, that we obtain from the experiment. Given $\mathcal{D}$, the objective of our system is to derive the posterior Bayesian probability distribution $p(\text{ACE}(D \to Y) \mid \mathcal{D})$. Although our system can be used to estimate the individual expectations $E_u[v_{y_1|d,u}]$, we concentrate on estimating the average causal effect because historically this has been the quantity of interest in clinical studies.

3. The Potential-Response Model

The graphical model presented in the previous section is attractive for representing the assumptions that underlie a given experimental design, but may not be convenient for computation. For example, the graph of figure 1 represents explicitly the assumptions that Z is randomized and that Z does not affect Y directly, while making no assumption about the relationship between subject compliance and the way subjects would respond to the treatment. However, leaving the domain of the unobserved variable U unspecified makes it difficult to derive the distribution of interest, namely, $p(\text{ACE}(D \to Y) \mid \mathcal{D})$.

As is done by Balke and Pearl (1994) and Heckerman and Shachter (1994), we exploit the observation of Pearl (1995c) that U can always be replaced by a single discrete and finite variable such that the resulting model is equivalent with respect to all observations and manipulations of Z, D, and Y. In particular, because Z, D, and Y are all binary variables, the state space of U divides into sixteen equivalence classes: each equivalence class dictates two functional mappings; one from Z to D, and the other from D to Y. To describe these equivalence classes, it is convenient to regard each as a point in the joint space of two four-valued variables C and R. The variable C determines the compliance behavior of a subject through the mapping:

$$d = F_D(z,c) = \begin{cases} d_0 \text{ if } c = c_0 \\ d_0 \text{ if } c = c_1 \text{ and } z = z_0 \\ d_1 \text{ if } c = c_1 \text{ and } z = z_1 \\ d_1 \text{ if } c = c_2 \text{ and } z = z_0 \\ d_0 \text{ if } c = c_2 \text{ and } z = z_1 \\ d_1 \text{ if } c = c_3 \end{cases}$$

Imbens and Rubin (1994) call a subject with compliance behavior c_0, c_1, c_2 and c_3, respectively, a *never-taker*, a *complier*, a *defier* and an *always-taker*. Similarly, the variable R determines the response behavior of a subject through the mapping:

$$y = F_Y(d,r) = \begin{cases} y_0 \text{ if } r = r_0 \\ y_0 \text{ if } r = r_1 \text{ and } d = d_0 \\ y_1 \text{ if } r = r_1 \text{ and } d = d_1 \\ y_1 \text{ if } r = r_2 \text{ and } d = d_0 \\ y_0 \text{ if } r = r_2 \text{ and } d = d_1 \\ y_1 \text{ if } r = r_3 \end{cases}$$

Following Heckerman and Shachter (1995), we call the response behavior r_0, r_1, r_2 and r_3, respectively, *never-recover*, *helped*, *hurt* and *always-recover*.

Let CR denote the variable whose state space is the cross-product of the states of C and R. We use cr_{ij}, with $0 \le i, j \le 3$ to denote the state of CR corresponding to compliance behavior c_i and response behavior r_j. Figure 2 shows the graphical model that results from replacing U from figure 1 by the sixteen-state variable CR. A state-minimal variable like CR is called a *response variable* by Balke and Pearl (1994) and a *mapping variable* by Heckerman and Shachter (1995), and its states correspond to the *potential response* vectors in Rubin's model (Rubin 1978).

Applying the definition of ACE($D \rightarrow Y$) given in equation 2, it follows that using the model of figure 2 we have:

$$\text{ACE}(D \rightarrow Y) = \left[\sum_{i=0}^{3} v_{cr_{i1}} \right] - \left[\sum_{i=0}^{3} v_{cr_{i2}} \right] \tag{3}$$

Equivalently, ACE($D \rightarrow Y$) is the difference between the fraction of subjects who are helped by the treatment ($R = r_1$) and the fraction of subjects who are hurt by the treatment ($R = r_2$).

As usual in experimental studies, we assume that the experimental condi-

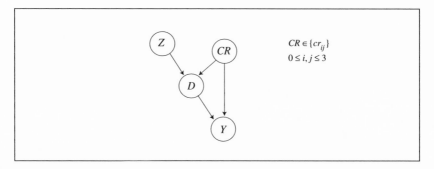

Figure 2, Potential-response model invoking a sixteen-state variable CR.

tions in themselves do not alter the physical response R of the subjects, and consequently the conclusions we draw from the experiment about ACE($D{\rightarrow}Y$) will be valid for the population as a whole. As we noted earlier, in contrast to the intent-to-treat analysis, we do *not* make the assumption that the compliance behavior of the subjects in the experiment will be the same as the compliance behavior in the population once the drug in question has been approved.

4. Learning the Causal Effect

Given the observed data $\mathcal{D}$ from the experiment, as well as a prior distribution over the unknown fractions v_{CR}, our system uses the potential-response model defined in the previous section to derive the posterior distribution for ACE($D{\rightarrow}Y$). In this section, we describe how this computation can be done. To simplify discussion, we introduce the following notation. Assume there are m subjects in the experiment. We use z^i, d^i and y^i to denote the observed value of Z, D, and Y, respectively, for subject i. Similarly, we use cr^i to denote the (unobserved) compliance and response behavior for subject i.

The posterior distribution of the causal effect can be derived using the graphical model shown in figure 3, which explicitly represents the independencies that hold in the joint (Bayesian) probability distribution defined over the variables $\{ \mathcal{D}, \{cr^1,\ldots, cr^m\}, v_{CR}, \text{ACE}(D{\rightarrow}Y)\}$. The model can be understood as m realizations of the potential-response model, one for each triple in $\mathcal{D}$, connected together using a node that represents the unknown fractions v_{CR}. The model explicitly represents the assumption that, given the fractions v_{CR}, the probability of a subject belonging to any of the compliance-response subpopulations does not depend on the compliance and response behavior of the other subjects in the experiment. From equation 3, ACE($D{\rightarrow}Y$) can be

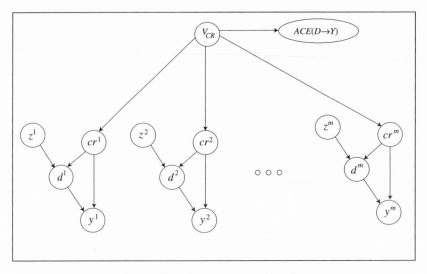

Figure 3. Model used to represent independencies in
$p(D, \{cr^1,..., cr^m\}, v_{CR}, ACE(D{\rightarrow}Y))$.

computed directly from v_{CR}, and consequently $ACE(D{\rightarrow}Y)$ is independent of all other variables in the domain once these fractions are known.

Determining the posterior probability for a node using a graphical model is known as performing *inference* in that model. In many cases, the independencies of the model can be exploited to make the process of inference efficient. Unfortunately, because the cr^i are never observed, deriving the posterior distribution for $ACE(D{\rightarrow}Y)$ is not tractable even with the given independencies. To obtain the posterior distribution, our system applies an approximation technique known as Gibbs sampling, which we describe in the following section.

5. Gibbs Sampling

Gibbs sampling is a well-known Markov chain sampling method that can be used to approximate the expected value of a function. The method can easily be applied to approximate the posterior density of $ACE(D{\rightarrow}Y)$ by exploiting the independencies in the model from figure 3.

Suppose we are interested in the expected value of some function $f(X)$ with respect to the distribution $p(X|Y)$:

$$E_{X|Y}[f] = \int_X f(X)p(X \mid Y)$$

In many cases, it may not be easy to solve the above integral analytically. However, we can approximate $E_{X|Y}[f]$ by repeatedly sampling values for X from the distribution $p(X|Y)$, and then taking an average. Assuming that N samples are taken and letting X^i denote the value for X on the ith sample we have:

$$E_{X|Y}[f] \approx \frac{1}{N} \sum_{i=1}^{N} f(X^i)$$

(4)

In practice, sampling points directly from $p(X|Y)$ may be difficult. The Gibbs sampling method draws points from the distribution by repeatedly sampling from the *conditional* distributions for the singleton components X_i of X. These conditional distributions are often very easy to derive in closed form. After initially setting all the values in X, the algorithm repeatedly unsets a single component X_i, and resamples that component according to the conditional distribution $p(X_i \mid X \setminus X_i, Y)$. It can be shown that as the number of iterations of the Gibbs sampler grows large, the sampled values for X are distributed as $p(X|Y)^2$.

We can use a Gibbs sampler to approximate the posterior distribution of ACE($D{\rightarrow}Y$) as follows. Let $f_{a,b}(v_{CR})$ denote the indicator function that is 1 if $a \le$ ACE($D{\rightarrow}Y$) $\le b$ and 0 otherwise. Then we have:

$$p(a \le ACE(D \rightarrow Y) \le b) = \int_{v_{CR}} f_{a,b}(v_{CR}) \cdot p(v_{CR} \mid \mathfrak{D})$$

After expanding the integral to include the unobserved compliance and response behavior for each of the subjects we have:

$$p(a \le ACE(D \rightarrow Y) \le b) = \int_{v_{CR}, cr^1, \dots, cr^m} f_{a,b}(v_{CR}) \cdot p(v_{CR}, cr^1, \dots, cr^m \mid \mathfrak{D})$$

Thus we can use the approximation of equation 4 in conjunction with the Gibbs sampler to estimate the probability that ACE($D{\rightarrow}Y$) falls within any interval $[a,b]$. The conditional distributions from which we sample are easily derived in light of the independencies depicted figure 3. In particular, letting $X=\{v_{CR}, cr^1, \dots, cr^m\}$, we have:

$$p(cr^i \mid X \setminus cr^i, \mathfrak{D}) = \alpha \cdot p(d^i, y^i \mid z^i, cr^i) \cdot v_{cr^i}$$

where α is the normalization constant. $p(d^i, y^i \mid z^i, cr^i)$ is either one or zero, depending on whether the observed values of z^i, d^i and y^i agree with the given compliance and response behavior. Note that we have used the fact that if the fractions v_{CR} are known, then the probability of cr^i is simply $v_{cr}{}^i$.

To update v_{CR}, we sample from the posterior distribution:

$$p(v_{CR} \mid X \setminus v_{CR}, D) = \beta \cdot \left[\prod_{i=0}^{3} \prod_{j=0}^{3} v_{cr_{ij}}{}^{N_{cr_{ij}}} \right] \cdot p(v_{CR})$$

where β is the normalization constant and $N_{cr_{ij}}$ is the number of times cr_{ij} occurs in X.

One choice of the functional form for $p(v_{CR})$ is particularly convenient for our application. In particular, if the prior $p(v_{CR})$ is a *Dirichlet* distribution, then both efficiently computing the posterior distribution in closed form and sampling from that distribution are easy. Assuming that the prior distribution for $p(v_{CR})$ is Dirichlet implies there exist exponents $N'_{cr_{00}}, ..., N'_{cr_{33}}$ such that

$$p(v_{CR}) = \gamma \cdot \prod_{i=0}^{3} \prod_{j=0}^{3} v_{cr_{ij}}^{N'_{cr_{ij}}-1}$$

where γ is the normalization constant. Let N'_{CR} be defined as follows:

$$N'_{CR} = \sum_{i=0}^{3} \sum_{j=0}^{3} N'_{cr_{ij}}$$

Having the given Dirichlet prior can be thought of as at some point being ignorant about the fractions v_{CR}, and then observing the compliance and response behavior of N'_{CR} subjects, $N'_{cr_{ij}}$ of which have behavior cr_{ij}. Using this simplifying assumption, we update v_{CR} by sampling from the following Dirichlet distribution:

$$p(v_{CR} \mid cr^1,...,cr^n) = \gamma \cdot \beta \cdot \prod_{i=0}^{3} \prod_{j=0}^{3} v_{cr_{ij}}^{N_{cr_{ij}}+N'_{cr_{ij}}-1}$$

For accurate results, the Gibbs sampler is typically run in two distinct phases. In the first phase, enough samples are drawn until it is reasonable to assume that the resulting Markov chain has converged to the correct distribution. These initial samples are commonly referred to as the *burn-in* samples, and the corresponding values of the function being estimated are ignored. In the second phase, the values of the function are recorded and are used in the approximation of equation 4. There are countless techniques for determining when a series has converged, and no single method has become universally accepted among researchers. Another complication of the Gibbs sampler is that successive samples in the second phase are inherently dependent, yet we use these samples to approximate independent samples from the distribution. As a consequence of the many different methods to address these problems, tuning a Gibbs sampler for the best results tends to be more of an art than a science.

The approach we took for the results presented in the next section can be explained as follows. We ran the Gibbs sampler for enough iterations to ensure a relatively smooth estimate of the distribution, always discarding a large number of the initial points sampled. We then repeated the same schedule, starting with a different random seed, and compared the resulting outputs. If the distributions were reasonably distinct, we repeated the process

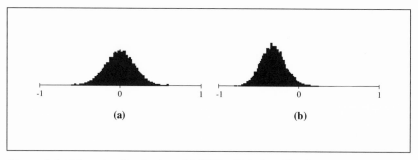

Figure 4. (a) The prior distribution of ACE(D→Y) induced by flat priors over the parameters v_{CR}, and (b) the distribution for ACE(D→Y) induced by skewed priors over the parameters.

using more samples. We emphasize that the any one of the many methods of data analysis can readily be applied to the output of our system.

6. Experimental Results

We have applied the Gibbs sampling algorithm to the model of figure 3 for various real and simulated data sets. Our system takes as input (1) the observed data D, expressed as the number of cases observed for each of the eight possible instantiations of $\{z, d, y\}$, and (2) a Dirichlet prior over the unknown fractions v_{CR}, expressed as the sixteen exponents $N'_{cr_{ij}}$. The system outputs the posterior distribution of ACE(D→Y), expressed as a histogram.

To investigate the effect of the prior distribution on the output, we ran all experiments using two different priors as input. The first is a flat (uniform) distribution over the 16-vector $\{v_{cr_{00}},..., v_{cr_{33}}\}$ that is commonly used to express ignorance about the domain. The second prior is skewed to represent a dependency between the compliance and response behavior of the subjects. Figure 4 shows the distribution of ACE(D→Y) induced by these two prior distributions. Note that the skewed prior of figure 4b assigns almost all the weight to negative values of ACE(D→Y).

In the following subsections, we present the output of our system using (1) a simulated data set for which the causal effect is identifiable, (2) a real data set from an experiment designed to determine the effect of cholestyramine on reduced cholesterol level, and (3) a real data set from a study to determine the effect of vitamin A supplementation on childhood mortality.

6.1 Simulated Data Example: Identifiable Causal Effect

As we noted in the introduction, Balke and Pearl (1994) have derived the

z	d	y	$v_{z,d,y}$
0	0	0	0.275
0	0	1	0.0
0	1	0	0.225
0	1	1	0.0
1	0	0	0.225
1	0	1	0.0
1	1	0	0.0
1	1	1	0.275

Table 1. Population fractions resulting in an identifiable ACE(Dk→Y).

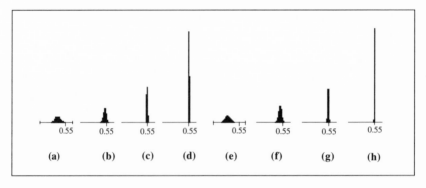

| (a) | (b) | (c) | (d) | (e) | (f) | (g) | (h) |

Figure 5: Output histograms for identifiable treatment effect using two priors. (a), (b), (c) and (d) show the posteriors for ACE(D→Y) using the flat prior and a data set consisting of 10, 100, 1000 and 10000 subjects, respectively. (e), (f), (g) and (h) show the posteriors for ACE(D→Y) using the skewed prior with the same respective data sets.

tightest bounds for ACE($D{\to}Y$) under the large-sample assumption. They show that for some distributions of Z, D and Y, the resulting upper and lower bounds collapse to a single point. We say that ACE($D{\to}Y$) is *identifiable* in this case. In this section, we show the output of our system when run on data sets derived from a distribution for which ACE($D{\to}Y$) is identifiable. One such distribution is shown in table 1, yielding ACE($D{\to}Y$) = 0.55.

Figure 5 shows the output of our system when applied to data sets of various sizes drawn from the distribution shown in table 1, using both the flat and the skewed prior. As expected, as the number of cases increases, the posterior distributions become increasingly concentrated near the value 0.55. In general, because the skewed prior for ACE($D{\to}Y$) is concentrated further from 0.55 than the uniform prior, more cases are needed before the posterior distribution converges to the value 0.55.

z	d	y	Lipid Study Observations
0	0	0	158
0	0	1	14
0	1	0	0
0	1	1	0
1	0	0	52
1	0	1	12
1	1	0	23
1	1	1	78

Table 2. Observed data for the Lipid study.

6.2 Real Data Example: Effect of Cholestyramine on Reduced Cholesterol

Consider the Lipid Research Clinics Coronary Primary Prevention data described in Lipid (1984). A portion of this data consisting of 337 subjects was analyzed by Efron and Feldman (1991) using a model that incorporates subject compliance as an explanatory variable; this same data set is the focus of this subsection.

A population of subjects was assembled and two preliminary cholesterol measurements were obtained: one prior to a suggested low-cholesterol diet and one following the diet period. The initial cholesterol level was taken as a weighted average of these two measures. The subjects were randomized into two groups: in the first group all subjects were prescribed cholestyramine (z_1), while the subjects in the other group were prescribed a placebo (z_0). During several years of treatment, each subject's cholesterol level was measured multiple times, and the average of these measurements was used as the post-treatment cholesterol level. The compliance of each subject was determined by tracking the quantity of prescribed dosage consumed.

We transformed the (continuous) data from the Lipid study to the binary variables D and Y using the same method as Balke and Pearl (1994). The resulting data set is shown in table 2. Using the large-sample assumption, Balke and Pearl (1994) use the given data to derive the bounds $0.39 \le \text{ACE}(D \rightarrow Y) \le 0.78$.

In figure 6 we show the posterior densities for $\text{ACE}(D \rightarrow Y)$ given the data. The density of figure 6a corresponds to flat priors (over the parameters) and the density of figure 6b corresponds to skewed priors. It is rather remarkable that even with only 337 cases in the data, both posterior distributions are highly concentrated within the large-sample bounds.

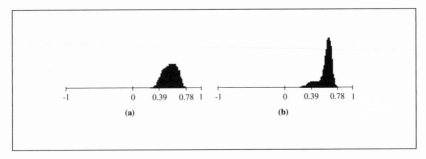

Figure 6. Output histograms for the Lipid data.
(a) Using flat priors and (b) using skewed priors.

6.3 Real Data Example:
Effect of Vitamin A Supplements on Child Mortality

In this section, we consider an experiment described by Sommer et al. (1986) designed to determine the impact of vitamin A supplementation on childhood mortality. In the study, 450 villages in northern Sumatra were randomly assigned to participate in a vitamin A supplementation scheme or serve as a control group for one year. Children in the treatment group received two large doses of vitamin A (d_1), while those in the control group received no treatment (d_0). After the year had expired, the number of deaths (y_0) were counted for both groups. The results of the study are shown in table 3.

Under the large-sample assumption, the method of Balke and Pearl (1994) yields the bounds: $-0.19 \leq \text{ACE}(D{\rightarrow}Y) \leq 0.01$. Figure 7 shows posterior densities for $\text{ACE}(D{\rightarrow}Y)$ given the data. The density of figure 7a corresponds to flat priors over the parameters, and the density of figure 7b corresponds to skewed priors over the parameters.

It is interesting to note that for this study, the choice of the prior distribution has a significant effect on the posterior. This suggests that the clinician should perform a careful assessment of the prior.

7. A Counterfactual Query

In addition to assessing the average treatment effect, the system is also capable (with only minor modification) of answering a variety of counterfactual queries concerning individuals with specific characteristics. In this section, we show the result of our system when modified to answer the following query: What is the probability that Joe would have had an improved cholesterol reading had he taken cholestyramine, given that (1) Joe was in the control group of the Lipid study, (2) Joe took the placebo as

z	d	y	Vitamin A Study Observations
0	0	0	74
0	0	1	11514
0	1	0	0
0	1	1	0
1	0	0	34
1	0	1	2385
1	1	0	12
1	1	1	9663

Table 3. Observed data for the vitamin A study.

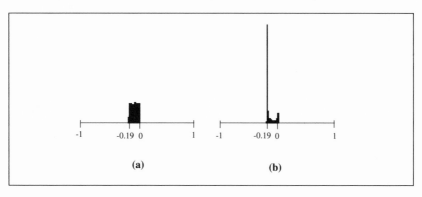

(a)   **(b)**

Figure 7: Output histograms for the Vitamin a supplementation data.
(a) Using flat priors and (b) using skewed priors.

prescribed, and (3) Joe's cholesterol level did not improve.

We can answer the above query by running the Gibbs' sampler on a model identical to that shown in figure 3, except that the function $ACE(D{\rightarrow}Y)$ (equation 3) is replaced by another function of v_{CR} that represents our query. If Joe was in the control group and took the placebo, that means that he is either a complier or a never-taker. Furthermore, because Joe's cholesterol level did not improve, Joe's response behavior is either never-recover or helped. Consequently, Joe must be a member of one of the following four compliance-response populations: $\{cr_{01}, cr_{02}, cr_{11}, cr_{12}\}$. Joe would have improved had he taken cholestyramine if his response behavior is either helped (r_1) or always-recover (r_3). It follows that the query of interest is captured by the function

$$f(v_{CR}) = \frac{v_{cr_{01}} + v_{cr_{11}}}{v_{cr_{01}} + v_{cr_{02}} + v_{cr_{11}} + v_{cr_{12}}}$$

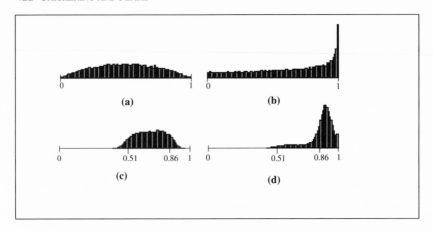

*Figure 8. Prior (a, b) and posterior (c,d) distributions for a subpopulation f(V_{CR})
specified by the counterfactual query "Would Joe have improved
had he taken the drug, given that he did not improve without it?"
(a) corresponds to the flat prior, (b) to the skewed prior.*

Figure 8a and figure 8b show the prior distribution over f(v_{CR}) that follows from the flat prior and the skewed prior, respectively. Note that whereas the skewed prior induces a prior over ACE($D{\rightarrow}Y$) that is concentrated on *negative* values, this same prior suggests that Joe would have *benefited* from receiving the drug. This result is an artifact of the skewed prior that we used in our experiments: the prior implies that we believe a large fraction of the population has the response behavior *hurt*; Joe, however, has response behavior *helped* or *never-recover*. Figure 8c and figure 8d show the posterior distribution p(f(v_{CR}) | 𝔇) obtained by our system when run on the Lipid data, using the flat prior and the skewed prior, respectively. From the bounds of Balke and Pearl (1994), it follows that under the large-sample assumption, 0.51 ≤ f(v_{CR}) ≤ 0.86.

Thus, despite 39% noncompliance in the treatment group, and despite having just 337 subjects, the study strongly supports the conclusion that, given Joe's specific history, he would have been better off taking the drug. Moreover, the conclusion holds for both priors.

8. Conclusion

This chapter identifies and demonstrates a new application area for network-based inference techniques—the management of causal analysis in clinical experimentation. These techniques, which were originally developed for medical diagnosis, are shown capable of circumventing one of the major problems in clinical experiments—the assessment of treatment efficacy in the face of imperfect compliance. While standard diagnosis involves purely probabilistic inference in fully specified networks, causal analysis involves partially specified networks in which the links are given causal interpretation and where the domain of some variables is unknown.

The system presented in this chapter provides the clinical research community, we believe for the first time, an assumption-free[3], unbiased assessment of the average treatment effect. We offer this system as a practical tool to be used whenever full compliance cannot be enforced and, more broadly, whenever the data available is insufficient for answering the queries of interest to the clinical investigator.

Acknowledgments

The research of D. Chickering was supported by NSF grant #IRI-9119825 and a grant from Rockwell International. The research of J. Pearl was supported by gifts from Microsoft Corporation and Hewlett-Packard Company. A preliminary version of this chapter appeared in the *Proceedings of the Thirteenth National Conference on Artificial Intelligence* (Menlo Park, Calif.: AAAI Press, 1996).

Notes

1 This approach is currently used by the FDA to approve new drugs.

2 The resulting Markov chain must be ergodic for this result to hold, a property that can be easily established for our application.

3 "Assumption-transparent" may be a better term, since the two basic assumptions in our analysis (i.e., randomized assignment and no-side-effects) are vividly displayed in the graph (e.g., figure 1), and the impact of the prior distribution is shown by histograms such as those of figure 4.

References

Angrist, J.; Imbens, G.; and Rubin, D. 1996. Identification of Causal Effects Using Instrumental Variables. *Journal of the American Statistical Association* 91(434): 444–472.

Balke, A., and Pearl, J. 1997. Bounds on Treatment Effects from Studies with Imperfect Compliance. *Journal of the American Statistical Association* 92(439)(September): 1171–1176.

Balke, A., and Pearl, J. 1994. Counterfactual Probabilities: Computational Methods, Bounds, and Applications. In *Proceedings of the Tenth Conference on Uncertainty in Artificial Intelligence,* 46–56. San Francisco, Calif.: Morgan Kaufmann.

Efron, B., and Feldman, D. 1991. Compliance as an Explanatory Variable in Clinical Trials. *Journal of the American Statistical Association* 86(413): 9–26.

Heckerman, D., and Shachter, R. 1995. Decision-Theoretic Foundations for Causal Reasoning. *Journal of Artificial Intelligence Research* 3:405–430.

Heckerman, D., and Shachter, R. 1994. A Decision-Based View of Causality. In *Proceedings of the Tenth Conference on Uncertainty in Artificial Intelligence*, 302–310. San Francisco, Calif.: Morgan Kaufmann.

Holland, P. W. 1988. Causal Inference, Path Analysis, and Recursive Structural Equations Models. In Sociological Methodology, ed. C. Clogg, 449–484. Washington, D.C.: American Sociological Association.

Imbens, G., and Rubin, D. 1997. Bayesian Inference for Causal Effects in Randomized Experiments with Noncompliance. *Annals of Statistics* 25(1): 305–327.

Lipid Research Clinic Program. 1984. The Lipid Research Clinics Coronary Primary Prevention Trial Results, Parts I and II. *Journal of the American Medical Association* 251(3): 351–374.

Pearl, J. 1995a. Causal Diagrams for Experimental Research. *Biometrika* 82(4): 669–710.

Pearl, J. 1995b. Causal Inference from Indirect Experiments. *Artificial Intelligence in Medicine Journal* 7(6): 561–582.

Pearl, J. 1995c. From Bayesian Networks to Causal Networks. In *Bayesian Networks and Probabilistic Reasoning*, ed. A. Gammerman, 1–31. London: Alfred Walter.

Rubin, D. 1978. Bayesian Inference for Causal Effects: The Role of Randomization. *Annals of Statistics* 7(1): 34–58.

Sommer, A.; Tarwotjo, I.; Djunaedi, E.; West, K. P.; Loeden, A. A.; Tilden, R.; and Mele, L. 1986. Impact of Vitamin A Supplementation on Childhood Mortality: A Randomized Controlled Community Trial. *The Lancet:* 1169–1173.

CHAPTER FOURTEEN

Estimating Latent Causal Influences

Tetrad II Model Selection and
Bayesian Parameter Estimation

Richard Scheines

1. Introduction.

This chapter presents an example of statistical causal inference in which two pieces of artificial intelligence technology proved crucial. The pieces are Tetrad II's Build module applied to a variable selection problem in linear regression, and Tetrad III's Gibbs sampler[1] applied to approximating the posterior distribution over the parameters of an "underidentified" linear model of the effect of lead exposure on IQ.

By measuring the concentration of lead in a child's baby teeth, Herbert Needleman was the first epidemiologist to use a reliable measure of cumulative lead exposure. His work helped convince the United States to eliminate lead from gasoline and most paint (Needleman et. al. 1979). Needleman's original statistical analysis of data he and colleagues collected on lead exposure and IQ scores (basically ANOVA) was criticized by the EPA (Grant et al. 1983), which concluded that his data neither supported nor rejected the conclusion that lead was toxic at the doses he recorded in asymptomatic children. Needleman reanalyzed his data with multiple regression, and found that even after controlling for five covariates, the estimated effect of lead on IQ was negative and significant (Needleman, Geiger, and Frank 1985).

This quieted the EPA, but aroused more sophisticated criticism from Steve Klepper, an economist at Carnegie Mellon (see Klepper 1988; Klepper,

Kamlet, and Frank 1993). Klepper correctly argued that Needleman's statistical model (a linear regression) neglected to account for measurement error in the regressors. That is, Needleman's measured regressors were in fact imperfect proxies for the actual but latent causes of variations in IQ, and in these circumstances a regression analysis gives a biased estimate of the desired causal coefficients and their standard errors.

Unfortunately, an errors-in-all-variables model that explicitly accounts for Needleman's measurement error is "underidentified" and thus cannot be estimated by classical techniques without making additional assumptions. Klepper, however, had worked out an ingenious technique to bound the estimates, provided one could reasonably bound the amount of measurement error contaminating each measured regressor (Klepper 1988; Klepper, Kamlet, and Frank 1993). The required measurement error bounds vary with each problem, however, and those required in order to bound the effect of actual lead exposure below 0 in Needleman's model seemed wholly unreasonable. Klepper concluded that the statistical evidence for Needleman's hypothesis was indeed weak.

Reanalyzing Needleman's data and regression model, I used Tetrad II to eliminate three spurious covariates that Needleman's backwards step-wise procedure had erroneously included. In fact the variables that Tetrad II eliminated were precisely those which required unreasonable measurement error assumptions. With the remaining regressors, I specified an errors-in-all-variables model to parameterize the effect of actual lead exposure on children's IQ. This model is still underidentified, but instead of trying to bound the coefficients of interest, I put a prior distribution over the parameters in the model and used a Gibbs sampler (Smith and Roberts 1993; Scheines, Hoijtink, and Boomsma 1995) to do a Bayesian estimation of the model. Under several priors, nearly all the mass in the posterior was over negative values for the effect of actual lead exposure—now a latent variable—on measured IQ.

2. Variable Selection with Tetrad II

In their 1985 article in *Science*, Needleman, Geiger and Frank gave results for a multivariate linear regression of children's IQ on lead exposure. Having started their analysis with almost forty covariates, they were faced with a variable selection problem to which they applied backwards eliminative regression, arriving at a final regression equation involving lead and five covariates. The covariates were measures of genetic contributions to the child's IQ (the parent's IQ), the amount of environmental stimulation in the child's early environment (the mother's education), physical factors that might com-

Correlations

	lead	fab	nlb	med	mab	piq	ciq
lead	1.00						
fab	-.08	1.00					
nlb	.11	.39	1.00				
med	-.14	.02	-.18	1.00			
mab	-.15	.85	.47	.003	1.00		
piq	-.06	.17	.03	.53	.16	1.00	
ciq	-.23	-.0003	-.17	.41	.05	.40	1.00

p-values

	lead	fab	nlb	med	mab	piq
fab	.23					
nlb	.10	.00				
med	.04	.78	.01			
mab	.02	.00	.00	.96		
piq	.39	.01	.70	.00	.02	
ciq	.00	.99	.01	.00	.43	.00

Table 1. Correlations and p-values (N = 221).

promise the child's cognitive endowment (the number of previous live births), and the parent's age at the birth of the child, which might be a proxy for many factors. The measured variables they used are as follows, with the correlations among these variables and the significance of each correlation given in table 1.

ciq – child's verbal IQ score   *piq* – parent's IQ scores

lead – measured concentration in baby teeth   *mab* – mother's age at birth

med – mother's level of education in years   *fab* – father's age at birth

nlb – number of live births previous to the sampled child

The standardized regression solution[2] is as follows, with *t*-ratios in parentheses. Except for *fab*, which is significant at 0.1, all coefficients are significant at 0.05, and $R^2 = .271$.

$$ciq = -.143 \, lead + .219 \, med + .247 \, piq + .237 \, mab - .204 \, fab - .159 \, \text{nl}$$
$$\quad\quad (2.32) \quad\quad (3.08) \quad\quad (3.87) \quad\quad (1.97) \quad\quad (1.79) \quad\quad (2.30)$$

The intuition behind statistically "controlling" for covariates in a multivariate regression intended to estimate causal influence is scientifically appealing but can be wrong. It stems from the following plausible story: a sizable unconditional association between X and Y might not be due to a direct causal link from X to Y, but rather at least partly from confounders (common causes of X and Y), or intermediate causes; statistically controlling for covariates leaves only the true causal association between X and Y. In the case of linear regression, β_i (the regression coefficient of the outcome Y on X_i) is statistically significant just in case the partial correlation of Y and X_i controlling for all of the other regressors is significant.

Linearity is not the issue, rather it is whether a significant association between X and Y, controlling for *all* the other potential confounders, is the right test for a direct causal connection between X and Y. Clearly Needleman (and Klepper after him) considered the variable selection problem settled by the significance test for coefficients in the multivariate regression, and this seems to be standard operating procedure in the social science and epidemiological community. Unfortunately, the general principle is wrong, and this data set is an exemplar of why.

In the general setting of multivariate regression, linear or otherwise, an outcome Y and a set of regressors $\mathbf{X}$ is specified. Assuming that $\mathbf{X}$ is prior to Y, in which case Y cannot cause any $X \in \mathbf{X}$, we say that X is causally adjacent to Y relative to the set $\mathbf{X}$ just in case either X is a direct cause of Y relative to $\mathbf{X}$, or there is a Z not in $\mathbf{X}$ such that Z is a common cause of X and Y. Two assumptions improve upon regression in detecting whether any $X_i \in \mathbf{X}$ is causally adjacent to Y relative to $\mathbf{X}$ from population data: the causal Markov condition and faithfulness.[3] The causal Markov condition amounts to assuming that every variable X is independent of all variables that are not its effects conditional on its immediate causes (Spirtes, Glymour, and Scheines 1993). The causal Markov assumption is satisfied necessarily by recursive structural equation models with independent errors (Kiiveri and Speed 1982) and seems to be relatively uncontroversial. Faithfulness amounts to assuming that all independencies true in a population determined by a causal structure are due to the absence of causal connection and not due to parameter values that produce independencies by perfect cancellation.

Although versions of this assumption are used in every science (Spirtes, Glymour, and Scheines 1993), it is not uncontroversial, and has been generally challenged by Robins and Wasserman (1996). Allowing these two assumptions, it turns out that X is causally adjacent to Y if X and Y are dependent conditional on *every subset* of $\mathbf{X} - \{X,Y\}$ (Spirtes, et al. 1993). Contrast this criterion with the one used in multivariate regression: X and Y are dependent conditional on *exactly the set* $\mathbf{X} - \{X_i,Y\}$. The model in figure 1, in which $\mathbf{X} = \{X_1, X_2, X_3\}$ and Z is unmeasured, makes the error in the regression criterion vivid.

The model does not entail that X_2 and Y are independent when we condition on all the other regressors $\{X_1, X_3\}$. It is possible for the model to imply this independence, but only for unfaithful parameterizations. For all faithful parameterizations, a regression of Y on X will produce nonzero coefficients for all three regressors. Although it is not a sampling problem, it is easy to

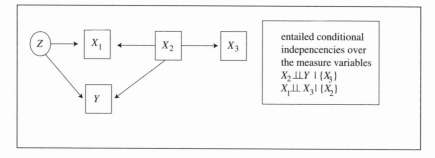

Figure 1: A model that fools regression.

verify that regression will mistakenly conclude that X_2 is causally adjacent to Y on sample data by randomly parameterizing this model, generating a pseudo random sample, and then running a regression.

It turns out that the regression criterion is reliable only when X is known to be prior to Y *and* the measured variables are known to be *confounder complete*,[4] i.e., all common causes of two variables in $\mathbf{X} \cup \{Y\}$ are already in $\mathbf{X} \cup \{Y\}$. Assuming confounder completeness in general seems entirely unrealistic, and clearly so for the lead data.

The FCI algorithm executed by the Build module in Tetrad II (Scheines et al. 1994) does not assume confounder completeness, and uses an improved criterion for causal adjacency under the causal Markov and faithfulness assumptions. Whereas edges included by the FCI will always be included by regression, in many cases FCI will correctly eliminate an edge when regression cannot, as in, for example, the graph in figure 1. It makes statistical decisions about independence by formulating null hypotheses, e.g., that $\rho_{X2,Y,X3}$ = 0, and accepting them if they cannot be rejected at a user set significance level. In the lead example, the variables are distributed approximately multivariate normal, so I use partial correlations to test for conditional independence. In figure 2 I show the relevant part of the output from the FCI algorithm on the lead data, with a significance level of .05, and temporal information such that *ciq* is not prior to lead, and lead is not prior to every other regressor. The output indicates that only lead, *med*, and *piq* are adjacent to *ciq*.

Tetrad II found that *mab, fab,* and *nlb* are *not* causally adjacent to *ciq*, contrary to Needleman's regression. In Needleman's data, these covariates are more highly correlated with *ciq after* conditioning on the other regressors than they are unconditionally. *Mab* and *fab*, for example, are completely uncorrelated with *ciq* unconditionally (see table 1), yet are *correlated* with *ciq* conditional upon all the other regressors. Whether *mab* and *fab* are measured with error or not, then under these assumptions they or the variables they are proxies for cannot be causally adjacent to *ciq* relative to this set. The regres-

```
List of vanishing (partial) correlations that made
TETRAD remove adjacencies.

Corr. :  Sample (Partial) Correlation
Prob. :  Probability that the absolute value of the sample
         (partial) correlation exceeds the observed value, on the
         assumption of zero (partial) correlation in the population,
         assuming a multinormal distribution.

Edge                (Partial)
Removed             Correlation              Corr.      Prob.
-------             -----------              -----      -----
fab -- ciq          rho(fab ciq)            -0.0003    0.9920
.
mab -- ciq          rho(mab ciq)             0.0540    0.4252
nlb -- ciq          rho(nlb ciq . med)      -0.1141    0.0914
-----------------------------------------------------------------
NOT assuming causal sufficiency
The Partial Ancestral Graph (PAG):
Significance Level =   0.0500

lead --> ciq
.
med o-> ciq
piq o-> ciq
```

Figure 2. Output from Tetrad II's Build Module on Needleman's data.

sor *nlb* is correlated with *ciq* unconditionally, uncorrelated with *ciq* when conditioned on *med* ($r_{nlb,ciq,med} = -.114$, $p = .1$), but once again correlated when conditioned on the entire set of regressors. Since the improved criterion for determining causal adjacency eliminates an adjacency between X and Y if they are independent conditional on *any* subset (including the empty set), Tetrad II eliminated the *fab-ciq* and *mab-ciq* adjacency because it accepted unconditional independence, and the *nlb-ciq* adjacency because it accepted the correlation between them as vanishing conditional on *med*. Asserting that the latent variable that *nlb* is a proxy for (e.g, mother's physical factors) is not causally adjacent to *ciq* is a little more delicate. We must assume there is a connection between *ciq* and *nlb* through *med*, which seems implausible, or that *med* is highly correlated with the latent it proxies (for environmental stimulation), and that *nlb* and *ciq* are uncorrelated conditional on environmental stimulation, which is plausible.

To finalize the variable selection phase, I did a regression of *ciq* on only those regressors found to be causally adjacent to *ciq*, namely *lead, med*, and *piq*.

$$ciq = - .177 \, lead + .251 \, med + .253 \, piq \qquad (2)$$
$$\quad\;\; (2.89) \qquad (3.5) \qquad\;\; (3.59)$$

The overall R^2 for the regression in equation 2 is .243, which is quite close to the R^2 of .271 from the full regression on all six variables in equation 1.

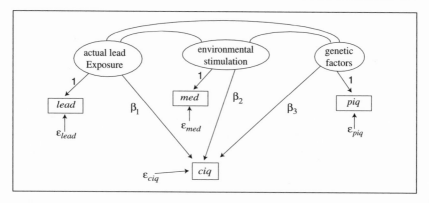

Figure 3. Errors-in-all-variables model for lead's influence in IQ.

All coefficients in equation 2 are significant at .01, as expected, and the coefficient on lead is slightly more negative than it was in equation 1.

3. Estimating the Parameters of an "Underidentified" Model

As Klepper (1988) and Klepper, Kamlet, and Frank (1993) point out, and rightly so, these measured regressor variables are really proxies that almost surely involve substantial measurement error. Measured *lead* is really a proxy for actual lead exposure, *med* is really a proxy for environmental stimulation, and *piq* is really a proxy for genetic factors related to IQ. Figure 3 shows a full errors-in-all variables specification for the variables included by Tetrad II. The task is now to estimate the coefficient β_1.

Although an errors-in-all-variables linear structural equation model seems a reasonable specification, this model is underidentified in the classical setting. That is, for any implied covariance matrix $\Sigma(\theta)$ that minimizes a discrepancy function of the implied and observed covariances, there are an infinity of parameterizations θ' such that $\Sigma(\theta) = \Sigma(\theta')$. In this case there are thirteen free parameters in the model but only ten data points in the covariance matrix for *ciq, lead, med,* and *piq;* thus the model is underidentified by three degrees of freedom.

Several strategies exist for identifying the model. One is to specify the exact proportion of measurement error for each measured independent variable. Since in this model Var(lead) = 1 = Var(Actual Lead) + Var(ε_{lead}), the proportion of measured lead's variance due to measurement error is just Var(ε_{lead}), which is between 0 and 1. Similarly for the other regressors. Using a linear regression to estimate β is equivalent to specifying a measurement error equal to zero for each regressor. We could also simply stipulate that the measurement error for lead is 0.20, or some other number.

Klepper and Leamer (1984) showed that in certain circumstances one can bound the actual coefficients, at least in sign, by putting upper bounds on the amount of measurement error. In 1988 and again in 1993 Klepper, Kamlet, and Frank argued that the upper bounds required by his method to solve this problem (with all six regressors) were unreasonable. For example, one had to bound the measurement error for *fab* (father's age at birth) at approximately five percent, which did not seem even remotely justifiable, considering *fab* is a proxy for physical, emotional, and intellectual factors present in the father that might influence a child's IQ score. Performing his analysis on the reduced set of regressors, one must be willing to bound the measurement of lead, *med*, and *piq* at .710, .465, and .457 respectively, a combination of bounds of which I am reasonably confident. Klepper's technique, however, provides sufficient conditions for bounding, not necessary, and cannot provide point estimates or standard errors.

The alternative I favor is Bayesian. By putting a prior distribution over the parameters and then computing the posterior, one can compute point estimates, e.g., the mean or median in the posterior (θ_{EAP} and θ_{MDAP}), standard deviations around the point estimates (SD(θ_{EAP})), percentiles that can be used to compute posterior credibility intervals ($\theta_{.025}$ and $\theta_{.975}$) and many other statistics of interest. If the posterior cannot be computed analytically, which is certainly the case for all but the most trivial structural equation models, then one can now compute a sample from the posterior by MCMC simulation methods with Tetrad III (Scheines, Hoijtink, and Boomsma 1995).[5] One can then use the sample from the posterior to estimate the posterior statistics from their sample counterparts, i.e., $\hat{\theta}_{EAP}$, $\hat{\theta}_{MDAP}$, SD($\hat{\theta}_{EAP}$), $\hat{\theta}_{.025}$, and $\hat{\theta}_{.975}$. For simplicity, I use a multivariate normal prior over the t parameters, i.e., $p(\theta) \sim N_t(\mu_0, \Sigma^2_0)$, and I enforce bounds on the parameters, e.g., variances are bounded below by 0, by rejecting sampled values outside of the legal parameter bounds.[6]

To apply the Bayesian solution to Needleman's problem, we must put a prior over the parameters. Needleman pioneered a technique of estimating cumulative lead exposure by measuring the accumulated lead in a child's baby teeth. From consultations with critics, I guess that between 0 percent and 40 percent of the variance in Needleman's proxy is from measurement error, with 20 percent a conservative best guess. For the measures of environmental stimulation and genetic factors, I am less confident, so I guess that between 0 percent and 60 percent of the variance in *med* and *piq* is from measurement error, with 30% as the best guess. Thus I began by specifying the multivariate normal prior over the model's thirteen parameters given in table 2, with

Parameter	Mean (μ_0)	Standard Deviation (σ_0)
$Var(\varepsilon_{lead})$	0.200	0.10
$Var(\varepsilon_{med})$	0.300	0.15
$Var(\varepsilon_{piq})$	0.300	0.15
$Var(\varepsilon_{ciq})$	0.757	4.00
Var(Actual Lead)	0.800	4.00
Var(Environ. Stim.)	0.700	4.00
Var(Genetic Factors)	0.700	4.00
β_1	-0.177	4.00
β_2	0.251	4.00
β_3	0.253	4.00
Cov(Act. Lead, Env. Stim)	-0.136	4.00
Cov(Act. Lead, Gen. Fac)	-0.058	4.00
Cov(Env. Stim, Gen. Fac)	0.527	4.00

*Table 2. Multivariate Normal prior distribution over
the parameters in the errors-in-all-variables model.*

no covariation between any of the model's parameters in the prior. Notice that the prior is only informative about the three error variances that parameterize the amount of measurement error in Needleman's original proxies. With a standard deviation of 4.0 around the other parameters, the prior is effectively uninformative everywhere else. The means the nonerror variances are set to the regression estimates from equation 2.

Using this prior, I produced 50,000 iterations with the Gibbs sampler in Tetrad III. The sequence converged immediately. Table 3 shows the results of this run, and the histogram in Figure 4 shows the shape of the marginal posterior over β_1, the crucial coefficient representing the influence of actual lead exposure on children's IQ. The results support Needleman's original conclusion, but do not require unrealistic assumptions about the complete absence of measurement error, or assumptions about exactly how much measurement error is present, or assumptions about upper bounds on the measurement error for the remaining regressors.

The Bayesian point estimate of the coefficient reflecting the effect of actual lead exposure on IQ is negative, and since the central 95% region of the posterior lies between -0.420 and -0.038, I conclude that exposure to environmental lead is indeed deleterious according to this model and my prior uncertainty over the parameters.

Although my uncertainty about the amount of measurement error associated with *med* and *piq*, which are proxies for environmental stimulation and genetic factors respectively, is not sufficient to make β_1 insignificant, it is

	$\hat{\theta}_{EAP}$	$\hat{\theta}_{MDAP}$	$SD(\hat{\theta}_{EAP})$	$\hat{\theta}_{.025}$	$\hat{\theta}_{.975}$
β_1	-0.215	-0.211	0.097	-0.420	-0.038
β_2	0.332	0.307	0.397	-0.358	1.252
β_3	0.321	0.304	0.391	-0.459	1.128

Table 3. Gibbs sample statistics for the
causal parameters in the errors-in-all-variables model.

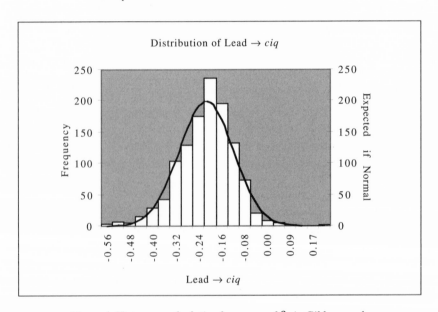

Figure 4. Histogram of relative frequency of β_1 in Gibbs sample.

sufficient to make β_2 and β_3 insignificant. That is, the central 95% of the
sample from the posterior over both β_2 and β_3 includes 0. Since these coefficients represent the effect of environmental stimulation and genetic factors
on a child's cognitive abilities, it seems reasonable to insist that they are at
least positive in sign. I thus reran the analysis, but imposed 0 as a lower
bound on β_2 and β_3. The posterior distribution over β_1 was slightly less diffuse, and centered over roughly the same value.

In fact I sampled from several posteriors corresponding to different priors,
and in each case I got similar results. Although the size of the Bayesian

Parameter	Mean (μ_0)	Standard Deviation (σ_0)
$Var(\varepsilon_{lead})$	0.05	0.05
$Var(\varepsilon_{med})$	0.10	0.10
$Var(\varepsilon_{piq})$	0.10	0.10
$Var(\varepsilon_{fab})$	0.05	0.05
$Var(\varepsilon_{mab})$	0.05	0.05
$Var(\varepsilon_{nlb})$	0.05	0.05

Table 4. Informative part of the prior in the errors-in-all-variables
model including all six original regressors.

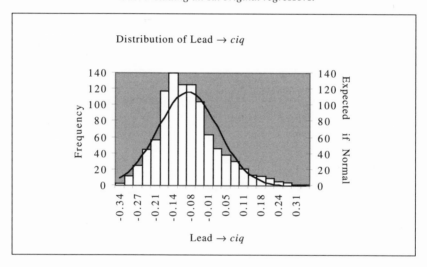

Figure 5. Gibbs sample from model with six regressors.

point estimate for lead's influence on IQ moved up and down slightly, its sign and significance (the 95% central region in the posterior over β_1 was always below zero) were robust.

I also ran the Gibbs sampler on an errors-in-all-variables model that included all six of Needleman's original regressors. In this case the bounds Klepper derived proved important. Recall that the measurement error on *fab* was required to be below .06. Using a prior in which substantial mass violated this bound, the sampler did not converge.

Using a prior that was uninformative except for the parameters I show in table 4, the histogram of values for β_1 in the Gibbs sample (figure 5) was substantially different than the one in figure 4.

A full Bayesian analysis would incorporate uncertainty over these and other model specifications, and in future work I intend to address this problem. Given the two errors-in-all-variables models I have considered here, however, I am highly inclined to favor the smaller model suggested by Tetrad II's analysis. Given this model, which is perfectly plausible, the data quite clearly support Needleman's conclusion.

Notes

1.Tetrad III is now under development. See the Tetrad project home page for details:http://hss.cmu.edu/philosophy/TETRAD/tetrad.html.

2. The covariance data for my reanalysis was originally obtained from Needleman by Steve Klepper, who generously forwarded it to me. In this and all subsequent analyses I use the correlation matrix.

3. For discussions of the reliability of regression for determining causal structure see Spirtes, Glymour, and Scheines (1993, chapter 8), Scheines (1995), and Glymour, Spirtes, and Scheines (1994).

4. In Tetrad II and many previous publications we use the terminology of "causal sufficiency" to mean what I define here as confounder completeness.

5. A Gibbs sampler for computing the posterior over the parameters of a structural equation model is now available in a beta version of Tetrad III. See the Tetrad project home page for details: http://hss.cmu.edu/philosophy/TETRAD/tetrad.html.

6. For details about the Gibbs sampler implementation see Scheines et al. (1995).

References

Casella, G., and George, E. I. 1992. Explaining the Gibbs Sampler. *The American Statistician* 46(3): 167–174.

Grant, L., et al. 1983. Draft Air Lead Criteria Document. Washington, D.C.: Environmental Protection Agency.

Glymour, C.; Spirtes, P.; and Scheines, R. 1994. In Place of Regression. In *Patrick Suppes: Scientific Philosopher, Volume 1,* ed. Paul Humphreys. Dordrecht, The Netherlands: Kluwer Academic.

Kiiveri, H., and Speed, T. 1982. Structural Analysis of Multivariate Data: A Review. *Sociological Methodology*, ed. S. Leinhardt. San Francisco, Calif.: Jossey-Bass.

Klepper, S. 1988. Regressor Diagnostics for the Classical Errors-in-Variables Model. *Journal of Econometrics* 37(2): 225–250.

Klepper, S., and Leamer, E. 1984. Consistent Sets of Estimates for Regressions with Errors in All Variables. *Econometrica* 52(1): 163–183.

Klepper, S.; Kamlet, M.; and Frank, R. 1993. Regressor Diagnostics for the Errors-in-Variables Model—An Application to the Health Effects of Pollution. *Journal of Environmental Economics and Management* 24(3): 190–211.

Needleman, H.; Gunnoe, C.; Leviton, A.; Reed, R.; Peresie, M.; Maher, E.; and Barrett, P. 1979. Deficits in Psychologic and Classroom Performance of Children with Elevated Dontine Lead Levels. *New England Journal of Medicine* 300: 389.

Needleman, H.; Geiger, S.; and Frank, R. 1985. Lead and IQ Scores: A Reanalysis. *Science* 227(4688): 701–704.

Robins, J., and Wasserman, L. 1996. On the Impossibility of Inferring Causation from Association without Background Knowledge, Unpublished manuscript, Department of Statistics, Carnegie Mellon Univ., Pittsburgh, Penn.

Scheines, R. 1993. Causation, Indistinguishability, and Regression. In *Softstat '93: Advances in Statistical Software 4*, 89–99. New York: Gustav Fischer.

Scheines, R.; Hoijtink, H.; and Boomsma, A. 1995. Bayesian Estimation and Testing of Structural Equation Models. Technical Report, CMU-PHIL-66, Department of Philosophy, Carnegie Mellon Univ., Pittsburgh, Penn.

Scheines, R.; Spirtes, P.; Glymour, G.; and Meek, C. 1994. *Tetrad II: Tools for Causal Modeling. User's Manual*. Hillsdale, N.J.: Lawrence Erlbaum.

Smith, A. F. M., and Roberts, G. O. 1993. Bayesian Computation via the Gibbs Sampler and Related Markov Chain Monte Carlo Methods. *Journal of the Royal Statistical Society* B(55): 3–23.

Spirtes, P.; Glymour, C.; and Scheines, R. 1993. *Causation, Prediction, and Search*. New York: Springer-Verlag.

PART FIVE

Applications

The value of a perspective on inquiry, and of the theoretical work it motivates, ought to be judged by the empirical results they are used to produce. The remaining chapters in this book describe applications of directed graphical representations and search techniques. The chapters cover a range of scientific domains: economics, physics, space science, biology, and educational research. These chapters illustrate the use of graphical representations and search in finding plausible explanations; they offer concrete comparisons of these methods with more conventional regression methods; and they compare predictions obtained with search methods with independently obtained information about cause and effect.

The separation of theory and application is partly false. Most of the "application" chapters that follow make original adaptations and modifications of the search methods described earlier in this volume, adaptations suggested or required by specific scientific contexts. That fact should lay to rest the very idea that the development of automated search procedures aims—or succeeds—at removing human ingenuity and insight from the process of inquiry.

CHAPTER FIFTEEN

Exploring Hypothesis Space: Examples from Organismal Biology

Bill Shipley

1. Introduction

It must seem curious that an evolutionary biologist would write a chapter in this book. After all, structural equations modeling is only just being discovered amongst evolutionary biologists and the axiomatic discovery procedures of Spirtes, Glymour, and Scheines (1993) are almost completely unknown to us. This curiosity is also, for me, tinged with irony. Sewall Wright, who invented the method of path analysis (Wright 1920, 1921), was one of the most influential evolutionary biologists of this century. Yet despite Wright's reputation amongst evolutionary biologists, his method of path analysis has been almost completely ignored by biologists until very recently, with the exception of a few scattered applications (e.g. Scott 1966, 1969, 1973; Li 1975 and references therein). I can only speculate on the reasons for this lack of interest, but these reasons must be addressed if we biologists are to reclaim our heritage. I suspect that Wright's method of path analysis appeared too subjective for biologists who were simultaneously being influenced by the rigorous inferential statistics of Fisher, based on the randomized experiment.

This subjectivity was twofold. First, there was no way of objectively testing the path model once it was parameterized; this problem has been solved with the advent of structural equations modeling (see Bollen 1989 for a brief history), but this is still largely unknown to most biologists. The second impression of subjectivity may have arisen because the development of the path model, independent of its testing, appeared to be a process of almost pure speculation. Organismal biology was (and still is) a largely empirical science without the quantitative theoretical foundations of physics or chemistry. Because our theoretical base is often weak we cannot be overly impressed by models derived from "theory." Fields such as sociology or psychology, which also lack a rigorous theoretical base but which have embraced structural equations modeling, at least deal with an organism which we all know intimately; an intuitive appeal to "causes" does not seem quite so outrageous when we study ourselves. A biologist studying grasshoppers or maple trees cannot appeal to such vicarious experiences. Our real challenge, as biologists, is not in fitting and testing our models, but rather in developing models that are worth testing. This is not a subtle distinction for the practicing biologist, although statistical methods are almost entirely concerned with testing, not developing, hypotheses. Methods of developing models that are worth testing is the theme of this chapter. My objective is to show, using two actual data sets, how the marriage of bootstrap resampling (Efron 1982) and the SGS (Spirtes, Glymour, and Scheines) algorithm of Spirtes, Glymour, and Scheines (1993) can help in this problem of hypothesis generation in the context of organismal biology.

2. The Biological Context

It is a common observation that the traits possessed by organisms often covary: sharp teeth tend to be associated with pointed claws, powerful leg muscles and acute senses. These attributes contribute to the evolutionary fitness of the organism, but the maximization of fitness by natural selection often requires tradeoffs between these attributes. Consider the phenomenon of photosynthesis in land plants, an example that I will explore in more detail later. Photosynthesis is the process by which plants convert atmospheric carbon dioxide into simple carbohydrates. In order to do this, the plant must adjust the size of small openings on the surface of its leaves ("stomates") to allow carbon dioxide into its intercellular spaces. However, as soon as these stomates open, water begins to escape from the moist tissues to a typically drier atmosphere. At its most basic level, photosynthesis in terrestrial plants can be thought of as a problem of maximizing carbon gain while minimizing water loss. Thus, we can imagine a whole set of leaf attributes that interact to "solve" this problem in a given environmental context. We would like to produce a mathematical model that can describe and predict how these attributes affect each other and thus determine the solution that natural selection has found to this problem. Such a mathematical model could be developed via structural equations modeling, but the challenge is less in testing our model than in finding a model worth testing. It is first a problem of discovery and only later a problem of inferential statistics.

3. The Philosophical Context

Structural equations modeling is an inferential technique. After obtaining (by whatever process) an hypothesized structure one can attempt to falsify it. The orthodox (and, I believe, largely correct) view is that one should not use the methodology of structural equations modeling as an exploratory technique to attempt to discover the structure that generated the data. The Monte Carlo studies described in Spirtes, Glymour, and Scheines (1993) show just how poorly the modification indices of LISREL IV (Joreskog and Sorbom 1984) or the Lagrange multiplier and Wald procedures of the EQS statistical program (Bentler 1995) are able to identify the correct model.

If one should not use the methodology of structural equations modeling to develop hypotheses concerning the structure that generated the data, how should this be done? The orthodox (and, I believe, much too stifling) view is that one should appeal only to independent "theory" and not to the data themselves. I have never been able to determine from where this strongly held opinion comes. I suspect that it comes from an over-zealous application of Popper's (1959) philosophy of falsificationism. In fact, Popper is quite neutral concerning how one generates hypotheses; these can be derived from preexisting theory, from patterns of correlation or even from self-flagellation, so long as these hypotheses are ultimately capable of falsification. Popper cannot be used to justify the orthodox view. The appropriate question then becomes: which methods of discovery are most useful in generating hypotheses in the form of structural relations?

To be slightly more concrete, consider a set of five attributes, whose values we have measured on a group of organisms, whose interactions we would like to model and which form a causally sufficient system (i.e., one in which there are no unmeasured variables that simultaneously cause the responses in more than two measured variables). There are approximately 59,000 different potential models. Any search strategy must be judged on the chances that such a strategy would hit upon the correct model. One search strategy is to simply choose one of the 59,000 possible models at random. This strategy would have a little less than two chances in 100,000 of hitting upon the correct model. Even in small data sets (say, 100 observations), the SGS algorithm, when coupled with bootstrap techniques, can have 3 chances out of 4 of finding the true model, based on the Monte Carlo studies of Shipley (1997). What are the chances of finding the true model, based on the orthodox method of appealing to "theory"? Clearly, this depends on the quality of the independent theory. To claim that one should only use "theory" in developing structural equations models is equivalent to claiming that this search strategy is always superior to any other. I am willing to entertain this claim, but my experience as a practicing scientist cautions me against it.

4. Bootstrapping and the SGS Algorithm

The SGS algorithm (Spirtes, Glymour, and Scheines 1993) is asymtotically reliable in discovering the causal structure underlying data drawn from homogeneous, acyclic, causally sufficient systems. This algorithm is based on the pattern of (conditional) independencies among the variables. Unfortunately, in finite samples, the algorithm can make errors because the sample correlation matrix deviates randomly from the population correlation matrix, and this problem is accentuated as the sample size decreases. Practical constraints often mean that evolutionary biologists have to make do with sample sizes (often below 100) that are much too small for the reliable use of the SGS algorithm. I have shown (Shipley 1997) that if this algorithm is imbedded within a bootstrap loop (Efron 1982), in which a random sample is drawn with replacement from the original data set and the SGS algorithm is applied to each bootstrap sample, the error rates are reduced and the true structure can often be reliably recovered from very small sample sizes (often below 50 observations). After each iteration of this procedure, the bootstrapped undirected or partially directed graph is obtained from the SGS algorithm. After a large number of interactions (300 is often sufficient) the average number of directed or undirected edges, and the frequency with which each potential edge occurs per bootstrapped graph, are counted. If there are an average of n edges (rounded to the nearest integer), then the n most frequent edges are used to determine the hypothesized structural equations model. All acyclic graphs having this topology are then tested against the data using the standard likelihood ratio chi-squared statistic.

I will illustrate this technique using two different data sets. These two data sets show both the promise and the problems that I have encountered.

5. Seed Dispersal in St. Lucie's Cherry

Jordano (1995) studied the interactions between various attributes that determine the relative number of seeds dispersed (mainly by birds) of different individual trees of a small Spanish tree, St. Lucie's Cherry *(Prunus mahaleb)*. The five measured variables in that paper were (1) the area of the tree canopy projection (a measure of total photosynthetic biomass), (2) the total number of ripe fruit produced per tree, (3) average fruit diameter, (4) average seed weight and (5) the number of seeds dispersed from the tree by birds. Data from 60 trees were available. Canopy projection area was transformed to its square root, and the other variables were transformed to their natural logarithms, to produce normality of their distributions.

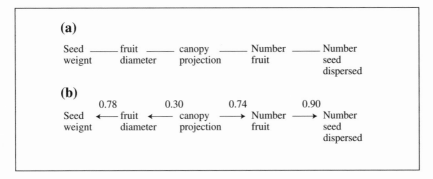

Figure 1 (a) The undirected graph of the relationships between five attributes of St. Lucie's Cherry affecting the number of seeds dispersed by birds. (b) The final path model (standardized variables) derived from the undirected graph.

The evolutionary question is the following: how do these five attributes interact and how do these attributes contribute to the reproductive output of a given tree? We wish to obtain a structural equations model that can reproduce the patterns of covariation between these five attributes and that can best predict the quantitative values of each. Although I could "propose" a model based on existing knowledge, any such hypothesis would not seem particularly compelling because the biology of these interactions is not well established. Since preexisting biological theory is not well developed for this phenomenon, there is little to be gained from testing it. Instead, I apply the bootstrapped version of the SGS algorithm to see if it can suggest a structure that is both consistent with this data and does not contradict what is known about the biology of seed production and dispersal.

Table 1 gives the relative frequency of each potential undirected edge among the five variables, based on 300 bootstrapped data sets and a rejection level of 0.4. There were an average of 4.2 edges per graph and figure 1a shows the undirected model obtained from choosing the 4 undirected edges with the largest relative frequencies from the summary graph. Note that all 4 undirected edges have relative frequencies of greater than 0.65 (i.e., they occurred in at least 195 out of the 300 bootstrapped graphs), while all others (except for the edge between canopy projection area and the number of seed dispersed, which equals 0.48) have relative frequencies of less than 0.12 (i.e. the occur in less than 36 of the 300 bootstrapped graphs). A total of eleven different directed acyclic graphs are both consistent with this topology and have a chi-squared statistic whose (asymptotic) probability is greater than 0.05.

Given this topology, basic biology can help to determine some directions. For instance, the number of seed dispersed by birds at the end of the growing period must depend on the number of fruits produced by the tree, not vice ver-

	Number of fruits per tree	Average fruit diameter	Average seed weight	Number of seeds dispersed
Canopy projection area	**0.82**	**0.65**	0.06	0.48
Number of fruits per tree		0.02	0.12	**1.00**
Average fruit diameter			**1.00**	0.01
Average seed weight				0.03

Table 1. The relative frequency of each undirected edge among five variables involved in seed dispersal in St. Lucie's Cherry by birds, based on the SGS algorithm applied to 300 bootstrap samples. No constraints were placed on the SGS algorithm.

sa, due to the time ordering of the process of seed dispersal. This reduces the number of alternate graphs to seven. Similarly, the total number of fruit produced is more likely determined by the total size of the canopy—and therefore the total amount of resources available to produce fruit—than vice versa. It is well known that photosynthates and nutrients are redirected from leaves or storage organs to developing fruit or seed. Furthermore, a lack of resources will cause the plant to abort seeds that have begun to form. Orientation of this edge reduces the number of alternate graphs to four. A similar argument can be made to orient the edge from total canopy size to average fruit diameter—it is more likely that the average size of a fruit is determined by the total amount of resources available to the tree than vice versa. This further reduces the number of alternate graphs to two. The final edge, between fruit diameter and seed weight, is the most problematic to orient. Orienting it from fruit diameter to seed weight produces a slightly better fitting model ($X^2 = 3.28$, $p = 0.78$, figure 1b) than the alternate one ($X^2 = 5.29$, $p = 0.51$) but this provides little reason to prefer one or the other. The edge between canopy projection and the number of seeds dispersed by birds had a relative frequency of 0.48. The addition of this edge to the final model does not significantly improve the fit of the model, but given the relatively high value of 0.48, this edge should be kept in mind when the model is tested against a larger data set. This is especially relevant since this edge has a plausible biological interpretation: the number of seeds dispersed by birds increases slightly as the size of the canopy increases even when trees have the same number of fruits. This may be because the size of the tree is a visual cue that first attracts birds.

This first example is a case in which there was not a body of preexisting theory to test and there were only a few empirical relationships that could be used to constrain alternate potential models. The application of the boot-strapped SGS algorithm produced a model which accords both with the available data and with preexisting empirical results. Because it has both of these qualities, it is, in my opinion, a model that is worth testing with independent data. The second example represents a case where there does exist a well-developed theoretical context and one which illustrates a potential problem with the SGS algorithm.

6. Interspecific Determinants of Gas Exchange

This second example involves the interactions of five plant attributes that affect net photosynthetic rate and the stomatal conductance to water vapor. The relevant variables are specific leaf mass (leaf area divided by the dry weight of the leaf), total leaf nitrogen concentration, stomatal conductance to water, net photosynthetic rate and the concentration of carbon dioxide within the leaf. As explained earlier, land plants are faced with a dilemma: in order to photosynthesize (i.e., convert atmospheric carbon to plant biomass), they have to open small pores ("stomates") on their leaves to let carbon dioxide into the intercellular spaces. This is a passive process of diffusion which is determined by the difference in the partial pressure of CO_2 between the external atmosphere and the intercellular spaces. The decreased partial pressure of CO_2 within the leaf is due to the fact that the plant is photosynthesizing and thus removing CO_2 from the air within the leaf. As soon as the stomates open, water also begins to passively diffuse out of the leaf. This is determined by the partial pressure of water vapor within and outside the leaf. The air within the leaf is always completely saturated with water vapor but (except when it is raining) the air outside the leaf is not saturated with water. So, the plant must accept a loss (in terms of water) in order to affect a gain (in terms of carbon). There is a well-developed theory of stomatal regulation (Cowan and Farquhar 1977) that describes the functional solution to this problem for a single leaf. This theory has been repeatedly tested and confirmed at the level of the individual leaf, and the interesting question for the biologist is simply whether this theory can also be used at an interspecific (evolutionary) level.

The data set consists of thirty-five observations. Each observation consists of the mean of each of the five variables for a different species; the means are based on approximately twelve plants per species. Martin Lechowicz and I are preparing details of this experiment, including the full data set and theoretical development of the model, for publication). Each mean value was transformed to its natural logarithm to obtain normality. Table 2 lists the rela-

	Stomatal conductance to water	Internal CO$_2$ concentration within the leaf	Leaf nitrogen concentration	Specific leaf mass
Net photosynthesis	**1.00**	0.12	0.13	0.03
Stomatal conductance to water		**0.99**	**0.58**	0.03
Internal CO$_2$ concentration within the leaf			0.04	0.02
Leaf nitrogen concentration				**1.00**

Table 2. The relative frequency of each undirected edge among five variables involved in leaf gas exchange based on the SGS algorithm applied to 300 bootstrap samples on the means of 35 species of plants. (No constraints were placed on the SGS algorithm.)

tive frequency with which each possible undirected edge occurred in 300 bootstrapped iterations of the SGS algorithm. There was an average of 3.9 edges per graph and figure 2a shows the resulting undirected graph obtained from the 4 most frequent edges. Only two alternate acyclic directed graphs both fit the data and are consistent with the undirected graph. Figure 2b shows the best fitting path model ($X^2 = 4.81$, $p = 0.569$). Neither of the two alternate models accord with the preexisting theory and both would be immediately rejected by any plant biologist. Why has the SGS algorithm produced a statistically acceptable, but biologically implausible, model?

Notice that there is no edge between net photosynthetic rate and internal CO$_2$ concentration (figure 2a). As already explained, the internal concentration of CO$_2$ within the leaf is determined by the equilibrium rate at which it is being removed from the intercellular air by photosynthesis (therefore photosynthetic rate is a direct cause of internal CO$_2$ concentration) and the rate at which it is diffusing into the leaf through the stomates (therefore stomatal conductance is also a direct cause of internal CO$_2$ concentration). We know that the internal CO$_2$ concentration is partly determined by the rate of photosynthesis, yet the SGS algorithm removed this edge in 88% of the bootstrapped graphs (table 2). The reason for this error is instructive. The first step in the SGS algorithm consists of determining the probability of the unconditional correlation between each pair of variables and, if any have a probability above the rejection level (0.4 in this example), the undirected

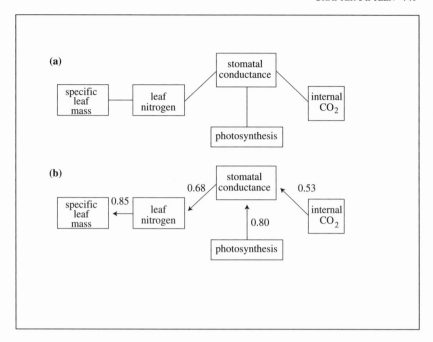

Figure 2 (a) The undirected graph of the relationships between five interspecific attributes affecting leaf gas exchange, based on the bootstrapped SGS algorithm without any constraints. (b) The best-fitted path model (standardized variables) derived fro the undirected graph. Although this model is not rejected by the data, it would be rejected by any plant biologist from basic biological knowledge.

edge is removed. In fact, the Pearson correlation coefficient between net photosynthetic rate and the internal CO_2 concentration in this data set was only 0.05 and so the edge between these two variables was almost always removed immediately by the SGS algorithm. I suspected that this was an example of an "empirical" zero correlation, that is, a weak absolute correlation due to the fact that alternate paths joining these two variables almost cancel each other. Indeed, the preexisting theory predicts that although increasing net photosynthesis should decrease the internal CO_2 concentration, net photosynthesis should also increase as the stomates open larger and as the stomates open larger the internal CO_2 concentration should increase. This implies two different treks, of opposite sign, between net photosynthetic rate and the internal CO_2 concentration.

If I again apply the bootstrapped SGS algorithm to these data, but constrain the algorithm to keep an undirected edge from each of stomatal conductance and net photosynthesis to the internal CO_2 concentration, then I obtain the results in table 3. Note that these two edges are justified by simple physical laws

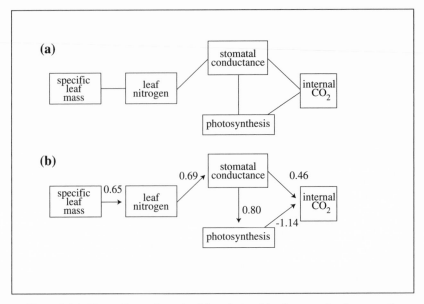

Figure 3 (a) .The undirected graph of the relationships between five interspecific attributes affecting leaf gas exchange, based on the bootstrapped SGS algorithm, after constraining the algorithm to keep the edges between internal CO_2 concentration within the leaf and each of net photosynthetic rate and stomatal conductance to water. (b) The best-fitting path model (standardized variables) derived from the undirected graph. This model is consistent with a well-established theory of leaf gas exchange.

of passive diffusion and by the well-known physiology and biochemistry of photosynthesis. There are now five alternate acyclic models that fit the data. One of the five (figure 3) is in fact the model that Martin Lechowicz and I had proposed based on the Cowan and Farquhar (1977) model of stomatal regulation, and this model provides a good fit to the data ($X^2 = 4.719$, 5 df, $p = 0.45$). The moral is that the SGS algorithm should be forced to either include or exclude edges that are based on well-established physical or biological principles.

7. Conclusions

I would like to conclude this chapter by returning to the philosophical context. The space of possible models of any phenomenon is defined by the number of variables chosen to describe it and the combinatorics of combining them. This space of possible models is huge, even for small numbers of variables. I like to think of the mathematical modeling of biological phenom-

	Stomatal conductance to water	Internal CO_2 concentration within the leaf	Leaf nitrogen concentration	Specific leaf mass
Net photosynthesis	**1.00**	**1.00**	0.13	0.03
Stomatal conductance to water		**1.00**	**0.58**	0.03
Internal CO_2 concentration within the leaf			0.04	0.02
Leaf nitrogen concentration				**1.00**

Table 3. The relative frequency of each undirected edge among five variables involved in leaf gas exchange, based on the SGS algorithm applied to 300 bootstrap samples on the means of thirty-five species of plants. The SGS algorithm was constrained to keep the undirected edge between internal CO_2 concentration within the leaf and each of net photosynthesis and stomatal conductance to water.

ena as a "search" through this space of possible models to identify those models that best predict and describe our empirical experience of the phenomenon. For the two data sets analyzed here, five variables define a possible universe of approximately 59,000 different models (and many more if one is willing to include unmeasured variables) and the efforts of biologists at proposing models and testing them against reality represent our collective "search" through this space of the possible. The advance of science depends on a dialectic between the generation of hypothetical models and our subsequent attempts to falsify them. How quickly we advance depends both on our ability to provide strong tests of our hypotheses and on our ability to generate hypotheses that efficiently explore those regions of "hypothesis space" that are closest to the "correct" model. Traditional statistics has concentrated on improving our ability to test hypotheses. We are only just beginning to devise methods of more efficiently exploring hypothesis space and therefore of finding hypotheses that are worth testing.

Both asymptotic proof and Monte Carlo simulations show that the search algorithms of Spirtes, Glymour, and Scheines (1993) for large data sets, or of its bootstrap version (Shipley 1997) for small data sets, can efficiently search though huge hypothesis spaces and identify models close to the true model in numerical experiments. It is impossible to know if this is also true when applied to real data because, by definition, the "true" model is unknown. The best that can be hoped for is that the models obtained by these search algorithms will be able to predict the patterns of covariation in independent data, including data obtained after manipulation, and are consistent with causal relationships when these are known.

References

Bentler, P. M. 1995. *EQS Structural Equations Program Manual.* Encino, Calif.: Multivariate Software.

Bollen, K. A. 1989. *Structural Equations with Latent Variables.* New York: Wiley.

Cowan, I. R., and Fraquhar, G. D. 1977. Stomatal Function in Relation to Leaf Metabolism Environment. In *Integration of Activity in the Higher Plant,* ed. D. H. Jennings, 471–505. Cambridge, U.K.: Cambridge University Press.

Efron, B. 1982. The Jackknife, the Bootstrap, and Other Resampling Plans. Phil., Penn.: Society for Industrial and Applied Mathematics.

Jordano, P. 1995. Furgivore-Mediated Selection on Fruit and Seed Size: Birds and St. Lucie's Cherry, *Prunus mahaleb. Ecology* 76:2627–2639.

Joreskog, K., and Sorbom, D. 1984. *LISREL IV User's Guide.* Moorseville, Ind.: Scientific Software.

Li, C. C. 1975. *Path Analysis—A Primer.* Pacific Grove, Calif.: Boxwood.

Popper, K. 1959. *The Logic of Scientific Discovery.* Fayetteville, Ark.: Hutchison.

Scott, D. 1973. Path Analysis: A Statistical Method Suited to Ecological Data. In *Proceedings of the New Zealand Ecological Society 20,* 79–95. Christchurch, N.Z.: New Zealand Ecological Society.

Scott, D. 1969. Determining the Type of Relationship between Plants and Environmental Factors. In *Proceedings of the New Zealand Ecological Society 16,* 29–31. Christchurch, N.Z.: New Zealand Ecological Society.

Scott, D. 1966. Interpretation of Ecological Data by Path Analysis. In *Proceedings of the New Zealand Ecological Society 13,* 1–4. Christchurch, N.Z.: New Zealand Ecological Society.

Shipley, B. 1977. Exploratory Path Analysis with Applications in Ecology and Evolution. *The American Naturalist* 149:1113–1138.

Spirtes, P.; Glymour, C.; and Scheines, R. 1993. *Causation, Prediction, and Search.* New York: Springer-Verlag.

Wright, S. 1921. Correlation and Causation. *Journal of Agricultural Research* 20:557–585.

Wright, S. 1920. The Relative Importance of Heredity and Environment in Determining the Piebald Pattern of Guinea Pigs. In *Proceedings of the National Academy of Science 6,* 320–332. New York: National Academy of Science.

CHAPTER SIXTEEN

In-Flight Calibration of Satellite Ion Composition Data Using Artificial Intelligence Methods

Joakim Waldemark and Patrik Norqvist

1. Introduction

Instruments aboard scientific satellites are usually unique and state of the art. However, such instruments are often extremely sensitive to the environment that they are supposed to operate in. This makes calibrations and preliminary tests of these instruments on earth difficult. To lower the risk of failure, scientists usually select well-known measuring techniques and instrumental design that already have been used on other missions. However, satellites or parts of satellites (at least civil satellites) are never "reused," so the actual instrument for a new mission has never been tested in space before launch. Everything from electronic devices, shielding material to mechanical systems can cause malfunction. Failure can actually occur only because some operator used a bad combination of instruments or other power-consuming systems on the satellite. Finally, regardless of how many tests, calibrations, calculations, or preparations that are made before launch of a satellite, no one can tell exactly how an instrument will perform until it is actually in orbit. All this means that calibrations and preparations made on the ground might not be valid once in the satellite is in operation. In fact, it is quite common that instrumental effects and operation capabilities cannot be investigated or even calibrated before the system is in orbit.

It would be useful if one could either confirm or improve calibrations of a satellite instrument made before launch, based on the actual measurements it makes in space. This chapter focuses on some of the cognitive analyzing techniques that are available and that might be useful for such a post calibration or validation of a satellite measurement system. As an example, these techniques are used to perform a postlaunch calibration of the three-dimensional ion composition spectrometer, TICS (Eliasson et al. 1994), on the Freja satellite was originally calibrated on earth; however, measurements made by TICS compared to other measurements made on the Freja satellite show that a recalibration is necessary. In section 5 TICS and its operation are briefly described. Further information can also be found in Norberg and Eliasson (1991).

TICS is a part of the "hot plasma" F3H experiment that includes both a magnetic imaging two-dimensional electron spectrometer (MATE) and an ion spectrometer, TICS, on the Freja satellite. TICS was designed to study ions in the lower magnetosphere and the upper ionosphere—especially the hot ions (i.e., ions that have energies in the range 1eV up to about 4keV). Ions in the ionosphere can have different origins; for example, hydrogen and helium ions that precipitate along the magnetic field lines in the keV energy range usually enter the earth's magnetosphere from solar wind, while oxygen ions originate in the atmosphere and are usually detected in the energy range of 1-100 eV. Different ions of different energies can thus be detected at different pitch angles (Pa) (we will discuss this further in section 5).

The TICS recalibration focused on three main tasks. The first was to identify the location of the different ion peaks (H^+, He^{++}, He^+, and O^+) in the ion mass spectra and thus define suitable integration points (section 5) to determine the actual numbers of a certain ion that is detected. The second was to determine the ion mass resolution capability during burst-mode measurements (section 5). The final task was to estimate a new set of sector sensitivity[1] coefficients for the TICS detection unit.

The IRF report is divided into two parts. Part I is about mass group identification and resolution, while part II is about the TICS sector sensitivity. This is a summary of the second report (Waldemark et al. 1995) —a joint project between Umea University Department of Applied Physics and Electronics and the Swedish Institute of Space Physics. Other published papers in this project are Waldemark and Norqvist (1995) and Waldemark (1996)

2. Identification of Ion Mass Spectra Components

An important question is whether ion mass data measured by TICS during burst mode actually show causality that corresponds to the original calibration of mass-channel integration points during other modes (i.e., normal high, see section 5). The different ion peaks originally expected to be identi-

Ion type:	Energy Step	Actual Energy level (Original) [eV]	H$^+$	He^{++}	He$^+$	O$^+$
	1	4300 (12500)	11..18	19..23	24..26	27..29
	2	3900 (8900)	8..15	16..22	23..25	26..29
	3	3000 (6350)	6..13	14..21	22..25	26..29
	4	2300 (4550)	5..12	13..19	20..24	25..28
Selected integration points	5	1900 (3250)	4..11	12..18	19..23	24..27
(masschannels)	6	1300 (2325)	3..10	11..17	18..22	24..27
	7	850 (1650)	2..9	11.16	17..21	23..27
	8	700 (1175)	2..8	10..16	17..21	23..27
	9	600 (850)	1..6	9..15	16..21	23..27
	10	500 (600)	1..6	9..15	16..21	23..27
	11	430 (430)	1..6	9..15	16..21	23..27
	12	310 (310)	1..6	8..13	15..20	22..27
	...	...	...	...	...	...
	32	1 (1.3)	1..6	8..13	15..20	22..27

Table 1. Selected integration points for each ion species.

fied in the TICS ion mass spectra were H$^+$, He$^+$, He^{++}, and O$^+$. The position of the ion peaks in the mass spectra depends on the energy of the ions, at least for high energies ($\approx$ above keV). The original intended energy range for TICS was 1.3 – 12500 eV, but, during final preparation, this range was lowered to 1 - 4300 eV. However, the calibration that was made to identify the integration points for each ion species was made for the original energy range. The eleven highest energy levels all had different settings of the various integration points. These settings were kept even when the energy range was changed (see table 1), because it was not possible to recalibrate TICS at that moment.

The ions are "post accelerated" by 4 kV (the acceleration voltage can under specific measurement modes be altered to 300 V or 0 V). That is, all ions are given an additional 4 keV energy before they are influenced by the permanent magnetic field inside TICS, which operates as a momentum analyzer (see section 5). This results in all ions that have an energy << 4 keV being deflected almost equally (only differing due to ion mass), with the possible exception of ions close to 4k keV. A fixed set of integration points should thus be possible to use for all energies without giving rise to large errors.

Each selected integration is supposed to measure a specific ion. This analysis aims to determine if studies of mass-channel causality can be used for identification of the position of the ion peaks (species) in the ion mass spectra. Furthermore, it aims to verify if the identified mass channels correspond to the original calibration of TICS, i.e., verify if the integration points below energy level 11 can also be used for the high energies. If not, it should suggest a new set of fixed integration points that lowers the measured ion density errors.

Two independent methods were used. One is the Tetrad II method developed at Carnegie Mellon University in Pittsburgh. Pennsylvania (Glymour et al. 1987 and Spirtes et al. 1993). The other is the principal component method. Theory regarding principal components can be found in many textbooks, such as Chatfield and Collins (1992).

2.1 The Principal Components Method

A measurement system is defined as a set of indicators that measure a set of features in a system, e.g. a set of microphones measuring different sound frequencies or different mass channels in an ion mass spectra. The measured data are usually represented in a data matrix, where each row is one complete measurement and columns represent each sensor output value in this specific measurement. It is possible to estimate a significant number of latent roots or latent variables (latent sources and production mechanism) that exist in a measurement system by using principal component analysis. This method separates the sensor outputs into independent orthogonal components called principal components.

The significant latent variables in a data matrix can be found by studying the latent roots (eigen values) of the matrix, or more correctly the explanation value (EV) for each latent root. The explanation value is the value of each latent root expressed in percent of total variance, that is, how much of the total variance in the data that each principal component (PC) explains. In complex problems it may be helpful to compare the measured data PC-EV with those which would be obtained from a pure random noise measurement system (a matrix of random noise).

Compare the explanation value for each principal component in a measurement system A to the explanation value of the principal component for a system B of pure random noise. If the explanation value for a principal component in A is larger than the explanation value in B, then this principal component in A is considered significant. A significant principal component indicates a high correlation. For example, a significant principal component can represent the source of the input variables (the indicators or the sensor outputs) correlated to that principal component. Component loading can be used to identify the specific input variables that are correlated to a certain principal component. Component loadings are, for standardized variables, the correlation coefficients between the input variables and the corresponding principal component. The principal component method is a linear separation of components, and each significant principal component found is independent and orthogonal to the other principal component found for the same measurements system. However, natural production mechanisms need not necessarily be independent; thus correlated latent variables may not be identified using the principal component method.

2.2 The Tetrad II Method

The Tetrad II method can be used to determine causality among the indicators in a measurement system (see definition above). This can, for example, be used to identify those mass channels in an ion mass spectra that have a common ion source. The analysis of TICS ion mass spectra will reveal if the identified "common source" mass channels actually are in a sequence on the micro-channel plate (MCP), e.g. channels 1 through 7 belong to one source (ion species), channel 19–25 belongs to another source, etc. Then we can reasonably believe first that the internal magnetic field of TICS is not damaged; second that TICS probably has an adequate shielding, i.e., the ion actually enters through the spherical top hat, not directly through the walls; and third that the ion energy separation, the electrostatic analyzer, is in operation.

If this is the case, then the sources (ion species) can be identified by the fact that light ions (H^+, He^{++}, He^+) are more deflected into the inner part of the MCP and heavier ions (mostly O^+) pass more or less undeflected by the internal magnetic field of TICS. Each and every sector on the MCP (and the anode system) can be—and indeed must be—treated as an individual. However, to program one measurement-mode of TICS, a set of fixed (equal for all sectors) ion mass spectra integration points is preferred, in order to shorten the programming sequence.

When studying a measured ion mass spectra from TICS, a first approximation is to assume that each mass-channel represents a specific ion weight and that the mass channels represent ion mass from light to heavier or vice versa. A measurement system that produces such a spectra can be represented by a one-dimensional linear (1D) model. A 1D-model is called pure if each dependent variable is affected by only one latent variable. The correlation matrix between the mass channels (the dependent variables, or indicators) can be calculated and the causal relations can be extracted from it.

A measurement model is a complete graph over all the causal relations between the dependent, latent variables and error signals. An example of a pure measurement model (M1) is shown in figure 1. The indicators $x1$ through $x8$ in figure 1 represent the measured values; at TICS they would be the mass channels. The signals $e1$ through $e8$ correspond to error signals, and $T1$, $T2$ are the latent variables, or the two sources that the indicators are measuring. The model is believed to be pure because no indicator is affected by more than one source. The causality is shown by *directed* and *undirected* edges. If a clear casual relationship is found by Tetrad II between two indicators or indicators/latent variables, then a directed edge (arrow) is drawn in the figure. If a causality is found but the direction cannot be established (given a specified probability) then an undirected edge is drawn (dotted lines, for example figure 2).

The Build function in Tetrad II calculates from the correlation matrix the causal relations that apply for the given significance and population size.

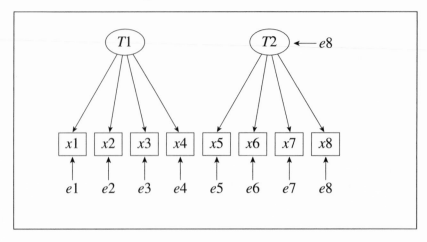

Figure 1. M1, a pure measurement model (one-dimensional)
in which indicators x1..x8 measure only one latent variable, T1 or T2.

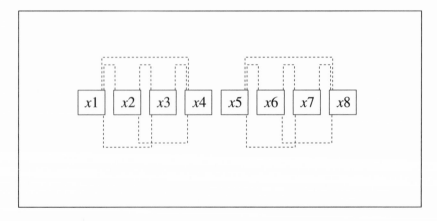

Figure 2. The causal model K1 of the pure measurement model
M1 having two latent variables (assuming causal sufficiency).

Build assumes causal sufficiency in the system, i.e., that no latent variables (common causes) are present. The two latent variables *T1* and *T2* in M1 will still affect the Build command. The causal model K1 calculated from M1 using Build is shown in figure 2. K1 appears to have two groups of causal connected indicators, but no connections between them.

If the measurement model is impure, e.g. M2 in figure 3, then one or more indicators are affected by more than one latent variable. The Build command will indirectly indicate impure indicators as shown in the corresponding causal model K2 of M2 in figure 4.

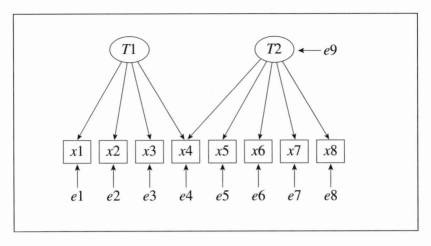

Figure 3. An impure measurement model, M2; the impure indicator is x4.

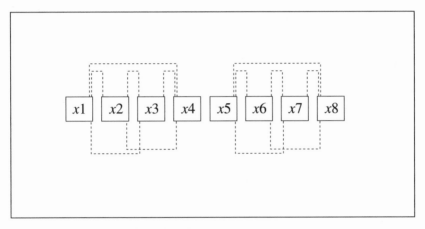

*Figure 4. The causal model K2 of the impure measurement
model M2 (assuming causal sufficiency).*

The causal model, K2, indicates two causally connected groups. However, x4, is strongly connected to both. This is logical since x4 actually is affected by both latent variables.

The Tetrad II method gives a tool to analytically determine if a group of indicators, e.g. mass channels in TICS, are measuring data of one unique source or species. The technique that has been used is to repeat the calculations for a range of significance levels and if possible also different population sizes. If a group of mass channels is causally connected, then this will occur in almost all significance levels.

One problem is that if a group of mass channels actually represents a "pure measurement model" but the latent sources are highly correlated, then Tetrad II will present this as one source and not two. This might be the reason why He⁺⁺ cannot be distinguished from the H⁺ measurements in this analysis, since hydrogen and helium in fact often[2] share the same source, the solar wind, and enter the earth's magnetosphere because of interactions between the magnetosphere and the solar wind. One can imagine that it would be possible to separate He⁺⁺ from He⁺ when the source is solar wind, since He⁺ and He⁺⁺ then have the same velocity and He⁺⁺ should therefore have twice the energy as He⁺. However, the mass spectrum analysis must include energy level while the task was to treat all energies alike (fixed set of integration points for all energies). Using all energies, the causal connections within this group of mass channels (He⁺ and He⁺⁺) will have a high probability of appearing as if there were only one source.

2.3 Result of Principle Component Analysis

The principal component (principal component) method applied on all selected TICS burst orbits data (see section 3.1) implies two strong latent roots or sources or species. All burst orbits analyzed were also summarized into one file, called Freja total or "total." A selection of principal component results, including Freja total, is shown in figure 5, where the latent roots of the first eight principal components, are plotted and compared to the latent root values of a matrix containing pure random noise (dotted line).

The component loadings (correlation coefficients between principal components and the indicators) vary from orbit to orbit. However, they all indicate one principal component correlated to the inner part (light ion mass channels) and the other principal component correlated to the outer part (heavy ions) of the spectra. Figure 6 shows the average correlation between PC1, PC2, and the mass channels for Freja orbit 2398es.

2.4 Results of Tetrad II Analysis

The Tetrad II analysis was first focused on the actual TICS mass resolution. TICS uses thirty-two mass channels, but the difficulties in tuning the anode system will affect the resolution. The number of exclusive burst orbits, i.e., burst measurements that use all thirty-two mass channels and that also contain enough statistics (data) to be analyzed using Tetrad II, is limited to only four orbits. However, the result is consistent; a strong crosstalk between nearest neighbors among the mass channels is confirmed. That is, a registration at one specific mass-channel and sector address is not distinct in the registration anode system. The anode system gives an uncertainty in exact ion detection location ,and this results in all ion detection addresses overlapping.

This crosstalk of mass channels (and sectors) is mostly due to the anode

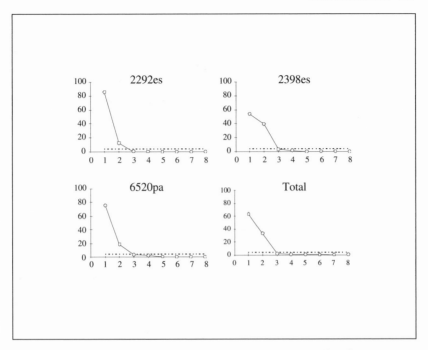

*Figure 5. X-axis. Principal components 1..8, Y-axis: percent of total variance
explained, explanation value (EV) by component. Solid line: the
EV for Freja (burst) orbit 2292es, 2398es, 6520pa and Freja total.
Dotted line (4%) results from a system of random noise.*

system in TICS, and the result was expected since the tuning of the anode
system was made such that the channels would overlap each other. A good
example is Freja orbit 2398es, since it is one of the "best" exclusive burst orbits found. The causal model (only for closest and second closest neighbors)
is shown in figure 7.[3]

The Tetrad II causal analysis of TICS mass channels was made by calculating several causal models for different levels of significance and numbers
of measurements for several burst orbits (see data selection). All the causal
graph figures shown in this report summarize calculations made on two different numbers of measurements for each orbit, and four different significant
levels in Tetrad II (0.01, 0.5, 0.1, 0.2), giving a maximum of eight possible
causal connections (edges) between two variables. Each population of measurements will give one set of edges for each significance level. The interpretation of such a summarized causal model graph is as follows.

1. If a set of strongly correlated mass channels exists, then this group

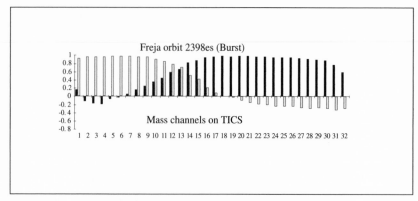

*Figure 6. The component loadings for PC1 and PC2 of
Freja orbit 2398es, exclusive burst.*

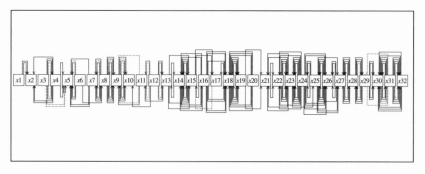

*Figure 7. Causal model for Freja orbit 2398es exclusive burst,
i.e. all 32 mass channels are used, only closest and second closest
connections to neighboring channels are shown.*

of channels will have a large set of edges (connections) among
themselves.

2. Further, if this group of channels also is distinguished (disconnected) from the other sensors—that is, only few edges connect the
group to the surrounding channels—then it is possible to suggest
(at high probability) that this group of channels is affected by one
latent variable.

In the case of TICS, a group of casually connected mass channels will indicate that this group of channels measures strongly correlated ions, i.e., ions
of the same species, or ions having the same production mechanism.

The principal component analysis has already indicated two latent roots,
species, or sources, in the mass spectra measured by TICS, figure 5. The

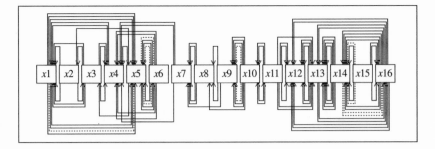

Figure 8. The causal model of Freja orbit 6520pa, normal burst.

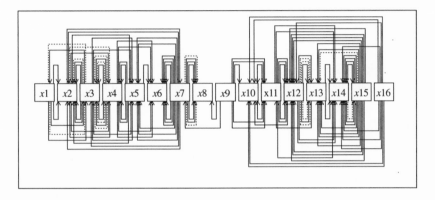

Figure 9. The causal model of Freja total.

Tetrad II analysis also indicates two causally connected groups of mass channels. An example of this is the causal model graph of Freja orbit 6520pa, shown in figure 8.

One Freja burst orbit does not produce enough statistics to present a set of general integration points. However all selected bursts were studied in the same manner. The Freja total file was also studied using Tetrad II/Build. The causal model of the Freja total is shown in figure 9.

Two well-defined, causally connected blocks of mass channels can be identified in all orbits analyzed: some are more diffuse as a result of a lack of data. These two blocks cover light ion and heavy ion mass channels in TICS. The block of mass channels in between are not strongly causally connected and they are also not distinctly correlated to one certain principal component (see figure 6). This indicates that this set (group) of sensors is *impure*. Sensors that are impure measure events produced by more than one source or la-

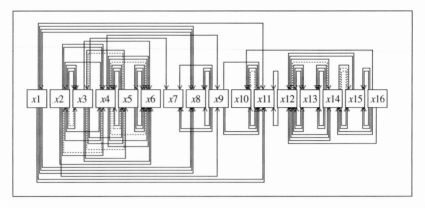

Figure 10. The causal model of orbit 6441pa, all energies used.

tent variable. The impure mass channels in TICS are channels that, for example, measure more than one ion species, e.g. both He^{++} and He^+.

2.5 Helium Ions Can be Distinguished

The ion mass-channel calibration in this report was made to find one *general* set of integration points equal for all sectors, all energy levels and *all orbits*. The Tetrad II analysis has not generally been able to distinguish helium ions from hydrogen, especially when all energies are studied. However, there are unique orbits where it is possible to distinguish helium from hydrogen. This chapter does not focus on this capability, but an example is Freja orbit 6441pa. Figure 10 depicts Tetrad II results for all energies shown.

It is clear that the two main clusters are $x2–x6$ and $x12.–x16$. This represents hydrogen and oxygen ions respectively. In this case, helium ions are not possible to detect distinctly, because helium is only a fraction of the amount of oxygen and also because the mass channels in between hydrogen and oxygen are slightly "impure." Impure channels measure ion counts of several species. It is simply difficult to resolve helium when compared to oxygen and hydrogen.

Figure 10 also shows another interesting occurrence: $x1$ seems to be strongly connected to the mass channels in the middle, especially $x8$ and $x11$. This is even more obvious if the causal model is optimized, i.e., all variables are rearranged so that all connections (edges) are as close as possible, as in figure 11. The optimization is made using a genetic algorithm focusing to minimize the edge distances. The result of $x1$ confirms that detected ions cannot always be correctly addressed on the MCP. This result can be explained from the construction of the register unit (the anode system) in TICS.

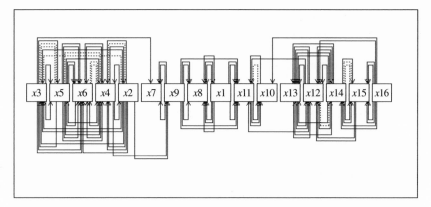

Figure 11. The causal model of orbit 6441pa, all energies used. The mass-channel order is rearranged compared to figure 10 in order to minimize the edge distances.

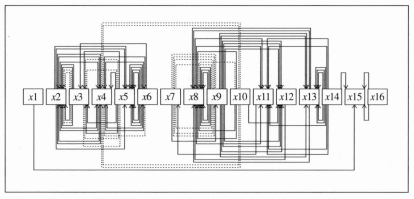

Figure 12. The causal model of orbit 6441pa, only high energies (above 220 eV) used.

When an ion reaches the MCP, then the anode system needs to detect the exact location. This process is, however, not trivial. The detection unit is a resistive anode system, both in angle (sector) and radial (mass-channel) direction. If an ion cannot be located by the anode system in the radial direction, then the registration unit will place the measurement in either the lowest or highest channel, depending on the type of error.

For example look at figure 11, orbit 6441pa. Channel $x1$ (the lowest channel) is mixed together with channel $x8$–$x11$, according to minimizing edge distances. A large number of measured ions could not be correctly detected (i.e. the correct mass channel could not be identified) during this orbit and were therefore addressed to channel $x1$. However, the correlation matrix and Tetrad II analysis show that a majority of measured counts on channel $x1$ correlate strongly with measurements in channel $x8-x11$. Thus, the counts in channel $x1$ should be added to the counts in channel $x8-x11$ to provide a correct estimate of the mass spectrum. Now three "almost" disconnected groups of mass channels can be distinguished. These are believed to represent hydrogen, helium, and oxygen ions.

The helium part of the mass spectra can be even better distinguished if only high energies (above 220 eV) are studied, then the spectra is dominated by hydrogen and helium, and only small fractions of oxygen exist. A Tetrad II analysis of orbit 6441pa high energies is shown in figure 12, where two strongly correlated groups of mass channels can be distinguished, in this case hydrogen and helium. As previously explained, H^+ and H^{++} should be possible to distinguish if only a suitable part of the energy range is studied. This result also shows that correlated mass channels do actually vary as a function of energy level, and the task to find *one* set of integration points independent of energy is not trivial. Thus an energy dependent analysis could be useful and give a more correct calibration.

3. Sector Sensitivity Calibration

The ion detection unit in TICS consists of a micro channel plate (MCP) and an anode system. The MCP is divided into thirty-two angular sectors. All sectors on the MCP have a unique ion detection sensitivity (C) (cm^2sr keV / keV) due to the construction of the MCP, the anode system and the attachment of the MCP inside TICS. The original C values were calibrated before launch using mainly argon as calibration ion and all C values were assumed to be constant for each sector in the radial direction of the MCP.

However, studies of the actual ion density, measured by TICS, compared to the theoretically determined ion density based on the plasma frequency (the plasma frequency can be determined from the electric field measurements made by other instruments on Freja show a significant large difference in obtained results. In fact comparing results between "measured total ion counts" (all sectors summarized) and "expected total ion counts" generally differ by a factor of four to five. Preliminary studies of the actual *relative* difference of counts between the sectors compared to the anticipated difference due to the originally determined calibration of C values (table 1) also showed a great difference. Furthermore, a radial variation of sensitivity within a sector is most likely to exist as well as the variation between sectors. The recalibration of the sector sensitivity was based on actual measurements during burst mode (section 5) made by TICS and reference measurements of the plasma frequency made by the field experiment on Freja. A set of norm-cumulative back-propagation (BP) neural net filters was used in order to apprehend the no-linear mapping between measurements made by TICS and the actual ion environment in the plasma.

3.1 Method and Data Selection

First the *relative* calibration of all sectors was needed in order to determine the new *absolute C* values. The relative calibration was determined by using a set of BP filters. These BP filters were trained so that a given mass spectra of one sector, after passing through the BP filter, was normalized to sector 22. That is, the BP filters were trained to nonlinearly transform a given mass spectra of a sector so that it appeared to be measured by sector 22. One BP filter was made for each sector. The BP filters use a mass spectra of sixteen discrete values (normal burst mode, see section 5) as inputs. The desired output during training is the normalized mass spectra, measured by sector 22.

The selection of sector 22 as a reference sector was made under careful consideration. The selected sector needed to have low interference with other parts of the instrument, good pitch angle coverage and good measuring response; i.e., the ion mass spectra should have distinguished spectral peaks corresponding to different ion masses. Sector 22 fulfills all desired conditions.[4]

Data selection was made so that data from different sectors could be compared independent of pitch angle. The data needed to be in high resolution burst mode, and also reasonably large ion fluxes were desired. Data were accumulated for the whole burst, i.e., 30s. In order to minimize pitch angle, dependencies' data were only accumulated when a sector was close to perpendicular with the magnetic field line. Furthermore, only the sixteen highest energy levels of data were used to avoid any interference from satellite velocity. Low energy ions moving slowly compared to the satellite velocity (about seven km per second) will, due to the speed of the satellite, reach an energy level that allows them to enter TICS low energy levels—so called ram-flow effects. This is true for oxygen ions but not for hydrogen ions, due to the fact that oxygen is much heavier than hydrogen. Finally, and most importantly, the ram-flow effects will not affect all sectors equally. Therefore, low energy measurements will not be correct if we do not compensate for the effects of the satellite speed. This is, at the moment, not possible to do at high enough accuracy for this task.

3.2 The Neural Net Filter System

The neural net filter system was developed so that each sector could be filtered through a neural net and then give the same ion mass spectral response as sector 22 would give if it was used for the same measurement and in the same position.

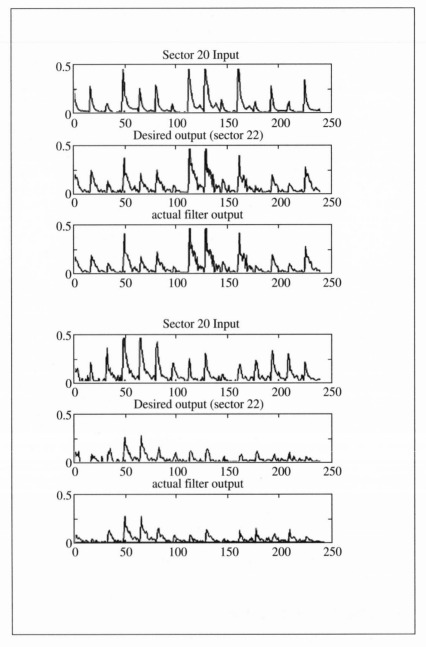

Figure 13. Filtering results compared to desired result for sector 3 and 4, notice that the filter is damping the input spectra. Observe the change in (y-axis) scale for sector 3.

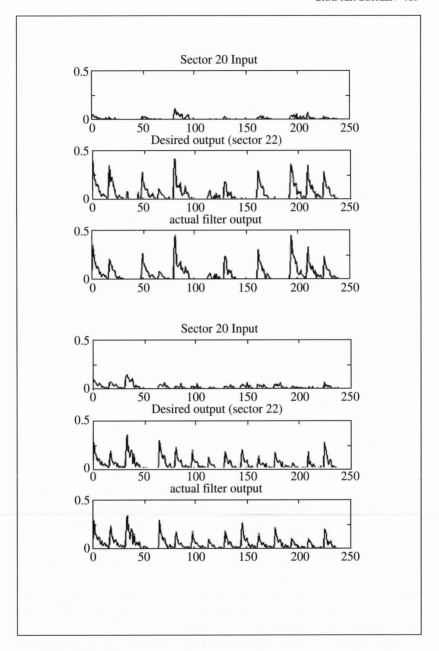

Figure 14. Filtering results compared to desired result for sector 14 and 20, notice that the filter is amplifying the input spectra. Sector 14 and 20 are shadowed by booms used in the construction of TICS.

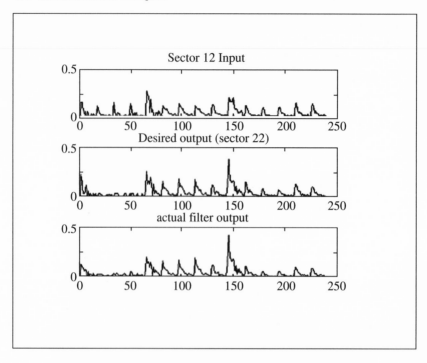

Figure 15. Filtering results compared to desired result for sector 12, notice that the input-output absolute level is almost the same only the shape of the spectra is changed.

A set of regular norm-cumulative back-propagation neural net filters (BP filters) was used. Each BP filter uses sixteen inputs, twenty-five hidden neurons, and sixteen outputs. Burst mode gives measurements from every second sector channel (this corresponds to sixteen values since each sector has a total of thirty-two channels). Thus, the BP filters are design to have sixteen inputs and sixteen outputs. The BP filters also used a momentum term and an epoch. The BP filters were trained using seventy-five percent of the available data; the remaining twenty-five percent was used for evaluation. Training was made by using the mass spectra of the sector that should be filtered as input and presenting the corresponding mass spectra of sector 22 as desired output. The mapping accuracy after training, i.e., the difference between actual filter output and desired filter output, was better than an RMSE (root mean square error) of ten percent, for all filters.

Three examples of filter capacity are shown in figures 13–15. Each figure unit consists of three graphs. The top graph is 15 input spectra side by side, giving a total of 240 values since each spectra is 16 values long (16 x 15 = 240). The middle graph is the desired filter output, i.e., the spectral values as

Ion type:	$H^+ (+ He^{++})$	He^+	O^+
Selected integration points (masschannels)	1..13	14..21	22..31

Table 2. New set of integration points for TICS.

they should appear according to sector 22. Finally the bottom graph shows the actual filter output from the BP neural network.

Figure 13 shows examples of input spectra of sectors 3 and 4, the response of sectors 3 and 4 is usually about two times higher than that of sector 22. Consequently, it is necessary for the filter to damp the input spectra and also to reshape it. Figure 14, is an example of two sectors that are affected, or shadowed by, the mechanic units holding the MCP in position. Sectors 14 and 20 receive very few particles compared to sector 22; therefore a large amplifying capacity is needed by the filter as well as a reshaping capacity. Finally figure 15, shows the filter examples of sector 12. Here, no modification of absolute level is needed, only reshaping of the spectra.

Obviously, the best way to chose a set of sector calibration values is to actually use the set of the neural-net filters. However, the neural-net filters are too complex to use in practical data analyzes, and each neural-net filter is developed for mass spectra using sixteen discrete mass values. The TICS instrument runs in many different measurement modes (see section 5). It is therefore far more useful to substitute the neural net filters with a set of proportionality constants, C—one for each ion species. The derivation of the relative and absolute C values are not shown here, but can be studied in detail in Waldemark and Norqvist (1995). The new set of calibration values C is thus a function not only of sector S but also of ion mass (hydrogen or oxygen).

3.3 Summary, Part I

The evaluation of the ion mass spectra measured by TICS, especially focusing on the causality among the channels in radial direction on each sector, show that there is strong crosstalk for closest and possible even second closest neighboring channels. As a result, TICS radial resolution is decreased to about eight to sixteen levels. The aim of this analysis was to find *one general* set of integration points to be used for all sectors, energies and orbits. The different ion peaks originally expected to be identified in the ion mass spectra was H^+, He^+, He^{++}, and O^+. However, the physical interpretation of the two analysis methods (the principal component and Tetrad II analyses) is that two ion species, most probably H^+ and O^+, dominate the measured ion mass spectra. The fact that crosstalking among the mass channels is large, and that each sector is in fact individually tuned because the anode system (section 5), makes it difficult, if not impossible, to distinguish He^+ from H^+. Exceptions do exist, as shown in section 5.

It is possible that He^+ would be more clearly identified if the analysis was made on only one sector at a time. A third species, e.g. He^+, cannot be analytically identified in either the principal component analysis nor the Tetrad II analysis. A principal component analysis of TICS data may only compute one principal component to model both H^+ and He^{++}, since He^{++} is strongly correlated to H^+ (as previously explained). This can then appear as if only one light ion species exists. Because of this fact, and also because H^+ and He^{++} often have the same source (solar wind), Tetrad II will fail to separate them. It is most natural to believe that the group of mass channels in between the light ion (hydrogen) group and the heavy ion (oxygen) group will represent helium, especially He^+, ions. That is, three regions in the ion mass spectra can be identified, two directly and the third indirectly. This third group can be more directly identified in orbits such as 6441pa as shown in section 5. The three identified mass-channel groups are believed to correspond to H^+ (that may also include He^{++}), He^+, and O^+ measurements, respectively. A new set of integration points (table 2) and the assumed corresponding ion species are shown in table 2.

This change of integration points will use the available mass channels on TICS more optimally. Furthermore it will also affect the number of ion counts detected. The statistics in ion mass measurements will (according to preliminary studies) increase about ten to twenty percent for H^+, 20-30% for He^+ and as much as sixty percent for O^+.

This pilot investigation has also proved that this type of recalibration made on measured results is possible and that the Tetrad II and the principal component method can be successfully used for measurement evaluation.

3.3 Summary, Part II

A set of back propagation neural nets has successfully been used to normalize the measuring response of all angular sectors in the TICS instrument. The neural networks were then used to determine two new sets of sector sensitivity values, C_1 and C_2, one for light ions and one for heavy ions.

The reason neural networks were used to transfer (normalize) the ion mass spectra was that the sector sensitivity depends not only on the angular position of the sector, but also on the radial direction within the sector, but not linearly. That is, we needed a nonlinear transformation. Furthermore, by using nonlinear back propagation neural nets both the large variation of the sector sensitiv-

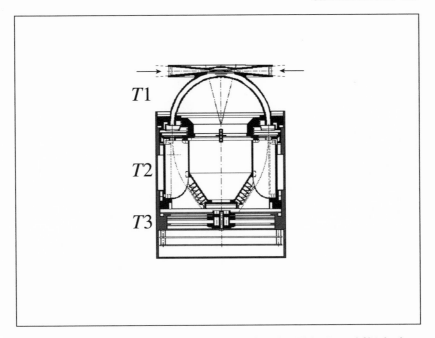

Figure 16. A cross section of TICS, The spherical top hat T1 having a 360 inlet for ions and operates as a electrostatic analyzer, the permanent magnetic chamber T2 which deflect ions in the radial direction depending on the weight of the ion, and finally the ion detection plate, MCP, T3 and the underlying anode system that identify the location of a detected ion on the MCP.

ity and the desire to normalize all measurements could be treated simultaneously. The conclusion of this evaluation is that neural net-filters are suitable to use for nonlinear transformations of spectra, such as the ion mass spectras in TICS. The system can transform any sector spectra to appear as sector 22 within ten percent accuracy. After the neural net-filters are developed or trained, the system can be used not only for ion mass spectra transformation, but also for simulation of measured response for given events.

The final evaluation of TICS performance (Waldemark and Norqvist 1995,) showed that TICS is more than four times as sensitive as expected by the original, earth-based, calibration.

4. General Conclusion and Discussion

This experience from the work in this report has shown that cognitive statistical methods, such as artificial neural networks and Tetrad II, are useful

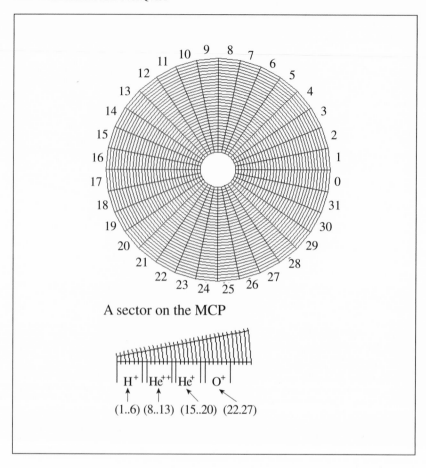

Figure 17. A schematic drawing of the MCP in TICS, left picture shows all 32 sectors and mass channels, right picture shows one sector and marks out the integration points for each of the four ion species H+, He++, He+ and O+ , the marked channels represent originally determined integration points for energy levels below 600 eV, integration points for other energy levels are listed in table 1.

tools in analysis of satellite data. This has been shown through the two different applications described in sections 2 and 3.

The Tetrad II method was used to successfully identify spectral components in ion mass spectra measured by TICS on the Freja satellite. The results of Tetrad II were also confirmed by a principal component analysis. The Tetrad II method generally needs good statistics about the system analyzed, but this was not always the case in this study. Nevertheless, results shows

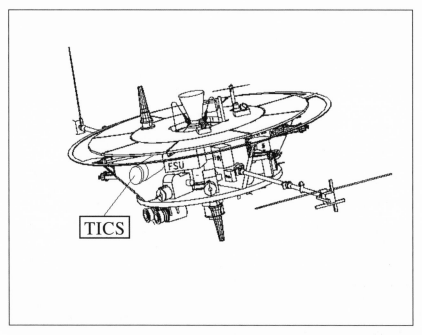

Figure 18. The Freja satellite and the position of TICS, it will be moved out (radially) by an sliding arm to avoid shielding. The ion inlet (T1 in figure A1) is parallel to the satellite spin axis, thus TICS will detect ions from all directions due to the satellite rotation.

that it is possible to obtain important information regarding a measurement system using Tetrad II even when available data do not meet all desired Tetrad II conditions.

Artificial neural networks were used as nonlinear filters in order to normalize ion mass spectra measured by different angular detection sectors in TICS. A general conclusion is that feed-forward neural networks are simple and fast when used for nonlinear transformations and filtering. It is also relatively simple to use a neural network as a transformation function, once it has been trained. That is, a trained network can be "ported" to regular run-time c-code routine. This routine can then easily be addressed in data analysis.

We believe that neural networks can be used to perform more complex nonlinear operations onboard a satellite. The neural net can either be trained on-line on board the satellite or be trained in batch mode (off-line) on ground and updated by downloading a new set of weights to the satellite computer—as simple as downloading a new look-up table. Neural networks can be implemented as hardware units if calculation speed is essential. However, to our knowledge, no "civil" neural network chip checked for used in space environments exists.

1772pa	2292es	2318es	2398es	2450pa
2531pa	2621pa	2805pa	3156pa	3169pa
3628es	5565pa	6037pa	6441pa	6520pa

Table 3 The Burst orbits considered for this work. A Freja total file was also created, it contained all Burst orbits above was averaged into one file. "Pa" and "es" is data received at ground station Prince Albert, Canada, and Esrange, Sweden respectively.

Examples of neural net systems that could be both trained and used for on-line classification are adaptive resonance theory, developed by Carpenter and Grossberg (1987) (Grossberg 1987), and self organizing map nets developed by Kohonen (1987). Off-line systems could, for example, be back propagation neural nets, Radial basis function nets (RBF) or a rule based system (fuzzy logic systems, not described here). Both the on-line and off-line monitoring systems could also be used to select data that should be stored and transmitted to ground, and what data should be trashed. That is, such systems cannot only perform better triggering but also reduce the memory and telemetry capacity needed on a satellite .

5. A Brief Description of TICS, Its Operation and Data Selection

A cross section of the three-dimensional ion composition spectrometer, TICS, instrument is shown in figure 16. The figure is divided into three parts: a spherical "top hat" and circular inlet for ions (*T*1), a cylinder passage with a strong permanent magnetic field perpendicular to the ion path (*T*2), and finally the microchannel ion detection plate, MCP (T3). The spherical top hat allows ions to enter from 360 degrees in one plane.

The spherical top hat also operates as an electrostatic analyzer, i.e., only ions of a specific energy will be allowed to pass. The energy is swept from one eV up to 4300 eV in thirty-two steps. One complete energy sweep takes 0.4s in total. The permanent magnetic field in the cylinder section (*T*2) is perpendicular to the ion path and results in a Lorenz force $\mathbf{F} = q(\underline{v} \times \underline{\mathbf{B}})$ on the ion, where $\underline{v}$ is velocity, q is the charge, and $\underline{\mathbf{B}}$ is the internal magnetic field. This force will deflect the ions in the radial direction; light ions will be more deflected than heavy ions. It will therefore be possible to distinguish an ion mass spectrum on the MCP (*T*3) in the radial direction.

The MCP is divided into thirty-two angular sectors (figure 17) and each sector is divided into thirty-two mass channels in the radial direction. Not all angular sectors on TICS are used. Sectors 0 and 1 are excluded, and sector 31 is used as a waste sector for detections that could not be correctly identified by the anode system. Thus, a total of twenty-one sectors are used for data analysis.

Each sector is divided up into thirty-two channels in the radial direction. The radial channels are divided into four ion groups corresponding to the assumed target positions of the four ion species H^+, He^{++}, He^+, and O^+. The actual locations where these ion were expected to hit the MCP were determined during calibration before launch (table 1). Each ion group is identified by two integration points; for example summarizing detected counts on mass-channel 1 through 6 and 22 through 27 are believed to represent H^+ and O^+ measurements.

An anode system is used to determine the position (sector and mass-channel) of a detected ion on the MCP. This gives a total of 29 x 32 x 32 measured values in one single energy sweep. The instrument position on the satellite, figure 17, allows measurements in both the spherical co-ordinate angles relative to the earth's magnetic field lines, i.e., the pitch angles (Pa), and the azimuth angles (Az). The Pa is the angle between the ion velocity vector and the direction of the geomagnetic field. For Freja data obtained in the northern hemisphere pitch angles of 0 and 180 corresponds to down- and up-going particles, respectively. All Pa and Az angles will be covered within 3s due to the rotation of Freja (one spin is 6s); thus the whole 3-dimension velocity space is covered every half spin.

TICS can be used in a number of operation *modes,* e.g. normal high, burst and exclusive burst. Each mode measure data in different resolutions. Normal high is the most used operation mode, it has been used for over ninety-eight percent of TICS measurements. The description below of different operation modes refer to the specification of the modes before this investigation started (February 1994).

Normal high (NrmH) gives only the summarized ion mass-channel group data for all sectors used, the odd sectors (3, 5, 7 ....) give two values (H+ and O+) and the even sectors give all four ion measurements (H+, He++, He+ and O+). That is, normal high gives H+ and O+ for all sectors, but He++ and He+ are only given for every second sector.

Burst (BstN) normal mode gives 16 mass values for every sector (no integration as in normal high mode occurs). That is, counts on every second mass-channel e.g. mass-channel 1, 3, 5, ... is given.[5]

Exclusive burst (BstX) mode gives thirty-two values for every sector. That is, all mass channels are given for all sectors. This mode was only used during orbit 2248-2570.

5.1 Selected Orbits, Measurement Modes and Comments

In order to make this analysis, only burst mode data could be used. Furthermore, bursts containing large data gaps or only a few measured ions, i.e., low ion flux, could not be used. Therefore, a visual selection of suitable intense burst orbits were made using xlook. The selected bursts were then analyzed and checked so that they fulfilled some trivial conditions.

Data were accumulated during a whole burst, 6 spins or 30s, but only for measurements near perpendicular to the magnetic field, 22.5 (total 45). Therefore, each selected burst needed to have a good pitch-angle coverage[6] so that as many sectors as possible could reach this near perpendicular condition as often as possible. One accumulated measured value was stored for each mass-channel, energy and sector used. To allow comparison between all sectors, each value was normalized to the number of possible measurement occasions that each sector had in the near perpendicular region. Each stored value therefore represented "particle per measurement."

Part I. All orbits listed in table 3, all energy levels, and all available mass-channel were used in part I. The detailed analysis of mass-channel crosstalking was concentrated to orbit 2292es and 2398es. These two orbits are "exclusive burst" orbits with extremely high ion flux.

Part II. In part II, a more rigorous orbit selection condition was needed. Only high energy data were used to avoid ram-flow effects and also only burst orbits with reasonably large ion fluxes and where sector 22 fulfilled the near perpendicular condition were used. These criteria allowed only a subset of the generally selected bursts to be used (1772, 2292, 2318, 2398, 2450, 2805, 3156, 3628 and 5565). The available data were even less for specific sectors, since not all sectors necessarily fulfilled all conditions. The task in part II, was too focused on the sector sensitivity relationship. A special "shuffle and deal" accumulation technique was used in part II in order to create a larger set of training and testing examples. This was made randomly, but equally, for each sector pair (sector X and 22) select number of orbits and energies to accumulate the data from.

For example, a training case might be: *Use burst 1772 and 2398 with energy 5, 6, and 9 for both sector X and 22 to create the next case.* The available data were multiplied into approximately 900 examples by randomly merging data in this manner.

A commonly used technique in neural net, and also traditional modeling, when the number of training/testing data is too low is to simply add some random noise to each case to create "new ones." Then only a few cases can be multiplied. However, in part II this was not necessary because each measurement is attached by a unique measurement error. Therefore, using the shuffle and deal accumulation technique creates new cases in a similar manner to the above technique, but without having to introduce more noise.

Acknowledgement

This work was financially supported by the Swedish National Space Board, the Swedish Institute of Space Physics (IRF) Kiruna division, and the Faculty of Mathematical and Natural Science together with the Department of Applied Physics and Electronic at Umeå University. We also wish to thank our colleagues at the Space Physics division at the Department of Physics Umeå University and the staff at the IRF—Laboratory for Mechanical Waves. Thanks also to the Department of Philosophy at Carnegie Mellon University Pittsburgh, Pennsylvania, for their support on the Tetrad II method.

Finally, special thanks to L. Liszka (IRF Umeå, Sweden) for his encouraging support, good advice and useful discussions in preparing this report.

Notes

1. The circular ion detection unit in TICS is divided up into several angular sectors (section 5). These sectors all have different sensitivity due to its construction.

2. The source of hydrogen ions can also be the ionosphere and not only the solar wind.

3. All figures in this report except figure 7. are based on "normal" burst data, i.e., data when only every second mass-channel is stored, thus only 16 sensor values will be displayed in the figures.

4. The selection of sector 22 was made together with Laila Andersson, Swedish Institute of Space Physics, Kiruna, Sweden.

5. This has been changed so that burst mode measurements on later Freja orbits gives the sum of every two mass channels.

6. Near perpendicular angle between the spin axis and the geomagnetic field.

References

Carpenter, G., and Grossberg, S. 1987. A Massively Parallel Architecture for Self-Organizing Neural Pattern Recognition Machine. *Computer Vision, Graphics, and Image Processing* 37(37): 54–115.

Chatfield, C., and Collins, A. 1992. *Introduction to Multivariate Analysis*. New York: Chapman & Hall.

Eliasson, L.; Norberg, O.; Lundin, R.; Lundin, K; Olsen, S.; Borg, H.; André, M.; Koskinen, H.; Rihelä, P.; Boehm, M.; and Whalen, B. 1994. The Freja Hot Plasma Experiment-Instrument and First Results. *Space Science Reviews*. 70(3–4): 563–576.

Glymour, C.; Scheines, R; Spirtes, P.; and Kelly, K. 1987. *Discovering Causal Structure—Artificial Intelligence, Philosophy of Science, and Statistical Modeling*. San Diego, Calif.: Academic.

Grossberg, S. 1987. Competitive Learning: From Interactive Activation to Adaptive Resonance. *Cognitive Science* 11: 23–63.

IRF. 1993. The Freja Scientific Satellite. Scientific Report 214, IRF, Kiruna, Sweden.

Kohonen, T. 1987. *Self-Organization and Associative Memory.* Second ed. New York: Springer-Verlag.

Liszka, L. 1995. Causal Modeling of Spectral Data: A New Tool to Study Non-Linear Processes, Scientific Report 218, IRF, Kiruna, Sweden.

Norberg, O., and Eliasson, L. 1991. The Hot Plasma Spectrometers on Freja. In Proceedings of the Tenth ESA Symposium on European Rocket and Balloon Programmes and Related Research, ESA SP-317.

Pandel, D. 1994. Compression of Particle Data Measured by the TICS Instrument on the Freja Satellite. Internal Note 027, IRF, Kiruna, Sweden.

Spirtes, P.; Scheines, R.; Glymour, C.; and Meek, C. 1993. TETRAD II: Tools for Discovery, Unpublished manuscript, Department of Philosophy, Carnegie Mellon University, Pittsburgh, Penn.

Swedish Institute. *Freja F3H User Handbook.* Kiruna, Sweden: Swedish Institute of Space Physics.

Waldemark J. 1996. Investigation of Suitable Computer Intelligence Methods for Automated Analysis of Multivariate Satellite Data, Scientific Report 232, IRF, Kiruna, Sweden.

Waldemark, J., and Norqvist, P. 1995. In-Flight Calibration of Satellite Ion Composition Data Using Artificial Intelligence Methods. Scientific Report 226, IRF, Kiruna, Sweden.

Waldemark, J.; Dovner, P.-O.; and Karlsson, J. 1995. Hybrid Neural Network Pattern Recognition System for Satellite Measurements. In *Proceedings of IEEE- International Conference on Neural Networks,* 1, 195–199. Washington, D.C.: IEEE Computer Society.

CHAPTER SEVENTEEN

Causal Modeling of Spectral Data: A New Tool to Study Nonlinear Processes

Ludwik Liszka

1. Introduction

Most processes in nature are nonstationary. The nonstationarity is usually a manifestation of the nonlinearity in the system. It means that, for example, when studying a time series from a nonlinear dynamic system, there will be an energy transport between different intervals of the frequency spectrum. Making a common assumption about the stationarity of the process, almost all spectral data in science are, at present, averaged. Time averaging is the most commonly used averaging technique. As the energy transport between the different parts of the spectrum is reflected in fluctuations of the covariance between spectral channels, time averaging will destroy this type of information.

There is another type of information destroyed by the averaging process. If a spectrum is produced by more than one generating mechanism, each generating mechanism, usually nonlinear, will produce a specific temporal pattern of variance. A statistical study of original sequences of spectra may thus be used to identify different generating mechanisms in spectral data.

In spectral data, variables (spectral channels) have a fixed order. The position of a variable (spectral channel) in the spectrum is determined by its index. Causal relations between nearby located spectral channels are in general more probable than between distant channels. There will, in general, be two different types of causal relations observed in the spectral data. The first type is relations between the spectral channels introduced by imperfections in the measurements and data processing. The second type is relations between the spectral channels originating from the source or from the medium between the source and the measuring device.

In this chapter, I will give some examples that will show how to interpret causal models of spectral data for both frequency spectra and energy spectra.

2. Causal Modeling Methodology

When studying physical phenomena, in order to understand them, it is essential to know what is the cause and what is the effect, i.e., to establish the causal relation between the phenomena. When we try to explain the phenomena we must state why they happen. This is equivalent to recognizing a causal relation between occurring events. As the causal relations between physical events in complex systems may be very difficult to establish, the explanation is usually limited to analytical or statistical models which are compared with the observed data. Very seldom is a full statistical proof for the proposed explanation given, although a variety of methods for model testing may be found in the literature. During recent years, a technique for investigating causal relations in measured data has been developed (Glymour et al. 1987 and Spirtes et al. 1993): the Tetrad method. This achievement should open new possibilities in the areas of physical sciences.

The Tetrad method starts with a correlation or covariance matrix of multivariate data assuming linear relations between variables. The latest version of the software based upon the tetrad method, Tetrad II, consists of 10 modules designed for different operations in the search for causal structures in data. A few of those modules, needed for studies of causal relations in spectral data, will be discussed.

The Build module makes a series of decisions about independence and conditional independence relations among the measured variables. This information is used to search for a class of models that cannot be distinguished by conditional independence relations alone and that are compatible with user-entered background knowledge.

The multiple indicator model builder (MIMbuild) module work on normally distributed linear structural equation models with latent variables, and uses assumptions provided by the user together with statistical decisions about vanishing correlations and tetrad differences to estimate the features of the causal structure.

When studying a complex system, we are often measuring a number of variables (indicators), which, we assume, are controlled by unmeasured, latent variables. This type of system may be represented by linear structural

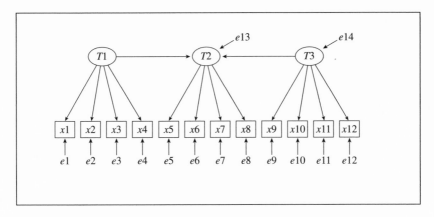

Figure 1. An example of a multiple indicator model with error terms.

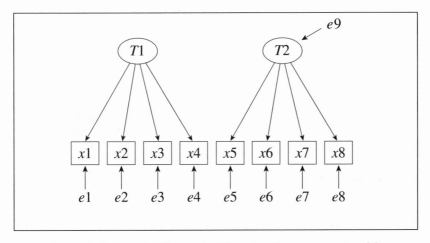

Figure 2. An example of a pure (unidimensional) measurement model.

equation models with latent variables described by Bollen (1989). The MIM-build module is able to locate unidimensional measurement models and to specify the structural equations among latent variables which have a unidimensional measurement model. An example of a multiple indicator model with error terms is shown in figure 1.

If each indicator is controlled by only one latent variable, the model is pure (unidimensional); see figure 2.

If one indicator is controlled by two latent variables (see figure 3), the model is impure. In order to establish relations between the latent variables in the model, the Tetrad II command MIMbuild may be used.

A problem with the MIMbuild command is that a measurement model (a

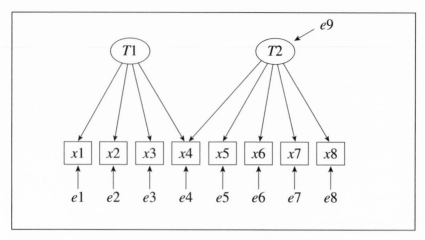

*Figure 3. An example of an impure measurement model
(x4 measures both T1 and T2).*

list of causal relations between latent variables and indicators) is needed to
run it. With no a priori information about the model, there is a need for a
method which can help to establish a preliminary measurement model.

A possible method to establish a preliminary measurement model is to use
the principal component analysis of the input data matrix. The number of
significant latent roots of the matrix will indicate the number of possible
common causes (latent variables) in the model. An example of latent roots
for the model shown in figure 2 is shown in figure 4.

By clustering component loadings calculated from the input data matrix
for the significant principal components, it is possible to establish which indicators are controlled by which common causes. As an example, the component loadings for the first two principal components for a data set corresponding to the model of figure 2 are shown in figure 5. In this example it
may be clearly seen that the loadings of indicators 1–4 are clustered in one
group and the loadings for indicators 5–8 in another group. A preliminary
measurement model may thus be established. Using the Purify module, the
impure indicators may now be pinpointed and removed from the model. The
MIMbuild will confirm the model and identify causal relations between the
latent variables.

The Makemodel and Monte modules provide a Monte Carlo simulation
package. Makemodel takes an unparameterized causal structure and parameterizes it and writes a fully parameterized statistical model to a Tetrad II file.
The Monte module can then be used to generate samples of any size from
such a model.

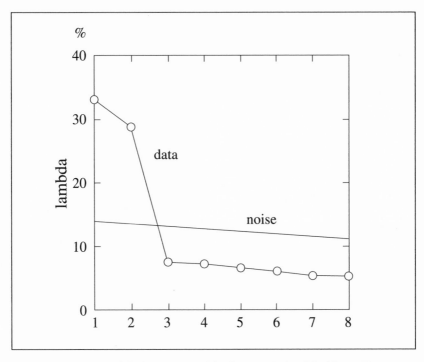

Figure 4. The values of the latent roots of the data matrix (model of figure 2) expressed in percent of the total variance. The second set of latent roots corresponds to a data matrix containing simulated random noise.

For data with a large number of indicators, as in the case of spectral data, it may be difficult to get a general impression of relations between the variables if conventional causal diagrams, as those in figures 1–3, are constructed for the data. A manual generation of causal diagrams may also be very tedious for a large number of variables. A software for automatic generation of causal diagrams from the Build module output files has been developed at the Swedish Institute of Space Physics. Further improvement of the lucidity of the diagram may be achieved by changing the order of variables. The above-mentioned software also provides a possibility of ordering the variables using the genetic algorithm (Goldberg 1989) minimizing the total length of edges between variables. Another facility of the software is a two-dimensional presentation of models. In this type of presentation, cause variables are shown on the horizontal axis and the effect variables are shown on the vertical axis. The type of the edge is indicated by a symbol at the corresponding point of the cause-effect plane. An example showing a two-dimensional causal plot of a 32-variable data set is shown in figure 6.

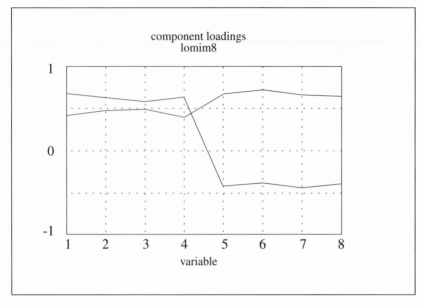

*Figure 5. The component loadings for the first two principal components
for the data corresponding to the model of Figure 12;
PC1 with a solid line, PC2 with a dashed line.*

3. Causal Modeling of Frequency Spectra

In a frequency spectrum, a certain quantity (for example, the oscillation amplitude) is displayed as a function of frequency. When studying a process, it
may be of interest to know whether all observed spectral components are
generated by the same source. For sound waves, the source (or sources) may
be identified using a direction-finding device together with the spectrum analyzer. However, on some occasions, it may be difficult or even impossible.
As it was mentioned above, the principal component analysis and causal
modeling of the spectra may be used to determine if all observed spectral
components are generated by the same source. How many sources (common
causes) are needed to explain the observed spectral data may also be determined. Also interesting is whether any energy transport occurs between the
spectral channels. That information may be obtained by studying causal relations between spectral channels.

One purpose of developing the present technique of statistical analysis of
spectral data, was to obtain an efficient tool to study infrasonic spectra. The recently developed infrasonic recording equipment at the Swedish Institute of
Space Physics (Waldemark 1997) collects large quantities of original, unaveraged, spectral data from three microphones together with direction-finding da-

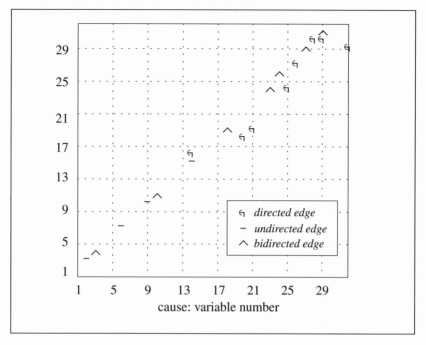

*Figure 6. A two-dimensional plot of edges on the cause-effect plane
for a thirty-two-point frequency spectrum. Observe the energy leakage
between the adjacent spectral channels.*

ta. The equipment works in the window 0.3 to 4.0 or 8.0 Hz, where most of the long distance signals are observed. The 0.3 Hz high-pass filter is used to decrease the wind noise. Most of the long distance sources are man-made. In some cases, infrasonic noise from meteorological sources can be observed.

In the example demonstrated here, the infrasonic noise from an industrial plant, located about 450 kilometers from the recording station, is analyzed. Data from 90 minutes of recording on July 16, 1994, between 1330 and 1500 UT, altogether about 990 frequency spectra, are investigated.

Figure 7 shows averages of amplitudes in all spectral channels except for channel 1, which is a DC-channel. The amplitude scale used is linear. The averages are plotted by the solid line. The range corresponding to +/- one standard deviation is shown by broken lines. The frequency difference between two adjacent channels is 0.28124 Hz, which means that channel 32 corresponds to 8.72 Hz. The bandpass 0.3 to 8.0 Hz—the result of the filters used—is clearly seen.

Because the actual infrasonic noise lasted for several hours, it is difficult to establish the actual background level between 1330 and 1500 UT. Usually, a coherent signal from a point source may be discovered when its level is

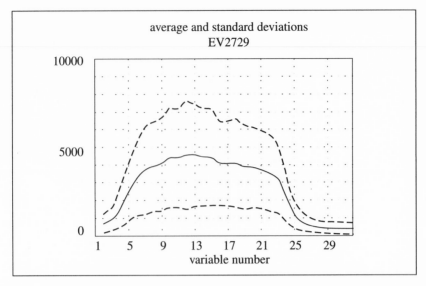

Figure 7. The linear amplitude scale for average amplitudes in all spectral channels except for channel 1, which is a DC-channel.

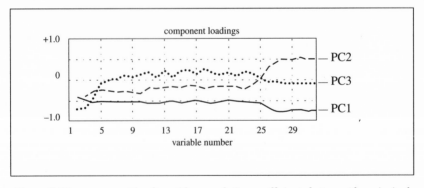

Figure 8. The component loadings (the correlation coefficients between the principal components and the spectral channels) for all three principal components.

above -6 dB re background level, i.e., half the background amplitude, depending on the signal frequency and the nature of the source.

The results of the principal component analysis show that there are probably three different sources of the infrasonic noise in figure 7. There are three significant latent roots for the correlation matrix derived from the complete spectral data matrix (990 spectra, 32 spectral channels). The data may thus be adequately described by three principal components, each corresponding to one common cause. The component loadings, being correlation coeffi-

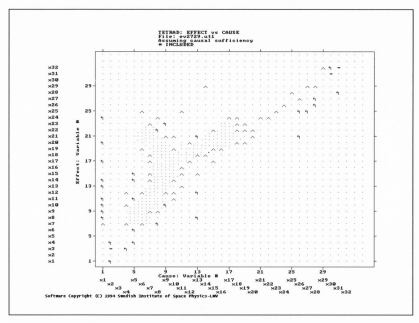

Figure 9. A two-dimensional causal diagram for infrasonic spectral data during 1330 - 1500 UT, July 16, 1994.

cients between the principal components and the original variables (spectral channels) are shown in figure 8.

It may be seen that the channels 2 and 3 are controlled by the cause described by PC3 (cause 3). Channels 4–25 are controlled by the dominating cause 1 described by PC1 (largest latent root). The amplitudes in channels 26–32 are due to both cause 1 and cause 2 (corresponding to PC2). Cause 1 is the distant man-made source; cause 2 is the local, high frequency infrasonic noise strong enough to pass the low-pass filter; cause 3 is atmospheric noise.

More information about the signal may be obtained by analyzing the correlation or covariance matrix by means of the Build module of Tetrad II. Because of a large number of variables (spectral channels), a conventional causal plot may be to complex to be surveyable. A pattern of causal relations between variables may be easier seen in the two-dimensional causal diagram. Results for the same infrasonic data from the Build module, are given in figure 9. The two-dimensional plot shows that the DC level in the spectrum (channel 1) is influenced by a number of high amplitude channels, which is probably an instrumental effect. There is evidence, which cannot be confirmed in the linear spectrum of figure 7, that there is a tone with a fundamental frequency in the channel 5 generating a few harmonics (directed edges towards higher channel numbers). The positions of the directed edges indicate that the frequency of the tone must be about 1.32 Hz. An interesting phenomenon, frequently observed in infrasonic spectra, is that there is no energy transport between certain combinations of close channels (see shaded area of figure 9). More studies are needed to fully understand the information contained in the causal models of spectral data. In order to increase the significance of causal models, the experimental strategy must be changed to collect the largest possible amount of unaveraged frequency spectra.

4. Causal Modeling of Particle Energy Spectra

A new type of information may be obtained when causal modeling is applied to energy spectra. When studying the particle energy spectra, particles with different energies are counted within the respective energy intervals. Also, in this case counting is performed during long time intervals so that large enough count numbers are obtained. A considerable fraction of temporal variations, and thus the important information contained in them, will be lost. In order to preserve the information about the covariance of different spectral channels, high counting rates must be guaranteed by detector characteristics and not by long measuring intervals. The present technique will be applied to particle energy spectra measured on board the Swedish satellite Viking (Hultqvist 1988).

The data used here contains electron and ion energy spectra between 0 and 40 keV collected by the satellite during the passage of the polar cusp region. In order to obtain a satisfactory number of energy spectra during a single satellite passage, the energy spectra were accumulated within a 10 seconds interval. Two populations of energy spectra were studied: those collected at low pitch angles (Pa < 30 degrees, i.e., particle detector looking upwards along the geomagnetic field lines) and those collected at high pitch angles (Pa > 150 degrees i.e., particle detector looking downward along the geomagnetic field lines). The energy spectra used for the analysis contains sixteen energy channels with a logarithmic energy scale in the interval 0–40 keV. The average counts for electrons and ions in pitch angle ranges >150 degrees are shown in figure 10.

An interesting question is whether different parts of the energy spectrum are generated by the same process and if there are any relations between electrons and ions which may be confirmed by statistical methods. In order to test the above questions, the spectral data for both electrons and ions were combined in a single matrix, side by side. The principal component analysis performed on the combined data shows that three principal components are needed to explain the variance in both electron and ion data. The component

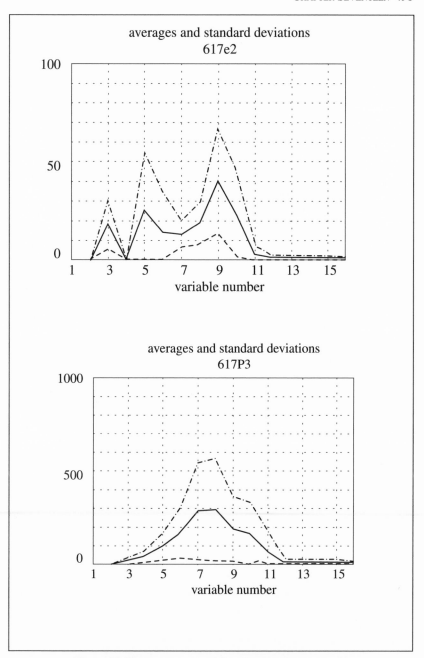

*Figure 10. The average counts for electrons (upper graph)
and ions (lower graph) for pitch angles > 150 degrees together
with the ranges of double standard deviations.*

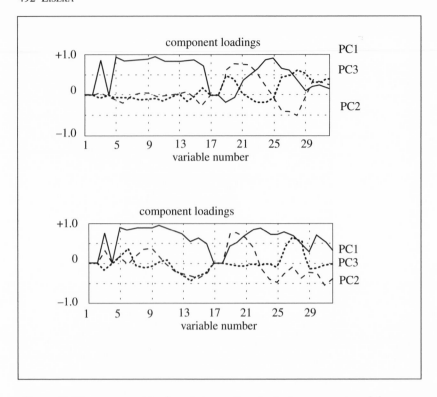

Figure 11. The component loadings between the principal components and the average counts in the spectral data shown for both pitch angle intervals.

loadings between the principal components and the average counts in the spectral data are shown for both pitch angle intervals in figure 11.

In the component loadings diagrams, the first sixteen variables correspond to the electron energy spectrum. Variables 17–32 correspond to the ion energy spectra. It may be clearly seen that the electron energy spectra in both pitch angle directions may be explained, for this particular satellite orbit, by only one principal component. In the ion energy spectrum the situation is much more complicated. There are three common causes needed to explain the variance in the data. One of the common causes is identical to the one responsible for the electron energy spectrum. For PC2, negative component loadings are observed at high ion energy channels. The negative component loading for a given variable (channel) and a given PC means that the amplitude of that particular channel is negatively correlated with that of the channel with positive component loading. PC1 is always the most important principal component. There is a significant difference between the distribution of

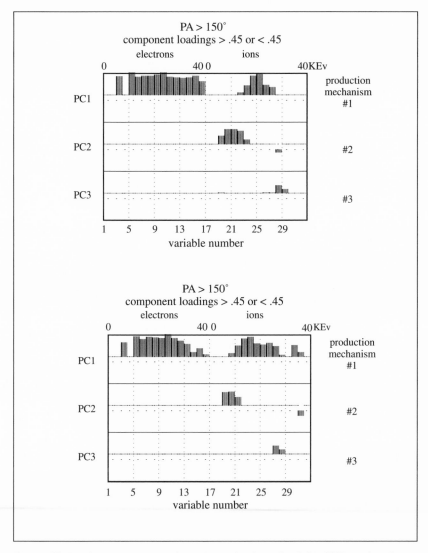

Figure 12. Another presentation of component loadings for Orbit #617, earlier shown in figure 11. Here only loadings >0.45 or > – 0.45 are plotted. The distribution of spectra into different causes (production mechanisms) is clearly seen.

common causes between the energy channels for low and high pitch angles.

A different method for presentation of the results in figure 11 is shown in figure 12. Here only loadings > 0.45 or < –0.45, corresponding to a significant correlation coefficient, are plotted.

Applying the Tetrad II Build module to these data, interesting information

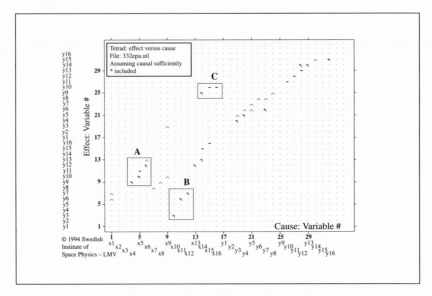

*Figure 13. A two-dimensional causal diagram for particle energy spectra
(electrons channels x1 - x16 and ions channels y1 - y16) during orbit # 332.
The regions of the diagram showing electron acceleration and deceleration are
marked with (A) and (B): The region (C) is where ions are causally
connected or correlated with energetic electrons.*

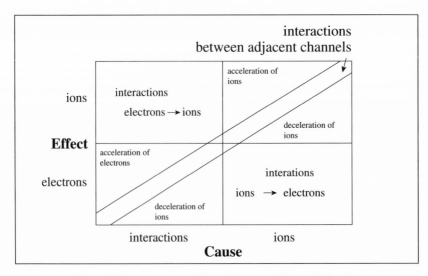

*Figure 14. Interpretation of two-dimensional causal plots for
joint electron & ion energy spectra.*

about energy transport in both spectra may be obtained. It may be expected that a causal diagram for an energy spectrum will not only reflect instrumental effects (energy resolution, angular resolution) but will also contain information about the acceleration processes controlling the measured particle flux. It may be expected that, for example, if an acceleration process takes place, there will be an energy transport in the spectrum directed towards channels with a higher energy. As the direction of influences between electron and ion spectra may be detected here, a larger amount of measurements, compared with the principal component method, is needed in order to obtain significant results. An example of joint causal diagrams for both electron and ion energy spectra and for all pitch angles is shown in figure 13. The regions of the diagram showing electron acceleration and deceleration are marked with (A) and (B): The region (C) is where ions are causally connected or correlated with energetic electrons.

Interactions between remote channels may, of course, also be due to instrumental effects. In that case, the interactions would be seen the whole time, or at least always when the equipment is operated in that particular mode. It is most likely that the features of figure 13 are not instrumental effects. In general, the two-dimensional causal plots for joint electron and ion energy spectra may be interpreted as shown in figure 14.

When particles are accelerated or decelerated by nonlinear processes, their energy spectra may be studied using the present technique. Completely new information may be obtained directly from the described analysis—information that, until present, was obtained only through indirect arguments.

To study this type of relations, it is necessary to increase the number of significant spectra per time unit (shorter sampling time). Normally it would cause a smaller number of counts/energy channel and decrease the significance of the data. Therefore, at the same time, the sensitivity of the detectors must be increased and the time constants decreased.

5. Conclusions

Important information may be obtained studying the variance of spectral data. That may be done by applying the Tetrad method and the principal component analysis to the correlation or covariance matrix derived from the original (unaveraged) spectral data. The principal component analysis gives an indication about the presence of latent variables, which may be confirmed using the Tetrad II modules Build and Purify. The MIMbuild module may then be used to search for possible relations between latent variables. Relations between the spectral channels may be identified using the Build module. Finally, a graphical interface presents the results of the Build module, showing variables either in alphabetical order, or in the order optimized using a genetic algorithm so that the total length of all edges in the model is a minimum. An alternative method of presentation, especially convenient when there are many variables in the problem, is the two-dimensional plot.

Acknowledgements

I am indebted to Clark Glymour and Peter Spirtes at Carnegie Mellon University for invaluable discussions concerning interpretation of Tetrad results.

References

Bollen, K. 1989. *Structural Equations with Latent Variables*. New York: Wiley.

Glymour, C.; Scheines, R.; Spirtes, P.; and Kelly, K. 1987. *Discovering Causal Structure—Artificial Intelligence, Philosophy of Science, and Statistical Modeling*. San Diego, Calif.: Academic.

Goldberg, D. 1989. *Genetic Algorithms*. Reading, Mass.: Addison Wesley.

Hultqvist, B. 1988. Scientific Results from the Swedish Viking Satellite: A 1988 Status Report. IRF Scientific Report 196, Swedish Institute of Space Physics, Kiruna, Sweden.

Spirtes, P.; Glymour, C.; and Scheines, R. 1993. *Causation, Prediction, and Search*. Lecture Notes in Statistics. Berlin: Springer-Verlag.

Spirtes, P.; Scheines, R.; Glymour, C.; and Meek, C. 1993. Tetrad II: Tools for Discovery, Unpublished manuscript, Department of Philosophy, Carnegie Mellon University, Pittsburgh, Penn.

Waldemark, K. 1997. High-Resolution Infrasonic Recording Equipment. IRF Scientific Report 242, Swedish Institute of Space Physics, Kiruna, Sweden.

CHAPTER EIGHTEEN

Modeling Corn Exports and Exchange Rates with Directed Graphs and Statistical Loss Functions

Derya G. Akleman, David A. Bessler,
and Diana M. Burton

1. Introduction

The role of exchange rates in the commodity price "boom" of the early 1970s is considered by Schuh (1974). He suggested that the U.S. dollar's 1952-71 overvaluation had made U.S. farm prices high (relative to competitors) on world markets. This led to a decrease in world demand for American farm products. He argued that the two devaluations of the dollar by the Nixon Administration in the early 1970s and the resulting realignments of world currencies decreased the dollar's value relative to other major world currencies. This, in turn, made U.S. agricultural products more competitive in world markets, increasing demand, resulting in higher prices (Schuh 1974, p. 10-11).

Several papers which considered the role of the exchange rate in world trade were published in the two decades following Schuh's initial study. A partial list includes: Kost; Vellianitis-Fidas; Johnson, Grennes, and Thursby; Fletcher, Just and Schmitz; Shei and Thompson; Bredahl, Meyers and Collins; Collins, Meyers and Bredahl; Chambers and Just; Longmire and Morey; Batten and Belongia; Orden; Bessler and Babula; and Babula, Ruppel and Bessler.

Perhaps the most frequently cited numbers from this literature are the esti-

mates obtained by Chambers and Just (1981). Based on a "structural" econometric model, they estimated exchange rate elasticities of soybeans, corn,
and wheat prices of –2.6, –1.9, and –1.2, respectively (percentage change in
soybean, corn or wheat price divided by the percentage change in exchange
rates). Further, demand elasticities for soybeans, corn, and wheat exports of
–1.31, –5.23, and –2.05, respectively, were reported.

An "alternative literature" has developed which questions the "exchange
rates matter" position. Under a pure purchasing power parity story, exchange
rates serve to adjust the real purchasing power of currencies and thus have no
real effect. Accordingly, sales and shipments of agricultural products should
not be expected to respond to changes in exchange rates. Advocates of the
"exchange rates matter" position argue that the purchasing power parity argument is a long run argument that will hold after differential inflation rates
run their courses, after trade barriers are lifted, and after all other market imperfections are accounted for (Machlup 1980). Given a world with nontrivial
trade barriers and other market imperfections, we ought to discount the purchasing power parity story, and see commodity flows between countries as a
result of changes in exchange rates. The agricultural economics literature
generally follows this latter argument.

Consistent with the "alternative literature," Bessler and Babula (1987)
and Babula, Ruppel, and Bessler (1995) find empirical evidence (observational data) that exchange rates have little effect on wheat and corn sales or
shipments, but do influence wheat and corn prices. Bessler and Babula
(1987) studied the lag relation between exchange rates and wheat export
sales, wheat price, and wheat shipments using Akaike's final prediction error
(FPE) and Schwarz's loss function to specify subset vector autoregressions.
They found wheat sales data were useful in forecasting wheat shipments, and
real exchange rates seemed to have an impact on real wheat prices. They
found little evidence that exchange rates cause export sales and shipments of
U.S. wheat. Babula, Ruppel and Bessler consider the same questions
(whether exchange rates cause sales and shipments) related to U.S. corn data.
Similar results, questioning the importance of exchange rates in determining
corn sales and shipments, were found in this more recent study.

This chapter considers the use of directed graphs, as described in Spirtes,
Glymour, and Scheines (1993), of exchange rates, corn price, corn export
sales, and corn export shipments. The consideration of graphical models is
important, as they offer an alternative to regression-based procedures for
model specification. It is well known that regression-based procedures can
(under certain conditions) yield improper results when applied to observational data. Spirtes, Glymour, and Scheines (1993, p. 15) write: "when a regressor X and an outcome variable Y have an unmeasured common cause, the
estimate of the influence on Y of every other regressor that directly influences
X or has a common unmeasured cause with X will likewise be unreliable."

Graphical models seek to avoid this problem through the use of sequential tests of conditional independence and direction of causal flow between variables through sepset conditions (defined below). Algorithms written by Scheines, et al (1994) and distributed as the software Tetrad II apply these conditional independence tests. The two procedures (regression-based search and graphical methods) may give different models for the same data; thus we construct models of export sales and shipments and judge each relative to the other through out-of-sample forecasts of data not used to construct each.

Some readers may argue that the question of exchange rates and exports is a question that has been laid to rest, one way or the other, by the a priori arguments of Schuh (1974), the empirical estimates of Chambers and Just (1981), or the forecasting results of Bessler and Babula (1987). It is our position that it is precisely these cases, where we "think we know the answer," that call for study with new methods.

This chapter is presented in five additional sections. First, we offer a discussion of the data. Second, a brief summary of Tetrad II algorithms is presented. Third, the data are modeled using the algorithms as described in Spirtes, Glymour and Scheines (1993). Fourth, subset vector autoregressions are built on the same data using the well-known search procedure introduced by Hsiao (1979a). The resulting models are presented and discussed. Comparisons of forecast performance on out-of-sample observations (data not used to specify the model) are made in section five using both the graphical and the Hsiao-specified models. The final section of this chapter offers a discussion of the results.

2. Data

The same corn market data used in Babula, Ruppel, and Bessler (1995) are used here. These are four monthly (observational) time series observed over the period January 1976 to December 1992: real exchange rates relative to currencies of U.S. corn importers, U.S. corn export sales, real corn prices (U.S. gulf price deflated by the PPI), and U.S. corn export shipments. The U.S. Department of Agriculture (USDA), under Congressional mandate, began to collect data on export sales and export shipments of major U.S. agricultural commodities in late 1973 (Ruppel 1987). Unanticipated Soviet wheat and corn purchases of 1972 and dramatic price increases in U.S. food and feed markets in the months following these purchases were the motivation for the legislation. The purpose of the legislation was to provide agricultural commodity markets with more up-to-date information on worldwide demand.

Exporters of designated agricultural commodities were required to report weekly to USDA's Foreign Agricultural Service in detail (including destinations and intended delivery dates). Shipments reflect physical movement of previously sold product and can respond to transportation rates and capacities, weather constraints, and desired delivery rates (Ruppel 1987). The data, once reported to the USDA, are summarized and released to the public in USDA trade and outlook publications on a monthly and quarterly basis.

Corn is a storable commodity, which is generally sold before it is shipped (as opposed to some perishable commodities which may actually be shipped before they are sold). The real exchange rate is represented by the real index of corn-import-weighted currencies of major U.S. corn importers relative to the U.S. dollar compiled by the U.S. Department of Agriculture, Economic Research Service, as described in Stallings (1988). The real price of corn is the deflated (by the wholesale price index) U.S. gulf price of corn compiled by the Economic Research Service of the USDA (ERS/USDA). Data are studied in logarithms.

Babula, Ruppel, and Bessler (1995) found evidence of a structural change in February 1985. The 1985 Farm Bill (Food Security Act of 1985) was passed in late 1985; debate and discussion on the bill was ongoing early in the year and is perhaps (partially) responsible for the change in structure. The goal of that bill is described in Lin, Riley, and Evans (1995):

> The FSA (Food Security Act) of 1985 was developed under the agricultural economic conditions that demanded a change in direction for U.S. farm programs. The goal was 'market orientation', and for the first time, legislation provided for future, planned reductions in annual target price minimums.

The FSA was an attempt to make U.S. exports more competitive on world markets, and thus we may expect that if exchange rates do have an influence on corn prices, export sales and export shipments, this second period should offer its strongest showing. Accordingly, the sample is studied in two periods: February 1978 to January 1985 (period one); and February 1985 to December 1992 (period two).

Dickey-Fuller (Dickey and Fuller 1979) and Durbin-Watson (Sargen and Bhargava 1983) tests are performed on logarithms of levels and first differences of logarithms of levels in both periods. The results are listed in table 1. Both tests indicate the logarithms of the levels of sales and shipments and first differences of the logarithms of price and exchange rates are stationary. Additional tests on cointegration are described in Babula, Rupel, and Bessler (1995). They find no cointegration in both time periods.

3. Tetrad II—A Brief Summary

Tetrad II is a program for helping to discover causal structure. While it does have capability for estimating parameters of a causal model, we constrain our discussion of Tetrad II to model specification.

A number of different kinds of graphs are used: directed graphs, undirected graphs, inducing path graphs. All contain a set of vertices (variables) and a set of edges (the causal flow from one variable to another signified by a directed line segment).

A graph is an ordered triple <**V, M, E**> where **V** is a nonempty set of vertices (variables), **M** is a nonempty set of marks (symbols attached to the end of undirected edges), and **E** is a set of ordered pairs. Each member of **E** is called an edge. Vertices connected by an edge are said to be adjacent. If we have a set of vertices {*A, B, C, D, E*}: (1) the undirected graph contains only undirected edges (e.g., *A — B*); (2) a directed graph contains only directed edges (e.g., *B → C*); (3) an inducing path graph contains both directed edges and bidirected edges (*C ↔ D*); (4) a partially oriented inducing path graph contains directed edges (→), bidirected edges (↔), nondirected edges (o—o) and partially directed edges (o→). A directed acyclic graph is a directed graph that contains no directed cyclic paths (an acyclic graph contains no vertex more than once). Only acyclic graphs are used in this chapter.

3.1 PC Algorithm

The PC algorithm is an ordered set of commands which begins with a general unrestricted set of relationships among variables and proceeds step-wise to remove edges between variables and to direct "causal flow." Edge removal and direction of causal flow are based on independence or conditional independence (or lack thereof) as represented by zero correlation or partial correlation. The algorithm is described in detail in Spirtes, Glymour, and Scheines (1993 p. 117–118). More advanced versions (refinements) of the PC algorithm are described as the modified PC algorithm (Spirtes, Glymour, and Scheines, p. 166–167), the causal inference algorithm (p. 183–184), and the fast causal inference algorithm (p. 188–189). As the basic definition of a sepset is used in all and the PC algorithm is the most basic, we restrict our discussion to the PC algorithm.

Briefly, one forms the complete undirected graph C on the vertex set **V**. The complete undirected graph shows an undirected edge between every variable of the system (every variable in **V**). Edges between variables are removed based on zero correlation or partial correlation (condition/correlation). The conditioning variable(s) on removed edges between two variables is called the sepset of the variables whose edge has been removed (for vanishing zero order conditioning information the sepset is the empty set). Edges are directed by considering triples $X — Y — Z$, such that X and Y are adjacent, as are Y and Z, but X and Z are not adjacent. Direct edges between triples $X — Y — Z$ as $X → Y ← Z$ if Y is not in the sepset of X and Z. If $X → Y$, Y and Z are adjacent, X and Z are not adjacent, and there is no arrowhead at Y, then orient $Y — Z$ as $Y → Z$. If there is a directed path from X to Y and an edge between X and Y, then orient $X — Y$ as $X → Y$.

The Tetrad II program allows the researcher to consider the possibility that he or she has not a complete or "causally sufficient" set of information variables. In the summary presented above, we made the implicit assumption that the set of variables are causally sufficient; which is, of course, untenable. The PC algorithm is modified to allow for the possibility that a third (unknown variable or set of variables) may be responsible for correlations between variables. The fast causal inference algorithm (Spirtes, Glymour, and Scheines 1993, p. 188) is an extension of the PC algorithm that does not make the causal sufficiency assumption. To indicate that an unmeasured variable may be connecting two variables, the mark "o" is used. The fast causal inference algorithm removes edges and records subset vertices based on vanishing covariance and conditional covariance, just as in the PC algorithm. However, before directing edges, in triples of vertices, it orients each edge as o—o. It then directs edges using the same sepset arguments as does PC. For example, the correlation pattern between x_t, x_{t-1} and x_{t-3} may result in an edge x_{t-1} o→ x_t, indicating that an unknown variable may be responsible for the "apparent" causal flow from x_{t-1} to x_t (see Spirtes, Glymour, and Scheines, 1993, p. 183–84). Continue until no more edges can be oriented. These sequential procedures are programmed and available in software Tetrad II (Scheines, et al. 1994).

4. Graphical Models of Corn Exports

Four stationary series, log shipments, log sales, first differences of log price, and first differences of log exchange rates are used. Following Glymour and Spirtes (1988, p. 195), we treat X measured at different times, x_t, x_{t-1}, and x_{t-2}, as separate variables (vertices). As the likelihood ratio test described in Babula, Ruppel, and Bessler (1995) suggested a lag length of two in an unrestricted vector autoregression, we consider current values and two lags of each variable as separate vertices, making our Tetrad search over twelve vertices — four variables each defined at lag zero, lag one and lag two: log sales (SA_t, SA_{t-1}, SA_{t-2}); log shipments (SP_t, SP_{t-1}, SP_{t-2}); first differences of log corn price (ΔP_t, ΔP_{t-1}, ΔP_{t-2}); and first differences of log exchange rates (ΔE_t, ΔE_{t-1}, ΔE_{t-2}). Assuming time ordering (the future cannot cause the past), we proceed without any background knowledge, other than the correlation matrix of 12 variables (all series at lags t, $t - 1$ and $t - 2$ for 57 observations in period one and 71 observations in period two). The correlation matrices (tables 4 and 5) are calculated from stationary data (levels of log shipments, levels of log sales, first differences of log price and first differences of log exchange rates) for which seasonality has been removed using ordinary least squares regression of each series on eleven dummy variables and a constant. These correlation matrices are the inputs (in each period) to our application of the Tetrad II program.

Our application of Tetrad II to a particular data set makes the implicit assumption that the data are generated by a multivariate normal process. Violations of this assumption will thus make any model tentative or approximate (but still perhaps useful). Jarque-Bera tests (1980) of normality were applied to each series. Exchange rates for both periods, prices for the first period, sales for the second period, and shipments for the first period pass these normality tests at usual levels of significance. The most serious violations of normality were found in the sales data over the first period. We reject the null of normality for these data at a 0.000 significance level.

The resulting graph on the first time period (February 1978 – January 1985), allowing for latent common causes, is shown in figure 1a. Notice that the three vertices on exchange rates are separated from the remaining vertices of the graph (the graph is not connected as there is no path between any of the exchange rate vertices and the price, sales and shipment vertices). There are edges between price and sales in contemporaneous time; however, the "o" marker on these indicates that we are unsure whether an arrowhead belongs at the vertex or some omitted "third" variable belongs in the model. There is an edge connecting shipments in period t and sales in period $t - 2$; however, the arrowhead on each vertex of this edge indicates the presence of an omitted variable. The fact that Tetrad II picked up a two period delay between sales and shipments is interesting, as previous studies and industry knowledge suggest that a delay between one and two months between sales and shipments is to be expected (Ruppel 1987).

When we do not allow for latent variables the resulting graph for the first period is given as figure 1b. Here, the basic patterns of variable interrelationships remain as in figure 1a. The ambiguity in directing edges between price and sales is gone (price causes sales in period t and $t - 1$). In addition, the ambiguity between sales in period $t - 2$ and shipments in t is cleared up—past sales cause current shipments—the two-period lag remains. The three exchange rate vertices remain disconnected from the shipments, sales and price vertices.

Since we compare forecasting ability of directed graphs with more tradi-

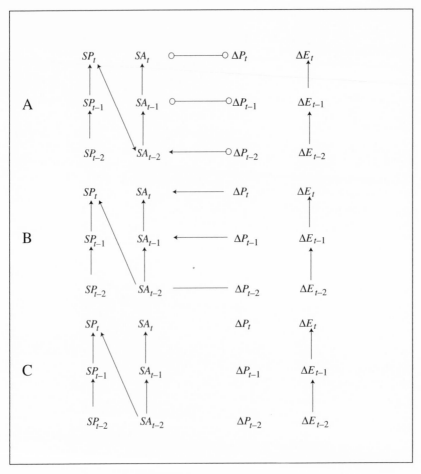

*Figure 1. Graphic representations under (A) no casual sufficiency; (B) causal suffi-
ciency, and (C) no contemporaneous causality on corn export shipments (SP$_t$); corn
export sales(SA $_t$); changes in corn price (ΔP_t); and changes in exchange rates
(ΔE_t)—February 1978 – January 1983 monthly data; 5% significance level.*

tional time series identification procedures on these data, a final directed
graph, under the assumption of causal sufficiency and no contemporaneous
relations is considered. The resulting graph for the first time period is given
as figure 1c. Notice here that prices and exchange rates are disconnected
from sales and shipments, with the latter two connected through a directed
edge from sales in period $t-2$ and shipments in period t.

The graphic representation under a no causal sufficiency assumption for period two (February 1985 – December 1992) is given as figure 2a. Again (as in figure 1), exchange rates are not connected to the corn price, sales, and shipments vertices. Edges connect contemporaneous price and sales; however, the "o" marks at the price vertices indicate that a possible omitted variable may account for the price — sales edges. Once again we see a bidirected edge between SA_{t-2} and SP_t. Two additional edges between sales and shipments appear in figure 2a, which were not present in the first period (figure 1a): the bidirected edge between SA_{t-1} and SP_t and the directed edge from SP_t to SA_t. The former is certainly feasible — that grain could be shipped one month after it is sold. The new edge, flowing from current shipments to current sales, is harder to understand; to our knowledge, current shipments do not cause current sales. Technically, the directed edges $SP_t \rightarrow SA_t \leftarrow \Delta P_t$ arise because the first order correlation (the partial correlation) between shipments in t and price in t, given shipments in $t - 1$ is not significantly different from zero ($\rho(SP_t, \Delta P_t \mid SP_{t-1}) = .23$; p-value is .055). As correlations between SP_t and SA_t and SA_t and ΔP_t are significantly different from zero ($\rho(SP_t, SA_t)$ = .55 and $\rho(SA_t, \Delta P_t)$ = .35)), SA_t is not in sepset SP_t and ΔP_t and thus the resulting directed edges: $SP_t \rightarrow SA_t \leftarrow \Delta P_t$. Actually we need only increase our marginal significance level slightly to 0.055 for this not to be so and for the "bothersome" directed edge ($SP_t \rightarrow SA_t$) not to show up.

The directed graph found under the assumption of causal sufficiency in the second period is given in figure 2b. Most importantly, notice that exchange rates remain disconnected under causal sufficiency. In addition, we observe some interesting directed edges not observed in figure 2a. Notice that, while in figure 2a there are no edges running from price in t, price in $t - 1$ and price in $t - 2$, there are such edges in figure 2b. We remove edges $\Delta P_t — \Delta P_{t-1}$ and $\Delta P_{t-1} — \Delta P_{t-2}$, in figure 2a based on some marginally insignificant conditional correlations ($\rho(\Delta P_t, \Delta P_{t-1} \mid SP_{t-1}, SA_{t-1}, SA_{t-2})$ = .23, p-value =.057 and $\rho(\Delta P_{t-1}, \Delta P_{t-2} \mid SP_{t-1}, \Delta E_{t-1}, SA_t)$ = .24, p-value = .053) . These remain in the graphic representation under the assumption of causal sufficiency. Our inability, in figure 2a to place an arrowhead at ΔP in the edges $SA_t \leftarrow o \; \Delta P_t$, $SA_{t-1} \leftarrow o \; \Delta P_{t-1}$, and $SA_{t-2} \leftarrow o \; \Delta P_{t-2}$ is resolved in (perhaps) an unsatisfactory manner with the edges $SA_t \leftrightarrow \Delta P_t$, $SA_{t-1} \rightarrow \Delta P_{t-1}$, and $SA_{t-2} — \Delta P_{t-2}$. Our disappointment here is that the seemingly consistent results obtained under the assumption of no causal sufficiency are confused under the stronger assumption of sufficiency. In addition, under causal sufficiency (figure 2b), we see paths from past sales to future shipments, just as in figure 2a. Finally, we note contemporaneous relations between sales and shipments at periods $t - 1$ and $t - 2$, which are not present under a no causal sufficiency assumption.

Under the assumption of causal sufficiency and no contemporaneous causation (our predictive model), we see that exchange rates and price are both not connected to sales and shipments. There are paths from sales in t –

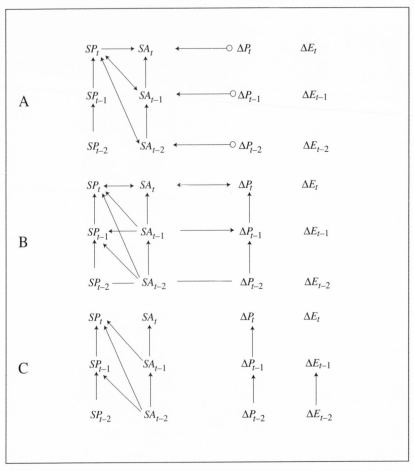

*Figure 2. Graphic representation under (A) no casual sufficiency; (B) causal suffi-
ciency, and (C) no contemporaneous causality on corn export shipments (SP$_t$); corn
export sales (SA$_t$); changes in corn price (ΔP$_t$); and changes in exchange rates
(ΔE$_t$)—February 1985 – December 1990 monthly data; 5% significance level.*

1 and $t - 2$ to shipments in periods t and $t - 1$, respectively.

Summarizing the directed graphs over the two periods (figures 1 and 2),
we note: (1) exchange rates are disconnected from the other variables studied; (2) relationships do exist between price and sales; however, these relationships are contemporaneous; (3) there are paths (relationships) running
from past sales to future shipments.

The graphs offered in figures 1 and 2 are built under a 5% significance level. Some may wish to consider relationships under lower or higher signifi-

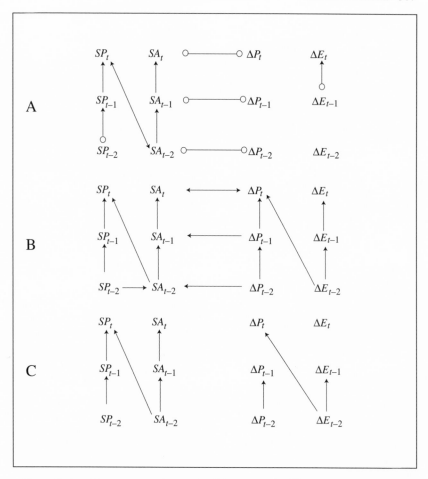

Figure 3. Graphic representations under (A) no casual sufficiency; (B) causal suffi-ciency, and (C) no contemporaneous causality on corn export shipments (SP₁); corn export sales (SA₁); changes in corn price (ΔP₁); and changes in exchange rates (ΔE₁)—February 1978 – January 1983 monthly data; 10% significance level.

cance levels. Figures 3 and 4 are summaries of "reruns" of figures 1 and 2, respectively, under a 10% significance level. Under no causal sufficiency the graphs are quite similar (figure 1, 5% is similar to figure 3, 10%). Exchange rates remain disconnected from the remaining vertices in each time period. In the first period the edge $SA_{t-2} \leftarrow\!\!\!\text{o}\; \Delta P_{t-2}$ found using a 5% significance level is replaced by the edge $SA_{t-2}\; \text{o}\!\!-\!\!\text{o}\; \Delta P_{t-2}$ at 10% and the path $\Delta E_t \leftrightarrow \Delta E_{t-1}$ $\leftarrow\!\!\text{o}\; \Delta E_{t-2}$ is replaced by $\Delta E_t \leftarrow\!\!\text{o}\; \Delta E_{t-1}\; \Delta E_{t-2}$.

Under causal sufficiency at a 10% significance level, we find a directed edge

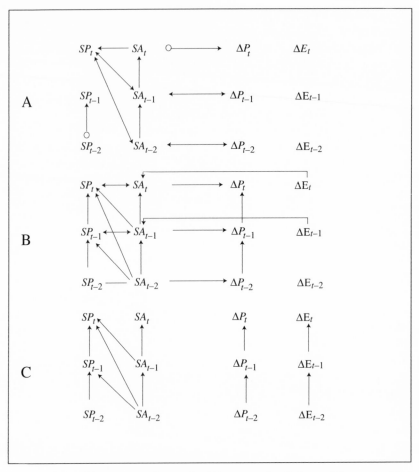

*Figure 4. Graphic representations under (A) no casual sufficiency; (B) causal suffi-
ciency, and (C) no contemporaneous causality on corn export shipments (SP$_t$); corn
export sales (SA$_t$); changes in corn price (ΔP$_t$); and changes in exchange rates
(ΔE$_t$)—February 1985 –December 1990 monthly data; 10% significance level.*

from exchange rates in $t - 1$ to prices in period t. This is the first evidence of
causal flow from exchange rates to any of the other variables considered. In addition to this new edge in period 1, increasing the significance level from
5–10% shows another new edge between $SP_{t-2} \rightarrow SA_{t-2}$, a difficult edge to explain (as discussed above). Finally, the edges $SA_{t-2} — \Delta P_{t-2}$, $SA_{t-1} \leftarrow \Delta P_{t-1}$ and
$SA_t \leftarrow \Delta P_{t-1}$ found at 5% are marked as $SA_{t-2} \leftarrow \Delta P_{t-2}$.

From figure 4b, we note a new contemporaneous flow out of exchange rates to sales at the 10% significance level. Other differences between figures 4 and 2 are: directed edges flowing out of sales and into price in contemporaneous time, which clears up a confusion noted in our discussion of figure 2, and the directed edge $SP_{t-2} \leftarrow SA_{t-2}$ found at 5% is bidirected at 10%. Otherwise, the graphic representation under 5% significance looks quite similar to the graphic representation under a 10% significance level for period one. $SA_{t-1} \leftarrow \Delta P_{t-1}$ and $SA_t \leftrightarrow \Delta P_{t-1}$ at 10% significance.

When contemporaneous causes are prevented, the 10% graphs in both periods look similar to the 5% graphs, with the notable exception of the directed edge from exchange rates in $t-2$ to price in t, found in period one.

We could present additional graphic representations under different levels of significance, with the result generally being that as we increase the level of significance (say going from 10% to 20%) we see additional edges or if we lower the level of significance we see fewer edges. In terms of the substantive question of whether exchange rates "cause" real commodity export flows for corn, the answer from directed graphs is: "it depends." It depends on the significance level one assumes for analysis and whether the assumption of causal sufficiency is permitted. Assuming causal sufficiency and a 10% level of significance, one finds directed edges from exchange rates to price (over period one data) and from exchange rates to sales (over period two data). If the chosen level of significance is dropped to 5%, these directed edges vanish. Under the assumption of no causal sufficiency, one has to go to even higher levels of significance (higher than 10%) to find edges running from exchange rates to prices and quantities of corn.

5. Hsiao Search

The directed graph algorithms of Spirtes, Glymour, and Scheines (1993) are offered as an alternative to regression-based search procedures for placing zero restrictions on relationships among a set of variables. One such procedure which has attracted considerable attention in economics is the search procedure introduced in a series of articles by Hsiao, (1979a, 1979b, and 1981). This routine employs a statistical loss function, final prediction error (FPE), for finding zero coefficients in a vector autoregression. The procedure has been applied often; for example, Hsiao (1979a) and Hsiao (1981) have over 100 *Social Sciences Citation Index* citation entries each through 1995. As we will see below, the procedure offers informative competition for directed graphs.

Briefly, one selects a set of variables $(x_1, x_2, ..., x_n)$ based on the problem under study and prior theory. For each series under study, the following steps are to be performed. Call the series under study x_1. Hsiao suggests that one first transform it to a covariance stationary series (possibly through log and first difference operations). The following steps are to be followed:

First, determine the order of the univariate autoregressive process for each series using the final prediction error. Here $K_1(1) < K^{\max}$, where $K^{\max}$ is the upper bound over which search takes place, determined by prior theory. Record the minimum FPE statistic from this search as FPE(1).

Second, based on prior theory introduce the most likely next important series into the multivariate determination of series one and search over $K^{\max}$ lags of that series (call this series $x_{2,t}$) in the x_{1t} equation, holding fixed the $K_1(1)$ lags of x_{1t} determined in step 1. Find that lag $K_1(2)$ that minimizes FPE loss over all K^* lags of series two in the series one equation. Compare the resulting FPE loss statistic from the second step, FPE(2 | 1), with that calculated in step 1. If FPE (2 | 1) is less than FPE(1) then keep variable 2 in the variable 1 equation with $K_1(2)$ lags. If FPE(2 | 1) > FPE(1) then do not include lags of series two in the $x_{1,t}$ equation. In either case, relabel FPE(2 | 1) at the end of step 2 as min FPE(1) or FPE(2 | 1).

Third, proceed on with the next most important series for variable 1 (call this series three) and calculate the FPE loss metric for including lags of that series in the x_{1t} equation, including lags of series one and two, as determined in step 2. If that statistic (FPE[3 | 1, 2]) is less than FPE(2 | 1), then include $K_1(3)$ lags of series three in the $x_{1,t}$ equation. If this statistic (FPE[3 | 1, 2]) is greater than FPE(2 | 1), then do not include series three in the autoregressive representation of series one. At the end of step 3, label FPE(3 | 1, 2) as the minimum of FPE(2 | 1) and FPE(3 | 1, 2).

Fourth, continue this search for lagged values of the additional variables (there are now $n-3$ variables to search over for inclusion in the $x_{1,t}$ equation) in the autoregressive representation of series one; this gives numbers $K_1(1)$, $K_1(2)$, ..., $K_1(n)$, the number of lags on variables 1, 2, ..., n in the $x_{1,t}$ equation.

Fifth, having completed this one direction search (call this the forward-looking search) through all n variables, as candidates for inclusion as "explanatory variables" for $x_{1,t}$, hold fixed the lags of the last $n-1$ variables (as determined in the previous steps) and research over lags of variable 1 (label this the *re*-search). If this statistic, FPE(1 | 2, 3, ..., n), is less than FPE(n | 1, 2, ..., —1) refit the lags of series $x_{1,t}$ in the $x_{1,t}$ equation at the level determined in this step (this statistic will equal FPE(n | 1, 2, 3, ..., $n-1$) at lag $K_1(1)$). Label the FPE statistic at the end of step 4 as FPE(2, 3, 4, ..., n | 1), which is given as the minimum of FPE(1, 2, 3, ..., n) and FPE(2, 3, 4, ..., n | 1). Continue to research sequentially over lags of variables 2, 3, ..., , n in an analogous manner, holding lags of variables determined later fixed and research over lags of variables determined earliest. Label the minimum of the forward search and the re-search for $x_{1,t}$ as FPE(1, 2, 3, ..., n). This model will have lags $K_1(1)$ of variable 1, $K_1(2)$ of variable 2, ..., and $K_1(n)$ of variable n in the autoregressive representation of series $x_{1,t}$, some of which may well be zero.

Sixth, apply the same sequential search procedure to variables 2, through n.

Hsiao (1979a, 1979b, and 1981) recommended using FPE as the loss metric for his search procedure. The literature, much of which comes after his initial papers, especially in economics, has generally agreed that FPE overfits (Geweke and Meese 1981). Hsiao recognizes this and offers an argument, that (in some instances) we may prefer a metric which overfits, as overfitting may be less of a serious mistake in model-building than underfitting (Hsiao 1979, p. 355). However, in order to recognize this tendency of FPE to overfit, we apply Hsiao's procedure with both FPE and Schwarz loss. The latter has been shown to not overfit (Geweke and Meese 1981).

Consistent with our work on directed graphs, we applied Hsiao search for building vector autoregressions (subset vector autoregressions) over the two time periods. We constrained our search to two lags of each of the four variables (corn export shipments, corn export sales, first differences of corn price, and first differences of exchange rates) on the same monthly data. Resulting graphs are given in figures 5 and 6. Figure 5 gives FPE and Schwarz-loss constructed graphs for the time period February 1978 – January 1985. The first point to notice from the figure is that FPE clearly fits a larger model than does Schwarz loss. FPE-generated paths from corn shipments in $t - 1$ and $t - 2$ to corn sales in period t and $t - 1$ respectively are particularly difficult to understand. The two paths running from corn shipments in $t - 1$ and $t - 2$ to price changes in period t and $t - 1$, respectively, generate questions as well. For example, why wouldn't the paths run from corn sales to price changes, rather than from corn shipments, as corn is generally sold before it is shipped. Notice that FPE does show edges running from changes in exchange rates in $t - 1$ and $t - 2$ to price changes in period t and $t - 1$, respectively. We saw a similar result from the Tetrad II –generated directed graphs, at a 10% significance level (figure 3).

The Schwarz-loss generated graph (for time period one) appears to be parsimonious, relative to the FPE generated graph. As we saw in Tetrad II generated graphs at 5% level, exchange rates are not connected to the other three variables. Under Schwarz-loss we see a flow from price changes in $t - 1$ and $t - 2$ to corn export sales in t and $t - 1$ respectively, edges not found by Tetrad II at 5%.

Figure 6 gives the Hsiao-search graphs on February 1985 – December 1992 data. Again, FPE finds a more complex model relative to that found using Schwarz loss. Edges running from price to exchange rates, and from shipments to price are difficult to understand. Schwarz loss shows changes in exchange rates and price not connected with corn sales and shipments.

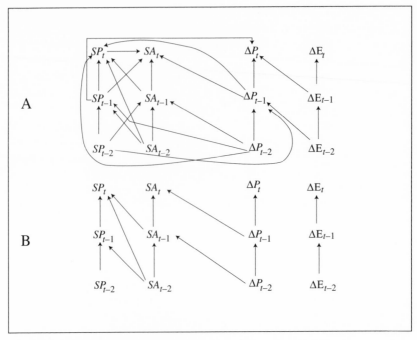

Figure 5. Directed graph from Hsiao-search on corn export shipments (SP$_t$); corn export sales (SA); changes in corn price (ΔP); and changes in exchange rates (ΔE) using (A) FPE loss and (B) Schwarz loss on February 1978 – January 1985 monthly data.

In fact the Schwarz loss graph looks very similar to the Tetrad II directed graph at 5% significance. The only difference between figure 2c and figure 6b is the omission of a directed edge $\Delta E_t \leftarrow \Delta E_{t-1}$ from the former.

5.1 Forecasting

To further test the usefulness of these directed graphs (Tetrad II under no contemporaneous causality and causal sufficiency at the 5% significance level and Hsiao-search using both FPE and Schwarz loss), we considered out-of-sample forecasting over the period of time immediately following the period of specification. Tables 2 and 3 give root mean squared error (RMSE) measures associated with forecasts at horizons of one, two, three, six and twelve steps ahead, for February 1983 – January 1985 and January 1991 – December 1992 data (other horizons are available from the authors, but these five suffice to tell the story, which does not change when intervening horizons are filled in).

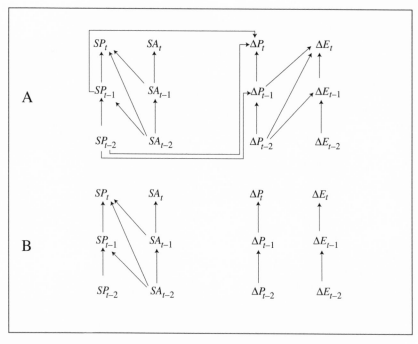

Figure 6. Directed graph from Hsiao-search on corn export shipments (SP_t); corn export sales (SA); changes in corn price (ΔP); and changes in exchange rates (ΔE) using (A) FPE loss and (B) Schwarz loss on February 1985 – December 1992 monthly data.

The measures show (quite clearly) problems with the FPE-specified models in both periods. Where FPE disagrees with Tetrad II or Schwarz loss, it (FPE) loses, almost always. Tetrad II yields lower RMSE on export sales and on three of the four horizons on export shipments over the first forecast period. Schwarz loss offers lower RMSE on corn price over the first period.

RMSE metrics from Schwarz loss and Tetrad II agree over the second period (as both procedures found the same model).

6. Conclusions

This chapter presents an application of directed graphs, as presented in Spirtes, Glymour and Scheines's (1993) and as modeled through Tetrad II programs for modeling relationships between variables in the U.S. corn export market. A substantive economic question associated with this market is

Period	Series	D-F	D-W
December 1978 to January 1985	*logged:* Exchange Rate	0.207	0.0222
	Sales	−6.432*	1.3054*
	Price	−1.556	0.1266
	Shipment	−5.416*	1.0490*
	first differenced logged: Exchange Rate	−6.687*	1.4585*
	Sales	A	A
	Price	−6.993*	1.4824*
	Shipment	A	A
February 1985 to December 1992	*logged:* Exchange Rate	−2.549	0.0251
	Sales	−7.087	1.3986*
	Price	−2.111	0.1491
	Shipment	−4.449	0.6886*
	first differenced logged: Exchange Rate	−7.598	1.5977*
	Sales	A	A
	Price	−6.970*	1.3609*
	Shipment	A	A

Table 1. Dickey-Fuller (D-F) and Durbin-Watson (D-W) tests for unit roots.

D-F stands for the Dickey-Fuller test and lists the coefficient estimates and t-statistics. The test is a quasi t-test on the coefficient of levels lagged one period in an ordinary least squares regression of the first difference of the series on a constant and one lag of the levels of the series. Dickey and Fuller (1979) describe the test. An approximate 5% critical value is −2.89, reject for t-statistics smaller.

D-W indicates the Durbin-Watson test. This test is described in Sargen and Bhargava (1983). An approximate 5% critical value is 0.259. Reject the null of nonstationarity for DW-statistics greater than the 5% critical. The "*" indicates the 5% significance and an "A" indicates that is not applicable

whether exchange rates (changes in exchange rates) cause export sales and shipments. Previous research has offered conflicting results on the question. At a 5% level of significance, our Tetrad II models suggest that the answer to this question is that exchange rates do not cause export sales or shipments. At higher levels of significance (10%, in particular), Tetrad II graphs offer some support that changes in exchange rates cause changes in corn price

Horizon	Number of observations	Hsiao-Search		
		Directed Graph	FPE	Schwarz
		(Shipments)		
1	24	.258	.268	.253
2	23	.258	.275	.265
3	22	.246	.260	.257
6	19	.265	.284	.273
12	13	.298	.314	.296
		(Sales)		
1	24	.311	.342	.336
2	23	.346	.387	.364
3	22	.337	.384	.365
6	19	.365	.374	.379
12	13	.417	.415	.414
		(Price)		
1	24	.048	.049	.048
2	23	.072	.070	.070
3	22	.095	.093	.091
6	19	.146	.150	.142
12	13	.173	.175	.169
		(Exchange Rates)		
1	24	.015	.015	.015
2	23	.022	.022	.022
3	22	.026	.026	.026
6	19	.037	.037	.034
12	13	.019	.019	.019

Table 2. Root mean squared error on forecasts of corn export shipments, corn export sales, corn price, and exchange rates over the period February 1983 – January 1985, by modeling technique.

All forecasts were made based on models specified using either directed graph or Hsiao-search procedures on February 1978 – December 1983 data. The model parameters were updated recursively over the "out-of-sample" period (February 1983 – January 1985) using the Kalman filter.

and/or corn export sales, although here one must make the assumption of causal sufficiency.

We compared our Tetrad II directed graphs with models found using the familiar search routine introduced by Hsiao. The models found using Hsiao-search with the Schwarz loss metric look very similar to the Tetrad II models

Horizon	Number of observations	Directed Graph	Hsiao-Search		
				FPE	Schwarz
(Shipments)					
1	24	.153	.153		.153
2	23	.214	.214		.214
3	22	.244	.244		.244
6	19	.234	.234		.234
12	13	.216	.216		.216
(Sales)					
1	24	.365	.365		.365
2	23	.284	.284		.284
3	22	.295	.295		.295
6	19	.306	.306		.306
12	13	.320	.320		.320
(Price)					
1	24	.042	.044		.042
2	23	.075	.079		.075
3	22	.093	.099		.093
6	19	.084	.083		.084
12	13	0.99	.110		.099
(Exchange Rates)					
1	24	.018	.019		.018
2	23	.030	.031		.031
3	22	.039	.040		.039
6	19	.042	.044		.042
12	13	.039	.040		.039

Table 3. Root mean squared error on forecasts of corn export shipments, corn export sales, corn price, and exchange rates over the period January 1991 – December 1992, by modeling technique.

All forecasts were made based on models specified using either directed graph or Hsiao-search procedures on February 1978 – December 1983 data. The model parameters were updated recursively over the "out-of-sample" period (February 1983 – January 1985) using the Kalman filter.

found using a 5% significance level. The Hsiao-search models found using the FPE loss metric are considerably more complicated than our Tetrad II models. The FPE specified models do a poorer job in forecasting out-of-sample observations.

Tetrad II directed graphs offer the researcher more than traditional search procedures, as they allow him to condition on alternative levels of knowl-

	1	2	3	4	5	6	7	8	9	10	11	12
1	1.0											
2	.488	1.0										
3	.315	.496	1.0									
4	.211	-.061	-.071	1.0								
5	.248	.200	-.083	.327	1.0							
6	.411	.261	.227	.224	.302	1.0						
7	.046	-.067	-.148	.386	.074	.067	1.0					
8	.218	.048	-.071	.294	.382	.069	.225	1.0				
9	.057	.210	.029	.159	.299	.361	.140	.223	1.0			
10	-.110	-.093	-.043	-.081	-.096	-.083	.022	.041	-.018	1.0		
11	-.149	-.107	-.076	-.062	-.084	-.081	-.163	.028	.040	.289	1.0	
12	-.060	-.159	-.090	-.035	-.058	-.063	-.244	-.150	.036	.083	.279	1.0

Table 4. Correlation matrix between current and lagged values of corn export shipments (SP), corn export sales (SA), changes in corn price (ΔP), and changes in exchange rates (ΔE), using February 1978 - January 1985 data.

Data are correlations between variable listed across the top of the table and down the leftmost column. Series numbers, represent series names as follows: $1 = SA_t$, $2 = SA_{t-1}$, $3 = SA_{t-2}$, $4 = SP_t$, $5 = SP_{t-1}$, $6 = SP_{t-2}$, $7 = \Delta P_t$, $8 = \Delta P_{t-1}$, $9 = \Delta P_{t-2}$; $10 = \Delta E_t$, $11 = \Delta E_{t-1}$ and $12 = \Delta E_{t-2}$. Seasonality was removed from each series with monthly dummy variables and ordinary least squares regression.

	1	2	3	4	5	6	7	8	9	10	11	12
1	1.0											
2	.674	1.0										
3	.528	.688	1.0									
4	.553	.206	.191	1.0								
5	.641	.548	.219	.418	1.0							
6	.676	.629	.526	.247	.429	1.0						
7	.348	.274	.203	.420	.218	.073	1.0					
8	.248	.357	.272	.019	.431	.203	.325	1.0				
9	.102	.245	.349	-.059	.024	.431	-.146	.319	1.0			
10	.205	.175	.186	.317	.074	.103	.226	.156	-.003	1.0		
11	.079	.219	.173	.165	.330	.053	-.084	.225	.148	.223	1.0	
12	.241	.090	.232	.150	.161	.311	-.146	-.073	.219	-.067	.236	1.0

Table 5. Correlation matrix between current and lagged values of corn export shipments (SP), corn export sales (SA), changes in corn price (ΔP), and changes in exchange rates (ΔE), using February 1985- December 1992 data.

Data are correlations between variable listed across the top of the table and down the leftmost column. Series numbers, represent series names as follows: $1 = SA_t$, $2 = SA_{t-1}$, $3 = SA_{t-2}$, $4 = SP_t$, $5 = SP_{t-1}$, $6 = SP_{t-2}$, $7 = \Delta P_t$, $8 = \Delta P_{t-1}$, $9 = \Delta P_{t-2}$; $10 = \Delta E_t$, $11 = \Delta E_{t-1}$, and $12 = \Delta E_{t-2}$. Seasonality was removed from each series with monthly dummy variables and ordinary least squares regression.

edge — in particular, one can easily investigate how his model would change assuming he doesn't have a complete set of information (no causal sufficiency). Further, they do not require a priori ranking of importance of lags of each "other variable" on the right-hand side of the autoregressive representation of current values of each variable (as the Hsiao search procedure requires).

Directed graphs have generated considerable discussion in the literature, as they are being offered as an alternative to other model specification procedures. Some (if not most) of the recent discussion does not center on the underlying mathematics, but rather on the actual performance of directed graphs in real world applications. Imbens and Rubin's discussion of a recent paper by Pearl (1995) crystalizes the concern (Imbens and Rubin 1995, p. 694):

> Although, (these models are) formidable tools for manipulating directed acyclic graphs, (they) can easily lull the researcher into a false sense of confidence in the resulting conclusions. Consequently, until we see convincing applications to substantive questions, we remain somewhat skeptical about its general applicability as a conceptual framework for causal inference in practice.

We offer our analysis of directed graphs of the corn export market as positive evidence of the type called for by Imbens and Rubin.

Acknowledgments

We would like to thank Teddy Seidenfeld for his suggestion, several years ago, to study directed graphs for sorting-out causal flows with empirical data. Further, Sir David Cox's 1994 Hartley Lectures at Texas A&M University were also helpful in motivating our early study of directed graphs

References

Babula, R. A.; Ruppel, F.; and Bessler, D. A. 1995. U.S. Corn Exports: The Role of the Exchange Rate. *Agricultural Economics* 13(1): 75–88.

Batten, D. S., and Belongia, M. T. 1986. Monetary Policy, Real Exchange Rates, and U.S. Agricultural Exports. *American Journal of Agricultural Economics* 68(2): 422–427.

Bessler, D. A., and Babula, R. A. 1987. Forecasting Wheat Exports: Do Exchange Rates Matter? *Journal of Business and Economic Statistics* 5(3): 397–406.

Bredahl, M. E.; Meyers, W. H.; and Collins, K. J. 1979. The Elasticity of Foreign Demand for U.S. Agricultural Products: The Importance of the Price Transmission Elasticity. *American Journal of Agricultural Economics* 61(1): 58–63.

Chambers, R., and Just, R. 1981. Effects of Exchange Rate Treatment in Agricultural Trade Models. *American Journal of Agricultural Economics* 63(1): 32–46.

Collins, K. J.; Meyers, W. J.; and Bredahl, M. E. 1980. Multiple Exchange Rate

Changes and U.S. Agricultural Commodity Prices. *American Journal of Agricultural Economics* 62(4): 657–665.

Dickey, D., and Fuller, W. 1979. Distribution of the Estimators for Autoregressive Time Series with a Unit Root. *Journal of the American Statistical Association* 74(366); 427–431

Fletcher, S. M.; Just, R. E.; and Schmitz, A. 1977. The Impacts of Exchange Rates and Other Factors on North American Wheat Export Demand. Working Paper, 12, California Agricultural Experiment Station, Giannini Foundation, University of California, Berkeley.

Geweke, J., and Meese, R. 1981. Estimating Regression Models of Finite but Unknown Order. *International Economic Review* 15(1): 55–70.

Glymour, C., and Spirtes, P. 1988. Latent Variables, Causal Models, and Overidentifying Constraints. *Journal of Econometrics* 39(1, 2): 175–198.

Hsiao, C. 1981. Autoregressive Modeling and Money-Income Causality Detection. *Journal of Monetary Economics* 7(1): 85–106.

Hsiao, C. 1979a. Autoregressive Modeling of Canadian Money and Income Data. *Journal of the American Statistical Association* 74(367): 553–560.

Hsiao, C. 1979b. Causality Tests in Econometrics. *Journal of Economic Dynamics and Control* 1(4): 321–346.

Imbens, G. W., and Rubin, D. 1995. Discussion of Causal Diagrams for Empirical Research by J. Pearl. *Biometrika* 82(4): 694–695.

Jarque, C. M., and Bera, A. K. 1980. Efficient Tests for Normality, Heteroscedasticity, and Serial Independence of Regression Models. *Economic Letters* 6(3): 255–259.

Johnson, P.; Grennes, T.; and Thursby, M. 1977. Devaluation, Foreign Trade Controls, and Domestic Wheat Prices. *American Journal of Agricultural Economics* 59(4): 619–625.

Kost, W. 1976. Effects of an Exchange Rate Change on Agricultural Trade. *Agricultural Economic Research* 28(3): 99–106.

Lin, W.; Riley, P.; and Evans, S. 1995. Feed Grains: Background for 1995 Farm Legislation. In United States Department of Agriculture, Economic Research Service *Agricultural Economic Report* 714, April. Washington, D.C.: Government Printing Office.

Longmire, J., and Morey, A. 1983. Strong Dollar Demand for U.S. Farm Exports. In United States Department of Agriculture, Economic Research Service *Foreign Agricultural Economic Report* 193, December. Washington, D.C.: Government Printing Office.

Machlup, F. 1980. Explaining Changes in Balances of Payments and Foreign-Exchange Rates: A Polemic without Graphs, Algebra, and Citations. In *Flexible Exchange Rates and the Balance of Payments*, eds. J. Chipman and P. Kindleberger, 99–112. New York: North-Holland.

Orden, D. 1986. A Critique of Exchange Rate Treatment in Agricultural Trade Models: Comment. *American Journal of Agricultural Economics* 68(4): 990–993.

Pearl, J. 1995. Causal Diagrams for Empirical Research. *Biometrika* 82(4): 669–710.

Ruppel, F. J. 1987. Agricultural Commodity Export Data: Sales and Shipments Contrasted. *The Journal of Agricultural Economics Research* 39(2): 22–38.

Sargan, J. D., and Bhargava, A. 1983. Testing Residuals from Least Squares Regression for Being Generated by the Gaussian Random Walk. *Econometrica* 51(1): 153–174.

Scheines, R.; Spirtes, P.; Glymour, C.; and Meek, C. 1994. *TETRAD II Tools for Causal Modeling: User's Manual and Software.* Hillsdale, N.J.: Lawrence Erlbaum.

Schuh, G. E. 1974. The Exchange Rate and U.S. Agriculture. *American Journal of Agricultural Economics* 56(1): 1–14.

Shei, S. Y., and Thompson, R. 1979. Inflation and U.S. Agriculture: A General Equilibrium Analysis of the Events of 1973. Paper presented to the American Agricultural Economics Association, Pullman, Washington, 29 July–1 August.

Spirtes, P.; Glymour, C.; and Scheines, R. 1993. *Causation, Prediction, and Search.* Lecture Notes in Statistics. New York: Springer-Verlag.

Stallings, D. 1988. Exchange Rate Volatility and Agricultural Trade. In United States Department of Agriculture, Economic Research Service *Agricultural Outlook* 146:16–23. Washington, D.C.: Government Printing Office.

Velliantis-Fidas, A. 1976. The Impact of Devaluation of U.S. Agricultural Exports. *Agricultural Economics Research* 28(3): 107–116.

CHAPTER NINETEEN

Causal Inferences from Databases: Why Universities Lose Students

Marek J. Druzdzel and Clark Glymour

1. Introduction

The procedures appropriate for database mining depend on the aims of the search. In many cases—as in information retrieval—the aim is to find cases that meet some criterion. In others, the aim is to learn to recognize a property, or values of a variable property, from other properties or variables. In still other applications, the aim is to learn about causal relations among features recorded in the data base. Information about causal relations can then guide actions or policies. A database might, for example, be studied in the hope of learning something about the factors that influence consumer electricity demand, or the causes of poverty, crime or other social variables of interest, or the causes of anomalous signals from a measuring instrument aboard an Earth satellite, or about the causal relations among evoked response potentials measured at various sites on the skull, and so on.

A conventional opinion in statistics is that, despite the potential value of causal information to business, government, medicine and research, uncontrolled sample data of the kind usually collected in large databases cannot provide reliable information about causal dependencies. The reasons given vary in their seriousness. For example, it is sometimes objected that while causation is asymmetric, correlation is a symmetric relation between two variables, so that correlation cannot be inferred from correlation. The objection overlooks the elementary fact that a *collection* of instances of pairwise symmetric relations among a set of objects can determine asymmetric relations between pairs of objects. Otherwise the theory of undirected graphs would be a much less interesting subject. A more serious objection concerns the possibility that associations found in a database may be due to unrecorded or unsampled variables rather than to any causal relations among the recorded variables. The second objection is especially problematic for standard statistical search methods, such as linear and logistic regression, that assume information about causal order is available and that all possible confounding variables have been recorded.

In contrast to this skepticism, work in computer science in the last decade has investigated the possibility of algorithms that make causal conjectures from sample data. These procedures represent causal hypotheses by directed graphs whose nodes are variables or features and whose directed edges represent hypothetical causal influences. We will identify graph vertices with corresponding random variables. The graphs are also taken to encode restrictions on probability relations in the form of conditional independence constraints that require one variable to be independent of another conditional on any values of a further set of variables. Specifically, the variable represented by any vertex V in a graph is assumed to be independent of any of its nondescendants conditional on the set of its parent vertices. This assumption—sometimes called the Markov condition—is used throughout experimental design: in the simplest case, a treatment variable is randomized to ensure there are no common causes of treatment and outcome, and if the outcome is then found to be independent of treatment, the hypothesis that treatment does not influence outcome is confirmed.

Since distinct graphs can encode the same constraints on independence relations, and so can equally well accommodate the same data, the search procedures must output a description of the features shared by an equivalence class of graphs. The equivalence relations between graphs that entail the same conditional independence relations (according to the Markov condition) are well understood and can be decided in time polynomial in the number vertices (Freydenberg 1990, Pearl 1988).

Three kinds of search strategies have been recently investigated: conditional independence searches, Bayesian searches, and mixed searches. The first (Pearl and Verma 1991; Spirtes, Glymour, and Scheines 1990, 1993) use standard statistical tests in a nonstandard way (null hypotheses that are not rejected are accepted) to determine conditional independence relations, and find a class of graphs consistent with those relations. The second (Cooper and Herskovits 1992; Heckerman, Geiger, and Chickering 1995) use relations between graphs and the data to score (or give a posterior probability to) graphs or equivalence classes of graphs, and search for the graph or equivalence class that maximizes the score. Mixed strategies (Spirtes and Meek 1995) find an initial graph using conditional independence relations and then search for modifications that maximize a scoring function. Searches based on scoring functions are heuristic and typically involve some greedy algorithm that examines stepwise small perturbations of an initial graph. The conditional probability searches have a proof of asymptotic correctness, assuming the Markov condition and also assuming that all conditional independence relations result from the Markov condition applied to the (usually unknown) true graph. In simulation studies, however, mixed strategies have proved superior either to pure scoring procedures with greedy search or to conditional independence searches.

It is important to inquire whether these search procedures can give useful results from empirical databases as well as from simulated data. It is most important to apply these search methods to cases in which conclusions can be tested on new samples and, even better, to cases in which independent experiments can test the causal conjectures extracted from the database. Only for procedures based on tests of conditional independence are there available proofs of asymptotic correctness or feasible searches that allow the possibility of unrecorded common causes. A single search procedure of this kind, the Tetrad II (we will abbreviate the name of the program to Tetrad in the remainder of the chapter) program (Scheines, et al. 1994), is publicly available. The search procedures in that program have been used, for example, to make predictions from psychometric tests (Spirtes, Glymour, and Scheines 1993), to recalibrate a malfunctioning mass spectrometer aboard a satellite (Waldemark and Norqvist 1995), and to study plant genetics (Shipley 1995). In this chapter we report the application of some of the Tetrad search procedures to data on graduation rates at colleges and universities in the United States, using two databases collected by *U.S. News and World Report* for two separate years. We found the conjectures drawn from the first year essentially the same as those obtained from data for the following year. The results lead to qualitative predictions of the effects on retention rates of various kinds of university policies. Subsequent policy changes at one of our universities confirm the predictions.

The remainder of the chapter is structured as follows. Section 2 gives a brief overview of the Tetrad program and an example demonstrating its search algorithm. Section 3 presents the problem addressed by our study: student retention in U.S. universities. We describe the analyzed data sets in section 4. Section 5 summarizes our assumptions about this data and prior information about the problem. Section 6 presents the results of Tetrad's search for possible causal structures that may have generated the data, and section 7 reports the results of applying simple regression to selected interactions identified by Tetrad. Section 8 contains a discussion of these results and policy suggestions.

2. Tetrad II

The Tetrad program contains several search modules as well as programs for estimating parameters in models of categorical data and procedures for

Monte Carlo studies. The search procedures include programs for determining whether a set of recorded variables is "unidimensional" or "purified" in the sense that the variables are linear functions of a single, usually unrecorded variable plus uncorrelated noises particular to each recorded variables. Another procedure searches for linear dependencies among hypothetical, unrecorded variables, each uniquely associated with a purified set of measured variables. The most general search procedure among the Tetrad programs, the Build module, constructs a class of directed graphs from raw data or covariance or correlation matrices and assumptions provided by the user. The Build program contains switches permitting the analysis either of discretely valued variables, as with categorical data, or of continuous variables under a general linear model. The procedure also permits the user either to assume, or not to assume, that there are no unrecorded common causes of recorded variables. The user can specify both positive and negative restrictions on possible causal structures, and these restrictions are satisfied in the output and used to make the search more efficient. The complexities of the search procedures are described in Spirtes, Glymour, and Scheines (1993); in summary, the search is feasible for large (e.g., 100 or more) numbers of variables when it is assumed there are no unrecorded common causes, the true graph is sparse, and there is adequate data. When unrecorded common causes are allowed, the search is worst case exponential even on sparse graphs, but the expected complexity is not known.

The Build procedure tests a sequence of hypotheses of independence or conditional independence, and uses the results to construct an equivalence class of graphs. Because the number of possible conditional independencies is exponential in the number of variables, and the power of tests decreases with the number of variables conditioned on, the procedure uses an algorithm that uses smaller conditioning sets before larger conditioning sets, stops automatically, and minimizes the necessary conditional independence tests.

The Build procedure that permits unrecorded variables can be illustrated with a simple case. Suppose the actual structure is that depicted in figure 1 with three independences: X, Y; X, U given Z; Y, U given Z. The procedure first forms the complete undirected graph shown in figure 2.

The procedure then tests each pair of variables for independence, eliminating the corresponding edge if the variables are found to be independent. As the only pair of unconditionally independent variables is X, Y, this yields figure 3.

Next the procedure checks, for each pair of adjacent variables—for example X and U—whether they are independent conditional on any single variable adjacent to either of them. If so, the corresponding edge is removed, and the set of variables conditioned on are stored in memory. The result in this case is figure 4.

The procedure then checks whether any pair of adjacent variables are in-

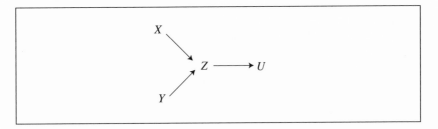

Figure 1. Tetrad Build procedure—the actual causal structure.

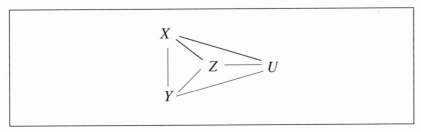

*Figure 2. Tetrad Build procedure—the complete
undirected graph connecting the four measured variables.*

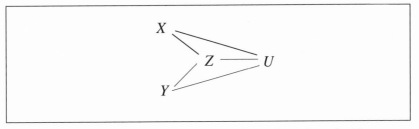

*Figure 3. Tetrad build procedure—the complete undirected graph with arc
between X and Y removed to reflect independence between X and Y.*

dependent conditional on any two variables jointly adjacent to either member
of the pair. In this case no edges are removed and the edge removal procedure stops. The remaining edges are marked at both ends, e.g., with small
"o" symbols (figure 5).

For any three variable such as X, Z, Y, with X adjacent to Z, Z to Y and X, Y
not adjacent, if Z is not in the set conditioned on to remove the X, Y edge, the
"o" symbols at Z are removed and replaced by arrowheads, yielding figure 6.

Finally, the algorithm applies the same condition to triples such as
$X*{\rightarrow}Zo{-}oU$ and if X, U are independent conditional on Z, orients them as
$X*{\rightarrow}Z{\rightarrow}U$. So the final output is figure 7.

The output represents an infinite collection of directed graphs all having
the feature that there is a directed path out of Z into U, and either a directed

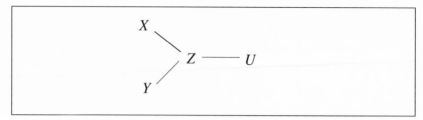

Figure 4. Tetrad Build procedure—the complete undirected graph with arcs X–U and Y–U removed to reflect conditional independence at X and U, Y and U.

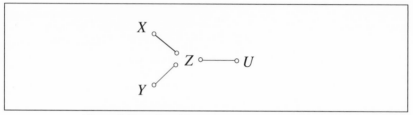

Figure 5. Tetrad Build procedure—graph with direct probabilistic dependencies reflected by undirected arcs.

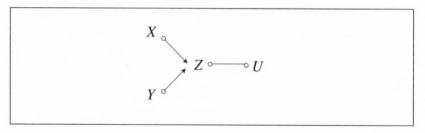

Figure 6. Tetrad Build procedure—orienting arcs.

path from X (and Y) to Z or a directed path from an unrecorded variable to X and to Z, and likewise a directed path from an unrecorded variable to Y and to Z, or both, but there are no directed paths, or pairs of directed paths from unrecorded variables, to any other pairs from among X, Y, Z, and U.

In other cases, the search procedure will indicate the presence of unrecorded common causes. For example, if the actual unknown structure is that in figure 8a, from the conditional independence constraints implied by this structure, Tetrad will output figure 8b, where the double-headed arrow indicates that there is no direct causal connection between Z and U, but the variables share at least one unrecorded common cause. The details of Tetrad's search algorithm are given in Spirtes, Glymour, and Scheines (1993).

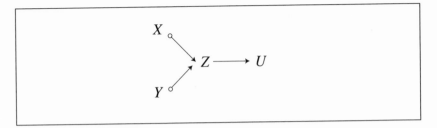

Figure 7. Tetrad Build procedure—final output of the algorithm.

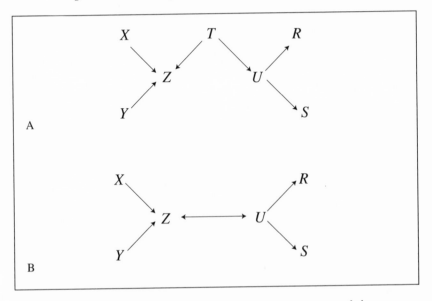

Figure 8. Tetrad Build procedure indicating the presence at unrecorded common causes: actual causal structure (A) and Tetrad output (B).

3. The Retention Problem

Low student retention is a major concern for many U.S. universities. Even though some American universities achieve a student retention rate of well over 90%, the mean retention rate tends to be close to 55% and in some universities fewer than 20% of the incoming students graduate (see figure 9 for the distribution of graduation rates across U.S. national universities for years 1992 and 1993). It should be noted here that the data include both academic and nonacademic dropouts (e.g., students who dropped out because of financial reasons or those who transferred to other schools). Low student retention usually means a waste in effort, money, and human potential. Retention rate

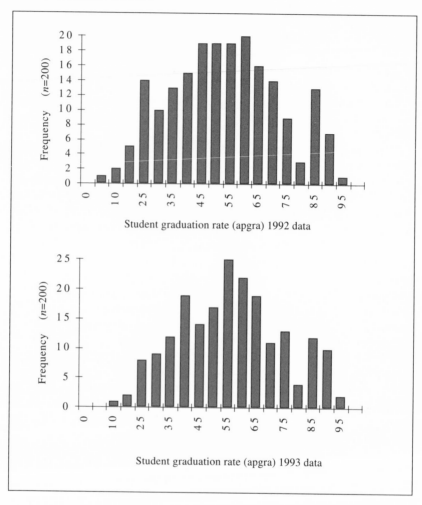

*Figure 9. Histograms of the 1992 and 1993 graduation
rates for U.S. national universities.*

is often thought to indicate student satisfaction with their university program
and, hence, indirectly, the quality of the university. Indeed, a significant correlation can be observed between university ranking and retention rate—universities close to the top of ranking lists tend to have high retention rates. Is a
university's low student retention rate an indication of the quality of education, facilities available to students, tuition costs, university's location, or
perhaps wrong admission policies? More importantly, what action can the
university take to improve the student retention rate? Can such actions as
higher spending on student facilities, increasing the student/faculty ratio, in-

creasing quality standards for teaching faculty, or modifications to admission policies make a difference?

As university-wide experiments testing causes of low retention may be too expensive, ethically suspect, or otherwise impractical, research on this problem must rely mainly on observations. The analysis has to be practically limited to extracting patterns from large collections of measurements of relevant variables. This is where, we believe, Tetrad search procedures are very useful.

This chapter describes a preliminary effort to see what, if anything, aggregate data for many U.S. universities can tell us about the problem. Our analysis involved data concerning U.S. national universities collected annually by the *U.S. News and World Report* magazine for the purpose of their college ranking.[1] While we are far from giving decisive answers to all of the questions posed above, we believe that our analysis provides some interesting insight into the problem. The available data suggest that the main factor in student retention among the studied variables is the average test scores (or other measures of academic ability) of incoming students. The test scores of matriculating students are a function of the quality of the applicants and the university's selectivity. High selectivity leads to high average test scores of the incoming students and effectively to higher student retention rates. Factors such as student-faculty ratio, faculty salary, and university's educational expenses per student do not seem to be directly causally related to student retention. We will consider later what this means for university policies.

4. The Data

The data used in our study consists of a set of records concerning U.S. national universities collected by the *U.S. News and World Report* magazine for the purpose of college ranking. To prepare the data for its annual ranking of colleges, *U.S. News and World Report* each year goes through a laborious process of data collection from over a thousand U.S. colleges. The data are collected from various university offices, such as admissions or business office, by means of surveys prepared by outside companies. The information obtained from each of the colleges is subsequently verified by the school's representatives. The process of collecting the data and combining them into the final college ranking is described in Morse (1992).

The data for national universities provided by *U.S. News and World Report* contains over 100 variables measured for each of the 204 U.S. national universities and national liberal arts colleges defined as major research universities and leading grantors of doctoral degrees. There are compelling reasons for reducing the number of variables studied. First, the power of statistical tests and the reliability of Tetrad's search depend on the ratio of the number of sample points to the number of variables: the higher the ratio, the better. Second, the complete data sets contained considerable redundancy, as many of the variables are analytical derivatives of other variables (e.g., retention rate is simply the ratio of graduating seniors to incoming freshmen, both numbers included separately in the data along with the numbers covering dropouts in every semester of the freshman year and every subsequent year).

A related issue is that of missing values. Including variables with missing values and calculating covariances by skipping a particular unit for a particular variable would undermine the theoretical reliability of statistical tests. Testing partial correlations involves multiple correlations from the correlation matrix, and since these would not be based on a fixed sample size, the sample size used in the tests would be indeterminate. Hence variables for which there are a great many missing values are to be avoided if possible.

We selected the following eight variables as those most relevant to our analysis in the available data sets:

- *apgra* average percentage of graduation, i.e., the fraction of the total number of entering students who make it through the graduation
- *rejr* rejection rate, i.e., the fraction of the applicants who are given an admission offer
- *tstsc* average standardized test scores of the incoming students[2]
- *top10* class standing of the incoming freshmen, which is a fraction of the incoming freshmen who were in top 10% of their high school graduating class
- *pacc* percentage of those students who accept the university's offer from among those who are offered admission
- *spend* total educational and general expenses per student, which is the sum spent on instruction, student services, and academic support, including libraries and computing services
- *strat* student-faculty ratio
- *salar* average faculty salary.

Describing each of over 100 remaining variables and discussing why we have not considered them for our analysis would make this chapter unacceptably long. We limit ourselves to a few remarks. The values of a large number of the variables were included indirectly in the eight chosen variables. Average test scores of incoming students (*tstsc*), for example, is a normalized compilation of values of fourteen variables, including a breakdown of average results for various parts of SAT and ACT tests. Average percentage of graduation (*apgra*) expresses the essence of fourteen variables concerning student retention, such as breakdown of dropout rates across all semesters of the freshman year. Rejection rate (*rejr*) and percentage of admitted students

	spend	apgra	top10	rejr	tstsc	pacc	strat	salar
University 1	9855	52.500	15	29.474	65.063	36.887	12.0	60800
University 2	10527	64.250	36	22.309	71.063	30.970	12.8	63900
University 3	6601	57.000	23	11.296	67.188	40.289	17.0	51200
University 4	15287	65.250	42	26.913	70.750	28.276	14.4	71738
University 5	16848	77.750	48	26.690	75.938	27.187	9.2	63000
University 6	18211	91.000	87	76.681	80.625	51.164	12.8	74400
...	...	...	...	...	...	...	...	...

Table 1. Example records from our database.

who accept university's offer (*pacc*) express, along with the average test scores (*tstsc*) and class standing (*top10*), selectivity of the school. We chose the total educational and general expenses per student (*spend*), student-teacher ratio (*strat*), and average faculty salary (*salar*) as indicators of the quality of school's teaching and its financial resources.

From the complete set of 204 universities, we removed 26(31)[3] universities that had missing values for any of the eight variables of interest. This resulted in a set of 178(173) data points. Table 1 lists a few records from the database to give the reader an idea of what the raw data looked like.

As with almost any data set relevant to socioeconomic policy, the variables under study contain a large amount of noise, attributable to a variety of reasons. Because *U.S. News and World Report* seems to do a very thorough job in collecting and verifying the data, we believe that the main source of noise in this data set may be due to latent factors that take part in the interactions among the variables under study, but are not measured. Because of large residual variances, rule-based approaches to studying the data would face considerable difficulty. Finally, we did not consider data for 1994 because the set available to us through the American Statistical Association did not include percentile ranking on standardized test scores.

The correlation matrices for the 170(159) data points of the 1992(1993) data sets are reproduced in tables 2 and 3 respectively.

Each of the variables is related to the graduation rate (*apgra*), with correlations ranging between – 0.3028 and 0.7822 and the absolute magnitude always larger than 0.3.

5. The Assumptions

Although Tetrad's algorithms are independent on the actual distribution of the variables, they rely on the outcomes of a series of statistical tests. The necessary tests are especially powerful if we can assume normally distributed, linearly related variables. We studied how reasonable this assumption is

	spend	apgra	top10	rejr	tstsc	pacc	strat	salar
spend	1.0000							
apgra	0.6012	1.0000						
top10	0.6756	0.6425	1.0000					
rejr	0.6335	0.5149	0.6432	1.0000				
tstsc	0.7149	0.7822	0.7988	0.6286	1.0000			
pacc	−0.2367	−0.3028	−0.2075	−0.0715	−0.1642	1.0000		
strat	−0.5617	−0.4583	−0.2478	−0.2836	−0.4652	0.1318	1.0000	
salar	0.7118	0.6358	0.6376	0.6068	0.7155	−0.3752	−0.3477	1.0000

Table 2. Matrix of correlations among the
analyzed variables (1992 data set, 170 data points).

	spend	apgra	top10	rejr	tstsc	pacc	strat	salar
spend	1.0000							
apgra	0.5455	1.0000						
top10	0.6381	0.5879	1.0000					
rejr	0.4766	0.4720	0.5674	1.0000				
tstsc	0.6732	0.7403	0.7655	0.5813	1.0000			
pacc	−0.3807	−0.4237	−0.2498	−0.0810	−0.2985	1.0000		
strat	−0.7713	−0.3867	−0.3099	−0.2721	−0.4688	0.1909	1.0000	
salar	0.6954	0.6328	0.6025	0.4885	0.6515	−0.5159	−0.3737	1.0000

Table 3. Matrix of correlations among the analyzed variables
(1993 data set, 159 data points).

spend, strat, salar
rejr, pacc
tstsc, top10
apgra

Table 4. Temporal order among the variables under study used as prior information
in TETRAD search: spend, strat, and salar precede rejr and pacc,
which precede tstsc and top10. The average graduation rate
(apgra) is assumed not to precede any variables.

for the available data set by plotting histograms of each of the eight variables. From visual inspection of the histograms, we removed 8(14) additional data points that appeared to be outliers. The resulting data set, consisting of 170(159) data points, reasonably satisfied the normality assumptions. No formal tests of normality were conducted. All histograms were close to symmetric unimodal distributions (see figures 9 and 10 for example), with the exception of two positively skewed variables, spend and strat.

An important assumption made by Tetrad is that the causal structure that

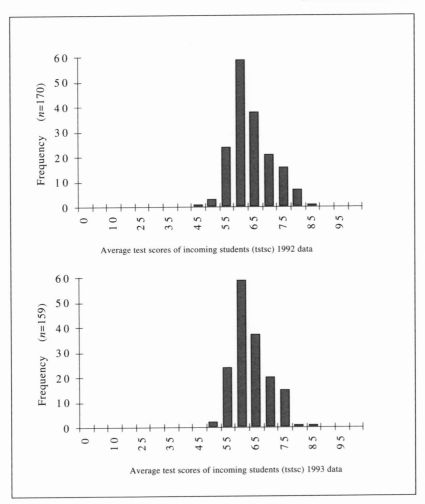

Figure 10. Histograms of the test scores tstsc (1992 and 1993 data).

generated the data points is not a feedback process. This assumption was not necessarily true in our data set. For example, most of the variables considered influence the image of the university. That image, in turn, may influence all of the eight variables. We believe, nonetheless, that the assumption is reasonable for this data set, as all feedback processes that we can think of in this context are very slow—on the order of decades—in comparison to the interaction between the measured factors and graduation rate, which takes place over four years.

An assumption frequently made in causal modeling is that the analyzed variables form a self-contained structure—there are no latent common causes. (Equivalently, for covariance studies, that all error terms are independent.) As it is unlikely that the selected variables form a self-contained structure, we have run Tetrad under the assumption that latent variables may be present. Several control runs imposing instead the assumption that the measured variables are causally sufficient did not reveal anything that would put our main conclusions in question.

One way that Tetrad can be aided in its search for the set of causal structures that could have generated the data is by an explicit encoding of prior knowledge about causal relations. Tetrad allows for specifying temporal precedence among variables, information about presence or absence of direct causal connections between pairs of variables, and information about absence of common causes between pairs of variables. With respect to the available data set, we believe that the average spending per student (*spend*), student-teacher ratio (*strat*), and faculty salary (*salar*) are determined based on budget considerations and are not influenced by any of the five remaining variables. Rejection rate (*rejr*) and percentage of those students who accept the university's offer from among those who are offered admission (*pacc*) precede the average test scores (*tstsc*) and class standing (*top10*) of incoming freshmen. The latter two are measures taken over matriculating students. Finally, our only assumption about graduation rate, *apgra*, was that it does not cause any of the other variables. These assumptions are reflected in the temporal ordering in table 4, which was the only prior knowledge (in addition to the raw data) given to Tetrad.

6. The Results

This section presents the results of our analysis for two data sets, measurements for the years 1992 and 1993. The analysis of the 1992 data was conducted before we had access to the 1993 data set.

Depending on the significance level used in independence tests, Tetrad's individual statistical decisions regarding independence may be different and a different class of causal structures may result. It is, therefore, a good practice to run the program at several significance levels. We ran Tetrad with the following four significance levels: $p = 0.2, 0.1, 0.05$, and 0.01. Our earlier simulation studies have indicated that a level of 0.05 is appropriate for data sets, and numbers of variables, of the sizes available for our problem. The danger of making p too small is that Tetrad will reject weak dependences as insignificant and, in effect, delete arcs that represent weak but genuine causal influences. Making p too large will introduce spurious arcs. Classes of the graphs proposed by Tetrad for the above significance levels are presented in figure 11. The edges of the graphs have the following meaning: A single ar-

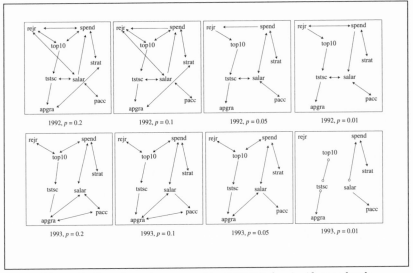

Figure 11. Causal graphs proposed by TETRAD for significance levels ranging from p = 0.2 through p = 0.01.

row (→) denotes a direct causal influence. A double headed arrow (↔) between two variables denotes presence of a latent common cause of these two variables. A single arrow with a circle at one end (o→) expresses Tetrad's inability to deduce whether there is a direct influence between the two variables (→) or a latent common cause between them (↔). An edge with circles at both ends (o—o) expresses Tetrad's inability to deduce whether there is a direct influence between the two variables and, if so, what is its direction (→ or ←), or a latent common cause between them (↔). The core of the structure, i.e., how *apgra* is related to the remaining variables, shows a slight sensitivity to changes in significance, but the dependence on test scores is robust. Variations in the interactions among the remaining variables can be attributed to the relatively small size of our data set and are not of interest in any case since we make no conjectures about them.

In the graphs in figure 11, as well as in all other graphs suggested by Tetrad, any connection between *apgra* and variables like *spend, strat,* or *salar* is through *tstsc.* The "latent common cause" connection between *salar* and *apgra* (1993 data), shown in figure 11 for $p = 0.05$, disappears at $p <$ 0.04. All graphs proposed by Tetrad contained a direct causal connection between the average test scores and student graduation rate.

Tetrad's algorithms are much more reliable in determining existence of direct causal links than in determining their orientation. Therefore, prior knowledge supplied to Tetrad may be critical for the orientation of edges of the graph. We used the temporal sequence described in section 5, but we also

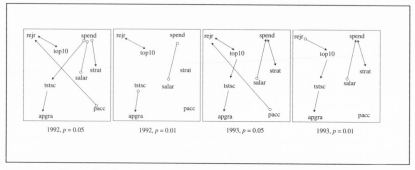

Figure 12. Causal graphs proposed by TETRAD for significance
levels p = 0.05 and p = 0.01 for the top fifty universities.

checked the robustness of our result to temporal ordering by running Tetrad
with no assumptions about temporal precedence. Although Tetrad proposed
different orderings of variables, all direct links, and the direct link between
test scores and graduation rate in particular, were the same in both cases.

To check whether the causal structure is the same for the top research universities, we prepared additional data sets for Tetrad with universities among
the top 50 universities with respect to their academic ranking by *U.S. News
and World Report*. Figure 12 shows classes of graphs suggested by Tetrad for
this restricted data set and various significance levels. The results are similar
to those from the complete data sets. Any differences between graphs concerned influences among variables different than *apgra* and can be partially
attributed to a small number of data points and, hence, susceptibility to
chance variations.

7. Linear Regression

We applied linear regression to the relation between the main indicator of the
quality of incoming freshmen, *tstsc* (average test scores), and *apgra* (graduation rate) to obtain a quantitative measure of the strength of these interactions.

In the full data set of 170(159) data points, linear regression applied to *apgra* on *tstsc* resulted in the following equations:

1992: *apgra* = −77.4 + 2.03 *tstsc*, R-sq(adj) = 60.9%
1993: *apgra* = −64.9 + 1.89 *tstsc*, R-sq(adj) = 54.5%

In the restricted set of 50 top ranked research universities, the regression
equations were:

1992: *apgra* = −84.6 + 2.13 *tstsc*, R-sq(adj) = 70.0%

1993: $apgra = -63.6 + 1.88\ tstsc$,   R-sq(adj) = 64.5%

While the regression coefficients for the top universities are similar to those for the entire data set, the average test scores of incoming freshmen explain more (as much as 70%(64.5%)!) variance in graduation rates.

Theoretically, it is possible to use the regression coefficients between average test scores and retention rate obtained in this study to predict the impact of improvement in the average test scores of incoming students on student retention. There are, however, potential problems with making predictions of an intervention at one institution, as the coefficients of the regression equations do not need to be identical for each institution.

We emphasize that we used regression only to estimate the coefficients in a linear model obtained by the Tetrad search. If regression were used instead to search for the variables influencing student retention, the results would include variables that Tetrad finds have no direct influence on the outcome, and that are conditionally independent of the outcome variables. Some of the reasons for the unreliability of regression as a search procedure are explained in chapter 8. We regressed $apgra$ on the remaining seven variables to illustrate the difference in results. For the 1992 data set, regression indicated three predictors to be significant: $tstsc$ ($p < 0.001$), $pacc$ ($p < 0.003$), and $strat$ ($p < 0.023$). For the 1993 data set, four predictors were significant: $tstsc$ ($p < 0.001$), $pacc$ ($p < 0.002$), $salar$ ($p < 0.012$), and $spend$ ($p < 0.059$).

8. Discussion

One limitation in our study is that the available *U.S. News* data do not disaggregate academic from nonacademic dropout. We predict that internal data will show a difference between average test scores of dropouts (academic and nonacademic) and graduates. Another limitation is that our data do not disaggregate between different departments. Some departments may have many academic dropouts, others few. Also, the available data set did not include other variables that may have been relevant, such as geographical location (climate, urban/rural, etc.), tuition costs, available academic support, financial situation of the students, prominence of athletics on campus, etc.

It is possible to apply alternative prior models of interaction of the variables in our data set. One alternative suggested to us posits one latent variable influencing all eight measured variables studied. This model, however, would not account for the strong conditional independencies observed in the data, and is in fact rejected in the 1992 data set—the only one we checked—by the standard f ratio test (chi square of 356 with 27 degrees of freedom).

It seems that none of the variables in the data set were directly causally related to student retention except for standardized test scores. This conjecture, based on the fact that graduation rate is nearly independent of all remaining variables conditional on average test scores, seems to be robust across varying significance levels, availability of prior knowledge, and data set size. The average test scores seem to have a high predictive power for student retention. For the top fifty ranking research universities, average test scores explain as much as 70% (64.5%) of the variance in graduation rate.

The average test score of incoming students can be viewed as indicators of the academic preparation of the incoming student body. It seems that retention rate in an individual university can be improved by increasing the quality of the incoming students. This, in turn, can be improved by increasing the number and the quality of applicants. Altering factors such as faculty salary, student-teacher ratio, or spending per student may influence graduation rates, but if our analysis is correct, only because such manipulations somehow influence the average test scores (or whatever academic preparation the average test scores are a proxy for). We do not have data on student academic assistance programs, tutoring, mentoring and the like, and for all we know such programs may influence retention rates, but they are unlikely to account for the preponderance of the variance in retention.

Universities have available several mechanisms for improving the academic preparation of beginning students. One method is for universities to take an active role in elementary and secondary schools to improve student preparation and establish an early association between children, their parents, and the university. A cheaper, more direct mechanism, which we regret to say is likelier to be used, is to alter financial aid packages to provide support based partly on measures of academic ability.

Carnegie Mellon University changed its financial aid policies in 1994 to assign a portion of its scholarship fund on the basis of academic merit. This resulted in an increase in the average standardized test scores of matriculating freshmen classes and thus far an increased freshmen retention rate. As most students who leave the university do so in their freshmen year, one can expect a subsequent increase in the graduation rates.

Acknowledgments

Considerable data collection effort and generosity in making the collected data available on the part of *U.S. News and World Report* made this study possible. Steven Klepper, Chris Meek, Richard Scheines and Peter Spirtes contributed to our work with valuable suggestions. We thank Felicia Ferko, Kevin Lamb, and Jeffrey Bolton from Carnegie Mellon University's Office of Planning and Budget for enabling us to access the data files and providing insightful background information. Support for this work has been provided by ONR and NPRDC under grant N00014-93-1-0568 to Carnegie Mellon University.

Notes

1. The data available to us is for the years 1992 and 1993.

2. We owe an explanation for readers who are not familiar with the admission procedure to U.S. universities. Practically every U.S. university requires a prospective student to take a nationwide test, administered by a private educational testing institution. The most popular test is SAT (Scholastic Achievement Test), but there are others, such as the ACT (American College Test), required for specialty schools, such as law or management schools. The score on such a standardized test gives a reasonable measure of the preparation of the applicant and is an important factor in admissions.

3. In the sequel, we will report the counts for the 1992 data followed by the counts for the 1993 data in parentheses.

References

Cooper, G. F., and Herskovits, E. 1992. A Bayesian Method for the Induction of Probabilistic Networks from Data. *Machine Learning* 9(4): 309–347.

Freydenberg, M. 1990. The Chain Graph Markov Property. *Scandinavian Journal of Statistics: Theory and Applications* 17(4): 333–353.

Heckerman, D. E.; Geiger, D.; and Chickering, D. M. 1995. Learning Bayesian Networks: The Combination of Knowledge and Statistical Data. *Machine Learning* 20(3): 197–243.

Morse, R. J., ed. 1992. U.S. News & World Report's America's Best Colleges Rankings: How It's Done. U.S. News Internal Report, May 8.

Pearl, J. 1988. *Probabilistic Reasoning in Intelligent Systems: Networks of Plausible Inference.* San Francisco, Calif.: Morgan Kaufmann.

Pearl, J., and Verma, T. S. 1991. A Theory of Inferred Causation. In *KR–91, Principles of Knowledge Representation and Reasoning: Proceedings of the Second International Conference,* eds. J. A. Allen, R. Fikes, and E. Sandewall, 441–452. San Francisco, Calif.: Morgan Kaufmann.

Scheines, R.; Spirtes, P.; Glymour, C.; and Meek, C. 1994. TETRAD II: *Tools for Discovery* (with Software). Hillsdale, N.J.: Lawrence Erlbaum.

Shipley, B. 1995. Structured Interspecific Determinants of Specific Leaf Area in 34 Species of Herbaceous Angiosperms. *Functional Ecology.* 9(1): 312-319.

Spirtes, P., and Meek, C. 1995. Learning Bayesian Networks with Discrete Variables from Data. In *Proceedings of the First International Conference on Knowledge Discovery and Data Mining,* 294–299, Menlo Park, Calif.: AAAI Press.

Spirtes, P.; Glymour, C.; and Scheines, R. 1993. *Causation, Prediction, and Search.* New York: Springer-Verlag.

Spirtes, P.; Glymour, C.; and Scheines, R. 1990. Causality from Probability. In *Evolving Knowledge in Natural Science and Artificial Intelligence,* eds. J. Tiles et al., 181–199. London: Pitman.

Waldemark, J., and Norqvist, P. 1995. In-Flight Calibration of Satellite Ion Composition Data Using Artificial Intelligence Methods. IRF Scientific Technical Report 226, Department of Applied Physics and Electronics, Umea University, Umea, Sweden.

Index

effect of covariates on conditional distributions, 78–79
Markov assumption and, 522
observeability of, 78–79
randomization and, 78
Explanation, causal, 9

Faithfulness assumption
in causal discovery, 103, 143
in constraint-based causal discovery, 30–33
in criticisms of inferring causal relationships, 313
in DCGs, 263–265
deducing absence of causal relations with,
309
as exclusion of unfaithful distributions, 309
in graphical models, 73–74
model specification and, 182
observeability and, 78–79
for PAGs, 217
population inference assumption and,
235–236
pros and cons of, 319
sample causal faithfulness assumption and,
345
SEMs and, 182
statement of, 181
in variable selection, 428
weak sample causal faithfulness assumption
and, 345
Fast Causal Inference (FCI) algorithm. see FCI
algorithm
FCI algorithm
adjacency phase of, 225–229
constructing PAGs with, 224–225
convergence results of, 52
estimating latent causal influences with,
429–431
evaluating performance of, 54
generating RSEMs with correlated errors,
188–191
orientation phase of, 229–232
possible improvements to, 234–235
simulation studies with, 232–234
Fisher consistency, 303
Fisher, R. A.
causal role of smoking in lung cancer, 80
on randomized experiments, 441
Frequency spectra, measuring, 489–490
Front-door criterion, 110–112
applying to smoking and genotype theory,
112–114
definition of, 112
equations for, 111
theorem for, 112

Galles and Pearl, 133
Gaussian approximation, 154–156
approximating marginal likelihood with, 155
comparing with Monte-Carlo methods, 154
equations for, 154–155
G-computation algorithm formula, 361–362
Geman and Geman, 153

GES algorithm. see Greedy equivalence search
(GES) algorithm
Gibbs sampling
applying to subject noncompliance, 409,
414–417
estimating latent causal influences with,
433–436
as Markov chain sampling method, 414
as Monte-Carlo sampling method, 153–154
phases of, 416
Glymour, Spirtes, and Richardson
on causal inference, 306
on pros and cons of Robins-Wasserman argument, 330
questioning plausibility of Robins-Wasserman prior, 324–327
questioning professional use of the Robins-
Wasserman prior and loss function,
327–330
responding to Robins-Wasserman rejoinder,
343–345
restating Robins-Wasserman on Tetrad II inference, 323–324
see also Robins and Wasserman
Graphical models, 73–75, 95–133
as alternative to Bayesian method, 126–127
applying to subject noncompliance,
409–411
causal discovery in, 101–103
confounding arcs in, 119–121
confounding bias in, 107–114
extending functionality of, 125–126
faithfulness assumption and, 73–74
finding conditional-independence constraints with, 97–101
identifiying models and, 122–124
intervention calculus for, 114–119
limitations of, 125
manipulation assumption and, 74
Markov assumption and, 73
modeling interventions with, 104–107
nonidentifying models and, 124–125
notational standards for, 126–127
notation of d-separation with, 99–100
overview of, 95–98
structural equations and, 131
testing identifiability with, 119–125
translating into Rubin's framework, 131
see also Causal diagrams
Graphs
combining with Rubin's framework and
structural equations, 129–133
directed graphs (DGs), 254–257
theoretical definitions for, 76
undirected graphs, 278
see also Directed acyclic graphs (DAGs);
Directed cyclic graphs (DCGs)
Greedy equivalence search (GES) algorithm,
53–54
Greedy search algorithms
GES algorithm as example of, 53–54
model selection with, 146
overview of, 47–49
Greedy search algorithms on essential graphs, 49